Interpretations of American History

Patterns and Perspectives

Fourth Edition

**Gerald N. Grob &
George Athan Billias**

**Volume II
since 1865**

THE FREE PRESS
A Division of Macmillan Publishing Co., Inc.
NEW YORK

Collier Macmillan Publishers
LONDON

The Free Press
A Division of Macmillan Publishing Co., Inc.
866 Third Avenue, New York, N.Y. 10022

Collier Macmillan Canada, Inc.

Library of Congress Catalog Card Number: 81-69222

Printed in the United States of America

printing number

6   7   8   9   10

Library of Congress Cataloging in Publication Data
Main entry under title:

Interpretations of American history.

    Includes bibliographical references and indexes.
    Contents: v. 1. To 1877 -- v. 2. Since 1877.
    1. United States--History--Addresses, essays,
lectures. 2. United States--Historiography--Addresses,
essays, lectures. I. Grob, Gerald N.
II. Billias, George Athan   III. Title.
E178.6.I53 1982   973   81-69222
ISBN 0-02-912690-8 (v. 1)   AACR2
ISBN 0-02-912700-9 (v. 2)

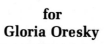

for
Gloria Oresky

CONTENTS

PREFACE TO THE FOURTH EDITION

This two-volume book of essays and readings is based upon our philosophy of teaching American history to advanced students. Simply stated, this philosophy holds to four premises: (1) the approach to history should be analytical, not factual; (2) students should be exposed to the newest viewpoints as well as to traditional interpretations; (3) readers should be provided with a brief historiographical background in order to appreciate more fully the selections assigned for outside readings; and (4) reading assignments should be exciting intellectual adventures rather than dull chores.

The first purpose of this work, then, is to bring together selections that approach American history from an analytical point of view. In most instances these readings represent interpretive pieces that illuminate different problems and periods in America's past. Students will be struck, however, by a single thread that runs through both volumes and ties together the diverse readings. The selections reproduced here underscore one major theme: that the view of American history has been a constantly changing one.

Generally speaking, new interpretations in American history have arisen for two reasons. First, the perspective of American historians of a given generation has been shaped in large measure by the sweep of events in the external world—occurrences outside the scholar's study. Scholars, in short, have tended to reflect either consciously or unconsciously in their works the problems and predilections of the age in which they have written. Each succeeding generation, therefore, seems to have rewritten American history to suit the felt needs of its time. Some selections in this work are indicative of this generational change. We have sometimes sought to show how the age in which the historian was writing often influenced starting assumptions, the gathering of evidence, and the interpretation of events. In recent years, for example, the consciousness of historians has been influenced by distinctive social changes reflecting the forces of racism, sexism, war, violence, and economic and urban problems that have profoundly affected the lives of most Americans.

The second reason for the constantly changing picture of our nation's past has come from internal intellectual changes within the historical profession itself—inside the scholar's study, so to speak. History like most other academic disciplines, seems to have a built-in tendency toward self-generating change. When scholars sense that they have reached the outer limits in applying the tenets of what has become an accepted interpretation, they do one of two things: introduce major revisions to correct the prevailing point of view, or strike off in new directions. Some articles in this work, therefore, represent the writings of scholars who seek to revise some of the more traditional interpretations; other selections reflect the work of a current generation of historians who apply concepts borrowed from the social and behavioral sciences, or employ quantitative techniques. The decades of the 1960s and 1970s were marked by attempts to create a "new social history," a "new political history," and a "new economic history." These efforts have focused primarily, though not exclusively, on the study of group behavior, with the group being defined by a set of variables that often lend themselves to quantification. Other efforts of a non-quantitative nature were either cross-disciplinary in purpose, or have resorted to new methodological approaches.

To meet the needs of our third premise, we have written chapter-length introductions for each group of selections. These introductions will enable students to approach the readings with greater ease and understanding by providing a historiographical context for the topic under discussion.

Finally, we have searched the literature for selections that have a lively literary style. It is our firm conviction that the readings represent spirited writing as well as sound scholarship. Much of the exciting work in American history has been done by scholars who possess a real literary flair. Students will discover the rewards of history when they read in these pages the selections by Perry Miller, Darrett Rutman, Bernard Bailyn, Daniel Boorstin, Gordon Wood, Edward Pessen, Stanley Elkins, Allan Nevins, Eric Foner, Gabriel Kolko, Dexter Perkins, Arthur Link, Arthur M. Schlesinger, Jr., Frederick Jackson Turner, Eugene Genovese, William A. Williams, and John Kenneth Galbraith.

In preparing this work, we have drawn upon the help of several friends. In particular, we should like to thank four of them, Milton M. Klein of the University of Tennessee and Ronald Formisano, Ronald Petrin, and Frank Couvares of Clark University.

G.N.G.
G.A.B.

1

Introduction

"Every true history is contemporary history." Thus wrote Benedetto Croce, the great Italian philosopher and historian, over a half century ago. By his remark Croce meant that history—as distinguished from mere chronicle—was meaningful only to the degree it struck a responsive chord in the minds of contemporaries who saw mirrored in the past the problems and issues of the present.

Croce's remark has special relevance to the writing of American history. Every generation of American scholars has reinterpreted the past in terms of its own age. Why is this so? One compelling reason, no doubt, has been the constant tendency of scholars to reexamine the past in light of the prevailing ideas, assumptions, and problems of their own day. Every age has developed its own climate of opinion—or particular view of the world—which, in turn, has partially conditioned the way it looks upon its own past and present. Thus, each succeeding generation of Americans has rewritten the history of the country in such a way as to suit its own self-image. Although there were other reasons for this continual reinterpretation of American history, the changing climate of opinion more than any other single factor caused historians to recast periodically their view of the past.

Changing interpretations arose also from the changing nature of American historians and their approach to the discipline. The writing of history in America, broadly speaking, has gone through three distinct stages. In the first stage—the era of Puritan historians during the seventeenth century—historical writing was dominated by ministers and political leaders of the Puritan colonies who sought to express the religious justification for their New World settlements. The second stage—the period of the patrician historians—saw the best history being written by members of the patrician class from the early eighteenth century to the late nineteenth century. Patrician historians—often gentlemen of leisure with private incomes—normally had little or no connection with the church or other formal institutions, as had the Puritan historians. They were stirred to write history by a strong sense of social responsibility that characterized the class from which they sprang, and by a personal conviction that each individual had a moral obligation to employ his best talents for the betterment of mankind. Their works, as a general rule, reflected the ideology and preconceptions of their class. Although they were amateur scholars for the most part, many patrician writers succeeded in reaching a high level of literary distinction and accuracy. The third stage—the period of the professional scholars—began during the 1870s and may properly be called "the age of the professional historians." These scholars qualified as professionals on several counts: they were specifically trained for their craft; they supported themselves by full-time careers of teaching, writing, and research at colleges and universities; and they looked to their professional group to set the standards of achievement by which historical studies were evaluated. Their work has been characterized by constant revisionism: They attempted to correct one another, to challenge traditional interpretations, and to approach old historical problems from new points of view.[1]

During each of these three stages of historical writing, the intellectual milieu in America was distinctly different. In the seventeenth century, the best histories were written by Puritan ministers and magistrates who saw history as the working out of God's will. Theirs was a Christian interpretation of history—one in which events were seen as the unfolding of God's intention and design. Borrowing the concept of a Chosen People from the ancient Hebrews, they viewed the colonization of America in Biblical terms. They cast the Puritans in the same role as the Jews in the Old Testament—as a regenerate people who were destined to fulfill God's purpose. New England became for them New Canaan— the place God had set apart for man to achieve a better way of Christian living. Massachusetts, therefore, was more than simply another colony. In the words of John Winthrop, it was to be a "city upon a hill"—a model utopia to demonstrate to the rest of the world that the City of God could be established on earth along the lines set forth in the New Testament.

The major theme of most Puritan historians, whether they were ministers or lay leaders, was the same—to demonstrate God's special concern for His Chosen People in their efforts to build a New Canaan. New England's history served their purposes best because it was here that God's mercy could be seen more clearly than in any other part of the globe. To the Puritans, New England's history was one long record of the revelation of God's providence toward His people. Their disasters as well as their triumphs were seen only in relation to God, and the setbacks they suffered were viewed as evidence of God's wrath and displeasure.

Of all the Puritan histories, William Bradford's *Of Plimouth Plantation* was, perhaps, the preeminent work of art. Written in the 1630s and 1640s while Bradford was governor of the colony, this book recounted

---

[1]John Higham *et al., History* (Englewood Cliffs, N.J., 1965), pp. 3-5.

the tale of the tiny band of Pilgrims who fled first to Holland and then to the New World. No other narrative captured so perfectly the deep feeling of religious faith of New England's early settlers. None illustrated better the Puritan ideal of a plain and simple literary style, or mastered so well the rhythms of Biblical prose. Yet, like most Puritan literature, it was written during the few spare moments that Bradford could find from his more important activities as a governor of a new community in the wilderness.

The patrician historians of the eighteenth century replaced the Puritan historians when the church ceased to be the intellectual center of American life. The Christian theory of history with its emphasis on supernatural causes increasingly gave way to a more secular interpretation based upon the concepts of human progress, reason, and material well-being. Influenced by European Enlightenment thinkers, American historians came to believe that man, by use of his reason, could control his destiny and determine his own material and intellectual progress in the world.

The patrician historians were profoundly influenced also by ideas derived from the writings of Sir Isaac Newton. This seventeenth-century English scientist, by applying a rational, mathematical method, had arrived at certain truths, or "natural laws," concerning the physical universe. Newton's systematization of scientific thought led many men to conclude that the same mathematical-scientific method could be employed to formulate similar natural laws in other fields. In order to develop a theory of history in keeping with Newtonian thought, writers began to postulate certain natural laws in the field of history. Thus, patrician historians abandoned the Christian theory in which God determined the events for a view of the universe in which natural laws were the motivating forces in history.

This shift from a Christian interpretation of history to a more secular approach was reflected in the change of leaders among American historians. Minister-historians were increasingly replaced by members of the patrician class—political leaders, planter-aristocrats, merchants, lawyers, and doctors.[2] In the eighteenth century, for example, America's outstanding historians included Thomas Hutchinson, member of the Massachusetts merchant aristocracy and royal governor of that colony; William Smith of New York, doctor, landowner, and lieutenant governor of that colony; and Robert Beverley and William Byrd of Virginia, who were planter-aristocrats, large landowners, and officeholders. Most of these men possessed a classical education, a fine private library, and the leisure time in which to write. With the growth of

---

[2]Harvey Wish, *The American Historian* (New York, 1960), p. 25.

private wealth and the opening up of new economic opportunities, more members of the upper classes were in a position to take up the writing of history as an avocation.[3]

The reaction against the Christian interpretation of history was particularly evident in the writings of Thomas Jefferson. In his *Notes on the State of Virginia*, first published in 1785, Jefferson stressed reason and natural law instead of divine providence as the basis for historical causation. Jefferson believed also that men were motivated by self-interest, and he employed this concept as one means of analyzing the course of historical events. As he wrote in his history of Virginia, "Mankind soon learn to make interested uses of every right and power which they possess, or may assume."

Jefferson's history showed the impact of yet another major influence—nationalism—which affected historical writing after 1776. As author of the Declaration of Independence, Jefferson felt a fierce, patriotic pride in the free institutions that emerged from the Revolution. He was convinced that America as a democratic nation was destined to pave the way for a new era in world history. A whole new generation of patrician historians sprang up after the Revolution, writing in a similar nationalistic vein—David Ramsay, Mercy Otis Warren, Jeremy Belknap, and Jared Sparks. They likewise contrasted America's free institutions with what they considered to be Europe's corrupt and decadent institutions.

During the first three quarters of the nineteenth century, the writing of history continued to be dominated by patrician historians. The influence of the romantic movement in the arts with its heightened appreciation of the past, emphasis upon pictorial descriptions, and stress upon the role of great men, caused history to be viewed increasingly as a branch of literature. Many outstanding literary figures—Washington Irving, Francis Parkman, Richard Hildreth, William H. Prescott, and John Lothrop Motley—wrote narrative histories about America, other lands, and other times, in a romantic style calculated to appeal to a wide reading public. Such authors were often part of a trans-Atlantic literary culture, for many English historians were writing in the same vein.

America's patrician historians, however, were not always content to provide only a colorful narrative. Writing within a developmental framework, they sought to reveal some of the underlying principles which they believed lay behind the rational evolution of historical events. For the most part, their writings reflected certain assumptions that were common to many historians on both sides of the Atlantic in the first half of the nineteenth century—the idea that history was essentially the story of liberty; that man's record revealed a progressive advance toward greater human rights down through the ages; and that peoples

---

[3]Higham, *History*, p. 3.

of Anglo-Saxon origin had a special destiny to bring democracy to the rest of the world.

Many of these American historians, influenced by the pronounced nationalism of the period, used such broad assumptions within a chauvinistic framework. They felt a responsibility to help establish the national identity of the new United States. Thus, they employed history as a didactic tool to instruct their countrymen along patriotic lines and presented America's story in the best light possible. Running through their writings were three basic themes: the idea of progress—that the story of America was one of continuous progress onward and upward toward greatness; the idea of liberty—that American history, in essence, symbolized the trend toward greater liberty in world history; and the idea of mission—that the United States had a special destiny to serve as a model of a free people to the rest of mankind in leading the way to a more perfect life. The last theme, in effect, was nothing more than a restatement of the idea of mission first set forth by the Puritan historians.

George Bancroft, the most distinguished historian of the mid-nineteenth century, organized his history of the United States around these three themes. After studying in Germany in the 1820s, Bancroft returned to America determined to apply Teutonic ideas of history to the story of his own country. Bancroft believed in the progressive unfolding of all human history toward a future golden age in which all men would eventually achieve complete freedom and liberty. This march of all mankind toward a greater freedom was in accordance with a preordained plan conceived by God. One phase of God's master plan could be seen in the way that a superior Anglo-Saxon people developed a distinctive set of democratic institutions. The United States, according to Bancroft, represented the finest flowering of such democratic institutions. American democracy, then, was the fruition of God's plan, and the American people had a unique mission in history to spread democracy throughout the rest of the world. Such was the central theme of Bancroft's famous twelve-volume work, *History of the United States from the Discovery of the American Continent*, written between 1834 and 1882.

Francis Parkman, a patrician historian from New England, held many views similar to those of Bancroft. Writing about the intercolonial wars in his work, *France and England in North America*, Parkman portrayed the American colonists as democratic Anglo-Saxons of Protestant persuasion whose superior qualities enabled them to conquer authoritarian-minded French Catholics in Canada. But in many other ways the two writers were quite different. Parkman was more representative of the gentlemen-historians of the nineteenth century who, being drawn from the upper classes, usually reflected an aristocratic bias in their writings, advocated a conservative Whig philosophy, and were distrustful of the American masses. Bancroft, on the other hand, eulogized the common man and was a Jacksonian in politics; his history was distinctly democratic in outlook.

By the 1870s two profound changes began to influence the writing of American history. The first was the change in leadership from amateur patricians to professional historians. Until the last quarter of the nineteenth century, American history had been written almost exclusively by men who had received no special training as historians—except, of course, for a few individuals like Bancroft. From this point on, however, the writing of history was dominated by professionally trained scholars educated in the universities of America and Europe. Professionalization in the field was made possible by developments in higher education as graduate schools appeared in increasing numbers in America to train college history teachers. In the last three decades of the century, this trend proceeded at a rapid rate: the Johns Hopkins University, the first institution devoted to graduate study and research, began its activities in 1876; the American Historical Association was founded in 1884; and the *American Historical Review* made its appearance in 1895.

The advent of professional historians brought about a marked transformation in the field. No longer was historical writing to be vested mainly in the hands of amateurs—though it should be emphasized that many patrician historians had been superb stylists, creative scholars, and researchers who made judicious use of original sources. Nor would historians be drawn almost exclusively from the patrician class in the Northeast, particularly from New England. Professional scholars came from all walks of life, represented a much broader range of social interests than the patricians, and hailed from different geographic regions. Finally, instead of being free-lance writers, as many patricians had been, professionals made their living as teachers in colleges and universities.

The second major development affecting the writing of American history was the emergence of a new intellectual milieu that reflected the growing dominance of novel scientific ideas and concepts. Influenced by Darwinian biology and its findings in the natural sciences, historians began to think of history as a science rather than as a branch of literature. Why couldn't the historian deal with the facts of history in much the same way that the scientist did with elements in the laboratory? If there were certain laws of organic development in the scientific field, might there not be certain laws of historical development? What historian, wrote Henry Adams, with "an idea of scientific method can have helped dreaming of the immortality that would be achieved by the man who should successfully apply Darwin's method to the facts of human history?"[4]

---

[4]Henry Adams, "The Tendency of History," *Annual Report of the American Historical Association for the Year 1894* (Washington, D.C., 1895), p. 19.

The first generation of professional historians—who held sway from about 1870–1910—was best exemplified by two outstanding scholars, Henry Adams and Frederick Jackson Turner. Henry Adams, a descendant of the famous Adams family that contributed American presidents, statesmen, and diplomats, turned to history and literature as his avocation after his hopes for high political office were dashed. In 1870 he was invited to Harvard and became the first teacher to introduce a history seminar at that institution. Adams pioneered in training his students in the meticulous critical methods of German scholarship, and searched for a time for a scientific philosophy of history based on the findings in the field of physics. His nine-volume history of the United States during the administrations of Jefferson and Madison was destined to become one of the classics of American historical literature. Although he left Harvard after a few years, his career symbolized the transformation from patrician to professional historian and the changing intellectual climate from romanticism to a more scientific approach in the writing of American history.

While Henry Adams was attempting to assimilate history and physics, Frederick Jackson Turner—perhaps the most famous and influential representative of the scientific school of historians in the first generation of professional historians—was applying evolutionary modes of thought to explain American history. Born and reared in a frontier community in Wisconsin, Turner attended the University of Wisconsin, received his Ph.D. from the Johns Hopkins University, and then went on to a teaching career first at Wisconsin and later at Harvard. Like Adams, Turner believed that it was possible to make a science out of history; he attempted, therefore, to apply the ideas of Darwinian evolution to the writing of history. Turner emphasized the concept of evolutionary stages of development as successive frontier environments in America wrought changes in the character of the people and their institutions. As one frontier in America succeeded another, each more remote from Europe than its predecessor, a social evolutionary process was at work creating a democratic American individualist. The unique characteristics of the American people—their rugged individualism, egalitarianism, practicality, and materialistic outlook on life—all resulted from the evolutionary process of adapting to successive frontier environments. Turner's famous essay "The Significance of the Frontier in American History," written in 1893, remains a superb statement of one approach that was employed by the scientific school of historians.

Between 1910 and 1945, a second generation of professional scholars—the Progressive historians—came to maturity and helped to transform the discipline by introducing new ideas and methodologies. Many of them were influenced by the Progressive movement of the early 1900s—a period when the future of American democracy appeared to be threatened by new economic and social forces arising from the rapid industrialization of American society. Rejecting the views of the older and more conservative patrician historians, the Progressive scholars viewed history as an ideological weapon that might explain the present and perhaps help to control the future. In sympathy with the aims and objectives of the Progressive movement between 1900 and 1920, these scholars continued to write history from a Progressive point of view even after the decline of the Progressive movement following the First World War.

Unlike the New England patrician historians of the nineteenth century, the Progressive scholars tended to hail more from the Midwest and South. These Progressives complained that in the past American history had been presented mainly as an extension of the history of New England. American civilization, they argued, was more than a transplanted English and European civilization that had spread out from New England; it had unique characteristics and a mission all its own. But while the Progressive historians were as nationalistic as the patrician school, their nationalism was different in nature. The patricians had conceived of nationalism as a stabilizing force, preserving order and thus assuring the continued ascendancy of the aristocratic element in American life. The Progressives, on the other hand, considered nationalism a dynamic force. To them the fulfillment of democracy meant a continued and protracted struggle against those individuals, classes, and groups who had barred the way to the achievements of a more democratic society in the past.

In changing the direction of American historical writing, Progressive scholars drew upon the reform tradition that had grown out of the effort to adjust American society to the new demands of an urban-centered and industrialized age. This tradition had originated in the 1890s and reached maturity in the early part of the twentieth century with the Progressive movement. Drawing upon various sources, the adherents of the Progressive movement rejected the idea of a closed system of classical economic thought which assumed that certain natural laws governed human society. Society, these reformers maintained, was open-ended and dynamic; its development was determined not by immutable laws, but by economic and social forces that grew out of the interaction between the individual and his environment.

Reacting against the older emphasis upon logic, abstraction, and deduction, these reformers sought a meaningful explanation of human society that could account for its peculiar development. Instead of focusing upon immutable laws, they began viewing society and individuals as products of an evolutionary developmental process. This process could be understood only by reference to the past. The function of the historian, then, was to explain how the present had come to be, and then to try and set guidelines for future developments. As a result of this approach, history and the other social sciences drew together, seeking to explain the realities of social life by emphasizing the interplay of economic, technological, social, psychological, and political forces.

History, according to its Progressive practitioners, was not an abstract discipline whose truths could only be contemplated. On the contrary, historians had important activist roles to play in the construction of a better world. By explaining the historical roots of contemporary problems, historians could provide the knowledge and understanding necessary to make changes which would bring further progress. Like the Enlightenment *philosophes*, historians could reveal prior mistakes and errors, and thus liberate men from the chains of tyranny and oppression of the past. When fused with the social sciences, history could become a powerful tool for reform. "The present has hitherto been the willing victim of the past," wrote James Harvey Robinson, one of the greatest exponents of Progressive history; but "the time has now come when it should turn on the past and exploit it in the interests of advance."[5]

Clearly, the sympathy of this school lay with change and not with the preservation of the status quo. Committed to the idea of progress, they saw themselves as contributing to a better and more humane world for the future. Consequently, they rejected the apparent moral neutrality and supposed objectivity of the scientific school in favor of a liberal philosophy of reform. In so doing, they rewrote much of American history, greatly widening its scope and changing its emphasis. Instead of focusing on narrow institutional studies of traditional political, diplomatic, and military history, they sought to delineate those determinant forces that underlay human institutions. In their hands American history became a picture of conflict—conflict between polarities of American life: aristocracy versus democracy; economic "haves" versus "have-nots"; politically overprivileged groups versus those underprivileged; and between geographical sections, as the East versus West. In short, the divisions were between those dedicated to democratic and egalitarian ideals and those committed to a static conservatism.

Believers in inevitable progress, the Progressive historians assumed that America was continually moving on an upward path toward an ideal social order. Not only was American society growing in affluence, but in freedom, opportunity, and happiness as well. The primary determinant of progress was the unending conflict between the forces of liberalism and those of conservatism. Thus all periods in American history could be divided into two clear and distinct phases: periods of active reform and periods of conservative reaction. As Arthur M. Schlesinger,

---

[5]James Harvey Robinson, "The New History," *The New History: Essays Illustrating the Modern Historical Outlook* (New York, 1912), p. 24.

Sr., wrote in 1939: "A period of concern for the rights of the few has been followed by one of concern for the wrongs of the many."[6]

Turner, a transitional figure between the scientific and Progressive historians, with Charles A. Beard and Vernon L. Parrington best presented the Progressive point of view. After his epochal essay on the frontier in 1893—an essay that emphasized unity rather than conflict— Turner's interest turned elsewhere, particularly to the idea of sectional conflict. From the late 1890s until his death in 1932, he elaborated and refined his sectional conflict hypothesis. Turner and his students attempted to understand not only how a section came into being, but also the dynamics of conflict that pitted the East against West, North against South, labor against capital, and the many against the few. Under Turner's guiding hand, American scholars wrote a series of brilliant monographs as well as broad interpretive studies that emphasized the class and sectional divisions in American society. Although a few favored the conservative side, the overwhelming majority of historians made clear their preference for democratic liberalism and progress.

While Turner was developing and elaborating his sectional approach, Charles A. Beard was applying the hypothesis of an overt class conflict to the study of American institutions. His book, *An Economic Interpretation of the Constitution,* written in 1913, was perhaps the most influential historical work of the twentieth century. Beard attempted to demonstrate that the Constitution, far from representing a judicious combination of wisdom and idealism, was actually the product of a small group of propertied individuals who were intent upon establishing a strong central government capable of protecting their interests against the encroachments of the American masses. In a series of books, climaxed by *The Rise of American Civilization* in 1927, Beard argued that American history demonstrated the validity of the class conflict hypothesis between "haves" and "have-nots." Time and again, he showed the paramount role that economic factors played in determining human behavior. Fusing his ardent faith in progress with a qualified economic determinism, Beard made clear that his sympathies lay with the forces of democracy as opposed to those of reaction and privilege.

The culmination of the Progressive interpretation came with the publication of Vernon L. Parrington's *Main Currents in American Thought.* Using literature as his vehicle, Parrington portrayed American history in clear and unmistakable terms. The two central protagonists of Parrington's work were Jefferson and Hamilton. Jefferson stood for a decentralized agrarian democracy that drew its support from the great masses of people. Hamilton, on the other hand, represented a privileged and aristocratic minority seeking to maintain its dominant position. Ameri-

---

[6]Arthur M. Schlesinger, Sr., "Tides of American Politics," *Yale Review* 29 (December 1939):220.

can history, according to Parrington, had witnessed a continual struggle between the liberal Jeffersonian tradition and the conservative Hamiltonian one. Underlying Parrington's approach was one major assumption that had also governed the thought of Turner and Beard, namely, that ideology was determined by the materialistic forces in history. Like Turner and Beard, Parrington clearly preferred the forces of reform and democracy, but there were times when he was much less certain of their eventual triumph than his two intellectual companions.

The Progressive point of view generally dominated the field of American historical scholarship down to the end of World War II. Class and sectional conflict, Progressive historians implied, was a guarantor of progress. Even during those eras in American history when the forces of reaction triumphed—as in the post–Civil War period—their victory was only temporary; ultimately the forces of progress and good regrouped and thereby gained the initiative once again. Such an approach, of course, led to broad and sweeping interpretive syntheses of American history, for the basic framework or structure was clear and simple, and the faith of historians in the ultimate triumph of good over evil remained unquestioned.

Beginning in the 1930s, however, some American scholars began to question the idea of progress that was implicit in this view. The rise of Nazism in the 1930s and 1940s, and the menace of communism in the 1950s and 1960s, led to a questioning of older assumptions and generalities. How, some asked, could one subscribe to the optimistic tenets of liberalism after the horrors of Auschwitz, Buchenwald, Hiroshima, Nagasaki, and the threat of modern totalitarianism? Indeed, had not American historians, through their own optimistic view of history and their faith in progress, failed to prepare the American people for the challenges and trials that they would face during the middle of the twentieth century? Parrington himself had recognized as early as 1929 that the Progressive faith was under attack by those who did not subscribe to its basic tenets. "Liberals whose hair is growing thin and the lines of whose figures are no longer what they were," he wrote, "are likely to find themselves today in the unhappy predicament of being treated as mourners at their own funerals. When they pluck up heart to assert that they are not yet authentic corpses, but living men with brains in their heads, they are pretty certain to be gently chided and led back to the comfortable armchair that befits senility. Their counsel is smiled at as the chatter of a belated post-Victorian generation that knew not Freud, and if they must go abroad they are bidden take the air in the garden where other old-fashioned plants—mostly of the family *Democratici*—are still preserved."[7]

---

[7]Vernon L. Parrington, *Main Currents in American Thought*, 3 vols. (New York, 1927–1930), 3:401.

Following the end of World War II, a third generation of professional historians appeared on the scene to challenge the Progressive point of view. They were sometimes called neoconservatives because they seemed to hark back to the conservative historical position that had prevailed prior to Turner and Beard. Their rise was partly a result of pressures—both external and internal—upon the historical profession in the postwar era.

External pressures resulting from changing political conditions in the world at large brought about a major change in the mood of many Americans. Some neoconservative historians reflected, either consciously or unconsciously, an outlook that prevailed in the United States as the nation assumed the sober responsibility of defending the world against the threat of communism. During the Cold War era, when the country felt its security endangered from abroad, these scholars wanted, perhaps, to present an image to the rest of the world of an America that had been strong and united throughout most of its history. Hence, the neoconservative scholars pictured American history in terms of consensus rather than conflict.

Internal pressures within the profession itself likewise brought changes. Particular points of view expressed in any academic discipline seem to have an inner dynamism of their own. After subscribing to a given interpretation for a time, scholars often sense that they have pushed an idea to its outermost limits and can go no farther without risking major distortion. A reaction inevitably sets in, and revisionists begin working in a different direction. Such was the case of the Progressive interpretation of history. Having written about American history from the standpoint of conflict and discontinuity, scholars now began to approach the same subject from an opposite point of view—that of consensus and continuity.

One way this new group of scholars differed from the Progressives was in their inherent conservatism. Progressive historians had had a deep belief in the idea of progress. Neoconservative historians, on the other hand, often rejected progress as an article of faith. Skeptical of the alleged beneficial results of rapid social change, they stressed instead the thesis of historical continuity.

Given their emphasis on continuity, the neoconservatives were less prone to a periodized view of American history. Progressive scholars had seen American history in terms of class or sectional conflicts marked by clearly defined turning points—the Revolution, the Constitution, the Jeffersonian era, the Jacksonian period, the Civil War, and so forth. These periods represented breaks, or discontinuities, from what had gone on before. For the Progressives, American history was divided into two distinct phases that followed one another in a cyclical pattern: periods of reform or revolution when the popular and democratic forces in society gained the upper hand and forced social changes, and periods of reaction and counterrevolution, when vested interests resisted such changes. For the neoconservative scholars, however, the enduring and unifying themes in history were much more significant. To them the continuity of common principles in American culture, the stability and longevity of institutions, and the persistence of certain traits and traditions in the American national character represented the most powerful forces in history.

Consensus, as well as continuity, was a characteristic theme of the neoconservative historians. Unlike the Progressives, who wrote about the past in terms of polarities—class conflicts between rich and poor, sectional divisions between North and South or East and West, and ideological differences between liberals and conservatives—the neoconservatives abandoned the conflict interpretation of history and favored instead one that viewed American society as stable and homogeneous. The cement that bound American society together throughout most of its history was a widespread acceptance of certain principles and beliefs. Americans, despite their differences, had always agreed on the following propositions: the right of all persons in society to own private property; the theory that the power of government should always be limited; the concept that men possessed certain natural rights that could not be taken from them by government; and the idea of some form of natural law.

One of the foremost neoconservative historians writing in the 1950s was Louis Hartz. In his book, *The Liberal Tradition in America*, Hartz took issue with those Progressive historians who had viewed the American Revolution as a radical movement that fundamentally transformed American society. America had come into being after the age of feudalism, Hartz claimed, and this condition had profoundly shaped its development. Lacking a feudal past, the country did not have to contend with the established feudal structure that characterized the *ancien régime* in Europe—a titled aristocracy, national church, national army, and the like. Hence, America was "born free" and did not require a radical social revolution to become a liberal society—it was one already. What emerged in America, according to Hartz, was a unique society characterized by a consensus upon a single tradition of thought—the liberal tradition. The absence of a feudal heritage enabled the liberal-bourgeois ideas embodied in the political principles derived from John Locke to flourish in America almost unchallenged. "The ironic flaw in American liberalism," wrote Hartz, "lies in the fact that we have never had a conservative tradition."[8]

What, then, of the "conservatives" in American history about whom

---

[8]Louis Hartz, *The Liberal Tradition in America* (New York, 1955), p. 57.

the Progressive scholars had written? When viewed within the context of comparative history, Hartz said, American conservatives had much more in common with their fellow American liberals than with their European counterparts. Many of the presumed differences between so-called American "conservatives" and "liberals" was in the nature of shadow-boxing rather than actual fighting, he concluded, because both groups agreed on a common body of liberal political principles. The Federalists, for example, were not aristocrats but whiggish liberals who misunderstood their society; they misread the Jeffersonian Democrats as being "radicals" rather than recognizing them as fellow liberals. What was true of the Federalists and Jeffersonians held for the other political confrontations in American history; if measured in terms of a spectrum of thought that included European ideologies, the American conflicts took place within the confines of a Lockean consensus.

Daniel J. Boorstin, another major neoconservative historian, also offered a grand theory which pictured American history in terms of continuity and consensus. Boorstin, like Hartz, stressed the uniqueness of American society, but he attributed this development to other causes. A neo-Turnerian, Boorstin postulated an environmental explanation of the American national character. To him the frontier experience was the source of America's conservatism.

In two books written in the 1950s—*The Genius of American Politics* and *The Americans: The Colonial Experience*—Boorstin denied the significance of European influences and ideas upon American life. Boorstin's premise was that the Americans were not an "idea-centered" people. From the very beginning Americans had abandoned European political theories, European blueprints for utopian societies, and European concepts of class distinctions. Americans concerned themselves instead with concrete situations and the practical problems experienced by their frontier communities. Thus, they developed little knack for theorizing or any deep interest in theories as such. The "genius of American politics" lay in its emphasis on pragmatic matters—its very distrust of theories that had led to radical political changes and deep divisions within European societies.[9]

The American way of life which evolved during the colonial period, wrote Boorstin, set the pattern for the nation's later development. That pattern placed a premium on solutions to practical problems, adaptations to changing circumstances, and improvisations based upon pragmatic considerations. Lacking a learned class or professional traditions,

---

[9]Daniel J. Boorstin, *The Genius of American Politics* (Chicago, 1953) and *The Americans: The Colonial Experience* (New York, 1958). Boorstin further elaborated on his views in two more volumes: *The Americans: The National Experience* (New York, 1965) and *The Americans: The Democratic Experience* (New York, 1973).

the colonists were forced to create their own ways of doing things in the areas of education, law, medicine, science, diplomacy, and warfare. During this process the "doer" dominated over the "thinker" and the generalist over the specialist. Over the course of time, this nontheoretical approach developed into a distinctive American life style—one characterized by a naive practicality that enabled Americans to unite in a stable way of life and to become a homogeneous society made up of undifferentiated men sharing the same values.

The "cult of the 'American Consensus,'" as one scholar called it, made the nation's past appear tame and placid; it was no longer a history marked by extreme group conflicts or rigid class distinctions.[10] The heroes in America's past—Jefferson, Lincoln, Wilson, and Franklin D. Roosevelt—became less heroic because there occurred no head-on clash between individuals on the basis of ideology since all Americans shared the same middle-class Lockean values. Conversely, the old villains— Hamilton, Rockefeller, and Carnegie—became less evil and were portrayed as constructive figures who contributed much to their country. The achievements of the business community in particular were glorified. Without the material achievements of American entrepreneurs, according to some scholars, the United States could not have withstood the challenges to democracy during World War I and World War II. The underdogs in American history—the reformers, radicals, and working class—were presented as being less idealistic and more egocentric as neoconservative scholars sought to demonstrate that the ideology of these elements in society was no less narrow and self-centered than that of other elements. The "cult" of the neoconservatives continued into the 1960s—though "cult" was perhaps too strong a term, and implied a unanimity rarely found in the historical profession.

Besides Boorstin and Hartz, other neoconservative scholars published specialized studies which revised the Progressive point of view in virtually every period of American history. The neoconservative trend, marked by a new respect for tradition and a de-emphasis on class conflict, brought many changes in American historiography: the revival of a sympathetic approach to the Puritans; the treatment of the American Revolution as a conservative movement of less significance; the conclusion that the Constitution was a document faithfully reflecting a middle-class consensus; the favorable, if not uncritical, attitude toward the founding fathers of the new republic; the diminution of the traditional ideological differences between Hamiltonianism and Jeffersonianism; the consensus interpretation of the Jacksonian era; the enhanced reputation of America's business tycoons; a renewed apprecia-

---

[10]John Higham, "The Cult of the 'American Consensus': Homogenizing Our History," *Commentary* (February 1959): pp. 93–100.

tion of such controversial political leaders as Theodore Roosevelt; the inclination to play down the more radical aspects of the Progressive and New Deal periods; the predisposition to support the correctness of America's recent foreign policy; and the tendency to view American society as being satisfied, unified, and stable throughout most of the nation's history. Implicit in the neoconservative approach was a fear of extremism, a yearning to prove that national unity had almost always existed, and a longing for the security and way of life America presumably had enjoyed before becoming a superpower and leader of the free world.

During the decades of the 1960s and 1970s, the assumptions and conclusions of the neoconservative historians were rudely overturned by two major developments. First, the mood of the American people shifted markedly as the seemingly placid decade of the 1950s was succeeded by tumultuous events in America's foreign and domestic affairs. Second, within the historical profession itself a reaction to the neoconservative point of view led to the rise of many revisionist interpretations. The result was a pronounced fragmentation in the field of American historiography.

The prevailing mood among the American people shifted dramatically in the 1960s and 1970s because of a series of shattering events on the domestic scene. Gone were the complacency, national self-confidence, optimism, and moral composure that seemed to have characterized the 1950s. Many historians were stirred by the great social upheavals that undermined previously held assumptions. A marked trend toward racial divisions within American society appeared with the newfound militancy among blacks during the civil rights movement. The resulting hostility to integration among many whites showed that American society was hardly as homogeneous as had been previously believed. At the same time, an increased tendency toward violence during the urban riots in the 1960s indicated that Americans were not always committed to the idea of peaceful compromise. President Kennedy's assassination in 1963 followed by that of Martin Luther King and Robert Kennedy revealed that the United States was as vulnerable to political terrorism as other societies. There was also a renewed awareness of poverty with the economic downturn in the 1970s, and some scholars began voicing doubts about the supposed social mobility within American society, the virtues of technological change, and the benefits of economic growth.

The appearance of numerous social-protest movements during those two decades also made many American historians more conscious of the importance of minority groups in the nation's past. Having witnessed protest movements by the blacks, the poor, and the women's liberation movement, some scholars took a greater interest in black history, women's history, and to protest groups like the Populists and IWW. Generally speaking, historians became more sympathetic to the role of the underdog in American history.

Changes in America's foreign affairs during these decades similarly had a profound effect on the writing of history. The Vietnam War, above all, divided the American people. Students participated in large-scale antiwar demonstrations, and college campuses were transformed into centers of political protest and activism. Many intellectuals grew disenchanted with the government's military policy and became increasingly suspicious of the political establishment in general. The Vietnam War also exposed the dangers of what one historian termed the imperial presidency. President Nixon and the Watergate scandal revealed further the threat posed to constitutional government by this concept of the presidency. As some historians grew more critical of America's foreign policy, they began to question the credibility of the government both in the present and past.

During the course of the 1960s and 1970s, scholars were affected also by sweeping intellectual changes within the historical profession itself. Some began by challenging the traditional approach to history—one that assumed the discipline was separate and self-contained. Acting on the premise that the other social sciences—psychology, sociology, anthropology, and political science—could contribute to the study of history, they turned more to an interdisciplinary approach. In doing so, these historians applied concepts, laws, and models from other social sciences in order to understand the conduct of individuals and social groups in the past. This interdisciplinary approach could hardly be called new for it had been employed during the first half of the twentieth century. Still, there was a stronger tendency among scholars to apply social science techniques during these two decades.

A second major development was the use of new methodological approaches to the study of history. Some historians began relying more on quantitative techniques in their efforts to derive scientifically measurable historical data to document their studies. Other scholars turned to a comparative history approach—comparing entire societies or segments of societies—to illuminate the American past. Quantitative and comparative history were but two of a number of methodological approaches which were employed with greater frequency in the 1960s and 1970s.

It was within this general context that there arose a significant challenge to the neoconservative historians in the 1960s from a group of younger radical scholars known as the New Left. Like the older Progressives, these historians sought to fuse historical scholarship with political activism, and might be called "neo-Progressives." Unlike the neoconservatives who emphasized consensus, continuity, and stability, the New Left saw social and economic conflict as the major theme in

American history. Of all historians, the individuals identified with the New Left were the most disenchanted with the course of events in recent American history. As a result they presented a radical critique of American society and took a more jaundiced view of the American past.

These scholars reinterpreted American history along more radical lines and insisted that their colleagues pay far greater attention to the lower classes and minority groups of all kinds. Members of the New Left were exceedingly critical in particular, of those neoconservative scholars who tended to celebrate the virtues and achievements of the American people. Because the neoconservatives had excluded conflict in their interpretation, the New Left argued, the American people were unprepared to cope with the social upheavals that occurred in the 1960s. These younger historians declared that the resort to violence by social groups to achieve their goals was a theme that had deep roots in the American past. The New Left historians sought to create a "usable past"—a history that would account for the country's social problems such as racism, militarism, economic exploitation, and imperialism, and would serve as the basis for reforming American society. American history had too often been written from "the top down"—that is, from the point of view of elites and the articulate like Washington, Lincoln, and Franklin D. Roosevelt. History, they argued, should be written "from the bottom up," a perspective which would reflect the concerns of the common people, the inarticulate masses, and nonelites. Viewing history in this way, scholars would discover the radicalism inherent in the American past.

In their treatment of America's foreign policy, for example, the New Left developed a much more critical interpretation than previous historians. America from its beginnings, they argued, had been an aggressive, expansionist, and imperialist nation. It expanded first at the expense of the Indians, and then later at the expense of its weaker neighbors like Mexico. The United States turned subsequently to an overseas imperialist foreign policy based on its need for foreign markets, raw materials, and investment opportunities. This expansionist foreign policy had global ramifications, the New Left claimed. America had played a major role in precipitating two world wars and was primarily responsible for bringing about the Cold War. The Vietnam War, according to the New Left, was simply a logical extension of America's aggressive and expansionist foreign policy.

The New Left view of American history never attained the importance or cohesion of either the Progressive or the neoconservative interpretation. One reason was that few Americans were prepared to accept either the analysis or the solutions proposed by these radical historians. Another was that the American withdrawal from Vietnam and the economic downturn of the 1970s brought a halt to most radical protest movements. Although New Left scholarship failed to develop the potential many had expected of it, some of its insights and concerns were absorbed by nonradical historians seeking to break out of the mold and limitations of the neoconservative approach of the 1950s.

A more significant challenge to both the neoconservatives and the older Progressive scholars was the "new social history" of the 1960s and 1970s. This group of scholars, in general, were concerned with defining the nature of America's social structure and its changes over time. They were called the "new social historians" to distinguish them from the old social historians who had been occupied primarily with descriptive and narrative history which dealt with the manners and mores of the common people.

The "new social historians" criticized both the neoconservatives and Progressives for their choice of subject matter and use of evidence. These historians claimed that previous scholars had focused too narrowly upon political, diplomatic, and institutional matters. Older scholars, moreover, were interested in describing isolated historical events. The "new social historians" hoped to widen the scope of history by showing that the relationship between social, economic, and political events inevitably involved changes in the social structure.

These scholars claimed also that earlier historians had sometimes made generalizations based on vague and limited evidence. Historical evidence, according to the "new social historians," should be more precise and approached in a more scientific manner. If at all possible, evidence should be expressed in quantifiable terms so that it might be measured to provide a greater degree of precision. It should be subjected also to systematic analysis in order to test broad conceptual hypotheses about human behavior advanced by the other social sciences. Their hope for history was likewise more ambitious than that of their predecessors. They aimed to create a "new social history" that would illuminate America's social structure and explain social change throughout all of American history.

The growing interest of American historians in the "new social history" was the result of several influences. First, French scholars since the 1930s had been moving away from narrow political and institutional studies and raising new questions which employed novel methodologies. The most significant outlet for the work of these European scholars was the *Annales*, a French publication. The aim of this distinguished journal was to break down the traditional disciplinary barriers and to create a new and unified approach to the understanding of the totality of human activity within a given society or geographical region. Under the editorship of two French scholars, Lucien Febvre and Marc Bloch, the *Annales* became the acknowledged leader in creating the new field of social history or historical sociology. Continuing its innovative beginnings after World War II, the *Annales* increasingly served scholars employing quantitative and demographic techniques, or resorting to multidisciplinary approaches. Slowly but surely, the influence of this French scholarship made itself felt in the United States.

A second influence shaping the "new social history" was the proliferation of work in the social and behavioral sciences after World War II on contemporary problems that vitally affected the lives of many Americans. Among these were included the issue of race relations, family problems, patterns of social and geographical mobility, crime, and educational as well as economic opportunities. Inevitably American historians began to examine the historical roots and antecedents of these social problems.

The final influence was the increased use of the computer and new quantitative techniques which permitted these newer scholars to analyze historical evidence from heretofore unusable sources. Before the advent of the computer, scholars found it difficult, if not impossible, to collect and analyze massive amounts of data. Historians, for instance, were now able to make use of the manuscript census schedules which formed the basis for the published federal and state censuses. These census schedules, which provided much information about individuals and households in the past, had remained unused for the most part because of problems encountered in reducing such a mass of discrete bits of information to usable form. Computer technology made it possible to gather and manipulate these data, while new quantitative techniques enabled researchers to analyze the information in more meaningful ways.

Although the "new social historians" were more or less unified in their desire to examine social structure and social change, their approaches to these problems led them in many different directions. The fragmentation characteristic of American history in general during this period was especially true among these scholars. It manifested itself in the appearance of a number of separate groups of historians who focused upon specific problems all of which came under the general heading of the "new social history."

The so-called "new economic historians" were among the first to employ quantitative techniques and computer technology. Their outstanding characteristic was the use of historical data to test hypotheses derived from economic theories. One of their main interests was to describe and explain the patterns of America's economic growth. They hoped also to identify in a more precise manner the forces that had shaped the complex pattern of the economy, the role of entrepreneurs, and the development of different kinds of labor groups and systems.

The "new political historians" represented another fragment group. These scholars were especially influenced by the behavioral approach of the political scientists. Unlike earlier scholars, these newer historians were less concerned with describing presidential elections and political developments in traditional terms. These scholars were interested instead in quantitative analyses of voting behavior, roll-call analyses of legislatures, and shifts in public opinion on political issues. In studying political behavior, they introduced new techniques for the collection and measurement of data, and developed and refined concepts for analyzing the political process. In doing so, they moved political history closer to social history by seeking to portray the social bases of political behavior.

Yet a third group consisted of the "new urban historians" who studied many processes that occurred within a city setting. These scholars examined such diverse topics as the process of urbanization, growth of suburbs, development of neighborhoods, educational systems, and the rise of political bosses and machines. In approaching these topics, these scholars also made use of computer technology and quantitative techniques to analyze new sources such as manuscript census schedules, city directories, and municipal records. At the same time, many of them resorted to multidisciplinary approaches which drew heavily from concepts of the social and behavioral sciences.

These three groups represent only a few of the new departures undertaken by the "new social historians." In their attempts to understand the American social structure and social change over time, still other scholars in this tradition turned to demography—the study of population in terms of statistical analyses of rates of births, deaths, and marriages. Many of these demographic studies focused upon the family and the community as units of analysis, and led to the establishment of two subfields within the "new social history"—family history and community studies. Others examined the experiences of ethnic and racial groups, giving rise to what was sometimes called an ethnocultural approach to American history. Still others turned to a study of the social, economic, and geographical patterns of mobility in order to identify the conditions that led to success or failure within American society.

Concern with social structure and social change led also to a greater interest in previously neglected social groups. In researching the history of welfare and dependency, scholars studied the ways American society had responded to these groups. The means of caring for the poor, the unemployed, the sick and infirm, the insane, and the aged were subjected to close scrutiny. This interest was accompanied by a corresponding concern for the history of crime and delinquency as historians sought to deal with the experiences of the less fortunate and less successful elements in American society.

The fragmentation of American history so obvious in the many manifestations of the "new social history" was marked by the emergence of four approaches to the discipline which continued along more traditional lines. First of all, as mentioned previously, the old Progressive tradition was continued after World War II by the group of historians called "neo-Progressives." These scholars, including the New Left and others, approached the study of American history in ways similar to the older tradition but modified the Progressive interpretation in many ways.

Another development along similar lines was the extension of the work of Perry Miller and other older intellectual historians into the post–World War II era by the so-called "new intellectual historians." Like Miller and others, these more recent scholars placed more emphasis on analyzing rather than describing ideas. Many of these historians reflected a different orientation from the Progressives because they stressed the primacy of ideas as determinants in history.

The two other developments—comparative history and the organizational school of scholars—likewise represented a continuation of the more traditional approaches to history. The comparative historians usually studied the histories of two or more countries in search of similarities or dissimilarities in national experiences. At other times they compared ideas and concepts like *democracy, nationalism,* or *imperialism* to discover to what extent these concepts were the same or different within diverse historical settings. The organizational school of scholars, on the other hand, developed new syntheses to explain American history since the advent of industrialism. They regarded the rise of bureaucratic structures in society and the acceleration in professionalization as the most significant influences shaping American life since the closing of the frontier in the 1890s. These scholars emphasized that the behavior of individuals might be better understood when seen within an organizational context.

What have been the effects of fragmentation within the discipline of history during the 1960s and 1970s? For one thing, it has prevented the rise of any new major synthesis comparable to that of the neoconservative or the older Progressive interpretations. Diversity and disagreement characterized the historical profession as the decade of the 1970s came to a close. Scholars could only agree that America's past was infinitely more varied and complex than earlier generations of historians had imagined. It may well be that the writing of American history in the future—given the diverse social backgrounds and varied interests of its practitioners—may never again attain the degree of unity it sometimes had achieved in the past.

Another effect of fragmentation has been the pronounced trend toward overspecialization. To be sure, greater specialization has resulted in the proliferation of historical works, and led to new methodologies and more sophisticated interpretations. At the same time, however, it has caused some historians to divorce artifically the "new economic history" from traditional political history and the "new social history" from intellectual history. Overspecialization, moreover, has posed a problem for those scholars seeking to maintain the integrity of the discipline as a whole.

Fragmentation was also evident in the concept of *community* recently employed by some historians. Many current scholars seemed to agree that their neoconservative predecessors had overemphasized national unity and consensus throughout American history. As scholars de-emphasized consensus, it might have been expected that they would return to conflict as a major theme. A number of historians applied instead the concept of community within different contexts in order to understand how certain institutions might have served to bring about greater cohesion and unity in a pluralistic nation. John Higham noted in the mid-1970s that the "exciting advances in contemporary scholarship have more to do with understanding cohesive structures: the New England town, the family, the ethnic subculture, the professional and trade associations, the political machines." Higham went on to warn, however, that the study of these different kinds of communities could lead to an even more fragmented view of America's past.[11]

To sum up, this introduction has postulated two major assumptions regarding the writing of American history: that "every true history is contemporary history" because external pressures of contemporary events have tended to color to some degree the view of scholars writing about the past; and that scholars have been affected also by internal pressures within the historical profession itself which led them to re-evaluate and revise their points of view periodically. If these premises were valid in the past, we may be certain that our view of American history is destined to undergo changes in the future.

[11]John Higham, "Hanging Together: Divergent Unities in American History," *Journal of American History* 61 (June 1974):5.

2

The Reconstruction Era

Constructive or Destructive?

To students of American history, the Civil War years stand in sharp contrast to those of the Reconstruction era. The war years represented a period of heroism and idealism; out of the travail of conflict there emerged a new American nationality that replaced the older sectional and state loyalties. Although the cost in lives and money was frightful, the divisions that had plagued Americans for over half a century were eliminated in the ordeal of fire. Henceforth, America would stand as a united country, destined to take its rightful place as one of the leading nations in the world.

The Reconstruction era, on the other hand, conjures up a quite different picture. Just as the war years were dominated by heroism, the postwar period was characterized as being dominated by evil, power-seeking scoundrels intent upon pursuing their narrow self-interest regardless of the cost to either the South or the nation. The result was a tragedy for all Americans—Northerners, Southerners, whites and blacks alike. Nothing short of a revolution, it seemed, could displace the forces of evil from power and restore the South and the nation to its rightful rulers.

Between 1890 and 1930 few historians would have disagreed with this contrast of the two periods. If anything, most scholars during these years characterized Reconstruction in even harsher terms. Led by Professor William A. Dunning of Columbia University—who literally founded the school of Reconstruction historiography that still bears his name—the historical profession set out to prove that the years following the Civil War were marked by tragedy and pathos because men of good will were momentarily thrust out of power by the forces of evil. This period, in the words of one historian, "were years of revolutionary turmoil.... The prevailing note was one of tragedy.... Never have American public men in responsible positions, directing the destiny of the Nation, been so brutal, hypocritical, and corrupt.... The Southern people literally were put to the torture."[1]

---

[1]Claude G. Bowers, *The Tragic Era: The Revolution After Lincoln* (Cambridge, 1929), pp. v–vi.

Underlying the interpretation of the Dunning school were two important assumptions. The first was that the South should have been restored to the Union quickly and without being exposed to Northern vengeance. Most Southerners, it was argued, had accepted their military defeat gracefully and were prepared to pledge their good faith and loyalty to the Union. Secondly, responsibility for the freedmen should have been entrusted to white Southerners. Blacks, these historians believed, could never be integrated into American society on an equal plane with whites because of their former slave status and inferior racial characteristics.

Working within the framework of these two assumptions, historians in the Dunning school tradition proceeded to study Reconstruction in terms of a struggle between elements of good and evil. On one side stood the forces of good—Northern and Southern Democrats and Republicans of the Andrew Johnson variety. These men, recognizing the necessity for compassion and leniency, were willing to forget the agonies of war and to forgive the South. On the opposing side were the forces of evil—scalawags, carpetbaggers, and above all, a group of radical and vindictive Republicans intent upon punishing the South by depriving the native aristocracy of their power and status, thereby ensuring the dominance of the Republican party in that section. Caught in the middle of this struggle were the helpless, impotent, and ignorant blacks, whose votes were sought for sinister purposes by Radical Republicans who had little or not real concern for the welfare of the freedman once he had left the ballot box.

The result of such a political alignment in the South, according to the Dunning school, was disastrous. The Radical carpetbag state governments that came into power proved to be totally incompetent—in part because they included illiterate blacks who were unprepared for the responsibilities of self-government. Still worse, these governments were extraordinarily expensive because they were corrupt. Most of them, indeed, left nothing but a legacy of huge debts. "Saddled with an irresponsible officialdom," one Dunning school historian concluded, "the South was now plunged into debauchery, corruption, and private plundering unbelievable—suggesting that government had been transformed into an engine of destruction."[2]

The decent whites in the South, the Dunning argument continued, united out of sheer desperation to force the carpetbaggers, scalawags, and blacks from power. In one state after another Radical rule was eventually overthrown and good government restored. By the time of the presidential campaign of 1876 only three states remained under Radical

---

[2]E. Merton Coulter, *The South During Reconstruction 1865–1877* (Baton Rouge, 1947), p. 148.

control. When the dispute over the contested election was resolved, Hayes withdrew the remaining federal troops from the South, and the three last Radical regimes fell from power. Thus the tragic era of Reconstruction came to an end.

For nearly three decades after the turn of the century the Dunning point of view was dominant among most American historians. Many monographs on the history of individual Southern states were published, but most of them simply filled in pertinent details and left the larger picture virtually unchanged. All of these studies, despite their individual differences, agreed that the Reconstruction period had been an abject and dismal failure. Not only had Reconstruction destroyed the two-party system in the South; it had left behind an enduring legacy of bitterness and hatred between the races.

The first selection by Albert B. Moore is a good example of a historian writing about Reconstruction within the Dunning tradition. The events between 1865 and 1877, Moore argues, had the effect of converting the South into a colonial appendage of the North. To put it another way, the Reconstruction period was simply one phase of the process whereby the North attempted to remake the South in its own image; it was an attempt by a victor to punish the vanquished. Rejecting completely the assertion that the North was lenient, Moore emphasizes property confiscations, mental torture, and vindictive military rule. The political enfranchisement of blacks, which laid the basis for carpetbag government, is to Moore perhaps the most incredible event of an incredible era. The result was the continued exacerbation of Southern economic, political, and social problems. The South, he concludes, was still paying for the dark legacy of Reconstruction in the twentieth century.

In the late 1920s, however, historians began to look at the events between 1865 and 1877 from a new and different perspective. These revisionists—a term that distinguishes them from followers of the Dunning school—were much less certain that Reconstruction was as bad as had been commonly supposed. Influenced by the Progressive school of American historiography—which emphasized underlying economic factors in historical development—the revisionists began to restudy the entire Reconstruction period. As a result, they posed a sharp challenge to the Dunning school by changing the interpretive framework of the Reconstruction era.

Generally speaking, the revisionists accepted most, if not all, of the findings of the Dunning school. The disagreement between the two groups, therefore, arose from their different starting assumptions and the consequent interpretation of data rather than over disputed empirical data as such. Unlike the Dunningites, the revisionists could not view events between 1865 and 1877 in terms of a morality play that depicted Reconstruction as a struggle between good and evil, white and black, and Democrats and Radical Republicans. Nor were the revisionists will-ing to accept the view that responsibility for the freedmen should have been entrusted to native white Southerners. Given these differences, it was understandable that the revisionist interpretation should differ sharply from that of the Dunning school.

In 1939 Francis B. Simkins, a distinguished Southern historian who published with Robert Woody in 1932 one of the first revisionist studies, summed up some of the findings of the revisionist school. Pointing out that the overwhelming majority of Southerners lived quietly and peace-fully during these years, he emphasized many of the constructive achievements of this era. Simkins, as a matter of fact, denied that the Radical program was radical within the accepted meaning of the word; indeed, the Radicals failed because they did not provide freedmen with a secure economic base. Past historians, he concluded, had given a dis-torted picture of Reconstruction because they had assumed that blacks were racially inferior. The result was a provincial approach to Recon-struction that was based on ignorance and priggishness. Only by aban-doning their biases could historians contribute to a more accurate under-standing of the past, thereby making possible rational discussion of one of the nation's most critical dilemmas.[3]

While the revisionists often disagreed as much among themselves as they did with the Dunning school, there were common areas of agree-ment that gave their writings a certain unity. Most revisionists viewed the problems of American society during these years in a broader context and concluded that they were national rather than sectional in scope. Corruption, to cite but one example, was not confined to the South. It was a national phenomenon in the postwar era and involved all sec-tions, classes, and political parties alike. To single out the South in this regard was patently unfair and ahistorical.[4]

Revisionist historians attempted also to refute many of the familiar assertions of the Dunning school. In the first place, they denied that the Radical governments in the South were always dishonest, incompetent, and inefficient. On the contrary, they claimed, such governments ac-complished much of enduring value. The new constitutions written dur-ing Reconstruction represented a vast improvement over the older ones and often survived the overthrow of the men who had written them. Radical governments brought about many long-needed social reforms, including state-supported school systems for both blacks and whites, a

---

[3]Francis B. Simkins, "New Viewpoints of Southern Reconstruction," *Journal of Southern History* 5 (February 1939): 49–61.

[4]For a revisionist synthesis see J. G. Randall and David Donald, *The Civil War and Reconstruction* (2d ed.: Boston, 1961). The first edition, written by Randall in 1937, was in the Dunning school tradition.

revision of the judicial system, and improvements in local administration. Above all, these governments operated—at least in theory—on the premise that all men, white and black alike, were entitled to equal political and civil liberties.

Second, the revisionists drew a sharply different portrait of blacks during Reconstruction. They denied that developments in the postwar South resulted from black participation in government or that the freedmen were illiterate, naïve, and inexperienced. In no Southern state, they pointed out, did blacks control both houses of the legislature. Moreover, there were no black governors and only one black state supreme court justice. Only two blacks were elected to the United States Senate and fifteen to the House of Representatives. Such statistics hardly supported the charge that the supposed excesses of Reconstruction were due to political activities of black Americans.

Indeed, the revisionists maintained that blacks, as a group, were quite capable of understanding where their own interests lay without disregarding the legitimate interests of others. The freedmen were able to participate at least as intelligently as other groups in the American political process. As Vernon L. Wharton concluded in his pioneering revisionist study of the Negro in Mississippi after the Civil War, there was "little difference... in the administration of... counties [having blacks on boards of supervisors] and that of counties under Democratic control. .... Altogether, as governments go, that supplied by the Negro and white Republicans in Mississippi between 1870 and 1876 was not a bad government. .... With their white Republican colleagues, they gave to the state a government of greatly expanded functions at a cost that was low in comparison with that of almost any other state."[5]

If black Americans were not the dominant group in most Radical governments, where did these governments get their support? In attempting to answer this question, revisionists again endeavored to refute the Dunning school contention that these governments were controlled by evil, power-hungry, profit-seeking carpetbaggers and renegade scalawags who used black votes to maintain themselves in power. The stereotype of the carpetbagger and scalawag, according to revisionists, was highly inaccurate and far too simplistic. Carpetbaggers, to take one group, migrated to the South for a variety of reasons— including the lure of wider and legitimate economic opportunities as well as a desire to serve the former slaves in some humanitarian capacity. The scalawags were an equally diverse group. Within their ranks

---

[5]Vernon L. Wharton, *The Negro In Mississippi 1865–1890* (Chapel Hill, 1947), pp. 172, 179–180. See also Willie Lee Rose, *Rehearsal for Reconstruction: The Port Royal Experiment* (New York, 1964), and Joel Williamson, *After Slavery: The Negro in South Carolina During Reconstruction 1861.-1877* (Chapel Hill, 1965).

one could find former Southern unionists and Whigs, lower-class whites who sought to use the Republican party as the vehicle for confiscating the property of the planter aristocrats, and businessmen attracted by the promise of industrialization. The Radical governments, then, had a wide base of indigenous support in most Southern states.[6]

Finally, the revisionists rejected the charge that the Radical governments were extraordinarily expensive and corrupt, or that they had saddled the South with a large public debt. It was true that state expenditures went up sharply after the war. This situation was due, however, to understandable circumstances and not to inefficiency or theft. As in most postwar periods, the partial destruction of certain cities and areas required an infusion of public funds. Deferring regular appropriations during the war years also meant that a backlog of legitimate projects had accumulated. Most important of all, the South for the first time had to provide certain public facilities and social services for its black citizens. Southern states and communities had to build schools and provide other facilities and services for blacks which did not exist before the 1860s and for which public funds had never been expended prior to this time. It is little wonder, then, that there was a rise in spending in the Reconstruction era.

In examining the financial structure of Southern governments between 1865 and 1877, the revisionists also found that the rise in state debts, in some instances, was more apparent than real. Grants to railroads promoters, which in certain states accounted for a large proportion of the increase in the debt, were secured by a mortgage on the railroad property. Thus, the rise in the debt was backed by sound collateral. The amount of the debt chargeable to theft, the revisionists maintained, was negligible. Indeed, the restoration governments, which were dominated by supposedly honest Southerners, proved to be far more corrupt than those governments controlled by the Radicals.

Although revisionists agreed that the Dunning interpretation of Reconstruction was inadequate—if not misleading—they had considerable difficulty themselves in synthesizing their own findings. If there was one idea on which the revisionists were united, it was their conviction that economic forces, which were related to the growth of an urban and industrialized nation, somehow played a major role during this period. Beneath the political and racial antagonisms of this era, some revisionists argued, lay opposing economic rivalries. Anxious to gain an advantage over their competitors, many business interests used politics as the vehicle to further their economic ambitions—especially since the

---

[6]See Otto H. Olsen, "Reconsidering the Scalawags," *Civil War History* 12 (December 1966): 304–20, and Allen W. Trelease, "Who Were the Scalawags?," *Journal of Southern History* 29 (November 1963): 445–68.

South, like the North and West, was ardently courting businessmen. The result was that economic rivalries were translated into political struggles.

Revisionists also emphasized the crucial issue of race. During Reconstruction many former Whigs joined the Republican party because of its probusiness economic policies. These well-to-do- conservatives, at first, were willing to promise blacks civil and political rights in return for their support at the polls. Within the Democratic party, however, lower-class whites, fearful of possible encroachments by blacks upon their social status and economic position, raised the banner of race. Conservatives found their affiliation with the Republican party increasingly uncomfortable, and they slowly began to drift back into the Democratic party. The fact that both parties were under the control of conservatives made it easier for former Republicans to shift their political allegiance. One result of the political alignment was that it left Southern blacks politically isolated and without allies among the whites. When the move to eliminate them from political life in the South got started, blacks could find little support among Southern whites. This political move came at a time when Northerners were disillusioned by the failure of the Radicals to achieve many of their idealistic aims for the freedmen. Tired of conflict and turmoil, Northerners became reconciled to the idea of letting the South work out its own destiny—even if it meant sacrificing the black people. Northern businessmen likewise became convinced that only Southern conservatives could restore order and stability and thus create a favorable environment for investment.

The result was both a polarization of Southern politics along racial rather than economic lines, and the emergence of the Democratic party as the white man's party. For whites of lower-class background, the primary goal was to maintain the South as a white man's country. Upper-class whites were also contented with the existing one-party political structure because they were permitted the dominant role in determining the future economic development of their section.

The end of Reconstruction, according to the revisionists, was closely related to the triumph of business values and industrial capitalism. When the contested presidential election of 1876 resulted in an apparent deadlock between Rutherford B. Hayes, the Republican candidate, and Samuel J. Tilden, his Democratic opponent, some prominent Republicans saw an opportunity to rebuild their party in the South upon a new basis. Instead of basing their party upon propertyless, former slaves, they hoped to attract well-to-do former Whigs who had been forced into the Democratic party as a result of events during the Reconstruction. To accomplish this goal, a group of powerful Republican leaders began to work secretly to bring about a political realignment. If Southern Democratic congressmen would not stand in the way of Hayes's election and also provide enough votes to permit the Republicans to organize the House of Representatives, these leaders were willing to promise the South federal subsidies—primarily for railroads—and also to name a Southerner as postmaster general.

The "Compromise of 1877," as this political deal was called, was not fully carried out, but its larger implications survived unscathed. As C. Vann Woodward, the revisionist historian who propounded the thesis of such a political bargain, concluded, the compromise "did not restore the old order in the South, nor did it restore the South to parity with other sections. It did assure the dominant whites political autonomy and nonintervention in matters of race policy and promised them a share in the blessings of the new economic order. In return the South became, in effect, a satellite of the dominant region. So long as the Conservative Redeemers held control they scotched any tendency of the South to combine forces with the internal enemies of the new economy— laborites, Western agrarians, reformers. Under the regime of the Redeemers the South became a bulwark instead of a menace to the new order."[7]

After the early 1950s, a new school of Reconstruction historiography called the neorevisionists emerged. These historians emphasized the moral rather than the economic basis of Reconstruction. The differences between the revisionists and neorevisionists were often minimal since the latter frequently relied upon the findings of the former to reach their conclusions, and it is difficult, if not impossible, to categorize certain historians as belonging to one group or another. Generally speaking, while the neorevisionists accepted many findings of the revisionists, they rejected the idea of interpreting Reconstruction in strictly economic terms. The Republican party, the neorevisionists maintained, was not united on a probusiness economic program; it included individuals and groups holding quite different social and economic views.[8]

In interpreting Reconstruction, the neorevisionists stressed the critical factor of race as a moral issue. One of the unresolved dilemmas after the Civil War, they claimed, was the exact role that blacks were to play in American society. Within the Republican party, a number of factions each offered their own solution to this question. Andrew Johnson, who had been nominated as Lincoln's running mate in 1864 on a Union party ticket despite his Democratic party affiliations, spoke for one segment of the party. To Johnson blacks were incapable of self-government. Con-

---

[7]C. Vann Woodward, *Reunion and Reaction: The Compromise of 1877 and the End of Reconstruction* (Boston, 1951), p. 246.

[8]Robert Sharkey, *Money, Class, and Party: An Economic Study Study of the Civil War and Reconstruction* (Baltimore, 1959), and Irwin Ungar, *The Greenback Era: A Social and Political History of American Finance, 1865–1879* (Princeton, 1964).

sequently, he favored the state governments in the South that came back into the Union shortly after the end of the war under his own plan of reconstruction, and went along with the Black Codes that denied black Americans many of their civil rights.

Although Johnson was president as well as titular head of the Republican party, there was a great deal of opposition to his policies by a group known as the Radicals. Who were the Radical Republicans and what did they stand for? To the Dunning school the Radicals were a group of vindictive politicians who were utterly amoral in their quest after power; they were merely interested in the black man for his vote. To revisionists the Radicals represented, at least in part, the interests of the industrial Northeast—men who wanted to use black votes to prevent the formation of a coalition of Western and Southern agrarian interests against the industrial capitalism of the Northeast.[9]

To the neorevisionists, on the other hand, the Radicals were a much more complex group. Many of the Radicals, they claimed, joined the Republican party in the 1850s for moral and idealistic reasons—their antislavery zeal—rather than for economic motives. These men, seeking to eradicate all vestiges of slavery, were consistent in their demands before and after the war that blacks be given the same rights as white Americans. Their beliefs, of course, brought them to a face-to-face confrontation with President Johnson in the postwar period. In the ensuing struggle, the President, because of his political ineptness, soon found himself isolated. Taking advantage of the situation, the Radicals first won the support of conservative Republicans and then set out to remake Southern society by transferring political power from the planter class to the freedmen. The program of the Radicals, therefore, was motivated in large measure by idealism and a sincere humanitarian concern.[10]

In 1965 Kenneth M. Stampp published an important synthesis that emphasized the moral dimension of the Reconstruction years. Stampp rejected the traditional stereotype of the average Radical as a figure motivated by vindictive considerations. He argued that the issues of the 1860s were not artificial ones as the Dunning school had claimed. The central question of the postwar period was the place of the freedmen in American society. President Johnson and his followers believed in the innate racial inferiority of blacks; therefore they rejected any program based upon egalitarian assumptions. The Radicals, on the other hand, took seriously the ideals of equality, natural rights, and democracy.

---

[9]This point of view was best expressed by Howard K. Beale, one of the fathers of the revisionist school, in *The Critical Year: A Study of Andrew Johnson and Reconstruction* (New York, 1930).

[10]See James H. McPherson, *The Struggle for Equality: Abolitionists and the Negro in the Civil War and Reconstruction* (Princeton, 1964), and Hans L. Trefousse, *The Radical Republicans: Lincoln's Vanguard for Social Justice* (New York, 1969).

Indeed, most of these men had been closely associated with the antebellum abolitionist crusade. Stampp did not deny that the Radicals had other motives as well, for he admitted that they saw black Americans as valuable additions to the Republican party. But most politicians, he insisted, identify the welfare of the nation with the welfare of their party. To argue that the Radicals had invidious and selfish motives, Stampp concluded, does them a severe injustice and results in a distorted picture of the Reconstruction era.

The Radicals, according to the neorevisionists, ultimately failed in their objectives. Most Americans, harboring conscious and unconscious racial antipathies, were not willing to accept blacks as equals. By the 1870s the North was prepared to abandon blacks to the white South for three reasons: a wish to return to the amicable prewar relations between the sections; a desire to promote industrial investment in the South; and a growing conviction that the cause of black Americans was no longer worth further strife. The tragedy of Reconstruction, the neorevisionists maintained, was not that it occurred, but that it had ended short of achieving the major goal sought by the Radicals.

The struggle over Reconstruction, nevertheless, had not been in vain. In addition to the many achievements of the Radical governments, the Radicals had succeeded in securing the adoption of the Fourteenth and Fifteenth amendments. These amendments, in Stampp's words, "which could have been adopted only under the conditions of radical reconstruction, make the blunders of that era, tragic though they were, dwindle into insignificance. For if it was worth four years of civil war to save the Union, it was worth a few years of radical reconstruction to give the American Negro the ultimate promise of equal civil and political rights."[11]

In the second selection in this chapter, Allen W. Trelease sums up the neorevisionist interpretation of Reconstruction. Given a commitment to racism that by 1865 was deeply embedded in the minds of a majority of white Americans, Trelease argues that Southerners could hardly be expected to abandon their antipathies toward blacks after emancipation. Although blacks were simply seeking the same rights enjoyed by whites, the latter were unable to accept the former as equals. Seeing the race question as crucial, Trelease insists that Radical Reconstruction failed because the seed of biracial democracy was planted on barren ground in the South. Moreover, the federal government failed to nurture the seeds of democracy. Despite significant achievements in the years following the end of slavery, most Radical state governments were quickly overthrown by a society committed to inequality.

---

[11]Kenneth M. Stampp, *The Era of Reconstruction* (New York, 1965), p. 215.

The heroic (though tragic) interpretation of Reconstruction offered by Stampp and, to a lesser extent, by Trelease did not remain unchallenged. Given the internal strife engendered by the continued existence of economic, political, and legal inequality, and the seeming resurgence of a radical critique of American institutions and society in the 1960s, it was not surprising that historians associated with the New Left would slowly begin to reevaluate the events of the postwar years in a way that took sharp issue with scholars such as Stampp. Staughton Lynd, for example, argued that it was pointless to debate endlessly the issue whether Northern policy was too hard or too soft following the end of the Civil War. Historians should focus instead on the discussion of strategies of planned social change that might have succeeded in avoiding the tragedies that followed. Conceding that Reconstruction failed and that American society during the succeeding century would reflect this failure, Lynd concluded "that the fundamental error in Reconstruction policy was that it did not give the freedman land of his own. Whether by confiscation of the property of leading rebels, by a vigorous Southern homestead policy, or by some combination of the two, Congress should have given the ex-slaves the economic independence to resist political intimidation."[12]

Nor were the New Left scholars alone in rejecting the revisionist or neorevisionist views of Reconstruction. Although not sufficiently in agreement to constitute a specific school, some individual historians began to place specific events during Reconstruction within a somewhat different structural setting. In his study of the presidential election of 1876, for example, Keith I. Polakoff came to conclusions that were partly at variance with those expressed by C. Vann Woodward some twenty-five years before. Woodward assumed that national political parties were centralized organizations under the control of their leaders. Polakoff, on the other hand, was influenced by the work of more recent social and political historians. Where Woodward saw centralized authority, Polakoff saw structural weakness; he insisted that American political parties at this time were decentralized.

> Not only was factionalism practically the central characteristic of both parties, but the precise balance existing between the various factions remained remarkably stable; and no wonder: each faction had its own little constituency on which it could always depend. The diffuseness of power in the Republican and Democratic parties was merely a reflection of the remarkable diversity of the American electorate. If there was one thing nineteenth-century parties did well, it was to represent their constituents. In the process rational

---

[12]Staughton Lynd, ed., *Reconstruction* (New York, 1967), p. 8. See also Lynd's article, "Rethinking Slavery and Reconstruction," *Journal of Negro History* 50 (July 1965): 198–209. For reasons that are not clear, New Left historians tended to ignore Reconstruction.

programs of government action were trampled underfoot. . . . The resulting
irrelevance of much of the political process was actually one of its principal
sources of strength. Because the stakes involved were more symbolic than
substantial, much like the outcome of the Army-Navy football game a century
later, politicking served as a means of transcending the dull routine of
everyday life, a means of identifying with the distinctive democratic greatness
of the United States while socializing with like-minded men.[13]

During the 1970s there was no indication that interest in the Reconstruction period was diminishing. On the contrary, neorevisionist
scholars continued to debate the same issues and problems as their
predecessors. To what degree were Americans committed to an equal-
rights ideology? Why were black Americans left in a defenseless position? What was the nature of such political events as the impeachment of
Andrew Johnson? Why did Reconstruction come to an end far short of
achieving its goals?[14]

To these and other questions historians gave varied answers that
demonstrated that few differences had been conclusively resolved.
Michael Les Benedict, for example, argued that Andrew Johnson was
impeached because he seemed to be violating the principle of separation
of powers and because he failed to carry out some key provisions in
legislation pertaining to Reconstruction.[15] Hans Trefousse emphasized
the degree to which Johnson thwarted radical policies and strengthened
conservative forces, thereby facilitating their eventual triumph in the
1870s. Michael Perman insisted that in the context of the political tensions that prevailed in the immediate postwar era, the very moderation
and conciliation that marked presidential and congressional Reconstruction was doomed to fail; only a coercive policy could have succeeded. Of
three recent studies of Andrew Johnson, two (by Patrick W. Riddleberger
and James E. Sefton) emphasized his commitment to sometimes incompatible principles which rendered him impotent, and one (by Albert
Castel) accentuated the degree to which his inordinate ambition and
desire for power helped to destroy him.[16] In a broad study of national

---

[13]Keith I. Polakoff, *The Politics of Inertia: The Election of 1876 and the End of Reconstruction*
(Baton Rouge, 1973), pp. 320–22. See also Allan Peskin, "Was There a Conpromise of
1877?," *Journal of American History* 40 (June 1973): 63–75; C. Vann Woodward, "Yes, There
was a Compromise of 1877," *ibid.* 40 (September 1973): 215–23; and M. Les Benedict,
"Southern Democrats in the Crisis of 1876–1877: A Reconsideration of *Reunion and Reaction*," *Journal of Southern History* 46 (November 1980): 489–524.

[14]For a descriptive analysis of black Americans after slavery that does not deal with
Reconstruction as a political event, see Leon F. Litwack's important *Been in the Storm So
Long: The Aftermath of Slavery* (New York, 1979).

[15]Michael Les Benedict, *The Impeachment and Trial of Andrew Johnson* (New York, 1973).
See also Benedict's *A Compromise of Principle: Congressional Republicans and Reconstruction,
1863–1869* (New York, 1974) and *The Fruits of Victory: Alternatives in Restoring the Union,
1865–1877* (Philadelphia, 1975).

[16]Hans L. Trefousse, *Impeachment of a President: Andrew Johnson, the Blacks, and Recon-*

politics, William Gillette noted that Reconstruction was so easily reversed because it had always been "fragmentary and fragile."

> From the very beginning, reconstruction had no more than tenuous support and had been wracked by chronic crises, marred by profound uncertainties, unsettled because of inner tensions, riddled through with unsolved ambiguities involving race relations and public policy, and blighted by the latent contradictions in the Republicans' attitudes and actions. Moreover, all these problems had been compounded by necessary compromises and incessant change, both of which are inherent in the democratic process itself. Clearly, the American people, their presidents, and their government had not been persevering or resourceful enough to see reconstruction through; and since the Republican governments in the South, with their numerous and supreme crises, had been unable or would not govern, their regimes were inevitably and inexorably replaced by those of Democrats, who did govern, but in accordance with their own rules.
>
> Thus reconstruction—which had been neglected, discredited, and deserted by many of its friends—fell an easy prey to its enemies.[17]

At the same time that interest in national politics remained high, historians also continued to write monographic studies dealing with individual states. Here too the traditional dichotomy appeared; some emphasized the degree to which Reconstruction succeeded while others pointed to its failures.[18] In a somewhat novel study of black political leadership in South Carolina that utilized quantitative techniques, Thomas Holt provided a somewhat novel thesis. Holt emphasized the continued persistence of class and caste, but argued that the Afro-American population of South Carolina was not an unvariegated classless mass. Black leaders were divided among themselves; their divisions contributed to the fall of the Republican party in the state. On the other hand, his profile of black leadership demonstrated that most owned property and were literate, and 10 percent were professionally or college trained.[19]

To a considerable extent, the differences between the various schools of Reconstruction historiography grew out of the milieu in which each had grown to maturity. The Dunning point of view, for example, origi-

stuction (Knoxville, 1975); Michael Perman, *Reunion Without Compromise: The South and Reconstruction, 1865–1868* (New York, 1973); Patrick W. Riddleberger, *1866: The Critical Year Revisited* (Carbondale, 1979); James E. Sefton, *Andrew Johnson and the Uses of Constitutional Power* (Boston, 1980); and Albert Castel, *The Presidency of Andrew Johnson* (Lawrence, 1979).

[17]William Gillette, *Retreat from Reconstruction 1869–1879* (Baton Rouge, 1979), p. 380.

[18]Jerrell H. Shofner, *Nor Is It over Yet: Florida in the Era of Reconstruction, 1863–1877* (Gainesville, 1974); Joe Gray Taylor, *Louisiana Reconstructed, 1863–1877* (Baton Rouge, 1974); William C. Harris, *The Day of the Carpetbagger: Republican Reconstruction in Mississippi* (Baton Rouge, 1979).

[19]Thomas Holt, *Black over White: Negro Political Leadership in South Carolina during Reconstruction* (Urbana, 1977).

nated in the late nineteenth century and flowered in the early part of the twentieth. During these years the vast majority of white Americans assumed that blacks constituted an inferior race, one that was incapable of being fully assimilated into their society. Most Southerners had come to this conclusion well before the Civil War; many Northerners arrived at the same conclusion after the debacle of Reconstruction seemingly vindicated this belief. Racism in America was buttressed further by the findings of the biological and social sciences in the late nineteenth century. Influenced by evolutionary concepts of Darwinism, some scientists argued that blacks had followed a unique evolutionary course which resulted in the creation of an inferior race. The racial prejudices of many Americans thus received what they believed to be scientific justification.

Given these beliefs, it is not difficult to understand why the Dunning school interpretation gained rapid acceptance. The attempt by the Radicals to give equal rights to a supposedly inferior race did not appear to be sensible; state governments that included black officials and held power in part through black votes were bound to be inefficient, incompetent, and corrupt. Moreover, the Southern claim that responsibility for black people had to be entrusted to whites seemed entirely justifiable. The findings of the Dunning school that Reconstruction was a tragic blunder doomed to failure from its very beginning came as no surprise to early-twentieth-century Americans, most of whom were prepared to believe the worst about black Americans.

The revisionist school, on the other hand, originated in a somewhat different climate of opinion. By the 1920s American historiography had came under the influence of the Progressive, or New History, school. This school, growing out of the dissatisfaction with the older scientific school of historians that emphasized the collection of impartial empirical data and eschewed "subjective" interpretations, borrowed heavily from the new social sciences. The New History sought to explain historical change by isolating underlying economic and social forces that transformed institutions and social structures. In place of tradition and stability, it emphasized change and conflict. Progressive and democratic in their orientation, Progressive historians attempted to explain the present in terms of the dynamic and impersonal forces that had transformed American society.

The revisionists, then, rejected the moralistic tone of the Dunning school. They sought instead to identify the historical forces responsible for many of the developments following the Civil War. Economic and social factors, they maintained, were basic to this era. The real conflict was not between North and South, white and black; it was between industrial capitalism and agrarianism, with the former ultimately emerging victorious. Thus, the question of the status of black people in American society was simply a facade for the more basic conflicts that lay hidden beneath the surface. Reconstruction, they concluded, was the first phase in the emergence of the United States as a leading industrial and capitalist nation.

The neorevisionist school, although owing much to the revisionists, was influenced by the egalitarian emphasis of the 1940s and the period following the Second World War. Indicative of changing attitudes toward blacks was the publication in 1944 of the monumental study by Gunnar Myrdal and his associates, *An American Dilemma: The Negro Problem and Modern Democracy.* Myrdal, a distinguished Swedish sociologist, was commissioned by the Carnegie Foundation in the late 1930s to undertake a comprehensive study of black people in the United States. Although emphasizing that a variety of complex factors were responsible for the depressed condition of American blacks, Myrdal argued that the problem was basically a moral one. Americans, he wrote, held a political creed that stressed the equality of all men. This ideal, however, was constantly confronted with the inescapable reality that in the United States white citizens refused to accept blacks as their equals. Thus many Americans were caught in a dilemma between theory and practice, causing them to suffer an internal moral conflict. Myrdal's work anticipated, in part, the thinking behind the civil rights movement of the 1950s.

In evaluating events between 1865 and 1877, neorevisionist historians began to shift the focus of previous schools. The issue of equal rights for blacks, neorevisionists maintained, was not a false one, even though it was complicated by economic and other factors. In a real sense, the fundamental problem of Reconstruction was whether or not white Americans were prepared to accept the freedmen as equal partners. Even though the Radicals ultimately failed in achieving their egalitarian goals, they left an enduring legacy in the form of the Fourteenth and Fifteenth amendments. These amendments gave black people citizenship, promised them equal protection under the laws, and gave them the right to vote. That America did not honor these promises in the decades after Reconstruction in no way detracted from the idealism of those responsible for these amendments. Indeed, the importance of these amendments took on a new meaning as they gave legal sanction to civil rights after the Second World War.

Historians of the New Left on the other hand, saw Reconstruction as a failure because Americans had not faced up to the problems arising from the end of slavery. Reflecting their own disillusionment and dissatisfaction with contemporary America, they condemned the post–Civil War generation for its failure to restructure society and thereby give blacks (and other poor groups as well) an equitable share of America's wealth. Reconstruction, they argued, represented but another unhappy chapter of American history; the past as well as the present merely revealed the widespread hypocrisy and corruption of ruling groups in the United States.

Although it is possible to demonstrate that particular interpretations grew out of and reflected their own milieu, historians must still face the larger and more important problem of determining the accuracy or inaccuracy of each interpretation.[20] Was Reconstruction, as the Dunning school argues, a tragedy for all Americans? Were the revisionists correct in stressing the achievements as well as the partial failures of this period, and emphasizing the fundamental economic factors? Were the neorevisionists justified in insisting that the major issue during Reconstruction was indeed a moral one? Or were New Left historians correct in their assessment of the general failure of Reconstruction and American society? Did the particular structural form of state and national politics preclude effective governmental action in dealing with the problems growing out of emancipation?

To answer these questions, historians must deal also with a number of subsidiary issues. Should the North have forgotten that it had taken four years of bloody and expensive conflict to keep America united and welcomed the South back into the Union in 1865 with open arms? Or was it proper for Northern Republicans to lay down certain conditions to ensure that slavery, legal or implied, would never again exist within the United States? What should have been the proper policy for both the federal and state governments to follow with regard to black Americans, and how were the voices of blacks to be heard during policy formation and implementation? Were Southerners justified in their belief that blacks were incapable of caring for themselves and that their future should be left in the hands of white men? Or were the Radicals correct in insisting that blacks had to be given the same legal and political rights that all Americans enjoyed?

The answers to some of these questions will, in large measure, determine the broader interpretive framework of the Reconstruction era. Although that period is a century away from our own, some of the basic conflicts common to both remain unresolved and are as pressing as ever. Time and circumstance may have changed; new leaders may have emerged; yet the fundamental dilemma of what role black people should play in American civilization remains a controversial and crucial one.

---

[20]For a discussion and an implicit condemnation of most schools of Reconstruction historiography see Gerald N. Grob, "Reconstruction: An American Morality Play," in *American History: Retrospect and Prospect*, ed. George A. Billias and Gerald N. Grob (New York, 1971), pp. 191–231. See also Richard O. Curry, "The Civil War and Reconstruction, 1861–1877: A Critical Overview of Recent Trends and Interpretations," *Civil War History* 20 (September 1974): 215–38, and Michael Les Benedict, "Equality and Expediency in the Reconstruction Era: A Review Essay," *ibid.* 23 (December 1977): 322–35.

Albert B. Moore

ALBERT B. MOORE (1887–1967), taught at the University of Alabama from 1923 to 1958, where he also served as Dean of the graduate school and Chairman of the Department of History. He was the author of several books on the history of the South. The selection reprinted here was his presidential address before the Southern Historical Association in 1942.

The South has long been, and to some extent still is, in the throes of being reconstructed by forces operating from outside the region. Ramifications of this reconstruction process account in large degree for certain conditions in the South today and for its place in the nation. They explain how the South has acquired a colonial status, not only in the economic system but also in the psychology, sentiment, culture, and politics of the nation.

While this address is concerned primarily with the reconstruction of the South after the Civil War, it takes cognizance of the fact that the reconstruction of the South by the North has been going on more than one hundred years. Prior to the Civil War it took the form of a savage attack upon slavery and Southern society, though it had other connotations. The Northeast with its western extensions, possessed of what one writer has called "egocentric sectionalism"—that is, the conviction that it was not a section but the whole United States and that, therefore, its pattern of life must prevail throughout the country—undertook after 1830 to reconstruct the South into conformity and into a subordinate position. With furious denunciations and menacing gestures and actions it drove the South into secession and war, destroyed its power, and reconstructed it with a vengeance and violence remarkable in the history of human conflict. This is not to give the South a clear bill of health; but whatever the rights and wrongs of the controversy, the Civil War, broadly speaking, was the tragic drama of a movement to reconstruct the South.

We have formed the habit of examining the phenomena of the reconstruction of the South after the Civil War—that is, the period 1865–1877—in a very objective, almost casual, way and with little regard to

"One Hundred Years of Reconstruction of the South," *Journal of Southern History* 9 (May 1943): 153–65. Copyright 1943 by the Southern Historical Association. Reprinted without footnotes by permission of the managing editor.

their essence and their significance in Southern and national history. While avoiding the emotional approach one should not forget that it was, after all, a settlement imposed by the victors in war, and should be studied in all its effects, immediate and far reaching, on its victims. An investigation of the effects on the victors themselves would also be an interesting adventure. It is a chapter in the history of the punishment of the defeated in war. The observations of a competent historian from another country, coming upon the subject for the first time, taking nothing for granted and making a critical analysis of its severity compared with the punishment of losers in wars in general, would make interesting reading.

The war set the stage for a complete reconstruction of the South. Furious hatred, politics, economic considerations, and a curious conviction that God had joined a righteous North to use it as an instrument for the purging of the wicked South gave a keen edge to the old reconstruction urge. The victories of bullets and bayonets were followed by the equally victorious attack of tongues and pens. Ministers mounted their pulpits on Easter Sunday, the day following President Lincoln's tragic death, and assured their sad auditors that God's will had been done, that the president had been removed because his heart was too merciful to punish the South as God required. An eminent New York divine assured his audience that the vice-regent of Christ, the new president, Andrew Johnson, was mandated from on high "to hew the rebels in pieces before the Lord." "So let us say," with becoming piety and sweet submissiveness he enjoined, "God's will be done." Whether the ministers thought, after they discovered that Johnson was opposed to a reign of terror, that the Lord had made a mistake is not a matter of record. As Professor Paul H. Buck has said, "It was in the churches that one found the utmost intolerance, bitterness, and unforgiveness during the sad months that followed Appomattox." Henry Ward Beecher, one of the more moderate Northern preachers, thought the South was "rotten." "No timber," said he, "grown in this cursed soil is fit for the ribs of our ship of state or for our household homes." The newspapers spread abroad the preachers' gospel of righteous vindictiveness and expounded further the idea that drastic punishment of the South was essential for the security of the Union.

Many unfriendly writers invaded the South, found what they wanted, and wrote books, articles, and editorials that strengthened the conviction that the South must be torn to pieces and made anew. Books, journals, and newspapers stimulated the impulse to be vigilant and stern, to repress and purge. A juggernaut of propaganda, stemming from the various sources of public instruction, prepared the way for the crucifixion of the South. The South of slavery and treason, of continuous outrages against the Negroes and Northerners, of haughty spirit and stubborn conviction, and of superiority complex, must be humbled and made respectable or be annihilated, so that it could never become again a strong factor in national politics.

The South did little or nothing to neutralize Radical Northern propaganda. To be sure, a few journalists, like A. T. Bledsoe, complained about "the cunningly devised fables, and the vile calumnies, with which a partisan press and a Puritanical pulpit have flooded the North," but their vituperative responses to vituperative attacks did more harm than good. There was, in the very nature of things, little that the South could do to disabuse the Radical Northern mind that was disposed to believe evil of it. There was simply no escape for Southerners from an awful scourge. Even more courage and fortitude than they had displayed on the battlefield would be required to endure what was in store for them.

As much as Reconstruction has been studied in this country it should not at this late hour be necessary to point out its severity, its permanent effects upon the South, and its influence upon various aspects of our national history. Yet few have examined critically the harshness of it and its persistent and manifold effects. While crucifying the South, the dominant Radical group of the North, thanks to the blindness of hatred, believed it was being lenient. Because no lives were taken—but there are some things more agonizing than death—for the "crimes of treason and rebellion," the North has prided itself on its magnanimity; and its historians have been strangely oblivious of property confiscations and mental tortures. It seemed to the late James Ford Rhodes "the mildest punishment ever inflicted after an unsuccessful Civil War." But this was no ordinary civil war, if indeed, it should be classed as a civil war. The thesis of leniency has oddly persisted. When the Germans protested to high heaven against the severity of the Versailles Treaty they had sympathizers in this country who compared the generosity of the North in its treatment of the South with the harshness of the Versailles Treaty. But the late Professor Carl Russell Fish of the University of Wisconsin, in his article on "The German Indemnity and the South," discredited the theory of generosity on the part of the North. He showed that the South was punished more than Germany, though he touched upon only a few phases of the South's burdens.

Professor Buck in his delightful and highly informative book, *The Road to Reunion,* recognized Reconstruction as "disorder worse than war and oppression unequalled in American annals," but made a serious error when he stated that "virtually no property" was confiscated. He overlooked the confiscation of large quantities of cotton—estimated in the minority report of the Ku Klux Klan Committee at two million bales—then selling for a very high price and most of which belonged to private citizens. The abolition of slavery wiped out about two billion dollars of capital and reduced the value of real estate by at least that amount. This was confiscation of property, and the repudiation of Confederate currency, the Confederate bonded debt, and the war debts of the states, all amounting to no less than $3 billion, was confiscation of property rights. As inevitable as much of this was, it represented a frightful confiscation of property.

The freeing of the slaves not only cost the South $2 billion but it also forced upon that section an economic and social revolution. It subverted a mode of life almost as old as the South itself. The repudiation of its debts impoverished the South and destroyed its financial relationships. While the South lost its debts, it had to pay its full share of the Northern debts which amounted to about four-fifths of the total Northern war expenses. The money for this debt was spent in the North for its up-building. It paid also its share of the $20 million returned by the federal treasury to the Northern states for direct taxes collected from them during the war, and of extravagant pensions to Union soldiers. Professor James Sellers estimates that the South paid in these ways an indemnity of at least a billion dollars to the North.

The South accepted the results of the war—the doom of slavery and the doctrine of secession—as inevitable and its leaders sought to restore their respective states as speedily as possible to their normal position in the Union. But despite its acceptance in good faith of the declared aims of the North, the South was forced through the gauntlet of two plans of Reconstruction. The people conformed in good faith to the requirements of President Johnson's plan, but Congress repudiated this plan and forced the South to begin *de novo* the process of Reconstruction. Pending its restoration, it was put under the heel of military authority, though there was no problem that exceeded the power of civil authority to handle. Objectively viewed, it is a singular fact that it took three years to restore the South to the Union. It is little short of amazing that for a dozen years after the war federal troops were stationed in the South among an orderly people who had played a leading role in the building and guidance of the nation since colonial times, and who now sought nothing so much as peace and surcease from strife. For much of the period government was a hodgepodge of activities by the civil authorities, the army, and the Freedmen's Bureau, with the president of the United States working through any or all of these agencies. Most of the serious problems of government were precipitated by outside influences and conspiracies.

The political enfranchisement of four million Negroes, from whose necks the yoke of slavery had just been lifted, is the most startling fact about Reconstruction, and a fact of tremendous impact in Southern history. There is nothing in the history of democracy comparable to it. To give the Negroes the ballot and office—ranging from constable to governor—and the right to sit in state legislatures and in Congress, while depriving their former masters of their political rights and the South of its trained leadership, is one of the most astounding facts in the history of reconstruction after war. It was a stroke of fanatical vengeance and design. The basic purpose of this sort of political reconstruction was to vouchsafe for the North—while chastising the South—the future control of the nation through the Republican party. The South was never again to be allowed to regain the economic and political position which it had occupied in the nation prior to 1860.

Negro voting laid the basis for the carpetbag regime. For eight years Radical Northern leaders, backed by the Washington authorities and the army and aided by some native whites, pillaged and plundered and finished wrecking the South. Northern teachers who invaded the South to reconstruct its educational and social system, and Northern preachers who came down to restore the unity of the churches by a reconstruction formula that required Southerners to bend the knee and confess their sins helped the politicians, the Freedmen's Bureau, and the Loyal League to undermine the Negroes' confidence in their white neighbors. The reconstruction policy of the churches did its part in stirring up both racial and sectional enmities. The *Nation* remarked, in 1879, the "Churches are doing their full share in causing permanent division." Reconstruction affected the religious life of the country for fifty years and more after the Radicals were overthrown. The character of the carpetbag-scalawag-Negro governments was well stated by the *New York Herald* which said the South is "to be governed by blacks spurred on by worse than blacks. . . . This is the most abominable phase barbarism has assumed since the dawn of civilization. . . . It is not right to make slaves of white men even though they have been former masters of blacks. This is but a change in a system of bondage that is rendered the more odious and intolerable because it has been inaugurated in an enlightened instead of a dark and uncivilized age."

It would be safe to say that the people of the North never understood how the South suffered during the Radical regime. The Radicals who controlled most of the organs of public opinion were in no attitude of mind to listen to Southern complaints, and most people were too busy with the pursuit of alluring business opportunities that unfolded before them to think much of what was going on down South. In some respects conditions in the South at the end of the Radical regime remind one of the plight of the Germans at the end of the Thirty Years' War.

The South staggered out of the Reconstruction, which ended *officially* in 1877, embittered, impoverished, encumbered with debt, and discredited by Radical propaganda. It had won after many frightful years the right to govern itself again, but there were still white men who could not vote and for many years there was danger of the federal regulation of elections and a resurgence of Negro power in politics.

The tax load had been devastating. The lands of thousands upon thousands had been sold for taxes. Huge state and local debts, much of which was fraudulent, had been piled up. So many bonds, legal and illegal, had been sold that public credit was destroyed. The people stood, like the servant of Holy Writ, ten thousand talents in debt with not one farthing to pay. They had to solve the paradoxical problem of scaling down public debts—a bewildering compound of legal and illegal and far too large to be borne—while restoring public credit. Northern hands had imposed the debts and Northern hands held the repudiated bonds. Repudiation became another source of misunderstanding between the sections and another basis for charges of "Southern outrages."

Reconstruction profoundly and permanently affected the political life of the South. It gave the South the one-party system. The white people rallied around the Democratic party standards to overthrow the Radical regime, and their continued cooperation was necessary to prevent the Negroes from acquiring again the balance of power in politics. The terrible record of the Republican party during the Radical regime was an insuperable obstacle to its future success in the South. Hostility toward this party promoted devotion to the Democratic party. The complete domination of the latter party not only invested Southern politics with the disadvantages of the one-party system, but proved to be costly to the South in national politics. The Democratic party has been out of power most of the time in national politics and the Republican party naturally has not felt under obligation to do much for the South when it has had control of the national government. Even when the Democratic party has been in power the South has not had its share of patronage and appropriations, or of consideration in the formulation of national policies. The inequitable distribution of federal relief funds between the states since 1930 is an illustration in point. Political expediency has been the controlling consideration and not gratitude for party loyalty, which calls to mind an old Virginian's definition of political gratitude. Political gratitude, he said, is a lively appreciation of favors yet to be received.

Radical Reconstruction corrupted Southern politics, and the prejudice aroused against Negro participation in politics led ultimately to the disfranchisement of most of the Negroes. Political habits formed in counteracting carpetbag machinations and the presence of Negro voters continued to influence politics. Fraudulent methods were employed to control the Negro votes and when factions appeared among the whites they employed against each other the chicanery and frauds which they had used against the Radicals.

Reconstruction contributed to the proscription of the South in national politics and to provincialism in Southern politics. Southerners so feared a recrudescence of Reconstruction in some form or other that for a generation they generally shrank from active participation in national affairs. Their attitude, generally speaking, was that if the North would leave them alone it could direct national affairs. This begat provincialism and made the continued proscription of the South easier. Such a situation was not good for either the South or the North.

Race friction and prejudice were engendered by Reconstruction, which was an unfortunate thing for both races and especially for the Negroes. It caused greater discriminations against the Negroes in politics and education, and in other ways. The Negroes had been so pampered and led as to arouse false notions and hopes among them and to make them for many years lame factors in the rebuilding of the South. The Negro after Reconstruction, and in large degree because of it, continued and continues to be a source of division between the North and South. The North either could not or would not understand the necessity of race segregation, and the idea that the Negro must have a definite place in the scheme of life was obnoxious. Disfranchisement of the Negro, occasional race riots, and the sporadic mobbing of Negroes accused of heinous crimes gave rise to continued charges of "Southern outrages." Criticisms from the North, generally based upon a lack of understanding of the problem, seemed more a matter of censure than of true interest in the Negro. Thus, those who expected to see sectional strife over the status of the Negro disappear with the emancipation of the slaves were disillusioned.

The Negro has been the cause of more misunderstanding and conflict between the sections than all things else. The North freed the Negro from slavery but by repressing and exploiting the South it has contributed much to conditions that have deprived him of some of the opportunities that a free man should have. If Southern whites have suffered the pangs and restraints of poverty, the lot of the Negro has inevitably been worse. The shackles upon the Negro's economic and cultural advancement have been formidable and deadening in their effects. Their inescapable lack of educational opportunities has been epitomized by the saying that the South has had the impossible task of educating two races out of the poverty of one.

In some respects the South has not pursued an enlightened policy toward the Negro. In ways it has exploited him. In the struggle for existence the Negro too often has been overlooked. Prejudice, too, resulting to a large extent from Reconstruction experiences, has done its part. Southerners, determined that the political control of Negroes back in the old Reconstruction days shall not be repeated, and probably too apprehensive about the breaking down of social barriers between the two races, have been conservative and slow to see adjustments that need to be made and can be made for the good of both races. Northerners with little information, but sure of their superior understanding, have scolded and denounced after the fashion of the old abolitionists.

They have protested and cast sweeping aspersions without making constructive suggestions or troubling themselves to procure information
upon which such suggestions could be based. Occasional violence
against Negroes by ignorant mobs and discriminations against the Negroes in the enforcement of laws have evoked brutal and indiscriminat-
ing attacks from the Northern press that remind one of journalism in the
old Reconstruction days. Needless to say, such criticisms have contributed nothing to the Southern Negro's welfare or to national unity.

The growing political power of the Negro in the North is adding to
the Negro problem in the South. Many Northern politicians to gain the
political support of the Northern Negroes—and, eventually, those of the
South—are now supporting radical Negro leaders in their demand for a
sweeping change in the status of the Negro in the South. But efforts to
subvert the social system of the South will lead to more friction between
the North and South and to bitter racial antagonisms.

The impoverishment of the people by Reconstruction and the heavy
debt load imposed by it were most serious impediments to progress.
They hindered economic advancement and educational achievement.
Vast hordes of children grew to maturity unable even to read and write.
It is impossible to measure the cost to the South of illiteracy alone resulting from the war and Reconstuction. Conditions brought about by Reconstruction also caused a tremendous loss of manpower. They caused a
large exodus of the white people of the South to diverse parts, and made
the Negroes unfit to apply their productive powers. The loss of whites is
well illustrated by Professor Walter L. Fleming's statement that Alabama
lost more manpower in Recontruction than it lost in the war.

The poverty attending Reconstruction laid the basis for the crop lien
system and promoted sharecropping, and these more than all things
else have hindered rural progress. Hundreds of thousands of both the
landless and the landed had nothing with which to start life over and the
only source of credit was cotton. Merchants, with the assistance of eastern creditors, advanced supplies to farmers upon condition that they
would produce cotton in sufficient quantity to cover the advances made
to them. The merchant charged whatever prices he chose to and protected himself by taking a lien upon the cotton produced. Under the
system the great mass of farmers became essentially serfs. To throw off
the shackles required more resources than most of them possessed.

Even at present a majority of Southern tenant farmers depend for
credit on their landlords, or on the "furnish merchants" for their
supplies. The landlord, moreover, who stakes all on cotton or tobacco, is
a bad credit risk. For this reason he pays interest rates as high as 20
percent, and naturally his tenants pay more. It has been estimated that
those who depend on the merchant for supplies pay as much as 30
percent interest even on food and feed supplies. Credit unions and the

Farm Security and Farm Credit Administrations have helped many of the farmers, but farm credit facilities are still sadly lacking in the South. Louis XIV's remark that "Credit supports agriculture, as the rope supports the hanged" has been abundantly verified in the South.

Thus, Reconstruction made a large contribution to the development of a slumfolk class in the rural South. The sharecropper-crop-lien farm economy of the South has produced a human erosion system more costly than soil erosion. In fact the two have gone hand in hand. These things always come to mind when in this day of national championships the South is referred to as the nation's "Economic Problem No. 1."

Reconstruction and its aftermath prevented the flow of population and money into the South. The 37 million increase in population between 1870 and 1900 was largely in the North. The South's increase, except in Florida and Texas, was principally native and, as has been observed, it lost part of this increment. Northerners who moved and the millions of Europeans who came in either flocked to the industrial centers of the North or settled down on expansive fertile lands between Ohio and Kansas, made available by the Homestead Act. Most of the nation's capital and credit resources were put into railroad building and industrial and business pursuits north of the Mason and Dixon line. By 1890 the railroad pattern was laid and most of the roads had been built to feed the North. In every phase of economic activity the South was a bad risk compared with the North. Not the least of the things that kept men and money out of the South were its debt load and the stigma of debt repudiation. Northern newspapers and journals lambasted the South for the sin of repudiation and warned investors and emigrants to shun the South. In addition to other risks, they would find, the *Nation* said, that in the South the "Sense of good faith is benumbed, if not dead," and if they had anything to do with the South they would make themselves a part "of a community of swindlers." Even Henry Clews, who had conspired with the carpetbag racketeers to sell shoddy Reconstruction bonds to gullible buyers in the North and Europe, railed out against the spectacle of "Southern robbery." The notion of Southern depravity was long-lived.

Between 1865 and 1900 a new republic of tremendous wealth and productive power was forged and concurrently there was a great educational development and a general advance in culture throughout the North. The South was a mere appendage to the new nation advancing through these epochal transformations; Reconstruction had assigned it a colonial status in all its relations with the North. J. M. Cross of New York City, for example, wrote to John Letcher of Virginia on March 8, 1867, that "Northern civilization must go all the way over the South, which is only a question of time." Some of those who had wanted to make the Northern way of life the national way lived to see their wish a *fait accompli.* The patterns of national life were forming and henceforth were to be formed in the North and national unity was to be achieved by the conformity of the South to these patterns. Northerners have made little or no distinction between the North and the nation. The idea has become deeply imbedded throughout the country. For example, Professor Buck unconsciously expresses this attitude when he says, "The small farm worked in countless ways to bring Southern life into closer harmony with the major trends in national life"—that is, Northern life. The same idea is carried in one of the chapter titles—"Nationalization of the South"—in Professor William B. Hesseltine's recent *History of the South.* When the South has failed to conform it has been stigmatized as backward, provincial, and sectional.

By 1900 the Old South was largely a thing of memory. Yearning for some of the good things of life, impulsive young men rejected antebellum traditions as inadequate to the needs of the New South which must be built. They sneered at "mummies," "mossbacks," and "Bourbons" who cherished the Old South. Others, just as avid about the future of business and industry, hoped to bring over into the New South of their dreams the best of the old and thus merge "two distinct civilizations" into a compound that some good day would surpass anything the North could show. They would leaven the lump of crass materialism with the leaven of graceful living. But to the older generation it seemed that those who were breaking loose from old moorings were bending "the knee to expediency" with little or no regard for principle.

Allen W. Trelease

ALLEN W. TRELEASE (1928–   ) is professor of history at the University of North Carolina, Greensboro. He is the author of several books, including *Indian Affairs in Colonial New York: The Seventeenth Century* (1960), *Reconstruction: The Great Experiment* (1971), and *White Terror: The Ku Klux Klan Conspiracy and Southern Reconstruction* (1971).

After promoting for a generation and more the idea of innate Negro inferiority in order to justify slavery, Southerners could hardly be expected suddenly to abandon it with the coming of emancipation, especially in the wake of military defeat. The newly freed slave, regarded as occupying an intermediate stage between humanity and the lower orders of animal life, fell into a niche already prepared for him—that of the antebellum free Negro. As such, he was not a citizen and had no civil or political rights except those which the white community deemed proper to confer. "He still served, we still ruled," as Cable pointed out a few years later; "all need of holding him in private bondage was disproved.... Emancipation had destroyed private, but it had not disturbed public, subjugation. The ex-slave was not a free man; he was only a free Negro." In effect Negroes were now the slaves of every white man. As subordination and discipline had been enforced by the lash before, it continued to be so now, but without the restraining influence of the slaveholder's self-interest. "The pecuniary value which the individual negro formerly represented having disappeared," Carl Schurz reported in 1865, "the maiming and killing of colored men seems to be looked upon by many as one of those venial offenses which must be forgiven to the outraged feelings of a wronged and robbed people." Most whites, he said, appeared to believe that Negroes existed for the special purpose of providing for their needs. If Schurz exaggerated, the history of the Ku Klux Klan will show that he did not do so very much. Certainly whipping and corporal punishment were regarded as the white man's right and duty, emancipation or no emancipation; organized regulators or vigilantes took up this task with the advent of emancipation, and the Klan further institutionalized the practice.

Negroes often suffered by their liberation.

> As a slave [a Mississippi official pointed out in 1871], the negro was pro-
> tected on account of his value; humanity went hand in hand with the interest
> of the owner to secure his protection, to prevent his being overworked,
> underfed, insufficiently clothed, or abused, or neglected when sick. But as a
> free man, he was deprived of all the protection which had been given to him
> by his value as property; he was reduced to something like the condition of a
> stray dog.

For all the talk of white suffering during the Reconstruction era, it was
the black man who experienced the greatest deprivation and mistreatment, first and last. But it was a rare freedman who regretted emancipation; stories to the contrary could almost invariably be traced to white
men's rationalizations of slavery.

Negroes wanted the same freedom that white men enjoyed, with
equal prerogatives and opportunities. The educated black minority emphasized civil and political rights more than the masses, who called most
of all for land and schools. In an agrarian society, the only kind most of
them knew, landownership was associated with freedom, respectability,
and the good life. It was almost universally desired by Southern blacks,
as it was by landless peasants the world over. Give us our land and we
can take care of ourselves, said a group of South Carolina Negroes to a
Northern journalist in 1865; without land the old masters can hire us or
starve us as they please. A major failure of Reconstruction was that,
except for a favored few, they never got it. Not only did they lack money
or credit, but the government made no substantial effort to help them
obtain it. Whites in many areas refused to sell, or even rent land to
Negroes when they did not have the means to buy, and often actively
conspired to keep them from acquiring it. Negro landownership would
have enhanced the economic and social well-being of the entire section,
but it smacked too much of equality and independence. Some Negroes
who did acquire farms of their own were driven off by mobs or the Ku
Klux Klan. A Negro state senator in Florida believed that there was a
general understanding among whites to deprive blacks of a great part of
the income and property they had rightfully acquired. In many places
this was correct.

The desire for education was reflected in the avidity with which
blacks of all ages took advantage of the limited schooling made available
to them immediately after the war. Knowledge and literacy too were
associated with freedom. Some of this enthusiasm was transitory, particularly among the elders, but parents continued to send their children
to schools, where they existed, and to cry for their establishment where
they did not.

Although a minority of Negroes moved to town—occasionally driven there by white terrorism—the overwhelming majority stayed on the land as wage laborers and sharecroppers. There was little motivation to work harder than they had under slavery. Many whites repeated the stock attitudes regarding Negro character: they were lazy, irresponsible, wasteful, and careless of property; they procrastinated, lacked forethought or perseverance, and derived no satisfaction from a job well done; they engaged in petty thievery and had no sense whatever of right and wrong or truth and falsehood. These characterizations were valid in varying measure—the natural defense mechanisms generated by a life of slavery. One well-disposed Northerner trying to cope with a Georgia cotton plantation reiterated nearly all of these traits from experience with his own laborers, but pointed out that the one thing which seemed to overcome Negro heedlessness was the desire to own their own land. Native Southerners admitted, however, that Negroes were performing far better than they had had any reason to expect at emancipation. A few proclaimed Negro labor the best in the world. The truth seems to be that, after a brief exultation with the idea of freedom, Negroes realized that their position was hardly changed; they continued to live and work much as they had before.

But white men generally agreed on the Negroes' good behavior after the war, and it was for many a matter of pleasant surprise; they had assumed that slavery alone could keep the blacks in good order. Most freedmen were as submissive and deferential to white men as before the war. The great majority were totally dependent upon white favor for a livelihood, and self-interest dictated subservience as a matter of second nature. If some aggressive souls—usually a minority of younger Negroes and other free spirits—talked back or refused to give up the sidewalk, this "insolence" was rare. Seldom were Negroes willing to stand up to a white man and resist or defy him to his face; those who did automatically incurred the wrath of the white community, and risked their lives. Concerted resistance was almost never successful and was apt to prove fatal. Whites were more numerous in most areas, and better armed. More important, they were used to commanding and the blacks to obeying. Next to poverty and economic dependence, this was the freedman's greatest handicap in asserting real freedom during the Reconstruction era.

When Negroes did strike back or defy the master race it was more often the product of impetuosity and extreme aggravation than forethought and planning. Whites commonly ascribed Negro violence, whether directed against them or (more often) among the blacks themselves, as the product of a congenitally passionate nature. The blacks were like children, it was said, who flared up without thought of consequences and then almost as quickly subsided. Negroes seemingly committed fewer murders than whites in proportion to their number, and most of these were crimes of passion in which other Negroes were the victims. Certainly black men were more often the victims than the perpetrators of interracial violence.

A partial exception to the rule of Negro passivity was the crime of arson. The fires almost invariably occurred at night, with barns, gin houses, and other outbuildings the chief targets, and the culprits were seldom discovered. This was, in fact, one of the few relatively safe ways Negroes had of evening the score with white terrorism, although the fire victims were not always those guilty of the terror. Whites frequently imagined incendiary plots when there were none, just as they had long imagined servile insurrections.

But the chief crime complained of was petty thievery. Most thefts occurred after dark, with no witnesses, and it was almost impossible to discover the culprits. Cotton and corn were stolen from the fields, hams were abducted from smokehouses, tools and equipment disappeared from sheds and barns. Occasionally cows, sheep, and hogs were stolen and slaughtered. Some planters who had raised their own meat supplies before the war now gave up trying to keep livestock. Negro larceny, too, was a legacy of slavery: a poverty-stricken people, systematically denied the fruits of their labors and having no property of their own to consider sacred, appropriated what they needed to make life more livable. . . .

Whites of every class united in opposition to what they called social equality—a completely integrated society—as leading inevitably to intermarriage and degeneration of the white race. In that event, a South Carolinian declared, "we shall become a race of mulattoes . . . another Mexico; we shall be ruled out from the family of white nations. . . . It is a matter of life and death with the Southern people to keep their blood pure." A Republican of Georgia pointed out, "If you talk about equality, they at once conclude that you must take the negro into your parlor or into your bed—everywhere that you would take your wife. They seem to be diseased upon that subject. They do not seem to consider that he is merely to be equal before the law, but take it, I suppose designedly, to mean equality in the broadest sense; and hence they stir themselves up and lash themselves into a fury about it."

Emancipation increased the Southern white rape complex because freedom presumably stimulated the Negro's innate passion for white women and removed external restraints. This was the supreme taboo, which evoked white supremacy in its most virulent form. Whether or not Negro rape of white women actually increased during Reconstruction, it certainly was not widespread; more important was the fact that whites *thought* it was on the increase. The only penalty sufficient to deter the tendency was violent and speedy death—lynching without the delay and dignity of formal trial. The *Fayetteville* (Tennessee) *Observer* echoed widespread opinion when it condoned the lynching of an alleged Negro rapist in 1868: "The community said amen to the act—it was just and right. We know not who did it, whether Ku Klux or the immediate neighbors, but we feel that they were only the instruments of Divine vengeance in carrying out His holy and immutable decrees." Here too the Ku Klux Klan helped to institutionalize a practice which preceded and long outlived it.

The physical and psychological necessities of keeping Negroes in subordination led to the wildest inconsistencies of attitude and expression. On the one hand the black man was best fitted by nature and temperament for a life of servility and happiest in his carefree dependence on white protectors. On the other hand he was only a degree removed from the wild beasts of the jungle, and the most constant surveillance was needed to keep him from bursting the bonds of discipline and turning upon his friends and protectors in a bloody insurrection. The first theory was necessary to rationalize slavery and the ensuing peonage, but as it never fully squared with the facts, the second argument served to justify necessary repressive measures. Both reinforced Negro subordinance. . . .

Northern Reconstruction policy evolved against this background of myths and realities. Again, the race question was crucial. The North began fighting the Civil War to defeat secession and ended by abolishing slavery as well. Emancipation brought the unavoidable problem of defining the freedmen's status. Northern Democrats generally shared the racial views of the white South and sanctioned the most minimal adjustments required by the ending of legal servitude. This was also the tendency of Abraham Lincoln and of Andrew Johnson afterward. Most Republicans fell between this conservatism and the Radicals' advocacy of full legal and political equality at war's end, but they were gradually driven toward egalitarianism by the course of events between 1865 and 1867. And as theirs was the majority party in the North, that drift determined federal government policy.

Lincoln had assumed the right to reorganize the South and guide her back into the Union, largely on his own authority as commander in chief. During the war, therefore, he sponsored new Loyal, or Unionist, state governments in Virginia, Tennessee, Louisiana, and Arkansas. Following Appomattox and Lincoln's death, Andrew Johnson took advantage of a congressional recess to organize the remaining seven states of the late Confederacy. Seemingly all that remained was for Congress to seat the senators and representatives chosen under these governments. But Congress delayed and ultimately refused to do so.

While the Lincoln and Johnson regimes were dominated in the South by men who had taken a back seat in the secession movement, or opposed it altogether, and who accepted the end of slavery as a price of military defeat, they subscribed as a matter of course to the view that white men must continue to rule in the South. To this end they enacted a series of Black Codes in 1865 and 1866 which clearly and deliberately relegated the Negro to a second-class citizenship. No state extended the right to vote to black men, even to the few who might be educated or well-to-do. Nor was any hope extended for equality someday in the future.

When new horizons did open up for the Negro, as they soon did, it was because of the Republican majority in Congress. Just as the war closed, Congress created a Bureau of Refugees, Freedmen, and Abandoned Lands, attached to the Army, primarily to care for the newly freed black population. The Freedmen's Bureau, as it was called, always suffered from inadequate funds and personnel to perform the tasks assigned it, but the services it did provide were indispensable. Under the direction of General O. O. Howard it distributed food and clothing to those of both races who needed them, protected Negroes against the most blatant forms of exploitation and mistreatment, arranged labor contracts with employers, and attempted with some success to enforce these contracts against infractions on either side. It established hospitals, schools, and colleges for its black charges with the cooperation of Northern charitable agencies.

The bureau represented an unprecedented extension of federal authority, regulating the economic, social, and legal affairs of individual persons within the respective states. Intended as an emergency device to cope with wartime and immediate postwar conditions, it was due to expire a year after the war ended. But the needs it was created to meet showed no sign of disappearing. Negroes were continually subjected to exploitation, discrimination, and outright violence, which they were powerless to combat alone. The new state governments not only failed to protect them or to assume the educational and other responsibilities of the Freedmen's Bureau, but their Black Codes actually perpetuated many of the hallmarks of slavery. So far as the Northern war effort had become a crusade to free the slaves, the victory seemed in danger of becoming undone. Thus the Republicans pushed through Congress in July 1866, over President Johnson's veto, a law continuing the bureau for two years more.

In the same spirit were the Civil Rights Act and its sequel, the Fourteenth Amendment, which the Republican majority enacted over the President's objections in April and June of 1866. The former measure defined United States citizenship to include Negroes and extended to them the basic civil rights to sue and to testify in the courts, to hold and convey property, and most importantly, to enjoy equal benefit of the laws with white people. The Fourteenth Amendment, which was ratified and went into effect in 1868, incorporated the provisions of the

Civil Rights Act into the Constitution; it also set forth a program for Southern Reconstruction which represented a compromise between the quick restoration favored by the white South and President Johnson and the stricter requirements (such as Negro suffrage) advocated by Radical Republicans. . . .

A basic assumption behind the Reconstruction acts was that the Negro freedmen would support congressional Reconstruction and would vote for the party which had freed them and granted them civil rights and the ballot. The assumption proved sound, for Negroes backed the Republican party overwhelmingly as long as they had the chance to do so. In fact they provided the bulk of the Republican electorate; in most states white supporters were more important for their leadership than for their numbers. No matter how dependent the freedmen were upon their former masters, or how much they continued to trust and confide in them as individuals, only a tiny minority of Uncle Toms willingly cast their ballots for the party of white supremacy.

Negroes were elected to office in every state, leading Conservatives in moments of bitter abandon to characterize the whole policy as one of "Negro rule," an accusation made partly for political effect but also arising from the common conviction that racial sovereignty was indivisible. If whites did not rule blacks, it must therefore be the other way around. The charge of Negro rule was absurd, for blacks never held office in proportion to their total number and they rarely held the most prominent posts. This situation resulted in part from the race prejudice which white Republicans shared, or which they sought to appease in nominating attractive party slates. But equally important was the plain fact that slavery was a poor training ground for the responsibilities of public office. The quality of those Negro officeholders high and low who did pass the barrier was not notably better or worse than that of white men who held comparable posts at that time, before, or later. Some, especially in the lower levels, were illiterate, but so were some of their white counterparts of both parties. Incompetent and illiterate officials did not begin or end with Reconstruction, nor were they typical of that period.

The so-called carpetbaggers—Northerners who settled in the South during and after the war and affiliated with the Republican party—were only a tiny minority numerically. They had great influence, however, particularly in the deep South where the Negro population was heavy and there was no significant native white Republican element to provide leadership. The term *carpetbagger* was another canard. These men supposedly descended on the South like a swarm of locusts, bringing no more than they could carry in a carpetbag; their purpose was to prey on the defenseless region through political manipulation of the gullible freedmen. Actually most of these persons moved South by 1866, well before Radical Reconstruction was conceived or the Republican party was even organized in most of the South. Some were stationed there by the Army or Freedmen's Bureau, but most moved South for the same reasons of economic betterment that led greater numbers to go West. When the Republican party was organized and new governments were in process of formation these men filled a need for educated and occasionally experienced leadership. In fact, they usually raised the caliber of Radical government rather than lowering it. Of course, their motives, abilities, and accomplishments ran the usual human scale; along with the incompetent or corrupt there were honest and highly able men whom posterity would have celebrated under other circumstances. Active Republicans required a tough skin and often great physical courage to withstand the social ostracism, economic boycott, verbal abuse, character assassination, and physical violence to which they were commonly subjected by Southern whites. In a few cases at least, this courage was inspired by a high degree of dedication. "That I should have taken a political office seems almost inexplicable," wrote General Adelbert Ames a quarter-century after he had been forced out of the governorship of Mississippi:

> My explanation may seem ludicrous now, but then, it seemed to me that I had a Mission with a large M. Because of my [earlier] course as Military Governor, the colored men of the State had confidence in me and I was convinced that I could help to guide them successfully, keep men of doubtful integrity from control, and the more certainly accomplish what was every patriots' [sic] wish, the enfranchisement of the colored men and the pacification of the country.

Men of Northern origin were to be found in local and subordinate offices here and there, and they served conspicuously in Congress, as governors, and in other high offices.

The native white Republicans—scalawags to their enemies—were drawn from every walk of Southern life. Some had been Democrats and others were Whigs before the war. A few had served the Confederacy in conspicuous fashion, but most were wartime Unionists; the more uncompromising their Unionism had been, the more apt they were to embrace the Republican party afterward. Although they could be found at least as isolated examples, throughout the South, most white Republican voters were concentrated in the hilly and mountainous regions where slavery had gained little foothold. The Appalachian highlands from western Virginia to northern Alabama and the Ozark Mountains of Arkansas were the major strongholds of white Republicanism during Reconstruction and for generations afterward. The term *scalawag* was of course another form of political abuse; the personal character of Southern Republicans did not suffer by comparison with their accusers. Many joined the Republican party because it was the Unionist party and it opposed the planter interest as they themselves had done for years. Most of them shared in some measure the racial views common to the white South, and this helped make the Republican coalition unstable, but for the most part they lived in regions where the Negro was hardly more of a factor locally than in the North. In such places they commonly filled all of the political offices and supplied nearly all of the Republican votes. At the state level, particularly in the upper South, they filled many of the higher offices as well. A few members of the antebellum ruling class, usually ex-Whigs who had not been enthusiastic secessionists, also joined the Republican party, hoping to hold it to a moderate course and exercise a paternalistic rein on the Negroes while profiting by their strength at the polls. Such men carried great prestige and were given some of the highest offices in an effort to make the party more appealing to the white population generally, but the number of these converts was small. Governor James L. Alcorn of Mississippi belonged to this class, as did former governors Lewis E. Parsons of Alabama and James L. Orr of South Carolina.

In terms of ideology, Republicans were clearly the democratic party of the Reconstruction South. Unquestionably there was an element of political expediency involved in the raising of Negroes to civil equality with white men, but a great many believed in it as a matter of principle. The *Charleston Daily Republican,* a voice of moderation and a critic of corruption and ineptitude within the party in South Carolina, attacked Democratic predictions that white men must at some near day control the state again.

> Such talk is as wickedly idle as for colored men to say that their race shall have complete control. It is not to be a matter of race at all. It is to be a matter of citizenship, in which colored and white are to have their rights and their due share of power; not because they are white, not because they are colored, but because they are American citizens. By-and-by we shall stop talking of the color of a man in relation to citizenship and power, and shall look at his wealth of mind and soul.

Radicalism was also aimed less spectacularly at raising the status of poorer whites. Within limits the Republican party was a poor man's party which sought to obliterate racial lines as much as popular prejudice made it politically safe to do. Democrats defeated the effort, as they later did when the Populists tried it, by crying "nigger"; most Southern whites placed white supremacy above all other issues.

Many public offices which had been appointive were now made elective, sometimes at the cost of efficiency. In some states, but not all, more home rule was extended, making local government more responsive to local wishes and less subject to central control. Property qualifications for officeholding, where they still existed in 1867, were removed. Legislatures were reapportioned to provide more equal representation, although Negro counties in some states were slighted. By far the most important democratic extension was the granting of Negro suffrage. This had been required by the Reconstruction acts, and it was incorporated in all the new constitutions.

The only exception to universal manhood suffrage lay in the partial and temporary disfranchisement of ex-Confederates. This provision had been written into the Reconstruction acts to help ensure further that the new state governments would be organized by Unionists, but state law governed the matter thereafter. Where disfranchisement survived as a significant factor—in Tennessee and Arkansas—Republicans felt themselves outnumbered and regarded it as a continuing necessity to keep the former rebels and the Democratic party from taking control. However dubious this policy may have been in those states, a free and unfettered majority rule permitted Republican victories in most states, and disfranchisement was abandoned either at once or very soon. Much the same was true of eligibility for public office, which was more nearly determined by federal law. By 1872 Congress had removed the disqualifications of all but a relative handful of ex-Confederate leaders. The Radical governments made no effort to outlaw the Conservative opposition or create a dictatorship. On the contrary, they were too lenient in enforcing law and order against those who used force to overthrow them.

There was corruption, electoral as well as financial, in nearly every state during the period of Republican control. Conservatives at the time succeeded in pinning on the Radical regimes a blanket charge of dishonesty which has never worn off, but the actual picture was not so simple. Corruption was rampant throughout the country after the war, and Democrats North and South were about as guilty as Republicans. The Tweed Ring in New York City supposedly stole more than all Southern politicians combined, if only because New York had more to steal. Within the South corruption varied widely from state to state. It flourished most in South Carolina, where it had been comparatively unknown, and in Louisiana, where it was endemic. In South Carolina the Republicans at least partially cleaned their own house under Governor Chamberlain after 1874. In Louisiana both parties were corrupt and remained so for generations. In Mississippi an honest Republican administration gave way to less honest Democratic regimes after 1875. During the period of Republican control moreover, minority Democratic officials were sometimes as venal as their Republican counterparts, and Democratic businessmen sometimes offered the bribes that Republicans accepted. In the matter of electoral, as opposed to fiscal, corruption generalization is easier. Republicans were occasionally guilty of manipulating election returns, but these practices paled in comparison with the massive campaigns of fraud and intimidation, symbolized by the Ku Klux Klan, with which Democrats sought to return to power in nearly every state. It was largely owing to these methods that they did assume power in one state after another during the 1870s. . . .

Radical egalitarianism for the Negro was primarily political and legal, but it also extended to economic and social matters. Republican governments repealed nearly all of the earlier laws requiring racial discrimination, and in some states it was specifically forbidden. A few states enacted laws to prevent racial segregation in railroad cars, theaters, restaurants, and hotels, but compliance was never complete and actual practice varied widely. It is mistaken to say that segregation did not begin until well after Reconstruction, although positive laws requiring it certainly were hostile to Republican policy. Both constitutional and legal enactments guaranteed racial equality before the law.

The greatest and most enduring achievement of the Radical governments was the establishment of a functioning public school system for the first time in Southern history. As in politics, the greatest change lay in the fact that Negroes were included in the new dispensation. Building on the work of the Freedmen's Bureau and various charitable agencies before 1868, they created school systems which could not compare with most of those in the North, but which represented a great accomplishment in the light of Southern traditions and resources. Straitened finances and the difficulty of securing qualified teachers plagued the new school systems in every state. Economy was hampered further by the fact that almost everywhere separate schools were established for the two races—Negroes seldom demanded integrated facilities, which were opposed even by most white Republicans. Often churches or other buildings were converted to school purposes, and many schools were erected by groups of individuals on their own initiative, sometimes, in the case of Negro schools, with financial aid from interested whites. Local whites served as teachers of both white and Negro schools; literate Negroes also taught in Negro schools, as did white men and women from the North. Most who taught in Negro schools did so at the price of social ostracism and sometimes physical danger; they required a high degree of dedication and a high resistance to poverty, given the pay scales. The new state governments provided support for higher education for both races. In some cases this meant the creation of Negro colleges and universities, and in others it entailed efforts, largely unsuccessful, to desegregate existing institutions.

New hospitals, orphanages, insane asylums, poorhouses, and other institutions were created, and older facilities enlarged. Jails and penitentiaries were built on a larger scale than before. Negro emancipation had rendered all of this necessary, for as slaves they had been under the wardship of their masters and rarely used public facilities. Moreover, the Radicals were somewhat readier than their predecessors to assume public responsibility for the welfare of citizens of both races, in many respects adopting attitudes and precedents which had been gaining headway in the North for a generation or more but which had lagged in the South.

The Radical regimes generally shared the old Whig-Republican willingness to use government power to stimulate business activity and economic growth, especially in the field of transportation. As elsewhere in the country, the major beneficiaries of public aid were railroads, although a good deal of money was spent on roads, bridges, levees, and other public works. These projects were expensive, taken collectively, and some states assumed greater debts than the returns justified. Everywhere, North and South, politics and personal profiteering motivated some of these expenditures. For the most part, however, they were relatively sound, and in the South they decidedly enhanced the region's economic growth and prosperity. Some of the projects were essential to repair wartime deterioration and destruction.

Radical governments did comparatively little to alter the conditions of labor or raise the incomes of citizens of either race; no governments did in nineteenth-century America. The Freedmen's Bureau continued most of its operations through 1868 and then gradually closed down because of congressional nonsupport, suspending altogether in 1872. This was a misfortune, especially for the Negroes, as the state governments lacked the funds, personnel, and legal power to advise and protect them as effectively in relations with the white community. Even in Republican-controlled localities, the scales of justice were weighted against the impoverished freedmen. A number of states did enact laws, however, to protect persons against foreclosures of all their property for debt. These homestead exemptions were designed to appeal to both races, and some Democrats found them to be embarrassingly popular with poorer whites.

One of the most cogent criticisms of Radical Reconstruction is that it failed to distribute land to the freedmen while it was giving them the ballot. Continuing economic dependence on the whites endangered every other right the Negro received. Some halting steps were taken by the federal government and the state of South Carolina to provide land to Negroes on easy terms, but they came to almost nothing, requiring as they did a social concern and an expenditure of tax money which most people in that generation did not have or were unwilling to make. At the same time, Southern whites were suspicious of Negro landownership and continued to discourage it, sometimes by outright violence. This was another service rendered by the Ku Klux Klan.

The Radical governments spent more money and levied higher taxes than Southerners had been used to, as it was. But public needs were also unprecedented. Even the Johnson governments had raised taxes and expenditures to repair war damage, but left much yet to be done. The necessary new social services, and especially the schools, were extremely costly by previous governmental standards. When the aid extended to railroads is also added in, it is no wonder that both taxes and public debt rose unprecedentedly at every level of government. States, counties, and municipalities all raised what money they could and then mortgaged the future to meet immediate needs and finance improvements which required time to repay themselves. If debts occasionally climbed beyond a prudent level this was by no means universal; Democrats sometimes raised them further when they returned to power in the 1870s.

Even with these increases the Southern tax level remained considerably below that which prevailed in the North. The average tax rate in the eleven ex-Confederate states in 1870, including all state, county, town, and city taxes, was 1.57 percent of assessed valuation; the comparable figure in all the remaining states was 2.03 percent. The Southern states were much poorer than the Northern, and less able to afford improvements and services; but this poverty was usually reflected in lower assessed valuations and hence a lower tax return at the same rate. Taxes levied by the Radical governments were extravagant only by comparison with the section's previous parsimonious standards.

Equally controversial as the level of taxes and debts was the matter of who paid the taxes and who derived the benefits. Landowners, who had previously governed the South in their own interest, now found themselves bearing the major tax burden while the benefits went in large measure to businessmen and Negroes. Republican fiscal policies thus further infuriated the old ruling class and convinced them that civilization had given way to barbarism.

Republicans were often accused of partiality in law enforcement, winking at black criminality. Law enforcement was always difficult in the sparsely settled South, and lawlessness increased with the unsettled conditions that prevailed during and after the war. Negro criminality, chiefly petty theft, may well have grown temporarily, but it was always comparatively easy to convict Negro criminals when they were known. Republican officials (including Negroes) usually leaned over backward to demonstrate their impartiality in this respect. Republican governors were also accused of pardoning Negro criminals indiscriminately. This charge too was exaggerated if not wholly false. Whatever substance it may have had probably derived from the fact that some pardons were granted (after proper investigation) to redress the manifest injustices of many Southern courts against Negroes in interracial cases. White Conservatives often recommended such pardons in individual cases, but collectively it was easy to accuse the Radicals of yet another outrage against white civilization.

Actually it was white men who committed most of the violence, and much of it was racially and politically inspired. When these overtones were not present, it was punished about as effectively, or ineffectively, in areas of Republican control as Democratic, and as was true in earlier and later periods of Southern history. A great deal of violence was deliberate and organized, however, committed by mobs and by armed bands in and out of disguise. A disproportionate share was directed at Negroes and white Unionists, partly to avenge real or imaginary injuries arising from the war, partly to keep the Negro "in his place" economically and socially, and partly to overthrow the Republican party by intimidating, exiling, or assassinating its members. The Ku Klux Klan exemplified this kind of violence in the most spectacular way, but it extended far beyond the Klan. The greatest short-run deficiency of the Republican regimes—it would soon prove fatal—was their physical weakness. In the face of implacable white resistance they proved unable to preserve law and order, or their own existence, against attempts at violent overthrow. In certain parts of the South the authorities were almost paralyzed by organized lawlessness.

When conspiracies to obstruct justice assumed this dimension the only solution was armed force. Republican officials repeatedly called on the Army for help in suppressing combinations which they could not handle by the usual means, but the results were usually discouraging. In the first place, too many troops were mustered out of service too quickly amid the euphoric celebration of victory in 1865. Only 20,000 troops remained on duty in the South by the fall of 1867, and this number gradually fell to 6,000 by the fall of 1876; moreover, one-quarter to half of these were stationed in Texas, chiefly on frontier duty. A much larger occupation force would have had trouble in maintaining order throughout the South. Furthermore, the traditional constitutional and legal safeguards against military power now sharply restricted the Army's peacekeeping potential. Its political and legal jurisdiction disappeared as soon as the new state governments were recognized by Congress. The military were limited thereafter to intervention only on application from, and in subordination to, the civil authorities. Where the latter did not act effectively, through incapacity, fear, or sympathy with the outlaws, the soldiers had little more than symbolic value.

For this reason most of the states organized militias, the traditional standby in times of emergency. But this weapon too was of doubtful value under the peculiar circumstances of Reconstruction. A militia composed in large part of the very white men who were engaged in lawlessness, or were sympathetic with it, seemed worse than useless. The only safe recruits were white Unionists and Negroes, but mobilizing these was equivalent to arming one political party against the other. The arming of Negroes in particular inflamed Conservatives and added fuel to the fire it was intended to quench. It summoned up the old fear of Negro insurrection and portended a race war which no Southern official was prepared to be responsible for. In the Deep South, where white Republicans were few and far between, militia were seldom mobilized and they played a negligible peacekeeping role. Governors in the upper South organized white Unionist recruits, for the most part, to stamp out Democratic terrorism, a tactic that was relatively effective but highly dangerous politically, for it fed Conservative charges of military despotism.

In the last analysis, Radical Reconstruction failed because the seed of biracial democracy which it planted fell on barren ground in the South, and the artificial nurture it received from the federal government was soon discontinued. Democracy has always required a high degree of popular homogeneity and consensus, a precondition which was altogether lacking in the South. Conservative opposition to Reconstruction was about as deeply felt as political opposition ever gets. As South Carolina whites expressed it in a protest to Congress in 1868:

> Intelligence, virtue, and patriotism are to give place, in all elections, to ignorance, stupidity and vice. The superior race is to be made subservient to the inferior.... They who own no property are to levy taxes and make all appropriations.... The consequences will be, in effect, confiscation. The appropriations to support free schools for the education of the negro children, for the support of old negroes in the poor-houses, and the vicious in jails and penitentiary, together with a standing army of negro soldiers [the militia], will be crushing and utterly ruinous to the State. Every man's property will have to be sold to pay his taxes.... The white people of our State will never quietly submit to negro rule.... By moral agencies, by political organization, by every peaceful means left us, we will keep up this contest until we have regained the heritage of political control handed down to us by honored ancestry. That is a duty we owe to the land that is ours, to the graves that it contains, and to the race of which you and we are alike members—the proud Caucasian race, whose sovereignty on earth God has ordained....

Such views contrasted sharply with the vision of a biracial democracy quoted already from the *Charleston Daily Republican*.

Conservatives mercilessly pilloried the Negroes, carpetbaggers, and scalawags who staffed and supported the Republican regimes. The Democratic newspaper press—which far outstripped the Southern Republican press in numbers and circulation—played a vital role in stimulating and disseminating hatred of all things Radical. The wildest allegations and *ad hominem* arguments were at least half believed and unblushingly broadcast because they fit preconceived notions. Moreover, character assassination and slander were resorted to even when editors did not believe them, because they "served a good end" in discrediting the enemy. The *Little Rock Daily Arkansas Gazette,* for example, characterized the state constitutional convention of 1868 as "the most graceless and unconscionable gathering of abandoned, disreputable characters that has even assembled in this state, outside of the penitentiary walls . . . a foul gathering whose putridity stinks in the nostrils of all decency." Altogether the whole tone of Southern government had been debased, Conservatives felt, and they proceeded to debase the tone of political discourse correspondingly. "So far as our State governments is [*sic*] concerned, we are in the hands of camp-followers, horse-holders, cooks, bottle-washers, and thieves," declared General James H. Clanton of Alabama. "We have passed out from the hands of the brave soldiers who overcame us, and are turned over the tender mercies of squaws for torture. . . ." Negroes were characterized as unfit to vote, much less hold office, and Democrats excoriated the federal and state enactments which had brought these things to pass. Few Southern Democrats in public life had any constructive proposal to make in behalf of the freedman. The whole thrust of their policy was to "put him back in his place" economically, socially, and politically. Some Conservatives disapproved in principle of universal manhood suffrage, even among whites, regarding it as a denial of character and intelligence in government and a threat to property; Negro suffrage was simply the ultimate outrage. An increasing number of so-called New Departure Democrats, like Benjamin H. Hill of Georgia, reluctantly accepted Negro suffrage as a *fait accompli* and hoped to control the black vote as they controlled black labor, but a majority rejected the idea out of hand and pledged themselves to repeal or nullify it at the earliest opportunity.

To Conservatives, Republican affiliation was itself a sign of moral turpitude which only the flimsiest additional evidence sufficed to confirm. The laws of libel had no practical existence in that day, and such evidence was commonly embroidered or manufactured to suit the occasion. Those Republicans who mingled socially with Negroes were morally depraved; those who refused to do so were hypocrites who betrayed their own political teachings. Those who came from the North were outlanders having no ties of knowledge or sympathy with the land and people they despoiled; those who were native to the South were traitors to their race and section and therefore equally unworthy of trust or confidence. Those who had owned slaves were now discovered to have treated them cruelly; those who had not owned them were the dregs of society who would never have risen to the surface in decent times. The greatest opprobrium was always heaped on those who associated most with the freedmen or who had substantial Negro followings. Eric Hoffer has remarked that hatred requires a vivid and tangible devil. Conservative Southern whites conjured them up by the hundreds.

But although Radical policies were condemned as a matter of course, Democrats in fact supported some of them unobtrusively. This was true of the exemption of homesteads from foreclosure, and also a great proportion of the railway expenditures. Opinion was divided on the subject of public schooling, especially for Negroes, but most Democrats accepted the policy and continued it when they later assumed power. Opposition was strongest in Mississippi, as noted earlier, but schools were unpopular with many rural people everywhere. The major complaints arose from the unprecedented cost of establishing and maintaining them and from the fact that Republicans sponsored the policy. Many persons objected less to Negro schools per se than to the Negro and Yankee teachers who staffed them. Most of these were advocates of racial equality, and some were quite militant about it. Hence Southerners resented them as they did the political carpetbaggers—outside agitators whose main purpose and effect was to alienate Negroes from the white population and make them less docile. H. C. Luce, a Northerner living in western North Carolina who had never engaged in politics at all, wrote of threats he received after establishing a school for local Negro children: "It is one of the perils of a Northern man residing in such a community that, however unexceptionable his conduct may be, if he is kind to the negroes and tries to help them, a report will very soon be put in circulation that he is inciting the negroes to revenge, and the chances are against him if he does not promptly and publicly convince his neighbors of their mistake in believing the report." Like countless teachers or sponsors of Negro schools across the South, Luce became a target of the Ku Klux Klan.

In general, Conservatives advocated retrenchment and economy at the expense of many social services favored by the Radicals. Apart from white supremacy, their most popular and effective cry was for economy in government and lower taxes—a cry that often came from the heart as they compared present and past tax bills. The position of most Democrats on most issues was plainly reactionary. They appealed largely to a rural, agrarian, racist past which had become increasingly hostile to new ideas, and except for the most minimal accommodations required by the war's outcome they proposed to return to it. Later, after the Radicals had been swept aside, they were to become more enamored of the vision of an industrialized New South.

The bitterest opposition was always reserved for those Radical policies that portended racial equality. This was the supreme Radical sin. Laws enacted for that purpose "have no binding force or moral sanction," the *New Orleans Times* declared in July 1868, "and will be disregarded and declared null and void as soon as the inalienable rights of the people are again recognized. . . . No privilege can be secured to the negro to which his white neighbors do not consent, and if he attempts to enforce privileges on the strength of carpetbag authority he will simply destroy his claims of future peace, and heap up wrath against the day of wrath." Political and legal equality for the Negro was rendered all the more noxious by the common assumption that it would lead inevitably to social mixing. "[If] I sit side by side in the Senate, House, or on the judicial bench, with a coloured man," one gentleman inquired indignantly, "how can I refuse to sit with him at the table? . . . If we have social equality we shall have intermarriage, and if we have intermarriage we shall degenerate; we shall become a race of mulattoes; . . . we shall be ruled out from the family of white nations."

The Radical revolution, as some contemporaries on both sides regarded it, was only a halfway revolution. Within the South, Radical Reconstruction was clearly revolutionary in its overthrow of the old ruling class and above all in its establishment of political and legal equality for Negroes; hence the bitterness of the Conservative reaction. But economically and socially there was far less change, and most blacks remained a landless peasantry subject to manifold discrimination. In the larger national context, Radical Reconstruction reflected a revival of the old nationalistic constitutional doctrine of Hamilton and Marshall submerged by the state rights creed of Jefferson, Jackson, and their successors before 1860. The Radicals were not revolutionary by traditional American standards; if they appeared to be so it was chiefly because of the archaic social and political structure of the South. Nor did most of them regard themselves as revolutionaries. Southern Republicans, in trying to broaden their base of support at home, denied the charge and sought repeatedly to identify themselves with established political traditions. They claimed to stand for state rights within the higher national context and for the liberation doctrines expressed in the Declaration of Independence. The Fourteenth and Fifteenth Amendments, the Reconstruction acts, the civil rights legislation, and other related laws attempted to guarantee Negro rights and a loyal South within the accepted federal framework set forth in the Constitution. National authority and military rule were applied only partially and temporarily after 1865, and often reluctantly at that. The chief reliance in day-to-day government rested on the existing civil authorities. When the new state governments were formed after 1867, national and military control were withdrawn and the new regimes had to rely for their survival on customary legal institutions.

The experiment failed, and these regimes were overthrown in a few years because the ideas underlying them had become alien to the South during a generation or more of defending slavery, and because the

Radicals' adherence to traditional forms weakened their resistance to attack. Radical regard for the civil liberties of ex-Confederates enabled the latter to sabotage the Reconstruction program almost from the start. Democrats had full access to the polls almost everywhere after 1868 and controlled hundreds of county and local governments throughout the period; they exercised the right to express themselves freely on every occasion, and they controlled the great majority of the section's newspapers. When they were charged with illegal activity and violence they had full access to the courts—in fact often dominated them. In such cases it was often impossible to get grand juries to indict, prosecutors to prosecute, or petit juries to convict, even if sheriffs were willing to arrest or judges to try them. This was even true in Republican-controlled localities. All of the safeguards for the accused in the Anglo-Saxon system of justice were mobilized to enforce the higher law of white supremacy. The Republicans themselves insisted upon certain limits to federal authority, and this was another source of weakness. Conservative violence against Negroes and Radicals involved crimes which had always fallen within state rather than federal jurisdiction, and as a result the federal government refused to intervene soon enough or strongly enough to check the error effectively. Thus the Radicals were defeated within a few years by their very conservatism and unwillingness to employ more than halfway measures.

3

The American Businessman

Industrial Statesman or Robber Baron?

For many students of American history, the problems of war and peace appear to be the dominant ones in the years from 1850 to 1877. Yet during this same period the country was undergoing an industrial and urban transformation that inevitably resulted in profound changes in the structure of American society. Few individuals or institutions remained unaffected by the forces at work and the nation as a whole was destined to experience fundamental changes which enabled it to emerge as a leading world power by the close of the nineteenth century. "The old nations of the earth," Andrew Carnegie observed in 1886 with considerable pride, "creep on at a snail's pace; the Republic thunders past with the rush of the express. The United States, [in] the growth of a single century, has already reached the foremost rank among nations, and is destined soon to outdistance all others in the race. In population, in wealth, in annual savings, and in public credit; in freedom from debt, in agriculture, and in manufactures, America already leads the civilized world."[1] Industrial growth and the accumulation of wealth, Carnegie suggested, would lay the cornerstone of a better America: Ultimately, material progress would lead to spiritual and intellectual progress.

Although this new burst of industrialism gave the United States one of the highest standards of living in the world, it was not always greeted with unrestrained enthusiasm. To some the new industrialism was destroying the very traits that had given America immunity from class strife, internal divisions, and rivalries that had long plagued Europe.

---

[1]Andrew Carnegie, *Triumphant Democracy* (New York, 1886), p. 1.

71

Others feared the greed and ugliness that accompanied the industrial transformation. Walt Whitman, in *Democratic Vistas*, summed up the opposition. "The depravity of the business classes of our country is not less than has been supposed but infinitely greater. The official services of America, national, state, and municipal, in all their branches and departments, except the judiciary, are saturated in corruption, bribery, falsehood, mal-administration; and the judiciary is tainted. The great cities reek with respectable as much as non-respectable robbery and scoundrelism. . . . In business, (this all-devouring modern word, business) the one sole object is, by any means, pecuniary gain. . . . [M]oney-making is our sole magician's serpent, remaining to-day sole master of the field. . . . I say that our New World democracy, however great a success in uplifting the masses out of their sloughs, in materialistic development, products, and in a certain highly deceptive superficial popular intellectuality, is, so far, an almost complete failure in its social aspects, and in really grand religious, moral, literary, and esthetic results."[2] In short, America was adversely affected by the material forces at work.

The differences between the views of Carnegie and Whitman were by no means atypical; Americans have always been ambivalent in their attitudes toward material affluence. While emphasizing the virtues of acquisitiveness, individualism, and competition, they have been unable to throw off the influence of their religious heritage and the sense that the nation as a whole has a mission. At times this dual heritage has created an internal conflict because attempts to harmonize American materialism and idealism have not always succeeded. Some Americans have dealt with this conflict by proclaiming that material well-being is a prerequisite of spiritual and intellectual achievement; others have criticized a system that emphasizes material values at the expense of other values; still others have insisted that America's abundance was proof of its superior moral character.

This ambivalent attitude toward our heritage has exercised a profound impact on the writing of American history. Historians, on the whole, have also displayed divided attitudes when studying the rise of industry and its implications for American society. Nowhere can this dichotomy of thought be better seen than in the changing image of such great entrepreneurs as Rockefeller and Carnegie. To many historians, these captains of industry represented more than the rise of industrialism; they symbolized some of the basic characteristics of modern American culture.

The first attempts to evaluate the achievements of these industrial

---

[2]Walt Whitman, "Democratic Vistas," in *Prose Works 1892*. Floyd Stovall, ed. 2 vols. (New York, 1963–1964), 2:370.

giants occurred at the beginning of the twentieth century. Many of the early studies took their cue from the writings of Henry Demarest Lloyd. A journalist and a scholar, Lloyd, until his death in 1903, played a significant part in reform movements that developed out of the social and economic unrest of that era. Critical of laissez faire corporate monopoly, he insisted that the American people were confronted with a choice between reform or revolution. Public ownership of monopolies and an increased role for government were absolutely necessary, according to Lloyd, if the American people were to avoid the fratricidal class struggles that had wracked other nations in the Western world.

In 1894 Lloyd spelled out his case in *Wealth Against Commonwealth*, a book that anticipated the writings of later muckrakers and Progressive journalists and also set the stage for much of the controversy among historians over the captains of industry. The book ostensibly was a study of the Standard Oil Company and the techniques used by John D. Rockefeller to gain a virtual monopoly over the petroleum industry. Actually *Wealth Against Commonwealth* was an indictment of the entire capitalistic system as it then existed. Businessmen, wrote Lloyd, paid lip service to the ideal of competition, but their true purpose was to achieve monopoly. If the captains of industry continued to have their way, the result would probably be a violent and bloody class struggle. There was little time to act, declared Lloyd, for the nation was already faced with "misery, plagues, hatreds, [and] national enervation."[3]

While Lloyd's principal purpose was to issue a call for national regeneration, he had drawn an unfavorable yet influential portrait of the typical industrial tycoon to make his point. His stereotype of the American businessman was in many respects similar to the one held by other American reformers, including the Populists, as well as many Progressives. Much of the debate over reform in the years from 1900 to 1917, indeed, centered about the unbridled power and selfishness of the captains of industry—a group, many claimed, who were motivated only by a desire to amass great wealth regardless of the cost to the American people. The specific political issues of the Progressive era—monopolies, trusts, federal regulation—were all based upon the proposition that Americans could no longer afford to permit these autocratic barons to shape the nation's destiny.

Many of the studies dealing with the American businessman written prior to the First World War were done not only by historians, but by social scientists and, to a lesser extent, socialists seeking to prove that the system of capitalism was identified with social and individual selfishness and egoism. Among the social scientists were economists and

---

[3]Henry Demarest Lloyd, *Wealth Against Commonwealth* (New York, 1894), p. 517.

sociologists like Thorstein Veblen and E. A. Ross, who implicitly denounced the predatory, profit-seeking, amoral businessman for refusing
to recognize the pressing needs of society. In the latter category were
Gustavus Myers and Algie Simons, who portrayed businessmen as
malefactors of wealth and looked forward to their eventual extinction as
the historical process reached its inevitable destiny in the emergence of a
socialist utopia.

While the interpretation of the businessman as robber baron was
being etched in the public's imagination, historians, under the influence
of the New History, were themselves beginning to inquire into the economic realities of capitalism in order to buttress their own predilection
for democracy and reform. But not until the 1920s—a decade that was
notable for the debunking activities of a small group of intellectuals—did
historians turn their full attention to the study of the rise of American
industry. With the publication in 1927 of Charles and Mary Beard's *Rise
of American Civilization* and the first volume of Vernon L. Parrington's
monumental *Main Currents in American Thought,* the scene was set for a
radical reevaluation of the role of the businessman in American history.

Although the Beards refrained from any direct or outward condemnation of the industrial tycoon in their panoramic study of American
civilization, their description suggested the analogy of a medieval
baron—an individual who was despotic and autocratic within his own
sphere. The story of American industry, they wrote, is "the story of
aggressive men, akin in spirit to military captains of the past, working
their way up from the ranks, exploiting natural resources without restraint, waging economic war on one another, entering into combinations, making immense fortunes, and then, like successful feudal chieftains or medieval merchants, branching out as patrons of learning, di-
vinity, and charity. Here is a chronicle of highly irregular and sometimes
lawless methods, ruthless competition, menacing intrigues, and pitiless
destruction of rivals."[4]

Parrington, on the other hand, was much clearer and far less ambiguous in his description of postwar industrial developments. Writing
within a Jeffersonian agrarian framework which stressed individualistic
values, he sought to defend his particular vision of liberalism. In Parrington's eyes the predatory and materialistic tycoon of industry represented the greatest threat to those humane and democratic values that
had made America great. Businessmen had created the America of the
present, with "its standardized life, its machine culture, its
mass-psychology—an America to which Jefferson and Jackson and Lincoln would be strangers." These giants of industry, Parrington wrote in

---

[4]Charles and Mary Beard, *The Rise of American Civilization,* 2 vols. (New York, 1927),
2:177.

colorful and emotion-laden terms, "were primitive souls, ruthless, predatory, capable; singleminded men; rogues and rascals often, but never feeble, never hindered by petty scruple, never given to puling or whining—the raw materials of a race of capitalistic buccaneers."[5]

The debunking atmosphere of the 1920s and depression years of the 1930s provided a favorable climate of opinion for the growing idea of the businessman as a robber baron. For decades the business community had taken great pains to convince the American people that the nation's greatness rested on the achievements of ambitious and energetic entrepreneurs. A. C. Bedford, a tycoon in the oil industry, made this point very clear in 1925. In his eyes, work was even of more importance than love, learning, religion, or patriotism. "I have come to the conclusion," he wrote, "that industry is the fundamental basis of civilization. The high office of civilization is to train men to productive efforts."[6] Other business leaders during the 1920s echoed Bedford's observations; if anything, they were even more ecstatic in extolling the contributions of business to American civilization. With the exception of a dissenting minority of reformers, many Americans agreed with President Coolidge's dictum that "The business of America is business."

Having taken credit for the apparent prosperity of the 1920s, the business community, ironically enough, was forced to accept responsibility for the catastrophic depression of the 1930s. The capitalist free enterprise system, which supposedly accounted for the greatness of America, seemingly failed in 1929. Millions who sought work were unable to find jobs; bankruptcies increased at an astounding rate; and many Americans even faced a real threat of starvation. Indeed, the United States appeared to be on the threshold of disaster. For once the business community found that the time-honored cliché that wealth was the product of ambition, talent, and drive, no longer held true. Capitalism and free enterprise perhaps had come to the end of the road, many argued, and new approaches were required if the needs of a modern, complex industrial society in America were to be satisfied.

Given these conditions, it was not surprising that much of the historical scholarship of the 1930s took an antibusiness turn. Beard and Parrington had anticipated this development; their writings during the late 1920s echoed some of the critical literature of this era. Sinclair Lewis's unforgettable portrait of Babbitt, while not wholly intended to debunk businessmen, contributed to a stereotype already widely held. The massive attack on the image of the American businessman, however, came

---

[5]Vernon L. Parrington, *Main Currents in American Thought*, 3 vols. (New York, 1927–1930), 3:12,26.

[6]Quoted in James W. Prothro, *The Dollar Decade: Business Ideas in the 1920's* (Baton Rouge, 1954), p. 67.

in the Great Depression. During the 1930s, the robber baron idea came to full bloom.

In presenting a highly unfavorable portrait of the industrial tycoon, most writers in this tradition were implicitly attacking an economic system that they thought had failed to live up to its promises and expectations. Oddly enough, many—though not all—of the critical studies during the 1930s were written by nonacademic figures who were critical of capitalism rather than by academic historians. Thus Lewis Corey, a socialist, in his book *The House of Morgan* (1930), detailed the techniques whereby a major banking and investment concern exercised near dictatorial control over corporations having assets well in excess of twenty billion dollars. His lesson was not lost upon his readers. It was Corey's purpose to marshal as much evidence as possible to demonstrate the evil, selfish, and corrupting nature of industrial and finance capitalism. Other historical and literary writers, attracted by Marxian ideas, lent support to the growing body of critical studies of the American economic system.

The book that did the most to fix in American historical scholarship the enduring stereotype of the late nineteenth-century industrialist, however, was Matthew Josephson's brilliantly written *The Robber Barons: The Great American Capitalists 1861–1901,* which appeared in 1934. Fittingly enough, Josephson dedicated his book to Charles and Mary Beard, who themselves had interpreted American history in terms of a struggle between haves and have-nots, debtors and creditors, agrarians and industrialists, workers and capitalists. Josephson set the tone of his work in his introduction. "This book," he began, "attempts the history of a small class of men who arose at the time of our Civil War and suddenly swept into power.... These men more or less knowingly played the leading roles in an age of industrial revolution.... Under their hands the renovation of our economic life proceeded relentlessly: large-scale production replaced the scattered, decentralized mode of production; industrial interprises became more concentrated, more 'efficient' technically, and essentially 'cooperative,' where they had been purely individualistic and lamentably wasteful. But all this revolutionizing effort is branded with the motive of private gain on the part of the new captains of industry. To organize and exploit the resources of a nation upon a gigantic scale, to regiment its farmers and workers into harmonious corps of producers, and to do this only in the name of an uncontrolled appetite for private profit—here surely is the great inherent contradiction whence so much disaster, outrage and misery has flowed." Josephson conceded that the robber barons had many imposing achievements to their credit. On the other hand, the debits far outweighed the credits. Ultimately, he concluded, the "extremes of management and stupidity would make themselves felt.... The alternations of prosperity and poverty would be more violent and mercurial, speculation and breakdown each more excessive; while the inherent contradictions within the society pressed with increasing intolerable force against the bonds of the old order."[7] The implications of Josephson's ideas were obvious.

The unfavorable portrait of the American businessman persisted as a theme in American historical writing. In the first selection in this chapter John Tipple notes that a relatively small number of late-nineteenth-century entrepreneurs used the corporate form of organization to amass great wealth, and in so doing contributed to the decline of individualistic institutions and values. Critics of businessmen, he suggests, were generally correct in their assessment of the negative consequences that followed the rise to dominance of such figures as John D. Rockefeller and Andrew Carnegie. Special privilege and the corporation went hand in hand; the result was the transfer of power to a relatively small economic elite.

At the same time that the robber baron concept was reaching maturity, another school of thought was emerging. Although it is difficult to give this school a particular name, the designation "business history" is not wholly inaccurate. The foundation of business history had already been laid by the 1930s. As a result of the work of Norman S. B. Gras and others at the Harvard Graduate School of Business Administration as well as the publication of a number of sympathetic biographies of individual business leaders, some historians and economists began to depart from the unfavorable stereotype of the American industrialist. Business history, however, was not merely a reevaluation of the contributions of industrialists; it represented a radically new approach to the study of American economic history. Indeed, business historians by the 1950s—because of their differences with other academic historians—had created their own professional organization, developed a new vocabulary and research techniques, published their own journal, and in some cases had even founded new departments within the university separate from regular history departments.

Generally speaking, business historians insisted that the careers of industrial leaders were far more complex than earlier scholars had realized. Business leaders were not predatory money seekers. Indeed, in many cases they were talented individuals whose creative contributions to the economy—and to American society as a whole—were very great. Allan Nevins, who published a major revisionist biography of John D.

---

[7]Matthew Josephson, *The Robber Barons: The Great American Capitalists 1861–1901* (New York, 1934), pp. vii–viii, 453. For a discussion of the robber baron theme, see Hall Bridges, "The Robber Baron Concept in American History," *Business History Review* 32 (Spring 1958): 1–13.

Rockefeller in 1940, argued that much of the blame heaped on this man was unwarranted. It was true, Nevins conceded, that Rockefeller used methods that were of dubious moral character. On the other hand, the kind of monopoly control attained by Standard Oil was a natural response to the anarchical cutthroat competition of the period and reflected the trend in all industrial nations toward consolidation. To Nevins, Rockefeller was not a robber baron; he was a great innovator who imposed upon American industry "a more rational and efficient pattern." Rockefeller's objective was not merely the accumulation of wealth; he and others like him were motivated by "competitive achievement, self-expression, and the imposition of their wills on a given environment."[8]

Thirteen years later Nevins pushed this thesis even further when he published a second biography of Rockefeller. He was, Nevins forcefully argued, an "innovator, thinker, planner, bold entrepreneur." Taking a confused and disorganized industry, Rockefeller organized it with completeness, efficiency, and constructive talent; in his philanthropy he set a model for all to follow. Had it not been for men like him—men who helped to create within a brief span of time great and powerful industrial units in steel, oil, textiles, chemicals, electricity, and automotive vehicles—"the free world might have lost the First World War and most certainly would have lost the Second."[9]

The points that Nevins made about Rockefeller were not fundamentally different from those made by other students of business history. The great nineteenth-century entrepreneurs, business historians emphasized, actually played a vital role in making the United States the greatest industrial power in the world and giving its people the highest standard of living. Far from being immoral, unethical, or evil individuals—although sometimes their methods involved questionable tactics—these industrial statesmen stepped into a disorganized, unstructured, anarchic economy, restored order and rationality, created giant organizations that were in a position to exploit fully the great natural resources of the nation, and took full advantage of the potentialities of the American economy.

Like students in the robber baron tradition of American historiography, business historians began with certain underlying assumptions that undoubtedly influenced the way in which they approached their subject. It is quite clear that they rejected the hostile critique of Progressive historians who believed that the social and economic costs of late

---

[8]Allan Nevins, *John D. Rockefeller: The Heroic Age of American Enterprise*, 2 vols. (New York, 1940), 2:707–14.

[9]Allan Nevins, *Study in Power: John D. Rockefeller, Industrialist and Philanthropist*, 2 vols. (New York, 1953), 1:viii–ix; 2:436. For a direct confrontation of views see the enlightening article, "Should American History be Rewritten? A Debate Between Allan Nevins and Matthew Josephson," *Saturday Review* 37 (February 6, 1954):7–10, 44–49.

nineteenth-century industrialization could have been far lower and less painful and degrading to the great mass of Americans, and that the result need not have been a dangerous centralization of economic power that ostensibly threatened freedom and democracy. On the contrary, business historians tended to eulogize rather than to disparage the American economic system. Did not the growth and development of the large corporation, they maintained, give the American people the highest standard of living in the world and make possible the victory against totalitarianism? Was not America's industrial capacity responsible for the strength of a large part of the free world in the struggle with communism? To put it another way, these historians concluded that the large corporation, despite its monopolistic and oligopolistic position, was far more of an asset than a liability. Unlike Progressive historians who defined the problem in terms of a tension between democracy and the menace of the concentration of economic power in the hands of a few, business historians minimized the threat of such dangers and opposed efforts to employ historical analysis as an ideological anticorporation weapon.

Perhaps the most sophisticated example of recent developments in business history is the work of Alfred D. Chandler, Jr. Unlike Nevins, Chandler was essentially disinterested in the biographical approach that sought to vindicate the career of an individual against his detractors. He was more concerned in the process whereby new forms, methods, and structures came into being in the late-nineteenth and twentieth centuries. In a major work issued in 1962 Chandler identified four stages in the development of large industrial enterprise. First came a period of expansion and the accumulation of resources. During the second period these resources were "rationalized." In the third phase the organization expanded its operations to include new products in order to ensure the most efficient use of existing resources. In the fourth and final phase new structures were created to promote effective use of resources in order to meet immediate and long-range demands. Borrowing heavily from work in the social sciences, Chandler saw large corporations as complex economic, political, and social systems with common administrative problems. He insisted, moreover, that most large firms went through similar stages of development. "Strategic growth," he noted, "resulted from an awareness of the opportunities and needs—created by changing population, income, and technology— to employ existing or expanding resources more profitably. A new strategy required a new or at least refashioned structure if the enlarged enterprise was to be operated efficiently."[10] The result was the large, decentralized, multidivisional corporation.

---

[10]Alfred D. Chandler, Jr., *Strategy and Structure: Chapters in the History of the Industrial Enterprise* (Cambridge, 1962), p. 15.

Less interested in the moral dimensions of industrial entrepreneurship, Chandler attempted to analyze the forces that led businessmen to
develop new products, new markets, and new sources of raw materials.
By 1900, he pointed out, these industrial leaders had created the modern
corporation, which integrated the functions of purchasing, manufacturing, marketing, and finance. Each of the major processes was managed
by a separate department, and all were coordinated and controlled by a
central office. Such a complex organization was a response to the
emergence of the urban market that followed the creation of a national
transportation system. Minimizing the role of technological innovation,
Chandler concluded that entrepreneurs like Rockefeller and others were
successful because they accurately analyzed the economic situation and
responded in a creative manner. Their contributions, he suggested,
played an important role in the dramatic growth of the economy and the
creation of an affluent society.[11]

In a subsequent book that won a Pulitzer Prize, Chandler analyzed
the manner in which the development of large-scale vertically organized
corporations altered the American economy between the Civil War and
depression of the 1930s. He once again emphasized the crucial role of
management and business executives in guiding these changes, and
even suggested that Adam Smith's concept of the market as the decisive
element in the economy was no longer applicable to the present.[12]

In the second selection in this chapter Harold C. Livesay examines
the role of individuals in modern economic development. Rejecting the
allegation that the rise of bureaucratic structures stifles the creative and
innovative processes that are the hallmark of capitalism and free enterprise, Livesay focuses on the careers of three business leaders—Andrew
Carnegie, Henry Ford II, and the lesser-known Howard Stoddard—who
used the bureaucratic form of organization as a means of innovation.
Bureaucracy, he concludes, does not necessarily obliterate the entrepreneurial spirit nor does it blur (as Joseph Schumpeter suggested) the
differences between mature capitalist and socialist systems. Some individuals make institutions; in this sense human beings are not helpless
captives of impersonal social and economic systems and structures.

Business historians tended to see the large corporation as essentially
an economic organization. Other scholars, however, were less concerned with understanding the corporation in structural and functional
terms; they were more concerned with the political aspects of business

[11]Alfred D. Chandler, Jr., "The Beginnings of 'Big Business' in American Industry,"
Business History Review 33 (Spring 1959):1–31.

[12]Alfred D. Chandler, Jr., *The Visible Hand: The Managerial Revolution in American Business* (Cambridge, 1977). For a brief and clear summary of the findings of business historians see Glenn Porter, *The Rise of Big Business, 1860–1910* (New York, 1973).

and the threat to democratic institutions posed by such huge conglom-
erations. This concern took two different forms in the 1950s and 1960s.
The first was a sophisticated body of scholarship that examined business
in a critical vein, though not with a view that sought the end of
capitalism and the establishment of a socialist society. Typical of this
approach was the work of Carl Kaysen, an economist who also served
for a time as the Director of the Institute for Advanced Study in Princeton, New Jersey. Kaysen noted the overwhelmingly disproportionate
importance of large corporations in the economy. Because of their size,
these large units were less influenced by changes in economic activity
and exercised considerable power over their smaller suppliers and customers. Their investment decisions and research activities, moreover,
had important implications for society. The bigger market power that
absolute and relative size gave to the large corporation also resulted in
political and social as well as economic power. Kaysen noted that
American society possessed three alternate ways of controlling business
power: the promotion of competitive markets; control by agencies external to business; and institutionalization within the firm of responsibility
for the exercise of power. Traditionally the United States relied on the
first in the form of antitrust activities, although far more could have been
done along this line. Kaysen's conclusions were equivocal, for he felt
that effective control of business power remained an unfinished task. [13]

Scholars like Kaysen were essentially in a reform tradition; they
sought to eliminate imperfections in American society rather than overthrow it. By the early 1960s, however, a small but growing number of
scholars in a variety of disciplines were coming to the conclusion that
American society was fundamentally immoral and that a radical change
in its structure was required. This point of view was best expressed by
historians associated with the New Left. War, poverty, racism, they
argued, were direct outgrowths of American capitalism. If this were so,
then only the abolition of capitalism could make possible the establishment of a just and peaceful society. This belief, of course, led to a
rejection of those scholars who had defended business as well as those
who were critical of it but did not seek its destruction.

One of the first monographs embodying a New Left approach was
Gabriel Kolko's *The Triumph of Conservatism: A Reinterpretation of American History, 1900-1916,* which appeared in 1963. Kolko argued that the
distinctive feature of American society—what he designated as political
capitalism—dated only from the first two decades of the twentieth
century. Rejecting the belief that large-scale business enterprise was
inevitable, Kolko maintained that competition was actually increas-

---

[13]Carl Kaysen, "The Corporation: How Much Power? What Scope?," in *The Corporation
in Modern Society,* ed. Edward S. Mason (Cambridge, 1959), chapter 5.

ing at the turn of the century. Even the merger movement and the capitalization of new combinations on an unprecedented scale failed to stem the tide of competitive growth. Corporate leaders, therefore, turned to government to control competition and to prevent the possibility of a formal political democracy that might lead to a redistribution of wealth. The result was a synthesis of business and government, with the former emerging as the dominant element. In contrast to Chandler, Kolko believed that large-scale units turned to government regulation precisely because of their inefficiency. The lack of a viable alternative to political capitalism at that time made its victory a certainty, for neither the Populists nor the Socialists (who themselves accepted the necessity of centralization) understood that the Progressive movement—far from being antibusiness—was actually a movement that defined the general welfare in terms of the well-being of business.[14]

Kolko's controversial thesis did not persuade other scholars, many of whom rejected his radical ideological assumptions and questioned his conclusions. Shortly after Kolko published his study of railroad regulation in 1965, Edward A. Purcell, Jr., criticized his thesis that businessmen favored government regulation because they feared competition and desired to forge a government-business coalition in which they would be the dominant partner. In an examination of the attitudes of businessmen during the passage of the Interstate Commerce Act of 1887, Purcell came to a quite different conclusion. Rejecting the idea that the actions of businessmen grew out of a particular ideology, he insisted that entrepreneurs and managers were more interested in solving particular problems than they were in adhering to any coherent body of thought. Hence some favored regulation while others opposed it. In general, Purcell concluded, diverse economic groups who felt threatened by the new national economy and rate discrimination turned to the federal government in the hope of protecting their interests. Political control of the economy was not their ultimate goal; they simply wanted to protect their own interests.[15]

In assessing businessmen and corporations since the late-nineteenth century, it is important to understand that differing interpretations often reflect diverging viewpoints regarding the very nature of economic development. Ironically enough, adherents of the robber baron and

---

[14]In addition to *The Triumph of Conservatism: A Reinterpretation of American History, 1900–1916* (New York, 1963), see Kolko's *Railroads and Regulation 1877–1916* (Princeton, 1965) for an illustrative case study of his interpretation.

[15]Edward A. Purcell, Jr., "Ideas and Interests: Businessmen and the Interstate Commerce Act," *Journal of American History* 54 (December 1967):561–78. See also Albro Martin, "The Troubled Subject of Railroad Regulation in the Gilded Age—A Reappraisal," *ibid.* 61 (September 1974):339–71, and *Enterprise Denied: Origins of the Decline of American Railroads, 1897–1917* (New York, 1971).

New Left school implicitly (and sometimes explicitly) extol the virtues of a competitive economy when they criticize the monopolistic objectives of most entrepreneurial and financial leaders. Business historians, on the other hand, tend to argue that the movement toward consolidation arose out of a cutthroat and disorganized economy whose productive potential could never have been realized without the large, decentralized, multidivisional corporation. Still others see the problem within a far more complex framework; decisions made by individuals often gave rise to results that were not anticipated.

Which of these viewpoints is correct? Was consolidation a necessary prerequisite for the emergence of a complex industrial economy? Is bigness synonymous with efficiency? On both these issues opposing schools of thought give very different answers. The upholders of the robber baron and New Left approach insist that the monopolistic control that often accompanies large productive units frequently reflects the inability of those units to meet the challenges of smaller competitors who do not have high overhead and fixed costs. Thus, consolidation actually reflects inefficiency rather than efficiency. Some of these historians, moreover, argue that the movement toward consolidation was the result of bureaucratic business reorganizations rather than an effort to increase efficiency. Most business historians, on the other hand, reject this interpretation. They tend to correlate consolidation with order and efficiency; thus the great entrepreneurs are viewed as creative individuals interested not in profit alone but in productive efficiency as well.

In the final analysis, any interpretation of the careers and accomplishments of American industrialists and the role of the large corporation will depend in large measure on the starting assumptions and values of the individual making the particular judgment. Despite claims of objectivity, it is difficult, if not impossible, for historians to divest themselves of beliefs and standards that influence their analysis of this problem. In some ways an evaluation of business and businessmen is even more controversial than other problems in American history. For underlying such an evaluation is the larger problem of the quality and meaning of the American experience. To some historians the significance of America is directly related to its productive capacity. America, they maintain, has demonstrated to the world that an affluent society is possible to achieve within a democratic capitalist framework. Thus the American economy—a creation of industrial pioneers and bold entrepreneurs—has far more to its credit than many have admitted. Other historians, however, argue in a much different vein. The social costs of industrialism, they maintain, could have been far lower had it not been for the greed and quest after power that marked this process. By placing a premium on acquisitive and amoral values, by creating a system of great inequality of wealth, they conclude, these entrepreneurs and large corporations contributed to the narrowness and materialism of American life. Political capitalism, moreover, was responsible for continued war, racism, and poverty in the twentieth century. Any judgment on this historical problem, then, often becomes a judgment on the nature and quality of American civilization itself.

John Tipple

JOHN TIPPLE (1916–   ) is professor of history at California State University in Los Angeles. He has compiled *The Capitalist Revolution: A History of American Social Thought, 1899–1919* (1970) and *Crisis of the American Dream: A History of American Social Thought, 1920–1940* (1968).

It is more than coincidence that the beginning of the robber baron legend, the portrayal of the big businessman as a warlike brigand cheating and plundering his way to millions, was contemporaneous with the inauguration of the corporation as the major instrument of business control in the United States. After the Civil War, the large corporation began to dominate the American economic scene. In those same years, Charles Francis Adams, Jr., launched his first assault against the "Erie robbers," and his brother, Henry Adams, warned of the day when great corporations, "swaying power such as has never in the world's history been trusted in the hands of mere private citizens," would be controlled by one man or combinations of men who would use these new leviathans to become masters of the nation.[1]

Such dangerous potentialities were not recognizable prior to the Civil War because the majority of businesses operated as local enterprises, usually as individual proprietorships, partnerships, or as small closed corporations in which ownership and control were almost invariably synonymous.[2] Under most circumstances, the power and influence of the businessman were limited to the immediate environs of operation and seldom extended beyond state boundaries. Equally important, there existed among most businessmen of prewar days a nearly universal desire and a practical necessity for community esteem. This governed their conduct, kept their ventures well within the limits of individual liability, and tended to restrain irresponsible profiteering. Antebellum criticisms of the businessman therefore were few and sporadic. Disap-

---

From *The Gilded Age*, revised and enlarged edition, edited by H. Wayne Morgan (Syracuse: Syracuse University Press, 1970). Copyright © 1970 by Syracuse University Press. Reprinted by permission.

[1] Charles F. Adams, Jr., and Henry Adams, *Chapters of the Erie and Other Essays* (Boston, 1871), p. 134.

[2] Adolph Berle, Jr., and Gardiner Means, *The Modern Corporation and Private Property* (New York, 1932), pp. 10–17.

proval usually focused on the speculator or stock gambler, and was often inspired by an agrarian distrust of big-city ways.[3]

The bloody struggles of the Civil War helped bring about revolutionary changes in economic and political life. War needs created almost insatiable demands for goods—arms, munitions, clothing—and offered some manufacturers unsurpassed opportunities to make fortunes. More important, the stimulus of massive military demands alerted entrepreneurs to new concepts of the power and possibilities of large-scale enterprise: "The great operations of war, the handling of large masses of men, the influence of discipline, the lavish expenditure of unprecedented sums of money, the immense financial operations, the possibilities of effective cooperation, were lessons not likely to be lost on men quick to receive and apply all new ideas."[4] Though the war prevented general economic expansion, the new ideas were profitably applied to the peacetime economy.

With the rich resources of the trans-Mississippi West open to private exploitation, the businessman had singular opportunities to become wealthy. Before him spread an immense untapped continent whose riches were his virtually for the taking; new means to turn these resources to profitable account were at hand. A host of new inventions and discoveries, the application of science to industry, and improved methods of transportation and communication were ready to assist the businessman. But all these aids would have been valueless without effective means to put them to work. The practical agency to meet these unprecedented entrepreneurial demands on capital and management proved to be the corporation. The stockholding system provided immense capital beyond the reach of any individual, and the corporate hierarchy presented a feasible solution to the greatly augmented problems of management.

The corporation was no novelty. It had served political as well as economic purposes in seventeenth-century America; as an instrumentality of business its use antedated the discovery of this continent. Seldom before in American history, however, had the corporation been used on such a large scale. From a relatively passive creature of legalistic capitalism, it was transformed by fusion with techniques into a dynamic system spearheading economic expansion.

The impact of the newborn corporation on American society was almost cataclysmic. In the first few decades of its existence the modern corporate system enabled the nation to develop more wealth more

---

[3]Cf. Frederick Jackson, *A Week in Wall Street by One Who Knows* (New York: n.p., 1841); James K. Medbery, *Men and Mysteries of Wall Street* (Boston, 1870).

[4]Adams and Adams, *Chapters of Erie*, p. 135.

rapidly than in any period since the discovery. But it also menaced hollowed economic theories and usages, threatening to ride like a great tidal wave over the traditional democratic social and political beliefs. Its size alone was sufficient to change fundamental social and economic relationships. Of the newly formed United States Steel Corporation an awed commentator wrote at the turn of the century: "It receives and expends more money every year than any but the very greatest of the world's national governments; its debt is larger than that of many of the lesser nations of Europe; it absolutely controls the destinies of a popula-tion nearly as large as that of Maryland or Nebraska, and indirectly influences twice that number."[5] Moreover, this concentrated economic power normally gravitated into the hands of a few, raising up a corpo-rate ruling class with great economic authority.[6]

Though the meteoric rise of the so-called robber baron to unheralded positions of power was inseparably bound to the large corporation, there were other factors behind his sudden emergence into popular view as the outstanding phenomenon of nineteenth-century business life. One of the most important of these was a stable government dedicated to the preservation of private property and devoted to an ambiguous concept of laissez faire. Through political alliances, principally with the Republican party, the big businessman consolidated his economic triumphs. Although in the past the commercial and manufacturing interests of the North had received favors from the federal government in the form of bounties to fisheries and protective tariffs, after the defec-tion of the South they were in the envied position of a pampered only child. With almost incestuous concern, a dotingly partisan Congress bestowed upon them lavish railroad subsidies, new and higher tarriffs, and a series of favorable banking acts.

The economic supremacy of the North had been guaranteed by mili-tary victory in 1865, but it was doubly insured by the actions of the Radical Republicans during the process of Southern reconstruction. The Fourteenth Amendment, whether intended for such purposes or not, was used by the courts to protect the corporation and to prevent at-tempts by the states to undermine its position of power.[7] The election of General Grant to the presidency in 1868 and 1872, backed by the leading representatives of the business community, the great financiers, and speculators, politically secured the issue of northern prosperity. Despite the panic of 1873, there were obvious signs that the business of the

---

[5]Ray Stannard Baker, "What the United States Steel Corporation Really is and How it Works," *McClure's* 18 (1901):6.

[6]Berle and Means, *The Modern Corporation*, pp. 2–6.

[7]Charles Wallace Collins, *The Fourteenth Amendment and the States* (Boston, 1912).

country had, as the *Nation* put it, "adapted itself to the situation created for it by Republican legislation."[8]

Within this artificial paradise, private profits were sacred. The inheritance tax had expired in 1870, the income tax was abandoned in 1872, and an attempt to revive it in 1894 was invalidated by the Supreme Court in 1895.[9] Corporate or excess profits taxes did not exist. By 1890, the bulk of government revenue was derived from customs duties and excises on liquor and tobacco, all taxes upon the nation's consumers.[10] Under such conditions, stock market volume attained the million-share mark in December, 1886, and industrial capital almost doubled itself every ten years.[11]

The dedicated businessman could make money on an unprecedented scale. Though John D. Rockefeller never quite became a billionaire, his fortune in 1892 reportedly amounted to $815,647,796.89.[12] Andrew Carnegie did nearly as well. The profits from his industrial empire in the decade 1889 to 1899 averaged about $7,500,000 a year and, in 1900 alone, amounted to $40,000,000.[13] In the following year he sold out his interest for several hundred million dollars.[14] Such fortunes, exceptional even for those days, emphasized the wealth available to the big businessman. In 1892, two New York newspapers engaged in a heated contest to count the number of American millionaires, the *World* uncovering 3,045 and the *Tribune* raising it to 4,047.[15] Regardless of the exact total, millionaires were becoming fairly common. By 1900, for instance, the Senate alone counted twenty-five millionaires among its members most of them well-paid agents of big business—a notorious fact that led some suspicious folk to dub that august body the "Rich Man's Club" and the "House of Dollars."[16]

This sudden leap of big businessmen into new positions of wealth and power caught the public eye. To Americans accustomed to thinking primarily of individuals, the big businessman stood out as the conspicu-

---

[8]The *Nation*, September 30, 1880, p. 232.

[9]*Pollock vs. Farmers' Loan and Trust Co.*, 157 U.S. 429, 158 U.S., 601.

[10]*Annual Report of the Secretary of the Treasury 1890* (Washington: GPO, 1890), p. xxi.

[11]*Commercial and Financial Chronicle*, Dec. 18, 1886, p. 739; *U.S. Census 1910* (Washington: GPO, 1913), 8, 32–33; Willard Long Thorp, *Business Annals* (New York, 1926), pp. 129–30.

[12]Allan Nevins, *A Study in Power: John D. Rockefeller, Industrialist and Philanthropist*, 2 vols. (New York, 1953), 2:613.

[13]James H. Bridge, *The Inside History of the Carnegie Steel Company* (New York, 1903), p. 295.

[14]*Ibid.*, p. 364.

[15]*Tribune Monthy* 4 (1892): 92; Sidney Ratner, ed., *New Light on the History of Great American Fortunes* (New York, 1953), pp. xviii–xxiii; Ida M. Tarbell, *The Nationalizing of Business* (New York, 1936), p. 113.

[16]David Graham Phillips, *The Shame of the Senate*, reprint from *Cosmopolitan*, 1906, 2, 94.

ous symbol of corporate power—his popular image encompassing not only his personal attributes and failings but combining also the more amorphous and impersonal aspects of the business organization by which he had climbed to fortune. Just as the diminutive Andrew Carnegie came to represent the entire steel-making complex of men and decisions which bore his name, so the lean, ascetic John D. Rockefeller personified Standard Oil, and the prominent nose and rotund figure of J. P. Morgan signified the whole of Wall Street with its thousands of operators, its ethical flaws, and its business virtues.

Big businessmen were usually attacked not for personal failings, though they had them as well as the lion's share of wealth, but as the recognizable heads of large corporations. When Carnegie and Rockefeller gave up business careers and became private citizens, the rancor against them almost ceased. Instead of being censured for past actions, which had been widely and vehemently criticized, they were praised as benefactors and good citizens. Public castigation of the steel trust was shifted from "Little Andy" to the broader shoulders of Charles Schwab. The odium of monopoly which had surrounded his father was inherited by John D. Rockefeller, Jr. Only as the active and directive heads of great corporations, and not as subordinates or members of a business elite, were big businessmen branded "robber barons" and indicted for alleged crimes against society.[17]

If the big businessman was not resented as an individual but as a power symbol wielding the might of the great corporation, the provocative question arises of why there was such resentment against the corporation. The answer is that the large industrial corporation was an anomaly in nineteenth-century America. There was no place for it among existing institutions and no sanction for it in traditional American values.

Institutions and values had been built around the social and political concept of the free individual. Born to the natural rights of life, liberty, and property, he was originally subject only to the law of nature. By being or becoming a member of society, the individual did not renounce his natural rights (because this gift of God could not be alienated) but submitted to certain restraints beyond those imposed by nature for the evident good of the whole community. The basis of this ideology was the presumed constancy of nature in moral as well as physical operations, and the universal efficacy of its laws. By asserting that these inevitable laws of nature constituted truth, and by setting out from the will of God or nature, eighteenth-century Americans sought to erect an inviolable system proceeding from natural causes and therefore not subject to human error. Fanciful as they seemed, these were the generally

---

[17]See John Tipple, "Who Were the Robber Barons?" (forthcoming).

accepted premises of government and society inherited by Americans of the nineteenth century.

In such a closed system there was no ready place for the large industrial corporation which was neither an individual nor a natural manifestation. As an artificial person created by charter and comprising many individuals and their wealth, the corporation was infinitely greater in size and power than the isolated individual about whom American society had been conceived. Unlike the individual, the corporate body was not ordinarily exposed to natural hazards of decay and death, having in effect been guaranteed immortality by the society which fathered it. Where individual accumulation of wealth and power was limited to a lifetime, corporate possibilities were almost limitless. Freed from death, and incidentally from death dues and inheritance taxes, the corporation waxed strong upon the accummulated lifetimes and earnings of many individuals.

A further complication, the hazard of which increased directly in proportion to corporate size and power, was that the corporation as an unnatural creation was born without natural reason—"the common rule and measure God hath given mankind"—and was therefore not intrinsically subject to the governance of nature. In ideological terms, the corporation, since it could not be counted upon to follow the moral precepts of nature, was an outlaw to the society which spawned it.

What was to be done with such a monster? Either the corporation had to be made to conform to American institutions and principles or those institutions and principles had to be changed to accommodate the corporation. This was the dilemma first seriously confronted by Americans during the Gilded Age, and the issue that set off the great movement of introspection and reform which activated the American people for the next fifty years.

Most flagrantly apparent was the destructive effect of the large corporation upon free competition and equal opportunity. According to the accepted theory, which was a projection of the doctrines of liberal democracy into the economic sphere, the ideal economy—the only one, in fact, sanctioned by nature—was made up of freely competing individuals operating in a market unrestricted by man but fairly ruled by the inexorable forces of natural law. The ideal polity was achieved by bargaining among free and equal individuals under the benevolent eye of nature. It was assumed that, in economic affairs, impartial rivalry between individual entrepreneurs and free competition would automatically serve the best interests of society by preventing anyone from getting more than his fair share of the wealth.

In early nineteenth-century America, this self-regulating mechanism seemed to work. Where businesses and factories were small, prices and output, wages and profits, rose and fell according to supply and demand. Every man appeared to have equal opportunity to compete with every other man. Even after the war, the individual businessman was forced, in the interests of self-preservation, to observe the common rules of competition. Ordinarily his share of the market was too small to permit any attempt at price control unless he joined with others in a pool, a trade association, or another rudimentary price-fixing agreement. The average businessman eschewed trade agreements, not out of theoretical considerations but for the practical reason that such coalitions did not work very well, often suffering from mutual distrust and the pursuit of centrifugal aims.

But what was true in a world of individual proprietors and workers was not necessarily correct for the corporation. It possessed greater unity of control and a larger share of the market and could either dictate prices or combine successfully with other corporations in monopolistic schemes. [18] By bringing to bear superior economic force which to a great extent invalidated the tenets of the free market, the large organization put the big businessman in the favored position of operating in an economy dedicated to the idea of freely competing individuals, yet left him unhampered by the ordinary restrictions. Under such auspicious circumstances, he soon outdistanced unorganized rivals in the race for wealth.

This unfair advantage did not go unchallenged. As the earliest of the large corporations in the United States, the railroads were the first to come under concentrated attack. The immense extension of railways after 1865, and the crucial nature of their operations as common carriers, exposed their activities to public scrutiny and subjected their mistakes or misdeeds to considerable publicity. Popular resentment against the railroads in the early 1870s grew hottest in the farming states of the Midwest, but indignant reports from all over the country accused railroads of using monopoly power against equal opportunity.

A most frequent criticism, common to both East and West, was that railway superintendents and managers showed unreasonable favoritism by discriminating between persons and places, offering rate concessions to large shippers, charging more for short than long hauls, and giving preferential treatment to large corporations in the form of secret rebates and drawbacks. That these preferential rates might sometimes have been forced upon the railroads by pressure from business made little difference. The popular consensus was that this elaborate system of special rates denied the little man equal opportunity with the rich and influential, breaking the connection between individual merit and suc-

---

[18]*Commercial and Financial Chronicle* 43 (March 27, 1886):393.

cess. The ultimate effect extended further monopoly by preventing free competition among businesses where railway transportation was an important factor.[19]

The Standard Oil Company seemed to be the outstanding example of a monopoly propagated in this manner, the charge being that the determining factor behind Rockefeller's spectacular conquest of the oil business had been this railway practice of secrecy and favoritism which had aided his company and ruined others. By collecting rebates on their own shipments and drawbacks on those of competitors, Standard had gained virtual control of oil transportation. It then could regulate the prices of crude oil, with the detrimental result, so Henry Demarest Lloyd charged, that by 1881, though the company produced only one-fiftieth of the nation's petroleum, Standard refined nine-tenths of the oil produced in the United States and dictated the price of all of it.[20]

As the whipping boy among trusts, Standard undoubtedly got more than its share of criticism, yet by contemporary standards of competition, the corporation was fairly adjudged a monopoly. Through the testimony of H. H. Rogers, an executive of the company, the Hepburn Committee in 1879 was able to establish that 90 to 95 percent of all the refiners in the country acted in harmony with Standard Oil.[21] In 1886, the monopolistic proclivities of the oil trust were attested to by the Cullom Committee:

> It is well understood in commercial circles that the Standard Oil Company brooks no competition; that its settled policy and firm determination is to crush out all who may be rash enough to enter the field against it; that it hesitates at nothing in the accomplishment of this purpose, in which it has been remarkably successful, and that it fitly represents the acme and perfection of corporate greed in its fullest development.[22]

Similar convictions were expressed by a New York Senate committee before which Rockefeller and other executives testified in 1888.[23] Four years later, in 1892, the Supreme Court of Ohio declared that the object of the Standard Oil Company was "to establish a virtual monopoly of the business of producing petroleum, and of manufacturing, refining and dealing in it and all its products, throughout the entire country, and

---

[19]James F. Hudson, *The Railways and the Republic* (New York, 1886), pp. 25–66; A. B. Stickney, *The Railway Problem* (St. Paul, 1891), pp. 27–35; Frank Parsons, *The Railways, the Trusts, and the People* (Philadelphia, 1906), pp. 25–56.

[20]Henry Demarest Lloyd, *Lords of Industry* (New York, 1916), p. 2; Ida M. Tarbell, *The History of the Standard Oil Company*, 2 vols. (New York, 1904), 2:111.

[21]*Report of the Special Committee on Railroads* (Albany, 1879), pp. 49–50 (*Hepburn Report*).

[22]Senate Reports, 49th Congress, 1st Session, no. 46, p. 199 (*Cullom Report*).

[23]*New York Senate Report*, no. 50 (1888), p. 10.

by which it might not merely control the production, but the price, at its pleasure."[24]

These findings were reaffirmed by new investigations. In 1902, the United States Industrial Commission reported that Standard, through its control of pipe lines, practically fixed the price of crude oil. In 1907, the commissioner of corporations supported and amplified this conclusion. The company might fall short of an absolute monopoly, the commissioner pointed out, but its intentions were monopolistic.[25] In 1911, the United States Supreme Court confirmed this allegation, observing that "no disinterested mind" could survey the history of the Standard Oil combination from 1870 onward "without being irresistibly driven to the conclusion that the very genius for commercial development and organization... soon begot an intent and purpose... to drive others from the field and to exclude them from their right to trade and thus accomplish the mastery which was the end in view."[26]

Far from regarding the intricate system of business combination he had developed as a monster to be curbed or destroyed, a big businessman such as Rockefeller looked proudly upon his creation as a marvel of beneficence, an extraordinary and distinctive expression of American genius. And Carnegie contended "not evil, but good" had come from the phenomenal development of the corporation. He and others pointed out that the world obtained goods and commodities of excellent quality at prices which earlier generations would have considered incredibly cheap. The poor enjoyed what the richest could never before have afforded.[27]

The big businessman supported his actions as being entirely in keeping with the business requisites of the day. Rather than engaging in a conscious conspiracy to undermine equal opportunity, he had sought only the immediate and practical rewards of successful enterprise, rationalizing business conduct on the pragmatic level of profit and loss.

Instead of deliberately blocking free competition, big businessmen maintained that their actions were only natural responses to immutable law. Charles E. Perkins, president of the Chicago, Burlington and Quincy Railroad Company, denied deliberate misuses of power in establishing rates, and claimed that the price of railroad transportation, like all other prices, adjusted itself. Discriminatory practices were viewed as

[24]*State of Ohio vs. Standard Oil Company*, 49 Ohio State, p. 137.

[25]*Report of the Commissioner of Corporations on the Petroleum Industry* (Washington: GPO, 1907), 1:xvi (*Smith Report*).

[26]*Standard Oil Co. of New Jersey et al. vs. United States*, 221 U.S., 1.

[27]Andrew Carnegie, "Wealth," *North American Review* 168 (June 1889):657, 654; *The Gospel of Wealth* (New York, 1900), p. 5.

part of an inevitable conflict between buyer and seller, a necessary result of competition.[28] The payment of rebates and drawbacks was simply one method of meeting the market. In answer to the accusation that the railroads had made "important discriminations" in favor of Standard Oil, an executive of that company replied: "It may be frankly stated at the outset that the Standard Oil Company has at all times within the limits of fairness and with due regard for the law sought to secure the most advantageous freight rates and routes possible."[29] Rockefeller went on record as saying that Standard had received rebates from the railroads prior to 1880, because it was simply the railroads' way of doing business. Each shipper made the best bargain he could, hoping to outdo his competitor.

Furthermore, Rockefeller claimed this traffic was more profitable to the railroads than to the Standard Oil Company, stating that whatever advantage the oil company gained was passed on in lower costs to the consumer. Just as his company later justified certain alleged misdemeanors as being typical of the sharp practices prevailing in the oil fields in the early days, so Rockefeller exonerated the whole system of rebates and drawbacks on the grounds that everybody was doing it, concluding cynically that those who objected on principle did so only because they were not benefiting from it.[30]

Yet despite his public rationalizations, the big businessman's attitude toward competition was ambivalent. He lauded it as economic theory, but denied it in practical actions. Theoretically, there was no such thing as an absolute monopoly; there was always the threat of latent competition. Whenever a trust exacted too much, competitors would automatically appear.[31] Competition as a natural law would survive the trusts. "It is here; we cannot evade it," declaimed Carnegie. "And while the law may be sometimes hard for the individual, it is best for the race, because it insures the survival of the fittest in every department."[32]

In practical matters, however, the big businessman acted as if the law had long since become outmoded, if not extinct. Progressive opinion in the business world heralded the growing monopolistic trend as a sign of economic maturity. Increased concentration in capital and industry was defended as necessary and inevitable.[33] Monopolistic practices in gen-

---

[28]*Cullom Report*, appendix, pp. 213–15.

[29]Ralph W. and Muriel E. Hidy, *Pioneering in Big Business 1882–1911* (New York, 1955), pp. 678–79; cf. p. 43.

[30]John D. Rockefeller, *Random Reminiscences of Men and Events* (New York, 1909), p. 112.

[31]John Bates Clark, "The Society of the Future," *Independent* 53 (July 18, 1901): 1 649–651.

[32]Carnegie, "Wealth," *North American Review* 168 (June 1889):655.

[33]John Moody, *The Truth About the Trusts* (New York, 1904), p. v.

eral were upheld in business circles on the grounds that they prevented disastrous competition. In the long run they benefited, rather than plundered, the public by maintaining reasonable rates and prices.[34] "There seems to be a great readiness in the public mind to take alarm at these phenomena of growth, there might rather seem to be reason for public congratulation," announced Professor William Graham Sumner of Yale. "We want to be provided with things abundantly and cheaply; that means that we want increased economic power. All these enterprises are efforts to satisfy that want, and they promise to do it."[35] Many big businessmen believed that, practically at least, the trust proved the superiority of combination over competition.

Though the claim was not always true, the business virtues of economy and efficiency were allegedly the trust's chief advantages. The combination was spared the folly and wastefulness of unrestrained competition, and gained huge savings in cross freight, advertising, sales, and executive expenses. The survival of only the most productive forms of business resulted in greater efficiency and cheapened production which in turn meant higher wages and lower prices.[36] In this respect, Standard Oil was represented as a model trust. According to its supporters, it was formed to curb speculation, waste, and overproduction. As Standard took pains to inform stockholders, the company owed its success not to illegal or reprehensible methods but to efficient organization.[37]

In his account of the birth of America's first great trust, Rockefeller advanced a generalization common to big businessmen, that combination arose in response to economic necessity. It was accurate up to a point, but not universally applicable. Rockefeller's description of the founding of Standard Oil was an interesting description of the genesis of monopoly from the big businessman's viewpoint. In the beginning, Rockefeller related, because refining crude petroleum was a simple and easy process and because at first the profits were very large, all sorts of people went into it—"the butcher, the baker and the candlestick maker began to refine oil." The market was soon glutted, and the price fell until the trade was threatened with ruin. At that moment "It seemed absolutely necessary to extend the market for oil . . . and also greatly improve

[34]See appended testimony to *Cullom Report*.

[35]William Graham Sumner, "The Concentration of Wealth: Its Economic Justification," *Essays of William Graham Sumner,* 2 vols. (New Haven, 1934), 2:166.

[36]This view had extensive support in the business world. For a useful compendium see James H. Bridge, *The Trust: Its Book* (New York, 1902). See also Jonathan P. Dolliver, "Facts About Trusts: Arguments for Protection," *American Industries* 2 (May 16, 1904); Franklin Head, ed., *Chicago Conference on Trusts* (Chicago, 1900).

[37]J. C. Welch and J. N. Camden, "The Standard Oil Company," *North American Review* 136 (February 1883):181–200; Hidy and Hidy, *Pioneering in Big Business*, pp. 658, 680.

the processes of refining so that oil could be made and sold cheaply, yet with a profit." So, "We proceeded to buy the largest and best refining concerns and centralize the administration of them with a view of securing greater economy and efficiency."[38] Though the birth pangs of Standard Oil obviously have been softened and somewhat simplified in the telling, it was on essentially this same basis that Carnegie explained the genesis of trusts in manufactured articles.[39]

Clearly, the operative point of view that consolidation of capital and industry was indispensable to the successful execution of the tasks which had developed upon modern business was the one embraced by big businessmen. In principle most of them agreed with the blunt statement of America's leading financier: "I like a little competition." J. P. Morgan was quoted as saying, "but I like combination better."[40] The choice was not between competition and monopoly, but between fighting to secure a monopoly by driving out competition in a bitter, destructive war and trying to obtain price control through industry-wide agreement.

Many, nevertheless, still paid lip service to the abstraction, though most had already rejected competition in practice.[41] This glaring incongruity between behavior and theory ridiculed the notion that such economic generalizations as free competition were natural "laws" timeless and placeless and entitled to sanctity. Rather than a competent expression of fact, the hedonistic theory of a perfect competitive system had turned out to be simply an expedient of abstract reasoning.

What in earlier and more halcyon days had been attributed to the benign operation of the law of competition was, in most instances, an absence of competition. Before the Civil War, competition was virtually dormant in many parts of the United States largely because of intervening geographical factors. Where it did exist, it usually operated on a local rather than a national scale, cushioning a large portion of the economy from the hardships of rigorous competition. The limitation of the nation's transportation system often allowed local businessmen a certain amount of monopoly power, and backward communications, particularly a lack of reliable market information, had a similar effect.[42] The trouble in many localities was that there was not always enough competition. These imperfections of competition in the antebellum period,

---

[38]Rockefeller, *Reminiscences*, pp. 81–82.

[39]Andrew Carnegie, "The Bugaboo of Trusts," *North American Review* 148 (February 1889):141–42.

[40]*Literary Digest* 45 (December 28, 1912):1213.

[41]Edward C. Kirkland, *Dream and Thought in the Business Community* (Ithaca, 1956), p. 27.

[42]Hans B. Thorelli, *The Federal Antitrust Policy* (Baltimore, 1955), p. 66.

however, tended to be eliminated by tremendous postwar advances in transportation and communication. Business rivalry also was intensified by the application of new technology to industry and nationalized by the substitution of the big interstate corporation for smaller local, individual, and partnership enterprises. The immediate outcome was competition with a vengeance, and the inauguration of a species of commercial warfare of a magnitude and violence unheard of in economic history. In the long run, the brutal realities of this cutthroat struggle were unpalatable to the public and big businessmen alike. But while the latter sought to shield themselves by erecting monopolistic barriers, the American people extolled the virtues of free competition and looked back fancifully to an earlier, more ideal state of economic affairs which, if anything, had been distinguished by a notable lack of competition.

The faith in the mythical virtues of competition prevailed widely. The majority of the American people took it for granted that competition was the normal way of life in business.[43] Henry Demarest Lloyd, an outstanding critic of big business, found it highly paradoxical that the American people who were so unalterably opposed to anarchy in politics advocated it in business. Worse yet, Americans had accepted industrial anarchy as their ideal of economic conduct.[44] Free competition was the shibboleth of practically all reform movements except that of the Socialists. It spurred the Grange, motivated the Single-Taxers and the Populists, and dominated the economic thought of the Progressives. Most of them desired, or thought they desired, free competition. On this matter there existed no clear partisan line. Members of Congress proclaimed "the norm of a free competition too self-evident to be debated, too obvious to be asserted."[45]

The belief in competition was an assertion of economic egalitarianism midway between the Gospel of Wealth and the Social Gospel, adopting neither the doctrine of stewardship by the chosen few nor the sweeping substitution of cooperation for competition.[46] It was a subtle interweaving of the Anglo-Saxon belief that the common law, as well as natural law, always favored competition over monopoly and native American opposition to privilege.[47] Some of the basic attitudes in this complex were clearly derived from classical economic theory. The economists whose works were most widely read were Adam Smith, John Stuart Mill, and David Ricardo; their laissez-faire attitude toward monopoly

[43]*Ibid.*, pp. 500–54.
[44]Henry Demarest Lloyd, *Wealth Against Commonwealth* (New York, 1899), p. 496.
[45]Walton Hamilton and Irene Till, *Antitrust in Action* (Washington: GPO, 1940), p. 6.
[46]Thorelli, *The Federal Antitrust Policy*, p. 556.
[47]Frederick Pollock, *The Genius of the Common Law* (New York, 1912), p. 95.

dominated the teaching of economics. "All our education and our habit
of mind make us believe in competition," said the president of Yale.
"We have been taught to regard it as a natural if not a necessary condition of all healthful business life. We look with satisfaction on whatever
favors it, and with distrust on whatever hinders it."[48] The Darwinian
theory of biological evolution was also generally interpreted as supporting popular notions about competition and individual initiative, although this was more apparent than real.[49] This ingrained habit of economic reasoning retarded public understanding of the new financial and
industrial order, but the belief proved more important than its actual
relevance. Sentiment, not fact, prompted American action against big
business.[50]

On the question whether the corporation had to be made to fit
American institutions and principles, or those institutions and principles
had to be changed to accommodate the corporation, the American
people almost unanimously declared for the first. If economic despotism
was the outcome of unchecked corporate growth, then the corporate
monster must be brought under control. The way out was the way back.
The economy must be restored to a former golden time of competitive
capitalism when the older individualistic values held sway, and the
common man was free from monopolistic pressures.

The way backward, however, was not to be all the way. Completely
breaking the trusts was rejected by the more realistic who wanted regulation. Somewhat paradoxically, they proposed to liberate competition
by imposing new restrictions in the name of freedom. They were not too
sure that unrestrained competition was the economic panacea they
sought. They justified the theoretical incongruity of their stand on the
moral grounds that such restrictions were to be imposed only to prevent
unfair competition. Apparently it never occurred to them that to acknowledge the defective working of natural law against corporate immorality was an ingenuous admission that the sacrosanct principle of
competition was invalid in the long run. Willfully blind to the logical
inconsistencies of this position, the majority clamored for governmental
regulation in the interests of equal opportunity: "We must either regulate . . . or destroy."[51]

---

[48]Arthur T. Hadley, *Railroad Transportation: Its History and Its Laws* (New York, 1885),
pp. 69–70.

[49]Richard Hofstadter, *Social Darwinism in American Thought, 1860–1915* (Philadelphia,
1945), p. 201.

[50]John Lydenburg, "Pre-Muckraking: A Study of Attitudes Toward Politics as Revealed
in American Fiction from 1870 through 1901" (unpublished Ph.D. Dissertation, Harvard
University, 1946), p. 59.

[51]Lloyd, *Wealth Against Commonwealth*, p. 496.

Responding to popular demand, Congress in 1890 passed the Sherman Act "to protect trade and commerce against unlawful restraints and monopolies," thus converting an economic myth into public policy. According to the ideology behind this law, there existed a direct cause and effect relationship between competition and monopoly. If the monopolistic obstacles in business were removed, the trend would immediately reverse itself; full and free competition would automatically return. Despite the stark realities of the growing trust and combination movement of the late 1880s, the public's confidence in the efficacy of this self-regulating mechanism set the tone of all subsequent federal action, whether for regulation or trust-busting.[52] Facts, however, proved otherwise. The Sherman Act, even when bolstered by later legislation, failed to halt or reverse the combination movement. It made evident the ineptitude of any legislation that regarded competition as a self-perpetuating and natural guarantor of economic justice rather than an intellectual hypothesis without institutional support.

The principal effect of legalizing the myth of competition was to encourage the growth of large combinations by deflecting the attack upon them into purely ideological channels. Since 1890, federal antitrust laws have symbolized the American democratic belief that "the only proper type of society is composed of unorganized competitive individuals." All attempts to curb big business by government action have been a ritual clash between an anachronistic ideal and a modern need, "the answer of a society which unconsciously felt the need of great organizations, and at the same time had to deny them a place in the moral and logical ideology of the social structure."[53]

Though the corporation had seemingly conformed to American institutions and principles under antitrust laws, those institutions and principles had really accommodated the corporation. By declaring the corporation to be an individual, with natural rights of life, liberty, and property, the Supreme Court in 1886 had seriously invalidated that basic concept of American society, the free individual.[54] This doctrine could be applied logically only to the individual as proprietor, partner, or even operating owner of a small company, but the jurists ignored the intrinsic conflict between the individualistic myth and the corporate reality, evoking the strained future efforts of the Supreme Court to dress "huge corporations in the clothes of simple farmers and merchants."[55]

---

[52]Senate Reports, no. 59, January 10, 1900; B and D, 951.

[53]Thurman W. Arnold, *The Folklore of Capitalism* (New Haven, 1937), p. 211.

[54]*Santa Clara Co. vs. Southern Pacific Railroad Co.*, 118 U.S., 394.

[55]Arnold, *The Folklore of Capitalism*, p. 189.

In establishing the legal fiction that the corporation was a person before the law, entitled to the rights and privileges of a citizen, the court undermined the ideal of the morally responsible individual by extending the individualistic ethic to the amoral impersonality of the modern corporation, and in the long run it subordinated the ideal to the right of property. To accord a legal robot equal rights with a living person in the holding and protection of property under the Constitution was to exalt corporate property above the individual person and to prevent the traditional faith in individualism into a juridical sophism. As the course of American legal history from 1886 to the 1930s amply disclosed, such was the ultimate effect of the personification of the corporation.

In condemning trusts as "dangerous to Republican institutions" and in branding corporate leaders as robber barons "opposed to free institutions and free commerce between the states as were the feudal barons of the middle ages," aroused Americans of the Gilded Age had clearly seized upon the major issue.[56] They had somehow recognized that American society with its individualistic traditions was engaged in a life-and-death struggle with the organized forces of dissolution.

The once-welcome business and industrial concentration threatened the foundations of the nation. There was more individual power than ever, but those who wielded it were few and formidable. Charles Francis Adams, Jr., denounced these "modern potentates for the autocratic misuse of that power":

> The system of corporate life and corporate power, as applied to industrial development, is yet in its infancy.... It is a new power, for which our language contains no name. We know what aristocracy, autocracy, democracy are; but we have no word to express government by monied corporations.... It remains to be seen what the next phase in this process of gradual development will be. History never quite repeats itself, and ... the old familiar enemies may even now confront us, though arrayed in such a modern garb that no suspicion is excited.... As the Erie ring represents the combination of the corporation and the hired proletariat of a great city; as Vanderbilt embodies the autocratic power of Caesarism introduced into corporate life, and neither alone can obtain complete control of the government of the State, it, perhaps, only remains for the coming man to carry the combination of elements one step in advance, and put Caesarism at once in control of the corporation and of the proletariat, to bring out vaunted institutions within the rule of all historic precedent.[57]

Yet the public already sensed that something had gone wrong with American institutions and values. With less understanding than Adams,

---

[56]See H. S. Commager, ed., *Documents of American History*, 2 vols. in 1 (New York, 1949), 2:78.

[57]Adams and Adams, *Chapters of Erie*, pp. 96–99.

they felt that somehow the old rules had been broken. Behind their growing animosity to the big businessman was the feeling that in some way he cheated his countrymen. The belief was becoming fairly common that extreme wealth was incompatible with honesty. "The great cities," Walt Whitman wrote in 1871, "reek with respectable as much as non-respectable robbery and scoundrelism."[58] There were undoubtedly moral men of wealth, but many Americans agreed with Thomas A. Bland, who in *How to Grow Rich* suggested: "In all history, ancient and modern, the examples of men of honest lives and generous hearts who have become rich... is so rare as to be exceedingly exceptional, and even these have invariably profited largely... by the labor of others."[59]

Very revealing in this regard was the portrayal of the big businessman in contemporary fiction. Socialist writers naturally depicted him as a "criminal of greed" or an "economic monster" who with other "business animals" preyed upon the life of the nation. Oddly enough, however, in an age when the corporation made unprecedented achievements in production and organization to the enrichment of countless people, when material success was widely favored as a legitimate goal, scarcely a single major novelist presented the big businessman as a hero or even in a favorable light. Except at the hands of a few hack writers, the business or industrial leader was consistently portrayed as powerful and capable, but nonetheless an enemy of American society.[60] This may have reflected the bias of the aesthetic or creative temperament against the pragmatic money-maker, but the big businessman was in disfavor with most of American soceity.

In the popular mind, the vices of lying and stealing were legendarily associated with Wall Street. The big businessmen who dominated "the street" were regarded by some as the ethical counterparts of the pirate and buccaneer. By the simple devices of "stock-watering" or the issuance of fictitious securities not backed by capital assets, speculators were generally believed to have stolen millions of dollars from the American people.[61] In the opinion of the more jaundiced, the men of Wall Street had barely escaped prison bars. "If the details of the great reorganization and trustification deals put through since 1885 could be laid bare," contended Thomas W. Lawson, a financier turned critic, "eight out of ten of our most successful stock-jobbing financiers would be in a fair way to get into State or federal prisons."[62]

[58]Mark Van Doren, ed., *The Portable Walt Whitman* (New York, 1945), p. 400.

[59]See Irvin G. Wyllie, *The Self-Made Man in America* (New Brunswick, 1954), p. 147.

[60]Edward Everett Cassady, "The Business Man in the American Novel: 1856 to 1903" (unpublished Ph.D. Dissertation, University of California, Berkeley, 1939), p. 199.

[61]Medbery, *Men and Mysteries*, p. 282; Fowler, 299.

[62]Thomas W. Lawson, *Frenzied Finance* (New York, 1905), p. 174.

The iniquity of Wall Street was not merely legendary, but had firm basis in fact. Though not all speculators were swindlers nor all speculation gambling, only a small number of the stock exchange transactions were unquestionably of an investment character. The vast majority were virtually gambling.[63] Many corporations, although offering huge blocks of stock to the public, issued only the vaguest and most ambiguous summary of assets and liabilities. While this was not iniquitous in itself, secrecy too often cloaked fraud.[64]

The men at the top who had used the corporate device to make millions did not see it this way at all. They justified their millions on the ground that they had fairly earned it.[65] Cornelius Vanderbilt, at the age of eighty-one, boasted that he had made a million dollars for every year of his life, but added that it had been worth "three times that to the people of the United States."[66] Others shared his belief. In *The Railroad and the Farmer*, Edward Atkinson made practically the same statement, asserting that the gigantic fortune of the older Vanderbilt was but a small fraction of what the country gained from the development of the railway system under his genius.[67] The Reverend Julian M. Sturtevant of Illinois College also envisioned the Vanderbilts and Astors of the world as "laborers of gigantic strength, and they must have their reward and compensation for the use of their capital."[68] Carnegie maintained that great riches were no crime. "Under our present conditions the millionaire who toils on is the cheapest article which the community secures at the price it pays for him, namely, his shelter, clothing, and food."[69]

Most Americans, however, did not so readily accept his evaluation. Some recognized that the big businessman in pursuing private ends had served national prosperity—the majority felt that he had taken extravagant profits entirely out of proportion to the economic services he had rendered. Rockefeller's millions were thought to be typical of the fortunes made by the robber barons, representing "the relentless, aggressive, irresistible seizure of a particular opportunity, the magnitude of which . . . was due simply to the magnitude of the country and the im-

---

[63]See *Report on Governor Hughes' Committee on Speculation in Securities and Commodities* (Albany, 1909), pp. 4, 15; Alexander D. Noyes, "The Recent Economic History of the United States," *Quarterly Journal of Economics* 19 (June 1905):167–209.

[64]Demarest Lloyd, *Lords*, p. 341.

[65]W. A. Croffutt, *The Vanderbilts and the Story of Their Fortune* (Chicago, 1886), p. 129.

[66]Francis A. Walker, "Democracy and Wealth," *Forum* 10 (September 1890):245.

[67]Joseph Dorfman, *The Economic Mind in American Civilization* (New York, Viking, 1949), 3:73.

[68]Andrew Carnegie, *The Empire of Business* (New York, 1902), p. 140.

[69]Henry George, *Progress and Poverty* (New York, 1880), pp. 174–75; Lyman Abbott, "Industrial Democracy," *Review of Reviews* 4 (June 1890):662.

mensity of the stream of its prosperous industrial life."[70] The feeling was general that the great fortunes of all the big business magnates—Vanderbilt, Gould, Harriman, Stanford, Carnegie, Morgan, and the rest—represented special privilege which had enabled them to turn the abundant natural resources and multitudinous advantages offered by a growing nation into a private preserve for their own profit.

The public at large was not clearly aware of it, but the chief instrument of special privilege was the corporation. Though public franchises and political favoritism played a large part in the aggrandizement of the robber barons, in the moneymaking world of late nineteenth-century America special privilege invariably meant corporate privilege. The corporation enabled Vanderbilt to unify his railroads while making large speculative profits on the side. The same device made it possible for men like Rockefeller to create and combine private enterprises embodying new technological and financial techniques while diverting enormous profits to themselves. The corporation was the constructive power behind the building of the cross-country railroads, but it was also the destructive instrument used by Jay Gould, Tom Scott, Collis P. Huntington, and others to convert them into quick moneymaking machines with no regard for their obligations as public carriers.[71]

The problem remained of establishing the relationship of big businessmen to the corporation. Judging by their conduct, they were not fully cognizant of the tremendous power placed in their hands by the corporation with single men controlling "thousands of men, tens of millions of revenue, and hundreds of millions of capital." Or they willfully exerted this prodigious force for private benefit regardless of consequences to the nation or ideals. Unhappily, most of those labeled robber baron by their contemporaries fell into the latter category.[72] Cornelius Vanderbilt held the law in contempt. Except where his own interests were involved, he had little regard for the consequences of his actions, manipulating and watering every corporate property he captured. One year after he took over the New York Central Railroad, he increased the capitalization by $23 million almost every cent of which represented inside profits for himself and friends. When admonished that some of his transactions were forbidden by law, he supposedly roared, "Law! What do I care about the law? Hain't I got the power?"[73] He confirmed

---

[70]Burton J. Hendrick, "The Vanderbilt Fortune," *McClure's Magazine* 19 (November 1908):46–62.

[71]New York State, *Assembly Documents*, 1867, no. 19, pp. 205–10.

[72]See John Tipple, "The Anatomy of Prejudice: The Critical Foundations of the Robber Baron Legend" (unpublished Ph.D. Dissertation, Stanford University, 1958), pp. 15–17.

[73]Frederick A. Cleveland and Fred W. Powell, *Railroad Promotion and Capitalization in the United States* (New York, 1909), p. 141.

this attitude in testimony before the committee on railroads of the New York State Assembly in 1869.[74] But Vanderbilt's methods were in no way exceptional. Most of the biggest businessmen made their millions in similar fashion. Twenty-four who because of notoriety and conspicuous power might be regarded as "typical" robber barons combined the role of promoter with that of entrepreneur. Stock manipulation along with corporate consolidation was probably the easiest way to wealth that ever existed in the United States. The exuberance with which promoters threw themselves into it proved that they were well aware of its golden possibilities.

As a consequence of these reckless corporate maneuverings, however, public opinion turned against the big businessman. While from a corporate point of view the conduct of the money-makers was often legal, although ethically dubious, the public often felt cheated. Puzzled and disenchanted by the way things had turned out, they questioned the way every millionaire got his money, and were quite ready to believe that a crime was behind every great fortune. While its exact nature escaped them, they felt they had been robbed. The classic statement of this feeling of outrage appeared in the Populist platform of 1892: "The fruits of the toil of millions are boldly stolen to build up colossal fortunes for a few, unprecedented in the history of mankind; and the possessors of these, in turn, despise the Republic and endanger liberty."[75]

The inchoate charges were basically accurate: too much wealth was being selfishly appropriated by a few. By the irresponsible use of the corporation, essentially a supralegal abstraction above the traditional laws of the land, they were undermining individualistic institutions and values. Big businessmen like John D. Rockefeller were attacked as robber barons because they were correctly identified as destroyers, the insurgent vanguard of the corporate revolution.

---

[74]New York State, *Assembly Documents, op. cit.*

[75]See Edward Stanwood, *A History of Presidential Elections* (Boston, 1892), pp. 474–78.

Harold C. Livesay

HAROLD C. LIVESAY is professor of history at the State University of New York at Binghampton. His books include *American Made: Men Who Shaped the American Economy* (1979), *Andrew Carnegie and the Rise of Big Business* (1975), *Samuel Gompers and Organized Labor in America* (1978), and (with Glenn Porter) *Merchants and Manufacturers: Studies in the Changing Structure of Nineteenth-Century Marketing* (1971).

Much of American economic and business history has become a bore, not only to the nonexpert audience, but also to many of its erstwhile enthusiasts, including a fair number of us who perpetrate it. This sad state of affairs results, I think, not from the split between so-called new and old economic historians (the terminology is sloppy and the distinction foolish in any case). The decline stems rather from the tendency to (1) focus on institutions instead of people; (2) inject heavy frameworks of economic theory and institutional model building, both propped up with aggregate statistics that sometimes must be fabricated before they can be analyzed; and (3) concentrate on the economic development and institutions of the colonial and antebellum periods. Relatively little energy has been expended on the emergence of modern industrial America.

Studies of individuals have fallen from favor for many reasons, some of them more symptomatic of changing fashions in historiography than of an increase in the sophistication of historians or their methodology. Researching individual lives is hard, lonely work, not readily susceptible to team efforts. Analyzing human behavior patterns uncovered by such research intimidates many historians who doubt their psychological qualifications for the task. Presenting such analyses cogently in print or in the classroom demands the literary grace of a novelist and the oratorical flair of an evangelist—neither skill conspicuously nourished in modern graduate schools. Finally, the current American environment tends to denigrate the effectiveness of individual efforts to shape, or even deflect history. . . .

"Entrepreneurial Persistence Through the Bureaucratic Age," *Business History Review* 51 (Winter 1977): 415–43. Reprinted with omissions by permission of the *Business History Review* and Harold C. Livesay.

Not suprisingly, this trend in the general society has been reflected in the rising popularity of such disciplines as sociology, which emphasizes "engineering" society as a whole or its constituent groups, and has meant heavy weather for history with its traditional focus on the role of the individual. Within the field of history itself, the response, as Louis Galambos predicted in 1970, has been a shift of attention from the study of people to analysis of groups and institutions. Not only does this kind of history seem trendy and therefore attractive, but it also solves—or at least avoids—the dilemmas associated with the study of individuals.

I favor a redirection of effort, not because I think that antebellum or aggregative questions are inherently less interesting, but rather because they seem to me of limited usefulness in explaining the most salient process associated with the development of the modern economy, the emergence of large bureaucratic institutions—public and private. Whether created by the citizens themselves, or by their governments, such institutions dominate the economic skyline of every developed society on earth, a primacy commonly recognized as an integral component of manufacturing societies but equally prevalent in developed agricultural nations such as Austria and New Zealand, where government agencies employ more than a third of the work force.

Despite this dominance of bureaucracies, we know too little about the dynamics of such institutions, either in terms of their internal behavior or in terms of their external relationships with other institutions or with society as a whole. This ignorance, much of it rooted in an absence of historical knowledge, prevails in the United States as well as elsewhere, despite widespread recognition of America as the preeminent business society. The remedy lies largely in the study of post–Civil War events, for, as Alfred D. Chandler, Jr., graphically illustrated in his presidential address to the Economic History Association some years ago, all the Americans who could have been described as "managers" in 1860 could easily have been housed in the Dupont Company's modern corporate headquarters building. Chandler argued that the American skyline, dominated by church steeples in the eighteenth century, by factory smokestacks in the nineteenth century, and by corporate office buildings in the twentieth century, symbolized a historical process poorly understood and little studied. There, in plain sight at every hand, lay *prima facie* evidence of the need for further research in more modern periods.

In this article I want to present some results of my research into the history of the dynamic relationships between individual entrepreneurs and business bureaucracies. These dynamics have played a major role in shaping capitalism's past and will surely do much to determine its future. Some of the material presented results from research focused on the careers of individuals; some derives from what began as institutional studies. All of it has reinforced my long-standing belief that individual people do make history and that understanding how they do it is what historians do best.

Schumpeter and Capitalism

In 1942 Joseph Schumpeter posed himself the question "Can capitalism survive?" "No, I do not think it can," he replied, going on to argue that capitalism's very success "inevitably creates conditions in which it will not be able to live." This contention he supported with observations on the historical evolution of capitalism, a process that he believed "strongly point[ed] to socialism as the heir apparent." Schumpeter's view obviously owed much to his study of Marx and to the statistical and cultural consequences of the recent worldwide depression. The core of his argument, however, depended upon his imaginative manipulation of two ideal types: Max Weber's conception of bureaucracy as the inevitable handmaiden of modernization, and Schumpeter's own view of the entrepreneur as the indispensable mainspring of capitalism.

According to Schumpeter, it was the entrepreneur's function "to reform or revolutionize the pattern of production" by exploiting some innovation in technology, production, management, or marketing. "This kind of activity," he argued, was "primarily responsible" for capitalism's energetic surges of growth; but one of the consequences of the process was the burgeoning of bureaucracies that replaced "individual action" with "bureau and committee work" and "reduced . . . innovation itself . . . to routine." Thus the inevitable outgrowth of successful capitalism was the destruction of its most essential component. The faster capitalism grew, the sooner it would die of hardening of the entrepreneurial arteries. . . .

I think there is ample evidence to posit a two-fold counter-thesis: first, that individuals sometimes do control bureaucracies—even massive, modern, industrial bureaucracies—so effectively that the organization becomes an instrument of personal will. In such cases, if the dominant person is talented, single-minded, and durable, his firm becomes a dynamic agency for growth in a capitalist economy because the inherent power of its bureaucratic management vastly multiplies, rather than stifles, the entrepreneurial spirit of its chief. I do not suggest that such individuals abound; obviously they are exceptional. Nor do I wish to imply that impersonal firms cannot generate dynamic innovations that propel the economy forward. Dupont's nylon, for example, was the handiwork of an experimental chemist buried far down in the company's organization chart. Enough similar examples exist to confound the notion that impersonal corporations inevitably stifle the entrepreneurial spirit of their minions. Indeed, such firms often exhibit enormous creative energy, sustaining economic growth in the United States and in some constructive cases, overseas as well. They have not done so alone, however, and what I want to show here is the continuing significance of firms in which authority functions in the older tradition, in the hands of a controlling owner. The success of these highly personalized enterprises shows that individual entrepreneurs have survived and prospered in an age characterized by anonymous bureaucracies. Together with other forms of business organizations, they have kept American capitalism vibrant and growing.

My second thesis is that while the passage of time adds many once-individualistic enterprises to the ranks of massive corporations run—and often run well—by cadres of anonymous managers, which dominate the American economy, new firms continue to appear and grow under the command of a controlling owner. I believe that this dual process has been a continuing feature of the American industrial economy. Its vitality suggests that capitalism contains not the seeds of its own destruction, but rather the seeds of its own regeneration, that its evolution is a cyclical one in which depersonalized, bureaucratic anonymity is a stage often occupied by individual firms, rather than the terminus of an inevitable linear progression carrying the whole society toward some form of bureaucratized socialism or fascism. . . .

A great many similar examples could be cited, but here I would like to focus on three: Andrew Carnegie and Carnegie Steel; Howard Stoddard and the Michigan National Bank; and Henry Ford II, his postwar revival of the Ford Motor Company, and his grand design for its overseas operations. All three demonstrate the competitive power that can be generated by a dynamic entrepreneur in control of a managerial bureaucracy. Because these examples span a century of time, involve powerful firms in three different industries, and include one nationwide, one statewide, and one multinational enterprise, they testify to the pervasiveness of entrepreneurial resiliency and to the tendency of capitalism to find in bureaucracy a source of renewal.

Andrew Carnegie

Andrew Carnegie's career as a steel manufacturer presents the prototypical case of an entrepreneur who used sophisticated bureaucratic controls to power an idea born of a market perception into a dominant manufacturing reality. In 1875 Carnegie's newly constructed rolling mill in Pittsburgh began to produce steel rails for the expanding American railroad system. Though he launched his firm in the midst of America's first industrial depression and had to steer it on a shakedown cruise through a period when, as one of his contemporaries observed, "you could not give away a rolling mill," Carnegie so successfully managed his enterprise that twenty-five years later it produced more steel than the entire British industry, and did so at a cost no competitor could match.

Carnegie's success rested upon his ability to transfer successfully into a manufacturing enterprise the techniques he had learned during his years (1852–65) on the Pennsylvania Railroad of J. Edgar Thomson and Thomas Scott. While on the Pennsylvania, regarded by most nineteenth-century observers as the epitome of efficient bureaucratic management, Carnegie learned two lessons fundamental to his subsequent success. First, he realized that American railroads offered an enormous potential market for rails, both for new construction and replacement, and that the future market would be for rails of steel, not iron. Second, he realized that competing successfully for this market would depend on the ability to turn out a high volume of product at low cost, which in turn required choosing and evaluating management personnel, knowing costs accurately at all times through constant attention to internal accounting, and reducing costs whenever possible through the introduction of technological improvements.

Carnegie began adapting his railroad skills to the problems of manufacturing management ten years before the first rail rolled out of Carnegie Steel. In 1862 he founded the Keystone Bridge Company to fabricate and erect iron bridges for the Pennsylvania and other railroads. In 1865 he assumed control of the Union Iron Company, a rolling mill and forge that produced plates, beams, and railroad axles. As he got into the iron business, he discovered that the accounting methods commonly used in the industry, like those of most American manufacturing firms of the time, had more in common with those of Medici-era merchants than they did with the modern systems Carnegie had learned on the Pennsylvania. From iron ore to finished product, the materials moved through a series of processes, but Carnegie "was greatly surprised to find that the cost of each of the various processes was unknown. Inquiries made of the leading manufacturers of Pittsburgh proved this. It was a lump business, and until stock was taken and the books balanced at the end of the year, the manufacturers were in total ignorance of the results. . . . I felt as if we were moles burrowing in the dark, and this to me was intolerable."

Not only did such antiquated methods keep managers ignorant of the costs of production, but they also provided no way to evaluate the performance of employees, and left unchecked workers' tendencies to waste, or even steal, the company's assets. The Pennsylvania's system functioned so well that, as a stockholders' committee reported, the cost of "a day's labor, of the purchase of a keg of nails, or the largest order goes through such a system of checks and audits as to make fraud almost an impossibility." In the iron business, on the other hand, Carnegie discovered owners "who, in the office, would not trust a clerk with five dollars without having a check upon him, were supplying tons of material daily to men in the mills without exacting an account of their stewardship by weighing what each returned in finished form."

This intolerable situation Carnegie at once assaulted. First, he "insisted upon such a system of weighing and accounting being introduced throughout our works as would enable us to know what our cost was for each process." This in turn made it possible, "by the aid of many clerks and the introduction of weighing scales throughout the mill," to achieve a situation where "responsibility for money or materials [could] be brought home to every man," and where individual performances could be evaluated by seeing "who saved material, who wasted it, and who produced the best results . . . what every department was doing . . . what each of the many men working at the furnaces was doing, and . . .compare one with another."

This cost-based method of management, pioneered in the 1840s and 1850s by railroad men such as Daniel McCallum of the Erie and J. Edgar Thomson and Tom Scott of the Pennsylvania, Carnegie employed throughout his career in manufacturing. From the nascent days of his small Pittsburgh rolling mill through the triumphant years when Carnegie Steel dominated its rivals, he demanded a continuous flow of cost data and used the results to make decisions about men and machinery. "Carnegie never wanted to know the profits," Charles Schwab reflected years later; "he always wanted to know the cost." "Show me your cost sheets," Carnegie demanded of his managers. "It is more interesting to know how well and how cheaply you have done this thing than how much money you have made, because the one is a temporary result, due possibly to the special conditions of the trade, but the other means a permanency that will go on with the works as long as they last."

Employees who reduced costs could expect rapid promotions, in some cases eventual elevation to partnership in the firm. Those who failed could expect no mercy. Carnegie summarized this credo once in commenting on a suggested promotion: "He may be just the man we need. Give him a trial. That's all we get ourselves and all we can give to anyone. If he can win the race, he is our racehorse. If not, he goes to the cart."

Carnegie's unremitting attention to cost reduction also lay behind his revolutionary attitude toward technological improvement. Holding down production expenses meant not only doing each stage of manufacturing as cheaply as possible, but also in forcing the largest quantity of material through the entire process in the shortest possible time. In addition, labor costs must be reduced or eliminated by every opportunity. All this meant using up-to-date machinery, and accepting the capital cost involved. Carnegie created the most modern plant that money could buy by hiring Alexander Holley, the world's foremost expert on Bessemer steel works, to design and build his mill. He stayed in the lead by a series of innovations in technique and by the constant replacement of obsolete machinery. Thus, Carnegie's firm pioneered in the integration of all stages of manufacturing from raw material to company-run sales offices, in the use of "hard-driving" in blast furnaces, in the use of the Bessemer method and the basic open-hearth process, and in the introduction of chemistry and metallurgy to improve production techniques. When more modern competitors such as Homestead and Duquesne appeared, he absorbed them intact into his complex.

Once convinced that a new process could save money, Carnegie never concerned himself with the capital costs, for he thoroughly understood economies of scale. On the railroad this had meant running big trains, heavily loaded, as fast as possible. In the steel business, he knew, "Cheapness is in proportion to the scale of production. To make ten tons of steel a day would cost many times as much per ton as to make one-hundred tons. . . . Thus the larger the scale of operation the cheaper the product." If new equipment could reduce the unit cost of product, it came cheap at any price. When the initial open-hearth using the Thomas Basic Process proved successful, Carnegie ordered six more furnaces constructed immediately, warning that "Every day's delay in building . . . is just so much clear profit lost." He once ordered Charles Schwab to rebuild a three-month-old rolling mill at once when Schwab said he had found a better design.

By adhering constantly to his principle of knowing costs and reducing them at every turn, Carnegie drove his firm to the top, beat back his competitors as swiftly as they emerged, and set a pattern of bureaucratic management that American industry copied widely. He did so even though he had "no shadow of claim to rank as inventor, chemist, investigator, or mechanician," and despite his habit of absenting himself for long periods. He made his main home in New York after 1867, and he punctuated his business career with world cruises and sabbaticals in Scotland. Although he relinquished some measure of control to Henry Frick and later to Charles Schwab, he always retained a majority share and exercised his power over the firm's destiny, including its final step, the merger into United States Steel in 1901.

That Carnegie's personal dynamism and policies permeated and dominated the firm's vast bureaucracy, few of his contemporaries doubted. Nor can one doubt his success. When he retired he was making more steel than any other company in the United States, and more than any other country in the rest of the world; he made it more cheaply than anyone else, knew the costs better on the last day of business than he had on the first, and beat the costs down so successfully that the last year's operation yielded a profit of $40 million. He molded his firm into such a perfect instrument of his will that a Morgan partner declared him "a threat and menace to the steel trade of the United States." Elbert Gary, who headed Federal Steel, one of Carnegie's competitors, before becoming chairman of United States Steel, thought that "the Carnegie Company [might] have driven entirely out of business every steel company in the United States." "I believe you would have captured the steel trade of the world if you had stayed in business," Congressman Stanley observed during his committee's hearings on United States Steel. "I am as certain of it as I can be ... of anything," Carnegie replied.

When Carnegie retired, his firm slipped into the bureaucratic anonymity of the United States Steel Corporation, but he quit because he wanted to, not because he had to. Had he continued, his individualistic company could easily have absorbed or destroyed its corporate competitors; and since he lived vigorously for twenty more years, there seems little reason to doubt that he could have gone on had he pleased, whatever Morgan partners and the rest of Wall Street might have thought about it. His passing from the scene meant simply the end of one man's career in building and controlling a massive enterprise; it did not signal the end of such opportunities, nor the last of the men who could seize them.

Howard B. Stoddard

Forty years almost to the day after Andrew Carnegie's retirement from business, Howard B. Stoddard announced the formation of the Michigan National Bank, with headquarters in Lansing, the state capital. At its inception, Michigan National amalgamated banks in six cities outside the Detroit area: Lansing, Flint, Battle Creek, Saginaw, Port Huron, and Marshall. Each of the constituent banks, while of considerable local importance prior to the merger, were of minor consequence to banking in the state as a whole—dominated as it was by the big Detroit and Chicago firms—and were insignificant on the national banking scene.

Despite these modest beginnings, within thirty years Michigan National attained a position of power and prestige, ranking fourth in the state—largest outside Detroit—and thirty-sixth in the nation in 1972. During this period, its rate of growth tripled the national average for banking firms, and Michigan National attracted industry-wide attention for a series of marketing innovations such as longer business hours (including full-service banking on Saturdays), drive-in windows, mobile home financing, bank credit cards, and an emphasis on home mortgages and consumer installment finance. The bank also pushed steadily ahead with internal structural modernizations such as centralized, computerized bookkeeping, and it followed Bank of America, the industry leader, in forging an expanding chain of offices across the state.

Stoddard, like Carnegie before him, created a bureaucracy to manage his firm's routine affairs, delegating considerable authority to subordinates. "We have pioneered in Michigan a system of branch banking," he said in 1952, "with centralization of policy but decentralization of operating responsibility and authority." Although he encouraged his subordinates' innovative spirit and often adopted their ideas, the firm remained solidly under his control. Its growth in size meant not a decline of his influence, but rather the perfection of an ever more potent instrument of his policy. In making that policy Stoddard, again like Carnegie, combined an accurate market perception with a clear vision of the kind of institution necessary to capitalize upon it, both acquired in previous experiences in the service of others. In addition, he embodied a restless drive to succeed, a single-minded dedication to his business, and an ability to maintain that drive throughout his career. That he succeeded so well despite the considerable handicap of having entered the money business with virtually no money of his own testifies to his determined character and his acute ability to learn from experience. Moreover, it shows that the opportunity to found an individual business and maintain control over its expanding bureaucracy still existed forty years after waves of mergers swept many family firms away into the anonymity of corporate Brobdingnag. What was needed, as always, was a man who could seize the chance and the time. Stoddard showed himself one such, notwithstanding the fact that much of the knowledge and many of the contacts that proved vital later, he acquired while in the service of what critics have often damned as the most initiative-stifling bureaucracy of them all, the federal government. . . .

When Stoddard died in 1971, his policies had proved their worth many times over, despite the fact that they often outraged his competitors and frightened the state bank examiners. Though his firm never expanded beyond Michigan boundaries, its innovative policies attracted the attention of banks everywhere, often receiving the ultimate compliment of imitation.

Like Carnegie before him, Stoddard adapted skills learned in the service of another, larger institution to the needs of his own enterprise and created a powerful combination of personal enterpreneurship and bureaucratic management. Unlike Carnegie who had no heir or successor, Howard Stoddard passed his domain on to his son, Stanford C. Stoddard, who has continued along the path his father laid out and has added goals of his own. Big, bureaucratized, but still personally run, Michigan National Bank continues to grow in size and efficiency, and shows no sign of disappearing or of being absorbed by its corporate competitors.

Henry Ford II

Henry Ford II's ability to shape the Ford Motor Company into an instrument of his personal policy and an embodiment of his world view presents the most astounding such case in the history of American business. Given the company's enormous size (consistently one of the ten largest corporations in the world), and the global scope of its operations (producing, assembling, or marketing in more than fifty countries, it sells more vehicles outside of North America than any other U.S. firm), Ford Motor Company obviously could not exist without a complex managerial bureaucracy to coordinate product development, purchasing, production, and sales. If ever a firm existed whose structure would appear to present an insuperable obstacle to individual domination, Ford would seem a prime candidate. In fact, the contrary situation prevails. Despite the obvious and necessary delegation of much authority to subordinate management, it remains clear both to industry observers and to company employees from the president in Dearborn, Michigan, to the plant manager in Wellington, New Zealand, that the boss is the man who sometimes reminds them, "my name is on the building."

Henry II's achievement looms even larger in light of the circumstances of his early years at the head of the company. In the fall of 1945, when he succeeded his legendary grandfather as president, Ford Motor Company was sliding rapidly down the razor blade of business life, headed toward an insignificant place in the industry, if not to bankruptcy or oblivion through sale to a competitor. It was not a matter of not being able to produce cars, but of not knowing what they cost. The company had no cost accounting system whatever; in its entire history it had employed no more sophisticated method of learning unit cost than dividing the number of units produced into the year's total expenditures. In fact, the company was run in 1945 the same way Carnegie had found the iron industry in 1865, as "a lump business."

For a long time, of course, there had not been any need to know costs; so long as new plants and bank balances kept going up, expenses were obviously well below income. Plenty of great fortunes have been made—by English textile manufacturers, for example—in blissful ignorance of costs. Henry Ford's was not the first, though it was surely the greatest and very likely the last. When the time arrived—probably during the declining auto market of 1920 and thereafter—when such information became important, the older Ford apparently did not care to know costs and did not try to find them out. For one thing Ford, like

Edison and many other contemporary industrialists, was not intrigued by money per se and was not motivated by it. For another, for all that he was a twentieth-century technician whose skills did much to modernize the world he lived in, and for all his prescience about economies of scale and the potential mass markets for automobiles, Ford had essentially a nineteenth-century, in some senses even an eighteenth-century, business mind. He focused his efforts on design and production of a utilitarian vehicle and let costs take care of themselves.

Such a system had served well enough in the halcyon days of the Model T but had grown increasingly inadequate under the competitive onslaught of General Motors, where Alfred Sloan and his associates had installed cost controls that Carnegie would have envied, and had added to them the techniques of forward planning based on market forecasting. Ford Motor Company not only had no market forecasting capability, but could not have used the information if it had. Prior to 1946, no one at Ford had any idea what it cost to produce a car. Moreover, above the plant manager level, where old hands like Meade Bricker kept production moving, the company's lines of authority disappeared into a chaos of untitled executives who had no clear-cut responsibilities and whose positions often depended not on ability but on their personal relationships with Harry Bennett. Bennett, who rose from head of Ford's notorious plant protection forces to a murky but powerful role as the elder Henry Ford's trusted confidante, had no ability to manage such an enterprise.

In such chaotic circumstances only the enormous cash reserves and the residual good will of dealers and customers, built up during the firm's prewar years, kept it afloat until the younger Henry Ford arrived at the top. It was, in fact, the frightening decline of those cash reserves that provided indisputable evidence of the company's disintegrating efficiency. That its products' popularity had already declined was shown by the fact that Ford Motor, which once made more cars than the rest of the industry combined, had slipped to third position behind General Motors and Chrysler. Complicating this toilsome situation was the fact that Ford faced the complex problem of reconverting to peacetime production quickly enough to take advantage of consumer demand dammed up through four years of war.

To confront this task Henry Ford II, then twenty-eight years old, had paper credentials that could only charitably have been called modest. Educated at Yale, he had switched from engineering to sociology because the former curriculum proved "too tough." He had come home to Detroit in 1940 and gone to work in the plant, learning the business as a "grease monkey in the experimental garage and a checker in the dynamometer room." In 1941 he entered the navy; in 1943 he returned to the company, where, like so many other Ford executives, he had no defined duties. Between his return in 1943 and his assumption of the presidency in 1945, young Ford, who declared himself "green and searching for the answers," apparently found much of what was wrong and pinpointed the source. Given his age and lack of experience, however, this knowledge scarcely qualified him technically for the necessary task of housecleaning and rebuilding.

What he did have, however, as he soon proved, were certain indefinable qualities. First, he had his heritage in the automobile business; he had been raised in it and had never expected to follow any other career. Detroit, where car-building is often called "a disease, not a profession," considers no amount of technical skill or bureaucratic finesse adequate unless there is a dose of gasoline in the blood, and this Henry II certainly had. Second, he had a goal—perhaps a vision would have been a more apt description under the circumstances—of returning his company to its former preeminent position in the industry, while retaining it firmly as a family concern. Third, he had a clear view of his abilities and limitations. He at once set out to do the things he could and hired the right people to do the rest.

As a first step he fired Harry Bennett and his cronies, then rounded up a stable of loyal Ford hands such as Meade Bricker, Jack Davis, Ernest Kanzler, and John Bugas to advise him and to begin the job of shoring up the structure. Reaching outside the organization, he engaged Earl Newsome, a public relations specialist, and Elmo Roper, the public opinion poller, to aid in the task of restoring the company's image. None of these, however, could tackle the most pressing task, that of installing a cost accounting system, analyzing the results, and applying tourniquets to the hemorrhages. What Ford Motor Company needed was a system like General Motors', and to get it Ford recruited a team of GM-trained executives. First came Ernest Breech, who left the presidency of Bendix Aviation to become, first, Ford's executive vice-president, and then president when Henry Ford II became chairman of the board. Breech and Ford then recruited Harold Youngren as chief engineer, Lewis Crusoe to handle finance, and Del Harder to take charge of production.

Crusoe at once set out to discover the company's costs, and soon determined that they added up to a loss of sixty-two dollars per car sold, an average of $10 million a month in the first half of 1946. Even this figure was an estimate, as the company's staff, unaccustomed to furnishing the necessary information, had to be retrained to the new policy. This took some time, so for many months Ford and Crusoe had to continue to rely on cash balances as the ultimate gauge of the company's fortunes.

As component costs became accurately quantified, Breech's team assaulted them across the board by revamping the company's plant with a dedication that Carnegie would have relished—spending $4 billion between 1945 and 1962—and by using comparative cost data to demand improved performance from management. By the end of 1946, the company had returned to a profit-making basis, although it was not until 1952 that Breech felt confident enough of the company's hold on costs to contemplate with equanimity the possibility of a price war with Chevrolet. By the time Breech retired in the summer of 1960, the company had become a solid, consistent profit maker, and had regained the number two position in the industry, even outselling Chevrolet in 1957 and 1959.

By the time Breech departed, the company's top echelons had become the province of a new generation of Ford executives. Some of the new men came from the so-called whiz kids who had joined Ford Motor as a team from the Army Air Force's statistical control unit after World War II. These included Robert McNamara and Arjay Miller, Breech's two immediate successors as president, and J. Edward Lundy, currently an executive vice-president. More important, Breech's retirement signaled the end of Henry Ford II's self-imposed apprenticeship at the head of his own company. As Breech himself said, "Henry doesn't need me any more." Even before Breech's departure, Ford had taken an active part in his company's affairs, not only in broad policymaking, but also at lower organizational levels, frequently intervening in personal decisions down to the third level of management, occasionally overruling his officers' recommendations in the process. On occasion he abandoned bureaucratic niceties to enforce a personal decision, such as telling Ford Division General Manager Donald Frey directly to abandon plans for a seven-passenger limousine, bypassing the three officers between him and Frey on the organization chart. Arjay Miller once observed, "The first thing you have to understand about the company is that Henry Ford is the boss. . . . He was always the boss from the first day I came in [1946], and he always will be the boss until he decides to retire."

After 1960, as his company continued to grow, Ford played an ever-more forceful role in its management. Some cases—his part in the meteoric rise of Lee Iacocca to the presidency, and the making and unmaking of Semon Knudsen, for example—have received wide publicity. Less well-known, but probably more significant to the company in the long run, has been his part in revamping the company's overseas operations into its current multinational structure. Throughout the 1950s, and increasingly after 1960, the firm's international strategy reflected his philosophy of global economics.

Ford Motor Company earned its first export dollar in 1903, and remained active outside the United States thereafter. The evolution of the company's overseas facilities was a complex one but the results can be summarized simply. By 1960 three companies, Ford of Canada (which owned subsidiaries in the British Commonwealth countries outside

Great Britain itself), Ford of England, and Ford of Germany existed as self-sufficient, essentially autonomous divisions, each producing its own line of cars, occasionally drawing on Dearborn for technological assistance, and submitting, sometimes reluctantly, to its coordination of export markets outside the three companies' defined domains. International sales had historically contributed an important share of the company's total business: 9 percent (by units sold), 1911–20; 12 percent, 1921–30; and 24 percent in each succeeding decade through 1960, as well as a significant share of its profits—20 percent in 1962, for example.

Despite this record, Ford felt that his company's international structure was inadequate for the future. It consisted, in his words, of "a collection of individual national organizations." Efficient as they might be, such organizations had horizons too limited to deal with "the day [which] might not be far off when organizations even of the scope of North America and Europe will prove too limiting." Furthermore, the national companies' facilities, all but a few of which were located in the industrialized countries of the world, could not hope to penetrate the potential markets of the underdeveloped world, where the people, "deeply committed to fast industrialization" demanded local manufacture or assembly as a prerequisite for doing business. "Whether we like it or not," Ford declared in 1961, "Africa, Latin America, and Asia are going all-out into the industrial age.... If we want to share in those markets, rich and vast as they will someday surely be ... we are going to have to go in with our tools and know-how and help them get the things they want."

In these statements and others, Ford revealed that he was more than a parochial American industrialist; he was an internationalist who saw the whole world as a potential market for Ford products. Widely traveled in the service of the company (he made trips to Europe in 1948 and 1952, and frequently thereafter traveled around the world to the company's facilities), he broadened his perspective as an alternate delegate to the United Nations in the early 1950s. Robert McNamara, speaking not only of his experiences with Ford at the company but also as head of the World Bank, declared, "there's no doubt that he's one of the best-informed businessmen in the U.S. on the rest of the world."

Like his grandfather's, Ford's world view envisioned a global market for automobiles; not a market in which American manufacturers could plunder less fortunate peoples, but rather one in which American industry stood to benefit from worldwide industrial prosperity in a climate of free trade. In the 1920s the elder Ford said, "We ought to wish for every nation as large a degree of self-support as possible. Instead of wishing to keep them dependent upon us for what we manufacture, we should wish them to learn to manufacture themselves and build up a solidly founded civilization." Forty years later, his grandson called upon

American firms "to go in with our tools and know-how and help them get the things they want." He had already publicly advocated free trade in an industrializing world: "I believe this country should step forth boldly and lead the world toward freer trade. . . . We need competition the world over to keep us on our toes and sharpen out wits. The keener the competition, the better it will be for us. . . . People cannot keep on buying from us unless we buy from them, and unless international trade can go on, our business will stagnate here at home."

In the 1960s Ford transformed the structure of his overseas affiliates according to his philosophy of maximizing the advantages of free trade and penetrating markets in the underdeveloped world by creating local manufacturing facilities. Specifically this resulted first in the coordination of Ford of England and Ford of Germany by Ford of Europe, and a unified product line and design to optimize the advantages of the emerging European free trade communities; and second, in the creation of Ford Asia-Pacific (FASPAC) to develop and produce vehicles for the Southeast Asian market including, if possible, Japan. Both organizations embodied a heavy dependence on a policy (called "complementation" by Ford Asia-Pacific) of cross-hauling components from specialized parts plants in various countries to strategically located assembly plants. Both organizations resulted from plans prepared by the Ford staff at Henry Ford II's instigation. He accepted the plans not because they offered the only alternatives (both General Motors and the Japanese manufacturers employ a different method), but because they combined the prospect of profit with a company structure consonant with his personal beliefs.

In implementing the plans for global organizations, the company benefited from steps already taken by its chairman. In 1948 Ford had instructed his overseas subsidiaries to sell worldwide in any market they could find. During the 1950s he began buying up the affiliates' stock, much of which had been sold to local investors during the 1920s. By 1962 the parent company owned 75 percent of Ford of Canada, 99 percent of Ford of Germany, and 100 percent of Ford of England. In 1961, already sure of unquestioned control of the subsidiaries, he took further steps toward an integrated global structure, stepping up overseas investment so that for the first time it exceeded domestic capital expenditure, and informing his subordinates that: "In order to further the growth of our worldwide operations, each purchasing activity of the company or an affiliated company should consider . . . sources of supply not only in its country but also sources located in other countries." To break down local resistance to the new policies, Ford dispatched American executives to key posts abroad. In 1962, for example, Americans headed eight of the twelve European sales, assembly, and manufacturing companies.

In Europe, Ford of England and Ford of Germany were in effect

super overseas operating divisions by 1966, still functioning highly au-
tonomously although plugged into the Dearborn staff for technical assistance. Each company produced a wide range of vehicles that duplicated
and competed, but that used no common parts. Each company operated
profitably and gave Ford Motor a viable entity in each of the European
free trade groups, the Common Market and the European Free Trade
Association (EFTA). Nevertheless, Henry Ford II found this arrangement wasteful and inadequate. He accepted a staff plan for reorganization and authorized Ford of Europe to coordinate the integration of the
European companies into a single unit, producing a single line of cars
assembled from common parts flowing from all over the region. "Implicit in this change," he said, "was a growing recognition that the entire
Company needed to think more and more in worldwide terms and that
the foreign subsidiaries no longer could be thought of as a collection of
individual national organizations. This was particularly true of Europe,
where eventual expansion of the common market seemed certain to
require a strongly integrated approach."

In the years since 1967, Ford of Europe has moved steadily toward its
goal of a product line built of nationally interchangeable parts. In doing
so it has adhered to the original assumptions on which the plan depended: that the European vehicle market would expand, that the
Common Market would survive and incorporate Britain and the rest of
EFTA, and that European consumers would accept cars that had no local
national identity. Manufacturing has become more decentralized with
the construction of single-product plants such as a transmission plant in
Bordeaux, France. Parts flow from these works to an expanding network
of assembly plants in Europe; the plants ship engines and transmissions
to Asia and the United States and supply, for example, major components for the American Pinto, fulfilling Ford's contention that "the entire
web of components and end products [will] become increasingly multinational. . . ."

Conclusion

These three men ran different kinds of businesses across a century of
time in domains ranging from statewide to national to global. Their
success, however, embodied several common factors. All of them saw a
market opportunity and moved to exploit it. All of them retained a
controlling ownership—Carnegie by means of his majority partnership,
Stoddard and Ford through a controlling share of their firms' stock. Each
of them exercised a centralized direction of his firm's policies, while
creating a managerial bureaucracy that translated policy into decentralized control of operations, generated new ideas, and furnished a

steady stream of information that enabled the owner to evaluate the cost-effectiveness of policies and people.

It can, of course, be argued that few such family firms remain, and that the opportunity for creating them has dwindled. But such arguments were made long ago, before Watson at IBM, Linowitz at Xerox, Land at Polaroid, and many others appeared. That such firms continue to appear seems to me self-evident; that they make a disproportionate contribution to the development of new technology seems likely. The question of how often it happens is a hard one to answer. Even harder is the question of how often it needs to happen for capitalism to survive. How many Carnegies did it take to "prove" the validity of the "American Dream"? Such people always constituted a tiny minority, but enough of them prevailed to rivet the dream of success into the American consciousness and fire the imaginations of men like Howard Stoddard. Enough individuals capable of turning bureaucracy to their own purposes continue to emerge to provide capitalism with a constant source of regeneration, confounding the expectations of Marx, Weber, Schumpeter, and others.

Bureaucracy, I think, has not inevitably obliterated the entrepreneurial spirit necessary to the maintenance of capitalistic business systems. In the hands of the right protagonists it has become an instrument to cope with the complexities of doing business in the modern world. Bureaucracy, then, has not inevitably proven the nemesis of the entrepreneur; it has rather become a necessary tool of this trade. The successes of men like Carnegie, Stoddard, and Ford, and the failures of so many others, demonstrate that the survival of the entrepreneurial spirit occurs because of bureaucracy, not in spite of it. Since such individuals and their institutions play so prominent a role in our past and present, and continue to provide a powerful impetus to capitalism, they seem to me worthy of determined study; and such study combines the realities of modern techniques of institutional and data analysis with the matchless excitment of traditional, personal history. People make institutions, and people's stories always have been and always will be the vital core of history.

4

American Imperialism

Altruism or Aggression?

During the last quarter of the nineteenth century the United States emerged as a world power. Its industrial and agricultural productivity, large size, growing population, and modern navy gave it a prominence that could not be ignored. The acquisition of an overseas empire added to America's stature. In 1898 and 1899 the United States suddenly acquired the Hawaiian Islands and gained control over Puerto Rico, the Philippines, and part of the Samoan archipelago. Within a year and a half America had become a dominant power in both the Caribbean and the Pacific.

Curiously enough, many Americans were ambivalent about their country's new role. Some feared that America's democratic institutions were incompatible with an overseas empire and the large military establishment that would be required to sustain it. Others rejected the concept of empire because they opposed bringing under the American flag groups they regarded as racial or social inferiors. Some Americans, on the other hand, favored the entry of the United States into world affairs, either because of a crusading zeal to spread American institutions or a desire to find new economic markets. Although the United States entered the twentieth century as a world power, its people remained divided over the wisdom or desirability of pursuing their new destiny.

These divisions among the public over foreign policy had their counterpart among diplomatic historians. Just as Americans debated the wisdom of particular policies, so historians disagreed about interpretations of past events. The historical debate, in reality, was not confined simply to an analysis of the past; implicit in many interpretations of diplomatic history was a vision of what America ought to be. To argue that the United States traditionally was a champion of freedom and democracy was to take a position on certain contemporary policies toward the nondemocratic world. Similarly, the argument that America was an imperialistic nation bent on imposing its economic and military power on the rest of the world had implications for contemporary foreign and domestic policy issues.

The historical literature dealing with the decade of the 1890s, which

123

culiminated in the Spanish-American War, is a case in point. Charles and Mary Beard, whose *Rise of American Civilization* symbolized the Progressive school of American historiography, implied that economic issues led President William McKinley to ask for a declaration of war. The Spanish government, after all, had practically acceded to his demands. McKinley, the Beards insisted, revised Cleveland's policy of neutrality, presumably because of the threat to American investments in and trade with Cuba. In the final analysis, war grew out of a desire to protect America's economic interests in that region. The ensuing acquisition of overseas territory provided further proof of the Beards's charge that the nation's business community played an important role in determining the country's foreign policy. Although the Beardian thesis was presented in somewhat qualified form, it clearly implied the primacy of economic forces.[1]

Relatively few scholars, however, followed the Beards's interpretation. To Samuel Flagg Bemis, whose synthesis of American diplomatic history appeared in 1936, the acquisition of an overseas empire represented a "great aberration." Before the war, Bemis noted, "there had not been the slightest demand for the acquisition of the Philippine Islands." A military victory, however, fanned imperialist sentiment. McKinley proved unable to resist jingoist sentiment, and he instructed his peace commission to demand the Philippine Islands, a demand that demonstrated "adolescent irresponsibility." McKinley's decision, concluded Bemis, was largely unplanned, and was not in accord with the traditional American aversion to imperialism.[2]

At the same time that Bemis's influential textbook appeared, Julius W. Pratt published his *Expansionists of 1898*. Also rejecting an economic interpretation of war causation, Pratt suggested instead that intellectual and emotional factors were responsible for the new expansionism. The emergence of social Darwinism, with its emphasis on competition and survival of the fittest, provided some people with an intellectual justification for expanding America's sphere of influence. Many argued that nations, like individuals, were engaged in a remorseless test of their fitness to survive. The criterion of success was dominion over others; failure to expand, on the other hand, meant stagnation and decline. Other expansionist-minded individuals were affected by religious and humanitarian concerns; they wished to bring American civilization and morality to less advanced peoples. Still others accepted the doctrines developed by Captain Alfred Thayer Mahan, who saw growing Ameri-

---

[1]Charles A. Beard and Mary R. Beard, *The Rise of American Civilization*, 2 vols., (New York, 1927), 2:369–82.

[2]Samuel Flagg Bemis, *A Diplomatic History of the United States* (1st ed. 1936; 4th ed., New York, 1955), pp. 463–75.

can sea power as the key to the nation's greatness. Sea power, however, required overseas naval bases. Pratt, interestingly enough, noted that the business community, which was still recovering from the depression that began in 1893, opposed intervention in Cuba for fear that it might block the road to economic recovery. With Admiral Dewey's dramatic victory in the Philippines, American businessmen became converted to the expansionist cause by the alluring prospect of dominating the potentially large Chinese market. These same businessmen now found it easy to apply to same rationale in the Caribbean and supported expansion in that area. The reasons why the United States went to war, therefore, were quite different from the reasons that led its government to acquire an overseas empire. Indeed, Pratt concluded, American imperialism consisted of a blend of religious, humanitarian, and economic components.[3]

These early historians agreed, at least in part, that foreign policy was to a significant extent determined by domestic considerations. There were significant differences, nevertheless, between their approaches. To the Beards the business community, with its emphasis on profits, pushed the nation into war. Bemis, on the other hand, saw the results of war as a repudiation of the traditional antiimperialist sentiment of Americans. To Pratt a variety of influences—domestic and foreign—came into play, although no one in particular exercised the decisive role. In general, two approaches ultimately came to dominate the writing of American diplomatic history. Those in the Beard tradition would interpet America's foreign policy primarily in terms of domestic considerations. A second tradition would emphasize, in addition, the importance of actions taken by foreign governments. Although the two approaches would on occasion come together in the work of an individual scholar, more often then not they would remain separate and distinct.

After the publication of Pratt's work in 1936, scholarly interest in American imperialism and the Spanish-American War tended to flag. Between the 1930s and 1950s diplomatic historians were primarily interested in illuminating the causes and consequences of the First and Second World Wars. But in 1959 William Appleman Williams published his influential book, *The Tragedy of American Diplomacy*, which had a profound impact on the writing of all diplomatic history. His book, indeed, became the starting point for the work of many revisionist and New Left historians, who believed that America's foreign policies were dominated by the narrow economic interests of a small elite.

The Williams thesis, briefly stated, rested on the premise that foreign

[3]Julius W. Pratt, *Expansionists of 1898* (Baltimore, 1936), and *America's Colonial Experiment: How the United States Gained, Governed, and in Part Gave Away a Colonial Empire* (New York, 1950).

policy was a function of the structure and organization of American society. During the depression of the 1880s and 1890s the business community had concluded that foreign markets were indispensable for America's well-being. These markets would help to avoid any internal problems that might arise from economic stagnation resulting from America's tendency to produce more goods than its people consumed. The result was a fundamental shift in the nation's foreign policy. Policymakers adopted what became known as the Open Door policy— an open door "through which America's preponderant economic strength would enter and dominate all underdeveloped areas of the world. . . . [T]he Open Door Policy was in fact a brilliant strategic stroke which led to the gradual extension of American economic and political power throughout the world."[4] Indeed, most of American diplomacy in the twentieth century, Williams insisted, was directed toward the goal of assuring the nation's economic supremacy on a global scale. Pursuit of this goal led to involvement in two world wars, the Korean and Vietnam conflicts, and the Cold War that pitted the Soviet Union and the United States against each other. In other words, Williams posited a continuity in American foreign policy from the late nineteenth century to the present.

The origins of modern American foreign policy, Williams argued, could be traced back to the economic crisis of the 1890s. During that decade a new national consensus was reached. Americans no longer debated whether or not an expansionist policy should be pursued, but rather what form expansion should take. This expansionist policy was based on the conviction that American diplomacy and prosperity went hand in hand and required access to world markets. Any restrictions on the flow of American goods and capital would lead to a depression and social unrest. Support for economic expansion, therefore, played a crucial role in precipitating the Spanish-American War and in the subsequent debate over the desirability of acquiring overseas possessions. The first selection in this chapter is an excerpt from *The Tragedy of American Diplomacy*.

In 1963 Walter LaFeber published a prize-winning volume on American expansionism from 1860 to 1898 that lent strong support to the Williams thesis. The Civil War, LaFeber noted, marked an important dividing line in America's expansionist policies. Before 1860 expansionism was confined to the American continent; it reflected the desire of an agrarian society to find new and fertile lands. Post–Civil War expansionism, on the other hand, was motivated by the belief that for-

---

[4]William Appleman Williams, *The Tragedy of American Diplomacy*, 2d rev. and enl. ed., (New York, 1972), pp. 45–46. See also Williams's *The Roots of the Modern American Empire* (New York, 1969).

eign markets were vital to America's well-being. By the 1890s the American business community and policymakers had concluded that additional foreign markets "would solve the economic, social, and political problems created by the industrial revolution." Given Europe's imperialist penetration in many regions of the world, Americans also concluded that their country needed strategic bases if they were to compete successfully. The diplomacy of the 1890s and the Spanish-American War grew out of these concerns. Indeed, LaFeber insisted that the debate between the imperialists and antiimperialists during this decade was a limited one; they differed over the tactical means that the United States should use in order to attain its objectives. "By 1899," concluded La Feber, "the United States had forged a new empire. American policy makers and businessmen had created it amid much debate and with conscious purpose. The empire progressed from a continental base in 1861 to assured pre-eminence in the Western Hemisphere in 1895. Three years later it was rescued from a growing economic and political dilemma by the declaration of war against Spain. During and after this conflict the empire moved past Hawaii into the Philippines, and, with the issuance of the Open-Door Notes, enunciated its principles in Asia."[5]

During the 1960s and 1970s many scholars continued to follow the Williams interpretation of American diplomacy. In 1967 Thomas McCormick published a book that traced the growing interest of Americans in the 1890s in the potentially large China market. Four years later Milton Plesur analyzed the origins of the "large policy" of the 1890s, which he located in the years between 1865 and 1890. The new diplomacy, he concluded, "was rationalized on the basis of racial and moral superiority, a sense of national mission, strategic considerations, enhancement of national prestige, and aversion to a worldwide imperialism from which we were excluded economically. Though originally not seeking territory for ourselves, we could not allow other powers to jeopardize what we thought were our legitimate interests." In a similar vein, Ernest N. Paolino emphasized the degree to which William H. Seward had laid the foundations for an expansionist policy during the 1860s.[6]

The Williams-LaFeber interpretation of the origins of modern America's foreign policy had a powerful appeal during the 1960s and 1970s,

[5]Walter LaFeber, *The New Empire: An Interpretation of American Expansionism 1860–1898* (Ithaca, 1963), pp. 412–17.

[6]Thomas McCormick, *China Market: America's Quest for Informal Empire 1893–1901* (Chicago, 1967); Milton Plesur, *America's Outward Thrust: Approaches to Foreign Affairs, 1865–1890* (DeKalb, 1971), pp. 235–36; Ernest N. Paolino, *The Foundations of American Empire: William Henry Seward and U.S. Foreign Policy* (Ithaca, 1973). See also Charles S. Campbell, *The Transformation of American Foreign Relations 1865–1900* (New York, 1976).

particularly as disillusionment with American society grew during the Vietnam conflict. The argument that the nation's diplomacy was based less on altruism, idealism, and antiimperialism and more on a desire to safeguard an international order that made possible America's economic supremacy, of course, had important implications for contemporary concerns. The Cold War, for example, rather than resting on a moral foundation that pitted freedom against communism, was seen as a product of America's continued insistence on structuring a world order along lines that preserved its liberal capitalist hegemony. Thus American foreign policy—which grew out of domestic institutions and developments—was allegedly responsible in large measure for initiating and perpetuating the Cold War and causing the Vietnam conflict.[7] Williams's work spawned a whole school of historians who proceeded to write revisionist accounts of the history of American foreign policy.

The Williams thesis, however, did not gain universal acceptance in historical circles. Not all scholars, for example, agreed with his portrait of American society. Others were critical of a viewpoint that emphasized the importance of domestic factors in the determination of foreign policy and belittled or ignored actions by other nations. In their eyes diplomatic policies were also influenced by the external actions and reactions of foreign governments. A more balanced approach, they argued, called for an understanding of the behavior of other governments, which, in turn, implied a multinational approach to diplomacy and multiarchival research. Rejecting the idea of American omnipotence in world affairs, they stressed other than economic factors and attempted to demonstrate that the purposefulness attributed to American policymakers was not justified by a critical examination of the sources.

Typical of this approach was Ernest R. May's *Imperial Democracy: The Emergence of America as a Great Power,* published in 1961. May argued that in the 1890s the United States had not sought to play a new role in world affairs. On the contrary, diplomatic problems concerning Hawaii, China, Venezuela, and Cuba had almost intruded upon the domestic issues in which most statesmen and political leaders were primarily interested. "Some nations," May observed, "achieve greatness; the United States had greatness thrust upon it."

President McKinley, for example, rather than being the harbinger of imperialism, was portrayed as a leader who was trying to keep his

---

[7]See LaFeber, *America, Russia, and the Cold War 1945–1966* (New York, 1967); Lloyd C. Gardner, "American Foreign Policy 1900–1921: A Second Look at the Realist Critique of American Diplomacy," in *Towards a New Past: Dissenting Essays in American History,* ed. Barton J. Bernstein (New York, 1968), pp. 202–31; David Healy, *U.S. Expansionism: The Imperialist Urge in the 1890s* (Madison, 1970).

nation out of war and at the same time to resolve the Cuban dilemma that had inflamed public opinion. His initiatives were ultimately doomed to failure, for Spain would neither grant Cuba autonomy nor suppress the rebellion. McKinley then gave Spain an ultimatum, which included American mediation in the event Spain and the Cubans could not reach some arrangement (a mediation that in all likelihood would have meant Cuban independence). To the Spanish government such an ultimatum was unacceptable. McKinley then faced a crucial choice. He could embark upon a war that he did not want or could defy public opinion and accept some compromise. The latter course might have led to the unseating of the Republican party if not the overthrow of constitutional government. "When public opinion reached the point of hysteria, he succumbed," said May.

Did McKinley accept the decision for war because of a need for foreign markets and strategic bases, as Williams argued? Most assuredly not, insisted May. "Neither the President nor the public had any aim beyond war itself. The nation was in a state of upset. Until recently its people had been largely Protestant and English; its economy predominantly rural and agricultural. . . . Now, however, the country was industrialized and urbanized. Catholics were numerous and increasing. People of older stock found themselves no longer economically or even socially superior to members of immigrant groups or to others. . . . The panic of 1893 made this new condition even more visible by depressing agricultural prices, rents, investment income, professional fees, and white-collar salaries. . . . In some irrational way, all these influences and anxieties translated themselves into concern for suffering Cuba. For the people as for the government, war with monarchical Catholic, Latin Spain had no purpose except to relieve emotion."[8]

In a certain sense May's thesis was anticipated a decade earlier by Richard Hofstadter. In 1952 Hofstadter published an article that rejected an economic explanation of American diplomacy in the 1890s and suggested instead that the hysteria and jingoism of this decade grew out of the anxieties occasioned by social and economic change. Indeed, shortly thereafter Hofstadter proposed a comparable explanation of the roots of McCarthyism. Although sympathetic to liberalism, Hofstadter's work in the 1940s and 1950s contributed to the emerging rejection of the basic tenets of the Progressive school of American historiography. In his eyes modern American liberalism reflected less a concern for the welfare of the masses of Americans and more the inner feelings of select middle-class groups alienated from their society because of economic

---

[8]Ernest R. May, *Imperial Democracy: The Emergence of America as a Great Power* (New York, 1961), pp. 268–70.

and technological change and a consequent decline in their social status. Foreign policy, implied Hofstadter, mirrored these irrational and noneconomic influences.[9]

In 1969 May published a second work in which he used concepts drawn from the social sciences in order to present a fuller portrait of the diplomacy of those years. In that work May examined the structure and role of public opinion in order to illuminate how the United States briefly became imperialistic in outlook and then even more quickly turned away from overseas expansion. After analyzing public opinion in terms of various categories involving elites with different interests and concerns, May argued that the anticolonialist consensus was briefly broken in 1898 and 1899, which resulted in the transfer of leadership to a wider circle. The outcome was a new consensus that accepted the desirability of acquiring foreign possessions and owed much of its inspiration to European, and especially British, opinion. Shortly thereafter the more traditional anticolonial view prevailed, especially after the difficulties faced by the British during the Boer War in South Africa and the growth of an antiimperialist movement in Britain. May concluded by insisting that the imperialist-antiimperialist debate could not be understood solely in terms of what Americans said or did, for they were members of a much broader Atlantic civilization.[10]

Another attack on the Williams school came from James A. Field, Jr. Much of the literature on American imperialism, Field charged, was a version of the Whig theory of history. Beginning with perceptions of American immorality in the twentieth century, Williams and his followers had interpreted the past with "the same perceptions of false continuities and imputations of sin." The historical literature dealing with the 1890s suffered from a number of failings: the adoption of a strictly rational explanation of events and a rejection of chance; the use of overly broad terms to describe complex situations; a treatment of diplomacy that was excessively ethnocentric; and a discussion that ignored "time, distance, costs, or technological feasibility."

Rejecting explanations of American imperialism based on the application of Darwinian theory, the psychic crisis of imperialism, the new navy, and the importance of the Pacific highway to Asia, Field proposed a new hypothesis. The new American navy that came into existence in the late nineteenth century was a defensive answer to European de-

---

[9]Richard Hofstadter, "Manifest Destiny and the Philippines," in *America in Crisis: Fourteen Crucial Episodes in American History*, ed. Daniel Aaron (New York, 1952), pp. 173–200.

[10]Ernest R. May, "American Imperialism: A Reinterpretation," *Perspectives in American History* 1 (1967): 123–283; also published as *American Imperialism: A Speculative Essay* (New York, 1968).

velopments; "its deployment reflected a shrunken perimeter." The search for bases was a response to the strategic problems of the proposed canal linking the Atlantic and Pacific oceans. The ideologists of that period, moreover, were of negligible importance. "What Americans, whether travellers or missionaries or businessmen, wanted of the outer world was the freedom to pursue happiness, to do their thing, to operate insofar as possible unhindered by arbitrary power or obsolete ideas. Proud of their own self-determined independence, they were sympathetic to similar desires on the part of Samoan chiefs, Korean kings, Egyptian khedives, Armenian Christians, Brazilians, Venezuelans, and Chinese. Most of all, because they were nearest and most visible and noisiest, it was the Cubans who engaged this sympathy." Indeed, Field suggested that the rapid deployment of the American navy headed by Admiral Dewey in the Pacific was largely a result of the rapidity of communication made possible by new cables linking nations and continents. Dewey's victory in turn focused public attention on the Far East; only then did an avalanche of publicity descend upon the American people. "Imperialism," according to Field, "was the product of Dewey's victory."[11]

The debate over the origins of American imperialism, of course, involved an evaluation of its consequences as well. To historians critical of the role of America in world affairs in the twentieth century, these consequences were largely negative. Williams, for example, argued that American foreign policy to a considerable degree rested on "a posture of moral and ideological superiority." Its leaders believed that underdeveloped nations had to be changed in order for the United States to harvest the fruits of expansionism. The goals of foreign policy (as compared with changing tactics) were to maintain markets for industrial exports, to control access to raw materials, and the right to take part in the economic life of other nations by establishing factories and other enterprises. Economic imperialism, in turn, led to efforts to establish political hegemony. Cuba, Williams noted, was a case in point. The United States "dominated the economic life of the island by controlling, directly or indirectly, the sugar industry, and by overtly and covertly preventing any dynamic modification of the island's one-crop economy. It defined clear and narrow limits on the island's political system. It tolerated the use of torture and terror, of fraud and farce, by Cuba's rulers. But it

---

[11]James A. Field, Jr., "American Imperialism: The Worst Chapter in Almost Any Book," *American Historical Review* 83 (June 1978):644–68. Following Field's article came two critical evaluations (and rejections) of his thesis by Walter LaFeber and Robert L. Beisner, and a reply by Fields. For this debate, see *ibid.*: 669–83. For a somewhat different rejection of the Williams interpretation, see Richard E. Welch, Jr., *Response to Imperialism: The United States and the Philippine–American War, 1899–1902* (Chapel Hill, 1979).

intervened with economic and diplomatic pressure and with force of arms when Cubans threatened to transgress the economic and political restrictions established by American leaders."[12]

Just as the Williams interpretation of the origins of the Spanish-American War came under criticism, so too did his view of twentieth-century American imperialism. Paul A. Varg, for example, argued that a careful examination of the specific actions of the United States in world affairs precluded any simple or facile generalizations about imperialism or America's world power status. China was *not* of major importance to American policy officials. Even the dominant role of the United States in the Caribbean was never pursued solely for economic considerations; strong opposition to any American intervention in that area arose during each crisis. In Varg's view, few American leaders pursued foreign policy concerns out of a conviction that the nation's welfare was dependent upon developments in other parts of the world. Although the United States did become a world power, it was not because of any master plan designed to control the destiny of other nations.[13]

The claim that American imperialism necessarily had a harmful impact on foreign nations was also challenged indirectly by Stanley Lebergott. Lebergott pointed to the relative insignificance of American foreign investment in Latin America from 1890 to 1929, and denied as well that it worked to the detriment of either workers or landowners in the nations that were affected. Indeed, American foreign investment increased the incomes of workers and peasants by expanding the need for labor; land values in many Latin American nations increased in value because of the opening of American markets to native products. Lebergott conceded that American business enterprise sometimes destroyed the vested interests of native business groups and their monopoly profits, and also created new entrepreneurial groups. The heart of the ensuing antiimperialist contest, he concluded, was not between America and Latin America, but between two capitalist groups, one native and the other foreign, each fighting over the spoils of progress. Lebergott's article is reprinted as the second selection in this chapter.

The debate among historians about the nature of late nineteenth- and early twentieth-century American diplomacy in part reflected visions not only of what American society was, but what it ought to have been. Charles A. Beard, writing within the Progressive school tradition,

---

[12]Williams, *Tragedy of American Diplomacy*, pp. 2, 59.

[13]Paul A. Varg, "The United States as a World Power, 1900–1917: Myth or Reality?," in *Twentieth-Century American Foreign Policy*, ed. John Braeman, Robert H. Bremner, and David Brody (Columbus, 1971), and *The Making of a Myth: The United States and China, 1897–1912* (East Lansing, 1968). For other examples of work in this tradition see Howard K. Beale, *Theodore Roosevelt and the Rise of America to World Power* (Baltimore, 1956), and Raymond A. Esthus, *Theodore Roosevelt and the International Rivalries* (Waltham, 1970).

tended to emphasize the role of economic factors. In the late 1940s he would spell out more precisely his belief that domestic reform and involvement in world rivalries were incompatible and benefitted relatively small groups of affluent elites. Samuel Flagg Bemis, on the other hand, wrote within an older patriotic tradition that emphasized the antiimperialist nature of the American people and their desire to avoid foreign adventures; hence he characterized the Spanish-American War as a "great aberration" and a war productive of no good. William Appleman Williams, a critic of American capitalism whose views became influential during the 1960s and 1970s, saw diplomacy as an extension of the need of American capitalism to dominate the world in an economic sense. The two world wars, the Korean and Vietnam conflicts, and the Cold War, he and his followers charged, were all products of internal flaws in American society; only by radical change could these flaws be eradicated. Recent critiques of the Williams approach were in part a reaction to his harsh criticisms of American society and in part a denial of American omnipotence. Events in other nations, as Ernest R. May noted, played a role in shaping American foreign policy, and a knowledge of the domestic determinants of policy, although indispensable, was insufficient by itself.

As long as Americans continue to discuss and fight over the proper role of their nation in world affairs, the events of the 1890s and early part of the twentieth century will continue to hold the interest of historians. In studying the origins and consequences of the Spanish-American War, scholars in all probability will continue to raise many of the same questions asked by their predecessors for nearly half a century. Did the United States go to war to resolve basic contradictions within its economic and social systems? Was the acquisition of an overseas empire a cause or a consequence of war? To what degree did moral, religious, and humanitarian sentiments play a role in the diplomacy of the 1890s? To what extent was American foreign policy a response to the diplomacy of other nations and events beyond its control? Did the United States in fact abandon its interests in empire after 1900, or did it create a new form of colonialism through the use of its economic power? Above all, did the United States become a world power because its leaders consciously recognized the importance of other regions to the nation's well-being, or did it simply stumble into its new status without a clear grasp of the underlying issues? Americans will struggle with these and other questions as long as they continue to debate foreign policy issues.

William Appleman Williams

WILLIAM APPLEMAN WILLIAMS (1921–   ) is professor of history at Oregon State University. He has written a number of major interpretive works on the history of American foreign policy, as well as a general interpretation of American history entitled *The Contours of American History* (1961).

Because of its dramatic and extensive nature, the crisis of the 1890s raised in many sections of American society the specter of chaos and revolution. Conservatives and reformers came to share the same conviction that something drastic had to be done, not only to solve the immediate problem, but to prevent the recurrence of such crises. That an expansionist foreign policy would provide such relief and prevention rapidly became an integral and vital part of all but an infinitesimal segment of the response to the general crisis. The issue that in a few years developed into what in the 1950s would have been called a Great Debate concerned *not* whether expansion should be pursued, but rather what *kind* of expansion should be undertaken.

This broad support for expansion, and particularly overseas economic expansion, rested upon agreement among conservatives and liberals (even many radicals joined in for a few years), and Democrats and Republicans, from all sections and groups of the country. A strong majority agreed that foreign policy could and should play an important—if not crucial—part in recovering from the depression of the 1890s and in forestalling future difficulties. . . .

The second idea about expansion was much broader and took account of the particular outlook of all special interests. It explained America's democracy and prosperity in the past as the result of expansion across the continent and, to a lesser degree, overseas into the markets of the world. Either implicitly or explicitly, depending on the form in which it was presented, the idea pointed to the practical conclusion

---

that expansion was the way to stifle unrest, preserve democracy, and restore prosperity. . . .

Such general and active support for economic expansion is often neglected when considering the coming of the Spanish-American War. It is customary to explain the war as a crusade to save the Cubans or to interpret it in psychological terms as a release for national frustrations arising from the depression. But while it may be granted that economic leaders preferred not to go to war as long as they could attain their objectives without it, and although it may be useful to talk about Americans developing a national compulsion to punish Spain for mistreating Cuba, it is equally apparent that such interpretations do not take account of several key aspects of the coming of the war. For one thing, it is clear that various groups saw war with Spain over Cuba as a means to solve other problems. They reached that conclusion, moreover, at the end of a conscious exercise in considering alternatives—not in a blind and irrational outburst of patriotic or ideological fervor. Many agrarians viewed it as a way to monetize silver at home and thus pave the way for a general expansion of their exports to the sterling areas of the world. Some labor groups thought it would ease or resolve immediate economic difficulties. Any many important businessmen, as contrasted with the editors of some business publications, came to support war for specific commercial purposes as well as for general economic reasons.

If there is any one key to understanding the coming of the war with Spain, it very probably lies in the growing conviction among top economic and political leaders that American military intervention was necessary in order to clean up the Cuban mess so that domestic *and other foreign policy* issues could be dealt with efficiently and effectively. It should be made clear, however, that in suggesting this explanation of the war there is no direct or implicit argument that other considerations were nonexistent or unimportant. Nor is it being hinted that the whole affair was the product of some conspiracy in high places. Consciousness of purpose is not conspiracy, even if those who are addicted to explaining everything in terms of irrational psychology often seem unable to distinguish between the two. There was consciousness of purpose in high places—as there should be, whatever one's individual judgment on either the goals or the means—but there was no conspiracy.

It likewise seems wise to emphasize the obvious, but nevertheless often overlooked, distinction between explicit economic motives and a more general economic estimate of the situation. Men have on occasion acted in certain ways because their pocketbook nerve prompted them to do so. They still do. Even historians have been known to change jobs (or their points of view) for more money, as well as for their egos or for better research facilities. And the actions of some influential figures during the period leading up to the war with Spain can only be understood in that light. They wanted intervention to save and extend their property holdings. In a similar way, other men can and do act on the basis of equally narrow political calculation. Some Americans wanted intervention on the ground that it would save their personal and party political fortunes.

Yet it is also quite possible, and not at all unusual, for men to act on the basis of a broader, more inclusive organization and integration of information and desires. Sometimes such a conception of the world—or *Weltanschauung,* as it is more formally called—orders data in such a way that political, religious, or cultural values are held to be the crucial factors. Thus some Americans undoubtedly supported war against Spain because according to their view of the world it was impossible to have peace or prosperity or good government in Cuba as long as it was ruled by Catholics.

To an extensive degree, however, American leaders of the 1890s entertained a *Weltanschauung* that organized data around economic criteria. They explained difficulties, and likewise advanced solutions and alternatives, by reference to economic phenomena. This did not make them economically motivated in the pocketbook sense, but it did lead them to believe that their objectives in the political and social realms could only be attained through economic means. To somewhat over-simplify the point to gain clarity, it can be summarized in this way.

Men like McKinley and other national leaders thought about America's problems and welfare in an inclusive, systematized way that emphasized economics. Wanting democracy and social peace, they argued that economic depression threatened those objectives, and concluded that overseas economic expansion provided a primary means of ending that danger. They did not want war per se, let alone war in order to increase their own personal fortunes. But their own conception of the world ultimately led them into war in order to solve the problems in the way that they considered necessary and best. These general remarks bearing on historical analysis and interpretation should be kept in mind. . . .

There are three central considerations to be evaluated and connected when explaining and interpreting the war against Spain. The first is that the basic policy of presidents Cleveland and McKinley was to secure the defeat of the revolution in Cuba and what they repeatedly and explicitly called "the pacification of the island" under Spanish rule. Both presidents wanted to get on with other domestic and foreign programs and policies; in particular, both were intensely concerned with vigorous overseas economic expansion into Latin America and Asia.

The outbreak of the Sino-Japanese War in 1894 upset Cleveland considerably, for example, and he formally warned the Congress and the country that the conflict "deserves our gravest consideration by reason of its disturbance of our growing commercial interests." Cleveland not only repeated the same general theme in his message of December 2, 1895, but explicitly tied that problem to the outbreak of revolution in Cuba that was "deranging the commercial exchanges of the island, of which our country takes the predominant share." Shortly thereafter, in March and April 1896, Secretary of State Olney told the Spanish that the United States wanted to help "pacify the island."

Speaking with "candor," Olney explained Cleveland's "anxiety," and bluntly repeated the president's "earnest desire for the prompt and permanent pacification of that island." The United States wanted to avoid "a war of races" within the island, and sought "the noninterruption of extensive trade relations [and]... the prevention of that wholesale destruction of property on the island which ... is utterly destroying American investments that should be of immense value, and is utterly impoverishing great numbers of American citizens."

After waiting eight months, Cleveland, on December 7, 1896, personally and publicly reiterated his desire for "the pacification of the island." America's concern, he bluntly pointed out, was "by no means of a wholly sentimental or philanthropic character. Our actual pecuniary interest in it is second only to that of the people and government of Spain." In the original draft of his message, Cleveland proposed to conclude with a warning strikingly reminiscent of the *Harper's* magazine remark of 1893 that "if we have fighting to do, it will be fighting to keep the peace." Cleveland originally put it this way: either Spain must end the rebellion promptly or "this government will be compelled to protect its own interests and those of its citizens, which are coincident with those of humanity and civilization generally, by resorting to such measures as will promptly restore to the Island the blessings of peace." He even added, again in the original draft, a deadline specified as "the coming of the New Year."

The increasing vigor and militance (and even self-righteousness) of Cleveland's approach to Cuban affairs cannot be explained or understood in isolation. The ever more threatening agitation of the agricultural businessmen was a major factor. So was the rising American concern about developments in the Far East. Japan's attack on China had thrown open the lid of Pandora's box of imperialistic rivalries, and American interests such as the American China Development Company (and other firms and banks) were caught and whipsawed in the resulting free-for-all between Japan, Russia, France, England, and Germany.

In the fall of 1896, however, China turned to the United States in an effort to protect its own position by aligning itself with a major power that had not indicated any significant interest in territorial concessions. At the same time they offered a railroad concession to Americans, a delegation of Chinese officials visited the United States. Received and entertained by public and private leaders, the Chinese clearly accomplished their initial objective of intensifying American interest in and concern over economic gains in Asia.

Cleveland's remarks on Cuba in the first draft of his December 1896 message would clearly seem to follow from that anticipated involvement in Asia—particularly since the president had called for the "gravest consideration" of that issue as early as 1894. But Cleveland had just been defeated by McKinley in the election of November 1896, and his position was obviously difficult. As a responsible politician, Cleveland no doubt realized that it would be unfair (and against tradition) to issue an ultimatum that would entrap his successor. He may even have been explicitly advised that McKinley had told Lodge that he "very naturally does not want to be obliged to go to war as soon as he comes in." Nor is it very likely that Cleveland judged it wise on second thought to go out of office as the man who gave the country a war as his farewell gift. In the message as delivered, therefore, he contented himself with the clear warning that "it can not be reasonably assumed that the hitherto expectant attitude of the United States will be indefinitely maintained."

Upon entering the White House, McKinley reiterated Cleveland's demand for prompt "pacification of the island." But in acting on that policy he began very quickly to squeeze Spain (and himself and the United States) into an ever more difficult position. To some extent, this pressure on Spain was prompted by the activity of various groups within the United States that insisted on more vigorous and dramatic action. This has led some historians to conclude that the prorebel newspaper campaign against Spain was primarily responsible for the war. Others have reduced the problem to a political issue, arguing that McKinley ultimately accepted war to sustain or save the influence and power of the Republican party (and his position within it).

These interpretations, which stress domestic pressure on the administration, do define and raise the second principal consideration in any evaluation of the war. But the wild and irresponsible press campaign initiated and directed by William Randolph Hearst and Joseph Pulitzer never succeeded in whipping up any sustained hysteria for war until early in 1898—*if even then*. The evidence is overwhelming that the psychological Rubicon was not crossed until a few weeks after the sinking of the battleship *Maine* on February 15, 1898. As for the argument that politics was the key to the war, that begs the real point about what provoked the political pressure. The agitation that scared metropolitan (and other) Republicans came from militant agriculturalists who wanted markets—and a symbolic and a real assault on autocratic European power throughout the world.

Several other factors appear far more significant in explaining McKinley's increasing pressure on Spain. One of them is intimately connected

with his continuation of Cleveland's policy of demanding prompt pacification. For along with other Americans, McKinley reacted against the
very ruthlessness that the thinly veiled warnings from the United States
encouraged Spain to employ. In insisting upon certain ends while pro-
hibiting the use of forceful measures, McKinley was more the victim of
his own irresponsibility than a puppet jerked about by the yellow press
of Pulitzer and Hearst.

Furthermore, McKinley was being increasingly pressured by metropolitan expansionists. Some of those men were economic entrepreneurs
acting on narrow interest-conscious motives. They wanted their property
protected and their opportunities secured. That outlook was typified by
Chauncey M. Depew of the New York Central Railroad; Alonzo B. Hepburn of the National City Bank; Edward F. Cragin of the Union League
Club, who had ties with the Nicaraguan Canal Company and Standard
Oil, Collis P. Huntington of the Southern Pacific Railroad; financier
August Belmont; and John S. McCook of New York, who was a railroad lawyer also active in organizing overseas economic ventures. Still
another group was made up of broad-gauged expansionists like Roosevelt and Lodge, who saw a war with Spain as a way to bring empire
to America by Caesarean section. "I have been hoping and working
ardently," Roosevelt candidly admitted, "to bring about our interference in Cuba."

Finally, McKinley himself made it precisely clear in July 1897, that he
was determined to finish up the Cuban crisis in order to proceed with
other matters. This became apparent in the long instructions given his
new minister to Spain (who was also a close friend). The document
should also serve to correct once and for all the mistaken impression that
McKinley drifted this way and that in response to whatever political
winds were blowing. He knew quite well what he desired to accomplish.
"The chronic disturbance in the social and political condition of our own
peoples. . . . A continuous irritation within our own borders injuriously
affects the normal functions of business, and tends to delay the condition of prosperity to which this country is entitled."

Though it was not unique in the archives of diplomatic history, this
assignment of responsibility for domestic welfare to a foreign power was
a very striking and unequivocal example of that approach. It revealed
beyond any possibility of misunderstanding the inner logic of all expansionist thought *whereby both opportunity and difficulty, good and evil, are
externalized.* As Frederick Jackson Turner once acknowledged in a moment of deep insight, the frontier itself was "a gate of escape" from
existing responsibilities; and when men began to act on the frontier
thesis they merely sustained that pattern of defining issues in such a
way that the solutions became progressively dependent upon external
factors. Stated as directly as possible, the point is that none of the for-

eign powers involved—either in Cuba or in Asia—actually threatened the United States, nor did they have any inherent primary responsibility for what McKinley called "the prosperity to which this country is entitled." It was only the definition of American well-being primarily in terms of overseas economic expansion, a definition formulated by Americans, that led to the conclusion that the foreign nations had such obligations.

The related consideration concerning the way that McKinley and other influential Americans envisaged the relationship linking prosperity, social peace, and foreign policy became increasingly clarified during the late summer and early fall of 1897. By August, for example, businessmen were generally convinced that recovery from the depression was being generated and sustained by overseas economic expansion. As a result, many of them began to change their earlier fears that intervention in Cuba would delay prosperity. Instead, they began to feel that it would be wise to remove that distraction so that the new frontier of exports could be given full attention.

In addition, many of those who had sympathized with or actively supported the rebels began to fear that a successful revolution would cause grave difficulties by bringing the lower class to power. McKinley was advised of this very explicitly by a correspondent who reported the growing anxiety that "the troublesome, adventurous, and nonresponsible class" would control the island "causing chaos, injury, and loss beyond redemption."

Probably even more important in strengthening the inclination to intervene to pacify Cuba was the renewed outbreak of trouble in the Far East. Germany's seizure of Kiaochow on November 14, 1897, intensified existing fears that Japan and the European powers were going to divide China among themselves. Whether they defined the issue in narrow interest-conscious economic terms, or in a broader analysis that stressed the need of the American economic *system* to expand overseas, American leaders became very disturbed. Most of them looked to Asia, and to China in particular, as the great market which would absorb the surplus. It is beside the point that this did not happen; at issue is the nature of American thought and action at the time.

The influence of these events in the late summer and fall of 1897 was revealed in many striking episodes. In September, for example, Roosevelt discussed personally with McKinley a memorandum in which he advocated war in November, *and specifically recommended that "we take and retain the Phillipines."* [Emphasis added.] In November, Senator Orville H. Platt and a member of the House of Representatives saw McKinley and added their advice that Manila was the key to the entire Asian crisis. In January 1898, a petition from over thirty-five leading New York businessmen (many of whom had raised their voices—and pens—as

early as May 1897) asked McKinley to intervene with "prompt and efficient measures" in Cuba to put an end to their "tremendous losses" and
restore "a most valuable commercial field." And in February other entrepreneurs of the New York State Chamber of Commerce asked for
similar action in Asia. Deeply concerned about the crisis in China and its
effect upon "the privileges enjoyed under existing treaty rights by
Americans," they "respectfully and earnestly" requested "prompt and
energetic defense" of such rights and "the preservation and protection
of their important commercial interest in that Empire."

These activities clarify the third central aspect of the coming of the
war: the McKinley administration knew that an important and growing
segment of the business community wanted prompt and effective action
in Cuba and Asia. Until some time in the latter part of March (or perhaps
even the first week in April), McKinley undoubtedly wanted to end the
Cuban affair without war. This seems quite clear despite his series of
ultimatums to Spain, which included a demand for independence
(under American guidance) if the United States thought it necessary.
But by the last ten days in March (by which time Germany had secured a
ninety-nine-year lease to Kiaochow with extensive economic concessions throughout the province of Shantung), the business community
was ready to accept war.

A special emissary sent by McKinley to sound out the New York area
reported that such key figures as John Jacob Astor, Thomas Fortune
Ryan, William Rockefeller, Stuyvesant Fish, and spokesmen for the
House of Morgan were "feeling militant." Then Lodge advised McKinley on March 21, 1898, that Boston economic leaders had concluded that
"one shock and then an end was better than a succession of spasms such
as we must have if this war in Cuba went on." And four days later, the
president received by telegram the following intelligence from a New
York correspondent. "Big corporations here now believe we will have
war. Believe all would welcome it as relief to suspense. . . . Don't think it
necessary now mince matters."

Now the purpose of all this analysis is not to argue or suggest that
McKinley went to war because important economic leaders told him to
do so. Neither is it to imply that the public clamor that arose after
the sinking of the *Maine* was insignificant. The point is quite different.
It is that American leaders went to war with Spain as part of, and as the
consequence of, a general outlook which externalized the opportunity
and the responsibility for America's domestic welfare; broadly in terms
of vigorous overseas economic expansion into Latin America and Asia;
and specifically in terms of Spain's inability to pacify Cuba by means
(and within time limits) acceptable to the United States, and the separate
but nevertheless related necessity of acting in Asia to prevent the exclusion of American interests from China. . . .

Discounted in recent years as a futile and naive gesture in a world of harsh reality, the Open Door policy was in fact a brilliant strategic stroke which led to the gradual extension of American economic and political power throughout the world. If it ultimately failed, it was not because it was foolish or weak, but because it was so successful. The empire that was built according to the strategy and tactics of the Open Door notes engendered the antagonisms created by all empires, and it is that opposition which posed so many difficulties for American diplomacy after World War II.

At the outset, it is true, the debate between imperialists and antiimperialists revolved around an actual issue—colonialism. Touched off by the specific question of what to do with Cuba and the Phillipines, the battle raged over whether they should be kept as traditional colonies or established as quasi-independent nations under the benevolent supervision of the United States. Though the differences were significant at the beginning of the argument, it is nevertheless clear that they were never absolute. The Open Door notes took the fury out of the fight. And within five years the issue was almost nonexistent. The antiimperialists who missed that changing nature of the discussion were ultimately shocked and disillusioned when Bryan became secretary of state and began to practice what they thought he condemned.

Such critics were mistaken in attacking Bryan as a backslider or hypocrite. Bryan's foreign policy was not classical colonialism, but neither was it antiimperial. He had never shirked his share of the white man's burden, though perhaps he did shoulder a bit more of the ideological baggage than the economic luggage. He was as eager for overseas markets as any but the most extreme agrarian and industrial expansionists. As with most other farmers, labor leaders, and businessmen, economic logic accounts for much of Bryan's anticolonialism. Looking anxiously for markets abroad as a way of improving conditions at home, all such men feared and opposed the competition of native labor. It was that consideration, as much as racism and Christian fundamentalism, that prompted Bryan to assert that "the Filipinos cannot be citizens without endangering our civilization."

Bryan's program for the Philippines symbolizes the kind of imperial anticolonialism that he advocated. Once the Philippine insurrection was crushed, he proposed that the United States should establish "a stable form of government" in the islands and then "protect the Philippines from outside interference while they work out their destiny, just as we have protected the republics of Central and South America, and are, by the Monroe Doctrine, pledged to protect Cuba." Opposition spokesmen gleefully pointed out that this was the substance of their own program. . . .

Though many of them felt that they had suffered a terrible defeat in the decision to retain the Philippines, the antiimperialists actually won their domestic war over fundamental policy with the issuance of the Open Door notes. Hay's dispatches of 1899 and 1900 distilled the conglomeration of motives, pressures, and theories into a classic strategy of noncolonial imperial expansion. Based on the assumption of what Brooks Adams called "America's economic supremacy," the policy of the open door was designed to clear the way and establish the conditions under which America's preponderant economic power would extend the American system throughout the world without the embarrassment and inefficiency of traditional colonialism. As Hay indicated with obvious anticipation and confidence in September 1899, the expectation was that "we shall bring the sweat to their brows."

Hay's first note of September 6, 1899, asserted the proposition that American enterpreneurs "shall enjoy perfect equality of treatment for their commerce and navigation" within all of China—*including the spheres of interest held by foreign powers*. That principle was soon extended to other underdeveloped areas. His second note of July 3, 1900, was designed to prevent other nations from extending the formal colonial system to China. That axiom was also applied to other regions in later years. Hay also circulated a third dispatch among the powers. Though rarely linked with the first two in discussions of the Open Door notes, it was nevertheless an integral part of the general policy statement. In that document, Hay made it plain that the United States considered loans to be an inherent part of commerce. The connection was always implict, if not rather obvious. "It is impossible to separate these two forms of business activity," as one businessman remarked at the time, "since it is axiomatic that trade follows the loan." The relationship was also and without any question in the minds of American policymakers when the first notes were written, since such loans were being sought and discussed as early as 1897. Hay's purpose was to close every formal loophole through which America's competitors might seek to counter the strategy of the open door.

The Open Door notes took the substance out of the debate between the imperialists and the antiimperialists. The argument trialed on with the inertia characteristic of all such disagreements, but the nation recognized and accepted Hay's policy as a resolution of the original issue. Former Secretary of State John W. Foster summarized this point quite accurately in the *Independent* at the end of 1900. "Whatever difference of opinion may exist among American citizens respecting the policy of territorial expansion, all seem to be agreed upon the desirability of commercial expansion. In fact it has come to be a necessity to find new and enlarged markets for our agricultural and manufactured products. We cannot maintain our present industrial prosperity without them."

It took some years (and agitation) to liquidate the colonial status of the territory seized during the war against Spain. It also required time to work out and institutionalize a division of authority and labor between economic and political leaders so that the strategy could be put into operation on a routine basis. And it was necessary to open the door into existing colonial empires as well as unclaimed territories. But the strategy that had been set was followed through the Potsdam Conference at the end of World War II, when President Harry S. Truman sought with considerable insistence to reestablish the open door for American economic and political influence in Eastern Europe and on the Asian mainland. . . .

The most dramatic confluence of these currents of ideological and economic expansion did not occur until the eve of American entry into World War I. For this reason, among others, it is often asserted that the United States did not take advantage of the Open Door policy until after 1917, and some observers argue that the policy never led to the rise of an American empire. In evaluating the extent to which Americans carried through on the strategy of the Open Door notes, there are two broad questions at issue with regard to statistics of overseas economic expansion, and they cannot be mixed up without confusing the analysis and the interpretation. One concerns the over-all importance of such expansion to the national economy. The answer to that depends less upon gross percentages than upon the role in the American economy of the industries which do depend in significant ways (including raw materials as well as markets) on foreign operations. Measured against total national product, for example, the export of American cars and trucks seems a minor matter. But it is not possible at one and the same time to call the automobile business the key industry in the economy and then dismiss the fact that approximately 15 percent of its total sales in the 1920s were made in foreign markets. . . .

In summation, the true nature and full significance of the Open Door policy can only be grasped when its four essential features are fully addressed.

First: It was neither a military strategy nor a traditional balance-of-power policy. *It was conceived and designed to win the victories without the wars.* In a truly perceptive and even noble sense, the makers of the Open Door policy understood that the war represented the failure of policy. Hence it is irrelevant to criticize the Open Door policy for not emphasizing, or not producing, extensive military readiness.

Second: It was derived from the proposition that America's overwhelming economic power could cast the economy and the politics of the poorer, weaker, underdeveloped countries in a pro-American mold. American leaders assumed the opposition of one or many industrialized rivals. Over a period of two generations the policy failed because some of those competitors, among them Japan and Germany, chose to resort to force when they concluded (on solid grounds) that the Open Door policy was working only too well; and because various groups inside the weaker countries, such as China and Cuba, decided that America's extensive influence in and upon their societies was harmful to their specific and general welfare.

Third (and clearly related to the second point): The policy was neither legalistic nor moralistic in the sense that those criticisms are usually offered. It was extremely hard-headed and practical. In some respects, at any rate, it was the most impressive intellectual achievement in the area of public policy since the generation of the Founding Fathers.

Fourth: Unless and until it, and its underlying *Weltanschauung*, were modified to deal with its own consequences, the policy was certain to produce foreign policy crises that would become increasingly severe. The ultimate failures of the Open Door policy, in short, are the failures generated by its success in guiding Americans in the creation of an empire.

Once these factors are understood, it becomes useful to explore the way that ideological and moralistic elements became integrated with the fundamentally secular and economic nature of the Open Door policy. The addition of those ingredients served to create a kind of expansionism that aimed at the marketplace of the mind and the polls as well as of the pocketbook.

Stanley Lebergott

STANLEY LEBERGOTT is professor of economics at Wesleyan University. He has
written several books, including *Manpower in Economic Growth: The American
Record Since 1800* (1964), and *The American Economy: Income, Wealth, and Want*
(1976).

Imperialism is a moderately ingenious system in which residents of
capitalist nations are forced to transfer income among themselves. The
transfer mechanism creates extraterritorial impacts as well. It increases
workers' incomes in colonial nations. It benefits their landowners. And
it strikes down their business monopolies. (That these benefits are conferred on developing nations helps distinguish imperialism from other
modes of subsidy to business such as tariff protection.) This process
creates an aura of generous patronage in the imperializing power. It
stimulates a sense of outrage in the colonial nation. And it speeds the
advancement of military leaders in both. Such lively consequences have
obscured the primary economic struggle under imperialism—which is
not between capitalists from the imperium and oppressed peasants, but
between different groups of capitalists.

We focus on foreign investment—Lenin's central component—for
the United States from 1890 to 1929. Part I considers how decisive such
investment was for prolonging the life of U.S. capitalism. Part II looks at
two specific interventions—Panama and Cuba—in terms of their overall
economic profitability. Part III, taking for granted the unwisdom of U.S.
interventions, goes on to consider the economic impact of U.S. foreign
investment on nations abroad. What did such investments do to returns
to Latin American labor, landowners and entrepreneurs?

I

Between the Civil War and 1897 American foreign investment rose from
a mere $75 million to $685 million; it then rose by nearly $20 billion from
1897 to 1929. "Under the old capitalism," Lenin wrote, "the export of
goods was a most typical feature. Under modern capitalism, when

Stanley Lebergott, "The Returns to U.S. Imperialism, 1890-1929," *Journal of Economic
History* 40 (June 1980): 229-49. Reprinted by permission of Stanley Lebergott and the
Economic History Association.

monopolies prevail, the export of capital has become the typical feature." Rosa Luxemburg declared, "Imperialism is the political expression of the accumulation of capital in its competitive struggle for what remains still open of the non-capitalist environment."

The increases in U.S. foreign investment were indeed impressive. But most numbers for continental economies look big, whether for the United States or China. How do they look when dimensioned against the entire flow of U.S. investment? Of all U.S. investment from 1869 to 1897, the foreign share accounted for 1 percent; and from 1900 to 1929, the heyday of marine intervention, it accounted for only 6 percent. Put another way: From 1900 to 1929 the entire increase of U.S. foreign investment all over the globe did not equal the increased investment in California alone.

Did so small a foreign commitment really offer a vent for surplus capital? Was it indeed the *unum porro necessarium* that enabled U.S. capitalism to create its twentieth-century hegemony?

Any approach as comprehensive as Marxism-Leninism deals comprehensively with capitalism. It does not offer a theory of Macy's profitability, or Gimbel's, or even United Fruit's. It deals with the complex, contradictory vastness of capitalism. That theory implies that U.S. investment abroad during 1890–1929 was critical in propping up the overall profit rate on U.S. capital. If so, it should have affected that rate significantly. But U.S. overseas investments from 1890 to 1929 pushed the rate of return on U.S. capital from a bit over 4.8 percent to a bit under 4.9 percent. Did so tiny an increase stave off the inevitable collapse of capitalism? Or change its character?

Most U.S. industries didn't bother to invest abroad. The aggregate impact on the profitability of the U.S. investment was small. What did occur was the seizure of lush investment opportunities in a handful of sectors. Which industries were involved? Cleona Lewis's data on U.S. investments abroad offer us a guide. Her rich detail indicates that U.S. firms made substantial investments abroad in several industry categories. For only three of these—agriculture, manufacturing, and metals—was the ratio of foreign-to-U.S. investment more than a tenth of 1 percent. (Nor did ratios of foreign-to-domestic investment even reach 2 percent for these categories.)

For five industry/product groups, an important (significant?) ratio of foreign-to-U.S. investment appears.

1. Bananas: There were no domestic sources. Latin America provided the entire supply.
2. Sugar: All foreign sources provided about one-fourth in 1897 and three-fourths by 1929.
3. Copper: The share of foreign to total U.S. copper mine investment rose to perhaps 20 percent around 1900 and continued to be very substantial.
4. Oil: The foreign share rose from 3 percent in 1897 to 7 percent in 1929.

5. Precious metals: Foreign sources accounted for under 5 percent of U.S. investment.

Is there a common denominator to these concentrations of increase in
U.S. foreign investment? Precious metal investment, indulged in by
states from ancient Greece and the Inca empire to Soviet Russia, hardly
requires any view on the theory of imperialism. The major categories—
bananas, sugar, copper and oil—however, may be linked to market
opportunities involving the trusts that developed in the period 1889–
1900.

For bananas and sugar, U.S. trusts integrated vertically. They thereby
protected themselves against combinations at the production level that
might skim off their monopoly profits. By investing in banana plantations United Fruit assured its supply, and prevented any combination
against it at either the farm or transport level. The American Sugar
Refining Company actually had been confronted by a developing alliance of American sugar producers. U.S. beet sugar producers had
expanded their output under the happy influence of the McKinley tariff.
They then joined with the Louisiana cane sugar producers to block the
Cuban Reciprocity Treaty. If successful they could then have raised
tariffs against both Hawaiian and foreign sugar, thereby forcing the trust
to divide its monopoly profits with a patriotic domestic cartel. By helping
to keep the reciprocity door open, then, the trust guaranteed its supply
of sugar and at the cost of only a minimum investment in Cuba by the
trust itself.

Amalgamated's 30 percent stock price increase from 1898 to 1899–
1901 had notified many investors of the potentially vast profits in copper. That point was italicized by the jump in its market yield (from about
2 percent in 1899 to 8 percent in the next two years). Moreover, dividends of the Michigan companies in 1899–1901 ran almost 50 percent
above their 1898 level. Such prospects led both Morgan and the
Guggenheims to invest heavily south of the border. They also induced
other ardent investors—among them, Hearst, Frick, Haggin, and
Ryan—to develop overseas copper mines. (Perhaps a more prudent
trust might not have ignored the Secretan fiasco.)

It would require a more comprehensive review to determine how
largely the actions of the new trusts were responsible for foreign investment in the turn-of-the-century years. For present purposes it may suffice to indicate that overseas investments by Americans in the period
1900 to 1929 do not seem particularly explicable by any general surplus
of funds seeking overseas outlets. What characterized U.S. foreign investment over these decades was, instead, the seizing of the local opportunities here and there as avid entrepreneurs saw profit potential. These
were pursued with no less zest than opportunities that appeared in
North Dakota or New Mexico. In addition, attention concentrated on a

few sectors (bananas, sugar and copper) where U.S. monopolies tried to protect future profit flows, or other entrepreneurs attempted to menace them.

II

CUBA

In April 1901 the occupying forces of the United States established a $1,000 prize to be known as "The Department of Agriculture stakes for Cuban bred horses and mares." General Wood, the American proconsul, was "acceding to the request of the 'Cuba Jockey Club'... [for] prizes at the horse races to be held at Buenavista, Havana course." And he expressed his fond hope "that the stakes will always be considered as the 'blue ribbon' of the Cuban turf."

This improbable but thoughtful gesture symbolized how varied were opportunities seized by special interests as they utilized the power and finance of the military government for their benefit. But what major U.S. economic interests benefited?

We take as our point of departure the example given in Lenin's succinct summary:

> Finance capital, concentrated in a few hands and exercising a virtual monopoly, exacts enormous and ever-increasing profits from the floating of companies, issues of stock, state loans, etc., tightens the grip of financial oligarchies and levies tribute upon the whole of society for the benefit of monopolists. Here is one example, taken from a multitude of others, of the methods of 'business' of the American trusts... the Sugar Trust set up monopoly prices on the market, which secured it such profits that it could pay 10 percent dividend on capital "watered" sevenfold.

Imperialism centrally involved foreign investment. Mere market possibilities were perhaps primary in earlier stages of capitalism, but, Lenin states, had taken a secondary position under imperialism. Indeed, a later review, by the major antiimperialist historian of "our Cuban colony," noted that American exports to Cuba actually had fallen after the Spanish-American War "as compared with those of Great Britain, France, and Germany.... Our occupation had not promoted Cuba as a market for goods.... It is a common notion that people with specific economic interests beset legislators and governments with pressure to do things that will make them money. No doubt many of them do. Others need to be aroused to the work of those governments. American manufacturers in many states in 1902 and 1903 were far from anxious about export markets, or about a privileged position." But pressure by Roosevelt and unspecified "industry" finally brought Congress to pass the Reciprocity Treaty. Of all the economic interest groups to be advantaged by this legislation, confirming the returns from the Cuban invasion, presumably the trust singled out by Lenin stood foremost.

Now what did the war with the Reciprocity Treaty do to the Sugar Trust and its profits? Did they increase the demand for sugar, thereby benefiting the trust? In 1899 U.S. consumers poured $190 million worth of sugar into their coffee, tea, and lemonade and bought a further $27 million to sweeten confectionary and soft drinks. The war, therefore, had not created the consumer's sweet tooth. Could it have shifted the demand curve for sugar in any significant fashion? There is no reason to think that it intensified the demand for Moxie. Nor did it increase the demand for other sugar products.

Did the war strengthen trust control of the U.S. market? As a tough enterprise the trust was already screwing as much out of the consumer as it could, war or no war. Its powers as a trust did not depend on either the Cubans or the war.

Gains to the Sugar Trust, therefore, must have been not on the demand but on the supply side. Jenks has written:

> On the face of the matter, the Reciprocity Treaty made a gift of .337 cents a pound on Cuban sugar to somebody from the United States Treasury.... (By 1910... this benefit amounted to a total of twenty million dollars.) No one seems then to have known exactly... where the .337 cents went. Most of it has gone... either to the ultimate consumers in the United States, or to the Atlantic refiners.

But Jenks's list includes those who did *not* benefit from the Reciprocity Treaty more surely than those who did.

Neither the war nor the treaty changed the supply of sugar. The Dutch were still producing in the East Indies. French, German, and American beet sugar producers were still producing. And the Hawaiians and Cubans were still producing. What the treaty did was award the Cubans a preferred market position. It cut the tariff margin between the price at which the Cubans sold and the price the American buyer had to pay.

If the American Sugar Refining Company had been the sole American purchaser of Cuban sugars it could have seized most, or all, of the reciprocity reduction. In fact, eight independent refining firms (some located on the West Coast) bought over one third of U.S. raw sugar. Moreover, transport and refining costs were not changed by any of this. Hence, the benefit should have accrued almost wholly to Cuban producers. American taxpayers had simply begun to make an annual gift to Cuban sugar producers.

This is precisely and explicitly what was intended. In the authoritative words of Elihu Root, that gift permitted Cubans "to live," for the war's destruction had largely cut Cuban sugar production, and thereby Cuban incomes, Root declared:

> The peace of Cuba is necessary to the peace of the United States; the independence of Cuba is necessary to the safety of the United States.... The same considerations which led to the war with Spain now require that a commercial agreement be made under which Cuba can live.

The impact was immediate. Between 1900 and 1903 Cuban exports to the United States tripled, rising by 1.7 billion pounds. Concurrently, U.S. imports of Dutch East Indies sugar fell by 0.3 billion pounds, and imports of European (beet) sugar fell by 0.6 billion.

The treaty, finest flower of American intervention in Cuba, had benefited neither the American consumer nor the Sugar Trust. It raised the gross receipts of Cuban sugar producers. These in turn had to pay increased rents to owners of Cuban land. For the price of land had immediately risen, capitalizing the value of the delightful new tariff advantage. Hence the true beneficiaries were the owners of Cuban resources. As one Cuban planter told Congress, since the average developed field yielded 2.5 tons of sugar, "if you took off the duty" (of about $34 a ton) you would give a bounty of about $75 to "every acre of available sugar land in Cuba." The continuing gift from the American taxpayer, therefore, increased the value of Cuban land. That capital gain was unquestionably skimmed off by landowners in subsequent years whenever they sold or rented their land.

Who owned the land in 1899, just before the war, and thereby became prime beneficiaries of the treaty? Not the trust. Indeed all Americans taken together controlled only 16 percent of the Cuban sugar crop as late as 1902.

The benefits of that advance could, of course, have been skimmed off of buyers had foreseen the passage of the treaty and had snapped up the land in advance. However, the Cuban mortgage law was changed in 1899 to prevent forced transfers of land in those turbulent times. And it kept the lands in the hands of its preinvasion owners. The land in 1902 remained "very largely in the hands of the people who had it on the 1st of January, 1899." It was, therefore, primarily the landowners as of 1899 who reaped the benefit of the revolution, invasion, and Reciprocity Treaty. And it was the owners of Cuban land not already in sugar who reaped the further benefits of continuing reciprocity as the sale of Cuban sugar in American markets expanded and expanded.

The prime economic beneficiaries of the Spanish-American War, in sum, were the Spaniards and the Cubans who owned Cuban sugar land at the start of the war. The generous donor of benefits to these gentlemen turned out to be the American taxpayer. For the latter's taxes had to make up for U.S. tariff revenue foregone by the Reciprocity Treaty.

THE PANAMA CANAL

"I took the Canal," declared Theodore Roosevelt at Berkeley. Discussion of American imperialism has been entangled ever since in this much (and appropriately) quoted declaration. But Roosevelt had a very high view of his prowess. One remembers the sardonic title Mr. Dooley gave to the president's egotistic memoir of the Spanish-American War: "Alone in Cuba." Roosevelt's intervention in Panama may well have been outrageous yet not as essential in detaching Panama from Colombia as he implied.

Two climactic events marked the outbreak of American intervention. First was the resumption in 1902 by Panamanians of the revolution that had been going on since 1899. Second was a sequence of volcanic explosions in Nicaragua, Martinique, and St. Vincent in 1902. That sequence had effectively removed the Nicaraguan route as an alternative for the canal across the isthmus. Colombia immediately recognized, and decided to monetize, its monopoly of available routes. With considerable moderation it demanded only $5 million above the $10 million provided for in the treaty to which it had already tentatively agreed. Hay responded with asperity, informing the Colombians (in July 1903) that "no additional payment... can hope for approval by the United States Senate" and that any amendment whatever "would imperil the treaty." Roosevelt (in his message of January 1904) restated the U.S. position: "We would give the terms that we had offered and no other; ... if such terms were not agreed to, we would enter into an agreement with Panama direct." This threatening attitude assisted those Panamanians who wished to resume their revolution.

The subsequent 1902 revolution guaranteed the United States a harvest of ill will. Moreover, it failed to save the United States the additional Colombian money claim, which irritated the impatient president. For in 1921 the United States paid the $25 million anyway. Such brilliance in achieving the worst of both worlds is more explicable by military than by commercial motivation. As a British engineer then working for Colombia wrote: "The Canal cannot be a paying concern for any other country except the United States, and for the United States it is a paying concern not from a commercial standpoint—it will therein be a loser—but on account of its Navy." After the Panamanian revolution, the navy's (unofficial) chief strategist, the president, could be confident that in the next war the U.S.S. *Oregon* need not be sent around Cape Horn before it could bring its weight to bear on the enemy.

Granting the military interests, what of the economic ones? U.S. taxpayers had made handsome expenditures for the canal by the end of 1929 (see Table 1).

What private economic interests benefited from this sequence of gifts

TABLE 1.   PANAMA CANAL: COSTS AND REVENUES TO U.S. TAXPAYERS, 1909–1929

ITEM	MILLION DOLLARS
Costs	
1. Construction outlays, 1902–1923	388
2. Construction interest, 1902–1920	155
3. Construction interest, 1921–1929	135
4. Payment to Colombia, 1921	25
5. "National defense" construction to 1924	113
Operating Revenues	
6. Revenues from canal operation (net)	110
Costs minus Revenue to 1929	706

by the American taxpayer? The U.S. payment of $10 million (by the act of 1902) to the New Panama Canal Company benefited few Americans. Most stockholders were French. (Of course, the Colombian government, as a major stockholder in the Canal Company, accepted its share of the $10 million—together with the $25 million the U.S. apologetically offered in 1921.) Hence the revolution in Panama redistributed wealth among Americans (from taxpayers to W. N. Cromwell and associates)— and gave some gifts to Frenchmen and Colombians.

What about American shippers? Building the canal tended to cut the real cost of ocean transport. Who then benefited? Was it the U.S. shipper? The Hay-Pauncefote Treaty of 1901 had stipulated that the canal "shall be open to all vessels . . . on terms of entire equality . . . [with] no discrimination . . . [on] charges of traffic." British ocean shippers, therefore, plus German, Dutch, and others, gained quite as much as American shippers—without their governments contributing one cent. American ocean shipping firms did benefit when some U.S. coast-to-coast traffic shifted its route, but only in the same proportion as American railroads were injured.

Shortly before the revolution in Panama a prominent Colombian lawyer estimated that the United States would profit by precisely $1,186,537,377 from the proposed canal concession. Who could deny (or demonstrate) that American military interests, as divined by Admiral Mahan, did indeed benefit in that amount, give or take a few dollars? That American economic interests benefited is far less likely. Americans had provided some three quarters of a billion dollars to build and run the canal to 1929 (plus a great deal more thereafter). They therefore contributed an international public work that benefited shippers throughout the world, that gave equal advantage to any nation that chose to use the canal. Had their money been well spent? As far as economic advantage is concerned, the gains are hardly obvious. They certainly were secondary to the moral drive described so sympathetically by Roosevelt's great Democratic opponent (after the United States had taken the Canal Zone): "We are a sort of pure air blowing in world politics. . . ."

III

What impact did American imperialism have on factor returns in Latin American nations in these years—the wages paid to labor, rents paid to landowners, interest rates paid to lenders, and entrepreneurial incomes? Since it is these returns that do much to determine the well-being of those who work and/or invest for a living, it is somewhat surprising that so little attention has been given explicitly to such a question. Perhaps the most extended discussion appears in the statement that

> . . . foreign investment often had limited benefits for the native population. In some cases it had almost no effect, positive or negative, as where it took place in an enclave. In Peru, the guano industry used European capital, Chinese labor, and foreign markets, hardly involving the local economy at all. In mines and plantations large amounts of local labor were used. Where foreign investors build railroads, they tended to serve the needs of foreign traders. . . .

We can say more than this. The economic consequences of American foreign investment and intervention can be inferred from various sources. We have chosen here to rely chiefly on the *Studies in American Imperialism* that appeared in the late 1920s. Sponsored by the American Fund for Public Service, they represent extended, careful, and tenaciously antiimperialist studies of American intervention in various Latin American nations. The case that U.S. investment injured labor, peasants, and landowners in Latin America could hardly have been put more persuasively than by these scholarly, and strongly antiimperialist, writers. What do their studies actually have to say on these points?

LABOR

We first turn to labor. The Marxist view is well known. As a recent Chinese textbook on economics states: "Colonies are the most profitable outlets for the capital exports of imperialism. In colonies, the monopoly organizations of the suzerain can exploit and enslave the laboring people more ruthlessly." Kwame Nkrumah found "imperialism is the most degrading exploitation and the most inhuman oppression of the millions of peoples in the colonies." It purpose: "to squeeze out superprofits." One of many American writers finds that "the workers and peasants in the colonies . . . countries . . . were the most oppressed owing to the fact that their labor was the source of capitalist superprofit." He refers to the "the superexploitation of labor through the export of capital."

What of labor in Cuba? How did the American occupation and the Reciprocity Treaty affect Cuban labor? From 1900 to 1903 Cuban cane exports responded to the treaty by tripling. Now tripling employment with little change in the population could only tend to drive up wages.

The obvious way for new American interests to nullify such pressures would have been to import low-cost contract labor from China. The Americans had done so in Hawaii. The Spaniards had once done so in Cuba. As Machado noted, however, Chinese labor "had been absolutely prohibited" for many years. Moreover, "public sentiment in Cuba would protest against introducing an inferior race, if any attempts were made to abolish the existing law." Did the U.S. military nonetheless impose such action at the behest of new American investors? On the contrary. Both Congress and the Executive sought to make Cuba the home of "the independent farmer and citizen," not of "the coolie": Contract labor (largely Chinese) was therefore to be forbidden. In may 1902 the military governor dutifully forbade the importation of contract labor. Moreover, when the Reciprocity Treaty was finally passed it required Cuba to enact "immigration laws as rigorous as those of the United States."

Given an expanding U.S. market for Cuban sugar, together with a law forbidding the import of cheap labor, an excess demand for Cuban labor was inevitable. Hence Cuban wage rates tended to rise. Apparently they did rise. In 1900–1901, the average daily farm wage in the major sugar province of Mantanzas was 76¢. By January 1902, according to Colonel Bliss, the island average for common labor was 85½¢ a day, a rise of over 10 percent. The "most inhuman oppression" should have led wage rates, and real income, to decline. The sequence of regulations, treaties, and investment by the American conquerors did not, however, yield such a decline.

What impact did "imperialist" investment have on labor conditions in other Latin American countries? The *Studies in American Imperialism* agree on one central point: American companies paid wages at least equal to those paid by native employers, and the Americans typically offered higher real wages and better working conditions. The studies agree on quite another point, with which the first is often confused: American companies did not pay wages anywhere near as high as the writers would have liked, nor as generous as workers would have preferred. (Nor did they scatter their bounties with a charitable and loving hand.)

Rippy's discussion of Colombia deals primarily with United Fruit. He notes that United Fruit bought most of its bananas from foreman-contractors, who in turn paid piece rates for bunches of bananas. Presumably they paid the same wage rates as those contractors who sold to native entrepreneurs. In his most comprehensive comment Rippy states:

Indeed, it appears safe to make the general statement that Colombian labor, whenever it is paid a stipulated wage, is better remunerated and granted more sanitary living quarters by foreigners than by natives, but the foreigners probably exact more systematic and strenuous effort.... Most of the mining is done by foreign companies who pay their laborers a better wage than they receive from the native capitalists.... American construction companies usually... [pay] the standard wage paid by the government on construction enterprises under its direct supervision and approximately the standard minimum given by native employers throughout the country. That the minimum wage allowed by the Tropical Oil Company [Standard Oil] and the United Fruit Company is considerably above this amount has already been noted, and it is believed that this is true of most other Yankee employers.

Since United Fruit paid part of the wages in scrip until 1929, it is necessary to check whether the higher real wages they paid were in fact nullified by above-market store prices. Rippy states, however, that just the opposite was true:

> Much of the clothing, food and other supplies consumed by the laborers is regularly brought into the region by the company.... The company store can usually sell supplies more cheaply than they can be bought from the local native merchants, who... often, lack(ing) a better source of supply, purchase their ware from the United Fruit Company itself.

Kepner's discussion of the United Fruit Company—primarily in Costa Rica, Guatemala, Honduras, and Colombia—states flatly: "The wages paid by the United Fruit Company before the world economic crisis... were high in comparison to money wages paid to agricultural workers elsewhere in Central America."

Knight's discussion of Santo Domingo declares that "Most of the Americans do not mistreat their labor. The complaints on this score in Santo Domingo have been directed mainly against the Italian estates." His comments on wages do not indicate that American enterprises paid below-average wages. His primary focus is on how Haitian immigration depressed Dominican wages.

> The Haitian profits by his seasonal move [to Santo Domingo] but his presence has a bad effect on wage levels in Santo Domingo.... Official sanitary reports show 70 percent or more of the population of Haiti to be suffering from venereal disease. Malaria is rife, and there are both amoebic and bacillic dysenteries.... the Dominicans would be glad to dispense with their 100,000 or so of annual Haitian visitors.... Cheap imported seasonal labor digs a pit of subsistence wages at the feet of the Dominican worker in the interest of the sugar business.

That both native and American employers allowed (or supported) the government in an open and loosely enforced immigration policy clearly is the center of Knight's concern. Unless foreign firms should be in the business of changing national immigration policy, however, Knight's discussion on labor policy is irrelevant to our focus of interest. Margaret Marsh's study of Bolivia provides a summary comment on wages paid in the metal mines, dominated by the Bolivian Patino interests and somewhat smaller American companies. She notes that the wages paid were "in keeping with" the "scale on which the free Indian throughout the plateau lives, and have been adjusted to a society in which it is possible to hire a fletero to trek seventy-five miles over a period of two and a half days, with a hundred pounds of coca on his back, for from six to eight bolivianos." The bulk of her discussion of labor conditions focuses on conditions of labor in Bolivia that were surely appalling by American standards, conditions that were—if anything—improved by the extension of mining as a result of American investment.

It turns out that these systematic and closely studied attacks on U.S. investment abroad agree on the impact of such investment on wages and working conditions in Central and Latin America. They find wages increased (insofar as they deal with the topic). Nowhere did that impact result from any plan to do good. We assume that, in fact, the companies paid market wages, or slightly better, only to attract the quality of labor they sought. The most explicit comment on the consequences of labor was made by Jenks, in his study of Cuba.

> The coming of American companies has made for regular wage payments, cash wages, improved housing, living conditions and facilities for recreation. . . . American capital . . . has brought standards of living which can be satisfied only with American goods. . . . One hears plenty of stories of sharp practice on the part of these American concerns. That this passes the limits of business methods daily resorted to in the States or by Cubans and Spaniards in their dealings with each other and with Americans—these are statements for which there is no evidence.

LAND

Did North Americans succeed in gouging Latin Americans by paying below-market values for their land? The query is not whether North Americans paid what the land might be worth fifty years later. Or what its inherent fertility or beauty warranted. Or whether the price was "very few dollars per acre." Imperialistic investment is assessed against the standards of national investment: Did the foreign investor pay less than the native investor?

We are fortunate to have the testimony of Charles Kepner, a knowledgeable antiimperialist (who wrote two books against the United Fruit Company, with its "domain of more than three million acres of tropical lowlands"). He focuses on the fact that United Fruit acquired these "vast areas of land . . . for trifling amounts of money or for nothing." How did United Fruit bring off such a coup? Kepner's answer is:

> Political unity, economic progress and social intercourse depend to a great extent upon efficient means of transportation. Hence for nearly a century national leaders have been anxious to connect their capital cities with the outside world. Unable, however, to finance such railway construction out of ordinary revenues these countries have sought to fulfill their aspirations by floating loans and encouraging private companies to build railroads. In exchange for promises of railroad construction, politicians have given away vast expanses of lands, which were of little immediate value to the nation.

Much of the land was also of little value to the companies: they relinquished much of the land given them in Costa Rica and Guatemala. Had the companies' power enabled them to pay below-market prices for the land they did buy? Kepner's detailed discussion suggests that it did not.

First the company had to compete with native land speculators. Second, United Fruit bought through intermediaries: "Many a landowner realizing that a fruit company wants his property will take advantage of the situation to ask a good figure for it. To avoid paying this the company frequently makes its purchases through intermediaries, who may be connected with the fruit company." But if the company bought "through intermediaries," it discarded the imposing bargaining advantage of declaring its connection with two governments, the local one and the one controlling the U.S. Navy.

Kepner's discussion, in fact, indicates the weakness of the foreign firm in the local land market. The effective monopolist was the native landowner whose land the company needed to fill out a run of land for a new railroad line or plantation. In this situation the local owner recognized his monopoly power, demanding more from the large company than the market price he could charge a small buyer. Thus, the powerful foreign company either paid local landowners more than the market price for their land, or—by covertly buying through intermediaries—paid only the market price.

In sum, investments by United Fruit increased prices paid to owners of Costa Rican, Honduran and Guatemalan land, first, because a demand shift resulting from increased fruit production tended to push up land prices; and, second, because the company (as a foreign target) had to pay market or above-market prices.

NATIVE ENTREPRENEURS

The classic attacks on American expansion cast a fitful light on how imperialism expanded the incomes of native workers and landowners. They reveal even less of the fate of those who supplied other factors of production. We can nonetheless infer that American expansion injured native capitalists.

Imperializing companies set up company stores. These, in Rippy's words, "usually sell supplies more cheaply than they can be bought from the local native merchants." Such price cutting may have served native workers and peasants admirably. But these stores destroyed monopolies once held by native entrepreneurs. What more hateful attack on native businessmen could occur?

Expanding foreign investment in this period often involved railway construction. Such construction inevitably menaced the local entrepreneurs who carted goods, drove cattle to market, ran stage coaches, or supplied tavern accommodations to travelers. Local shoemakers, blacksmiths, millers, suddenly found themselves forced to compete with goods introduced by the railway. To these entrepreneurs "the calamity of the railways" was created by foreigners. In China the porters, carters, and wheelbarrow men dispossessed by the Shanghai-Woosung Railroad actually got it torn up and shipped out of the country. In Latin America, however, the imperialists had their way, and the railroads wreaked their havoc on older transport and related entrepreneurs.

Incomes created by expanded production—whether of bananas, sugar or copper—induced doctors, lawyers, moneylenders, carpenters, builders, and millwrights to enter the areas affected. Such new entry ended monopolies once held by such entrepreneurs and skilled workmen. Yankee imperialism cut monopoly profits in many lines of local enterprise. The peasants benefited. The native entrepreneurial group eventually increased. But such results offered cold comfort to the monopolistic entrepreneurs thus injured.

A fourth threat was as infuriating as any. Opportunities seen by native entrepreneurs were seized by foreign ones. The clamor that resulted resembles the xenophobia voiced by American Populists when they saw Scots and Englishmen investing in American lands. True, the greatest Populist of them all, Bryan, fought to acquire the Philippines. But that foreigners should frustrate American entrepreneurs was quite another matter. In North and South America alike the simple motto was: Profits for the natives. Andre Gunder Frank quotes a 1911 Chilean writer:

> The foreign merchant strangled our commercial initiative abroad, and at home he eliminated us from the international trade. . . . The foreigner owns two thirds of our nitrate production and continues to acquire our most valuable copper deposits. The merchant marine . . . continues to cede ground to foreign shipping even in the coastwide trade. The majority of the insurance companies that operate among us have their head office abroad. The national banks . . . keep ceding ground to the branches of the foreign banks. . . .

Frank adds, "foreign capital acquired an importance that was almost equal to that of foreign trade in transforming . . . Latin America in a way that would consolidate the structure of its underdevelopment."

Native businessmen, and their supporters, inevitably mourned their lost profit opportunities.

One could merely dismiss such regrets. After all, with local interest rates at 10 and 30 percent it was hardly to be expected that they could engage in long-range development of mines and plantations. Profit seekers from lands where government bonds were paying 2 percent (as the United States) were a more likely source for long-term investment, in which profits were often deferred for years. For example, the Cerro de Pasco mine yielded net returns only after 15 years.

On the other hand, one might conclude such investment opportunities should have lain fallow until native businessmen were able to take advantage of them. Perhaps some inevitable historic sequence even requires the growth of a native bourgeoisie before its downfall and (with it) the advance of socialism. Or one might believe, with Felipe Pazos, that foreign investment only "brings with it ready-made development. . . . There is no wait for training of technicians and managers, nor for try-outs and for gaining of experience . . . it may inhibit the emergence . . . of local personnel . . . and institutions needed for self-sustaining development."

In any event, foreign investors seized opportunities that native entrepreneurs had been unable to seize. The unsuccessful investor, or lover, never wholly ceases to regret.

In summary, American imperialism after the Spanish-American War worked systematic effects on economic interest groups in Latin America. (1) It increased the income of workers and peasants because it expanded the demand for labor. Moreover, antiimperialist writers assure us that American companies in that expanding market paid wages that were average, and sometimes above average. (2) Workers' real wages often increased more than their money wages. The introduction of company stores ended monopolies once exercised by local general stores and taverns, thereby reducing the monopoly profits once provided by workers and peasants. (3) Imperialist investment increased the value of land held by local landholders, whether they held small plots of land or vast acreage. Such increases proved most substantial when the United States offered new and especially advantageous terms for native products entering the U.S. market (for example, as in Cuba). They also occurred whenever American companies bought land for plantations and railroads. The assertions by antiimperialist writers that the United Fruit Company sometimes bought land through intermediaries suggest that American companies generally paid at least the price for land that native buyers did (and whenever the identity of the company became known, the company presumably paid somewhat above market prices). (4)

American imperialism injured the vested interests of the existing native business group by destroying monopoly profits. The provision of general stores by American companies brought new competition to isolated farm and village areas. Such expansion inevitably menaced the monopoly profits of existing native entrepreneurs, even as it induced the creation of a new enterpreneurial group. Moreover, American investments would have snatched away opportunities that would-be native entrepreneurs saw, coveted, and sometimes might even have been able to finance. The heart of the antiimperialist struggle, then, may prove to be a squabble between two capitalist groups, one native and the other foreign, fighting over the spoils of progress.

5

The Progressive Movement

Liberal or Conservative?

The rise of American industry in the decades following the Civil War was a development whose impact can hardly be exaggerated. It involved more than a shift from a commercial and agrarian economy to an urban and industrial one; indeed, it effected fundamental changes in the nature and quality of American society. The far-reaching technological and industrial innovations forced Americans to reexamine their traditional values and beliefs, many of which seemed obsolete, if not irrelevant, to the problems of a new age.

Traditionally, Americans were accustomed to think in terms of individualistic values. The rise of industry itself was often rationalized in the ideology of the self-made man who claimed he attained success by virtue of his own talents, drive, and ambition. By the end of the nineteenth century, however, it was becoming more difficult to conceive of industrial progress solely in terms of the achievements of a few creative individuals. The growth of a national transportation and communications system, which led to the rise of a national market, had stimulated the formation of large industrial units. This organizational revolution, to use Kenneth Boulding's convenient phrase,[1] was to have profound implications. Americans at the turn of the twentieth century found that their nation was being increasingly dominated by large corporations whose establishment resulted in the partial curtailment, if not abolition, of competition—a development that collided sharply with the ideology of individualism and freedom.

The position of the individual within the nation's increasingly industrialized society became a major source of concern for many Americans. If America's greatness was related to individual achievement, what would happen as freedom and social mobility were more and more

---

[1]Kenneth E. Boulding, *The Organizational Revolution: A Study in the Ethics of Economic Organization* (New York, 1953).

circumscribed by giant corporations with their impersonal and machinelike qualities? Did not the emphasis of corporations on efficient production and material objectives distort the human qualities that had been responsible for America's rise to greatness? Was not the growing disparity between rich corporations and poor workingmen creating a situation akin to that existing in many European countries where there was open class strife? These and similar questions led many Americans to advocate reforms that would restore dignity to the individual and give meaning to his life.

The forces of reform gradually gathered momentum in the last quarter of the nineteenth century. Although critics of American society could not agree upon a specific diagnosis, let alone remedial measures, they were united in a common conviction that some changes would have to be made if the United States was to survive with its historic values intact. The solutions presented were often diffuse. Many were all-embracing panaceas that called for the preservation of a competitive and individualistic society, but, at the same time, did not sacrifice the affluence associated with technological progress. Henry George, for example, gained international fame by presenting his single tax scheme in 1879 in his book *Progress and Poverty*, while Edward Bellamy, in his utopian novel *Looking Backward* (1886), argued that only the nationalization of all the means of production and distribution would solve most of America's major problems. In a similar vein, many Protestant clergymen who were distrubed by the cleavages in American society offered their own answers in what came to be known as the Social Gospel. These religious critics argued that an immoral society was incompatible with the ideals of moral men. Society, therefore, would have to be remade in the form of a Christian socialist commonwealth, thereby offering individuals an opportunity to lead moral lives. Others, including the Populists, Socialists, advocates of civil service reform, and academic critics also contributed to the swelling chorus of reform.

Between 1900 and 1917, these uncoordinated efforts at reform were institutionalized in what came to be known as the Progressive movement. Pluralistic rather than unitary, the Progressive movement was actually a series of movements operating at the local, state, and national levels of government and society. The movement consisted of a loose coalition of reformers who sought a variety of goals: political reforms such as the initiative, referendum, recall, and the destruction of urban political machines and corruption; economic reforms such as the regulation of public utilities and the curtailment of corporate power; and social reforms such as the Americanization of the immigrant, the amelioration of the lot of the urban poor, and regulation of child and woman labor as well as many others. Among the symbolic leaders of the movement were two presidents, Theodore Roosevelt and Woodrow Wilson. These two men not only revived the moral authority and leadership-potential inherent in the presidency, but they supported the enactment of a series of laws embodying major social reforms.

Until the period after the Second World War, there was relatively little controversy among historians about the nature and character of the Progressive movement. Most American historians were writing within the tradition of the Progressive school. Consequently, they interpreted these reform movements and reformers within a liberal framework. In their eyes, the reformers in the movement had been challenging the dominant position of the business and privileged classes. The reformers' goals had been clear and simple: to restore government to the people; to abolish special privilege and ensure equal opportunity for all; and to enact a series of laws embodying principles of social justice. These reformers, Progressive historians emphasized, were not anticapitalist; they had not advocated the abolition of private property nor sought the establishment of a socialist society. On the contrary, they had taken seriously the American dream; their fundamental goal had been a democratic and humane society based on egalitarian ideals and social compassion. The real enemies of society were the businessmen, dishonest politicians, and "special interests," all of whom posed a serious threat to the realization of American democracy.

Such an approach put progressivism squarely within the American liberal tradition and on the side of the "people" as opposed to the forces of wealth, self-interest, and special privilege. Vernon L. Parrington, one of the best known Progressive historians, saw progressivism as a "democratic renaissance"—a movement of the masses against a "plutocracy" that had been corrupting the very fabric of American society since the Civil War. Thus, the movement concerned itself not only with political democracy, but with economic democracy as well. To Parrington progressivism was a broad-based movement that included members of the middle class, journalists, and scholars—men, in other words, whose consciences had been aroused by the "cesspools that were poisoning the national household," and who had set for themselves the task of reawakening the American people.[2]

Implicit in this point of view was the conviction that the course of American history had been characterized by a continuous struggle between liberalism and conservatism, democracy and aristocracy, and equal opportunity and special privilege. Most historians writing in the Progressive tradition believed that reformers, regardless of their specific goals or the eras in which they appeared, were cast in the same mold because they invariably supported the "people" against their enemies.

---

[2]Vernon L. Parrington, *Main Currents in American Thought*, 3 vols., (New York, 1927–1930), 3:406.

Such was the position of John D. Hicks, an outstanding American historian whose textbooks in American history were used by tens of thousands of high school and college students between the 1930s and 1960s. Hicks in 1931 published *The Populist Revolt*, the first major account of populism based on wide research in the original sources. To Hicks the Populists carried the banner of reform in the 1890s and represented the first organized protest of the masses against the encroachments of a monopolistic plutocracy. Although the Populist movement ultimately failed, it was victorious in the long run, Hicks held, because much of its program was taken over by later reformers and enacted into law during the first two decades of the twentieth century. To a large extent his thesis rested on the assumption that American reform efforts drew much of their inspiration from the Jeffersonian agrarian tradition which had survived intact among the nation's farmers and rural population.[3]

Not all historians were as friendly and well-disposed toward populism and progressivism as was Hicks. Those historians writing within a socialist and Marxian tradition, for example, were highly critical of progressivism because of its superficial nature and its refusal to adopt more radical solutions to meet the basic needs of American society. To John Chamberlain, a young Marxist who in 1932 published a devastating critique of American reform, the Progressive movement was an abysmal failure. Its adherents, claimed Chamberlain, were motivated by an escapist desire to return to a golden past where honesty and virtue had dominated over egoism and evil.[4]

Oddly enough, many of the detractors of the achievements of the reform movement from 1890 to 1917 were, like Chamberlain, within the Progressive school of history in that they accepted the idea that class conflict had been the major determinant of progress and social change in America. Many of them, particularly during the depression of the 1930s, condemned the Progressive reforms as being piecemeal and superficial in nature. The failure of the Progressive generation, these critics emphasized, had led to the reaction of the 1920s, which in turn had resulted in the disastrous depression of the 1930s. Disillusionment with the Progressive movement, however, did not necessarily imply disillusion with the efficacy of reform or with the aspirations and ideals of the liberal tradition in America. Even those intellectuals who flirted with Marxism during the depression did so out of their conviction that America could still be redeemed from the hands of its enemies.

---

[3]John D. Hicks, *The Populist Revolt: A History of the Farmers' Alliance and the People's Party* (Minneapolis, 1931).

[4]John Chamberlain, *Farewell to Reform* (New York, 1932).

Beginning in the 1940s, and continuing in the 1950s and 1960s, the mood of American historians began to change. The increasing homogeneity of American society began to dissolve the sectional, class, and ethnic groupings that had been employed by the Progressive school of history. No longer did historians have to vindicate the claims of the West against the East, the South against the rest of the nation, or to establish conclusively the contributions of the Puritans, the immigrants, the working class, or the businessmen. Such narrow loyalties appeared parochial in a milieu where national similarities seemed to be more significant than group differences.

The change in mood, however, was due to far more fundamental factors than a mere shift in the class and ethnic backgrounds of historians. Much more basic was the change in attitude and outlook that accompanied the revolutionary changes in the world since the 1940s. To scholars writing after 1940, the Progressive ideology appeared much too facile and simplified. Like many philosophers and theologians, they began to criticize Progressive historians for underestimating man's propensities for evil and for overestimating his capacity for good. In brief, these critics argued that the interpretation of the Progressive school of history rested on an unrealistic evaluation of human nature. The result, they concluded, was that Americans had been unprepared for the dilemmas and challenges that they faced in the Great Depression of the 1930s and the worldwide conflict of the 1940s because of their tendency to view history in terms of a simple morality play where good always triumphed over evil.

The challenge to democracy by communism since World War II gave rise to a new group of scholars—the neoconservative historians—who have been critical of the progressive school and who embarked upon their own reevaluation of the American past. Writing from a conservative point of view, these historians stressed the basic goodness of American society and the consensus that has characterized the American people throughout most of their past. Thus these scholars insisted that American history could not be written in terms of a struggle between democracy and aristocracy or the people against the special interests. On the contrary, they tended to stress the unity and homogeneity of the American past, the stability of basic institutions, and the existence of a monistic national character. While they did not deny that there have been conflicts and struggles between sections, classes, and special interest groups in the past, the neoconservative historians insisted that such struggles were always fought within a liberal framework and that the protagonists were never really in disagreement over fundamentals. Moreover, these scholars were also much less certain about the value or desirability of social change. Having witnessed the effects of revolutionary movements in other parts of the world, the

neoconservatives questioned whether conflict and change would necessarily lead to a better society.

The result of this changed outlook was a sharp shift in the way that
historians interpreted the Progressive movement. The Progressive
school of history had looked upon the Progressive era as but one phase
in the continuing struggle against special privilege and business. The
newer neoconservative school, in rejecting the older view, now began to
ask new and different questions. If progressivism was not in the Jeffersonian liberal tradition, in what tradition could it be placed? If Progressives were not necessarily moral individuals fighting on behalf of
the masses, who were they and what did they stand for? If they did not
democratize and reform America by their efforts, just what did they
accomplish? Such were the questions raised by historians who rejected
the older Progressive view.

The attack on the Progressive school interpretation was led by
Richard Hofstadter, the distinguished Columbia University historian.
Oddly enough, Hofstadter was writing within the Progressive tradition
and as a liberal partisan. Yet he could not find very many constructive
achievements to attribute to the American liberal tradition. Indeed,
he found the liberal ideology to be narrow and deficient in many
respects. In a number of brilliant books, Hofstadter attempted to expose,
by historical analysis, the shortcomings, the inadequacies, and the
failure of American liberalism.

In 1948 Hofstadter published *The American Political Tradition and the
Men Who Made It*. In this book he attempted to delineate the basic characteristics of the American political tradition by studying the careers of
nearly a dozen presidents and political leaders, including Andrew
Jackson, John C. Calhoun, Abraham Lincoln, Theodore Roosevelt,
Woodrow Wilson, and Franklin Delano Roosevelt. Hofstadter's thesis
was that the liberal tradition had failed because it was based upon the
idea of a return to an ideology that emphasized acquisitive and individualistic values. Thus, the Populists and Progressives had similar deficiencies; neither had faced up to the fundamental problems of an industrialized and corporate America. Even Franklin Delano Roosevelt,
who did not share the nostalgia common to the Progressive tradition,
was a pragmatist whose attraction lay in the force of his personality
rather than in any consistent ideology or philosophy.

Seven years later, Hofstadter spelled out his case in even greater
detail in *The Age of Reform: From Bryan to F. D. R.* The Populists, he
argued, were unsophisticated and simplistic reformers. Rather than approaching the farm problem within a broad national and international
context, they placed the blame for their difficulties upon elements of
American society which were alien to them—Easterners, Wall Street
bankers, Jews, and foreigners. Associated with populism, therefore,

was a combination of attitudes made up of a curious blend of racism, nativism, and provincialism—attitudes that helped to explain the fears of agricultural and rural America that later manifested themselves in national paranoic scares. "The Populists," Hofstadter emphasized, "looked backward with longing to the lost agrarian Eden, to the republican America of the early years of the nineteenth century in which there were few millionaires and, as they saw it, no beggars, when the laborer had excellent prospects and the farmer had abundance, when statesmen still responded to the mood of the people and there was no such thing as the money power. What they meant—though they did not express themselves in such terms—was that they would like to restore the conditions prevailing before the development of industrialism and the commercialization of agriculture."[5]

Nor were the Progressives, according to Hofstadter, very much more sophisticated. Traditionally, progressivism had been viewed by historians as a liberal reform movement aimed at readjusting American institutions to the imperatives of a new industrial age. To Hofstadter, on the other hand, progressivism was something quite different. Borrowing heavily from the work of behavioral scientists, he argued that progressivism was related to other influences, notably status anxiety. Playing down the role of economic factors in individual and group motivation, Hofstadter maintained that to a large extent American political conflicts reflected the drive of different ethnic and religious groups for a secure status in society. By the latter third of the nineteenth century, a number of groups—clergymen, lawyers, professors, older Anglo-Saxon Protestant families—were finding themselves displaced from the seats of power and their traditional positions of leadership by a dangerous plutocracy and new political machines under the control of alien elements. The response of this displaced elite was a moral crusade to restore older Protestant and individualistic values—the Progressive movement. This crusade was based on the simple idea that only men of character—the "right sort of people"—should rule. Few Progressive leaders, including Theodore Roosevelt and Woodrow Wilson, were realistic in their appraisals of and solutions to America's problems. "In the attempts of the Populists and Progressives to hold on to some of the values of agrarian life, to save personal entrepreneurship and individual opportunity and the character type they engendered, and to maintain a homogeneous Yankee civilization," Hofstadter wrote, "I have found much that was retrograde and delusive, a little that was vicious, and a good deal that was comic."[6] Blinded by their moral ab-

---

[5]Richard Hofstadter, *The Age of Reform: From Bryan to F. D. R.* (New York, 1955), p. 62.
[6]*Ibid.*, p. 11.

solutism and their righteous convictions, the Progressives were unable
to foresee that much of their ideology was narrow and undemocratic and
would prepare the groundwork for a later reaction that would threaten
the very fabric of American liberty.

The implications of Hofstadter's interpretation were indeed striking.
In brief, his line of thought led to the conclusion that American
liberalism was not a liberal movement, but a movement by fairly well-
to-do middle-class groups alienated from their society because of
technological and industrial changes. There is no doubt that Hofstadter
himself was writing from the left of the political spectrum, but it is clear
also that he felt strongly that the United States never had had a viable
and constructive liberal tradition. Implicit in his views, therefore, was
the assumption that American history occurred within an illiberal or
conservative mold, that a genuine struggle between classes—as portrayed by the Progressive historians—had never taken place.

Hofstadter's general interpretation of progressivism rested to a large
degree upon the research of others, particularly the work of George E.
Mowry. Author of a number of important books on Theodore Roosevelt
and the Progressive movement, Mowry was one of the first historians to
see progressivism as a movement by a particular class aimed at reasssert-
ing its declining position of leadership. Motivated by an intense faith in
individualistic values, these groups opposed the rapid concentration of
power in the hands of large corporate entities and the consequent
emergence of an impersonal society. The Progressives, Mowry concluded, sought to recapture and reaffirm the older individualistic values,
but they attempted to do so without undertaking any fundamental economic reforms or altering to any great extent the structure of American
society.[7]

While the specific formulations of the Mowry-Hofstadter thesis have
not been universally accepted,[8] most recent historians seem to agree that
the older interpretation of progressivism as a struggle between the
people and special interests is oversimplified, if not erroneous. Thus
Louis Hartz in his fascinating book *The Liberal Tradition in America: An
Interpretation of American Political Thought Since the Revolution* (1955) ar-

---

[7]George E. Mowry, "The California Progressive and His Rationale: A Study in Middle
Class Politics," *Mississippi Valley Historical Review* 36 (September 1949): 239-50.

[8]A number of historians have pointed to what they regard as a methodological flaw in
the Mowry-Hofstadter analysis. To argue—as Mowry and Hofstadter have done—that the
Progressives were a cohesive group requires that they show that the anti-Progressives
represented a quite different social and economic group. One recent historian who did a
study of the anti-Progressives in one state found that their social and economic and
ideological characteristics were almost identical with those of the Progressives. See
Richard B. Sherman, "The Status Revolution and Massachusetts Progressive Leadership,"
Political Science Quarterly 78 (March 1963): 59-65.

gued that because America never had a feudal tradition, it did not experience the struggles between conservatives, reactionaries, liberals, and Marxians that characterized the history of most European countries. On the contrary, the United States had a three-century-long tradition of consensus, wherein all Americans subscribed to the Lockean tenets of individualism, private property, natural rights, and popular sovereignty. The differences between Americans, Hartz maintained, have been over means rather than ends. Thus, Americans never had a conservative tradition in the European and Burkean sense of the term, because American liberalism, by virtue of its continuity, was a conservative tradition. To view American history in terms of class struggle, said Hartz, was to misunderstand the basic agreements that united all Americans.

As a result of the rise of the neoconservative school of historians, the Progressive movement has begun to be interpreted in a new and different light. Some of these scholars, for example, neatly reversed the Progressive school approach. Instead of seeing early twentieth-century progressivism as a liberal movement, they argued that it was essentially conservative in nature—a characteristic that was a source of strength rather than of weakness. Thus the historical stature of Theodore Roosevelt rose as historians such as John M. Blum saw him as a conservative though responsible president who was flexible enough to deal with the major issues of the day in a constructive yet practical manner. Conversely, the reputation of Woodrow Wilson among some historians tended to decline because of his righteous moralism. Wilson's New Freedom, they wrote, was unrealistic because of its worship of a bygone age where all individuals had equal opportunity in the economic sphere. His foreign policies also turned out to be dismal failures because they rested on an exclusively moral foundation that omitted any appreciation of the national interest or the realities of international affairs.[9]

Conversely, the reputation of many American reformers suffered as a result of the writings of neoconservative historians. Rather than writing about their contributions and achievements, historians have shown the shortcomings and failures of various reform leaders. They have exposed the personal and selfish factors that supposedly motivated the behavior of reformers and implicitly determined their unrealistic approach to contemporary problems. Above all, such historians scored the reformers for accepting an optimistic moralism based on their faith in progress. According to neoconservative scholars, Progressive reformers

---

[9]John M. Blum, *The Republican Roosevelt* (Cambridge, 1954). For a critical, but by no means unsympathetic, interpretation of Wilson see Arthur S. Link, *Woodrow Wilson and the Progressive Era 1910–1917* (New York, 1954).

tragically misunderstood man's propensity for evil. As a result, they failed to prepare Americans for the inevitable reaction that followed their failure to establish a democratic utopia at home and a peaceful international community of nations abroad in the first two decades of the twentieth century.

At the same time that neoconservative scholars were attempting to undermine the Progressive school emphasis on reform and class conflict, other historians were in the process of developing an entirely new synthesis to explain American history since the late-nineteenth century. Influenced by work in the social and behavioral sciences, they began to apply organizational theory to historical study. Building on the impressive contributions of Max Weber and others, organizational historians saw American society as being increasingly dominated by hierarchical and bureaucratic structures, which were accompanied by a sharp acceleration in the process of professionalization. Associated with these developments was a corresponding shift in the nation's value system. Through the mid-nineteenth century individualistic values remained dominant; after that time they were replaced by an orientation that stressed ideals of efficiency, order, rationality, and systematic control.[10]

The organizational model—as we have already seen—had been employed by business historians such as Alfred D. Chandler, Jr., to explain the emergence of large corporations. But such a model was also capable of being applied in a far more inclusive manner. A number of historians, for example, advanced the thesis that progressivism represented largely an attempt to govern society in accordance with the new ideals of scientific management and efficiency. The conservation movement, to take one concrete illustration, was not—as historians of the Progressive school had maintained—a struggle by the American people and their champions against special interests and large corporate enterprises bent on depriving the nation of its natural resources and despoiling the landscape. On the contrary, the conservation movement, according to Samuel P. Hays, was a movement of scientists and planners interested in "rational planning to promote efficient development and use of all natural resources." Frequently, large corporations—which were profoundly influenced by the ideals of scientific management—were ardent supporters of conservationist policies because of their interest in long-range resource planning. Conversely, small farmers, small cattlemen, homesteaders, and other groups that Progressive historians equated with the democratic masses, often opposed conservation because it conflicted with their hopes of becoming rich quickly. "The broader signifi-

---

[10]For a penetrating discussion of this problem see Louis Galambos, "The Emerging Organizational Synthesis in Modern American History," *Business History Review* 44 (Autumn 1970): 279–90.

cance of the conservation movement," Hays concluded, "stemmed from the role it played in the transformation of a decentralized, nontechnical, loosely organized society, where waste and inefficiency ran rampant, into a highly organized, technical, and centrally planned and directed social organization which could meet a complex world with efficiency and purpose."[11] Implicit in this approach was the assumption that conservation had little or nothing to do with the liberal-conservative categories of the Progressive school of historiography.

In stressing the role of the "expert" and the ideals of scientific management as basic to an understanding of the Progressive era, organizational historians also reinterpreted other aspects of early twentieth century American history. Many of the Progressive reforms, they stressed, were directed not at making the government more democratic and responsive to the wishes of the American people, but to making it and the economy more efficient. The movement for federal regulation of business was not, as the Progressive school of historians had argued, motivated by fear or hatred of large corporate enterprise. Its goal, according to these newer historians, was the elimination of senseless and destructive competition in the economic system by making business and government partners in the effort to eliminate the ups and downs of the business cycle. Progressivism, therefore, reflected the desire of various professional groups to substitute planning for competition, to raise the "expert" to a position of paramount importance, and to end the inherent defects of democratic government by making government conform to the ideals of efficiency and rational planning.

The decline of the older view of the Progressive era was also evidenced in the changing historical interpretation of business and businessmen. For a good part of the twentieth century, the liberal assumptions of most historians led them to portray the business community not only as monolithic in character, but as being made up of men who were grasping, selfish, and narrow in their outlook. In recent scholarship, on the other hand, the businessman has been studied within a quite different framework. Business historians found in the careers of great entrepreneurs a creative and constructive leadership that brought into being America's phenomenal industrial capacity. Similarly, a number of recent scholars have denied that the business community was necessarily reactionary or that all businessmen shared a common ideology. Instead, they attempted to demonstrate that businessmen divided into various groups with conflicting ideas and that many of the Progressive reforms of the early-twentieth century were actually introduced, sup-

---

[11]Samuel P. Hays, *Conservation and the Gospel of Efficiency: The Progressive Conservation Movement, 1890–1920* (Cambridge, 1959), pp. 2, 265. See also *American Political History as Social Analysis: Essays by Samuel P. Hays* (Knoxville, 1980).

ported, and endorsed by businessmen. In a study of the relationship between businessmen and the Progressive movement, for example, Robert H. Wiebe found a complex situation. Businessmen, he noted, rarely tried to improve the lot of low-income groups; they fought against unions and social insurance legislation; and while desiring to purify democracy, they opposed its extension. Economic regulation, on the other hand, aroused a quite different response, for "at least one segment of the business community supported each major program for federal control. In this area businessmen exercised their greatest influence on reform and laid their claim as progressives."[12]

In *Businessmen and Reform* (1962) Wiebe had referred to the Progressive era as an "age of organization." Businessmen, he averred, turned to organization as a means of survival in an impersonal and changing world. Five years later, in a major work, Wiebe carried his analysis much further and provided one of the first attempts to synthesize American history around an organizational core. For much of the nineteenth century American society was composed of autonomous and semiautonomous "island communities." The United States was a nation more in name than in fact, for most individuals resided in relatively small, personal centers, each of which managed its affairs independently of other communities. By the 1880s, however, these communities no longer functioned in their traditional manner, for technological and economic forces had undermined their cohesiveness and caused "dislocation and bewilderment." The result, according to Wiebe, was a "search for order." Some attempted to restore the local community to a position of significance; others turned to agrarian reform; still others joined moral crusades in the belief that a return to traditional values would solve many problems. Ultimately most Progressives turned to organization to bring a new order and equilibrium to American society. In such diverse fields as law, medicine, economics, administration, social work, architecture, business, labor, and agriculture—to cite only a few examples—a new middle class appeared, tied together by their conviction that their expertise and occupational cohesiveness provided the means of ordering a fragmented society. "The heart of progressivism," wrote Wiebe, "was the ambition of the new middle class to fulfill its destiny through bureaucratic means."[13] Slowly but surely America was brought "to the edge of something as yet indefinable. In a general sense, the nation had found its direction early in the twentieth century. The society that so many in the nineties had thought would either disintegrate or polarize had emerged tough and plural; and by 1920 the realign-

---

[12]Robert H. Wiebe, *Businessmen and Reform: A Study of the Progressive Movement* (Cambridge, 1962), p. 212.

[13]Robert H. Wiebe, *The Search for Order 1877–1920* (New York, 1967), p. 166.

ments, the reorientations of the Progressive era had been translated into a complex of arrangements nothing short of a revolution could destroy."[14]

Curiously enough, neoconservative, consensus, and organizational interpretations of the Progressive movement that grew in influence in the 1950s and 1960s were also echoed by New Left historians. Disillusioned by the continued existence of war, poverty, and racism, New Left scholars tended to write about the shortcomings and failures of American reform, a point of view that grew out of their own belief that only radical changes in the framework and structure of American society would solve these problems. Consequently, the New Left interpretation of early-twentieth-century progressivism was written within a partial consensus framework (although those individuals writing within this radical tradition clearly rejected the consensus on which this movement was based) and an awareness of the importance of organizations in twentieth-century America.

To New Left historians the Progressive movement was anything but a reform movement. In one of the most significant studies of early-twentieth-century American history, Gabriel Kolko argued that both major political parties shared a common ideology and set of values. This ideology—what Kolko called politcal capitalism—sought the elimination of a growing competition in the economy. Political capitalism, he noted, "redirected the radical potential of mass grievances and aspirations"; rather than federal regulation *of* business the norm became federal regulation *for* business. Between 1900 and 1916 a unique synthesis of economics and politics occurred. Progressivism, argued Kolko,

> was initially a movement for the political rationalization of business and industrial conditions, a movement that operated on the assumption that the general welfare of the community could be best served by satisfying the concrete needs of business. But the regulation itself was invariably controlled by leaders of the regulated industry, and directed toward ends they deemed acceptable or desirable. In part this came about because the regulatory movements were usually initiated by the dominant businesses to be regulated, but it also resulted from the nearly universal belief among political leaders in the basic justice of private property relations as they essentially existed, a belief that set the ultimate limits on the leaders' possible actions.

Since neither populism nor the Socialist party developed a specific diagnosis of existing social dynamics and relationships, Americans had no viable alternatives, for the two major political parties became the means through which business domination was institutionalized. "The Progressive Era," concluded Kolko, "was characterized by a paucity of al-

---

[14]*Ibid.*, pp. 301–02.

ternatives to the status quo, a vacuum that permitted political capitalism to direct the growth of industrialism in America, to shape its politics, to determine the ground rules for American civilization in the twentieth century, and to set the stage for what was to follow."[15] An excerpt from Kolko's book is included as the first selection in this chapter.

The reaction against the liberal interpretation of the Progressive movement, however, has not been shared by all historians. While admitting that older historians may have been wrong in their emphasis on a class conflict of the people versus the special interests, some scholars continue to see progressivism as an attempt to deal effectively with many social and economic problems that grew out of industrialism and the resulting concentration of power in the hands of a few individuals and groups. J. Joseph Huthmacher, for example, explicitly rejected the Mowry-Hofstadter idea that progressivism was a middle-class movement dominated by a system of values espoused by rural-Yankee-Protestant groups. On the contrary, Huthmacher maintained that progressivism was much more broadly based, and that lower-class groups played an important role in the movement. Implicitly rejecting the neoconservative thesis, Huthmacher argued that progressivism was an attempt to cope with the complex dilemmas of an urban-industrial society. Although he clearly rejected the Jeffersonian agrarian interpretation of progressivism, his point of view was essentially a modification and elaboration of the Progressive school that saw the reform movement of 1900–1920 as a continuing phase in the perennial struggle of liberalism versus conservatism.[16]

Nor was Huthmacher alone in reasserting a version of the older interpretation of progressivism. John C. Burnham, for example, pointed to the voluntaristic flavor of progressivism, and its effort to merge Protestant moral values with the hard facts of scientific and technological change. Indeed, Burnham insisted that moral commitment and immediacy lay at the heart of this movement, which left behind a number of specific achievements. Similarly, John D. Buenker pointed to the broad-based nature of progressivism that included middle- and lower-class elements.[17] An article by Buenker is included as the second selection in this chapter.

[15]Gabriel Kolko, *The Triumph of Conservatism: A Reinterpretation of American History, 1900–1916* (New York, 1963), pp. 2–3, 285, 305.

[16]J. Joseph Huthmacher, "Urban Liberalism and the Age of Reform," *Mississippi Valley Historical Review* 44 (September 1962): 231–41.

[17]John D. Buenker, John C. Burnham, and Robert M. Crunden, *Progressivism* (Cambridge, 1977) This volume is composed of three separate essays by three historians. Although there are important differences between them, the degree of similarity is also striking. See also John D. Buenker, *Urban Liberalism and Progressive Reform* (New York, 1973).

Increasingly the Mowry-Hofstadter thesis that status tensions and insecurity were central to the origins of progressivism came under attack as well. Using the state of Wisconsin as a case study, David P. Thelen could find no correlation between an individual's social characteristics and his political affiliation and ideology. Rejecting the sociological and psychological interpretation that progressivism was rooted in social tensions, he argued instead that its roots went back into the nineteenth century. The depression of the 1890s was of particular importance, for it dramatized the failures of industrialism and gave rise to a search for alternatives. Out of this search came a broad consensus on a series of reform programs that cut across class lines. All groups could unite on the urgent necessity for tax reform and the need to control "corporate arrogance." "When the progressive characteristically spoke of reform as a fight of 'the people' or the 'public interest' against the 'selfish interests,' he was speaking quite literally of his political coalition because the important fact about progressivism, at least in Wisconsin, was the degree of cooperation between previously discrete social groups now united under the banner of the 'public interest.' . . . Both conceptually and empirically it would seem safer and more productive to view reformers first as reformers and only secondarily as men who were trying to relieve class and status anxieties."[18]

Most interpretations of progressivism rested on studies of midwestern and eastern states. In a significant analysis of Alabama during the Progressive era, on the other hand, Sheldon Hackney found that many of the standard generalizations were open to question. He noted, for example, that there was little continuity between populism and progressivism in Alabama; following the demise of their party, Populists either voted Republican or else withdrew from politics. Holding a social philosophy that viewed society in static terms, they clearly preferred a minimal rather than an activist government; they were "primitive rebels." Nor were Progressives motivated by status anxiety or committed to producer values; they saw society in dynamic terms and insisted that economic opportunity could come about only through greater economic growth stimulated in part by positive governmental action. Unlike their forebears, Progressives were earnestly interested in changing southern society and bringing it into the modern industrial era. Indeed, Hackney found that Alabama Progressivism resembled more the eastern, urban Roosevelt brand than the western, rural Bryan variety.

But progressivism, as Hackney observed, also had sharp implications for the status of black Americans in Alabama. During the years from

---

[18]David P. Thelen, "Social Tensions and the Origins of Progressivism," *Journal of American History* 56 (September 1969): 323–41, and *The New Citizenship: Origins of Progressivism in Wisconsin, 1885–1900* (Columbia, Mo., 1972).

1890 to 1910, the pattern of race relations in that state was highly fluid; inconsistency was its primary characteristic. One manifestation of this uncertainty was the high frequency of lynchings. Stability came to Alabama only when the Constitutional Convention of 1901 in effect eliminated black citizens from political participation. Curiously enough, the movement for disfranchisement was led by opponents of reform. Their success helped Progressives to create a new coalition from the purged electorate that owed little to Populist antecedents. Progressivism in Alabama, therefore, rested on the institutionalization of legal and political inequality. Hackney's book raised significant questions about the nature of progressivism and gave little support to either liberal, conservative, or radical schools of historical interpretation.[19]

Oddly enough, virtually all historians, whether they are in the older Progressive or the newer neoconservative, organizational, or New Left traditions, seem to be in agreement on at least one major point; namely, that progressivism was an urban rather than a rural-centered movement. Once again, historians seem to have been reflecting their milieu. In the past many of the major historians had come out of an environment dominated by rural and agrarian values; their attitude toward cities was partly conditioned by the prevailing view that American democracy was the creation of a rural agrarian society. Within the past two or three decades, however, the majority of historians have tended to come from a society and regions of the country much more concerned with the problems of urban life. They do not share the antiurban attitudes held by many of their predecessors. As a result, these historians have written about the contributions of cities and growing urban areas to American history. In this respect, they have shared the mounting concerns of most present-day Americans with the problems of an urban society.

As the historiography of the Progressive movement shows, it is difficult to evaluate the specific contributions of the movement without dealing with certain moral values that inevitably influence the historical judgments of scholars studying the subject. To the Progressive school of historical scholarship, progressivism was one of the first efforts to adjust American values to an urban, industrialized society. The concentration of economic power was thwarting the workings of American democratic institutions as well as corrupting the moral fiber of its citizens. Since they agreed with the goals of reformers who were attempting to ameliorate this situation, the writings of the Progressive school of historians on the movement tended to be a favorable one. More recent scholars, on the other hand, operated within quite a different value structure. Business and other neoconservative historians, precisely because they emphasized the constructive achievements of American

---

[19]Sheldon Hackney, *Populism to Progressivism in Alabama* (Princeton, 1969).

business, did not see much good in a movement which they believed was based on superficial knowledge, amateurism, and demagoguery. Because these historians were more complacent, even proud, of the accomplishments of American society, they saw less need for radical reforms in America's past history. Hence, they either emphasized the conservative nature of progressivism or else pointed to its lack of realism or its optimistic illusions in order to show why the movement failed. Similarly, New Left scholars were equally hostile in their analysis of progressivism; they saw the movement as one dedicated to the control of government by business, giving it a reactionary rather than a reform character. Some historians who identified themselves with the liberal tradition also argued that American liberalism fell far short of enacting truly meaningful reforms during the Progressive era. Thus it was possible for neoconservative, liberal, and radical scholars to be critical of the Progressive movement from their respective viewpoints. And even organizational historians evidenced considerable ambivalence; they were not at all certain that a society based on bureaucratic values and structures was necessarily good.

The problem of evaluating the nature of the Progressive movement, therefore, is by no means easy or simple. Despite considerable research on this important era of American history, the divisions among historians are not necessarily disappearing. On the contrary, these divisions are in some respects growing sharper because of differences among historians pertaining to the nature and meaning of the American liberal tradition. In the final analysis, when historians are assessing progressivism, they are assessing also the ability of Americans to adapt themselves to new problems in any given era.

Aside from the ideological and philosophical conflicts among historians, there are several major questions and problems that must be dealt with in evaluating the Progressive movement. Was there a relationship between the Progressive movement and earlier as well as later reform movements, including populism and the New Deal? Who were the Progressives and what did they represent? Similarly, what groups opposed progressivism and why did they do so? Were the reforms that were enacted between 1900 and 1917 constructive? What impact, if any, did they have upon American life? What significance did progressivism have for black Americans and other minority groups? Why did the Progressive movement come to an end as an organized movement, or did it, indeed, come to an end at all?

These are only a few of the questions that historians have dealt with in an effort to understand the development of American society during the first two decades of the twentieth century. It is difficult, if not impossible, to avoid addressing oneself to these issues because of the bearing they have upon the larger question of understanding the nature of the American experience.

Gabriel Kolko

GABRIEL KOLKO (1932–   ) is professor of history at York University. He has
written a number of books on the history of domestic and foreign policy,
including *Railroads and Regulation 1887–1916* (1965) and *The Politics of War:
The World and United States Foreign Policy, 1943–1945* (1968).

Mergers and Promoters

At the turn of the century the vast majority of the businessmen who
defended monopoly and corporate concentration believed in it as a goal,
and often strove to attain it, but their beliefs were based on a very
limited experience which they thought would extend into the future.
Monopoly, however, was the exceptional and not the routine characteristic of most industries, and the use of the term "monopoly" or
"trust" by defenders of the status quo was based more on wish-
fulfillment than on economic reality. (By "trust" I mean effective control
of an industry by one firm or a working alliance of firms. Contemporary
usage of the term usually equated it with mere large size or concentration, without any specific reference to the extent of market control but
with the implicit assumption that large size could be equated with control.)

Many big businessmen, such as Elbert H. Gary, knew that monopoly
and the total concentration of economic power did not exist even as they
defended it as inevitable. What they were defending was concentration
and their monopolistic aspirations, aspirations that never materialized
despite their enthusiastic efforts. These key businessmen believed concentration and combination led to efficiency and lower costs, and therefore worked for them energetically. And although we might find this
inconsistency natural among the militantly unreflective, it can be
suggested that what these men were defending was the status quo, their
past actions and consolidation, their future actions and, hopefully, industrial domination.

Certainly it can be said that there was a revolution in the American
business structure from about 1897 on—a revolution caused by the sud-

den rise of a merger movement and the capitalization of new combinations on an unprecedented scale. But the revolution was abortive, whereas the intellectual conclusions based upon it were projected into the future and survived long after the revolution's death. Indeed, the preoccupation with monopoly, which seemed imminent at the turn of the century, led to general intellectual confusion as to the important distinction between monopoly and concentration, and this confusion has seriously interfered with subsequent efforts for a proper understanding of the nature of the American economy and politics in the Progressive era.

In 1895 only 43 firms disappeared as a result of mergers, and merger capitalizations were $41 million. In 1898, 303 firms disappeared, and merger capitalization was $651 million; and in 1899 the peak was reached when 1,208 firms disappeared as a result of mergers, and merger capitalizations soared to $2,263 million. In 1900 the movement declined precipitously to 340 firm disappearances, and a capitalization of $442 million, and in 1901 the last great merger movement, largely centered about the formation of United States Steel, occurred when 423 firms disappeared, and capitalization amounted to $2,053 million. But the merger movement declined sharply after 1901, despite the permanent impact it had on the modern American intellectual tradition. During 1895–1904 there was an annual average firm disappearance of 301 companies and a total annual average capitalization of $691 million. During 1905–1914 an average of only 100 firms disappeared each year, and average capitalization was $211 million. More important, from 1895 to 1920 only eight industries accounted for 77 percent of the merger capitalizations and 68 percent of the net firm disappearances. In effect, the merger movement was largely restricted to a minority of the dominant American industries, and that for only a few years.

The merger movement was caused primarily by the growth of a capital market for industrial stocks after the return of economic prosperity in late 1897. The railroad industry, which was the main preoccupation of European investors who had plunged $3.0 billion into the United States by 1890, was overexpanded and unprofitable. Capital invested in manufacturing increased 121 percent from 1880 to 1890, and despite the depression of 1893–1897 increased 51 percent over the next decade. In this context of shifting economic interests, the history of the 1890s is one of sharpening and extending the existing institutional structures for raising capital, and thereby creating movements for mergers, concentration, and, hopefully, monopoly in the American industrial structure.

The stock exchanges of the major financial centers had specialized in railroads until the 1890s, although the Boston Stock Exchange had a copper mine section in the early 1850s which helped establish that city's domination over the American copper industry until the end of the century. Boston, in addition to textiles, was also to dominate the capital market for the electrical and telephone industries until the turn of the century. In 1890 no more than ten industrial stock issues were quoted regularly in the financial journals. By 1893 the number increased to about thirty, and by 1897 to over two hundred.

Industrial capital until the late 1890s came mainly from short-term loans and self-financing out of profits, aiding instability and bankruptcies during the periods of economic decline or depressions. By the 1890s industrial shares became widely available as a result of the creation of new issues from mergers and the reconversion of many trusts, in the literal sense, into unified corporations. And many industrial leaders, ready to retire or diversify their fortunes—Andrew Carnegie is the most notable example—were anxious to develop outlets for their shares. Each new wave of mergers created new sources of capital in a sort of multiplier fashion, and, quite ironically, the very creation of mergers and new industrial combinations led to the availability of funds in the hands of capitalists which often ended, as we shall see, in the creation of competing firms.

The director and coordinator of this industrial metamorphosis was the promoter. To the extent that the dominant stimulus for the promoter was watered stock and his charge for the transaction, the economic concentration which took place at the turn of the century was based on factors other than technological elements inherent in any advanced industrial society. But even if not interested in the transaction fees per se, the promoter was invariably motivated by concern for his own profit position and financial standing, and merely regarded promotion as the means of maintaining or reestablishing it.

Promoters included in their ranks both members of firms being merged and outsiders seeking to stimulate consolidations in order to obtain a share of the profits of the merger. In a number of spectacular instances the insiders of a group of firms sought to interest outside promoters capable of financing or organizing the merger. Quantifications of the nature and source of all or a significant number of promotions do not exist, but some of the more important variations can be illustrated.

William H. Moore and his brother, James H. Moore, were among the three or four most significant promoters. It would be difficult to regard them as anything more than brilliant gamblers. In 1898 William H. Moore organized, at the request of a committee of manufacturers, the American Tin Plate Company out of a group of thirty-five to forty plants. He took options on the component companies and obtained loans to pay for them and provide working expenses. After choosing all officers and directors, he sold $18 million in preferred and $28 million in common stock to bankers and capitalists. Out of this sum he awarded himself $10 million. The Moore brothers were not always so fortunate, however. In 1899 they gave Andrew Carnegie $1 million for an option to try to raise $350 million from bankers to float the sale of Carnegie Steel. They failed, and Carnegie pocketed the money. Similar failures in 1896 forced the Moore brothers into insolvency.

Not infrequently a single manufacturer would turn promoter in order to try to eliminate competition or instability. John W. Gates successfully proved in a law suit that he earned less than $400,000 through underwriting profits and the exchange of shares in the promotion of American Steel and Wire Company in 1899. His only substantial profits were on his component properties that he turned over to the new firm. In the case of the Amalgamated Copper Company, formed in 1899 to gain effective control over the copper industry, outsiders and insiders united. Thomas Lawson, Henry H. Rogers, and William Rockefeller, none of whom had any special competence in the copper industry, cooperated with Anaconda Copper. J. P. Morgan, the largest single industrial promoter and the dominating figure in railroad mergers, resorted to nearly every variation of insider and outsider promotions. Morgan, the Moore brothers, John R. Dos Passos, Moore and Schley, and Charles R. Flint collectively probably accounted for a minority of the total mergers and less than half of the value of all mergers; in addition, there were innumerable single individuals and investment bankers involved in the merger movement.

If the merger movement as organized by promoters was the result of "inevitable" impulses within the capitalist economy, as well as technological imperatives to maximum efficiency, we should determine whether the organization of these new corporations was arranged in such a manner as to: (1) make the competitive entry of new firms increasingly difficult, and (2) avoid the accusation of being organized primarily to create the profits of promotion. It is understood that unless the merger of firms within an industry obtained control of a crucial raw material, patents, or trade advantage, it would have to maintain a reasonable price and profit level or else run the risk of attracting new competitors or allowing existing ones to grow, the risk being scaled to the capital requirements of successful entry. Overcapitalization of the stock of a merged firm, therefore, is an indication of the extent to which a merger was executed to obtain maximum industrial efficiency, control over the competitive annoyances of the industry, or the profits of promotion and speculation. Watered stock meant higher prices in order to pay dividends, and higher prices opened possibilities of new competitive entries.

It is significant, of course, that the heyday of the merger movement was restricted to a few years, and ended almost as abruptly as it began. There are now few academic defenders of the thesis that the merger movement was primarily the outcome of industrial rationality or a desire for control of economic conditions. Charles R. Flint, one of the more important promoters and organizer of twenty-four consolidations, naturally claimed that mergers were intended mainly to attack the evils of competition, and that the profits of promoters were greatly exaggerated by critics. Capitalization, he maintained, was not overinflated, and Flint published data showing that the average return on the *market value* of the stock of forty-seven merged firms was 13.6 percent.

The evidence is overwhelming, however, to indicate that the watering and overcapitalization of the securities of merged companies was the general rule. This fact was widely acknowledged at the time by economists, by most promoters, and by many businessmen. It was simply not generalized upon or related to contemporary theories on the necessity and inevitability of the trust. Indeed, the incompatibility between the obvious ulterior motives behind the merger movement and social theory was ignored even by those attacking the evils of watered stock. J. P. Morgan's lawyer, Francis Lynde Stetson, frankly admitted that he opposed any scheme for limiting overcapitalization that risked "taking away from men of enterprise their paramount motive for corporation organization. . . ."

A government study in 1900 of 183 industrial combinations shows that stocks and bonds valued at $3,085,000,000 were issued for plants with a total capital worth of $1,459,000,000. The Department of Labor, in the same year, claimed that a substantial group of combinations they studied issued stocks valued at twice the cost of reproducing active plants. Arthur S. Dewing, in a study of fourteen mergers, found that the average overcapitalization was well in excess of 50 percent of the assets. The large majority of mergers clearly capitalized their firms on the basis of preferred stock representing the cost of the real property or assets and common stock representing the costs of promotion, the expenses of amalgamation, and the expectations of future earnings as a result of the merger. John W. Gates, Henry O. Havermeyer, and John R. Dos Passos freely admitted that common stock represented the promoter's estimate of the potential earning power of consolidations. The profits of underwriters, in many instances, came exclusively from the sale of securities, not anticipated dividends, and this fact alone placed a premium on overcapitalization.

Seven of the combined firms that later entered the United States Steel merger paid out $63 million in stock as commissions to promoters, excluding bonuses and other forms of commission. The tangible assets and property of United States Steel on April 1, 1901, were worth $676 million, and the average market value of the shares it acquired was $793 million in 1899–1901. The total capitalization of the firm was $1,403 million, and the cost of promotion and underwriting consumed over $150 million of this amount. United States Rubber, in much the same way, based its capitalization on 50 percent watered stock, the common shares representing "the increased earning capacity by reason of the consolidation. . . ."

Promotion, with its premium on speculation to maximize its profits, soon extended its heady gambling mentality to the general stock market. Brokers emphasized the more profitable speculative stock orders rather than investment buying, and they directed their customers to the speculative issues. The commission rates on speculative orders made investment orders less profitable, and by no later than 1904–1907 the volume of transactions on the stock market far exceeded investment demand. This trend alarmed a number of more conservative capitalists primarily concerned with the means, not the ends, of the merger movement, and led to dire predictions, most of which were realized by 1932. Russell Sage wrote in 1901 that watered stock "has also . . . produced a feeling of unrest and disquiet, industrial and political, that threatens, sooner or later, to bring serious results." Henry Clews, the banker, was less restrained.

> Many of these [combinations] have been organized in disregard and defiance of legitimate finance, and have exposed the stock market and all the monetary interests depending upon them to risks and disastrous disturbances inseparable from organizations whose foundations rest largely on wind and water. . . .

J. P. Morgan persistently overcapitalized his promotion schemes whenever he was able to do so. His greatest triumph was United States Steel, but when the merger initiative came from insiders, as in the case of International Harvester, Morgan restricted himself to more limited, yet amply lucrative profits. In every case, however, Morgan sought to obtain substantial, if not total, managerial control or board representation.

Morgan's efforts were generally marked by success, and had he avoided managerial responsibilities his fortunes might have been larger and his reputation would certainly have been better. In the case of the formation of the International Mercantile Marine Company, Morgan became deeply involved in a grossly overextended venture. His firm initially received $5.5 million in preferred and common stock at par, and a share of the $22 million paid to bond underwriters. An additional $6 million went to shipper-promoters, and the new firm was burdened with a total of $34 million in merger fees on a preferred and common stock issuance of $120 million and $50 million in cash. But the company was poorly conceived and poorly managed: In the end the Morgan firm lost about $2 million, and International Mercantile Marine went out of business after World War I. In the case of American Telephone and Telegraph, Morgan fought for effective control of the board, which he managed to obtain in 1907. As part of an overall effort to replace New England management and financial connections, a Morgan-led syndicate obtained a $100 million bond flotation, but was able to dispose of only $10 million before giving up the effort in 1908. Although Morgan's philosophy of trying to obtain managerial control along with the profits of promotion was, on the whole, profitable, it is questionable whether he increased managerial or industrial efficiency. The primary goal of promotions was, as Francis Lynde Stetson admitted, profits. Insofar as Morgan's profits were not immediate or short-range, but tied to the managerial and profit performance of the new company, Morgan tended to do relatively poorly. And in several spectacular instances Morgan either lost money or, as in the railroad industry, bankrupted companies.

To the extent that promotions and mergers were organized among competing firms, the dominant causal factor behind the merger and consolidation movement can be said to have been the existence of internecine competition. A market for industrial securities did not exist in any significant form before 1897, but it most certainly continued after the decline of the merger movement in 1901, and the history of the movement must be explained by more than a market for securities. In the period 1897–1901 the merger movement was the unique result of the rise of a market for securities and an impetus to eliminate competition, and the success of outside promoters was dependent on both factors. But the decline of mergers was due to the collapse of the promises of stability, profits, and industrial cooperation. Save for the outside promoter who took his profit immediately and then broke his ties with the consolidation, the larger part of the mergers brought neither greater profits nor less competition. Quite the opposite occurred. There was *more* competition, and profits, if anything, declined. Most contemporary economists and many smaller businessmen failed to appreciate this fact, and historians have probably failed to recognize it altogether. This phenomenon, I maintain, is a vital key to understanding the political history of the period of reform preceding World War I.

Most important businessmen did not comprehend the general demise of the merger and consolidation movement save in their own industry, and were unable to understand the larger economic context in which they operated. Businessmen, as a group, are not prone to reflection, much less theoretical generalization, but they did act to ameliorate their own illnesses. Now and again, however, a business journal commented on the failure of the merger movement and on the real trends, as opposed to commonly accepted mythology, in the American economy as a whole. In late 1900 *The Iron Age* lamented:

Experience has shown that very few of the promises of the promoters of consolidations have materialized. That some of them are satisfactorily profitable is undoubtedly true.... Others are less so; some are conspicuously unprofitable; some have dissolved, and more will have to dissolve within the next two or three years. Before another wave of the consolidation movement overtakes us, if it ever does, the experiment will have proved itself by the test of time.

The first decades of this century were years of intense and growing competition. They were also years of economic expansion and, in a number of industries, greater internal concentration of capital and output. But neither of these phenomena was incompatible with increased competition. From 1899 to 1904 the number of manufacturing firms in the United States increased 4.2 percent, and from 1904 to 1909 they increased 24.2 percent—a growth of 29.4 percent for the entire decade. Of the nine manufacturing industries with a product value of $500 million and up in 1909, only one, the iron and steel industry, had less than 1,000 establishments, and the exception had 446. In the thirty-nine industries with products valued at $100–$500 million, only three had less than 100 establishments. The numbers of business failures from 1890 on followed the classic pattern of being high in depressions and low in periods of prosperity, and there is no evidence whatsoever that failures due to competition were any more numerous in 1900 than in 1925.

The new mergers, with their size, efficiency, and capitalization, were unable to stem the tide of competitive growth. Quite the contrary! They were more likely than not unable to compete successfully or hold on to their share of the market, and this fact became one of utmost political importance. The very motives behind the merger movement, and the concern with promotion of enterprises irrespective of the health of the component firms or the advantages of combination, led to an immediate apprehension among well-informed businessmen. "One question of great interest in relation to our new industrial combinations is whether a proper readjustment of their hugely inflated capital and excessive charges will place them permanently in a condition of efficiency, productiveness, solvency, and prosperity, or whether they will ultimately drift, one by one, into the hands of receivers..." said Henry Clews at the opening of the century.

This skepticism was more than justified by subsequent events, since the promises of the promoters were, by all criteria, mirages. Forty-eight pre–World War I manufacturing mergers studied by the National Industrial Conference Board had a nominal return on their net worth in 1903–1910 averaging 5.8 percent—no greater than the average to other firms. Arthur S. Dewing, studying thirty-five mergers of five or more firms in existence at least ten years before 1914, discovered that the steep fixed interest charges and contingent preferred stock dividends imposed by promoters led to a radical deflation of promoters' promises. The earnings of the premerger firms were about one-fifth greater than the ten-year average profits of the new consolidation. Promoter estimates of expected ten-year earnings turned out to be about twice the actual performance. Another study by Dewing reveals that heavy fixed changes on the basis of expected earnings, administrative difficulties, and continued competition caused ten mergers to earn an average of 65 percent of their preconsolidation profits. Shaw Livermore, in a study seeking to defend the success of 328 mergers formed during 1888–1905, nevertheless was forced to conclude that only 49 percent were "successes" in the sense that their rate of earnings compared favorably after 1918 to other companies in their field. Forty percent failed altogether, and 11 percent limped along at lower than average profit levels. He judged the main causes of failures to be poor judgment by promoters, dishonesty, and the decline of the industries.

The inescapable conclusion is that mergers were not particularly formidable and successful, and surely were incapable of exerting control over competitors within their own industries. "Mere bulk, whether of capital or of production, is not, *per se*, an element of strength," *The Iron Age* commented in 1900. "Some of the new plants are better equipped, carry less dead weight of unproductive assets and can produce more cheaply per unit of output than the consolidations can. So far as can be judged, the great industrial aggregations, instead of discouraging competition, have rather encouraged it." Most of the new mergers started out with less than monopoly control, and virtually all lost their initial share of the market. This failure, discussed in detail later in the chapter, was due to the rise of important new competitors and the significant economies of size attainable at lower production levels. Thirteen consolidations studied by Dewing controlled an average of only 54 percent of the output of their industries upon organization, and the U.S. Industrial Commission studied a sample with an average market share of 71 percent. Of seventy-two mergers listed by Ralph L. Nelson, twenty-one controlled 42.5 to 62.5 percent of their markets upon formation, twenty-five controlled 62.5 to 82.5 percent, sixteen controlled over 82.5 percent, and ten controlled "large" portions.

There is also data to suggest that very large corporations as a whole did poorly—and many of these were recent mergers. Alfred L. Bernheim studied the 109 corporations with a capitalization of $10 million and up in 1903. Sixteen of these failed before 1914 and were dropped from the list, leaving ninety-three. Only twenty-two of the remainder paid common stock dividends of over 5 percent during 1900–1914, and twenty-four paid nothing. Their average dividend on common stock over the period was 4.3 percent. The market value of common stock of forty-eight of the companies declined over 1900–1914, and rose in only forty-five instances.

In the light of such mediocre profit records it should not surprise one to discover that the mobility of giant firms out of the ranks of the largest hundred industrial corporations was high. Of the fifty largest companies in 1909, seven could not be found in the ranks of the top hundred in 1919, and twenty could not be found there in 1929; for the top hundred corporations in 1909 the figures are forty-seven dropouts by 1919 and sixty-one by 1929. By comparison, of the top one hundred industrials in 1937, only twenty-eight could not be found in that category in 1957. Bernheim studied the fate of the ninety-nine largest industrials of 1909 by 1924, and found that forty-seven of them could not be found among the largest two hundred corporations of every type. Of this forty-seven, seven had dissolved, three had written down their capital to realistic proportions and were disqualified, nine had become unable even to pay their preferred dividends in full, two had paid no common dividends, ten had merged or reorganized without loss, and sixteen had failed to grow fast enough after 1909.

Many large corporations soon found their overcentralization unprofitable, and tried to reduce plant sizes and distribute plants more widely throughout the nation. In the case of United States Steel, as we shall see, the organizational structure was centralized only at the very highest policy level, and autonomous operating units and specialized staffs have been a general trend in the large corporate structure since the turn of the century. To the extent that Joseph A. Schumpeter was correct in holding that each significant new innovation was embodied in a new firm and the leadership of new men in a still dynamic capitalism—and that firms that do not innovate die—it can also be said that important competitive trends were inherent in the economic structure. The growth in the number of individual patents issued until the peak year of 1916 indicates that innovation was very much a part of the American economy and technology until World War I. Even if organized corporate and government research and development now dominates the field, and many private patents are purchased just to be suppressed, or are infringed merely because most private inventors are economically helpless, enough individuals were able to break into established fields, or to create entirely new ones, to make a significant economic difference. For all of these reasons *The New York Financier*, in opposition to the vast majority of contemporary writers and modern historians, was correct when it observed in June 1900, that "The most serious problem that confronts trust combinations today is competition from independent sources. . . . In iron and steel, in paper and in constructive processes of large magnitude the sources of production are being multiplied, with a resultant decrease in profits. . . . When the papers speak of a cessation of operation in certain trust industries, they fail to mention the awakening of new life in independent plants. . . ."

Theory and the American Reality

The American experience justifies different theoretical conclusions than those reached by Marx, Weber, or Veblen. Any reasonable generalization on the phenomenon of progressivism must necessarily take into account the economic realities and problems of the period, and the responses that were set in motion. Yet the crucial factor in the American experience was the nature of economic power which required political tools to rationalize the economic process, and that resulted in a synthesis of politics and economics. This integration is the dominant fact of American society in the twentieth century, although once political capitalism is created a dissection of causes and effects becomes extraordinarily difficult. The economy had its own problems, dictated by technological innovation, underconsumption, crises, and competition. But these difficulties were increasingly controlled by political means to the extent that the consideration of economic problems outside their political context is meaningless. The "laws of capitalist development" were not self-contained imperatives in the technological, economic, or political sphere, but an inseparable unification of all three elements.

The object of such a combination was not merely capital accumulation, although it was that as well, but a desire to defend and exercise power through new media more appropriate to the structural conditions of the new century: the destructive potential of growing competition and the dangerous possibilities of a formal political democracy that might lead to a radical alteration of the distribution of wealth or even its total expropriation. Politics and the state become the means of attaining order in the economic sphere and security in the political arena. And they were accessible tools because the major political parties and leaders of the period were also conservative in the sense that they believed in the basic value of capitalist social relations—of some variation of the status quo. The resilience of capitalism, under these circumstances, becomes something that cannot be evaluated in isolated economic terms. Behind the economy, resting on new foundations in which effective collusion and price stability is now the rule, stands the organized power of the national government. The stability and future of the economy is grounded, in the last analysis, on the power of the state to act to preserve it. Such support does not end crises, nor does it eliminate antagonisms inherent in the very nature of the economy, but it does assure the ability of the existing social order to overcome, or survive, the consequences of its own deficiencies. The theory of the national government as a neutral intermediary in its intervention into the economic process is a convenient ideological myth, but such a contention will not survive a serious inquiry into the origins and consequences of such intervention. The rhetoric of refom is invariably different than its structural results.

Such mythology is based on the assumption that those who control the state will not use it for their own welfare.

It is important to stress that under conditions of political capitalism the form of the industrialization process, and of the political machinery of society, take on those characteristics necessary to fulfill the peculiar values, attributes, and goals of the ascendant class of that society. The rationalized, dominated, and essentially totalitarian decision-making process is not a consequence of forces inherent in industrialism, but in political capitalism in all its components. The organization of industry is based on the decisions of men whose motives have nothing whatsoever to do with inexorable destiny. Mergers, the scale of effective production, the nature of the production itself, and the direction given to the fruits of technology—all these were decisions made by men whose motives, interests, and weaknesses were peculiar to the basic capitalist assumptions upon which they operated. Their errors were many, as were the possibilities for their failure; but the national government stood behind them so that the consequences of their mistakes would not be calamitous. Perhaps industrialization would not have permitted democratic control and direct participation in the work process under any circumstances. All one can do is point to the large extent to which the concentration of industry in this period had nothing to do with considerations of efficient technology, and suggest that no effort whatsoever was ever made to democratize the work situation and industrial control, much less consider the desirability of reducing technological efficiency, if necessary, in such a way as to make decentralization of workers' control possible.

Nor is there any evidence to suggest that the bureaucratization of the political machinery of society, to the extent it took place, was as inevitable as the concentration of industry. It was perfectly logical for men who had spent years solving their economic problems or making their fortunes through political means to also welcome the intervention of a centralized state power to meet problems they could not solve themselves. Social forces, dynamic institutional factors, were the cause of bureaucratic developments in the form of new political agencies and the strengthening of many of the older ones. American capitalism was not merely interested in having law that operated like a piece of machinery, as Weber suggested, but in utilizing the state on terms and conditions which made bureaucratic functions class functions. Bureaucracy, in itself, needed a power base in order to operate in a roughly continuous, systematic fashion. Since it had no economic power itself, it had to support, and hence be supported by, powerful economic groups. This was especially true in a situation where the conditions of political activity were defined by political parties which in turn reflected economic interests, or where the idea of the bureaucracy originated with those operating in the very area in which the bureaucracy was to function.

The skeptical reader may ask whether political capitalism changed after 1916, or perhaps whether capitalism was made more socially responsible by virtue of the stability and rationalization it attained through political means. The question is a moot one, and would take at least one more volume to answer properly. All one can do is point to the continuity in the nature of the political parties and their key leaders, but, more important, to the perpetuation of the same distribution of wealth and the same social relations over the larger part of this century. The solution of economic problems has continued to take place in the political sphere, and the strength of the status quo is based ultimately on the synthesis of politics and economics. Crises have been overcome, or frozen, as much by the power of the state as by internal economic resources applied by business in isolation.

The question remains: Could the American political experience, and the nature of our economic institutions, have been radically different than they are today? It is possible to answer affirmatively, although only in a hypothetical, unreal manner, for there was nothing inevitable or predetermined in the peculiar character given to industrialism in America. And, abstractly regarding all of the extraneous and artificial measures that provided shape and direction to American political and economic life, and their ultimate class function, it would be possible to make a case for a positive reply to the question. Yet ultimately the answer must be a reluctant "No."

There can be no alternatives so long as none are seriously proposed, and to propose a relevant measure of fundamental opposition one must understand what is going on in society, and the relationship of present actions to desired goals. To have been successful, a movement of fundamental change would have had to develop a specific diagnosis of existing social dynamics and, in particular, the variable nature and consequences of political intervention in the economy. It would have, in short, required a set of operating premises radically different than any that were formulated in the Progressive era or later. Populism rejected, on the whole, the values of business even as it was unable to articulate a viable alternative. Intellectually it left a vacuum, and, more important, the movement was dead by 1900. The Socialist party suffered from the fetishistic belief in the necessity of centralization that has characterized all socialist groups that interpreted Marx too literally, and it had a totally inaccurate estimate of the nature of progressivism, eventually losing most of its followers to the Democrats. The two major political parties, as always, differed on politically unimportant and frequently contrived details, but both were firmly wedded to the status quo, and the workers were generally their captives or accomplices. No socially or politically significant group tried to articulate an alternative means of organizing industrial technology in a fashion that permitted democratic control over centralized power, or participation in routine, much less crucial, decisions in the industrial process. No party tried to develop a program that suggested democracy could be created only by continuous mass involvement in the decisions that affected their lives, if the concentration of actual power in the hands of an elite was to be avoided. In brief, the Progressive era was characterized by a paucity of alternatives to the status quo, a vacuum that permitted political capitalism to direct the growth of industrialism in America, to shape its politics, to determine the ground rules for American civilization in the twentieth century, and to set the stage for what was to follow.

John D. Buenker

JOHN D. BUENKER (1937–   ) is professor of history at the University of Wisconsin at Parkside. He is the author of a number of articles and *Urban Liberalism and Progressive Reform* (1973).

The first two decades of this century witnessed a flurry of reform activity unparalleled in American history up to that point. Reformers at all levels of government produced a myriad of legislation dealing with the complex political, economic, and social questions of the day. So intense was their activity that scholars have dubbed the period the Progressive era and hailed it as the watershed of modern day liberalism. Ever since that time, historians have labored to create an interpretation of progressivism which will adequately explain this phenomenon because, in the words of Richard Hofstadter, "it is the historian's business ... to assess the general direction of social movements in the past." As yet, however, no one has been able to construct a truly definitive interpretation, one which will account for the variety as well as the unity of the period.

Although the earliest interpreters stressed the agrarian origins of Progressive reform, seeing in it a fulfillment of the programs of the Grangers, Greenbackers, and Populists, the field has more lately been dominated by what is known as the status revolution theory. This view holds that there is a clearly definable movement known as progressivism and a readily identifiable group of people known as Progressives. The typical reformer of the period, according to Mowry, was a relatively young man of old American stock and British origins, economically secure, college educated, and molded by "the long religious hand of New England." Motivated thus by the heart and the head, rather than by the belly, Mowry's middle-class reformer acted "because he felt himself hemmed in, and his place in society threatened by the monopolistic corporation on the one side, and by organized labor and socialism on the other." In sum, California progressivism, and by implication progressivism in general, was "an expression of an older America objecting to the ideological and social drifts of the twentieth century."

John D. Buenker, "The Progressive Era: A Search for a Synthesis," *Mid-America* 51 (July 1969): 175–93. Reprinted with permission of *Mid-America*.

194

The status revolution interpretation was further elaborated upon by Hofstadter in his brilliant and provocative *Age of Reform*. Hofstadter saw the Progressives as the "spiritual sons of the Mugwumps," although they had broadened their view of society considerably. Basically, however, they were still motivated by an aristocratic revulsion over the excesses of the robber baron, the political boss, and the union leader, in about equal proportion. Their security and status threatened from above and below, the erstwhile gentry abandoned their customary distaste for political activity in order to restore the pristine tranquility of American life. Although making a few highly qualified admissions that other groups occasionally aided these reformers, Hofstadter still insisted that "progressive reform drew its greatest support from the more discontented of the native Americas, and on some issues from the rural and small town constituencies that surrounded the big cities."

There can be little doubt that this interpretation has made a highly valuable contribution to our understanding of the Progressive era and that it is a substantially true picture of the group with which it has been concerned, but it is equally certain that this view alone cannot begin to account for the vast outpouring of legislation which occurred during the first two decades of this century. In the words of Edwin Rozwenc, this "preoccupation with the syndrome of middle class anxieties and prejudices has served to distract attention from the content of progressive policies and the complex relations that composed the political process during the Progressive Era." Equally mindful of this situation, a considerable number of scholars have undertaken to sketch the attitude toward reform which was assumed by other segments of society. Most noteworthy have been the efforts of J. Joseph Huthmacher to chronicle the contributions of the urban, new stock wage earner and his political representative, the machine politican, to the cause of reform. While willing to acknowledge the role of the intellectual and the good government advocate, Huthmacher insists that few of the measures enacted in such industrial states as Massachusetts and New York could have been successful without the skill of the professional politicians and the votes of the urban masses.

This insistence upon the dynamism of what Huthmacher calls "urban, working-class liberalism" has been advanced in a somewhat different fashion by Richard Abrams. Although restricting the use of the term "progressive" to the people singled out by Mowry and Hofstadter, Abrams nonetheless sees the Boston Irish and other Massachusetts ethnic minorities as the major force for change in the Bay State:

> In Massachusetts, the truly insurgent groups—that is those who sought to break through the deep crust of tradition—did not derive from the middle class businessmen and professionals whom George Mowry and Richard Hofstadter, and other historians, have identified as the vital elements at the

core of the Progressive Movement. They came instead primarily from the large Irish-American segment of the population, who purported to represent the newer Americans generally, and, to a lesser extent, from the growing class of labor unionists.

In a somewhat similar vein, Irwin Yellowitz has produced a study of the activities of New York state labor organizations during the Progressive years which presents considerable evidence that labor's influence on reform legislation was more considerable than the status revolution interpretation would seem to allow.

At the other end of the economic scale, a great many scholars have also discovered that the business community was not monolithically opposed to all reforms. Robert Wiebe, for example, has produced a comprehensive study of the question and turned up evidence of substantial business support for even such supposedly antibusiness measures as the Federal Trade Commission and the Clayton Anti-Trust Act. In addition, both Samuel Hays and James Weinstein have documented the backing of many business leaders for such municipal programs as the city manager and commission forms of government. Much of this concern was doubtless due to enlightened self-interest, but it is nevertheless difficult to reconcile the stand of many businessmen on these issues with the contention that progressivism was essentially an antibusiness crusade.

In addition to the machine politician and the businessmen, reformist stirrings have also been uncovered in even more obscure places. It has been generally assumed that the Progressive urge was largely limited to the North, and especially the West and Midwest, with the South either implicitly or explicitly omitted. Recent findings, however, seem to establish considerable southern support for such important measures as the Clayton Act, the direct election of senators, the children's bureau, and workmen's compensation. It is also an axiom of the middle-class interpretation of progressivism that the reform impulse flowed essentially from a capitalist base. Howard Quint, however, argues that "much of the period's moral fervor had socialist origins," a point of view to which the author of this essay is willing to subscribe after studying the attitude of Illinois's Socialists toward the reform proposals of the era. Perhaps even more surprisingly, Philip Gleason has recently published a book which strongly indicates reformist tendencies among first and second generation German-American Catholics in the Midwest, despite their generally conservative orientation.

Taken together, all these works clearly demonstrate the inadequacy of the middle-class status revolution theory as an explanation for something as diffuse and variegated as Progressive reform—a condition which is made all the more apparent by the increasing number of historians calling for a more pluralistic approach. Probably the first to do so was the highly respected biographer of Woodrow Wilson, Arthur Link, in his famous essay on the persistence of progressivism in the 1920s. As part of his explanation for the apparent decline of the reform impulse during the war years, Link argued that "there were many 'progressive' movements on many levels seeking sometimes contradictory objects." Testing Link's thesis in California some years later, Jackson K. Putnam concurred that "the progressive movement embraced a hodge podge of disparate and often contradictory elements." Following the same line of reasoning, Paul Glad has also concluded that "the Progressive movement was nothing if not pluralistic and its very diffuseness should be a warning against a narrow conception of it."

The appreciation of the diverse character of the reform impulse of the Progressive years, however, has not obscured the fact that the period also possessed a measure of unity. A myriad of legislation was enacted, and this suggests strongly that the ideals and interests of a variety of groups must have coalesced on a number of issues. Huthmacher, for one, insists that forward-looking legislation, at least in such industrial states as New York and Massachusetts, "seems to have depended upon constructive collaboration, on specific issues, between reformers from both the urban lower class and the urban middle class (with the further cooperation at times of organized labor)." Link, in the article previously mentioned, talks of the "Coalition of 1916," which made possible the reelection of Woodrow Wilson and provided the major source of support for his programs. The almost legendary achievements of the La Follette years in Wisconsin, according to Robert Maxwell, owed themselves to the efforts of farm groups, labor leaders, and intellectuals, a union of "soil, shop and seminar." Indeed, even as far back as 1913, Walter Weyl recognized that certain issues might make common cause for a variety of people. "The Polish slag worker," he said, "the Boston sales girl and the Oshkosh lawyer have a similar interest (and a common cause of discontent) as consumers of national wealth."

The primary task for the historian who seeks to construct a comprehensive explanation for Progressive reform, then, is to delineate the vast divergence of forces demanding change in the era and to analyze the manner in which these forces coalesced in order to effect meaningful legislative results. To do this, one must perforce begin with a clear understanding of the nature of the complex problems which faced Americans at the turn of this century. In the main, these difficulties were the product of the interaction of three powerful catalytic agents which transformed American life in the nineteenth century—industrialization, immigration, and urbanization. Among other things, industrialization led eventually to the creation of huge business combinations which were fully capable of manipulating the so-called immutable laws of economics to suit their own design, a circumstance which put the small businessman, the laborer, the farmer, the white collar worker, and the consumer at a decided disadvantage. By virtue of this tremendous economic leverage, the corporation was able to wield political power far out of proportion to the numbers of its directors and officials, so much so that the American ideal of democracy was in serious danger of perversion.

Rapid industrialization also led to a serious maldistribution of the nation's wealth. By 1912, when the average worker rarely sported an annual income of $1,000, the income of John D. Rockefeller soared to an unbelievable $50 million and that of his son William to a scarcely more modest $35 million. The first income tax law in 1913 exempted all incomes under $4,000 per year, an estimated 95 percent of the population. The United States was probably never in any real danger of fulfilling Karl Marx's prediction of doom, but it was doubtless closer at that point than at any other in history. This gap between rich and poor in turn was a major contributing factor in the boom and bust business cycle which worked the nation's economic growth for over a century. The recurring threat of depression hung over all like the sword of Damocles, ready to drop financial ruin on capitalist and worker alike. Then, too, there were the other familiar results of industrialization—exploitation of resources, child labor, declining farm prices, and a myriad of other effects too numerous to delineate.

The consequences of massive immigration were more subtle, but no less perplexing. Excepting Negroes and Indians, Americans constituted a fairly homogenous society at the beginning of the nineteenth century. Upwards of 90 percent were of British antecedents, espousing some form of Protestant religion and entertaining similar notions concerning manners and morals. Then came the great influx of Irish, German, and Scandanavian immigrants before the Civil War, followed later by multitudes of Poles, Bohemians, Russian Jews, Italians, Orientals, and various other diverse nationalities. Here were peoples whose customs, traditions, standards of morality, and entire way of life deviated significantly from the established norm. The resultant clashes over these cultural differences were a vital, if unpleasant, fact of nineteenth-century life, and the conflicts grew in intensity as the twentieth-century wore on. At times, as in 1896, they threatened to rend the whole fabric of society.

Added to these two significant trends was the fact of urbanization. From a nation which was almost 90 percent rural in 1790, the United States had become by 1900 a country which was almost evenly divided between city dwellers and their country cousins. By 1920 the majority of Americans lived in urban areas for the first time in history. This almost even balance between city and country was a constant factor in the politics of the Progressive era, for both sides sought to advance their cause at the expense of the other. The cities, for example, strove for home rule to enable themselves to cope with the staggering problems of

sanitation, crime, transportation, and housing which plagued the burgeoning metropolises. The rural areas, aware of the population shifts,
sought fiercely to defend their prerogatives against the onrushing city
which they neither understood nor liked. In most states, the appoint-
ment system was still heavily weighted against the cities and this profoundly influenced the attitude which both groups took toward the various structural reforms considered during the period.

These developments deeply altered the lives of everyone in a variety
of ways. To the farmer they meant declining prices and slipping prestige. To the factory worker they meant long hours at low wages, under
very adverse conditions. To the gentry of Mowry and Hofstadter they
meant a crisis of status and a revulsion at the machinations of the newly
rich entrepreneurs. To all of these, and to the white collar worker and
the small businessman as well, they meant a growing inability to cope
with the circumstances of their new environment and a mounting frustration with their current lot in life.

Indeed, industrialization, immigration, and urbanization actually
contributed mightily toward dividing people into these various
categories. Not that America was in danger of becoming as rigidly
stratified as Europe, but it had become apparent by 1900 that our society
was no longer as fluid as it had been in preindustrial days. These divisions were primarily along the familiar economic lines—big business,
small business, skilled labor, unskilled labor, farmer, white collar
worker, and consumer. As previously indicated, however, divisions
along ethnic, religious, and even geographical lines were also significant. Conflicts between old stock and new stock, Protestant, Jew, and
Catholic were every bit as important and acrimonious as the economic
clashes of the period. These cultural distinctions naturally cut across
economic lines and often made bitter enemies of these who were natural
economic allies. Just as the race question in the South prevented effective cooperation between Negroes and lower-class whites, so too the
arguments over Sunday observance, the use of liquor, immigration restriction, and forced Americanization often nullified collaboration between economically disadvantaged northern groups.

These differences were actually reinforced by the geographical distribution of the nation, for the city was rapidly becoming the haven of the
new immigrant, while the country remained the bastion of the American
of old native stock. The recent immigrant was a peculiarly urban creature. Census figures for 1920 revealed that while the nation as a whole
was only 51 percent urban, the first and second generation American
was an almost 75 percent city dweller. This percentage was even higher
in the New England, Middle Atlantic, and North Central states, where
the new-stock American predominated. These combined cultural and
geographical discrepancies rendered any cooperation between the rural,
old-stock American and his urban, new-stock counterpart on economic

or political questions highly difficult. These differences particularly plagued the Democratic party, where the new-stock voter and politician tended to congregate. No matter what his stand on economic or political matters, an old-stock rural candidate like William Jennings Bryan could never hope to attract enough urban new-stock votes to be elected, while a hopeful from the latter environment such as Al Smith provoked bitter recriminations in the rural, old-stock heartland. Concrete issues like initiative and referendum often engendered attempts by each group to limit the influence of the other, while the direct election of senators found its most consistent support in the industrial states from the representatives of the urban new-stock areas as a means of bypassing the malapportioned legislatures.

Thus, America entered the Progressive era beset by severe problems and sharply divided along economic, cultural, and geographical lines. The logical response to this condition was organization, for the industrial system clearly put a premium on large-scale enterprise, a lesson which the success of the corporation and the trust eloquently taught. The example was not lost on the rest of society. Indeed, for them, as Samuel Hays so skillfully put it, it was a case of "organize or perish." And so a nation which boasted of its individualism undertook to organize itself into cooperatives and unions, trade associations, and national societies in order to defend its members against the hostile world outside.

At first, most of these organizations attempted to work in the private sector, pitting their own power against that of competing groups. The farmers established cooperatives which enabled them to sell their produce at higher prices and to buy manufactured goods at lower ones. Skilled labor, following the pure and simple trade unionism policy of Samuel Gompers, sought to achieve higher wages and better working conditions through the medium of private collective bargaining. Small businessmen tried to maximize their economic position by forming trade associations. National and religious societies like the Ancient Order of Hibernians, the Sons of Italy, the United Societies of Bohemia, the Polish American Society, the Knights of Columbus, and the B'nai B'rith combined to protect their traditions from native attack and to modify the shock of alienation suffered by the recent immigrant. Even the political machine, as Oscar Handlin has so well demonstrated, operated within the private sector by providing welfare in the form of jobs, food, and protection from the law for their disadvantaged constituents.

Ultimately, however, each of these groups found it necessary to enter the political arena and to seek legislative remedies for their plight. The farmer's alliances gave way to the Populists and their farm bloc descendants. Labor slowly abandoned its nonpartisan stance and began to back candidates committed to prolabor platforms. Nativist societies like the American Protective Association and the Anti-Saloon League lobbied for laws which would help to Americanize the immigrant and electioneered for candidates who would support them. The new stock groups retaliated by political activity against such measures as prohibition, Sunday blue laws, and immigration restriction. Representatives from urban areas were pressured by their constituents for proposals that would aid the burgeoning city in its fight for economic and political well-being, while those from rural areas were encouraged to defend the prerogatives of the country against the incursions of the city. The political machines found that their private welfare activities were no longer adequate to meet the needs of the urban masses and were forced to support schemes which would shift this burden to the states. Business, which had been in politics from the outset, intensified its efforts in the face of the flurry of activity engaged in by the rest of society. In short, the problems and divisions which plagued America in the real world finally came to be mirrored in the political world as well, and politics once more became relevant to American life. It was precisely this changeover from the unreality of the late-nineteenth-century politics which marked the beginning of the Progressive era.

Because none of these interest groups constituted more than a significant minority of the population, no single one could possibly hope to gain control of any segment of the government by itself. This necessitated the formation of coalitions in order to accomplish anything of note. In the multiparty states of Europe each group probably would have formed its own party and tried to develop the traditional coalition governments. In our two-party system, however, the parties themselves are essentially coalitions, featuring every shade of political opinion and economic interest imaginable. Legislative success, therefore, usually came through effective collaboration between various factions within the majority party, aided by elements of the opposition with similar interests and ideals. It is true that the Progressive period produced that American rarity, a viable third-party movement, but this was primarily a vehicle of the more liberal minority of the Republicans, who still were required to cooperate with like-minded Democrats, so the process was not altered in any fundamental manner.

It should be emphasized that support for a particular measure on the part of a number of factions did not necessarily indicate any basic, broad-gauged agreement on principle. Indeed, it is easy to conceive of different groups voting for (or against) the same bill for very dissimilar reasons. On an issue such as the regulation of child labor, for example, the middle-class intellectual was favorable because he believed the practice to be a moral evil, the machine politician because it adversely affected his constituent's children, and organized labor because it tended to lower wages and working standards. By the same token many businessmen opposed regulation of child labor because the practice was profitable, and they were sometimes joined in this by some representatives of the wage-earning classes for whom working children were a practical, if regrettable, way to make ends meet. Or take the case of immigration restriction, a highly charged emotional question of the period. The middle class, the intellectual, and the farmer sought, through such organizations as the American Protective Association, to restrict the flow of immigration in order to protect American life from alien influences. They were joined by organized labor, attempting not to protect cultural values but pay scales, on the grounds that immigrants drove down wages. They were opposed by businessmen seeking to preserve a source of cheap labor and the representatives of ethnic minorities fighting against an attempt to close the channels of opportunities for their fellow countrymen. In Rhode Island the issue of one day's rest in seven for laborers produced a unique coalition between the state's unions and a group of ministers, with the latter acknowledging that its motives were purely religious and differed from those of the workers. Other examples might be chosen but they would only serve to point up the fragile and transitory nature of the Progressive coalitions.

By all odds, it was easiest to obtain agreement in the area of economics, where there were so many groups who felt themselves to be disadvantaged. So great was the success of the finance capitalists and the industrial leaders that attempts to tax or regulate them, or to aid their adversaries, were readily welcomed by most other segments of the economy. The foremost economic reform of the era, the adoption of the federal income tax amendment, found tremendous support at all but the highest levels of society because it was so clearly an attempt to make the wealthy bear their fair share of the burden of government. Ironically enough, even the servants of the wealthy inadvertently contributed to this process by proposing a constitutional amendment permitting an income tax in order to forestall the immediate passage of a statutory tax in 1909. What they could not foresee was that the measure would attract so much support in the various state legislatures. In the South, the erstwhile Populists combined with the new urban middle-class reformers. In the West, it was largely the same combination, with a little more support from organized labor in the mining and coastal states. In the industrial Northeast it was the Democratic urban machines like Tammany Hall and the Boston Irish, representing the new-stock wage earner, who most vigorously pushed for ratification, aided by such middle-class Progressive governors as Eugene Foss in Massachusetts, Woodrow Wilson in New Jersey, and Judson Harmon in Ohio, plus the forces of organized labor.

Tax reform on the state level often required the effective cooperation of various factions. In Ohio, for example, one of the signal achievements of the Progressive era was the Warnes Tax Commission Act, which created a central commission for the assessment of taxes, removing it from the control of the local officials. The measure was drawn up by Milton Warnes, a well-known middle-class Progressive, but passed largely because of the support given it by the large Cleveland and Cincinnati delegations, who were mostly of working-class origins. A similar proposal in Illinois was first introduced by Governor Edward F. Dunne, the Irish Catholic former mayor of Chicago who was largely the representative of the state's urban new-stock citizens, but was finally enacted during the subsequent administration of Republican Frank Lowden, who was a more typical middle-class Progressive.

By the same token, proposals to curb the power of big business generally received large-scale backing. There was, of course, the well-known division between those who felt that trust-busting was the best solution and those who looked to regulation as the most effective remedy. In the case of public utilities, there was also a disagreement as to whether regulation or public ownership was the superior tactic, but generally small business, labor, white collar workers, and consumers were in a mood to curb the excesses of the giant corporation by the Progressive years. The most conspicuous example of this type of regulation, the Clayton Anti-Trust Act, was most certainly an accomplishment of Woodrow Wilson, who was almost the prototype of the middle-class Progressive, but it also had the backing in Congress of southern agrarians, urban machine politicians, some business organizations, and organized labor, for whom it became known as the "Magna Charta." Just a partial list of those pressure groups which lobbied for passage of the Clayton Act featured such unlikely bedfellows as the American Federation of Labor, the Railway Brotherhoods, the Chamber of Commerce, the Farmers Union, and the American Anti-Boycott Association. Wilson's famous laws for the regulation of corporations in New Jersey were also a triumph for the middle-class brand of progressivism as illustrated by the support which good government reformers like J. Warren Davis and James Fielder gave them. Without the votes of the huge bloc of urban working-class votes in the assembly, however, they could never have become a reality.

The myriad of labor and welfare measures adopted by the various industrial states during the Progressive era likewise depended upon effective cooperation between middle-class intellectuals, social welfare workers, organized labor, and the representatives of the great mass of unskilled, urban, new-stock wage earners. The successful collaboration between Tammanyites Al Smith and Robert Wagner, and social workers like Frances Perkins and Belle Moskowitz on the New York industrial code and other welfare measures is justly famous. Miss Perkins herself attributed the success of the factory code bill to the cooperation which she and other social workers received from Tammany, from organized labor, and from a few enlightened businessmen. The same observation has been made about welfare laws in other states. California's minimum wage law, for example, was a victory for the combined efforts of Progressive Republicans like Hiram Johnson, women's organizations, and a few of the weaker unions in the state over the opposition of the unlikely coalition of the State Federation of Labor and the Chamber of Commerce. Richard Abrams, as previously noted, attributes most of the accomplishments in this area in Massachusetts to the combined activities of the Boston Irish and the labor legislators. In Illinois, where a great deal of legislation in the labor and welfare area was adopted, including old age pensions, employers liability laws, child labor measures, women's hours and wages regulation, unemployment offices, and industrial codes, various factions coalesced to make a contribution. These included middle-class Progressives like Walter Clyde Jones and Medill McCormick, labor leaders like James Morris, the secretary of the Illinois Federation of Labor, and John Grunau of the railway workers, the large Chicago Democratic delegation to the legislature under the direction of Governor Dunne, and even a handful of Socialist lawmakers. Cooperation between middle-class governors like Wilson and Harmon and the representatives of the lower classes and organized labor in New Jersey and Ohio on matters relating to labor and welfare was also very much in evidence.

These economic coalitions were often difficult to maintain when it came to questions of political reform. Reformers like Franklin Roosevelt were able to cooperate effectively with machine politicians like Al Smith on economic matters, but when the former sponsored measures aimed at Tammany's prerogatives, the two parted company as Roosevelt's effort to block the election of "Blue-eyed Billy" Sheehan to the United States Senate amply demonstrated. Middle-class, good-government types could make a common ground with labor and the machines on welfare legislation, but when the former brought up questions like civil service or corrupt practices acts which struck at the machine's sources of power, the coalition fell apart. Rural politicians might share the enthusiasm of city representatives for business regulation, but oppose them bitterly on issues like legislative apportionment.

Still, meaningful political change was effected during the era, and this reflected the formation of other working coalitions. In Illinois, for example, initiative and referendum was strongly endorsed by Governor Dunne, and supported by a large number of other Chicago politicians, but it also was backed by such good-government advocates as Charles Merriam and the National Referendum League, by the state Grange, and by both the Chicago and the Illinois Federation of Labor. The fight for the direct election of senators enlisted the cooperation not only of the middle-class reformers identified by the status revolution historians, but also of such identifiable urban machine politicians as Smith, Wagner, Dunne, Roger Sullivan, Martin Lomasney, and Edwin Vare. Together they were able to overcome the formidable resistance of southern Democrats who feared federal interference in elections and conservative eastern Republicans of the Nelson Aldrich school who simply wished to defend the system which produced them. A similar coalition between good government groups and urban machines was largely responsible for the success of the women's suffrage amendment, once the latter organization had undergone a change of heart on the question. Various urban groups which opposed each other on economic issues often came together on such issues as home rule or reapportionment in the face of rural dominated legislature. Rural lawmakers of all parties and all walks of life sometimes formed a united front against the incursions of a great metropolis. All in all, the attitude assumed by most voters and lawmakers toward a particular issue usually depended more upon the merits of that one question than upon any well-defined philosophy of progressivism.

As sharp and bitter as these divisions over economic or political issues often were, however, they were mild when compared to the acrimony aroused by questions involving manners, morals, and religion. On these cultural matters, people tended to divide fairly faithfully along ethnic and religious lines, whatever their economic position or political affiliation. Certainly one of the most distasteful, but nonetheless integral, developments during the Progressive years was the attempt on the part of old-stock America to force the new-stock citizen to conform to the prevailing system of values. The so-called native, as Hofstadter and others have convincingly demonstrated, blamed a large portion of his declining status on the influx of alien peoples and cultures, which tended to erode the American way of life as he understood it. Consequently, he sought to allay that threat by a variety of legislative means. Just as the southern white reformer saw segregation as a solution to his difficulties, so too did many northerners, especially those of the old-stock middle class, envision immigration restriction and legislated Americanization as the answer to their problems. In this they were often joined by many rural Americans of similar lineage.

These cultural considerations, to a certain extent, even underlay the attack of the "native" reformer upon the political machine, for the latter organization rested upon the votes of large numbers of new-stock voters. This antagonism is certainly evident in Hofstadter's discussion of the conflicts between the "reformer-individualist-Anglo-Saxon complex" and the "boss-immigrant-machine complex." Similarly, many apparent urban-rural contests had strong cultural overtones since the residents of the cities were so overwhelmingly new stock. Divisions along ethnic lines were even more clearly in evidence on issues like Sunday blue laws or compulsory public school attendance—a move which was often an ill-disguised attempt to use the educational system as an agency for Americanization. In Illinois, one of the bitterest issues of the era was over the legalization of professional boxing—a proposal usually sponsored by the recent immigrant and opposed by the American of more ancient lineage.

The two questions which most nearly divided people along cultural lines, though, were prohibition and immigration restriction. The former issue had many ramifications, but basically it was a proposition to which people responded out of the depths of their cultural and religious heritage. The two latest studies on the adoption of prohibition, those of Andrew Sinclair and James Timberlake, both put great stress on the native Protestant strain in the reform movement itself as well as the new-stock non-Protestant character of the opposition. It is significant too that the Prohibition party regularly included planks on immigrant restrictions and Bible reading in the public schools in its platform. Most importantly, a study of the votes on ratification in the various state legislatures clearly reveals that the amendment was overwhelmingly advocated by the representatives of rural, old-stock, Protestant America and vigorously fought by those of urban, new-stock, non-Protestant America. This was especially noteworthy in Illinois where the opposition to ratification came almost entirely from lawmakers with minority group backgrounds, representing the major cities like Chicago, Peoria, and East St. Louis. Those few rural or small town legislators who voted "no" had ethnic and religious backgrounds similar to those from the major cities, and those few Chicago representatives who favored ratification were all old-stock Protestants.

Similarly, the issue of immigration restriction produced an old stock-new stock cleavage. The pressure for limitation steadily increased during the Progressive years as more and more "natives" began to despair of the possibility of assimilating the vast numbers of aliens into their midst, and the latter began to resist the process more vigorously. The most popular device during the first two decades of the century was the proposed literacy test, which, while not ostensibly based on national origins, nevertheless was capable of being used to discriminate against various ethnic groups. Twice a "native"-dominated Congress succeeded in passing the literacy test requirement over the vigorous objections of the representatives of the nation's polyglot districts, only to have it vetoed by President Wilson. Wilson himself was of old American stock and his earlier views had some racial overtones, but it must be remembered that as a Democratic president he was heavily dependent for votes upon the large urban machines with their constituencies of ethnic minorities.

These cultural divisions, then, seem to have been every bit as crucial as economic ones during the period and could well have had as much influence as the latter in many political struggles. In fact, it is entirely possible that one reason for the decline of the reform impulse was the fact that these cultural questions became so important that cooperation on economic and political matters was all but impossible. In a sense, the battle over prohibition was the death knell of the Progressive impulse. The First World War increased the tension between ethnic groups, and the carpings of the various hyphenate groups over the alleged defects of the Versailles Treaty completed the process, opening the door to the excesses of the National Origins Quota Act, the Ku Klux Klan, the Sacco-Vanzetti Case, and the Red Scare in the next decade. So strong were these ethnic and religious feelings in the twenties that any economic or political alliance between the disadvantaged of old stock and new stock was proscribed, as the bitter electoral struggles of 1924 and 1928 clearly indicate. It eventually took the shock of the Great Depression to effect a reconciliation as the economic question once again became paramount.

The dimensions which a comprehensive definition of the Progressive era ought to encompass, then, seem reasonably clear. It must first of all recognize that no one group or party could possibly have been responsible for the myriad of legislation which characterized the period. It must acknowledge that divisions along cultural and geographical lines were often as important as economic differences. It must admit that pragmatic coalitions based upon temporary harmonies of interest were more compelling considerations than any unified philosophical system of reform. In short, it must proclaim that there was really not one progressive movement, but several concurrent attempts at all levels of society by those seeking to cope with the circumstances of their new environment. There were perhaps a few very general unifying principles which can be discerned in the period, but they are too abstract really to order events. Nearly everyone seemed to feel that government at all levels should play a more active role in American life, for example, but there was no agreement upon the precise nature of that role nor the conditions under which it should be exercised. There seems to have been also a widespread feeling that government should be made more responsible to the people, but there was precious little consensus as to how best to accomplish this, or even who the people were, for that matter.

As previously suggested, no one has as yet been able to account for all of this diversity. About the nearest that anyone has come so far is the provocative analysis by Samuel Hays in *Response to Industrialism.* Hays sees the whole period from 1885 to the First World War as an attempt to come to grips with the problems created by industrialization, immigration, and urbanization. He demolishes the idea that it was merely a crusade against the corporation and the political machines. He even has a fairly good impression that groups like farmers, organized labor, and the unskilled immigrant workers have to be included within the purview of the era. In the end, however, Hays falls back on the middle class, the good-government reformer, the social worker, and the intellectual as the driving force behind most legislation, and thus fails to follow through effectively as he might on the implications of his thesis.

The twentieth century has produced phenomenal advances in coping with the problems which the nineteenth-century transformation of the United States created. Most of this progress can be legitimately attributed to a phenomenon roughly called twentieth-century American liberalism, a development which had its origins in the first two decades of this century. If we would seek to understand the evolution of this movement in order that we can better deal with the monumental problems which still face us, we must surely begin with a clear compreension of the era which spawned it.

6

America's Entry into World War I

Needless or Necessary?

For most Americans World War I posed a dilemma that conflicted sharply with what they felt was their national heritage. Traditionally Americans regarded themselves as a peace-loving nation destined to serve as a model for mankind. War itself was considered as an aberration from the normal course of events. After each of its previous foreign wars—the War of 1812, the Mexican War, and the Spanish-American War—bitter self-recrimination had followed as Americans sought to fix the blame on some person or party for involving this peace-loving nation in combat. How had the nation been drawn into conflict with foreign countries, when war itself seemed contrary to the cherished American ideal of peace? To this question many answers were given. Some pointed to blundering statesmen; some alleged evil conspiracies by groups that stood to benefit from war; and some argued that a strong sense of moralism blinded America's leaders to the realities of international affairs. But whatever answer was given, it was usually accompanied by a great debate concerning the proper role of the United States in world affairs—a debate that transcended the immediate specific issue of war causation or responsibility.

When armed hostilities broke out in the summer of 1914, most Americans, although concerned over events abroad, showed little or no inclination to become involved. President Wilson echoed the desires of most of his fellow citizens when he called upon them to remain neutral in thought as well as deed. Yet the hope of remaining neutral was soon to encounter formidable obstacles that placed a severe strain upon American diplomacy.

One of the basic problems confronting Wilson and his advisers was the fact that new weapons and total war had created a situation where past precedents and rules defining the duties, responsibilities, and rights of a neutral in time of war simply did not apply. In attempting to redefine the long-established rules of neutrality, Wilson soon found himself facing a dilemma. Both the Allies and the Central Powers sought to force America to adopt a policy of ostensible neutrality that would in fact be beneficial to their own national interests.

Britain, who controlled the seas by virtue of her predominant naval strength, wanted to exercise maximum restraint on neutral trade with the Central Powers. A naval blockade was established at the start of the war to intercept neutral vessels trading with Germany and the scope of the blockade was gradually expanded until it virtually covered all neutral commerce with the continent. To allow Britain to employ her naval might to this degree, America would be forced to relinquish some of its rights as a neutral, which was clearly to the disadvantage of Germany.

Germany, on the other hand, attempted to counter the impact of the British blockade by various means, which also raised problems insofar as America's neutrality was concerned. Submarines, then a novel means of naval warfare, soon became the center of the controversy. Being relatively defenseless on the surface, submarines dared not investigate neutral and belligerent shipping too closely, nor could they always make adequate provision for the safety of the crews and passengers. Under these conditions there was bound to be indiscriminate destruction of both ships and lives. Early in 1915 the German Admiralty announced a blockade of the waters around the British Isles, declaring that all enemy vessels in the area would be sunk without warning by German submarines. Given the manner in which submarine warfare was being conducted, there was no doubt that American lives would be threatened.

The policies of both belligerents places Wilson in a difficult position. If he accepted the British regulations, it would favor the Allied cause; if he obeyed the German blockade it would nullify Britain's naval advantage and favor Germany's strength on the continent. A total embargo against all belligerents would clearly redound to the advantage of the Central Powers because Britain rather than Germany was the beneficiary of the trans-Atlantic trade. Thus, genuine neutrality was virtually impossible and even an American embargo raised implications of an unneutral policy.

President Wilson ultimately decided that German submarine warfare presented America with a far greater danger than did the restrictions imposed by the British. When Germany decided at the end of 1916 that its national interests demanded a resumption of unrestricted submarine warfare against belligerent and neutral shipping, Wilson concluded that he had no real alternatives. Following the sinking of several American vessels, he went before Congress to ask for a declaration of war. Despite isolated opposition, Congress concurred with the president's request, and on April 7, 1917, the United States entered the war on the Allied side.

Although the overwhelming majority of citizens agreed with Wilson that the United States had no choice but to defend itself, there was some scattered opposition throughout the country. In Congress six senators and fifty representatives voted against the declaration of war. Outside Congress some intellectuals and Socialists also opposed America's participation. Nevertheless, the conformity brought on by the war resulted in silencing much of the opposition. It was only well after the war was over that serious discussion got under way regarding the reasons for America's involvement.

The debate in the early 1920s over America's entry into war did not reflect the traditional assumptions that had given rise to the Progressive school of historiography. One of the reasons for this was the fact that domestic issues played a relatively minor role in the decision for war. But like historians of the Progressive school, the diplomatic historians who wrote about America's entry into the First World War had their own set of assumptions. These assumptions usually revolved around such questions as the proper role of the United States in world affairs and the desirability of American involvements in foreign conflicts. More than anything else, the divisions among those historians who dealt with American diplomacy from 1914 to 1917 reflected differing views as to what America's policy should have been.

Generally speaking, most of the contemporary or near-contemporary accounts—none of which were based upon wide research in the sources simply because relevant manuscript materials were as yet unavailable— took a favorable view of America's diplomatic moves between 1914 and 1917. The two most widely read works in this regard in the 1920s were semiautobiographical accounts that dealt with the careers of Walter Hines Page, the American ambassador to England, and Colonel Edward House, Wilson's close friend and adviser. Both men had advocated intervention; both had shown concern lest America's policy obstruct the Allies; and both were of the opinion that German militarism would have represented a real threat to American democracy if the Central Powers had emerged victorious. When the United States entered the war, they argued, it did so for reasons of morality and self-interest, both of which coincided in 1917.[1]

The controversy over the Versailles peace treaty and the growing disillusionment with Wilsonian idealism, however, set the stage for a reexamination of the problem of America's entry into the war. During the 1920s a new school of historians known as the revisionists emerged to offer different explanations for America's involvement. John K.

---

[1]Burton J. Hendrick, *The Life and Letters of Walter Hines Page*, 3 vols. (Garden City, N.Y., 1922–1925); Charles Seymour, ed., *The Intimate Papers of Colonel House*, 4 vols. (Boston, 1926–1928).

Turner, a veteran Socialist writer who published a book entitled *Shall It Be Again?* in 1922, was among the first of the revisionists. Rejecting the interpretation that the United States had intervened to protect commerce and lives and to uphold national honor and international law, Turner argued that Wilson, a pseudo-liberal, had gone to war because of the greed of Wall Street bankers. His book, however, had little influence at the time of its publication, one possible reason being its polemical tone.[2]

A few years later a more significant statement of the revisionist point of view was presented by Professor Harry Elmer Barnes, who had become interested in the general problem of war guilt. In 1926 Barnes published his *Genesis of the World War* in which he repudiated the idea that Germany had been responsible for the outbreak of war in 1914. He contended that America's participation in the war had been a mistake brought about by Wilson's acquiescence in Britain's illegal maritime restrictions and his misguided desire to save the Allies from defeat. By throwing American power into the conflict on the side of the Allies, Wilson set the stage for the disastrous and one-sided Versailles peace settlement that followed.[3]

Barnes continued for over forty years to reiterate his belief that the United States should have stayed out of World War I. Implicit in his point of view was the assumption that America had had no stake in the European conflict and that a much fairer peace between the warring powers could have been negotiated had American power not thrown the balance in favor of England and the Allies. In the first selection in this chapter, Barnes spells out his case in detail. Wilson started off as a neutral, he argues, but his Anglo-Saxon perspective and the fact that most of his advisers were pro-Ally and distorted the case against Germany caused the President ultimately to take an unneutral stand. One of the reasons for Wilson's change of mind was the growing munitions trade with the Allies upon which America's prosperity rested, in part, at the time. This trade—which according to Barnes was unneutral and illegal—forced Germany to resort to unrestricted submarine warfare and led to America's involvement in the war. Because of our unneutral policy, Barnes concluded, the United States entered the conflict without any clear legal or moral basis for doing so.

During the 1920s and 1930s the revisionists continued to build up their thesis that America had entered the war because of Wilson's unneutral diplomacy. C. Hartley Grattan, one of Barnes's former students at Clark University, published a long and detailed revisionist work in 1929. Working on the assumption that neither the world nor the United

---

[2]John K. Turner, *Shall It Be Again?* (New York, 1922).

[3]Harry E. Barnes, *The Genesis of the World War: An Introduction to the Problem of War Guilt* (New York, 1926).

States had gained anything from the war, Grattan in his book *Why We Fought* examined in detail the circumstances that had led to American involvement. He pointed to Wilson's shift in policy from true neutrality to a pro-Allied position—a shift brought about by Anglophilism, the influence of capitalists, financiers, and munition makers who had an economic stake in an Allied victory, and the skill of British propagandists. In view of America's pro-English policy by late 1916, Grattan concluded, Germany had no choice but to counter with the submarine.[4]

The revisionists found a very receptive climate of opinion for their views in the 1930s because of the deterioration in the world situation. By this time it was evident that the international structure erected at Versailles and at various conferences in the 1920s was failing to keep the peace. In Italy Mussolini and the Fascists exercised dictatorial control; in Germany Hitler was well on the road to rebuilding Germany's war potential; and in the Far East Japan was already beginning its policy of expansion on the mainland of Asia.

To many Americans these developments were particularly distressing. After all, the United States had gone to war in 1917 not only to protect its own interests, but also, as Wilson had so eloquently put it, "to make the world safe for democracy." More than ever before, the rise of dictatorships abroad seemed to be making a mockery of the high idealism with which America had entered the First World War.

The disillusionment of the American people in the 1930s was reflected in their growing distrust and suspicion of foreign nations. As a result, the United States entered a period of semi-isolationism. In its foreign policy moves, America seemed to be intent upon cutting itself off from membership in the community of nations as much as possible. At the same time, steps were taken to prevent a repetition of the mistakes many felt had been made in the period prior to America's entry into the First World War. In the mid 1930s a series of neutrality acts were passed in an obvious effort to prevent history from repeating itself. For example, the Johnson Act of 1934 forbade American citizens from lending any money to a nation which was in default of its war debts to America. The intent of this act, in part, was to prevent the establishment of an American financial interest in the survival of any foreign country. The three neutrality acts written between 1935 and 1937 had other provisions to prohibit aid to belligerent nations in time of war.

The isolationist mood of the 1930s was further strengthened as a result of the Senate investigation of the American munitions industry. A Senate committee headed by Senator Gerald P. Nye of North Dakota was given the task in 1934 of investigating the influence of munition makers on American foreign policy. Although the evidence gathered by

---

[4]C. Hartley Grattan, *Why We Fought* (New York, 1929).

the committee came closer to refuting rather than supporting the thesis that the munitions industry had played a Machiavellian role in influencing foreign policy, the findings of the committee were used indirectly by some revisionist historians to buttress their case against Wilsonian diplomacy.

Coupled with the rise of isolationism was that of pacifism. The pacifist movement in this era was a potent force in shaping the minds of many Americans and creating an intense desire throughout the nation for peace. Many American citizens became convinced that war was to be avoided at all costs because of its immoral nature, its threat to civilization, and its failure as a means of achieving any worthwhile objectives.

The desire to avoid involvement in any future European war had the effect of reawakening interest in the reasons why America had entered World War I. How had America become involved in the war and who was responsible? In asking a question of this nature, many historians started with the assumption that America's entry into the war had been a gross error that could have been avoided. By revealing the process whereby the United States had undertaken a mistaken commitment, the revisionists hoped to provide contemporary statesmen and diplomats of the 1930s with the knowledge and wisdom to avoid similar pitfalls in the future.

Some of the revisionists deplored America's participation on different grounds. These historians felt that war and liberal reform were incompatible. War, they argued, always sounded the death knell of domestic reform and often inaugurated periods of conservatism or reaction. The First World War, for example, had weakened if not destroyed the commitment to liberal values that had been characteristic of the Progressive era.

Such was the thesis presented by Charles A. Beard during the 1930s. Although Beard did not write specifically on Wilsonian diplomacy, he was one of the most articulate of the antiwar critics. In his book *The Open Door at Home,* which was published in 1934, as well as in testimony before congressional committees, he argued that America's strength and character had derived from its relative isolation from European power politics and chicanery. Committed to a program of liberal reform, Beard staunchly opposed America's involvement in any future European war. His position seemed to support by implication the revisionist critique of American foreign policy between 1914 and 1917, though for different reasons.[5]

By the mid-1930s the writings of the revisionist school of historians had reached a peak. Edwin Borchard and W. P. Lage in an important

---

[5]Charles A. Beard, *The Open Door at Home* (New York, 1934) and *The Devil Theory of War* (New York, 1936).

book, *Neutrality for the United States*, written in 1937, attributed American involvement in 1917 to the failure of the Wilson administration to observe recognized rules of neutrality. "There is no doubt," they wrote, "that the administration desired to see the Allies win and declined to take any action even in defense of American neutral rights which would seriously interfere with that objective. Perhaps the objective is understandable... but to suggest that the objective was consistent with the maintenance of American neutrality is a travesty of the truth. We were unneutral and we paid the price."[6]

The most mature and complete revisionist account came when Charles C. Tansill published his massive work *America Goes to War* in 1938. In writing this book, Tansill explored a huge mass of manuscript and printed material. Tansill believed that there were multiple causes for America's entry into the war: He stressed the great growth of the munitions trade with the Allies; the unneutral biases of Lansing, House, and Page; and the inability of Wilson to cope with the pressures put on him. But above all, Tansill's argument rested mainly on one premise—that the United States had no valid reason for helping the Allies and opposing Germany and that a German victory would have been a lesser evil than American participation. Reflecting the disillusionment of the 1930s and the intense desire of the nation to avoid any future conflict, Tansill's work seemed to offer conclusive evidence for support of the revisionist thesis.[7]

There were a number of historians in the 1930s, however, who took issue with the revisionist point of view. The outstanding opponent of the revisionists was Professor Charles Seymour of Yale University, who edited *The Intimate Papers of Colonel House* (4 vols., 1926–1928), published *American Diplomacy During the World War* in 1934, and *American Neutrality, 1914–1917* in 1935. Unlike the revisionists, Seymour never discussed the issue of whether or not the United States *should* have gone to war; he approached the question of America's entry into the war as a historical problem rather than a moral issue. Nor were Seymour's writings in a didactic vein; he was not concerned with the problem of how America might stay out of a future conflict. Seymour succeeded, therefore, in ridding his work of the present-mindedness that had characterized the writings of many other historians on this issue.

As a result of his approach, Seymour came to certain conclusions regarding Wilson's diplomacy that differed sharply from those of the

---

[6]Edwin Borchard and William P. Lage, *Neutrality for the United States* (New Haven, 1937), pp. 33–34.

[7]Charles C. Tansill, *America Goes to War* (Boston, 1938). For a history of revisionism see Warren I. Cohen, *The American Revisionists: The Lessons of Intervention in World War I* (Chicago, 1967).

revisionists. Seymour admitted that Wilson and his advisers were pro-English in their sympathies, but he felt that the president made a determined effort to follow the principles of international law. Indeed, Seymour pointed out, there were periods when America's relations with the Allies were far more vexatious and troublesome than those with Germany. At certain times in the course of the war, Wilson had seriously considered the possibility of imposing economic sanctions against the Allies.

Seymour's major thesis, however, was that the United States had gone to war primarily because of Germany's decision to wage unrestricted submarine warfare. If Germany was permitted to have her own way, the economic well-being of neutral nations and the lives of their citizens would have been seriously threatened. Since Wilson was unwilling to surrender to German demands, Seymour concluded, he had no alternative—given Germany's intransigence on the submarine issue—but to ask Congress for a declaration of war.

The wide range of opinion that existed among historians during the 1930s regarding America's involvement in the First World War was lucidly demonstrated in the work of Walter Millis. A graduate of Yale and an editorial writer for the New York *Herald Tribune,* Millis became interested in American diplomacy between 1914 and 1917. In 1935 he published *Road to War: America, 1914–1917,* a book that caused a stir because the author refused to pinpoint with precision the reasons why America had entered the war. That same year Millis also published an article which was more explicit. After examining the events from 1914 to 1917, Millis concluded that a conspiratorial thesis about Wilson and his advisers simply could not be proved and that the problem of causation was far more complex than anyone had imagined. In discussing the work of other historians on this problem, Millis observed that their interpretations often depended in large measure upon their starting assumptions regarding the nature of the state and upon their philosophy of international relations. "The facts of the period from 1914 to 1917," he noted, "are complex enough to support almost any theory of historical causation that one may apply to them, at the same time that they are obstinate enough to resist almost any theory of how the ultimate entanglement could have been prevented. An examination of the facts must remain as an essential foundation of any policy designed to control a similar situation in the future. Yet it is to be suspected that before the facts can be of much use there will have first to be agreement upon many profound issues as to the ends which the control should serve, the proper philosophy of international relations, the real character and objects of the state in the international and domestic complex—issues the very existence of which seems to be scarcely realized as yet by most of those participating in the current debate. They have so far confined themselves to the problem of how the nation is to avoid entanglement in

another foreign war. The far more important question of whether the
nation (whatever they may conceive that to mean) will want to avoid
entanglement has hardly even been raised."[8]

The outbreak of World War II tended to quiet for a time the debate
over the reasons for America's participation in World War I. But one
work—Walter Lippmann's *U.S. Foreign Policy: Shield of the Republic,* published in 1943–touched upon the problem and cast the issue in a different light. Lippmann argued that America had gone to war in 1917
because a German victory ultimately would have threatened the nation's
security. When Germany embarked on its campaign of unrestricted
submarine warfare, Lippmann claimed, the United States responded by
declaring war because it was unwilling to risk an Allied defeat which
would have jeopardized America's safety. Lippmann admitted that Wilson had never educated the American people to the dangers involved in
an Allied defeat nor clearly defined America's national interests. But the
events of the Second World War were demonstrating that America could
not afford to stand idly by while the rest of the Atlantic community was
overrun by aggressors. With the United States fighting a two-front war
against Germany and Japan at the time his book was published, it is not
too difficult to understand why Lippmann wrote as he did.[9]

Lippmann's work foreshadowed the position many historians were
to take in the period after 1945 as well as to suggest some of the assumptions they would make. As a result of the epochal events in world affairs
between 1933 and 1945, historians and political scientists began placing
more emphasis upon power politics and the national interest as significant factors in the shaping of international relations. This tendency was
reinforced by the increasingly important role that the United States was
playing as leader of the free world after World War II. Many argued that
America's foreign policy had to be based upon realistic rather than moral
considerations and a keen appreciation of the national interest. Viewing
America's diplomatic moves in the period prior to 1917 in these terms,
some scholars were very critical of Wilson's foreign policy. Now Wilson
began to be criticized not because America had entered the war in 1917,
but because he had never clearly defined the reasons why the country
had gone to war. His excessive moralism, some scholars claimed, prevented Wilson from defining America's national interest and placed him
at a serious disadvantage when it came to writing a treaty of peace in the
postwar period.

Such was the argument advanced by two writers, George Kennan
and Hans Morgenthau, in 1951. According to both of these scholars,
America's national interest required the preservation of a balance of

---

[8]Walter Millis, "How We Entered the Last One," *The New Republic* 83 (July 31, 1935):
323–27.

[9]Walter Lippmann, *U.S. Foreign Policy: Shield of the Republic* (Boston, 1943).

power in Europe. If one accepted this premise, the United States indeed had had a vital interest in the outcome of World War I. America's national interest made it mandatory, as Kennan put it, that the war "be brought to an end as soon as possible on a basis involving a minimum maladjustment and as much stability as possible for the future."[10] Wilson's policy, on the other hand, had been founded on precisely the opposite assumption—that one of the aims of the war was to end once and for all the balance of power concept.

What was the result of the implementation of Wilson's policy? According to Kennan and Morgenthau, it resulted in diplomatic disaster for America. Wilson's policies fatally weakened the European balance of power and thereby prepared the way for the ultimate emergence of fascism and Nazism. Germany, bitter and resentful over its treatment at Versailles, found that the breakup of its traditional institutions brought about a decade of profound social unrest; Austria-Hungary was dismembered and carved up into a series of unstable nation-states; Russia was no longer a potential ally of France to help contain German power; and England and France lay weakened by the vicissitudes of war and unable to do much to maintain world peace. Wilson's insistence upon the total destruction of German power, plus his reliance upon abstract moral principles, had isolated him from reality and caused him to embark on a mistaken policy. "If Woodrow Wilson erred," one political scientist has concluded, "it was not because he led the United States into war but because he failed to do everything in his power to prepare the people to see their entrance into a foreign war as an act consistent with imperative principles of national self-interest, as well as with national ideals and sentiments. . . . Armed intervention might well have been the wisest alternative from the long-run standpoint of American ideals and interests, but the great majority of the people did not choose war upon mature deliberation; they simply drifted into war, guided largely by impulses—some noble, some mean—with but a tenuous relation to broad and enduring national policy. Consequently, it is little wonder that the motives which led to war seemed inadequate in the perspective of peace, and that America's vaunted moral leadership revealed itself once more as the irresponsible outburst of a nation physically mature but emotionally and intellectually adolescent—a quick-tempered, good-hearted giant of a nation, moved by impulses it would later regret, undertaking commitments it would not fulfill, and never quite comprehending either the circumstances or the consequences of its erratic behavior."[11]

[10]George Kennan, *American Diplomacy 1900–1950* (Chicago, 1951), p. 66.

[11]Robert E. Osgood, *Ideals and Self-Interest in America's Foreign Relations: The Great Transformation of the Twentieth Century* (Chicago, 1953), pp. 262–63.

Realists like Morgenthau and Kennan, of course, judged Wilson in the light of their own philosophy of international relations. In one sense, their works were primarily intended to serve as a message to Americans after the Second World War. They were less interested in understanding Wilson and the dilemmas that he faced than they were in showing that America's foreign policy during the First World War had been based too much on moral grounds. Unlike the revisionists, the school of realists represented by Kennan and Morgenthau was not critical of Wilson because he had taken the United States into war; they criticized him instead because he had taken the nation into war *for the wrong reasons.*

At the same time that the realists were evaluating Wilson in terms of what he should have done, other historians were following in the footsteps of Charles Seymour. Less interested in criticizing the diplomacy of 1914 to 1917, they sought to define the issues faced by the Wilson administration, the pressures imposed upon American leaders, and how these leaders responded to such pressures. These historians did not have to deal specifically with the issue of whether the United States should have stayed out of war in 1917 or whether it should attempt to avoid any future conflicts, because the problem of American intervention did not exist in the same form as it had at the time of the First World War. The profound change in America's international role and position after 1945 made any discussion of such an issue a meaningless one. Research by these recent historians was facilitated also by two other developments. The private papers of many public officials who played an active and important part in the Wilson administration became available with the passage of time, and materials in foreign archives were placed at their disposal. As a result, these historians were able to view the problem of America's entry into the First World War in a somewhat different light than earlier writers.

The picture drawn by these historians of the 1950s and 1960s—and since they did not establish a distinct school these scholars cannot be given a specific designation—wars far more complex than that of their predecessors. Rejecting a moralistic or conspiratorial approach, they viewed Wilson as a leader confronted with a variety of pressures—pressures that limited his choices of alternative policies. They sought to understand how Wilson responded to the foreign and domestic problems that arose in rapid succession after the outbreak of war in Europe in 1914. In so doing they sketched a portrait of a wartime leader that was both tragic and sympathetic, but by no means uncritical.

Unlike the revisionists of the 1930s or the realists of the 1950s—both of whom wrote under the assumption that Wilson had considerable freedom in determining the nation's foreign policies—these more recent historians have emphasized the complexity of events following 1914. The second selection in this chapter is from Arthur S. Link's *Wilson the*

Diplomatist, which was delivered as the Albert Shaw lectures at the Johns Hopkins University in 1956. Link's writings on this problem represent one of the best examples of this recent trend in historiography. Having spent over twenty years working on a multivolumed biography of Wilson, Link had mastered virtually every important source bearing on the period from 1914 to 1917.

The picture of Wilsonian diplomacy that Link drew was anything but simple. He pointed to the many factors with which the president had to contend: the desire of most Americans to remain neutral; the pressure for continued trade, particularly with the Allies; the existence of pacifist, interventionist, and preparedness groups; the growing restrictiveness of the British maritime system; and the challenges posed by German submarine policy. Added to these problems was the fact that Wilson ardently desired to act as a mediator between the warring European powers in order to bring about a just peace. To Link, Wilson was not as simple a figure as he had been presented by the revisionists or realists. On the contrary, Wilson was a complex individual who combined both idealistic and realistic traits. Given the circumstances that he faced and the numerous pressures that were piled upon him, Link implied that Wilson had far less freedom than had been supposed in determining the course of events. Many of the major decisions were beyond his control and were made by the English and German leaders. The result was that by the spring of 1917, according to Link, Wilson reached the tragic conclusion that the United States had no alternative but to intervene once the Germans had decided to sink all vessels bound for Allied ports.

Several other historians have also argued that the range of choices open to Wilson was limited from the very beginning and that as time went on the available alternatives grew fewer and fewer. Considering that neither the Allies nor the Central Powers were willing to accept a peace without victory in 1917 and that the Germans believed that unrestricted submarine warfare could defeat the Allies before American aid became effective, Wilson had to accept either the sinking of American ships and the loss of American lives or else defend his nation's rights. Reviewing the history of this period, Ernest R. May, a Harvard historian, wrote in the late 1950s: "One has a sense that it could not have ended otherwise. . . . There was no way out. Triumph for the immoderates was only a matter of time. . . . Despite its tragic ending, the struggle [for peace] was heroic."[12]

While Link and May were explaining American involvement in the First World War in more or less tragic terms, another group of historians during the 1950s and 1960s slowly began to shift the focus of the debate

---

[12]Ernest R. May, *The World War and American Isolation 1914–1917* (Cambridge, 1959), p. 437.

so as to take into account what they regarded as the basic ideological framework that governed the formulation of foreign policy. Their thesis, in its most simple form, rested on the premise that foreign and domestic policy were intimately entwined, and that the former reflected the latter. According to these scholars, many Americans—partly as a consequence of the depressions of the 1880s and 1890s—had come to the conclusion that foreign markets were indispensable for the economic well-being of the United States. Such markets would help to avoid the internal problems arising out of the economic stagnation associated with surplus productive capacity. The result was a fundamental shift in the direction of American foreign policy. American policymakers adopted what became known as the Open Door policy—an open door "through which America's preponderant economic strength would enter and dominate all underdeveloped areas of the world. . . . the Open Door Policy was in fact a brilliant strategic stroke which led to the gradual extension of American economic and political power throughout the world."[13] Much of twentieth-century American diplomacy, therefore, was directed largely toward the goal of assuring America's economic supremacy.

Such an interpretation reflected in part the rising disillusionment with American society that originated in the late 1950s and grew in intensity during the 1960s. The argument that American diplomacy was based less on altruism and idealism and more on a desire to safeguard an international order that made possible economic supremacy, of course, had major implications for contemporary concerns. For example, the Cold War, rather than resting on a moral foundation that pitted freedom against communism, was actually a product of America's continued insistence on structuring a world order along lines that preserved its capitalist hegemony. Thus American foreign policy—which grew out of its domestic institutions and policies—was responsible in large measure for initiating and perpetuating the Cold War and causing the Vietnam conflict. The most extreme statements of this thesis came from New Left historians such as Gabriel Kolko, whose previous work on early-twentieth-century progressivism had provided a hostile analysis of American society.[14] Nevertheless, a number of scholars, including William Appleman Williams, Walter LaFeber, and Lloyd C. Gardner,

---

[13]William Appleman Williams, *The Tragedy of American Diplomacy*, rev. ed. (New York, 1962), pp. 37–38. For similar points of view see Walter LaFeber, *The New Empire: An Interpretation of American Expansionism 1860–1898* (Ithaca, 1963), *America, Russia, and the Cold War 1945–1966* (New York, 1967); and Lloyd C. Gardner, "American Foreign Policy 1900–1921: A Second Look at the Realist Critique of American Diplomacy," in *Towards a New Past: Dissenting Essays in American History*, edited by Barton J. Bernstein (New York, 1968), pp. 202–31.

[14]Gabriel Kolko, *The Politics of War: The World and United States Foreign Policy, 1943–1945* (New York, 1968).

rejected both the conspiracy framework and some of the ideological presuppositions of the New Left.

Because revisionist scholars tended to be concerned with the sweep of American diplomacy, they produced no major reinterpretation of the problem of American entry into World War I. Yet in an analysis of Woodrow Wilson and world politics, N. Gordon Levin, Jr., argued that "Wilsonians laid the foundations of a modern American foreign policy whose main thrust, from 1917 on, may be characterized as an effort to construct a stable world order of liberal-capitalist internationalism, at the Center of the global ideological spectrum, safe from both the threat of imperialism on the Right and the danger of Revolution on the Left."[15] While Levin did not argue that the United States went to war in 1917 for economic reasons directly, he did imply that Wilsonian ideology, with its interest in a world order conducive to American economic interests, helped set the stage for America's participation in World War I.

Other scholars rejected the New Left interpretation of diplomatic history. Daniel M. Smith, for example, emphasized the importance of national interest in Wilson's mind when he made the decision for war. By 1917, according to Smith, Wilson feared that a probable German victory would upset the balance of power. Although he did not believe that a German victory would pose an immediate threat to American security, he did believe "that such a result would endanger his idealistic hopes for a just peace and the founding of a new and stable world order. He referred to Germany as a madman who must be restrained. He finally accepted the necessity for actively entering the war, it would appear, with the submarine as the precipitant, only because he believed that larger reasons of national prestige, economic interests, and future security so demanded, and above all because of his commitment to the cause of an enduring world peace."[16] Ross Gregory, on the other hand, denied that Wilson believed that a German victory was imminent, nor did he go to war to protect American security, if only because he did not see it in jeopardy. Wilson did go to war, Gregory concluded, to protect "American honor, rights, and general interest—for both moral and practical reasons. He saw no contradictions between the two. But Wilson's idea of right and interest grew out of what the nation was at the time, and the First World War made clear what had been true for some years: the United States was in all respects a part of the world, destined to profit from its riches and suffer from its woes."[17]

[15]N. Gordon Levin, Jr., *Woodrow Wilson and World Politics: America's Response to War and Revolution* (New York, 1968), p. 1.

[16]Daniel M. Smith, *The Great Departure: The United States and World War I, 1914–1920* (New York, 1965), p. 82. See also Smith's "National Interest and American Intervention, 1917: An Historical Reappraisal," *Journal of American History*, 52 (June 1965): 5–24.

[17]Ross Gregory, *The Origins of American Intervention in the First World War* (New York, 1971), p. 139.

In surveying the extensive literature covering America's entry into World War I, one is struck by the fact that the attitude taken by different generations toward war itself has played a significant role in determining the approach scholars have adopted in evaluating Wilson's diplomacy. The revisionists of the 1930s were persuaded that the United States had little to gain by foreign entanglements; thus they tended to project their beliefs back to the period from 1914 to 1917. War was the great enemy of progress, and in their eyes Wilson was either a dupe at best or part of an evil conspiracy. The realists of the 1950s, on the other hand, felt that war and the use of force was an integral part of the prevailing international system. Their criticism of Wilson, therefore, was not that he took the nation to war, but that he did not make clear why the national interests of the United States required this action. Even historians like Arthur S. Link and Ernest R. May—neither of whom was within the realist tradition—looked upon war as part of the tragic human condition; they emphasized the limitations of political leaders in dealing with international problems. Revisionists and New Left scholars of the 1960s and 1970s tended to see war as an outgrowth of America's concern with economic supremacy; either directly or indirectly, their historical contributions allocated a large share of the blame for the tragic events of the twentieth century to American foreign policy.

As long as Americans continue to debate the proper role of their nation in world affairs, the events from 1914 to 1917 will continue to hold interest for historians. In studying this problem, historians will continue to raise many of the same questions that their predecessors asked for nearly half a century. Should the United States have gone to war in 1917? Was America's national interest threatened by Germany? Did American involvement arise out of its unneutral policies, its misguided sentimentalism and utopianism, and its desire to maintain the integrity of the Atlantic community? Or was its true interest to preserve the balance of power in Europe? Was America's singular concern with a world order that was conducive to its economic interests responsible for the breakdown of neutrality between 1914 and 1917? These remain, in one form or another, the questions that will continue to be the object of future debate.

Harry Elmer Barnes

HARRY ELMER BARNES (1889–1968) taught at Clark University, Smith College, and the New School for Social Research. He was the author or more than a dozen books in history and sociology and was also considered to be one of the founders of World War I and World War II historical revisionism.

The United States could not have been more perfectly set up for neutrality than it was in July and August 1914. President Woodrow Wilson was a lifelong and deeply conscientious pacifist. His convictions in this matter were not emotional or impressionistic, but had been based upon deep study and prolonged reflection. Moreover, he was married to a woman noted for pacific sentiments and firm convictions on such matters. She strongly backed up her husband in his pacific beliefs and policies. As Secretary of State, we had in William Jennings Bryan the world's outstanding pacifist. His pacifism was notably courageous; he was willing to stick by his guns even in the face of malicious criticism.

Moreover, Wilson was almost uniquely well informed as to the essentials of the European situation before war broke out in the summer of 1914. He had sent his personal representative, Colonel Edward M. House, to Europe to study the international situation and to report to him upon it. Whatever his later mistakes, Colonel House sized up matters in Europe with almost perfect sagacity and understanding in May 1914. He concluded his observations with the statement that "whenever England consents, France and Russia will close in on Germany."

If one were to summarize, as briefly as this, the outcome of the years of scholarly study since 1918, with respect to responsibility for the World War, a more perfect estimate and verdict than Colonel House's phrase could not be rendered in the same number of words. Further, the colonel pointed out that whatever the Kaiser's emotional shortcomings he wished for European peace. On the other hand, he stated candidly that George V of England was "the most pugnacious monarch loose in these parts."

When war broke out, President Wilson's statements were a model of neutral procedure. He issued a formally correct neutrality proclamation

---

Harry Elmer Barnes, "The World War of 1914–1918," in Willard Waller, ed., *War in the Twentieth Century* (New York: The Dryden Press, 1940), pp. 71–82, 96–98. Reprinted by permission of Harry Elmer Barnes.

and went on to exhort his countrymen to be neutral in thought as well as in action. There is no doubt that he was completely neutral at heart in August 1914. Less than three years later, however, in April 1917, he went before Congress and told its members that "God helping her," this country could do no other than make war on Germany. Moreover, he returned from the Capitol to the White House and made statements to his secretary, Joseph P. Tumulty, indicating that, at the time of his war message, he had so far changed his attitude that he could not believe he ever had been neutral. He cited with approval an article by the correspondent of the *Manchester Guardian* stating that Mr. Wilson had always been sympathetic with the Allies and had wished to throw this country into war on their side just as soon as circumstances would permit.

We shall first briefly consider some of the reasons why Wilson altered his point of view, since no other set of circumstances could alone have forced us into the war, if Wilson had not been favorable to our entry by the spring of 1917.

First and foremost, we must take into account the fact that Wilson's intellectual perspective was predominantly Anglo-Saxon. He had little knowledge of, or sympathy with, continental European culture and institutions. His great intellectual heroes were such English writers as John Milton, John Locke, Adam Smith, and Walter Bagehot. He did his graduate work in the Johns Hopkins University Seminar under Herbert Baxter Adams, where the "Anglo-Saxon myth" reigned supreme. Wilson was a presistent student and admirer of the English constitution and frankly regarded the British system of government as superior to our own.

Then Wilson had in his cabinet and among his ambassadors men who were intensely pro-English or pro-Ally in their sympathies. Such were Secretaries Lindley M. Garrison and David F. Houston. Walter Hines Page, our ambassador in London, was even more intensely pro-English than Wilson. Indeed, he frequently went to such excesses as to annoy the president. When Bryan was succeeded by Robert Lansing, the most crucial post in the cabinet went to another vehemently pro-English sympathizer. The biases of Page and Lansing made it difficult to pursue forthright diplomacy with Great Britain.

Another major difficulty lay in the fact that President Wilson and Secretary Lansing did not formulate and execute a fair and consistent line of diplomatic procedure. They had one type of international law for England and the Allies, and quite another for Germany. They all but allowed Great Britain to run wild in the violation of international law and of our neutral rights, while they insisted on holding Germany "to strict accountability."

England started out in 1914 by making a scrap of paper out of the Declaration of London governing contraband in wartime. Next, we proceeded to allow her to make use of armed belligerent merchantmen as if they were peaceful commercial vessels. England violated our neutral rights far more extensively between 1914 and 1917 than she did before the War of 1812, even to the point of flying the American flag.

Wilson came to believe, however, that Great Britain was fighting for civilization and that so trivial a thing as international law must not be allowed to stand in her way. Wilson's attorney general, Thomas W. Gregory, tells of the rebuke which the president administered to certain cabinet members when they protested over the flagrant British violation of our neutral rights: "After patiently listening, Mr. Wilson said, in that quiet way of his, that the ordinary rules of conduct had no application to the situation; that the Allies were standing with their backs to the wall, fighting wild beasts; that he would permit nothing to be done by our country to hinder or embarrass them in the prosecution of the war unless admitted rights were grossly violated, and that this policy must be understood as settled." Bryan protested against our unfair and un-neutral diplomacy and ultimately resigned because he could not square his conscience with it.

Secretary Lansing admits in his *Memoirs* that he made no real pretense of holding England to the tenets of international law. He tells us that after the sinking of the *Lusitania* he thought we should be fighting on the side of the Allies and that he was determined to do nothing which would prove embarrassing to us when we later took up our position as a military comrade of the Allied powers. He persisted in this attitude, even though he was honest enough to write after the war that in 1917 we had as good, if not better, legal grounds for fighting Britain as for fighting Germany.

Ambassador Page even went so far as to collaborate with Sir Edward Grey in answering the protests of his own government, an unparalleled procedure which, when revealed, outraged even so pro-Ally a journal as the *New York Times*.

We thus encouraged and perpetuated the illegally extensive British blockade, which provoked the German submarine warfare. In time, we made war on the latter, though it was our unneutral diplomacy which contributed, in large part, to the continuance of both the British blockade and the German submarine activities.

Wilson was deeply affected by the criticisms to which he was subjected by prominent Americans sympathetic with the Allies and in favor of intervention on their side. He was stung by the famous speeches of Theodore Roosevelt on "The Shadows of Shadow Lawn," and by the latter's reference to Wilson's diplomatic statements as examples of "weasel words." He was particularly annoyed by the statement of Elihu Root that "first he shakes his fist and then he shakes his finger."

On the other hand, Wilson was human enough to take note of the praise which was showered upon him by the press when he made a bellicose statement or led a preparedness parade. This contrasted sharply with the bitter criticism he evoked when he made a statesmanlike remark, such as that a country might be "too proud to fight," or that the only desirable peace would be "a peace without victory."

Wilson was also profoundly moved by the British propaganda relative to German atrocities and territorial ambitions. This was particularly true after Lord Bryce lent his name to the prestige and veracity of the propaganda stories as to German savagery. Of all living Englishmen, Bryce was probably the man whom Wilson most admired and trusted. When Bryce sponsored the propaganda lies, Wilson came to believe that they must have a substantial basis in fact. This helped on his rationalization that England was fighting the battle of human civilization against wild beasts.

Personal matters also played their role in the transformation of Wilson's attitude. His first wife died and a strong pacific influence was removed. He then courted and married a dashing widow who was sympathetic with the Allied side and friendly with Washington military and naval circles. She was also bitterly resentful of the criticism to which Wilson was subjected on account of his refusal to be stampeded into intervention. She appears to have wished him to take a stronger stand for intervention. The domestic influence on the president was, thus, completely transformed in character as a result of his second marriage. The publication of Mrs. Wilson's *Memoirs* does not make it necessary to modify this statement.

When, as an outcome of these various influences, Wilson had been converted to intervention, he rationalized his change of attitude on the basis of a noble moral purpose. As he told Jane Addams in the spring of 1917, he felt that the United States must be represented at the peace conference which would end the World War if there was to be any hope of a just and constructive peace. But Wilson could be at the peace conference only if the United States had previously entered the World War.

It is still asserted by many writers, such as Professor Charles Seymour, that the resumption of submarine warfare by Germany was the sole reason for Wilson's determination to enter the war on the Allied side. But we know that he had been converted to intervention long before January 1917. A year earlier, he had sent Colonel House to Europe with a plan to put us in the war on the side of the Allies if Germany would not accept peace terms obviously unfavorable to her. But even such peace terms for Germany were rejected by the British leaders who felt sure of American aid anyway and were determined to crush Germany. Yet this British rebuff did not lead Wilson to lose heart in his efforts to put his country into the war.

His next step was taken in this country. Early in April 1916, Wilson

called into consultation Speaker Champ Clark of the House of Representatives and congressional leaders Claude Kitchin and H. D. Flood, and
sounded them out to see if they would support him in a plan to bring the
United States into the war on the side of the Allies. This was the famous
"Sunrise Conference" described later by Gilson Gardner in *McNaught's
Monthly* of June 1925. These men sharply refused to sanction any such
policy, and Wilson allowed the campaign of 1916 to be fought out on the
slogan, "He kept us out of war." Wilson did not dare to risk splitting the
Democratic party over entry into the war before the campaign of 1916
had successfully ended. The existence of the Sunrise Conference has
been fully verified by Professor A. M. Arnett in his scholarly book on
Claude Kitchin.

Wilson was convinced after the failure of the Sunrise Conference that
there was no hope of getting the country into war until after the election.
The sentiment of the nation was for peace. If he was elected as an
exponent of peace and then went into war the country as a whole would
believe that he had done his best to "keep us out of war." He would
have a united country behind him. Hence, he and Colonel House sent
Governor Martin Glynn of New York and Senator Ollie James of Ken-
tucky to the Democratic National Convention at St. Louis, in June 1916,
with instructions to make keynote speeches emphasizing Wilson's
heroic efforts to keep us out of war.

Thus was fashioned the famous slogan "He kept us out of war,"
which reelected Woodrow Wilson to the presidency almost a year after
Colonel House, following Wilson's directions, had declared that: "The
United States would like Great Britain to do whatever would help the
United States to aid the Allies."

The campaign and election of 1916 was a very real referendum on
war, and the people voted against war. This is illuminating as an illustration of the fallacy that a war referendum, such as the Ludlow Amendment, would, by itself alone, suffice to keep us out of war, but the
election of 1916 does offer definite proof that Wilson was not pushed
into war by popular demand.

The influence exerted by American finance upon our entry into the
World War has been revealed in Ray Stannard Baker's *Life and Letters of
Woodrow Wilson*, in the volumes of the Nye armament investigation, and
in Professor C. C. Tansill's *America Goes to War*.

At the outset, the international bankers were not by any means all
pro-Ally. Some, like the Morgan firm, were pro-British, and had been
for years, while others, like Kuhn, Loeb and Company, manned chiefly
by men of German derivation, were pro-German. But the financial
interests of all the bankers soon came to be pro-Ally, for credit and loans
to Germany were discouraged, while large loans were presently being
made to the Allied powers.

On August 15, 1914, at the beginning of the war, Bryan declared against loans to any belligerent, on the ground that credit is the basis of all forms of contraband. President Wilson backed him up. For the time being, his position did not operate seriously against the Allies, for the balance of trade and investment was against the United States, and the Allied countries could pay for their purchases by canceling the debts owed abroad by Americans. This situation took care of matters for a few months. But Allied war purchases became so great that, by the autumn of 1914, there was a credit crisis. The National City Bank addressed Robert Lansing, then counselor of the State Department, on this matter on October 23, 1914. Short-term credits to European governments were advocated. Lansing talked the matter over with President Wilson at once, and the latter agreed that the government would not interfere with such an arrangement. This information was transmitted orally to Willard Straight of J. P. Morgan and Company at the Metropolitan Club in Washington on the same night.

Shortly afterwards, H. P. Davison of the Morgan firm went to England and signed a contract to become the British purchasing agent in America. A similar contract was soon made with France.

The short-term loans sufficed for some months, but by the summer of 1915 Allied buying had become so extensive that the bankers saw that they must float loans here for the Allied countries if the latter were to continue to buy American munitions on a large scale. So they made strong representations to Colonel House and to the secretary of the treasury, W. G. McAdoo.

On August 21, 1915, McAdoo wrote a long letter to President Wilson, pointing out that great prosperity had come to the country as a result of the sale of munitions to the Allies, but that this prosperity could not continue unless we financed it through open loans to the Allies—i.e. selling Allied bonds in our own financial markets.

On September 6, 1915, Secretary Lansing argued similarly in a letter to President Wilson, stressing the crisis that faced American business if the earlier ruling of Bryan and the President on American loans to belligerents was not rescinded. Colonel House supported this position. McAdoo and Lansing won their point. On September 8, 1915, Wilson assented to loans and the Morgan firm was once more given oral information. Very soon, the first public loan, the $500 million Anglo-French loan, was floated.

The formal loans to the Allies—over $2.5 billion in all—financed their purchases for a little over a year, but their buying was so heavy that even the great investment banking houses could not take care of their needs. By January, 1917, the Allies had overdrawn their credit by nearly $500 million. Only Uncle Sam could save the great banking houses and the Allies. And Uncle Sam could help only if the United States were at war with Germany. We could not, as a government, lend money to a belligerent, unless we were at war with its enemy.

Just at this time the Germans renewed their unrestricted submarine warfare. The United States could now be led into the war, and the bankers would be repaid. They were repaid to the last cent. When the war was over, Mr. Thomas W. Lamont, of J. P. Morgan and Company, stated the facts relative to the attitude of his firm toward the World War and the belligerent powers:

> At the request of certain of the foreign governments the firm of Messrs. J. P. Morgan and Company undertook to co-ordinate the requirements of the Allies, and then to bring about regularity and promptness in fulfilling these requirements. Those were the days when American citizens were being urged to remain neutral in action, in word, and even in thought. But our firm had never for one moment been neutral: we didn't know how to be. From the very start we did everything we could to contribute to the cause of the Allies. And this particular work had two effects: one in assisting the Allies in the production of goods and munitions in America necessary to the Allies' vigorous prosecution of the war; the other in helping to develop the great and profitable export trade that our country has had.

Most American industrialists naturally shared the attitude of the bankers. Since England controlled the seas, our sales were mainly to the Allied powers. We wished to see the Allies continue the war and win it. Upon their purchases depended most of our sales and prosperity, and upon their success and solvency depended the prospect of their being able to pay us in the end. The trade in munitions carried us from a depression in 1914 to boom years in 1915 and 1916.

By abandoning his neutral financial and industrial policy in favor of the Allies, President Wilson made it possible for the Entente Powers to enjoy an enormous advantage over the Central Powers in getting war supplies. The only way for the Central Powers to overcome it was to resume unlimited submarine warfare and try to sweep from the seas the ships that were carrying these supplies to the Allies.

It was our unneutral financing of the Allies that led to the resumption of German submarine warfare, and it was the resumption of this warfare which furnished the "incident" that enabled the war party in this country to put us into the conflict, It is, thus, perfectly clear that economic and financial pressure was the crucial factor which led us into war in 1917.

But no one need hold that President Wilson was moved primarily by any tender sentiments for the bankers. Both McAdoo and Lansing argued that it was essential to American prosperity to finance the Allies.

It was this general consideration of continued prosperity in 1915 to 1916, and the relation of this to the prospects of the Democratic party in the election of 1916, rather than any direct banker pressure on the White House, that bore in on Wilson's consciousness in the late summer of 1915, when he let down the gates to financing the Allies.

Yet, it is downright silly to contend that the bankers had no influence on Wilson's policy. If he did not listen to the bankers himself, he did listen very attentively to those who did heed banker pressure, namely, McAdoo, Lansing, and House.

The active campaign for American preparedness and intervention was engineered by leaders of the war cult in the United States, such men as Theodore Roosevelt, Leonard Wood, Henry Cabot Lodge, "Gus" Gardiner, and the like. They led in the preparedness movement, the Plattsburg camp episode, and other steps designed to stimulate the martial spirit in America. The newspapers warmly supported this movement because of the circulation appeal which preparedness material supplied.

While there were notable exceptions, the majority of our newspapers were pro-Ally and pro-interventionist. Many of them were honestly sympathetic with the Allies. Others were deeply influenced by Allied propaganda. Some were heavily subsidized by the Allies. Still others were bought outright by Allied interests. Moreover, the Allies supplied all American newspapers with a vast amount of war-news material always favorable to the Allied cause. The newspapers also had a natural affinity for the bankers and industrialists who were their chief advertising clients. Finally, the newspapers were not unaware of the enormous circulation gains and increased advertising revenue which would follow our entry into the World War.

In the matter of propaganda the Allies had a notable advantage. They controlled the seas, the cables, and other means of communication. The Germans had only one crude and temporary wireless contact with the United States. Further, Allied propaganda was far better organized and more lavishly supported. It was also much more adroit than the German. As a result, a majority of Americans were led to believe in the veracity of the great batch of atrocity lies relative to the German invasion of Belgium, submarine warfare, and the like. This was particularly true after Lord Bryce put the force of his name and prestige behind the authenticity of such tales. Lord Northcliffe, who was in charge of British propaganda, in moments of unusual candor, stated that the Americans proved more gullible in such matters than any other people except the Chinese, and called us "a bunch of sheep."

The ministers of the gospel also joined heartily in the great crusade to put us into the World War. Lining up behind such a stalwart as Newell Dwight Hillis, they preached a veritable holy war. They represented the Allies as divinely-anointed promoters of international decency and justice and the Central Powers as the servants of evil and the agents of savagery.

The net result of all this was that we entered the World War in April 1917. We did so, even though there was no clear legal or moral basis for our so doing. If there ever was an instance in which the facts were clearly in accord with a neutrality policy it was in the spring of 1917. We should have fought both Germany and Britain or else neither. But the country went into war, with most of the citizens of the United States feeling that our self-respect and national honor demanded it. No other course seemed open to us. . . .

It was generally believed in 1917 and thereafter that the intervention of the United States in the World War on the side of the Allies saved human civilization. It was lauded as one of the most noble and fortunate episodes in the history of man on the planet. Today, there is a great deal of skepticism about any such judgment. There is a tendency now to see in American intervention one of the major calamities in modern history—a calamity for the Allies and the United States as well as for the Central Powers.

Let us assume the worst possible result of American neutrality in 1917 to 1918. If we had not gone into the war the worst imaginable result would have been a German victory. But no sane person can very well conceive that the world would be any worse off today if the Germans had won under the Hohenzollerns.

We used to picture the horrors of a Germany and a Europe dominated by the crown prince and his followers. But, compared to Hitler, Mussolini, and company, the crown prince and his crowd now appear to be cultivated gentlemen, urbane democrats, and sincere pacifists. A more warlike world than the present could hardly have been created as a result of German victory, and certainly the economic situation in Europe since 1918 would have been far better under a Europe dominated by monarchist Germany.

But there is hardly a remote possibility that Germany would have won the war, even if the United States had not come in on the side of the Allies. Germany was eager to negotiate a fair peace arrangement at the time when Lloyd George's "knock-out victory" interview with Roy Howard put an end to all prospect of successful negotiations. We now know that the Lloyd George outburst was directly caused by his assurance that the United States was surely coming in on the side of the Allies. Had Wilson remained strictly neutral, there is little doubt that sincere peace negotiations would have been actively carried on by the summer of 1916.

There is every reason to believe that the result of American neutrality throughout the European conflict would have been the "peace without victory," which Woodrow Wilson described in his most statesmanlike pronouncement during the period of the World War. We would have had a negotiated peace treaty made by relative equals. This would not have been a perfect document but it would certainly have been far superior to the Treaty of Versailles.

Had we remained resolutely neutral from the beginning, the

negotiated peace would probably have saved the world from the last two terrible years of war. Whenever it came, it would have rendered unnecessary the brutal blockade of Germany for months after the World War, a blockade which starved to death hundreds of thousands of German women and children. This blockade was the one great authentic atrocity of the World War period. In all probability, the neutrality of the United States would also have made impossible the rise of Mussolini and Hitler—products of postwar disintegration—and the coming of a second world war.

Not only was our entry into the World War a calamity of the first magnitude for Europe and contemporary civilization, it was also a serious disaster for the United States.

During the first Wilson administration an impressive program of social reform had been introduced, widely known as the New Freedom. Had this continued until March 1921, enormous and permanent improvements might have been made in the political and economic system of the United States. But when Wilson allowed himself to be slowly but surely pushed into war, the New Freedom perished overnight. Reaction and intolerance settled down on the country. Some of those who had earlier warmly supported Wilson's domestic policies were thrown into prison, and many others were bitterly persecuted.

The myth of a German menace and the crusading sanctity of the Allies was exploded by Wilson himself shortly before his death. On December 7, 1923, he told his friend James Kerney: "I should like to see Germany clean up France, and I should like to see Jusserand and tell him so to his face."

Arthur S. Link

ARTHUR S. LINK (1920–   ) is professor of American history at Princeton University. He is the author of many books on the Wilsonian era, including a multivolume biography of Woodrow Wilson. Link is also editor of Wilson's papers.

For Woodrow Wilson and the American people, who had a positive disinclination to play the game of power politics, events on the international stage intruded in an ironic, if fateful way from 1914 to 1917. By the spring of 1915 the United States was the only great power not directly involved in the war then raging from western Europe to the Far East. Desiring only to deal fairly with both sides and to avoid military involvement, the president soon found that neutrality, as well as war, has its perplexities and perils.

The way in which Wilson met the challenges to America's peace and security raised by the death grapple between the opposing alliances has never been fully explained, notwithstanding scores of books and articles. Too often, historians, in company with public men, have looked for culprits instead of facts. Too often they have misunderstood the facts even when they found them. Too often they have written as if Wilson and his advisers made policy in a vacuum independent of the interplay of conflicting pressures. If we can see the president's policies of neutrality in the light of his convictions and objectives, the pressures and events (both domestic and foreign) that bore constantly upon him, and the alternatives between which he was often forced to choose—if we can do this, then perhaps we will see that his task in foreign policy at this juncture was not as simple as it has sometimes been described.

Among the most pervasive pressures controlling Wilson's decisions throughout the period 1914 to 1917 were the attitudes and opinions of the American people concerning the war and America's proper relation to it. . . .

The dominant American sentiment throughout the period of nonintervention can be summarily characterized by the single adjective "neutral." This is not to say that Americans had no opinions on the merits of the war and the claims of the opposing alliances, or that there were no

From Arthur S. Link, *Wilson the Diplomatist* (Baltimore: Johns Hopkins Press, 1957), pp. 31–33, 35–50, 73–74, 82, 85–90. Reprinted by permission of the Johns Hopkins Press.

differences among the popular reactions. It is simply to state the fairly obvious fact that the preponderant majority, whose opinions played a decisive role in shaping Wilson's policies, did not believe that their interests and security were vitally involved in the outcome of the war and desired to avoid participation, if that were possible without sacrificing rights that should not be yielded. The prevalence and astounding vitality of neutralism, in spite of the severest provocations and all the efforts of propagandists on both sides, formed at once the unifying principle of American politics and the compelling reality with which Wilson had to deal from 1914 to 1917.

On the other hand, it would be a large error to imply that Wilson was a prisoner of the public opinion of the majority, and that his will to adopt sterner policies toward one group of belligerents or the other was paralyzed by the stronger counterforce of neutralism. Actually, the evidence points overwhelmingly to the conclusion that Wilson personally shared the opinions of the majority, in brief, that he was substantially neutral in attitude, and that his policies were controlled as much by his own convictions as by the obvious wishes of the people. . . .

All authorities, whether friendly or hostile to Wilson, would agree that the acid tests of his neutrality were the policies that he worked out and applied vis-à-vis the British from 1914 to 1917. He has been most condemned by that group of historians highly censorious of his policies, generally known as revisionists, on this score—for becoming the captive of pro-Allied influences within his administration, for condoning such sweeping British control of neutral commerce that the Germans were forced to resort to drastic countermeasures, for permitting American prosperity to become dependent upon loans and exports to the Allies, in short, for permitting a situation to develop that made it inevitable that the United States would go to war if the success of Allied arms was ever seriously threatened.

Like most fallacious arguments, this one contains a certain element of plausibility. Wilson did condone a far-reaching British maritime system. American neutrality did work greatly to the benefit of the Allies. The error arises in saying that these things occurred because Wilson and his advisers necessarily wanted them to occur. . . .

In view of the prevailing American sentiment at the outbreak of the war, a policy of strict official neutrality was the only possible course for the United States government. This fact prompted the president's official proclamations of neutrality, supplemented by his appeal to the American people for impartiality in thought; the subsequent working out by the State Department of the elaborate technical rules to preserve American neutrality; and the establishment of a Joint State and Navy Neutrality Board to advise the various departments upon the correct interpretation of international law.

One cannot read the records revealing how these policies were formulated without being convinced that their authors were high-minded in their determination to be fair to both sides. Indeed, Wilson and the man who chiefly influenced him in the formulation of the rules of neutrality, Secretary of State Bryan, were so intent upon being fair to the Germans that they adopted policies during the first months of war that were highly disadvantageous to the British, if not unneutral. One was to prevent the sale of submarine parts, and hence parts for any naval craft, by a private American firm to the British government, on the ground that such a sale would be "contrary to . . . strict neutrality." Wilson persisted in supporting Bryan in this matter, in spite of advice from Counselor Lansing and the Joint Neutrality Board to the effect that their position was contrary to international law.

Infinitely more damaging to the Allies was the administration's second effort to lean over backward in being "strictly," neutral—the ban of loans by American bankers to the belligerent governments that the president permitted Bryan to impose in August 1914. From a technical viewpoint, the ban was not unneutral, but it was highly prejudicial to the Allies because its effect was potentially to deny them their otherwise legal right to purchase supplies in the American market. These two incidents are not to be understood as revealing any anti-British bias on the part of Wilson and Bryan, although British officials at the time were convinced that they did. I mention them only to show what an important role the administration's desire to be impartial played in the formation of policies vis-à-vis the British during the early period of American neutrality.

The other pressure shaping American policies at this time was the force of combined demands at home for the virtually free transit of American ships and goods to the European neutrals and the belligerent Central Powers. So powerful were these demands, especially from cotton growers and exporters and their spokesmen in Congress, that Wilson personally sponsored two measures highly disadvantageous to the British and unneutral in fact as well as in spirit. One was a change in the ship registry law, put into effect by an act approved August 18, 1914, which made it easy for German or other foreign shipping firms to take out American registry for their vessels. The other was a plan to establish a federal corporation to purchase German ships in American ports and to use them to carry supplies to the belligerents, particularly to Germany. Wilson applied heavy pressure to obtain congressional approval of this, the so-called ship-purchase bill, during the short term from December 1914, to March 1915; he failed only because of a stout senatorial filibuster.

In negotiations with the British government during the early months of the war, Wilson fought hard in response to domestic pressures to keep the channels of international commerce open to American ships and goods. He did not go as far in defense of neutral rights as some of his predecessors, but he did suggest a code so sweeping that an enforcement of it would have meant almost total destruction of the British system of maritime controls. Specifically, the president first proposed on August 6, 1914, that the belligerents adopt the rules of naval warfare laid down in the Declaration of London of 1909, a convention never ratified by Great Britain or the United States, which permitted the free transit of all goods except those obviously contraband. When the British rejected this suggestion, the president came back on October 16, proposing a compromise that would have still seriously impaired the effectiveness of British sea power. When this effort also failed, Wilson then announced that his government would assert and defend all its rights under international law and treaties.

I have described these policies and proposals because they so clearly reveal Wilson's neutral intentions and what he would have done in matters of trade had he been able to make the rules himself. But he obviously could not follow his personal preferences alone or respond only to domestic pressures. In seeking to assert and defend American neutral rights he ran head-on into a reality as important as the reality of the pressures at home. It was the British determination to use sea power to prevent American ships and goods from going to the sustenance of the German economy and military forces.

British assumption of a nearly absolute control of the seas washing western Europe began with relatively mild measures in August 1914, and culminated in the suppression of virtually all commerce to the Central Powers in March 1915. For the British, this was not a question of adhering to the laws of blockade or of violating them, or of doing things merely to be nice to American friends. It was a question of achieving their supreme objective, to deprive their enemies of vital raw materials and goods, without risking the alienation of the United States. The controlling fact for the British was the necessity of preserving American friendship in order to assure the uninterrupted rhythm of the North Atlantic trade. . . .

The crucial question all along, therefore, was whether the United States, the only neutral power strong enough to successfully challenge the British measures, would acquiesce or resist to the point of threatening or using force. The American response during the formative period of neutrality was, in brief, to accept the British system and to limit action against it to a vigorous assertion of American legal rights for future adjudication. All this is too well known to require any further exposition. What is not so well understood are the reasons why Wilson and his advisers acquiesced in a solution that denied the objectives that they and a large segment of the American public demanded. These reasons may be briefly summarized as follows:

First, the British maritime system, in spite of American allegations to the contrary, enjoyed the advantage of being legitimate and usually legal, or nearly so, by traditional criteria. It was legitimate rather than fraudulent, and legal rather than capricious or terroristic, in its major aspects because the British did in fact hold undisputed sea supremacy and were therefore able to execute their controls in an orderly fashion. In asserting their own rights, the Americans could not well deny the advantages that accrued to the British by virtue of their sea power. The British, for example, had an undoubted right to establish a blockade of the Central Powers, and the American attempt to persuade the London government to use techniques effective only in the days of the sailing ship did not have much cogency in the twentieth century.

Second, much of the success of the British in establishing their control depended upon the way in which they went about it. Had they instituted their total blockade at the outset of the war, the American reaction would undoubtedly have been violent. Instead, the British applied their controls gradually, with a careful eye upon American opinion, using the opportunities provided by recurrent crises in German-American relations to institute their severest measures.

Third, the British were careful never to offend so many American interests at one time that retaliation would have been inevitable, or any single interest powerful enough by itself to compel retaliation. . . .

Fourth, there was great significance in the language and symbolism that the British Foreign Office used in defending the measures of the Admiralty and Ministry of Blockade. By justifying their maritime system in terms of international law and the right of retaliation, and (at least before the summer of 1916) by making an honest effort to meet American objections halfway when possible, the British made it almost inevitable that the Washington authorities would have to reply in the same language, thus giving a purely *legal* character to the issues involved and for the most part avoiding raising the issues of sovereignty and inherent national rights. The significance of this achievement can be seen in the conviction of Wilson and the majority of Americans that the Anglo-American disputes did involve only property rights, which should be vindicated only by an appeal to much-controverted international law. Moreover, by appealing to the American government and people in the name of friendship and by always professing their devotion to the cause of humanity, the British succeeded in evoking strong feelings of sympathy and understanding on the other side of the water.

Finally, the British were able partially to justify their own blockade measures as legitimate adaptations to a changing technology by pointing to precedents established by the Washington government itself during the American Civil War. To be sure, the British drew some incorrect analogies (as Lansing pointed out) between American and British practice; even so, their main contention—that the American government had also stretched the rules of blockade to allow for technological changes—was essentially correct.

Wilson's refusal to challenge the British maritime system, in short, to break the British blockade, was almost inevitable in view of the facts we have just reviewed, *if the president's objective was simply to maintain as best he could the neutral position of the United States.* An absolute neutrality was, in any event, impossible because of the total character of the war and America's importance in the world economy. It often happened that any action by the United States inevitably conferred a benefit on one side and thereby injured the other, at least indirectly. In these circumstances, neutrality often consisted of doing the things that would give the least unwarranted or undeserved advantages.

By this standard, it would have been more unneutral than neutral for Wilson to have broken the British maritime system by enforcing highly doubtful technical rights under international law. Judged by practical standards rather than by the often conflicting criteria of neutrality, Wilson's acceptance of the British system seems realistic and wise—indeed, the only choice that he could have made in the circumstances. This is true because the results of destroying the British blockade would have been the wrecking of American friendship with the two great European democracies and the probable victory of the Central Powers, without a single compensating gain for the interests and security of the United States. Only the sure achievement of some great political objective like a secure peace settlement, certainly not the winning of a commercial advantage or the defense of doubtful neutral rights, would have justified Wilson in undertaking a determined challenge to British sea power.

The second stage in Anglo-American relations, lasting from the summer of 1915 to the late spring of 1916, saw the development of the natural economic consequence of the American adjustment to tightening British control of the seas. That consequence was the burgeoning of an enormous war trade between the United States and the Allies. The United States became the storehouse and armory of the Allies neither because there was any conspiracy on the part of certain pro-Allied leaders in Washington to make American prosperity dependent upon an Allied victory, nor because American businessmen and bankers were willing to incur the risks of war in order to increase their profits. The United States became the storehouse of the Allies for the simple reason that Great Britain, and not Germany, controlled the seas.

The war trade itself was entirely neutral. Indeed, any action by the United States government to impede it, unless undertaken for overriding political motives, would have been grossly prejudicial and unneutral. If it had been permitted to develop in a normal way, this commerce would have raised no important problems in the relations of the United

States with the Allies. A problem of the first magnitude did arise, however, because the president, in the summer of 1914, had permitted Secretary Bryan to enforce his own private moral views by imposing a ban on loans by American bankers to the belligerents. . . .

Bryan's ban could not survive the development of the war trade on a large scale because, in the first place, it (like the embargo of 1808) was potentially nearly as disastrous to the United States as to the Allies. American material well-being was in large measure dependent upon foreign trade, and particularly upon trade with the Allied world. Such trade was possible during wartime only if American businessmen were willing to do for the Allies what they always did for solvent customers in temporary straits, namely, sell them goods on credit.

The most important reason that Bryan's embargo could not survive, however, was that it was an essentially unneutral policy that impeded the growth of the chief economic consequence of American neutrality, the legitimate war trade. The credit embargo and the war trade could not both survive. The former gave way because Wilson finally realized that it would be as unneutral to interfere with the extension of credit as it would be to stop the flow of goods. Bryan's ban was in a sense, therefore, a casualty chiefly of American neutrality. . . .

The second stage in Anglo-American relations also witnessed the apparent convergence of the diplomatic policies of the two countries on the high level. During the summer and autumn of 1915 Colonel Edward M. House, Wilson's confidant and principal adviser on foreign policy, conceived a plan by which the American and British leaders would join hands to press for an end to the war through Wilson's mediation. The British foreign secretary, Sir Edward Grey, replied that his government would cooperate only if the Washington administration were willing to go beyond simple mediation and would agree to join a postwar international organization established for the purpose of effecting disarmament, maintaining freedom of the seas, and preserving peace. Wilson hopefully consented, and House went to Berlin, Paris, and London in January 1916, to lay the diplomatic basis of mediation.

In London, House worked out in documentary form with Grey and the other members of the British cabinet the specific terms of Anglo-American cooperation. Initialed by House and Grey on February 22, 1916, and known as the House-Grey Memorandum, or Agreement, this document declared that President Wilson was ready, upon hearing from England and France that the time was ripe, to propose that a conference be called to end the war. Should the Allies accept and Germany refuse the invitation, the United States would "probably" enter the war against Germany. Should the conference meet and Germany refuse to accept a reasonable settlement, then the United States would also "probably" enter the war on the Allied side.

To the so-called revisionists the conclusion of the House-Grey Agreement is irrefutable proof that Wilson had abandoned neutrality and meant to take the country into war at the first opportunity. . . .

The revisionists are correct in asserting that the conclusion of the House-Grey Agreement marked the beginning of a new and epochal phase in Wilson's policies toward the belligerents. Otherwise they have missed the entire meaning of the affair, for the House-Grey Agreement was in Wilson's purpose *not an instrument of intervention, but a means of averting American involvement.* The truth of this important generalization will perhaps become evident when we recall the realities of the American diplomatic situation during late 1915 and early 1916, and when we understand Wilson's motives and intentions in devising a solution.

The overshadowing reality confronting the makers of American foreign policy at this time was the grave possibility of war with Germany over the submarine issue. It caused Wilson and Lansing, for example, to abandon ambitious plans for further intervention in Mexico. It speeded the American acquiescence in the British maritime system. Most important, it prompted the president and his advisers to search for ways to avert the rupture that might draw the United States into the maelstrom.

One way out of the predicament was to come to a full understanding with the German government over the issues involved in the submarine controversy. This is what Lansing attempted to do and almost succeeded in accomplishing during his negotiations over the *Lusitania* affair. Another way out and a surer means of averting the peril of American involvement in the future was to bring the war itself to an end through Wilson's mediation. It seemed at the time that the best hope of peace lay in Anglo-American cooperation for a peace of compromise, specifically in the kind of cooperation detailed in the House-Grey Agreement.

Thus Wilson approved this plan of mediation, but with a full realization that certain obligations and risks were involved. There was the necessity of giving positive assurances to the Allies, for they would have been at a fatal disadvantage in a peace conference without American support, in view of the strategic advantages that the Germans then enjoyed on the Continent of Europe. There was, moreover, the risk of war if the Germans refused to approve an armistice or proved to be unreasonable at a peace conference after agreeing to end the fighting. However, Wilson gave the necessary assurances in the belief that the risk of war involved was insignificant as compared to the greater danger of hostilities with Germany if he could not somehow bring the war to an end. This, then, was his dominant motive in sending House to Europe in January 1916, and in approving the House-Grey Agreement at the cost of Lansing's proposed compromise for submarine warfare.

In the final analysis, our judgment of Wilson's mediation plans must depend upon the kind of settlement that he had in mind and for which he was willing to run the risk of war in order to achieve peace. It is clear that Wilson envisaged a "reasonable" settlement based upon recognition that the war was a stalemate and upon a return for the most part of the *status quo ante bellum*. It meant, Wilson also hoped, the kind of settlement in which all the belligerents would forego annexations and indemnities, put aside past differences, and join hands with the United States to create a new international order. In his final discussions with the British cabinet, Colonel House made it clear that this, and this only, was the kind of settlement that Wilson was prepared to use the House-Grey Agreement to achieve. In other words, as House told the British leaders, the president would "throw the weight of the United States on the side of those wanting a just settlement—a settlement which would make another such war impossible. . . ."

In the circumstances prevailing during the late autumn and early winter of 1916–1917, the Germans had three possible choices of policy. These were, first, to join hands with Wilson in a drive for peace generally on the president's terms; second, to make a limited bid for victory by intensifying the submarine war at the risk of alienating the United States; and, third, to make a supreme bid for victory by instituting a total blockade of all commerce to the British Isles. The situation from the German point of view was such that this choice would not depend upon anything that Wilson did or said, unless, of course, the president could be used as a German pawn or was willing openly to support Germany's war objectives. The German decision would depend entirely upon a realistic evaluation of the possibilities of the military situation, that is, upon whether the Imperial army and navy were capable of imposing terms upon the enemies of the Reich.

Discussions of these possibilities had begun in Germany in earnest in mid-August 1916, as a consequence of the urgent demand of the Admiralty for permission to resume unrestricted submarine attacks in the near future. The civilian and military leaders rejected the demand at a conference at Pless Castle on August 31, 1916, on the ground that the navy did not have enough submarines to enforce a blockade and that it would obviously be foolhardy to risk American retaliation at this time. Actually, it was the new commanders of the army, Generals Paul von Hindenburg and Erich von Ludendorff, who made this decision. The military situation, they said, was too menacing to justify assuming the risk of war with America. There was heavy Allied pressure on the western front; above all, there was the grave danger of an Allied invasion of the Balkans, which might cause the collapse of Austria-Hungary.

Events of the late summer and early autumn combined inexorably to create a new situation in which a different decision would be made. First, the great British offensive on the Somme, aimed at tearing a huge hole in the German lines and a thrust into Belgium, failed; as a result, the German position in the west was again secure. Second, after dawdling in the matter for nearly two years, the Admiralty had finally launched a large program of submarine construction and the training of crews; by the end of the year it would be possible to talk in terms of dealing England a deathblow underseas. Finally, the army's counteroffensive against the Russians and its smashing victory over Rumania removed all cause for concern about the security of Austria-Hungary and the Balkans. . . .

Almost formless at the outset of the war, German war objectives had grown in a direct ratio to the progress of the Imperial armies in the field. By the late autumn of 1916 the military situation was so favorable and the potentialities of an effective submarine blockade were so great that the German leaders inevitably abandoned thought of a compromise peace and began to plan for a settlement that would remove all threats to future German security. As drawn up by Bethmann-Hollweg, amended by Hindenburg, and approved by the German and Austrian governments, the German peace terms were breath-taking in scope. They included, in the east, the establishment of a Polish kingdom under German control and German annexation of Lithuania and Courland on the Baltic; in the west, destruction of British naval supremacy, an indemnity from England and France, the annexation of strategic parts of France and Belgium, and the reconstruction of Belgium as a German vassal; and, overseas, the annexation of all or part of the Belgian Congo. To be sure, these were the maximum German objectives at the time; a realization of even part of them, however, would have secured German domination of Europe for years to come.

This was the kind of settlement that the German leaders were determined to obtain through peace negotiations. They knew that they could never obtain such terms, or even a large part of them, through Wilson's mediation. They knew that Wilson would demand, among other things, the restitution of a free and independent Belgium and perhaps the return of Alsace-Lorraine to France. Acceptance of Wilson's mediation and a compromise peace, even one based entirely upon the *status quo ante bellum*, would, in German eyes, be tantamount to defeat, for it would mean the frustration of everything for which so much German blood had been shed. As a consequence, no German leader, civilian or military, ever seriously considered accepting Wilson's *mediation*. During all the high-level discussions about peace plans, no German leader ever seriously mentioned such a possibility. On the contrary, all German diplomatic efforts were concentrated upon the goal of preventing Wilson's mediation, or "meddling," as the Germans called it.

This statement needs some clarification. The Germans were eager, almost desperately eager, to win the president's support for their peace plans. They wanted Wilson's help in forcing the Allies to the peace table at a time when all the odds favored the winning of a German peace. They were willing to give pledges of postwar disarmament and membership in a League of Nations, if this were necessary to win the president's support. But they did not want, indeed, they would not permit, Wilson's mediation or even his presence at the peace conference.

Wilson did not know these facts during the first stages of the peace discussions, but the truth finally came out in January 1917, when the president begged the Foreign Office in Berlin to come out frankly and fully in acceptance of his mediation. Then the German leaders had to say that they would welcome Wilson's cooperation only after the peace treaty had been signed, not at the conference of belligerents itself. Shrewdly perceiving the German intentions, Wilson refused to be a pawn in Berlin's game.

Wilson's refusal meant that the German leaders would now proceed to consider means of achieving through force what they had failed to win by their inept diplomacy. The high command had already made the decision by late December; it was confirmed by a conference of all leaders at Pless Castle on January 9, 1917. That decision was, in brief, to begin unrestricted submarine warfare against all shipping, belligerent and neutral, in the approaches to the British Isles and the eastern Mediterranean after January 31.

It was easily the most fateful decision made by any government during the course of the war, and the German records fully reveal the reasons for its adoption. It now seemed beyond all doubt that the navy had sufficient power to establish an effective submarine blockade of the British Isles, for it could send between twenty-five and thirty submarines into western waters by February 1, 1917, and a growing number after that date. Moreover, other circumstances, particularly a short wheat crop in the New World, augured well for the success of the blockade. Indeed, on a basis of elaborate calculations the Admiralty spokesmen guaranteed absolutely to reduce the British to actual starvation within five months after the submarine blockade began. If this were possible, then Germany had it within her power to win a total victory and a settlement that would establish the Reich in an unassailable position. To the military leaders, who had despaired of winning the war in the trenches, it was an opportunity that could not be refused.

Fear of American belligerency no longer had any effect on German policy in such an atmosphere of confident expectation. The German leaders all assumed that a wholesale attack on American maritime commerce would drive the United States into the war. These same leaders also concluded that American belligerency would not make any difference. On the contrary, American participation would have certain positive advantages, for it would mean the diversion of huge quantities of food and matériel to an American army in training during the very period when the U-boats would be winning the war on the seas. But in any event, American participation was, in the circumstances, necessary to the success of the German plans, because the submarine blockade could succeed only if it were total, that is, only if American as well as British ships were prevented from carrying life-giving supplies to the beleaguered British Isles. Of course, no German leader wanted recklessly to provoke an American declaration of war; all Germans, however, were prepared to incur American belligerency if they could win the war by so doing.

It was the only decision that seemed possible to the Imperial military commanders. No nation involved in a desperate war for survival will fail to use a weapon, whether it be the submarine or the atomic bomb, when that weapon promises to bring quick and overwhelming victory. But the submarine campaign brought catastrophic defeat to Germany and misfortunes unnumbered to the world because it destroyed all possibility of a peace of reconciliation. For this outcome, the political leaders in Berlin, particularly Chancellor Bethmann-Hollweg, were primarily responsible. Not once during the critical months of 1916 did they attempt to organize any movement for peace on a basis that could succeed. Not once did the Foreign Office make any serious effort to understand Wilson's motives and objectives. Not once during the final debates over submarine policy did the chancellor attempt to subject the Admiralty's dubious promises to any really searching scrutiny, to determine in a realistic way what the effect of American participation would be, or to inform the Reichstag of the consequences of failure of unlimited underseas warfare. It is true that the supreme high command, which now had the constitutional right to override the chancellor on submarine policy, might have proceeded as it did in any event. None the less, the fact remains that Bethmann-Hollweg simply made no serious effort to influence what was the most fateful decision confronting Germany's leaders since the formation of the empire. . . .

There was, however, only one decision that Wilson could now make. No great power could continue to maintain diplomatic intercourse with a government that promised to destroy its shipping and slaughter its citizens in violation of national and treaty rights and solemn pledges. Small neutral states like Holland and Norway had no choice but to suffer under protest, but a great nation like the United States had responsibilities commensurate with its power and influence. Continuing to maintain relations with Berlin after the issuance of the blockade proclamation of January 31 would have meant nothing less than Wilson's condoning of the German assault upon American rights and lives. The remarkable thing is not that Wilson severed diplomatic relations as he did on February 3, but that he hesitated at all. . . .

By the middle of March, therefore, it seemed that Wilson had made his decision in favor of a limited defensive war on the seas. "We stand firm in armed neutrality," he declared, for example, in his second inaugural address on March 5, "since it seems that in no other way we can demonstrate what it is we insist upon and cannot forego." Yet on April 2 (he had meanwhile convened Congress for this earlier date), scarcely more than a month after he had uttered these words, he stood before Congress and asked for a declaration of full-fledged war. What events occurred, what forces were at work, what pressures were applied during this brief interval to cause Wilson to make the decision that he had been trying so desperately to avoid? We should perhaps put the question in a less positive way as follows: What caused the president to abandon armed neutrality and to *accept* the decision for war?

There was first the fact that from the end of February to the end of March the Germans gave full evidence of their determination to press a relentless, total attack against all ships passing through the war zones that enveloped western Europe. The sinking of the British liner *Laconia* without warning on February 25 and with loss of American life, the ruthless destruction of three American merchantmen (*City of Memphis, Illinois,* and *Vigilancia*) on March 18, and the relentless attacks against the vessels of other neutral nations, to say nothing of the slashing attacks against Allied merchant shipping, removed all doubt in Wilson's mind about the deadly seriousness of the German intention to conduct total warfare against all commerce and human life within the broad war zones.

The more the character of the submarine blockade became apparent, the stronger the conviction grew in the president's mind that armed neutrality was neither a sufficient response physically, nor a proper or legally possible one.... It was simply that the German assault upon American lives and property was so overwhelming and so flagrant that the only possible way to cope with it was to claim the status of a belligerent in order to strike at the sources of German power. "I would be inclined to adopt ... [armed neutrality]," the president wrote only two days before he delivered his war message, "indeed, as you know, I had already adopted it, but this is the difficulty: ... To make even the measures of defense legitimate we must obtain the status of belligerents."

Certainly Wilson had convinced himself that this was true, but I have a strong suspicion that he would have stood doggedly by his first decision to limit American action to a defense of rights on the seas if this decision had not been overridden by convictions, events, pressures, and ambitions that were themselves decisive in Wilson's final shift from armed neutrality to war, in forcing him to the conclusion that the *immediate* circumstances left the United States with no choice but full-scale participation.

One of the most important of these factors was the subtlest and the one for which the least direct evidence can be adduced. It was Wilson's apparent fear that the threat of a German victory imperiled the balance of power and all his hopes for the future reconstruction of the world community. We must be careful here not to misinterpret his thoughts and motives. There is little evidence that he accepted the decision for war because he thought that a German victory would seriously endanger American security, because he wanted to preserve Anglo-American control of the North Atlantic sea lanes, or because he desired to maintain the traditional balance of European power because it served American interests. Nor is there any convincing evidence that Wilson's attitude toward the objectives of the rival alliances had changed by the time that he made his final decision.

On the other hand, there was now a great and decisive difference in the relative position of the belligerents: The Allies seemed about to lose the war and the Central Powers about to win it. This, almost certainly, was a governing factor in Wilson's willingness to think in terms of war. Germany, he told Colonel House, was a madman who must be curbed. A German victory meant a peace of domination and conquest; it meant the end of all of Wilson's dreams of helping to build a secure future.

As the president pondered America's duty at this juncture in history, the answer must have seemed obvious to him—to accept belligerency, because now only through belligerency could the United States fulfill its mission to insure a just and lasting peace of reconciliation. This could be accomplished only by preventing a German victory and only by the assertion of such power and influence among the Allies as would come to the United States by virtue of its sacrifice of blood and treasure. . . .

The combined weight of official and public opinion was another pressure meanwhile driving Wilson toward acceptance of the decision for war. It was a fact of no little consequence that by the end of March every important member of the administration, including those members of the cabinet who had heretofore opposed any bellicose measures, urged the president to admit that a state of war with Germany in fact existed. Public opinion had remained stubbornly pacific until near the end of February 1917. Then the publication of the Zimmermann telegram, in which the German government proposed to Mexico a war alliance against the United States, the sinking of the *Laconia*, and, above all, the destruction of American ships in the war zones after mid-March generated a demand for war that grew with mounting crescendo in all sections and among all classes, until it seemed beyond doubt to be a national and a majority demand. . . .

All this is said without any intention of implying that Wilson ever *wanted* war. The agony of his soul was great as he moved through the dark valley of his doubts. He had no illusions about the merits of the conflict into which he and his people were being drawn. He saw the risks of intervention, both to his own nation and to the world, with remarkable clarity. But he could devise no alternative; and he set aside his doubts in the hope that acting now as a belligerent, with all the power and idealism of the American people sustaining him, he could achieve objectives to justify the misery of mankind.

7

The 1920s

Decade of Decline or Destiny?

The decade of the 1920s occupies an ambiguous position in American history. Sandwiched between two exciting eras—the Progressive era and World War I on the one side and the New Deal on the other—the 1920s appear almost out of place. Certainly the presidents—Harding, Coolidge, Hoover—were not of the stature of men like the two Roosevelts and Woodrow Wilson. Few legislative landmarks or creative social experiments emerged from the decade of the postwar era. Indeed, Prohibition—the most significant social reform of the 1920s—did not survive. For these reasons, popular writers, movies, and television in recent years have depicted the decade in terms of a decline in morality, an orgy of financial speculation, a reaction against authority, an increase in organized crime, and a withdrawal from world affairs; in short, a time when established institutions and standards were in the process of disintegration. The popular designation of these years—the Roaring Twenties—sums up the traditional view.

Upon closer examination, however, the 1920s become far more complex than the picture presented in the popular stereotype. While Americans in later years looked back at the postwar era with distaste—even hostility—partly because it ended in the worst depression in American history—contemporaries viewed the period in a quite different light. One group in American society, the businessmen, felt that they were living in a new era. To them the twenties were marked not by conservatism but by change and innovation. The application of scientific procedures and new measures of efficiency in industry, businessmen believed, would bring about a level of prosperity that would eliminate poverty from the country completely. Under an enlightened and informed business leadership and a government sympathetic to business ideals, they predicted a new golden age for America.[1]

The optimistic outlook on the part of businessmen was expressed in a variety of ways. Spokesmen of industry never tired of proclaiming that

---

[1] See James W. Prothro, *The Dollar Decade: Business Ideas in the 1920's* (Baton Rouge, 1954).

the nation's greatness resulted from the labors of individual entrepreneurs who had raised America to a level of prosperity hitherto un-
matched in history. Perhaps the most spectacular glorification of business values and ideals was exemplified in a biography of Jesus by Bruce
Barton in 1925. Barton's book was ostensibly an effort to write about the
career of Jesus in a popular vein. But Barton's conclusion was cast in
business terms that were simple to understand: Jesus was the greatest
organizer and promoter in history because he had succeeded in "selling" Christianity to millions of persons over the centuries. As Barton put
it in his preface of the book:

> A physical weakling! Where did they get that idea? Jesus pushed a plane and
> swung an adze; he was a successful carpenter. He slept outdoors and spent
> his days walking around his favorite lake. His muscles were so strong that
> when he drove the moneychangers out, nobody dared to oppose him!
>
> A kill-joy! He was the most popular dinner guest in Jerusalem! The criti-
> cism which proper people made was that he spent too much time with
> publicans and sinners (very good fellows, on the whole, the man thought)
> and enjoyed society too much. They called him a "wine bibber and a glut-
> tonous man."
>
> A failure! He picked up twelve men from the bottom ranks of business
> and forged them into an organization that conquered the world. . . . [For the
> story of Jesus is] the story of the founder of modern business.[2]

Confidence in the 1920s was by no means confined to businessmen.
Even American historians, who were traditionally hostile to business
because of their liberal sympathies, saw much to praise. Charles and
Mary Beard, for example, were not particularly impressed with either
the Harding or Coolidge administrations when they published *The Rise
of American Civilization* in 1927. Yet they did not view the twenties as a
decade of reaction. Although the Beards admitted that Harding and
Coolidge were dealing with complex problems in much the same manner as William McKinley and Marcus A. Hanna of bygone days, they
noted that a large group of rebels in Congress fought the Republican
presidents and occasionally won an issue. But the outstanding development of the 1920s to the Beards was not the political battles; it was
rather the rapid growth of industry and mechanization in this era which
left its imprint on virtually every phase of American life. "The most
common note of assurance," they concluded in their work, "was belief
in unlimited progress. . . . Concretely it meant an invulnerable faith in
democracy, in the ability of the undistinguished masses, as contrasted
with heroes and classes, to meet by reasonably competent methods the
issues raised in the flow of time—a faith in the efficacy of that new and

---

[2]Bruce Barton, *The Man Nobody Knows: A Discovery of the Real Jesus* (Indianapolis, 1925),
Preface.

mysterious instrument of the modern mind, 'the invention of invention,' moving from one technological triumph to another, overcoming the exhaustion of crude natural resources and energies, effecting an even wider distribution of the blessings of civilization—health, security, material goods, knowledge, leisure, and aesthetic appreciation, and through the cumulative forces of intellectual and aesthetic reactions, conjuring from the vasty deeps of the nameless and unknown creative imagination of the noblest order, subduing physical things to the empire of the spirit—doubting not the capacity of the Power that had summoned into being all patterns of the past and present, living and dead, to fulfill its endless destiny."[3]

The sociologists, like the historians, also found much to be optimistic about during the decade. Although they were critical of many aspects of American life, most sociologists were confident that existing defects could be remedied. In the past, they argued, few statesmen or political leaders had possessed an adequate understanding of how American society functioned and judgments were often made on the basis of inadequate or misleading information. Only rarely had scientific methods been applied to social problems. What was required now, claimed the sociologists, was the gathering of quantitative and objective data that would enable leaders to define factors that governed society. Armed with the knowledge provided by sociologists, future statesmen would be able to make decisions in a truly enlightened manner.

As a general rule, sociologists during the 1920s were fond of emphasizing what they called a "cultural lag," that is, the condition wherein the institutions of a given society lagged behind the advances in technological and scientific knowledge. Such a lag was responsible for the internal tensions and difficulties in America, they maintained. The solution was obvious: existing institutions had to be brought up to date to conform to the findings of science. Once these institutions were modernized, the American millennium would begin. If American society would only accept the findings and recommendations of the social scientists, the sociologists claimed, a new utopia lay just ahead.

Sociologists, therefore, asserted with confidence that the 1920s represented the beginnings of a new era in American history. Even Thorstein Veblen, one of the most devastating commentators on the irrationality of the capitalistic profit system, seemed to think that most of society's pressing problems could be solved. All that was required, he concluded in *The Engineers and the Price System*, was a transference of power and authority from the businessman—who viewed industry in terms of profits rather than efficiency and social utility—to the engineer—an indi-

---

[3]Charles A. and Mary R. Beard, *The Rise of American Civilization*, 2 vols. (New York, 1927), 2:800.

vidual to whom productivity and efficiency were ends in themselves. Although Veblen had little confidence that America's leaders would seize upon opportunities presented to them, he did imply that possible solutions to America's major problems lay close at hand.[4]

One serious note of dissent in this chorus of optimism and self-congratulation was struck by the literary intellectuals of the 1920s. Many of them saw a decade of decline and degradation in America rather than one of destiny. They pictured Americans as being caught up in an irresistible surge of materialism—a people who had failed to grasp the meaning and significance of life. American society as a result lacked depth and was noted for the superficiality of its cultural, artistic, and intellectual achievements.

Among the earliest indictments by intellectuals was the symposium edited by Harold E. Stearns. Published in 1922 under the title *Civilization in the United States,* the book was a biting commentary on the superficial quality of American life. Stearns pointed out in his preface that each of the thirty contributors was a native American who had written his piece independently of the others, but that all had reached virtually the same conclusions. First, that hypocrisy was a major characteristic of American life; to most Americans the cardinal sin was not the immoral or dishonest act itself, but rather being found out or caught. Second, that America lacked a genuine sense of nationalistic self-consciousness—a fact that prevented the country from living up to its promise. Third—and most important—that America's social life was one of "emotional and aesthetic starvation," one in which "the mania for petty regulation, the driving, regimentating, and drilling, the secret society and its grotesque regalia, the firm grasp on the unessentials of material organization of our pleasures and gaieties are all eloquent stigmata." Could America be changed, asked Stearns? The answer was "yes." "There must be an entirely new deal of the cards in one sense; we must change our hearts. For only so, unless through the humbling of calamity or scourge, can true art and true religion and true personality . . . grow up in America to exorcise these painted devils we have created to frighten us away from the acknowledgement of our spiritual poverty."[5]

Most of Stearns's contributors agreed with his general indictment. To Lewis Mumford the American city was both an index of the nation's material success and a symbol of its spiritual failure. To H. L. Mencken the American politician was a cowardly and frightened individual whose primary concern was holding fast to his office. To Harold E. Stearns America's intellectuals were confined in a spiritual prison by a reg-

---

[4]Thorstein Veblen, *The Engineers and the Price System* (New York, 1921).

[5]Harold E. Stearns, *Civilization in the United States: An Inquiry by Thirty Americans* (New York, 1922), pp. vi–vii.

imented and standardized society. To John May the press was controlled by advertising and the public was gullible and uncritical in accepting at face value whatever appeared in their newspapers. The other chapters in *Civilization in the United States* included discussions of art, law, education, radicalism, business, advertising, and other aspects of American life, and all were equally critical in their approach. Most of the writers left the impression that America was a cultural wasteland and an intellectual desert with few redeeming features. So widespread was deception and hypocrisy, they concluded, that democracy itself seemed threatened.

Although many of the literary intellectuals were critical of American society in the twenties, few could agree upon a specific remedy, let alone a general diagnosis of its malaise. Some writers migrated to Paris in order to find an environment conducive to their art. Other artists congregated in Greenwich Village, in New York City, where they could remain aloof from the sordid materialism that seemed to permeate every nook and corner of American life. Still others related the decline in American civilization to the breakdown of Western civilization as a whole. Led by Irving Babbitt and Paul Elmer More, these "New Humanists," as they were called, insisted upon the necessity of man's "inner check" to control his desires and impulses. They emphasized the need for a "natural aristocracy" and scoffed at the idea of progress that was generally accepted by most Americans. Yet many of these alienated intellectuals—a group that included such outstanding figures as F. Scott Fitzgerald, Sinclair Lewis, Ernest Hemingway, John Dos Passos, and William Faulkner—were capable of creating a rich and enduring literature in the twenties and providing a cultural renaissance in America that perhaps had had no equal since the transcendentalist era of nearly a century before.

The Great Depression of the 1930s that began with the stock market crash in 1929, however, provided a new perspective from which to judge the previous decade. Now the optimistic outlook of the twenties seemed erroneous if for no other reason than the fact that America's prosperity had culminated in the worst economic disaster that the nation had ever known. With the seemingly imminent collapse of the capitalist system, business values and ideals were cast into disrepute. Businessmen who had been the heroes of the 1920s became the villains of the 1930s in the popular mind.

The view of the 1920s by the social scientists was less affected by the depression than was that of the businessmen. Having emphasized the application of intelligence and science to social problems in a period of prosperity, sociologists were even more adamant about taking such an approach during the depression. However, there was a growing realization among the social scientists that certain difficulties would impede the realization of their technocratic and scientific utopia. The famous report by the President's Committee on Social Trends in 1933, a project commissioned in 1929, came to the conclusion that the task of social understanding and control was far more complex than had been previously imagined. There were elements in American life to which concepts and projects involving mechanization, efficiency, and change simply could not be applied. What was required was not an outright rejection of older approaches to social problems, but a careful analysis of modern society that struck a correct balance between tradition and change.[6]

The interpretation of the twenties by historians was much more influenced by the depression than was that of the sociologists. However, this change in outlook was hardly surprising. Those historians who had written about the 1920s earlier had done so in a rather casual and superficial manner. For one thing, many of the sources required for an understanding of the so-called era of normalcy were only just becoming available by the end of the decade. But a much more basic reason for the shift in emphasis lay in the intellectual orientation of the profession itself. Having been reared in the liberal ideology of Progressivism, many historians of the Progressive school tended to interpret American history within the framework of a continuous class conflict that resulted in alternating periods of reform and reaction. Each era of liberal reform, they believed, was succeeded by a period of conservative consolidation or reaction. Caught up in the maelstrom of New Deal reform, these historians looked back at the 1920s as a time of reaction—a decade dominated by ultra-conservative presidents who reflected the selfish and narrow desires of the business community. In many respects such historians accepted at face value the claim by Franklin Delano Roosevelt that the New Deal was simply a continuation of America's traditional liberal values that had been momentarily subverted by the First World War and the ensuing era of disillusionment in the postwar period.

The typical interpretation of the twenties by such Progressive historians ran along the following lines. By 1920 the American people had tired of the moralistic fervor that had been characteristic of the Progressive era and of Wilsonian idealism. Having lived through two crusades lasting for over two decades—one for domestic reform and the other to make the world safe for democracy—the American people were ripe for a return to "normalcy," to use the word coined by Warren G. Harding during the presidential campaign of 1920. But normalcy turned out to be anything but normal. In contrast to both the Progressive and New Deal periods, which were exciting ones—if only because the American people and their leaders recognized and attempted to cope with the problems facing them and set out in a resolute and imaginative manner to come to

---

[6]President's Research Committee on Social Trends, *Recent Social Trends*, 2 vols. (New York, 1933).

grips with them—the twenties had a decidedly negative atmosphere. Under the conservative, and at times reactionary, Republican leadership, the American people abdicated their responsibilities. They withdrew from the efforts on the part of other nations to ensure lasting peace; they rejected Progressive attempts to grapple with the problems of an increasingly complex industrial society and retreated instead into an outdated idea of individualism; and they turned the affairs of state over to the business community which was interested only in the pursuit of the almighty dollar.

Given this negative interpretation, it is not difficult to understand the events and developments that Progressive historians chose to document their case. Generally speaking, they were prone to write about the suppression of dissent, the near prostration of the labor movement, and the relative decline in the economic position of the farmer and worker in American society. In their eyes the twenties was a period of bigotry marked by the rise of the Ku Klux Klan, the abandonment of the ideal of America as a haven for the oppressed peoples of the world, and the resurgence of anti-Catholicism and anti-Semitism. It was a time of corruption, symbolized by the scandals of the Harding administration; even the restoration of "honesty" under Coolidge simply meant a policy whereby the federal government turned many of its functions over to business. But worst of all, it was a time when idealism seemed sadly out of date—when the youth of America were alienated from their society and the homogeneity of the nation seemed threatened by competing group loyalties. If any one theme stood out in the writings of Progressive historians, it was their assumption that the 1920s had been an irresponsible decade.

The picture of the Roaring Twenties or the Jazz Age, to use designations that later became popular, was evident in the work of many historians. Vernon L. Parrington, writing within the Progressive tradition, sharply criticized the literary figures of the 1920s for throwing away their democratic-liberal heritage to emulate Europe's radical writers. To those historians writing within a Marxian framework—such as Lewis Corey or John Chamberlain—the decade was an exercise in futility—a period marked by the triumph of monopolistic capitalism which inevitably concluded with the worst depression in American history. Perhaps the most savage indictment of the decade appeared in John Dos Passos's brilliant trilogy, U.S.A. In this literary masterpiece, Dos Passos drew an unforgettable picture of the era. Using a variety of literary techniques to create an impressionistic view of a period, he emphasized the corrupting nature of materialism upon potentially "good" individuals.[7]

The critical approach to the 1920s continued to hold the allegiance of

_____

[7]Vernon L. Parrington, *Main Currents in American Thought*, 3 vols. (New York, 1927–1930), 3; Lewis Corey, *The Decline of American Capitalism* (New York, 1934), and *The Crisis of*

some leading contemporary historians writing within the Progressive tradition down to the 1950s and 1960s. Arthur M. Schlesinger, Jr., in *The Crisis of the Old Order 1919–1933* spelled out in great detail the failure of that period. Unlike other historians who had dealt with the 1920s before him, Schlesinger was in a position to write in an authoritative manner because of the greater mass of source materials that were available. Although Schlesinger took note of the intellectual and technological advances in the twenties, his picture of the period remained a relatively hostile one. In his view the 1920s were but a prelude to the New Deal.[8]

Similarly John D. Hicks, in *Republican Ascendancy 1921–1933* (1960), a volume in the New American Nation series, took much the same approach as Schlesinger. "It is not unfair," wrote Hicks in another essay, "to characterize the period . . . as an age of disillusionment. The high hopes with which the United States had entered World War I had been shattered; neither the League of Nations, nor the World Court, nor the disarmament program, nor the outlawry of war provided adequate guarantees of peace. . . . Politically speaking, the swing to conservatism had brought little comfort. The Harding scandals had left an ugly smell that even the puritanical Coolidge had found it difficult to eradicate; but for the ills of the times the Progressives under LaFollette could suggest only shopworn remedies of little relevance to the new age. American society was on the loose. . . . Then, despite business control of every aspect of American economic and political life, including a successful businessman in the White House, business had gone broke. Small wonder that the very bottom had fallen out of American confidence."[9]

The first selection in this chapter, by John Kenneth Galbraith, a Harvard economist and an individual active in a variety of liberal and reform movements, discusses the state of the American economy in the twenties. In presenting his argument, Galbraith makes a distinction between the stock market crash in October 1929, and the ensuing depression because the first did not automatically cause the second. The depression of the 1930s, he writes, followed the stock market crash because the American economy had been unsound. Being in a vulnerable position, the economy was unable to withstand the blow it received from Wall Street. Although Galbraith is by no means completely hostile toward the 1920s, his interpretation falls largely within the Progressive tradition of American historiography because of the picture it presents of a maldistribution of income and unsound corporate and banking structure, and a

---

the Middle Class (New York, 1935); John Chamberlain, *Farewell to Reform, Being a History of the Rise, Life and Decay of the Progressive Mind in America* (New York, 1932).

[8] Arthur M. Schlesinger, Jr., *The Crisis of the Old Order 1919–1933* (Boston, 1957).

[9] John D. Hicks, *Normalcy and Reaction 1921–1933: An Age of Disillusionment* (Washington, D.C., 1960), p. 21.

generally weakened economy in the world at large during the decade. Given these conditions, Galbraith concludes, the depression was a logical outgrowth of the economic developments that took place in the twenties.

The popular stereotype of the 1920s, however, had already begun to undergo a reevaluation in the late 1930s, and this changing view gained momentum in the 1940s. During the drab days of the depression, many persons and especially the youth of America looked back upon the gaiety and irresponsibility of the twenties with a strange fascination and even a longing as they contemplated the bleak present and uncertain future. But the major shift in interpretation came during the Second World War. Concerned with maintaining the nation's morale during the war, certain critics began to denigrate the literature of the 1920s for its negative outlook and its blanket condemnation of American society. In 1944 Bernard De Voto, the famous historian and literary critic, argued that American civilization had not been bankrupt in the twenties; the bankruptcy lay in the negative literary interpretation of that decade. Indeed De Voto found much that was appealing as well as constructive during the 1920s.[10]

While De Voto was condemning the literary rebels of the twenties for their negative and irresponsible outlook, other literary historians were beginning to approach the decade with a more appreciative eye. In 1955 Frederick J. Hoffman published his work *The Twenties: American Writing in the Postwar Decade*. After a thorough examination of the subject, Hoffman concluded that the writers of the 1920s had lived in a world that appeared to be cut loose from the past and therefore had sought to discover new ways of expressing the human condition. These literary artists, he continued, "had to invent new combinations of spirit and matter and new forms of expressing the human drama. They were not aided by any secure ordering of social or religious systems.... Their restless desire for the new was always motivated by their distrust of the old ... the 1920's were an opportunity and a challenge offered to a group of persons who were freshly and naively talented, anxious to learn *how* to restate and redramatize the human condition, morally preoccupied with the basic problem of communicating their insights into their present world."[11]

Although De Voto and Hoffman came to sharply divergent judgments about the literature of the 1920s, they were not very far apart in their general view of the period as a whole; both found much that was constructive and exciting during those years. Their break with the pre-

---

[10]Bernard De Voto, *The Literary Fallacy* (Boston, 1944).

[11]Frederick J. Hoffman, *The Twenties: American Writing in the Postwar Decade* (2d edition: New York, 1962), pp. 434–36.

vailing critical approach was soon echoed by other scholars. Indeed, shortly after the end of World War II, the pendulum began to swing away from the Progressive interpretation of the twenties. Rejecting the older and more critical view of the period, historians as well as other social scientists took a fresh look at the twenties, and in doing so offered a new perspective for understanding the events that transpired between 1921 to 1933.

The new view of the twenties was actually the joint product of scholars in a number of disciplines. George Soule, for example, an economic historian, concluded in his study of the 1920s that the economic picture traditionally drawn of the period was an erroneous one. It was true that the rich became richer in the 1920s, Soule wrote, but at the same time the poor were also getting richer—albeit at a slower rate. In his view the depression that began in 1929 had much more deeply rooted causes than those previously advanced. To Soule the depression grew out of a fundamental maladjustment of productivity and purchasing power—a maladjustment that was not indigenous to the 1920s but whose origins stretched back into American history for a good many decades.[12]

Other historians in the post–World War II era joined in the growing chorus of praise that celebrated the achievements of American capitalism rather than emphasizing its defects. They argued that it was America's productive capacity, after all, that had made possible the Allied victory during World War II and provided the free world with the means to resist the Soviet challenge after 1945. At the same time, American capitalism had given to the American people an affluent society hitherto unattainable and did so without resorting to a government-owned or managed economy. This new perspective was particularly evident in David M. Potter's challenging book, *People of Plenty: Economic Abundance and the American Character,* published in 1954. In this work Potter maintained that economic abundance had been the most important determinant in the shaping of the American character. Although Potter was not writing in terms of specific time periods, his interpretation placed the 1920s squarely within the mainstream of American history. In this context, the depression of the 1930s became the exception to the general rule of American prosperity. To put it another way, there was nothing unique or different about the twenties from an economic point of view.

The changing picture of the 1920s was reflected too in the way that historians began to look at the politics of the period. Arthur S. Link in a key article written in 1959 questioned whether the portrayal of the twen-

---

[12]George Soule, *Prosperity Decade* (New York, 1947).

ties as a reactionary decade actually fit the known facts. He argued that historians for too long had accepted uncritically the hypothesis that Progressivism had disintegrated at the end of World War I. Progressive ideals and Progressive leadership supposedly had been submerged by the rising tide of reaction and bigotry during the postwar era. This was not the case, said Link. Progressivism, after all, had never been a single national movement; it had been composed of a number of diverse reform movements operating at different levels of society. The war had shattered the coalition of Progressive reformers, but many of the individual reform efforts continued into the postwar period—albeit with less vigor. There were still many Progressive leaders in Congress in the twenties, Link maintained. This development was often obscured by the reactionary and conservative figures who were either elected to the presidency or dominated the executive branch of government. The apparent conservatism of the period concealed from public view the continued existence of progressive ideals that asserted themselves later in the New Deal era. Link implicitly rejected the Progressive historiography of the twenties which saw the decade as a reactionary one. Link's picture was far less negative because of his desire to redress the balance by stressing the achievements as well as the failures of the twenties.[13]

Other historians in the 1950s echoed the same view by stressing the continuity of social and cultural trends from the prewar years into the 1920s. Rather than representing a deviation in the normal course of American history, the decade was seen as a natural outgrowth of the country's past. Henry F. May in an article suggested that the breakup of America's traditional culture began closer to 1910 than to 1920. He argued that after the first decade of the twentieth century the upper-middle-class Protestant aristocracy that had largely dictated American mores gradually lost influence to other groups which gained power—the rising new middle class, working class, and ethnic minorities. The cultural disintegration of the 1920s—a movement synonymous with the decline of the old Protestant literary and moral tradition—was a complex development. To divine the true nature of the decade, May concluded, would require an examination not only of politics, economics, literature, and science of the period, but also of the relationship between them all. Much of the work since the 1950s has reflected May's call for new methods, as well as his argument along with that of Link, for continuity rather than reaction as the major theme of the 1920s.[14]

---

[13]Arthur S. Link, "What Happened to the Progressive Movement in the 1920's?" *American Historical Review* 64 (July 1959): 833–51. For a continuation of welfare reforms into the 1920s as evidence of the enduring force of Progressivism, see Clarke Chambers, *Seedtime of Reform* (Minneapolis, 1963).

[14]Henry F. May, "Shifting Perspectives on the 1920's," *Mississippi Valley Historical Review* 43 (December 1956): 405–427.

In a similar vein John C. Burnham attacked the popular view that Prohibition was a social experiment unique to the 1920s and a failure, or that it encouraged alcoholic consumption and crime. Well before 1920, Burnham noted, a number of states and localities had mandated prohibition; the enactment of the Eighteenth Amendment was simply an extension of what had already occurred. Nor did Prohibition increase the consumption of alcohol; per capita drinking dropped sharply, as did morbidity and mortality rates associated with excessive alcohol. Finally, crime statistics do not support the allegation that crime increased during the 1920s. Burnham's article is reprinted as the second selection in this chapter.

During the 1960s and 1970s, scholarly interest in the 1920s steadily mounted. Link in his article had called the decade "the exciting new frontier of American historical research." Burl Noggle, the leading historiographer on the twenties, writing in the mid-1960s agreed that more historians had been drawn to the decade.[15] The reasons for the growing interest were many. Papers of major public figures had become available, memoirs had been written, and scholars were able to view events with a sharper focus as a result of this new evidence. The question of whether the 1920s served as a bridge or a chasm to the 1930s continued to intrigue historians. Most important of all, historians began to employ new research strategies and to follow May's call for a cross-disciplinary approach to the period.

The "new social historians," for example, sought to find links between religion, prohibitionism, and nativism. These scholars were less inclined to view American society of the 1920s in the simplistic, dichotomous terms of the Progressives. They doubted that social conflict could be understood best in terms of polarized social groups or classes such as urban versus rural, working class versus middle class, Catholic versus Protestant, fundamentalist versus modernist, immigrant versus nativist, and "wet" versus "dry." These groups in their view were much more complex; they did not conform neatly to the definitions assigned them by earlier scholars. The "new social historians" sought to illuminate America's complex social structure and to study the social and political changes that took place not as isolated events but as closely related phenomena which had some continuity with social changes in earlier and later eras.

The concerns of the "new social historians" in these matters was evident in a series of essays that appeared in a volume entitled *Change and Continuity in Twentieth Century America: The 1920's*, published in 1968. Several scholars stressed the theme of anxiety as one that was common

---

[15]Link, "What Happened to the Progressive Movement in the 1920's?" p. 834, and Burl Noggle, "The Twenties: A New Historiographical Frontier," *Journal of American History* 53 (September 1966): 299–314.

to some social movements in the twenties, and used an interdisciplinary approach to study them. Paul A. Carter traced the fears and reactions of the Fundamentalists to the growing encroachment of secularism and science. Joseph R. Gusfield, a sociologist, applied the insights of his discipline to study prohibition. But the significance of anxiety as a motivating force and the methods used to study its nature could best be seen in Robert Miller's essay on the Ku Klux Klan.[16]

To Miller the Klan reflected a reaction to the tensions of what Klansmen considered to be an age of social revolution. The K. K. K. was a counterrevolutionary movement by citizens in all parts of the country—not only the South—to push back the changes in modern America and to restore its older and more pure past. Its membership was heterogeneous and made up of many splinter groups. Although its values were those of small-town rural America, it was based in urban as well as rural areas. Each Klansman identified change with a particular enemy. To some the enemy was the black who threatened a white man's country. To others it was the Catholics who endangered a Protestant America. The immigrant was seen by many Klansmen as polluting the purity of America's Anglo-Saxon blood. Foreign radicals, like Bolsheviks, could undermine American ways. What held the fragmented and amorphous Klan together, concluded Miller, was a "fellowship of belief" that the country faced a myriad of such enemies, as well as a shared anxiety about America's future and a longing to return to the past.[17]

Other social historians turned their attention to the nature of youth in the 1920s. In *The Damned and the Beautiful* Paula S. Fass studied middle-class college students during that decade. Although most were white and native born, Fass noted that all groups were influenced by the same broad social forces at work, including changes in family structure and educational institutions as well as new kinds of communication and mass consumerism. The result was that "youth" assumed its "modern" characteristics; the availability of peer groups made young Americans into products as well as agents of social change.[18]

One subgroup of the "new social historians"—the urban historians—were able to arrive at new insights by applying the term *urban* with greater precision as they studied more meticulously the changing distri-

---

[16]Paul A. Carter, The Fundamentalist Defense of Faith," pp. 179–214; Joseph R. Gusfield, "Prohibition: The Impact of Political Utopianism," pp. 257–308; and Robert M. Miller, "The Ku Klux Klan," pp. 215–56 in *Change and Continuity in Twentieth-Century America: The 1920's* ed. John Braeman et al. (Columbus, Ohio, 1968). See also Gusfield's book, *Symbolic Crusade: Status Politics and the American Temperance Movement* (Urbana, 1963).

[17]Miller, "The Ku Klux Klan," p. 217.

[18]Paula S. Fass, *The Damned and the Beautiful: American Youth in the 1920's* (New York, 1977).

bution of population. The 1920 census marked a significant change in the urban-rural ratio, showing for the first time that the majority of Americans lived in what were defined as "urban" areas—incorporated communities of twenty-five hundred persons or more. But urban historians were no longer content to use the city as a static unit of analysis. They employed imaginative techniques to study residential patterns—the growth of suburbs, zoning laws, and urban planning. By viewing the role of the city in a more dynamic way, they revised some old ideas. Charles Glaab discovered, for example, that many solutions applied in urban plans and programs in the 1930s had been actually worked out by the urban theorists in the 1920s. George E. Mowry in his book, *The Urban Nation, 1920–1960*, pointed out the profound impact urbanization had on shaping American society during the decade. He stressed the marked acceleration of this trend in succeeding decades, thereby tying the 1920s more closely to the period that followed.[19]

The work of the "new political historians"—another subgroup of the "new social historians"—was characterized by greater sophistication in the use of quantitative techniques which also shed new light on the 1920s. Samuel Lubell, the pollster, had advanced a thesis regarding the election of 1928 in a book written in the early 1950s in which he argued that Al Smith had brought about a critical realignment of voters in the Northeast. The "Al Smith revolution" attracted to the Democratic party the urban dwellers, second-generation immigrants, Catholics, and labor voters, all of whom identified with the candidate, and thereby setting into motion the train of events that led to the Democratic coalition resulting in Roosevelt's election in 1932. Lubell's thesis was strengthened by Richard Hofstadter's analysis of the same election written a few years later. But two scholars—Jerome Clubb and Howard Allen—who developed highly sophisticated quantitative techniques for studying election returns, came up with evidence contrary to the Lubell-Hofstadter hypothesis in the late 1960s after studying closely twenty major metropolitan areas over a long time span. Smith's appeal appeared to have little carry-over effect, and Roosevelt's election seemed to be rooted more in the depression of the 1930s than in the 1920s.[20]

Another fruitful area of research into the 1920s for the "new social

---

[19]Charles Glaab, "Metropolis and Suburb: The Changing American City," in *Change and Continuity in Twentieth-Century America: The 1920's*, pp. 399–437; George E. Mowry, *The Urban Nation, 1920–1960* (New York, 1965); and Burl Noggle, "Configurations of the Twenties," in *The Reinterpretation of American History and Culture*, ed. William H. Cartwright and Richard L. Watson, Jr. (Washington, D.C., 1973), pp. 470–71.

[20]Samuel Lubell, *Future of American Politics* (New York, 1952); Richard Hofstadter, "Could a Protestant Have Beaten Hoover in 1928?," *Reporter* (March 17, 1960), pp. 31–33; Jerome Clubb and Howard Allen, "The Cities and the Election of 1928: Partisan Realignment?," *American Historical Review* 74 (April 1969): 1205–1220.

historians" was sparked by the renewed interest in minority groups resulting from the tensions experienced in the 1960s and 1970s. The social protest movements in these decades—civil rights and women's liberation in particular—aroused a desire among some scholars to search deeper for the part that blacks and women had played in America's past. Books on black history dealing with the 1920s cast new light on some significant developments and personalities: the growth of the Harlem ghetto; the "Harlem Renaissance;" black leaders like Marcus Garvey; and the role of black intellectuals. The study of women's history in the same period, however, proved less extensive and less rewarding, perhaps because of the rapid disintegration of certain organizations after the achievement of women's suffrage in 1920. Scholars, nevertheless, studied the continuing though unsuccessful efforts of women to gain other rights and privileges in the feminist movement during the decade.[21]

Biographers recently have rehabilitated also the reputation of two presidents—Harding and Hoover—and in doing so have by implication dealt a blow to the idea of the 1920s as a decade of reaction and inertia. Robert K. Murray's biography of Warren G. Harding portrays him as a politically adept president and one who was quite competent in managing the nation's domestic and foreign affairs. More significant was the reevaluation of Herbert Hoover which reversed the image of his presumably inept presidency and gave him credit for starting policies supposedly inaugurated by the New Deal. Joan H. Wilson's study labeled Hoover a Progressive, and showed that he personified Progressive ideals while serving in the government during the early and mid-1920s. If these two presidents were, indeed, less conservative and more energetic than portrayed in the past, then the line of continuity between the 1920s and 1930s was more direct and less marked by abrupt change than previously supposed.[22]

The historians of the New Left, who figured more prominently in revising other periods of American history during the 1960s, all but ignored the 1920s. When they discussed the decade at all, their point of view—a reflection of their hostility toward and alienation from American society in the 1960s—was in many ways similar to that of the Pro-

---

[21]For studies in black history see Gilbert Osofsky, *Harlem: The Making of a Ghetto* (New York, 1966); Theodore G. Vincent, *Black Power and the Garvey Movement* (Berkeley, 1971); and Harold Cruse, *The Crisis of the Negro Intellectual* (New York, 1967). For women's history, see William L. O'Neill, *Everyone Was Brave: The Rise and Fall of Feminism in America* (Chicago, 1969) and J. Stanley Lemons, *The Woman Citizen: Social Feminism in the 1920's* (Urbana, 1973). For a work that studies blacks, women, and the peace movement in the twenties, see Paul A. Carter, *Another Part of the Twenties* (New York, 1977).

[22]Robert K. Murray, *The Harding Era* (Minneapolis, 1969); Carl Degler, "The Ordeal of Herbert Hoover," *Yale Review* 52 (Summer 1963): 564–83; and Joan H. Wilson, *Herbert Hoover: Forgotten Progressive* (Boston, 1975).

gressive scholars. Barton J. Bernstein in his essay on the New Deal described the 1920s as a period "more properly interpreted by focusing on the continuation of progressive impulses, demands often frustrated by the rivalry of interest groups, sometimes blocked by the resistance of Harding and Coolidge, and occasionally by Hoover. Through these years while agriculture and labor struggled to secure advantages from the federal government, big business flourished."[23]

Paradoxically, the more radical New Left historians were responsible for rehabilitating, in part, the reputation of the presumably conservative Herbert Hoover. William Appleman Williams (who helped to found the New Left school, but who was not always in agreement with its viewpoint), refurbished Hoover's reputation in foreign affairs because both men were critics of America's foreign policy as it developed along more imperialistic lines after 1890. Both men favored a more limited American intervention in global affairs, though for quite different reasons and from widely divergent perspectives.[24]

Other scholars besides the New Left have continued in the tradition of the Progressive school of historians in evaluating the 1920s as a decade of reaction. The application of social science concepts and techniques by recent historians sometimes tended to confirm the critical portrait of the decade etched by the Progressives. Paul L. Murphy, in his article written in the 1960s on the nature and sources of intolerance during the twenties, emphasized the impact of World War I in inaugurating measures of repression. After the war ended, repression continued because many Americans believed that a large number of domestic problems arose from the activities of groups and individuals who rejected the established order. Murphy argued also that the Americans who were most receptive to a movement directed at seemingly dangerous groups shared certain characteristics: they were rural or rural-oriented, homogeneous in their religious structure and values, adhered to traditional status arrangements, and exhibited a low social mobility. American society between 1919 and 1930, he concluded, was characterized by "intolerance and its shrewd manipulation."[25]

It should be noted, in conclusion, that some historians like Murphy

---

[23]Barton J. Bernstein, "The New Deal: The Conservative Achievements of Liberal Reform," in *Towards a New Past: Dissenting Essays in American History*, ed. Barton J. Bernstein, (New York, 1968), p. 265. In this same book, see the only essay by a New Left historian on the 1920s—Robert F. Smith, "American Foreign Relations 1920-1942," pp. 232-62.

[24]William A. Williams, *The Tragedy of American Diplomacy* (Cleveland, 1959); Wilson, *Herbert Hoover: Forgotten Progressive*, p. 276; and Selig Adler, "Herbert Hoover's Foreign Policy and the New Left," in *The Hoover Presidency* ed. Martin L. Fausold and George T. Mazuzan (Albany, 1974), pp. 153-63.

[25]Paul L. Murphy, "Sources and Nature of Intolerance in the 1920s," *Journal of American History* 51 (June 1964): 60-76.

have stressed the decade of the 1920s as one having unique characteristics that set it apart because of the extraordinary reaction against Progressive ideals and reforms. Other scholars have argued that there was a greater continuity between the politics and culture of the twenties and the Progressive era that preceded, and the New Deal that followed it. In trying to decide whether the decade was one of continuity or reaction, the student should keep in mind the following questions. Is it accurate to speak about the economic developments in the twenties in terms of presidential administrations? Indeed, can important economic changes be properly understood within such a restricted time span as a single decade? Would it not be more accurate for historians—as some have done—to study the emergence of a complex industrial economy in the twentieth century as a whole? Were the Progressives correct in understanding the nature of social conflict in terms of class and geographical differences? Or were the "new social historians" more accurate because of their stress upon sociological and psychological influences? Is it possible—or even desirable—to view the twenties as a decade apart? Or is it more plausible to emphasize the continuity between the twenties and the periods that went before and after it? These are only a few questions one must answer if the true nature of the 1920s is to be correctly assessed.

John Kenneth Galbraith

JOHN KENNETH GALBRAITH (1908–   ) was professor of economics at Harvard University until his retirement in 1975 and also served as ambassador to India under President John F. Kennedy. He has written a number of widely read and controversial works, including *American Capitalism* (1952), *The Affluent Society* (1958), *The New Industrial State* (1967), *Economics and the Public Purpose* (1973), and *Money, Whence It Came, Where It Went* (1975).

After the Great Crash came the Great Depression, which lasted, with varying severity, for ten years. In 1933, Gross National Product (total production of the economy) was nearly a third less than in 1929. Not until 1937 did the physical volume of production recover to the levels of 1929, and then it promptly slipped back again. Until 1941 the dollar value of production remained below 1929. Between 1930 and 1940 only once, in 1937, did the average number unemployed during the year drop below eight million. In 1933 nearly thirteen million were out of work, or about one in every four in the labor force. In 1937 one person in five was still out of work.

It was during this dreary time that 1929 became a year of myth. People hoped that the country might get back to twenty-nine; in some industries or towns when business was phenomenally good it was almost as good as in twenty-nine; men of outstanding vision, on occasions of exceptional solemnity, were heard to say that 1929 "was no better than Americans deserve."

On the whole, the great stock market crash can be much more readily explained than the depression that followed it. And among the problems involved in assessing the causes of depression none is more intractable than the responsibility to be assigned to the stock market crash. Economics still does not allow final answers on these matters. But, as usual, something can be said.

I

As already so often emphasized, the collapse in the stock market in the autumn of 1929 was implicit in the speculation that went before. The only question concerning that speculation was how long it would last. Sometime, sooner or later, confidence in the short-run reality of increasing common stock values would weaken. When this happened, some people would sell, and this would destroy the reality of increasing values. Holding for an increase would now become meaningless; the new reality would be falling prices. There would be a rush, pellmell, to unload. This was the way past speculative orgies had ended. It was the way the end came in 1929. It is the way speculation will end in the future.

We do not know why a great speculative orgy occurred in 1928 and 1929. The long accepted explanation that credit was easy and so people were impelled to borrow money to buy common stocks on margin is obviously nonsense. On numerous occasions before and since credit has been easy, and there has been no speculation whatever. Furthermore, much of the 1928 and 1929 speculation occurred on money borrowed at interest rates which for years before, and in any period since, would have been considered exceptionally astringent. Money, by the ordinary tests, was tight in the late twenties.

Far more important than rate of interest and the supply of credit is the mood. Speculation on a large scale requires a pervasive sense of confidence and optimism and conviction that ordinary people were meant to be rich. People must also have faith in the good intentions and even in the benevolence of others, for it is by the agency of others that they will get rich. In 1929 Professor Dice observed: "The common folks believe in their leaders. We no longer look upon the captains of industry as magnified crooks. Have we not heard their voices over the radio? Are we not familiar with their thoughts, ambitions, and ideals as they have expressed them to us almost as a man talks to his friend?" Such a feeling of trust is essential for a boom. When people are cautious, questioning, misanthropic, suspicious, or mean, they are immune to speculative enthusiasms.

Savings must also be plentiful. Speculation, however it may rely on borrowed funds, must be nourished in part by those who participate. If savings are growing rapidly, people will place a lower marginal value on their accumulation; they will be willing to risk some of it against the prospect of a greatly enhanced return. Speculation, accordingly, is most likely to break out after a substantial period of prosperity, rather than in the early phases of recovery from a depression. Macaulay noted that between the Restoration and the Glorious Revolution Englishmen were at a loss to know what to do with their savings and that the "natural effect of this state of things was that a crowd of projectors, ingenious and absurd, honest and knavish, employed themselves in devising new schemes for the employment of redundant capital." Bagehot and others have attributed the South Sea Bubble to roughly the same causes. In

1720 England had enjoyed a long period of prosperity, enhanced in part by war expenditures, and during this time private savings are believed to have grown at an unprecedented rate. Investment outlets were also few and returns low. Accordingly, Englishmen were anxious to place their savings at the disposal of the new enterprises and were quick to believe that the prospects were not fantastic. So it was in 1928 and 1929.

Finally, a speculative outbreak has a greater or less immunizing effect. The ensuing collapse automatically destroys the very mood speculation requires. It follows that an outbreak of speculation provides a reasonable assurance that another outbreak will not immediately occur. With time and the dimming of memory, the immunity wears off. A recurrence becomes possible. Nothing would have induced Americans to launch a speculative adventure in the stock market in 1935. By 1955 the chances are very much better.

II

As noted, it is easier to account for the boom and crash in the market than to explain their bearing on the depression which followed. The causes of the Great Depression are still far from certain. A lack of certainty, it may also be observed, is not evident in the contemporary writing on the subject. Much of it tells what went wrong and why with marked firmness. However, this paradoxically can itself be an indication of uncertainty. When people are least sure they are often most dogmatic. We do not know what the Russians intend, so we state with great assurance what they will do. We compensate for our inability to foretell the consequences of, say, rearming Germany by asserting positively just what the consequences will be. So it is in economics. Yet, in explaining what happened in 1929 and after, one can distinguish between explanations that might be right and those that are clearly wrong.

A great many people have always felt that a depression was inevitable in the thirties. There had been (at least) seven good years; now by an occult or biblical law of compensation there would have to be seven bad ones. Perhaps, consciously or unconsciously, an argument that was valid for the stock market was brought to bear on the economy in general. Because the market took leave of reality in 1928 and 1929, it had at some time to make a return to reality. The disenchantment was bound to be as painful as the illusions were beguiling. Similarly, the New Era prosperity would some day evaporate; in its wake would come the compensating hardship.

There is also the slightly more subtle conviction that economic life is governed by an inevitable rhythm. After a certain time prosperity destroys itself and depression corrects itself. In 1929 prosperity, in accordance with the dictates of the business cycle, had run its course. This was the faith confessed by the members of the Harvard Economic Society in the spring of 1929 when they concluded that a recession was somehow overdue.

Neither of these beliefs can be seriously supported. The twenties by being comparatively prosperous established no imperative that the thirties be depressed. In the past, good times have given way to less good times and less good or bad to good. But change is normal in a capitalist economy. The degree of regularity in such movements is not great, though often thought to be. No inevitable rhythm required the collapse and stagnation of 1930–1940.

Nor was the economy of the United States in 1929 subject to such physical pressure or strain as the result of its past level of performance that a depression was bound to come. The notion that the economy requires occasional rest and resuscitation has a measure of plausibility and also a marked viability. During the summer of 1954 a professional economist on President Eisenhower's personal staff explained the then current recession by saying that the economy was enjoying a brief (and presumably well-merited) rest after the exceptional exertions of preceding years. In 1929 the labor force was not tired; it could have continued to produce indefinitely at the best 1929 rate. The capital plant of the country was not depleted. In the preceding years of prosperity, plant had been renewed and improved. In fact, depletion of the capital plant occurred during the ensuing years of idleness when new investment was sharply curtailed. Raw materials in 1929 were ample for the current rate of production. Entrepreneurs were never more eupeptic. Obviously if men, materials, plant, and management were all capable of continued and even enlarged exertions a refreshing pause was not necessary.

Finally, the high production of the twenties did not, as some have suggested, outrun the wants of the people. During these years people were indeed being supplied with an increasing volume of goods. But there is no evidence that their desire for automobiles, clothing, travel, recreation, or even food was sated. On the contrary, all subsequent evidence showed (given the income to spend) a capacity for a large further increase in consumption. A depression was not needed so that people's wants could catch up with their capacity to produce.

III

What, then, are the plausible causes of the depression? The task of answering can be simplified somewhat by dividing the problem into two parts. First there is the question of why economic activity turned down in 1929. Second there is the vastly more important question of why, having started down, on this unhappy occasion it went down and down and down and remained low for a full decade.

As noted, the Federal Reserve indexes of industrial activity and of factory production, the most comprehensive monthly measures of economic activity then available, reached a peak in June. They then turned down and continued to decline throughout the rest of the year. The turning point in other indicators—factory payrolls, freight-car loadings, and department store sales—came later, and it was October or after before the trend in all of them was clearly down. Still, as economists have generally insisted, and the matter has the high authority of the National Bureau of Economic Research, the economy had weakened in the early summer well before the crash.

This weakening can be variously explained. Production of industrial products, for the moment, had outrun consumer and investment demand for them. The most likely reason is that business concerns, in the characteristic enthusiasm of good times, misjudged the prospective increase in demand and acquired larger inventories than they later found they needed. As a result they curtailed their buying, and this led to a cutback in production. In short, the summer of 1929 marked the beginning of the familiar inventory recession. The proof is not conclusive from the (by present standards) limited figures available. Department store inventories, for which figures are available, seem not to have been out of line early in the year. But a mild slump in department store sales in April could have been a signal for curtailment.

Also there is a chance—one that students of the period have generally favored—that more deep-seated factors were at work and made themselves seriously evident for the first time during that summer. Throughout the twenties production and productivity per worker grew steadily: between 1919 and 1929, output per worker in manufacturing industries increased by about 43 percent. Wages, salaries, and prices all remained comparatively stable, or in any case underwent no comparable increase. Accordingly, costs fell and with prices the same, profits increased. These profits sustained the spending of the well-to-do, and they also nourished at least some of the expectations behind the stock market boom. Most of all they encouraged a very high level of capital investment. During the twenties, the production of capital goods increased at an average annual rate of 6.4 percent a year; nondurable consumers' goods, a category which includes such objects of mass consumption as food and clothing, increased at a rate of only 2.8 percent. (The rate of increase for durable consumers' goods such as cars, dwellings, home furnishings, and the like, much of it representing expenditures of the well-off to well-to-do, was 5.9 percent.) A large and increasing investment in capital goods was, in other words, a principal device by which the profits were being spent. It follows that anything that interrupted the investment outlays—anything, indeed, which kept them from showing the necessary rate of increase—could cause trouble. When this occurred, compensation through an increase in consumer spending could not automatically be expected. The effect, therefore, of insufficient investment—investment that failed to keep pace with the steady increase in profits—could be falling total demand reflected in turn in falling orders and output. Again there is no final proof of this point, for unfortunately we do not know how rapidly investment had to grow to keep abreast of the current increase in profits. However, the explanation is broadly consistent with the facts.

There are other possible explanations of the downturn. Back of the insufficient advance in investment may have been the high interest rates. Perhaps, although less probably, trouble was transmitted to the economy as a whole from some weak sector like agriculture. Further explanations could be offered. But one thing about this experience is clear. Until well along in the autumn of 1929 the downturn was limited. The recession in business activity was modest and underemployment relatively slight. Up to November it was possible to argue that not much of anything had happened. On other occasions, as noted—in 1924 and 1927 and of late in 1949—the economy has undergone similar recession. But, unlike these other occasions, in 1929 the recession continued and continued and got violently worse. This is the unique feature of the 1929 experience. This is what we need really to understand.

IV

There seems little question that in 1929, modifying a famous cliché, the economy was fundamentally unsound. This is a circumstance of first-rate importance. Many things were wrong, but five weaknesses seem to have had an especially intimate bearing on the ensuing disaster. They are:

THE BAD DISTRIBUTION OF INCOME

In 1929 the rich were indubitably rich. The figures are not entirely satisfactory, but it seems certain that the 5 percent of the population with the highest incomes in that year received approximately one third of all personal income. The proportion of personal income received in the form of interest, dividends, and rent—the income, broadly speaking, of the well-to-do—was about twice as great as in the years following the Second World War.

This highly unequal income distribution meant that the economy was dependent on a high level of investment or a high level of luxury consumer spending or both. The rich cannot buy great quantities of bread. If they are to dispose of what they receive it must be on luxuries or by way of investment in new plants and new projects. Both investment and luxury spending are subject, inevitably, to more erratic influences and to wider fluctuations than the bread and rent outlays of the $25-a-week workman. This high-bracket spending and investment was especially susceptible, one may assume, to the crushing news from the stock market in October of 1929.

THE BAD CORPORATE STRUCTURE

In November 1929, a few weeks after the crash, the Harvard Economic Society gave as a principal reason why a depression need not be feared its reasoned judgment that "business in most lines has been conducted with prudence and conservatism." The fact was that American enterprise in the twenties had opened its hospitable arms to an exceptional number of promoters, grafters, swindlers, impostors, and frauds. This, in the long history of such activities, was a kind of flood tide of corporate larceny.

The most important corporate weakness was inherent in the vast new structure of holding companies and investment trusts. The holding companies controlled large segments of the utility, railroad, and entertainment business. Here, as with the investment trusts, was the constant danger of devastation by reverse leverage. In particular, dividends from the operating companies paid the interest on the bonds of upstream holding companies. The interruption of the dividends meant default on the bonds, bankruptcy, and the collapse of the structure. Under these circumstances, the temptation to curtail investment in operating plant in order to continue dividends was obviously strong. This added to deflationary pressures. The latter, in turn, curtailed earnings and helped bring down the corporate pyramids. When this happened, even more retrenchment was inevitable. Income was earmarked for debt repayment. Borrowing for new investment became impossible. It would be hard to imagine a corporate system better designed to continue and accentuate a deflationary spiral.

THE BAD BANKING STRUCTURE

Since the early thirties, a generation of Americans has been told, sometimes with amusement, sometimes with indignation, often with outrage, of the banking practices of the late twenties. In fact, many of these practices were made ludicrous only by the depression. Loans which would have been perfectly good were made perfectly foolish by the collapse of the borrower's prices or the markets for his goods or the value of the collateral he had posted. The most responsible bankers—

those who saw that their debtors were victims of circumstances far beyond their control and sought to help—were often made to look the worst. The bankers yielded, as did others, to the blithe, optimistic, and immoral mood of the times but probably not more so. A depression such as that of 1929–1932, were it to begin as this is written, would also be damaging to many currently impeccable banking reputations.

However, although the bankers were not unusually foolish in 1929, the banking structure was inherently weak. The weakness was implicit in the large numbers of independent units. When one bank failed, the assets of others were frozen while depositors elsewhere had a pregnant warning to go and ask for their money. Thus one failure led to other failures, and these spread with a domino effect. Even in the best of times local misfortune or isolated mismanagement could start such a chain reaction. (In the first six months of 1929, 346 banks failed in various parts of the country with aggregate deposits of nearly $115 million.) When income, employment, and values fell as the result of a depression bank failures could quickly become epidemic. This happened after 1929. Again it would be hard to imagine a better arrangement for magnifying the effects of fear. The weak destroyed not only the other weak, but weakened the strong. People everywhere, rich and poor, were made aware of the disaster by the persuasive intelligence that their savings had been destroyed.

Needless to say, such a banking system, once in the convulsions of failure, had a uniquely repressive effect on the spending of its depositors and the investment of its clients.

THE DUBIOUS STATE OF THE FOREIGN BALANCE

This is a familiar story. During the First World War, the United States became a creditor on international account. In the decade following, the surplus of exports over imports which once had paid the interest and principal on loans from Europe continued. The high tariffs, which restricted imports and helped to create this surplus of exports remained. However, history and traditional trading habits also accounted for the persistence of the favorable balance, so called.

Before, payments on interest and principal had in effect been deducted from the trade balance. Now that the United States was a creditor, they were added to this balance. The latter, it should be said, was not huge. In only one year (1928) did the excess of exports over imports come to as much as a billion dollars; in 1923 and 1926 it was only about $375 million. However, large or small, this difference had to be covered. Other countries which were buying more than they sold, and had debt payments to make in addition, had somehow to find the means for making up the deficit in their transactions with the United States.

During most of the twenties the difference was covered by cash—

i.e., gold payments to the United States—and by new private loans by the United States to other countries. Most of the loans were to governments—national, state, or municipal bodies—and a large proportion were to Germany and Central and South America. The underwriters' margins in handling these loans were generous; the public took them up with enthusiasm; competition for the business was keen. If unfortunately corruption and bribery were required as competitive instruments, these were used. In late 1927 Juan Leguia, the son of the president of Peru, was paid $450,000 by J. and W. Seligman and Company and the National City Company (the security affiliate of the National City Bank) for his services in connection with a $50 million loan which these houses marketed for Peru. Juan's services, according to later testimony, were of a rather negative sort. He was paid for not blocking the deal. The Chase extended President Machado of Cuba, a dictator with a marked predisposition toward murder, a generous personal line of credit which at one time reached $200,000. Machado's son-in-law was employed by the Chase. The bank did a large business in Cuban bonds. In contemplating these loans, there was a tendency to pass quickly over anything that might appear to the disadvantage of the creditor. Mr. Victor Schoepperle, a vice-president of the National City Company with the responsibility for Latin American loans, made the following appraisal of Peru as a credit prospect:

> Peru: Bad debt record, adverse moral and political risk, bad internal debt situation, trade situation about as satisfactory as that of Chile in the past three years. Natural resources more varied. On economic showing Peru should go ahead rapidly in the next 10 years.

On such showing the National City Company floated at $15 million loan for Peru, followed a few months later by a $50 million loan, and some ten months thereafter by a $25 million issue. (Peru did prove a highly adverse political risk. President Leguia, who negotiated the loans, was thrown violently out of office, and the loans went into default.)

In all respects these operations were as much a part of the New Era as Shenandoah and Blue Ridge. They were also just as fragile, and once the illusions of the New Era were dissipated they came as abruptly to an end. This, in turn, forced a fundamental revision in the foreign economic position of the United States. Countries could not cover their adverse trade balance with the United States with increased payments of gold, at least not for long. This meant that they had either to increase their exports to the United States or reduce their imports or default on their past loans. President Hoover and the Congress moved promptly to eliminate the first possibility—that the accounts would be balanced by larger imports—by sharply increasing the tariff. Accordingly, debts, including war debts, went into default and there was a precipitate fall in American exports. The reduction was not vast in relation to total output of the American economy, but it contributed to the general distress and was especially hard on farmers.

THE POOR STATE OF ECONOMIC INTELLIGENCE

To regard the people of any time as particularly obtuse seems vaguely improper, and it also establishes a precedent which members of this generation might regret. Yet it seems certain that the economists and those who offered economic counsel in the late twenties and early thirties were almost uniquely perverse. In the months and years following the stock market crash, the burden of reputable economic advice was invariably on the side of measures that would make things worse. In November of 1929, Mr. Hoover announced a cut in taxes; in the great no-business conferences that followed he asked business firms to keep up their capital investment and to maintain wages. Both of these measures were on the side of increasing spendable income, though unfortunately they were largely without effect. The tax reductions were negligible except in the higher income brackets; businessmen who promised to maintain investment and wages, in accordance with a well-understood convention, considered the promise binding only for the period within which it was not financially disadvantageous to do so. As a result investment outlays and wages were not reduced until circumstances would in any case have brought their reduction.

Still, the effort was in the right direction. Thereafter policy was almost entirely on the side of making things worse. Asked how the government could best advance recovery, the sound and responsible adviser urged that the budget be balanced. Both parties agreed on this. For Republicans the balanced budget was, as ever, high doctrine. But the Democratic party platform of 1932, with an explicitness which politicians rarely advise, also called for a "federal budget annually balanced on the basis of accurate executive estimates within revenues."

A commitment to a balanced budget is always comprehensive. It then meant there could be no increase in government outlays to expand purchasing power and relieve distress. It meant there could be no further tax reduction. But taken literally it meant much more. From 1930 on the budget was far out of balance, and balance, therefore, meant an increase in taxes, a reduction in spending, or both. The Democratic platform in 1932 called for an "immediate and drastic reduction of governmental expenditures" to accomplish at least a 25 percent decrease in the cost of government.

The balanced budget was not a subject of thought. Nor was it, as often asserted, precisely a matter of faith. Rather it was a formula. For centuries avoidance of borrowing had protected people from slovenly or reckless public housekeeping. Slovenly or reckless keepers of the public purse had often composed complicated arguments to show why balance of income and outlay was not a mark of virtue. Experience had shown that however convenient this belief might seem in the short run, discomfort or disaster followed in the long run. Those simple precepts of a simple world did not hold amid the growing complexities of the early thirties. Mass unemployment in particular had altered the rules. Events had played a very bad trick on people, but almost no one tried to think out the problem anew.

The balanced budget was not the only strait jacket on policy. There was also the bogey of "going off" the gold standard and, most surprisingly, of risking inflation. Until 1932 the United States added formidably to its gold reserves, and instead of inflation the country was experiencing the most violent deflation in the nation's history. Yet every sober adviser saw dangers here, including the danger of runaway price increases. Americans, though in years now well in the past, had shown a penchant for tinkering with the money supply and enjoying the brief but heady joys of a boom in prices. In 1931 or 1932, the danger or even the feasibility of such a boom was nil. The advisers and counselors were not, however, analyzing the danger or even the possibility. They were serving only as the custodians of bad memories.

The fear of inflation reinforced the demand for the balanced budget. It also limited efforts to make interest rates low, credit plentiful (or at least redundant) and borrowing as easy as possible under the circumstances. Devaluation of the dollar was, of course, flatly ruled out. This directly violated the gold-standard rules. At best, in such depression times, monetary policy is a feeble reed on which to lean. The current economic clichés did not allow even the use of that frail weapon. And again, these attitudes were above party. Though himself singularly open-minded, Roosevelt was careful not to offend or disturb his followers. In a speech in Brooklyn toward the close of the 1932 campaign, he said:

> The Democratic platform specifically declares, "We advocate a sound currency to be preserved at all hazards." That is plain English. In discussing this platform on July 30, I said, "Sound money is an international necessity, not a domestic consideration for one nation alone." Far up in the Northwest, at Butte, I repeated the pledge . . . In Seattle I reaffirmed my attitude . . .

The following February, Mr. Hoover set forth his view, as often before, in a famous letter to the president-elect:

> It would steady the country greatly if there could be prompt assurance that there will be no tampering or inflation of the currency; that the budget will be unquestionably balanced even if further taxation is necessary; that the Gov-

ernment credit will be maintained by refusal to exhaust it in the issue of securities.

The rejection of both fiscal (tax and expenditure) and monetary policy amounted precisely to a rejection of all affirmative government economic policy. The economic advisers of the day had both the unanimity and the authority to force the leaders of both parties to disavow all the available steps to check deflation and depression. In its own way this was a marked achievement—a triumph of dogma over thought. The consequences were profound.

V

It is in light of the above weaknesses of the economy that the role of the stock market crash in the great tragedy of the thirties must be seen. The years of self-depreciation by Wall Street to the contrary, the role is one of respectable importance. The collapse in securities values affected in the first instance the wealthy and well-to-do. But we see that in the world of 1929 this was a vital group. The members disposed of a large proportion of the consumer income; they were the source of a lion's share of personal saving and investment. Anything that struck at the spending or investment by this group would of necessity have broad effects on expenditure and income in the economy at large. Precisely such a blow was struck by the stock market crash. In addition, the crash promptly removed from the economy the support that it had been deriving from the spending of stock market gains.

The stock market crash was also an exceptionally effective way of exploiting the weaknesses of the corporate structure. Operating companies at the end of the holding-company chain were forced by the crash to retrench. The subsequent collapse of these systems and also of the investment trusts effectively destroyed both the ability to borrow and the willingness to lend for investment. What have long looked like purely fiduciary effects were, in fact, quickly translated into declining orders and increasing unemployment.

The crash was also effective in bringing to an end the foreign lending by which the international accounts had been balanced. Now the accounts had, in the main, to be balanced by reduced exports. This put prompt and heavy pressure on export markets for wheat, cotton, and tobacco. Perhaps the foreign loans had only delayed an adjustment in the balance which had one day to come. The stock market crash served nonetheless to precipitate the adjustment with great suddenness at a most unpropitious time. The instinct of farmers who traced their troubles to the stock market was not totally misguided.

Finally, when the misfortune had struck, the attitudes of the time kept anything from being done about it. This, perhaps, was the most disconcerting feature of all. Some people were hungry in 1930 and 1931 and 1932. Others were tortured by the fear that they might go hungry. Yet others suffered the agony of the descent from the honor and respectability that goes with income into poverty. And still others feared that they would be next. Meanwhile everyone suffered from a sense of utter hopelessness. Nothing, it seemed, could be done. And given the ideas which controlled policy, nothing could be done.

Had the economy been fundamentally sound in 1929 the effect of the great stock market crash might have been small. Alternatively, the shock to confidence and the loss of spending by those who were caught in the market might soon have worn off. But business in 1929 was not sound; on the contrary it was exceedingly fragile. It was vulnerable to the kind of blow it received from Wall Street. Those who have emphasized this vulnerability are obviously on strong ground. Yet when a greenhouse succumbs to a hailstorm something more than a purely passive role is normally attributed to the storm. One must accord similar significance to the typhoon which blew out of lower Manhattan in October 1929.

John C. Burnham

JOHN C. BURNHAM (1929–   ) is professor of history at Ohio State University. He has written many significant articles on late-nineteenth- and twentieth-century America, as well as a book, *Psychoanalysis and American Medicine, 1894–1918* (1967).

Recently a number of historians have shown that the temperance movement that culminated in national Prohibition was central to the American reform tradition. Such writers as James H. Timberlake have demonstrated in detail how the Eighteenth Amendment was an integral part of the reforms of the Progressive movement. Yet we commonly refer to the "Prohibition experiment" rather than the "Prohibition reform." This characterization deserves some exploration. The question can be raised, for example, why we do not refer to the "workmen's compensation law experiment."

One explanation may be that of all of the major reforms enacted into law in the Progressive period, only Prohibition was decisively and deliberately repealed. The Sixteenth and Seventeenth amendments are still on the books; the Eighteenth is not. For historians who emphasize the theme of reform, referring to Prohibition as an experiment gives them the option of suggesting that its repeal involved no loss to society. To characterize the repeal of Prohibition as a major reversal of social reform would seriously impair the view that most of us have of the cumulative nature of social legislation in the twentieth century.

We have been comfortable for many decades now with the idea that Prohibition was a great social experiment. The image of Prohibition as an experiment has even been used to draw lessons from history: to argue, for example, that certain types of laws—especially those restricting or forbidding the use of liquor and narcotics—are futile and probably pernicious. Recently, however, some new literature has appeared on Prohibition, whose total effect is to demand a reexamination of our customary view.

The idea that Prohibition was an experiment may not survive this renaissance of scholarship in which the reform and especially Progres-

John C. Burnham, "New Perspectives on the Prohibition 'Experiment' of the 1920's," *Journal of Social History* 2 (Fall 1968): 51–68. Reprinted by permission of the *Journal of Social History* and John C. Burnham.

sive elements in the temperance movement are emphasized. But it is profitable, at least for the purposes of this article, to maintain the image of an experiment, for the perspectives available now permit a fresh evaluation of the experiment's outcome.

Specifically, the Prohibition experiment, as the evidence stands today, can more easily be considered a success than a failure. While far from clear-cut, the balance of scholarly evidence has shifted the burden of proof to those who would characterize the experiment a failure. It is now becoming clear, moreover, how the myth of failure developed and why it flourished.

In order to understand how Prohibition came to be a Progressive reform measure, it is necessary to take into account turn-of-the-century class structure among Americans, their drinking habits, and particularly their liquor-by-the-drink retailing institution, the saloon. At that time, typical middle-class Americans did not drink, except sometimes wine. Respectable men were careful about being seen in or about a saloon. The saloon was for the most part a noxious institution, in fact inextricably bound up with prostitution, gambling, police corruption, and crime. The image of the respectable, old-fashioned saloon with its free lunch and manly conviviality was to a surprising extent the product of sentimental reminiscing. There were, it is true, many such delightful neighborhood institutions, but most saloons were disreputable places.

Although connected with social evils, the saloon did serve social needs of the working class, especially the first generation immigrants. The fact that the unfortunate and exploited were also the victims of the perniciousness associated with the saloon did not make them hate it, and when middle-class reformers took it away from them, the deprived opposed the reform. Wet voting strength, however, lay principally in highly localized parts of urban areas and was therefore ineffective.

The Progressive movement represented an alliance of upper and middle class reformers with two different groups. Many reforms, such as workmen's compensation laws, were achieved by a combination of urban labor elements and the reformers. Other reforms, of which Prohibition was the prototype, were achieved by the reformers only with the active aid of a part of the business community in its business capacity. For the Progressives, Prohibition, with its elements of moralism, social desirability, meliorism, and scientifically demonstrated need, provided a perfect vehicle for reform. Here was a means by which they could use law to change the personal habits of Americans in general in such a way that both the nation and the individual would profit. The viewpoint of the business elements was not so altruistic, but it was equally convincing. They believed that a sober, temperate worker was a more productive, a more stable, and a happier worker.

One of the sources of the concern of businessmen was the increasing use of machinery in industry. The intemperate worker, once merely inefficient, now became a veritable menace. For safety reasons, many industrial concerns did not employ problem drinkers. The best example of industrial Prohibition was "Rule G" of the American Railway Association, which called for the dismissal of operating employees who drank on duty or even frequented saloons. In the years before World War I some railroads enforced even stricter regulations. A number of other businesses followed suit, and there was widespread belief that sobriety and industrial safety were inseparable.

Employer groups were the sources of various opinions about the way in which both employee and employer benefitted from enforced sobriety. Not least striking was the argument that the money spent on liquor might go to pay for other consumer goods. While large segments of business, including industries economically dependent upon the liquor industry, opposed Prohibition or anything like it as government interference with business, a wealthy segment of the business community was committed, with the Progressives, to temperance reform. The brewers' blacklist of April 1915, for example, contained, in some cases without justification, the names of the Pennsylvania Railroad, United States Steel Corporation, John Wanamaker's, Pittsburgh Coal Company, Goodyear Rubber Company, and S. S. Kresge Company.

The American Prohibition experiment grew out of the transformation that the combination of Progressive reformers and businessmen wrought in the temperance movement. Beginning in 1907 a large number of state and local governments enacted laws or adopted constitutional provisions that dried up—as far as alcoholic beverages were concerned—a substantial part of the United States. The success of the antiliquor forces, led by the Anti-Saloon League, was so impressive that they were prepared to strike for a national Prohibition constitutional amendment. This issue was decided in the 1916 congressional elections, although the amendment itself was not passed by Congress until December 22, 1917. A sufficient number of states ratified it by January 16, 1919, and it took effect on January 16, 1920.

In actuality, however, Prohibition began well before January 1920. In addition to the widespread local Prohibition laws, federal laws greatly restricted the production and sale of alcoholic beverages, mostly, beginning in 1917, in the guise of war legislation. The manufacture of distilled spirits beverages, for example, had been forbidden for more than three months when Congress passed the Eighteenth Amendment late in 1917. The Volstead Act of 1919, passed to implement the amendment, provided by law that wartime prohibition would remain in effect until the amendment came into force.

The Eighteenth Amendment prohibited the manufacturing, selling, importing, or transporting of "intoxicating liquors." It was designed to kill off the liquor business in general and the saloon in particular; but at the same time the amendment was not designed to prohibit either the possession or drinking of alcoholic beverages. At a later time the courts held even the act of buying liquor to be legal and not part of a conspiracy. Most of the local and state prohibition laws were similar in their provisions and intent. The very limited nature of the Prohibition experiment must, therefore, be understood from the beginning.

At the time, a number of union leaders and social critics pointed out that the Eighteenth Amendment constituted class legislation; that is, the political strength of the drys lay among middle-class Progressives who wanted, essentially, to remove the saloon from American life. The amendment permitted those who had enough money to lay in all the liquor they pleased, but the impecunious workingman was to be deprived of his day-to-day or week-to-week liquor supply. The class aspect of Prohibition later turned out to have great importance. Most of the recent revisionist writers have concentrated upon the interplay between Prohibition and social role and status.

The primary difficulty that has stood in the way of properly assessing the Prohibition experiment has been methods of generalization. Evidence gathered from different sections of the country varies so radically as to make weighing of evidence difficult. In addition, there has been a great deal of confusion about time: When did Prohibition begin? What period of its operation should be the basis for judgment? The difficulties of time and place are particularly relevant to the fundamental question of enforcement.

As the country looked forward to Prohibition after the elections of 1916, widespread public support, outside of a few urban areas, was expected to make Prohibition a success both initially and later on. It was reasonable to expect that enforcement would be strict and that society both institutionally and informally would deal severely with any actions tending to revive the liquor trade. These expectations were realistic through the years of the war, when Prohibition and patriotism were closely connected in the public mind. Only some years after the passage of the Volstead Act did hopes for unquestionably effective enforcement fade away. In these early years, when public opinion generally supported enforcement, the various public officials responsible for enforcement were the ones who most contributed to its breakdown. This breakdown in many areas in turn led to the evaporation of much public support in the country as a whole.

Successive Congresses refused to appropriate enough money to enforce the laws. Through its influence in Congress the Anti-Saloon League helped to perpetuate the starvation of the Prohibition Bureau and its predecessors in the name of political expediency. Huge sums spent on prohibition, the drys feared, would alienate many voters—and fearful congressmen—more or less indifferent to Prohibition. The prohibitionists therefore made the claim that Prohibition was effective so that they would not have to admit the necessity of large appropriations for enforcement. A second act of irresponsibility of the Congresses was acquiescing in exempting the enforcement officers from Civil Service and so making the Prohibition Bureau part of the political spoils system. League officials who had written this provision into the Volstead Act hoped by using their political power to dictate friendly appointments, but the record shows that politics, not the League, dominated federal enforcement efforts. Not until 1927 did the Prohibition Bureau finally come under Civil Service.

The men charged with enforcement, the presidents of the 1920s, were, until Hoover, indifferent to Prohibition except as it affected politics. Wilson, although not a wet, vetoed the Volstead Act, and it was passed over his veto. Harding and Coolidge were notoriously uninterested in enforcing Prohibition. When Hoover took office in 1929 he reorganized the administration of enforcement, and his effectiveness in cutting down well-established channels of supply helped give final impetus to the movement for a reevaluation of Prohibition.

In some areas prosecutors and even judges were so unsympathetic that enforcement was impossible. Elsewhere local juries refused to convict in bootlegging cases. These local factors contributed greatly to the notable disparities in the effectiveness of Prohibition from place to place.

By a unique concurrent enforcement provision of the Eighteenth Amendment, state and local officials were as responsible for enforcement as federal authorities. The Anti-Saloon League, because of its power in the states, expected to use existing law enforcement agencies and avoid huge federal appropriations for enforcement. Contrary to the expectations of the League, local officials were the weakest point in enforcement. Most of the states—but not all—enacted "little Volstead" acts; yet in 1927 only eighteen of the forty-eight states were appropriating money for the enforcement of such acts. Local enforcement in many southern and western areas was both severe and effective; in other areas local enforcement was even more unlikely than federal enforcement. For years the entire government of New Jersey openly defied the Eighteenth Amendment, and it was clear that the governor was not troubled a bit about his oath of office. Some states that had enforced their own Prohibition laws before 1919 afterward made no attempt to continue enforcement.

With such extreme variations in the enforcement of Prohibition over the United States, judging the overall success of the experiment on the basis of enforcement records is hazardous. Bootlegging in New York, Chicago, and San Francisco clearly was not necessarily representative of the intervening territory, and vice versa.

An easier basis for generalizing about the effectiveness of enforcement is the impact that Prohibition had on consumption of alcohol. Here the second major complication mentioned crops up: the availability of liquor varied greatly from time to time and specifically from an initial period of effectiveness in 1919–1922 to a later period of widespread violation of the law, typically 1925–1927.

In the early years of national Prohibition, liquor was very difficult to obtain. In the later years, when the laws were being defied by well-organized bootleggers operating through established channels, the supply increased. By the late 1920s, for example, the domestic supply of hard liquor in northern California was so great that the price fell below the point at which it was profitable to run beverages in from Canada by ship. In the last years of Prohibition it became very easy—at least in some areas with large populations—to obtain relatively good liquor. Many people, relying on their memories, have generalized from this later period, after about 1925, to all of the Prohibition years and have come, falsely, to the conclusion that enforcement was neither real nor practical. Overall one can say that considering the relatively slight amount of effort put into it, enforcement was surprisingly effective in many places, and particularly in the early years.

Both so-called wet and dry sources agree that the amount of liquor consumed per capita decreased substantially because of Prohibition. The best figures available show that the gallons of pure alcohol ingested per person varied widely over four different periods. In the period 1911–1914, the amount was 1.69 gallons. Under the wartime restrictions, 1918–1919, the amount decreased to .97. In the early years of national prohibition, 1921–1922, there was still further decrease to .73 gallons. In the later years of Prohibition, 1927–1930, the amount rose to 1.14 gallons.

These figures suggest that great care must be used in making comparisons between "before" Prohibition and "after." Statistics and memories that use 1920 as the beginning of Prohibition are misleading, since not only were federal laws in force before then but there was also extensive state prohibition. The peak of absolute consumption of beer, for example, was reached in the years 1911–1914, not 1916–1918, much less 1919. The real "before" was sometime around 1910.

The best independent evidence of the impact of Prohibition can be found in the available figures for certain direct and measurable social effects of alcohol consumption. The decrease from about 1915 to 1920–1922 in arrests for drunkenness, in hospitalization for alcoholism, and in the incidence of other diseases, such as cirrhosis of the liver, specifically related to drinking was remarkable. The low point of these indexes came in 1918–1921, and then they climbed again until the late 1920s. Because of confusion about when Prohibition began, the significance of these well known statistics has seldom been appreciated: there is clear evidence that in the early years of Prohibition not only did the use of alcohol decrease but American society enjoyed some of the direct benefits promised by proponents of Prohibition.

Undoubtedly the most convincing evidence of the success of Prohibition is to be found in the mental hospital admission rates. There is no question of a sudden change in physicians' diagnoses, and the people who had to deal with alcohol-related mental diseases were obviously impressed by what they saw. After reviewing recent hospital admission rates for alcoholic psychoses, James V. May, one of the most eminent American psychiatrists, wrote in 1922: "With the advent of Prohibition the alcoholic psychoses as far as this country is concerned have become a matter of little more than historical interest. The admission rate in the New York state hospitals for 1920 was only 1.9 percent [as compared with 10 percent in 1909–1912]." For many years articles on alcoholism literally disappeared from American medical literature.

In other words, after World War I and until sometime in the early 1920s, say, 1922 or 1923, when enforcement was clearly breaking down, Prohibition was generally a success. Certainly there is no basis for the conclusion that Prohibition was inherently doomed to failure. The emasculation of enforcement grew out of specific factors that were not organically related to the Eighteenth Amendment.

Nor is most of this analysis either new or controversial. Indeed, most of the criticism of Prohibition has centered around assertions not so much that the experiment failed but that it had two more or less unexpected consequences that clearly show it to have been undesirable. The critics claim, first, that the Eighteenth Amendment caused dangerous criminal behavior; and, second, that in spite of Prohibition more people drank alcohol than before. If a candid examination fails to confirm these commonly accepted allegations, the interpretation of Prohibition as a failure loses most of its validity. Such is precisely the case.

During the 1920s there was almost universal public belief that a "crime wave" existed in the United States. In spite of the literary output on the subject, dealing largely with a local situation in Chicago, there is no firm evidence of this supposed upsurge in lawlessness. Two criminologists, Edwin H. Sutherland and C. H. Gehlke, at the end of the decade reviewed the available crime statistics, and the most that they could conclude was that "there is no evidence here of a 'crime wave,' but only of a slowly rising level." These admittedly inadequate statistics emphasized large urban areas and were, it should be emphasized, *not* corrected to reflect the increase in population. Actually no statistics from this period dealing with crime are of any value whatsoever in generalizing about crime rates. Apparently what happened was that in the 1920s the long existent "underworld" first became publicized and romanticized. The crime wave, in other words, was the invention of enterprising journalists feeding on some sensational crimes and situations and catering to a public to whom the newly discovered "racketeer" was a covert folk hero.

Even though there was no crime wave, there was a connection between crime and Prohibition, as Frederick Lewis Allen suggested in his alliterative coupling of "Alcohol and Al Capone." Because of the large profits involved in bootlegging and the inability of the producers and customers to obtain police protection, criminal elements organized and exploited the liquor business just as they did all other illegal activities. It would be a serious distortion even of racketeering, however, to emphasize bootlegging at the expense of the central criminal-directed activity, gambling. Since liquor related activities were not recognized as essentially criminal in nature by substantial parts of the population, it is difficult to argue that widespread violation of the Volstead Act constituted a true increase of crime. Nevertheless, concern over growing federal "crime" statistics, that is, bootlegging cases, along with fears based on hysterical journalism, helped to bring about repeal.

We are left, then, with the question of whether national Prohibition led to more drinking than before. It should first be pointed out not only that the use of 1920 as the beginning of Prohibition is misleading but that much of the drinking during the 1920s was not relevant to the prohibition of the Eighteenth Amendment and Volstead Act. Private drinking was perfectly legal all of the time, and possession of liquor that had been accumulated by the foresighted before Prohibition was entirely lawful. The continued production of cider and wine at home was specifically provided for also. Indeed, the demand for wine grapes was so great that many grape growers who in 1919 faced ruin made a fortune selling their grapes in the first years of the amendment. Ironically, many an old lady who made her own wine believed that she was defying Prohibition when in fact the law protected her.

We still face the problem of reconciling the statistics quoted above that show that alcohol consumption was substantially reduced, at one point to about half of the pre-Prohibition consumption, with the common observation of the 1920s that as many or more people were drinking than before.

What happened, one can say with hindsight, was predictable. When liquor became unavailable except at some risk and considerable cost, it became a luxury item, that is, a symbol of affluence and, eventually, status. Where before men of good families tended not to drink and women certainly did not, during the 1920s it was precisely the sons and daughters of the "nice" people who were patronizing the bootleggers and speakeasies, neither of which for some years was very effectively available to the lower classes. This utilization of drinking as conspicuous consumption was accompanied by the so-called revolution in manners and morals that began among the rebellious intellectuals around 1912 and reached a high point of popularization in the 1920s when the adults of the business class began adopting the "lower" social standards of their children.

We can now understand why the fact was universally reported by journalists of the era that "everyone drank, including many who never did before." Drinking, and often new drinking, was common among the upper classes, especially among the types of people likely to consort with the writers of the day. The journalists and other observers did indeed report honestly that they saw "everyone" drinking. They seldom saw the lower classes and almost never knew about the previous drinking habits of the masses. The situation was summed up by an unusually well-qualified witness, Whiting Williams, testifying before the Wickersham Commission. A vice-president of a Cleveland steel company, he had for many years gone in disguise among the working people of several areas in connection with handling labor problems. He concluded:

> ... very much of the misconception with respect to the liquor problem comes from the fact that most of the people who are writing and talking most actively about the prohibition problem are people who, in the nature of things, have never had any contact with the liquor problem in its earlier pre-prohibition form and who are, therefore, unduly impressed with the changes with respect to drinking that they see on their own level; their own level, however, representing an extremely small proportion of the population.
>
> The great mass who, I think, are enormously more involved in the whole problem, of course, in the nature of things are not articulate and are not writing in the newspapers.

The important point is that the "everyone" who was reported to be drinking did not include working-class families, i.e., the preponderant part of the population. Clark Warburton, in a study initiated with the help of the Association Against the Prohibition Amendment, is explicit on this point: "The working class is consuming not more than half as much alcohol per capita as formerly." The classic study is Martha Bensley Bruère's. She surveyed social workers across the country, and the overwhelming impression (even taking account of urban immigrant areas where Prohibition laws were flouted) was that working people drank very much less than before and further, as predicted, that prohibition had, on the balance, substantially improved conditions among low-income Americans.

Even in its last years the law, with all its leaks, was still effective in cutting down drinking among the workers, which was one of the primary aims of Prohibition. Here, then, is more evidence of the success of the Prohibition experiment. Certainly the Anti-Saloon League did succeed in destroying the old-fashioned saloon, the explicit target of its campaign.

Taking together all of this evidence of the success of Prohibition, especially in its class differential aspects, we are still left with the question of why the law was repealed.

The story of repeal is contained largely in the growth of the idea that Prohibition was a failure. From the beginning, a number of contemporary observers (particularly in the largest cities) saw many violations of the law and concluded that prohibition was not working. These observers were in the minority, and for a long time most people believed that by and large Prohibition was effective. Even for those who did not, the question of repeal—once appeals to the Supreme Court had been settled—simply never arose. Bartlett C. Jones has observed, "A peculiarity of the Prohibition debate was the fact that repeal, called an absolute impossibility for much of the period, became irresistibly popular in 1932 and 1933." Not even enemies of Prohibition considered absolute repeal as an alternative until quite late, although they upheld through all of these years their side of the vigorous public debate about the effectiveness and desirability of the Prohibition laws.

In the early days of Prohibition, the predominant attitudes toward the experiment manifested in the chief magazines and newspapers of the country were either ambivalent acceptance or, more rarely, impotent hostility. In 1923–1924 a major shift in the attitudes of the mass circulation information media occurred so that acceptance was replaced by nearly universal outright criticism accompanied by a demand for modification of the Volstead Act. The criticism was based on the assumption that Volsteadism, at least, was a failure. The suggested solution was legalizing light wines and beers.

The effectiveness of the shift of "public opinion" is reflected in the vigorous counterattack launched by the dry forces who too often denied real evils and asserted that Prohibition was effective and was benefiting the nation. By claiming too much, especially in the late 1920s, the drys discredited that which was really true, and the literate public apparently discounted all statements that might show that Prohibition was at least a partial success, partly on the rigidly idealistic basis that if it was a partial failure, it was a total failure.

Great impetus was given to sentiment hostile to Prohibition by the concern of respectable people about the "crime wave." They argued, plausibly enough given the assumptions that there was a crime wave and that Prohibition was a failure, that universal disregard for the Eighteenth Amendment was damaging to general respect for law. If the most respectable elements of society, so the argument went, openly showed contempt for the Constitution, how could anyone be expected to honor a mere statute? Much of the leadership of the "anti's" soon came from the bar associations rather than the bar patrons.

Coincident with this shift in opinion came the beginning of one of the most effective publicity campaigns of modern times, led by the Association Against the Prohibition Amendment. At first largely independent of liquor money, in the last years of prohibition the AAPA used all it could command. By providing journalists with reliable information, the AAPA developed a virtual monopoly on liquor and Prohibition press coverage. In the late 1920s and early 1930s it was unusual to find a story about Prohibition in small local papers that did not have its origin—free of charge, of course—with the AAPA.

The AAPA had as its announced goal the modification of the Volstead Act to legalize light wines and beers. The organization also headed up campaigns to repeal the "little Volstead" acts most states had enacted. By the late 1920s the AAPA beat the Anti-Saloon League at its own game, chipping away at the state level. State after state, often by popular vote, did away with the concurrent enforcement acts. Both the wets and the drys viewed state repeals and any modification of the Volstead Act as only steps toward full repeal. Perhaps they were correct; but another possibility does need examination.

Andrew Sinclair, in the most recent and thorough examination of the question, contends that modification of the Volstead Act to legalize light wines and beers would have saved the rest of the Prohibition experiment. It is difficult to differ with Sinclair's contention that complete repeal of the Eighteenth Amendment was unprovoked and undesirable.

When President Hoover appointed the Wickersham Commission, public opinion was almost unanimous in expecting that the solution to the Prohibition problem would be modification. The commission's report strengthened the expectation. Not even the Association Against the Prohibition Amendment hoped for more than that, much less repeal. But suddenly an overwhelming surge of public sentiment brought about the Twenty-first Amendment denouement.

The cause of this second sudden shift in opinion was the Great Depression that began about 1929. Jones has shown convincingly that every argument used to bring about repeal in 1932–1933 had been well known since the beginning of prohibition. The class aspect of the legislation, which had been so callously accepted in 1920, was suddenly undesirable. The main depression-related argument, that legalization of liquor manufacture would produce a badly needed additional tax revenue, was well known in the 1910s and even earlier. These rationalizations of repeal were masks for the fact that the general public, baffled by the economic catstrophe, found a convenient scapegoat: Prohibition. (The drys had, after all, tried to credit Prohibition for the prosperity of the 1920s.) The groundswell of public feeling was irresistible and the entire "experiment, noble in motive and far-reaching in purpose," was not modified but thrown out with Volsteadism, bathwater, baby, and all.

Because the AAPA won, its explanations of what happened were accepted at face value. One of the lasting results of Prohibition, therefore, was perpetuation of the stereotypes of the wet propaganda of the 1920s and the myth that the American experiment in Prohibition (usually misunderstood to have outlawed personal drinking as well as the liquor business) was a failure. Blanketed together here indiscriminately were all of the years from 1918 to 1933.

More than thirty years have passed since the repeal of the Eighteenth Amendment. Surely the AAPA has now had its full measure of victory and it is no longer necessary for historians to perpetuate a myth that grew up in another era. For decades there has been no realistic possibility of a resurgence of Prohibition in its Progressive form—or probably any other form.

The concern now is not so much the destruction of myth, however; the concern is that our acceptance of the myth of the failure of Prohibition has prevented us from exploring in depth social and especially sociological aspects of the Prohibition experiment. Recent scholarship, by treating Prohibition more as a reform than an experiment, has shown that we have been missing one of the most interesting incidents of twentieth-century history.

8

The New Deal

Revolutionary or Conservative?

Franklin Delano Roosevelt was perhaps the most controversial president ever to occupy the White House. For over twelve years he led the American people, first through the worst depression in their history and then through a war that encompassed virtually the entire globe. To his admirers he was an individual of heroic stature, a leader who firmly believed that it was possible to preserve free and democratic institutions by internal reforms without adopting authoritarian or totalitarian methods and overturning the basic structure of American society. To his enemies he was a misguided, even immoral, individual who mistakenly believed that he could save American democracy by taking the people down the road to the welfare state—a road that would eventually end in socialism and therefore the negation of individual freedom. Unlike some other presidents, Roosevelt had the uncanny ability to arouse strong passions. He was a person who was either loved or hated; few remained neutral toward him or reacted blandly to his personality or accomplishments.

Why did Roosevelt arouse such strong passions? The answer to this ostensibly simple question is anything but simple. Certainly there was little in his background or his accomplishments prior to 1933 that would explain the controversial nature of his presidential tenure. Even those friends and associates who worked closely with Roosevelt during his dozen years in the White House were not always able to grasp his many-sided personality or understand why he acted as he did. Frances Perkins, his long-time Secretary of Labor, described him as "the most complicated human being I ever knew," a comment that was echoed by others such as Henry Morgenthau and Robert E. Sherwood.

The controversy that surrounded Roosevelt's years in the White House has almost been matched by the quantity and quality of books written about him by friends, associates, and enemies. Unlike other presidents whose careers were not chronicled until decades after their death, Roosevelt has already been the subject of literally hundreds of books and articles. Part of the reason for this situation undoubtedly lies in the fact that much of the source material left by Roosevelt[1] and his associates was opened up to scholars within a surprisingly short time after his death in 1945. But part of the reason surely lies in the fascination with the New Deal and the changes that American society underwent during the years from 1933 to 1945. However the Roosevelt years are interpreted, it is difficult to avoid the conclusion that the United States was a very different nation in 1945 as compared with 1933.

It was the sheer magnitude of the New Deal innovations early in his presidential career that caused Roosevelt to become such a highly controversial figure. Although his victory in 1932 was relatively broadbased, he soon alienated many businessmen as well as other powerful interest groups. As a result, he came under increasingly harsh attacks as the 1930s progressed. Some accused him of subverting traditional American ideals of individualism and liberty by moving toward a welfare state that could end only in socialism and an omnipotent state. Such a staunch Democrat as Al Smith, for example, hotly argued during the presidential campaign of 1936 that Roosevelt was indeed taking the American people down the road to socialism. "It is all right with me if they [the Roosevelt administration] want to disguise themselves as Norman Thomas or Karl Marx, or Lenin, or any of the rest of that bunch," Smith shouted, "but what I won't stand for is allowing them to march under the banner of Jefferson, Jackson and Cleveland."[2]

The attack on Roosevelt's New Deal from the right was echoed also by the critics of the left. There were many who felt that the traditional American attachment to individualistic values had been rendered obsolete by the nation's industrial and technological advances. Rexford G. Tugwell, a professor of economics and one of the early New Deal "brain trusters," was one such critic. He was convinced that America's competitive economy had never worked well; to attempt to reform it with minor changes would prove hopelessly inadequate. What was required, Tugwell concluded, was thorough and effective governmental planning for all aspects of the economic system; only in this way could the economy be stabilized and future depressions avoided. Much to his disappointment, the New Deal seemed too pragmatic. Roosevelt, he finally concluded, was either unwilling or unable to plan in a rational and systematic manner. To the left of men like Tugwell stood the Socialist

---

[1]It has been estimated that Roosevelt's personal papers occupy more than 9,000 cubic feet at the Hyde Park Library; this figure does not include the papers of other important New Deal officials.

[2]Quoted in William E. Leuchtenburg, *Franklin D. Roosevelt and the New Deal 1932–1940* (New York, 1963), p. 178.

and Communist groups in America. Their criticism was that the New Deal was too conservative; the only proper approach to the depression was a complete overhaul of America's social and economic system and the establishment of a socialist state.

Thus, during the depression years the New Deal was attacked from many points of view. To some it was too radical; to others it was too conservative or reactionary. Still others viewed Roosevelt's policies as a series of pragmatic and expedient moves in response to specific events and deplored the fact that the president never seemed to give much thought to the overall dimensions of the crisis facing the American people. To be sure, many of these critics were reflecting to a large extent the passions and emotions of the age in which they were living. Faced with the problem of coming to grips with the greatest depression the country had ever known, they did not have the perspective nor the dispassionate attitude required to view the issues at stake in a detached or objective manner. Their criticisms, nevertheless, helped to establish the framework of reference with which later writers were to approach the New Deal. In brief, the question usually raised by contemporary commentators and later historians revolved around the role of the New Deal in American life. Was the New Deal simply an extension of the Progressive tradition, or did it involve a radical departure from the mainstream of American history?

For historians reared in the tradition of the Progressive school there was little doubt about the basic nature of the New Deal. Viewing America's past in terms of a conflict between liberalism and conservatism and the people versus the vested interests, they saw the New Deal as simply another phase in the struggle against monopoly, privilege, and special interests. To them the New Deal was related to earlier reform movements, including Jeffersonian and Jacksonian Democracy, populism, and progressivism, all of which had represented the people in their continuing struggle to achieve a greater measure of political, economic, and social equality. While they often referred to the revolutionary character of the New Deal, their use of the term "revolutionary" did not necessarily imply a sharp break with the past. Louis Hacker, although not squarely in the Progressive tradition, referred to the New Deal as the "Third American Revolution" in the mid-1940s. His description of the New Deal, however, was anything but revolutionary. Some of its policies, he wrote, were improvisations; some were descended from populism and progressivism; but always "there existed the thought that the responsibility of public authority for the welfare of the people was clear and that the intervention of the state was justifiable."[3] Hacker's last point, while by no means acceptable to all Ameri-

---

[3]Louis M. Hacker, *The Shaping of the American Tradition* (New York, 1947), pp. 1125–1126.

cans, was hardly novel; reformers and intellectuals had been urging government-sponsored reforms since the mid-nineteenth century.

To Henry Steele Commager, one of America's most distinguished historians, the relationship between the New Deal and earlier reform movements was obvious. Writing at the time of Roosevelt's death, Commager explicitly denied the revolutionary character of the New Deal. What was simply a new deal of old cards appeared radical for two reasons: the rapidity with which the New Deal program was enacted into law; and the fact that the movement contrasted so sharply with the do-nothing attitude of the Harding-Coolidge-Hoover administrations. If the New Deal was compared with the Progressive era rather than the 1920s, Commager maintained, "the contrast would have been less striking than the similarities. . . . [For] precedent for the major part of New Deal legislation was to be found in these earlier periods." The achievements of Roosevelt—the restoration of self-confidence, the reassertion of faith in democracy, and the rehabilitation of the nation's human and natural resources—all demonstrated the affinity of the New Deal to the earlier reform movements in American history.[4]

Perhaps the fullest and most eloquent argument favoring the idea that the New Deal was a continuation and extension of America's liberal past was advanced by the outstanding historian writing in the Progressive tradition. Arthur M. Schlesinger, Jr. A former professor at Harvard University, Schlesinger has been the most persuasive and brilliant historian writing within and in defense of America's liberal tradition. He was, of course, much more than a historian. A leading intellectual, important member of the Kennedy administration, and shrewd commentator on current affairs, Schlesinger has been an activist as well as a scholar. As a historian, Schlesinger since the close of World War II has championed a modified brand of American liberalism whose roots, he believed, go far back into the nation's history. Thus, his Pulitzer Prize-winning study, *The Age of Jackson* (1945), argued that Jacksonian Democracy was a liberal political movement based on a coalition of urban workers and other democratic groups in American society. Schlesinger attempted also to rebuild the intellectual foundations of the liberal ideology in his writings. His book *The Vital Center* (1948) incorporated Niebuhrian theology into the corpus of American liberalism so as to give the latter a more realistic and viable character. Taking cognizance of the reaction against liberal ideas since the 1940s, Schlesinger borrowed Reinhold Niebuhr's emphasis on original sin and reinterpreted the liberal ideology in order to purge that ideology of the charge that its utopian optimism had been unrealistic and its adherents had been incapable of meeting the challenge of totalitarianism since the 1930s.

---

[4]Henry Steele Commager, "Twelve Years of Roosevelt," *American Mercury* 40 (April 1945): 391–401.

All of American history, according to Schlesinger, was characterized by a cyclical movement which saw periods of liberal reform followed by alternate periods of conservative consolidation. In his eyes Jacksonian Democracy followed the decline of Jeffersonian Democracy, the Progressive era followed the age of the Robber Barons, and the New Deal came after the sterile conservatism of the 1920s. Indeed, Schlesinger argued, the New Frontier of John F. Kennedy and the Great Society of Lyndon B. Johnson were themselves reactions to the inaction of the Eisenhower years. The generative force behind this cycle was social conflict—conflict which arose from a constant accumulation of disquietude and discontent within American society. Schlesinger spelled out his thesis in a series of books and articles, one of which was *The Age of Roosevelt,* a multivolume study of the New Deal.[5]

In the first selection Schlesinger discusses the origins of the New Deal. To him the New Deal represented much more than a mere response to the depression. On the contrary, the New Deal was an integral part of the history of American liberalism; it was another phase of the liberal-conservative cycle in American history. By the 1920s, Schlesinger claimed, the nation had tired of the Progressive crusade. National disinterest in politics meant that power gravitated inevitably toward powerful economic interests, and government increasingly came under the control and influence of the business community. As a result of this shift in power, there was a progressive alienation of various groups from American society, including the farmers, workers, minority ethnic groups, and disenchanted intellectuals. Even without a depression, Schlesinger suggested, the New Deal was bound to have happened in one form or another. What the depression did was to give the New Deal its particular character—a political movement responding to the immediate problem of an impending economic collapse. The New Deal, he concluded, rejected the dogmatic absolutes and the simplistic dichotomies posed in contemporary ideologies such as communism and fascism. To Schlesinger the New Deal was a practical, energetic, and pragmatic movement based on the assumption that a "managed and modified capitalist order achieved by piecemeal experiment could combine personal freedom and economic growth."

Schlesinger's approach to the New Deal was echoed by other historians. Frank Freidel, author of what appears to be the most definitive multivolume biography of Roosevelt, wrote in much the same historiographical tradition as that of Schlesinger. Freidel, however, posed the discussion in quite different terms. To him the New Deal was basically the work of a number of persons who had grown to maturity during the

---

[5]Schlesinger has to date published three volumes of this study: *The Crisis of the Old Order, 1919–1933* (Boston, 1957), *The Coming of the New Deal* (Boston, 1958), and *The Politics of Upheaval* (Boston, 1960).

Progressive era and who still shared the moral fervor of that period. Like Roosevelt, they were conservative men whose primary goal was to save rather than to destroy the free enterprise system. These humanitarian reformers were willing to use the machinery and authority of government to improve the lot of the common man. Taken as a whole, the New Deal was based on "American objectives and experience in the Progressive Era and during the first World War."[6] To put it another way, Roosevelt's program was squarely within the American tradition; his goals were essentially to conserve the existing economic and social system by eliminating obvious defects rather than changing it by radical programs.

Historians such as Commager, Schlesinger, and Freidel were all favorably disposed to the New Deal because they identified themselves with the American liberal or Progressive tradition. This is not to imply that they were uncritical toward Roosevelt and the New Deal; in many instances they found much that was inadequate, wrong, or misleading about the goals, program, and administration of many New Deal experiments. Generally speaking, however, they wrote with approval of Roosevelt's pragmatism, his faith in American democracy, and his obvious distaste for totalitarian methods. The alternative to the New Deal, they hinted, might very well have been a dictatorship of the right or left if the nation had continued to drift along as it had under Hoover.

While such historians who identified themselves in the Progressive tradition were interpreting the New Deal in a favorable light, others, particularly those adhering to a conservative ideology, were writing in quite a different vein. Conceiving of individual freedom and competition in almost absolutist terms, they saw the New Deal as a violent departure from traditional American values. To them the New Deal was anything but a continuation of America's political tradition; it represented rather an outright rejection of everything that was good and desirable within that tradition. During the decade of the thirties, many critics, especially spokesmen of conservative social groups and businessmen, took this position on the New Deal. Former President Hoover, for example, sounded a note of warning in 1934 when he condemned the expansion

---

[6]Frank Freidel, *The New Deal in Historical Perspective* (2d ed.: Washington, D.C., 1965), p. 6. To date Freidel has published four volumes of his study of Roosevelt: *Franklin D. Roosevelt: The Apprenticeship* (Boston, 1952), *The Ordeal* (Boston, 1954), *The Triumph* (Boston, 1956), and *Launching the New Deal* (Boston, 1973).

In a recent study of Hoover, Roosevelt, the "Brain Trust," and the origins of the New Deal, Elliot A. Rosen argued that Roosevelt's domestic and diplomatic objectives were shaped in 1932 by a small group of advisers who gave the domestic economy priority. "A better distribution of income, achievement of the social minima, and federal intervention where necessary for social and economic purposes became part of our permanent past. This has remained the legacy of Roosevelt and the Brains Trust." Elliot A. Rosen, *Hoover, Roosevelt, and the Brains Trust: From Depression to New Deal* (New York, 1977), p. 380.

of the federal government's role and the subsequent regimentation of American life. "It is a vast shift," he wrote, "from the American concept of human rights which even the government may not infringe to those social philosophies where men are wholly subjective to the state. It is a vast casualty to Liberty if it shall be continued."[7]

Hoover's hostility was matched by other writers like John T. Flynn, a former liberal who had become progressively disillusioned by America's liberal tradition. Author of several books on Roosevelt, Flynn's antagonism against the New Deal reached a peak in his work *The Roosevelt Myth*. Specifically denying the achievements that liberal historians had credited to the New Deal, he argued that Roosevelt had substituted for the free enterprise system one that operated upon "permanent crises and an armament economy." In the process of implementing New Deal programs, the vigor of state governments had been sapped, the authority of Congress had been eroded, and unprecedented power had been concentrated in the hands of the president. One result of Roosevelt's New Deal policies was the appearance of a staggering federal debt; "a debt that can never be paid and which can be taken off our shoulders only by a great and devastating inflation."[8]

The charge by conservative writers that the New Deal represented a break with the past, interestingly enough, was echoed by some Progressive historians. One of these was Richard Hofstadter who, although writing within a liberal framework, was among the severest critics of America's liberal tradition. American liberalism, Hofstadter argued, had failed because of its moralizing tendencies and its inability to come to grips with the fundamental issues of the day. In *The Age of Reform: From Bryan to F.D.R.*, he insisted that the New Deal could not under any circumstances be interpreted as a continuation of the liberal-Progressive tradition. The section in his book devoted to the New Deal was appropriately entitled "The New Departure."

To Hofstadter the New Deal was markedly different from any other indigenous American political movement. Past reform movements, Hofstadter noted, had generally operated under the assumption that their purpose was to clear the way for new enterprises and new men—to smash established privilege and monopoly and to provide all Americans with an equal opportunity in life. Within this context, the national government was considered to be either negative in its nature or an obstacle in the way of success. Earlier reform movements had taken it for granted that American society was essentially a healthy society but one that needed further democratization to reach its full potential.

The New Deal, according to Hofstadter, was based on entirely dif-

[7]Herbert Hoover, *The Challenge to Liberty* (New York, 1934), p. 103.

[8]John T. Flynn, *The Roosevelt Myth* (rev. ed.: New York, 1956), pp. 414, 445.

ferent premises. Instead of viewing American society as healthy, New Deal reformers saw it as a sick society in need of changes that could only be instituted through federal action. Thus the New Deal accepted the idea of federal responsibility for the relief of the unemployed, supported legislation for social security, unemployment insurance, wages and hours, and public housing, and did not fear massive expenditures that resulted in deficit spending. Many of the traditional aims of past reform movements—to restore government to the people and to destroy big business and monopolies—were simply bypassed or ignored by Roosevelt. Considering the nature and magnitude of New Deal programs, Hofstadter concluded, the movement had to be considered a new departure in American life. "The New Deal, and the thinking it engendered," wrote Hofstadter, "represented the triumph of economic emergency and human needs over inherited notions and inhibitions. . . . At the core of the New Deal, then, was not a philosophy (FDR could identify himself philosophically only as a Christian and democrat), but an attitude, suitable for practical politicians, administrators, and technicians, but uncongenial to the moralism that the Progressives had for the most part shared with their opponents."[9]

The New Deal, Hofstadter pointed out with an ironic touch, represented a change of the usual ideological roles of American conservatives and reformers. The conservatives had traditionally prided themselves on their sense of realism, their distrust of abstract plans for remaking society, and their belief in the necessity for institutional continuity. Reformers, on the other hand, had invariably appealed to moral sentiments, denounced existing injustices, and aroused the indignation of the community. By the 1930s, however, the traditional roles of the two had become reversed. Reformers appealed not to moral abstractions, but to concrete grievances of specific groups—farmers without markets, unemployed men without bread, laborers seeking to organize in unions of their own choosing, and to those groups concerned with the soundness of banks, investment markets, and manufacturing enterprises. Conservatives were now in the position of moral critics—they denounced the New Deal precisely because of its violation of traditional rules, its abandonment of the nation's moral heritage, its departure from sound principles, and its imposition of a federal tyranny upon the American people.

Oddly enough, Hofstadter was unhappy with the efforts of both conservatives and reformers. The reformers from the New Deal on, according to him, had refused to think in terms of rational planning and remained content to respond in a pragmatic way to individual pressures

---

[9]Richard Hofstadter, *The Age of Reform: From Bryan to F.D.R.* (New York, 1955), pp. 314, 323.

and situations as they arose. The criticisms of the conservatives, on the other hand, were "hollow and cliché-ridden," the complaints of a class increasingly cut off from the world of reality. But all that Hofstadter could do—at least in his role as historian and contemporary critic—was to hope that a better understanding of America's past political tradition might help future politicians to formulate a more realistic philosophy.

A similar criticism was voiced by Rexford G. Tugwell, a Columbia University professor who had joined Roosevelt's administration in the early 1930s as a strong advocate of governmental economic planning. The old faith in a self-regulating market, he maintained, had never been justified; it was part of the American mythology of a free enterprise system. Distrustful of business and businessmen, Tugwell felt that only the federal government was in a position to control the economy in such a way as to make it run smoothly and efficiently.

After leaving government service to return to the academic world, Tugwell set out to write a biography of Roosevelt, which was finally published in 1957, although parts had appeared in a series of long articles somewhat earlier. The picture Tugwell drew of Roosevelt and the New Deal was a friendly one, but one also marked with a sense of disappointment. According to Tugwell, the productive capacity of the American economy by the late 1920s had far outrun purchasing power, thus giving rise to a fundamental maladjustment which resulted in the depression. The Republicans under Hoover initially denied that the economic situation was serious. Later they adopted halfway measures and encouraged private rather than public relief. When Roosevelt came to power, he was faced with a grave emergency but one which gave him an unprecedented opportunity such as no other president had had. Although he was a master improviser and politician, Roosevelt never conceived of New Deal measures in terms of rational planning. Many of the New Deal innovations, indeed, resulted from careful balancing between the claims of various competing pressure groups. Roosevelt, Tugwell concluded, was a political pragmatist with a progressive bent. Despite his essential greatness, he was unable or unwilling to seize the opportunity and institute far-reaching reform measures. Whether future historians would continue to look upon the New Deal in this manner, Tugwell admitted, was an open question.[10]

Both Hofstadter and Tugwell were critical of Roosevelt because of his political opportunism and his pragmatic approach to serious problems. Implicit in their writings was the belief that the New Deal could not be interpreted as a part of America's liberal tradition. Oddly enough, they

---

[10]Rexford G. Tugwell, "The New Deal in Retrospect," *Western Political Quarterly* 1 (December 1948): 373–85. See also Tugwell's full length study of Roosevelt, *The Democratic Roosevelt* (New York, 1957).

were in agreement with recent neoconservative historians who had also rejected the thesis that American history could be understood in terms of class and ideological conflict. In the eyes of these more recent historians, American history had been marked not by conflict and divisions, but by stability and unity. Domestic struggles in the United States, they maintained, were over means, never over ends. To look upon the politics of the 1930s as an expression of fundamental divisions among the American people, they concluded, was a mistake.

But if the New Deal did not reflect fundamental class and ideological divisions, what did it reflect? To Heinz Eulau, a political scientist at Stanford University writing in essentially a neoconservative vein, the New Deal defied ideological classification. It is true, he admitted, that many individuals associated with Roosevelt had their own particular blueprints for the reconstruction of American society. Taken as a whole, however, the New Deal had many sides, and for this reason was not the product of a cohesive and rational ideology. Nor did the New Deal articulate a faith in a better tomorrow; it did not call upon people to join a crusade to remake their society or to experiment with new and untried schemes. But if the New Deal was not an ideology, a faith, a crusade, an experiment, a revolt, or a charisma, what was it? To Eulau the answer to this question was clear. The New Deal, he suggested, was "both a symbol and evidence of the nation's political maturity"; it represented an effort to solve problems "through politics rather than through ideology or violence." In Eulau's eyes a mature politics involves adjustment, compromise, and integration. By this standard the New Deal symbolized a mature politics because it was seeking solutions to problems rather than imposing preconceived solutions on problems.[11]

By implication Eulau was agreeing with those neoconservative historians who rejected class and ideological interpretations of American history in favor of an approach that emphasized the stability of American institutions and the pragmatism of American culture. The distinguishing characteristic of American history, therefore, was a rejection of the unrealistic intellectual and ideological characteristics of European thought and the substitution in their place of common sense. To writers like Eulau the New Deal must be understood as part of the basic common-sense approach of most Americans and their rejection of the world of ideology. In this sense the New Deal was not comparable to earlier liberal movements; the New Deal was simply an attempt to cope with unique problems in a simple and sensible manner.

During the 1960s the stature of Franklin D. Roosevelt and the New Deal again began to change as younger scholars asked some searching

---

[11]Heinz Eulau, "Neither Ideology Nor Utopia: The New Deal in Retrospect," *Antioch Review*, 19 (Winter 1959–1960): 523–37.

questions. If the New Deal had modified and humanized American society, why did poverty and racism continue to exist? If the New Deal had truly reformed an unbridled capitalism and made it more responsive to the needs of people, why were so many different groups—blacks, Puerto Ricans, Mexican Americans, and middle-class youths—alienated from their society? If the New Deal had led to a change for the better in terms of America's role in world affairs, how had the nation become involved first in the Korean War and then in the Vietnam conflict? Given the tensions and crises of the 1960s, it was perhaps inevitable that the historical image of the New Deal would once again change.

Perhaps the sharpest critique—though by no means the only one—came from the pens of historians identified with the New Left. Many of these scholars were committed to radical changes in the structure of American society and they saw history as a discipline that would illuminate the present by a searching examination of the past. We have "sought explicitly," wrote the editor of a book of essays representing in part New Left scholarship, "to make the past speak to the present, to ask questions that have a deep-rooted moral and political relevance. In moving occasionally beyond description and causal analysis to judge significance, we have, by necessity, moved beyond objective history in the realm of values."[12]

Given their own values and commitment to social change, it was natural that radical historians would see the New Deal in an unfavorable light. In an essay discussing the place of the New Deal in American history, for example, Barton J. Bernstein argued that the liberal reforms of the 1930s had not transformed the American system; rather they conserved and protected corporate capitalism. Nor had the New Deal significantly redistributed power in any way, or granted any meaningful recognition to unorganized peoples. Even its bolder programs had not extended the beneficence of government beyond affluent groups or used the wealth of the few for the needs of the many. The New Deal followed essentially conservative goals, for it was intended to maintain the American system intact. "The New Deal," Bernstein concluded, "failed to solve the problem of depression, it failed to raise the impoverished, it failed to redistribute income, it failed to extend equality and generally countenanced racial discrimination and segregation. It failed generally to make business more responsible to the social welfare or to threaten business's pre-eminent political power.... In acting to protect the institution of private property and in advancing the interests of corporate capitalism, the New Deal assisted the middle and upper sectors of society. It protected them, sometimes, even at the cost of

---

[12]Barton J. Bernstein, ed., *Towards a New Past: Dissenting Essays in American History* (New York, 1968), p. xiii.

injuring the lower sectors. Seldom did it bestow much of substance upon the lower classes."[13]

From the vantage point of the political left, therefore, the New Deal was a failure. Committed to capitalism, it could not offer the lower classes anything but rhetoric and psychological comfort. So wrote even Paul K. Conkin in a penetrating analysis of Roosevelt and the New Deal. Judging the New Deal more from the perspective of a social democrat rather than a partisan of the New Left, he expressed considerable admiration for Roosevelt's political astuteness and charismatic qualities. Yet Conkin denied that Roosevelt was even a pragmatist, for his thought was too shallow and superficial and concerned largely with immediate issues. "For the historian," noted Conkin in his critical but compassionate summation, "every judgment, every evaluation of the past has to be tinged with a pinch of compassion, a sense of the beauty and nobility present when honest hopes and humane ideals are frustrated. He sees that the thirties could have brought so much more, but also so much worse, than the New Deal. The limiting context has to be understood— the safeguards and impediments of our political system, Roosevelt's intellectual limitations, and most of all the appalling economic ignorance and philosophic immaturity of the American electorate.... The New Deal solved a few problems, ameliorated a few more, obscured many, and created new ones. This is about all our political system can generate, even in crisis."[14]

Much of the historiography of the New Deal, therefore, reflected to some degree personal ideological commitments. To Progressive scholars Roosevelt was a hero; to conservatives he was too radical; and to radicals he was too conservative, if not reactionary. Each group, of course, judged Roosevelt in terms of the direction they felt America *should* have taken.

In a major study of New Deal economic policy, however, Ellis W. Hawley approached the problem quite differently. Americans, he noted, shared a commitment to two value systems that were not wholly compatible. On the one hand, they cherished liberty and freedom, which implied a competitive economic and social order. On the other hand, they valued order, rationality, and collective organization, and associated large business units and economic organizations generally with abundance, progress, and a rising standard of living. Yet the latter value posed a potential threat to the former; monopoly negated, at least in theory, freedom and competition. Much of twentieth-century American history, Hawley observed, revolved around the search for a solution

[13]Barton J. Bernstein, "The New Deal: The Conservative Achievements of Liberal Reform," in *ibid.*, pp. 264, 281–82.

[14]Paul K. Conkin, *The New Deal* (New York, 1967).

"that would preserve the industrial order, necessarily based upon a high degree of collective organization, and yet would preserve America's democratic heritage at the same time." New Deal economic policy mirrored this basic ambivalence; it vacillated between rational planning and antimonopoly, neither of which was completely compatible. Hawley's conclusion offered little support to any of the competing ideologies that underlay many of the historical interpretations of Roosevelt and the New Deal. "If the experiences of the nineteen thirties have any relevance at all," he wrote, "it is in illustrating the limitations of logical analysis, the pitfalls inherent in broad theoretical approaches, the difficulty of agreeing on policy goals, and the necessity of making due allowances for the intellectual heritage, current trends of opinion, and the realities of pressure-group politics."[15]

In the second selection in this chapter Hawley analyzes the nature of business-government relationships in the New Deal era. Rejecting either the glorification or denigration of the mixed economy created during the 1930s, Hawley emphasizes instead the tensions between organizational capitalism and the liberal-democratic ethos, as well as Franklin Delano Roosevelt's tendency to resist ideological systems. Nor does he accept the claim that business groups dominated policy making during the depression. What emerged from the New Deal, he concludes, "was the creation not of an omnipotent corporate elite but of a complex interaction between conflicting interest groups, resurgent liberal ideals, and the champions of competing reform models, all of which, after all, contemplated the salvation and stabilizing of corporate capitalism as well as the democratizing of it."

Considering, then, the many ways historians have written about the New Deal, is it possible to come to any sort of definitive conclusions about its essential nature? Can Roosevelt and the New Deal be positioned precisely in terms of their place within the American political tradition? In dealing with this question, it should be emphasized that many of the apparent differences between students writing about the New Deal are partly semantical in nature. When describing the operation of specific New Deal programs, for example, the differences of opinion between historians tend to narrow sharply. Thus, what the WPA, NRA, and other federal agencies *did* is often not a subject of dispute. The issue that invariably leads to conflict is the *intent* of the participants involved. The controversy involves not the relief activities of the 1930s, to cite one instance, but whether or not the concept of federal relief undermined the cherished American ideals of individualism and liberty.

---

[15]Ellis W. Hawley, *The New Deal and the Problem of Monopoly: A Study in Economic Ambivalence* (Princeton, 1966), p. 493.

The semantic difficulty may be seen in the various ways historians have used the word *pragmatic*. When Roosevelt was described as a "pragmatic leader," what did this mean? Actually the term was used in at least three different ways. Edgar E. Robinson, for example, has described Roosevelt's personal leadership as "pragmatic—an individual playing by ear." What Robinson meant by his characterization was that Roosevelt, in order to gain an immediate political advantage, never considered the long-range effects of his policies. "Roosevelt's failure," Robinson concluded, "lay in his unsuccessful attempt to justify the means or establish the ends he had in view." Underlying Robinson's thesis was the criticism that the New Deal resulted in an almost fatal concentration of power in the hands of the executive—a "power that could destroy the world or build it in the image of an entirely new scientific perspective."[16]

A second use of the term *pragmatic*, as we have already seen in Tugwell's case, involved the criticism that Roosevelt never even understood the need for long-range economic planning. Roosevelt limited himself to immediate problems and tended to neglect more fundamental issues. Consequently, he never took advantage of the unparalleled opportunity for reform that arose out of the greatest single economic crisis that the American people had ever faced. While New Deal measures were important in giving status and material benefits to groups in American society that had been hitherto neglected, relatively speaking, these reforms fell short of their real potential. This view of Roosevelt, which has been echoed by many writers, is based on the underlying assumption that New Deal pragmatism and rational governmental planning were incompatible.

The term *pragmatic* has been used in a third way to describe a mental attitude and frame of mind that rejected the dogmatic thinking of the 1930s and remained open and receptive to new ideas. William E. Leuchtenburg, a Columbia University historian, has argued that the pragmatism of the New Deal seemed striking only because the period as a whole was characterized by rigid ideological thinking. The New Deal was pragmatic, Leuchtenburg maintained, "only in contrast to the rigidity of Hoover and of the Left." Moreover, the movement was pragmatic in the sense that reformers themselves remained skeptical about final utopias and ultimate solutions and were always open to experimentation. To Leuchtenburg the New Deal was more than a movement to experiment or to improvise; it was a movement led by men who were committed to the proposition that it was possible to make human life more tolerable, that depressions were by no means inevitable events,

---

[16]Edgar Eugene Robinson, *The Roosevelt Leadership 1933–1945* (Philadelphia, 1955), pp. 383, 397, 408.

and that human affairs were not necessarily guided by inexorable deterministic laws.[17]

Because of the preoccupation with the New Deal as a national phenomenon, historians have generally not dealt with its actual impact on the lives of individuals. In a recent study of Boston during the 1930s, Charles H. Trout observed that the "New Deal's manifestations were treated piecemeal and were perceived by individuals and groups according to their particular needs." Indeed, many federal programs involving social and economic change were resisted by Bostonians precisely because of the weight of tradition and history; the concept "of a national or even a municipal communality of interest was seldom grasped."[18] From a local perspective, therefore, the accomplishments of the New Deal were limited and more remote.

The problem of understanding and assessing the achievements of the New Deal and its place in American history, therefore, is one whose answer will largely be determined by a series of prior assumptions about the nature of the American past and the nation's ideals in both the present and future. To those historians whose view is that America is founded upon an atomistic philosophy—that the nation's greatness arose from the achievements of talented and ambitious individuals and was not always related to the activities of government—the New Deal will always appear as a movement alien and hostile to traditional values. In this context the New Deal represents a new departure in American history that will end perhaps in a collectivistic and authoritarian government. On the other hand, to those scholars who adhere to a corporate philosophy—that society is more than a mere aggregate of private individuals and that a modern complex industrial economy requires a certain amount of public regulation as well as government-sponsored reform—the New Deal becomes a political movement inspired by proper ideals. Instead of being an aberration in terms of the American political tradition, the New Deal was a movement consonant with previous struggles for justice and equality. Finally, to those historians who maintain that only a radical restructuring of American society could eliminate poverty, racism, war, and inequality, the New Deal appears as a palliative or sham designed to gloss over fundamental defects.

The problem of judging the nature and accomplishments of the New Deal is, then, a difficult one, for it involves the entire fabric of the American past. Indeed, to avoid any broad judgments is in effect to render a judgment, albeit on an unconscious level. In the final analysis,

---

[17]William E. Leuchtenburg, *Franklin D. Roosevelt and the New Deal 1932–1940* (New York, 1963), pp. 344–45.

[18]Charles H. Trout, *Boston, The Great Depression, and the New Deal* (New York, 1977), pp. 321–22.

therefore, historians will continue to grapple with the place of the New Deal in American life. Was the New Deal a continuation of America's liberal tradition or was it a repudiation of that tradition? Did the New Deal reflect an attempt by corporate capitalism to maintain its power intact by forging a partnership with the federal government, with the latter in a subordinate position? Or did the New Deal give a significant voice to minority groups that in the past had been powerless? Can the New Deal even be understood in ideological terms or should it be viewed as a political movement characterized by an underlying pragmatism? Or were the alleged inconsistencies of the New Deal a reflection of the underlying commitment of Americans to the values of order and freedom, which in turn gave rise to ambivalent policies? These are only some of the broad questions that must be answered in order to assess the nature and significance of the New Deal.[19]

---

[19]For a penetrating analysis of the historical literature on the New Deal see Alfred B. Rollins, Jr., "Was There Really a Man Named Roosevelt?," in *American History: Retrospect and Prospect*, ed. George A. Billias and Gerald N. Grob (New York, 1971), pp. 232–70.

Arthur M. Schlesinger, Jr.

ARTHUR M. SCHLESINGER, JR. (1917–   ) is Albert Schweitzer Professor of the Humanities at the City University of New York. He was also a special assistant to President John F. Kennedy. Among his many published works are *The Age of Jackson* (1945), *The Age of Roosevelt* (1956–   ), *A Thousand Days: John F. Kennedy in the White House* (1965), and *Robert Kennedy and His Times* (1978).

In the background of any historical episode lies all previous history. The strands which a historian may select as vital to an understanding of the particular episode will vary widely according to his interest, his temperament, his faith and his time. Each man must unravel the seamless web in his own way. I do not propose here any definitive assessment of the sources of the New Deal. I doubt whether a final assessment is possible. I want rather to call attention to certain possible sources which may not have figured extensively in the conventional accounts, including my own—to the relation of the New Deal to the ebb and flow of American national politics and then its relation to the international dilemma of free society in this century.

Such relationships are speculative; nonetheless, an attempt to see them may perhaps cast light on some of the less discussed impulses behind the New Deal itself. To begin—and in order to make a sharp issue—let me ask this question: Would there have been a New Deal if there had been no depression? Without a depression, would we have had nothing but a placid continuation, so long as prosperity itself continued, of the New Era of the twenties?

I would answer that there would very likely have been some sort of New Deal in the thirties even without the depression. I think perhaps our contemporary thinking has come too unreflectively to assume depression as the necessary preliminary for any era of reform. Students of American history know better. The fight against depression was, to be sure, the heart of the New Deal, but it has not been the central issue of traditional American reform: it was not the heart of Jeffersonian Democracy nor of Jacksonian Democracy nor of the antislavery movement nor of the Progressive movement.

What preceded these other epochs of reform was an accumulation of disquietudes and discontents in American society, often noneconomic in character, and producing a general susceptibility to appeals for change—this and the existence within society of able men or groups who felt themselves cramped by the status quo and who were capable of exploiting mounting dissatisfaction to advance policies and purposes of their own. This combination of outsiders striving for status and power and a people wearying of the existing leadership and the existing ideals has been the real archetype of American reform.

The official order in the twenties presented perhaps the nearest we ever came in our history to the identification of the national interest with the interests, values, and goals of a specific class—in this case, of course, the American business community. During the generation before Harding, the political leaders who had commanded the loyalties and the energies of the American people—Theodore Roosevelt and Woodrow Wilson—expressed strains in American life distinct from and often opposed to the dominant values of business. They represented a fusion of patrician and intellectual attitudes which saw in public policy an outlet for creative energy—in Lippmann's phrase, they stood for mastery as against drift. In the service of this conception, they led the people into great national efforts of various sorts, culminating in the convulsive and terrible experience of war. Two decades of this—two decades under the glittering eyes of such leaders as [Theodore] Roosevelt and Wilson, Bryan and La Follette—left the nation in a state of exhaustion.

By 1920 the nation was tired of public crisis. It was tired of discipline and sacrifice. It was tired of abstract and intangible objectives. It could gird itself no longer for heroic moral or intellectual effort. Its instinct for idealism was spent. "It is only once in a generation," Wilson himself had said, "that a people can be lifted above material things. That is why conservative government is in the saddle two-thirds of the time." And the junior official to whom he made this remark, the young Assistant Secretary of the Navy, also noted soon after his unsuccessful try for the vice-presidency in 1920, "Every war brings after it a period of materialism and conservatism; people tire quickly of ideals and we are now repeating history." John W. Davis, the Democratic candidate in 1924, said a few years later: "The people usually know what they want at a particular time. . . . In 1924 when I was a candidate what they wanted was repose."

A nation fatigued with ideals and longing for repose was ready for "normalcy." As popular attention receded from public policy, as values and aspirations became private again, people stopped caring about poli-

ARTHUR M. SCHLESINGER, JR.   309

tics, which meant that political power inevitably gravitated to society's powerful economic interests—the government of the exhausted nation quite naturally fell to the businessmen. And for nearly a decade the business government reigned over a prosperous and expanding country.

Yet, for all the material contentment of the twenties, the decade was also marked by mounting spiritual and psychological discontent. One could detect abundant and multiplying symptoms of what Josiah Royce, after Hegel, used to call a self-estranged social order. The official creed began to encounter growing skepticism, and even opposition and ridicule, in the community at large. Able and ambitious groups, denied what they considered fitting recognition or opportunity, began to turn against the Establishment.

If the economic crash of 1929 astonished the experts, a spiritual crash was diagnosed well in advance. "By 1927," reported Scott Fitzgerald, "a widespread neurosis began to be evident, faintly signaled, like a nervous beating of the feet, by the popularity of crossword puzzles." In the same year Walter Lippmann pointed more soberly to the growing discrepancy between the nominal political issues of the day and the actual emotions of the people. If politics took up these real issues, Lippmann said, it would revolutionize the existing party system. "It is not surprising, then, that our political leaders are greatly occupied in dampening down interest, in obscuring issues, and in attempting to distract attention from the realities of American life."

What was wrong with the New Era was not (as yet) evidence of incompetence or stupidity in public policy. Rather, there was a profound discontent with the monopoly of power and prestige by a single class and the resulting indifference of the national government to deeper tensions. Those excluded from the magic circle suffered boredom, resentment, irritation and eventually indignation over what seemed the intolerable pretensions and irrelevances of their masters. Now it is the gravest error to underrate the power of boredom as a factor in social change. Our political scientists have pointed out convincingly how the human tendency toward inertia sets limits on liberalism; I wish they would spend equal time showing how the human capacity for boredom sets limits on conservatism. The dominant official society—the Establishment—of the twenties was an exceedingly boring one, neither bright nor witty nor picturesque nor even handsome, and this prodded the human impulse to redress the balance by kicking up heels in back streets.

All this encouraged the defection of specific groups from a social order which ignored their needs and snubbed their ambitions. Within the business community itself there were dissident individuals, especially in the underdeveloped areas of the country, who considered that opportunities for local growth were unduly restrained by Wall Street's control of the money market. The farmers felt themselves shut out from the prevailing prosperity. Elements in the labor movement resented their evident second-class citizenship. Members of foreign nationality groups, especially the newer immigration and its children, chafed under the prevalent assumption that the real America was Anglo-Saxon, Protestant, middle class, and white. In time some of the younger people of the nation began to grow restless before the ideals held out to them; while others, in accepting these ideals, acquired a smug mediocrity which even depressed some of their elders.

Gravest among the symptoms was the defection of the intellectuals: writers, educators, newspapermen, editors—those who manned the machinery of opinion and who transmitted ideas. The fact of their particular estrangement and discontent guaranteed the articulation, and thus, to a degree, the coordination of the larger unrest. The intellectuals put the ruling class in its place by substituting for it own admiring picture of itself a set of disrespectful images, which an increasing number of people found delightful and persuasive; the insiders, who had before been seen in the reverent terms of Bruce Barton and the *American Magazine,* were now to be seen less reverently through the eyes of H. L. Mencken and Sinclair Lewis. Satire liberated people from the illusion of business infallibility and opened their minds to other visions of American possibility. The next function of the intellectuals was precisely to explore and substantiate those other visions. They did so with zest and ingenuity; and the result was that, beneath the official crust, the twenties billowed with agitation, criticism and hope. Dewey affirmed man's capability for social invention and management; Beard argued that intelligent national planning was the irresistible next phase in history; Parrington insisted that Jeffersonian idealism had a sound basis in the American past, and indeed, expressed a truer Americanism than did materialism. Together the satirists and the prophets drew a new portrait of America—both of the American present and of the American promise—and the increasingly visible discrepancy between what was and what might be in America armed the spreading discontent.

The well of idealism was rising again; energies were being replenished, batteries recharged. Outsiders were preparing to hammer on the gates of the citadel. The 1928 election, in which an Irish Catholic challenged Yankee Protestant supremacy, illustrated the gathering revolt against the Establishment. And, though Hoover won the election, Samuel Lubell has pointed out that "Smith split not only the Solid South, but the Republican North as well." Smith carried counties which had long been traditionally Republican; he smashed the Republican hold on the cities; he mobilized the new immigrants. In losing, he polled nearly as many votes as Calvin Coolidge had polled in winning four years before. He stood for the vital new tendencies of politics; and it is likely that the prolongation of these tendencies would have assured a national Democratic victory, without a depression, in 1932 or certainly by 1936. And such a Democratic victory would surely have meant the discharge into public life of able and ambitious people denied preference under a business administration—much the same sort of people, indeed, who eventually came to power with the New Deal; and it would have meant new opportunities for groups that had seen the door slammed in their faces in the Twenties—labor, the farmers, the ethnic minorities, the intellectuals.

The suspicion that a political overturn was due even without a depression is fortified, I think, by the calculations of my father in his essay of some years back "The Tides of National Politics." In this essay he proposed that liberal and conservative periods in our national life succeeded themselves at intervals of about fifteen or sixteen years; this alternation takes place, he wrote, without any apparent correlation with economic circumstances or, indeed, with anything else, except the ebb and flow of national political psychology. By this argument, a liberal epoch was due in America around 1934 or 1935, depression or no.

In short, the New Deal was, among other things, an expression of what would seem—to use a currently unfashionable concept—an inherent cyclical rhythm in American politics. The depression did not cause the cycle: What the depression did was to increase its intensity and deepen its impact by superimposing on the normal cycle the peculiar and unprecedented urgencies arising from economic despair. One might even argue—though I do not think I would—that the depression coming at another stage in the cycle would not necessarily have produced a New Deal. It is certainly true, as I said, that depressions did not induce epochs of reform in 1873 or in 1893. I think myself, however, that the magnitude of the shock made a political recoil almost certain after 1929. Still, the fact that this recoil took a liberal rather than a reactionary turn may well be due to the accident that the economic shock coincided with a liberal turn in the political cycle.

In any event, the fact remains that the historical New Deal, whether or not something like it might have come along anyway, was after all brought into being by the depression. It assumed its particular character as it sought to respond to the challenge of economic collapse. And, in confronting this challenge, it was confronting a good deal more than merely an American problem. Mass unemployment touched the very roots of free institutions everywhere. "This problem of unemployment," as Winston Churchill said in England in 1930, "is the most torturing that can be presented to civilized society." The problem was more than torturing; it was something civilized society had to solve if it were to survive. And the issue presented with particular urgency was whether representative democracy could ever deal effectively with it.

Churchill, in the same Romanes lecture at Oxford in 1930, questioned whether it could: Democratic governments, he said, drifted along the lines of least resistance, took short views, smoothed their path with platitudes, and paid their way with sops and doles. Parliaments, he suggested, could deal with political problems, but not with economic. "One may even be pardoned," Churchill said, "for doubting whether institutions based on adult suffrage could possibly arrive at the right decisions upon the intricate propositions of modern business and finance." These were delicate problems requiring specialist treatment. "You cannot cure cancer by a majority. What is wanted is a remedy."

The drift of discussion in the United States as well as in Britain in the early thirties revealed an increasingly dour sense of existing alternatives; on the one hand, it seemed, was parliamentary democracy with economic chaos; on the other, economic authoritarianism with political tyranny. Even more dour was the sense that history had already made the choice—that the democratic impulse was drained of vitality, that liberalism was spent as a means of organizing human action. Consider a selection of statements from American writers at the time, and their mortuary resonance:

> The rejection of democracy is nowadays regarded as evidence of superior wisdom. (Ralph Barton Perry)
>
> The moral and intellectual bankruptcy of liberalism in our time needs no demonstration. It is as obvious as rain and as taken for granted. (Nathaniel Peffer)
>
> To attempt a defense of democracy these days is a little like defending paganism in 313 or the divine right of kings in 1793. It is taken for granted that democracy is bad and that it is dying. (George Boas)
>
> 'Liberalism is dead.' So many people who seem to agree upon nothing else have agreed to accept these three sweeping words. (Joseph Wood Krutch)
>
> Modern Western civilization is a failure. That theory is now generally accepted. (Louise Maunsell Fields)
>
> Why is it that democracy has fallen so rapidly from the high prestige which it had at the Armistice? . . . Why is it that in America itself—in the very temple and citadel of democracy—self-government has been held up to every ridicule, and many observers count it already dead? (Will Durant)

Only the most venerable among us can remember the creeping fear of a quarter of a century ago that the free system itself had run out of energy, that we had reached, in a phrase Reinhold Niebuhr used as a part of the title of a book in 1934, the "end of an era." What this pessimism implied for the realm of public policy was that democracy had exhausted its intellectual and moral resources, its bag of tricks was played out, and salvation now lay in moving over to a system of total control.

In affirming that there was no alternative between laissez-faire and tyranny, the pessimists were endorsing a passionate conviction held both by the proponents of individualism and the proponents of collectivism. Ogden Mills spoke with precision for American conservatives: "We can have a free country or a socialistic one. We cannot have both. Our economic system cannot be half free and half socialistic. . . . There is no middle ground between governing and being governed, between absolute sovereignty and liberty, between tyranny and freedom." Herbert Hoover was equally vehement: "Even partial regimentation cannot be made to work and still maintain live democratic institutions." In such sentiments, Hoover and Mills would have commanded the enthusiastic assent of Stalin and Mussolini. The critical question was whether a middle way was possible—a mixed system which might give the state more power than conservatives would like, enough power, indeed, to assure economic and social security, but still not too much as to create dictatorship. To this question the Hoovers, no less than the Stalins and Mussolinis, had long since returned categorical answers. They all agreed on this, if on nothing else: no.

As I have said, economic planning was not just an American problem. Great Britain, for example, was confronting mass unemployment and economic stagnation; moreover, she had had since 1929 a Labor government. In a sense, it would have been hard to select a better place to test the possibilities of a tranquil advance from laissez-faire capitalism to a managed society. Here was a Labor leadership, sustained by a faith in the "inevitability of gradualness," ruling a nation committed by tradition and instinct to the acceptance of empirical change. How did the British Labor government visualize its problem and opportunity?

The central figures in the Labor government of 1929 were Ramsay MacDonald, now prime minister for the second time, and Philip Snowden, his sharp and dominating chancellor of the exchequer. Both were classic Socialists who saw in the nationalization of basic industry the answer to all economic riddles. Yet in the existing political situation, with a slim Labor majority, nationalization was out of the question. With socialism excluded, MacDonald and Snowden—indeed, nearly all the Labor party leaders—could see no alternative to all-out socialism but nearly all-out laissez-faire. A capitalist order had to be operated on capitalist principles. The economic policy of the Labor government was thus consecrated as faithfully as that of Herbert Hoover's Republican administration in the United States to the balanced budget and the gold standard—and, far more faithfully than American Republicanism, to free trade.

Socialism across the Channel was hardly more resourceful. As the German Social Democrat Fritz Naphtali put it in 1930, "I don't believe that we can do very much, nor anything very decisive, from the point of view of economic policy, to overcome the crisis until it has run its course," In this spirit of impotence, the democratic Socialists of Europe (until Léon Blum came to power some years later) denied the possibility of a middle way and concluded that, short of full socialization, they had no alternative but to accept the logic of laissez-faire.

The assumption that there were two absolutely distinct economic orders, socialism and capitalism, expressed, of course, an unconscious Platonism—a conviction that the true reality lay in the theoretical essences of which any working economy, with its compromises and confusions, could only be an imperfect copy. If in the realm of essences socialism and capitalism were separate phenomena based on separate principles, then they must be kept rigorously apart on earth. Nor was this use of Platonism—this curious belief that the abstraction was somehow more real than the reality, which Whitehead so well called the "fallacy of misplaced concreteness"—confined to doctrinaire capitalists and doctrinaire socialists. The eminent Liberal economist Sir William Beveridge, director of the London School of Economics, braintruster for the Lloyd George welfare reforms before the First World War, spoke for enlightened economic opinion when he identified the "inescapable fatal danger" confronting public policy in the depression as "the danger of mixing freedom and control. We have to decide either to let production be guided by the free play of prices or to plan it socialistically from beginning to end. . . . Control and freedom do not mix." Beveridge, encountering Donald Richberg in Washington in the glowing days of 1933, asked a bit patronizingly whether Richberg really believed that there was "a half-way between Wall Street and Moscow." As for Britain, "there is not much that anyone can do now to help us," Beveridge said. "We must plan to avoid another crisis later. We shall not by conscious effort escape this one."

So dogma denied the possibility of a managed capitalism. But could dogma hold out in Britain against the urgencies of depression? Some Englishmen dissented from the either/or philosophy. In the general election of 1929, for example, John Maynard Keynes and Hubert Henderson had provided the Liberal party with the rudiments of an expansionist policy, based on national spending and public works. As unemployment increased in 1930, so too did the pressure for positive government action. That year Sir Oswald Mosley, a member of the Labor government, proposed to a cabinet committee on unemployment an active program of government spending, accompanied by controls over banking, industry and foreign trade. But he could make no impression on the capitalist orthodoxy of the Socialist leaders; Snowden rejected the Mosley memorandum. Another minister suggested leaving the gold standard; Snowden covered him with scorn. To the party conference of 1930, MacDonald said, "I appeal to you to go back to your Socialist faith. Do not mix that up with pettifogging patching, either of a Poor Law kind or Relief Work kind." In other words, socialism meant all or—in this case—nothing!

As economic pressure increased, more and more had to be sacrificed to the balancing of the budget; and the implacable retrenchment meant more governmental economy, reduction in salaries, reduction in normal public works, until in time, the frenzy for economy threatened the social services and especially the system of unemployment payments on which many British workers relied to keep alive. The summer crisis of 1931, after the failure of *Kreditanstalt*, weakened the pound; and to Snowden and the Labor government nothing now seemed more essential than staying on the gold standard. To keep Britain on gold required American loans; American loans would not be forthcoming unless satisfactory evidence existed of a determination to balance the budget; and the evidence most likely to satisfy J. P. Morgan and Company, which was arranging the American credit, was a cut in unemployment benefits.

In August 1931, MacDonald and Snowden confronted the cabinet with this dismal logic. Arthur Henderson made it clear that the whole cabinet absolutely accepted Snowden's economic theory: "We ought to do everything in our power to balance the Budget." But MacDonald's proposal for a cut in the dole seemed downright wrong; the Labor government fell. MacDonald soon returned to office as head of a National government. The new government, slightly more adventurous than its predecessors, took Britain off gold in a few weeks. Sidney Webb, Labor's senior intellectual, provided the Labor government its obituary: "No one ever told *us* we could do that!"

The Labor government having immobilized itself by its intellectual conviction that there was no room for maneuver, no middle way, now succeeded through its collapse in documenting its major premise. Then the experience of 1931 displayed the Right was too hardboiled ever to acquiesce in even the most gradual democratic change. "The attempt to give a social bias to capitalism, while leaving it master of the house," wrote R. H. Tawney, "appears to have failed."

If piecemeal reforms were beyond the power of the Labor government, as they were beyond the desire of a Tory government, then the only hope lay in the rapid achievement of full socialism; the only way socialism could be achieved seemed to be through ruthlessness on the Left as great as that on the Right. Such reasoning was responsible for the lust for catastrophic change that suffused the British Left and infected a part of the American Left in the early thirties. No one drew more facile and sweeping conclusions than Harold Laski. The fate of the MacDonald government, Laski wrote, was "tantamount to an insistence that if socialists wish to secure a state built upon the principles of their faith, they can only do so by revolutionary means."

From this perspective Laski and those like him quite naturally looked with derision on the advocate of the middle way. In December 1934, for the perhaps somewhat baffled readers of *Redbook* magazine, Laski debated with Maynard Keynes whether America could spend its way to recovery. Public spending, Laski said with horror, would lead to inflation or heavy taxation or waste; it would mean, he solemnly wrote, "an unbalanced budget with the disturbance of confidence (an essential condition of recovery) which this implies": it would bequeath a "bill of staggering dimensions" to future generations. "Government spending as anything more than a temporary and limited expedient," he concluded, "will necessarily do harm in a capitalist society." This was, of course, not only the argument of Ramsay MacDonald but of Herbert Hoover; Laski's novelty was to use it to defend, not a balanced budget and the gold standard, but—socialist revolution.

One way or another, the British Left began to vote against liberal democracy. Sir Oswald Mosley, who had championed the most constructive economic program considered within the MacDonald government, indicated the new direction when, with John Strachey and others, he founded the authoritarian-minded New Party in 1931. Mosley's excesses soon led him toward fascism and discredit; but plenty of others were reaching similar conclusions about the impossibility of reform under capitalism. Sidney and Beatrice Webb abandoned Fabianism for the mirage of a new civilization in the Soviet Union. All peaceful roads to progress seemed blocked. After a visit with Roosevelt in Washington, Cripps wrote, "My whole impression is of an honest anxious man faced by an impossible task—humanizing capitalism and making it work." "The one thing that is not inevitable now," said Cripps, "is gradualness."

Both Right and Left—Hoover and Stalin, John W. Davis and Mussolini, Ogden Mills and Stafford Cripps—thus rejected the notion of a socially directed and managed capitalism, of a mixed economy, of something in between classical free enterprise and classical socialism. And the either/or demonstration commanded considerable respect in the United States—self-evidently on the American Right; and to some degree on the American Left. So Laski had made clear in *Democracy in Crisis* that the American ruling class would be as tough and hopeless as any other:

> What evidence is there, among the class which controls the destiny of America, of a will to make the necessary concessions? Is not the execution of Sacco and Vanzetti, the long indefensible imprisonment of Mooney, the grim history of American strikes, the root of the answer to that question?

In 1932 both Right and Left thus stood with fierce intransigence on the solid ground of dogma. In so doing, they were challenging an essential part of the American liberal tradition. When Professor Rexford G.

Tugwell of the Columbia University economics department, on leave in Washington, revisited his campus in 1933, he rashly bragged of the New Deal's freedom from "blind doctrine," and the *Columbia Spectator*, then edited by a brilliant young undergraduate named James Wechsler, seized on this boast as the fatal weakness of Tugwell's argument and of the whole New Deal. "This is the crux of the problem," the *Spectator* said; "the blind stumbling in the most chaotic fashion—experimenting from day to day—without any anchor except a few idealistic phrases—is worthless. It is merely political pragmatism."

Merely political pragmatism—to ideologists, whether of Right or of Left, this seemed conclusive evidence of intellectual bankruptcy. As the conservatives had said that any attempt to modify the capitalist system must mean socialism, so the radicals now said that any attempt to maintain the capitalist system must mean fascism. "Roosevelt's policies can be welded into a consistent whole," wrote I. F. Stone, "only on the basis of one hypothesis ... that Mr. Roosevelt intends to move toward fascism." "The essential logic of the New Deal," wrote Max Lerner, "is increasingly the naked fist of the capitalist state."

Convinced of the fragility of the system, the radicals saw themselves as the forerunners of apocalypse. "American commercial agriculture is doomed," wrote Louis Hacker; capitalism was doomed, too, and the party system, and the traditional American way of life. In 1934 Sidney Hook, James Burnham, Louis Budenz, V. F. Calverton, James Rorty and others addressed "An Open Letter to American Intellectuals." "We cannot by some clever Rooseveltian trick," the letter warned,

> evade the unfolding of basic economic and political developments under capitalism. . . . Let us not deceive ourselves that we shall not have to face here also the choice between reaction, on the one hand, and a truly scientific economy under a genuine workers' democracy on the other.

In 1935 the *New Republic* stated with magisterial simplicity the argument of the radicals against the New Dealers, of New York against Washington, of the Marxists against the pragmatists.

> Either the nation must put up with the confusions and miseries of an essentially unregulated capitalism, or it must prepare to supersede capitalism with socialism. *There is no longer a feasible middle course.*

Both radicalism and conservatism thus ended in the domain of either/or. The contradictions of actuality which so stimulated the pragmatists of Washington, only violated the properties and offended the illusions of the ideologists. While they all saw themselves as hardheaded realists, in fact they were Platonists, preferring essence to existence and considering abstractions the only reality.

The great central source of the New Deal, in my judgment, lay precisely in the instinctive response of practical, energetic, and compassionate people to those dogmatic absolutes. This passion to sacrifice reality to doctrine presented a profound challenge to the pragmatic nerve. Many Americans, refusing to be intimidated by abstractions or to be overawed by ideology, responded by doing things. The whole point of the New Deal lay in its belief in activism, its faith in gradualness, its rejection of catastrophism, its indifference to ideology, its conviction that a managed and modified capitalist order achieved by piecemeal experiment could combine personal freedom and economic growth. "In a world in which revolutions just now are coming easily," said Adolf Berle, "the New Deal chose the more difficult course of moderation and rebuilding." "The course that the new Administration did take," said Harold Ickes, "was the hardest course. It conformed to no theory, but it did fit into the American system—a system of taking action step by step, a system of regulation only to meet concrete needs, a system of courageous recognition of change." Tugwell, rejecting laissez-faire and communism, spoke of the "third course."

Roosevelt himself, of course, was the liberal pragmatist *par excellence.* His aim was to steer between the extremes of chaos and tyranny by moving always, in his phrase, "slightly to the left of center." "Unrestrained individualism" he wrote, had proved a failure; yet "any paternalistic system which tries to provide for security for everyone from above only calls for an impossible task and a regimentation utterly uncongenial to the spirit of our people." He constantly repeated Macaulay's injunction to reform if you wished to preserve.

Roosevelt had no illusions about revolution. Mussolini and Stalin seemed to him, in his phrase, "not mere distant relatives" but "blood brothers." When Emil Ludwig asked him about his "political motive," he replied, "My desire is to obviate revolution. . . . I work in a contrary sense to Rome and Moscow." He said during the 1932 campaign:

> Say that civilization is a tree which, as it grows, continually produces rot and dead wood. The radical says: "Cut it down." The conservative says: "Don't touch it." The liberal compromises: "Let's prune, so that we lose neither the old trunk nor the new branches." This campaign is waged to teach the country to march upon its appointed course, the way of change, in an orderly march, avoiding alike the revolution of radicalism and the revolution of conservatism.

I think it would be a mistake to underestimate the extent to which this pragmatic attitude was itself a major source of New Deal vitality. The exaltation of the middle way seems banal and obvious enough today. Yet the tyranny of dogma was such in the early years of the Great Depression that infatuation with ideology blocked and smothered the instinctive efforts of free men to work their own salvation. In a world intoxicated with abstractions, Roosevelt and the New Dealers stood almost alone in a stubborn faith in rational experiment, in trial and error. No one understood this more keenly than the great English critic of absolutes; Keynes, in an open letter to Roosevelt at the end of 1933, stated the hopes generated by the New Deal with precision and eloquence. "You have made yourself," Keynes told Roosevelt,

> the trustee for those in every country who seek to mend the evils of our condition by reasoned experiment within the framework of the existing social system. If you fail, rational choice will be gravely prejudiced throughout the world, leaving orthodoxy and revolution to fight it out. But, if you succeed, new and bolder methods will be tried everywhere, and we may date the first chapter of a new economic era from your accession to office.

The question remains: Why did the New Deal itself have the pragmatic commitment? Why, under the impact of depression, was it not overborne by dogma as were most other governments and leaders in the world? The answer to this lies, I suspect, in the point I proposed earlier—in the suggestion that the New Deal represented, not just a response to depression, but also a response to pent-up frustration and needs in American society—frustrations and needs which would have operated had there been no depression at all. The periodic demand for forward motion in American politics, the periodic breakthrough of new leadership—these were already in the works before the depression. Depression, therefore, instead of catching a nation wholly unprepared, merely accelerated tendencies toward change already visible in the national community. The response to depression, in short, was controlled and tempered by the values of traditional American experimentalism, rather than those of rigid ideology. The New Deal was thus able to approach the agony of mass unemployment and depression in the pragmatic spirit, in the spirit which guaranteed the survival rather than the extinction of freedom, in the spirit which in time rekindled hope across the world that free men could manage their own economic destiny.

Ellis W. Hawley

ELLIS W. HAWLEY (1929–   ) is professor of history at the University of Iowa. He
is the author of *The New Deal and the Problem of Monopoly: A Study in Economic
Ambivalence* (1966).

As depicted by most American historians in the 1950s, the "mixed economy" of the United States was a superlative blend of two worlds, a
system that combined rational direction, organizational security, and
stable growth with a large measure of democratic decision-making, individual liberty, and local and private initiative. While bringing competitive excesses and harmful fluctuations under administrative control, it
had also developed a system of "countervailing powers," a "corporate
conscience," and a vigorous "inter-industry competition," all of which
had enabled it to retain the dynamism and safeguards associated with
free markets and competitive enterprise. And though it was still far from
perfect, its amazing productivity had all but solved the quantitative
problems of production and distribution, thus providing the material
base for a new type of qualitative and cultural reform. Looking back,
moreover, these writers credited Franklin D. Roosevelt and his New
Deal with much of the historical development responsible for this happy
state of affairs. By modernizing and defending the American political
system, they argued, and by using it to stabilize, democratize, and
humanize an unruly corporate capitalism, the pragmatic New Dealers
had provided the basic framework within which the nation's liberal-
democratic ideals could be preserved and realized.

More recently, as views of the economy have changed, this older
image of the New Deal has become somewhat tarnished. The central
development in recent American history, according to a new group of
institutionalist scholars, has been the rise of bureaucratic industrialism,
not the further advance of liberal democracy; and the chief impetus to
reform, they insist, has come from organizational elites in search of
stability and order, not from liberal democrats seeking equality and so-

---

All quotations from "The New Deal and Business," by Ellis W. Hawley, are from vol. 1 of
The New Deal, ed. John Braeman, Robert H. Bremner, and David Brody, and published in 2
vols. (1: *The National Level*; and 2: *The State and Local Levels*) in the *Modern America* series.
Copyright © 1975 by the Ohio State University Press. All rights reserved. Used by permission of the author, the editors, and the publisher.

cial justice. Hence, the New Deal was more the product of corporate capitalism rather than the shaper of it. In essence, it provided a threatened managerial elite market behavior, and solved the problems of aggregate demand and developmental capital. And the results, according to another group of younger and more radical scholars, have been tragic. Out of the failure of "reform," they contend, came a bastard liberalism, a "corporate" variety, which, in the name of "progress," built illiberal and undemocratic institutions that have, in effect, perpetuated social injustice and economic tyranny, required constant involvement abroad, and transformed what should be a free people into mindless bureaucrats and earnest consumers.

These divergent views, of course, may well tell us more about the 1950s and 1960s than about the 1930s. Yet, they do raise major questions concerning the nature of the political economy that was hammered out during the New Deal years, who it was that did the hammering, and how such conflicting estimates of it could be made. They also suggest that New Deal activities might be profitably explored within a broader perspective, one that would see them as part of a continuing but never wholly successful effort to resolve the tensions between bureaucratic industrialism and a liberal-democratic ethos. In the 1930s, as the political arena became a confusing battleground for conflicting industrial groups seeking stability and salvation, rival groups of reformers seeking to remedy a "defective" and "oppressive" economic structure, and competing models of how one could reconcile a technocorporate order with America's democratic heritage, the tensions became particularly acute. But the dilemma that underlay them was not new. Nor would it disappear with the passing of the New Deal.

For business-government relations, in fact, the period of the New Deal is probably best viewed as a time when one resolution of these tensions between organizational capitalism and the liberal-democratic ethos, the resolution that emerged in the 1920s, broke down, lost credence, and was rejected as being both unworkable and tyrannical. The result was an intense but confused search for another synthesis, one, so most agreed, that would necessarily involve a larger role for government. And New Deal policy, as it fluctuated between competing models and built new bureaucracies, did lay the groundwork for the point of resolution that was lauded in the 1950s. In this sense, it represented a new departure. Yet it was also tied to the past, both in the sense that it was trying to cope with a continuing problem, one that antedated the depression, and in the sense that most of the competing models offered as solutions derived from past experience, particularly from conflicting progressive visions, variants of the "planned economy" of World War I, or logical extensions of the cooperative associationalism that had been hailed as the answer during the New Era but found wanting after 1929.

Seen in perspective, the origins, formulation, and effects of New Deal policy fit into a broader framework of long-standing tensions and repeated efforts at resolution; and it is to the task of examining them within this framework that the remainder of this essay will be devoted.

In recent years, historians have disagreed sharply about business-government relations during the Progressive era. But from all they have said, two things seem to stand out. One was the rapid rise of an organizational economy, which brought with it large areas of "private government," new bureaucratic-scientific-professional values, and a persistent search for order and stability, primarily through the creation of ever larger associative and hierarchic structures, the infusing of these with a new set of managerial attitudes and group loyalties, and the use of the state, where necessary and expedient, to further the process. The other was an ambivalent cluster of reform efforts, striving in general to resolve the tensions between the new order and the liberal-democratic-village values that it threatened, yet deeply divided over the point at which this should take place, the degree of centralization needed, and the method by which liberty could best be advanced. Not surprisingly, different reform models appeared; and around these, as seekers of order and both "old" and "new" liberals clashed, compromised, and merged into one another, many of the period's debates swirled.

Four models, in particular, were significant. The first, best known as Wilson's New Freedom and best articulated by Louis Brandeis, held that bureaucratic centralism had gone beyond technological needs, that this "new tyranny" rested chiefly on special privilege and "unfair" or "unnatural" behavior, and that the state could best advance freedom by removing these aids to concentration and forging an economy that was not only modern and scientific but competitive, ethical, and decentralized as well. The second model, the New Nationalism of Herbert Croly and Theodore Roosevelt, held just the opposite: that concentration and cooperation did stem from technological needs, and consequently, to liberate and democratize, the state must forge national controls and use them to advance social justice, promote cooperation in the public interest, and provide the material base for a new and higher individualism. The third model, generally labeled the New Competition and associated particularly with the trade association promoter and spokesman for business progressivism Arthur J. Eddy, held that through self-regulating associations, codes of ethics, and schemes of "industrial betterment," the new economy was itself developing an "industrial democracy," a "purer" competition, a "higher individualism." Hence, it needed only encouragement and guidance, not regulation and restructuring. And finally, implicit in much agitation and explicit with a few theorists, was an incipient model of interest-group liberalism, one that would allegedly advance liberty by balancing groups against each other and allowing this to take the place of classical competition. . . .

The shift from Hoover to Roosevelt, then, did bring a new departure in business-government relations. After three years of deepening depression climaxed by a banking crisis, demands for change had become insistent; and under an administration committed to "doing something," the government's role in the economy quickly became a larger one. The novelty of this "new deal," however, has often been exaggerated. The shift was not from laissez-faire to a managed economy, but rather from one attempt at management, that through informal business-government cooperation, to another more formal and coercive attempt. The tensions that had reappeared, although altered somewhat by the economic situation and the relative decline of an older middle class of small capitalists and independent professionals, were essentially the same ones that earlier policy-makers had tried to resolve. And the guiding models for a new order were mostly inherited ones, not alien imports or instant improvisations. They derived from what innovators had envisioned during the Progressive period, from the experience during World War I, from agitation outside the consensus of the 1920s, and from what seemed to be the "lessons" of Hoover's experience or "logical extensions" of his approach.

The new administration, moreover, despite its critics' charges and its own claims of "pragmatism," was committed to change only within a relatively rigid "middle way," one that, to be sure, was broader than Hoover's, but at the same time was clearly limited by fixed ideological boundaries. Ruled out on one side were stabilizing arrangements involving the open avowal of a "closed," "authoritarian," or "monopolistic" system. Ruled out on the other were liberalizing or democratizing reforms that would seriously jeopardize capitalist incentives, constitutional safeguards, modern technology, or recovery prospects. And ruled out, even when they came within these limits, were programs whose implementation would require excessive conflict or some radically new type of politics or administration. The disposition, by and large, was to adjust differences, make accommodations, and build on existing institutions.

Still, within these elements of continuity, there was a commitment to change, or at least to "action." And once the government had changed hands, a variety of different types of activists began pushing their particular visions of what should replace the Hoover approach to business-government relations. Some, ranging from Rexford Tugwell on the left to Hugh Johnson on the right, were either national or business-oriented "planners." Deriving their models from either the New Nationalism, the war experience, or the vision of an associational

capitalism, they were ready now to accept an organizational as opposed
to a competitive system, restructure it somewhat in the interests of better "balance," and then "manage" it so as to insure sustained expansion
and make possible a reflowering of the liberal-democratic heritage. Others, including western "antimonopolists" like William Borah and Wright
Patman, Brandeisian-oriented lawyers like Thomas Corcoran and Benjamin Cohen, farm leaders like Edward O'Neal and John Simpson, and
spokesmen for urban labor like Robert Wagner, were either decentralizers or balancers. Heirs of the New Freedom or spokesmen for disadvantaged interest groups, they were insistent now that recovery and
freedom must come not by centralizing power but by dispersing it,
revitalizing the market system, or strengthening a previously exploited
group. And still others, men like the agricultural economist George
Warren, the Oklahoma inflationist Elmer Thomas, and the Utah banker
Marriner Eccles, were "reflationists," concerned not with structural reform but with using monetary-fiscal levers to "reflate" the economy or
"compensate" for its defects.

Within each camp, moreover, further divisions existed. Small-
business decentralizers of both the populist and Brandeisian types disagreed at times with those pushing consumer, farmer, or labor welfare;
permanent spenders clashed with "pump primers," "currency tinker-
ers," and "budget balancers"; and leftist "planners" differed sharply
with those of the center and right. "Planning," as men like Tugwell saw
it, must be done by "public men," not by corporate interests, who almost always opted for scarcity profits. But as envisioned by others,
particularly by a man like Adolf Berle, a "regenerated" business could be
used in the public interest. And for still others, men like Hugh Johnson,
George Peek, or Raymond Moley, all of whom seemed to believe that a
more powerful "private government" could deliver on the New Era
promises, the answer was a "partnership" with federal authority in a
supportive role.

On the business side, too, similar divisions existed. Now flirting with
corporate statism were substantial numbers of association officials,
former war chieftains, spokesmen for "sick" industries, and other leaders of the corporate "enlightenment." Included in their ranks, for example, were trade association lawyers like Benjamin Javits, Gilbert
Montague, and David Podell, economists like Edgar Heermance and
Philip Cabot, wartime administrators like Bernard Baruch and Howard
Coffin, corporate paternalists like Gerard Swope and Henry Dennison,
and prominent association officials like Charles Abbott of the Structural
Steel Institute, Wilson Compton of the National Lumber Manufacturers
Association, and Walker Hines of the Cotton Textile Institute. Yet these
people did not, as some revisionists would have it, constitute a united,
omnipotent elite moving confidently toward a corporate order. Among

themselves they frequently despaired of agreeing on a specific scheme. Unlike assured rulers, they worried constantly about creating an apparatus that might be used against them. And clearly, they did not speak for all businessmen, particularly not for those who tended to cling either to entrepreneurial modes of thought or to the dream of private coordination. Groups like the American Trade Association Executives, under the leadership of Leslie C. Smith, and the National Association of Manufacturers, with its long history of attacks on "big government" and business-labor cooperation, had not endorsed antitrust revision, chiefly for fear it would lead to unfriendly controls or powerful labor unions. Hard-pressed independents, especially in retail fields and the "sick" or chaotic industries, complained bitterly about their "monopolistic" rivals. Most of the talk about planning, as they saw it, amounted to schemes through which "predatory interests" hoped to join with "big government" and "big labor" to crush "independent enterprise." And intermingled with these views was a discordant medley of others, sentiments ranging from such stout defenses of "rugged individualism" and "natural law" as those set forth by the financier Albert Wiggin or the banking economist Benjamin Anderson to the support for "reflationary schemes" that emanated from James Rand's Committee for the Nation and to time-hallowed calls for tax relief, economy, union-busting, and tariff adjustment.

For a leader who valued consistency, such divided counsels might have required either a choice or a delay in the promised action. But for Roosevelt, with his penchant for resisting ideological systems, mixing opposites, and administering by conflict, the answer was to give "something" to everyone, institutionalize the divisions, and avoid, at least for the time being, a definite commitment to any one reform model. Consequently, what most of the recovery-reform program did as it took shape in 1933, was to create new administrative frameworks, give them vague or ambivalent mandates, and leave it to clashing administrators, competing ideologies, and conflicting pressure groups to fill in the details. This was true, for example, of the act creating the Tennessee Valley Authority, of the Emergency Transportation Act, of the farm law, and, to some extent, of the financial legislation. But it was true, above all, of the National Industrial Recovery Act. Its formulators, by setting forth vague goals, giving industrial code-makers a virtually blank check, and adding licensing provisions and public works, Section 7a for labor, and a mixture of antitrust exemptions with incantations against "monopoly," had provided an "economic charter" rather than a definite policy, a framework that different sets of administrators could use to build quite different versions of an "industrial democracy." Reform through administration, a route upon which the progressives had embarked, had seemingly come into its own. . . .

In practice, though this brand of business-government cooperation, like Hoover's earlier brand, failed to generate expansion and was therefore quickly charged with being tyrannical and oppressive. Perhaps, if the public works side had been rapidly expanded, if business had been massively subsidized with cheap credit and guarantees against loss, or if the initial psychological lift could have been sustained, the outcome would have been different. But this was not the way it happened. On the contrary, "reflation" was stymied by a mixture of fiscal orthodoxy, excessive red tape, and unsuccessful attempts at currency tinkering; expectations of rising sales and profits quickly evaporated; and under the circumstances, the codes were used to raise prices along with wages and restrict new investment rather than encourage it. What seemed for a moment to be the making of a new consensus quickly dissolved. Like Hoover's system, "business planning" had been tried and found wanting; and though industrialists reacted by asking for greater autonomy and blaming the failure on "chiselers," bureaucrats, and labor, they could no longer convince large numbers of their fellow citizens that the approach was either workable or the "American way." With increasing support, advocates of other approaches were soon demanding major changes. And since Roosevelt, unlike Hoover, had not committed himself to one model, he could let others take the blame for the initial failure, watch over the resulting policy debates, and wait for another version of "industrial democracy" to take shape.

In 1934, then, the gap between promise and performance brought the New Deal's initial approach, that embodied in the NRA codes, under increasing attack, particularly from farm and labor leaders, dissident businessmen, "market restorers," and "national planners." Measures like the Securities Exchange Act, the Air Mail Act, and the new trade law, based as they were on competitive models and ideals, were all indications that this initial approach was in retreat. So were the opening shots in a campaign to dismantle the "power trust." And within the NRA, the shift in sentiment and political pressure was reflected in drives to scrap the price and production provisions, strengthen the labor clauses, and restructure the code authorities. A coherent alternative, however, was slow to emerge. Throughout 1934, the conflicting thrusts—the battles between internationalists, nationalists, and intranationalists in trade policy, between regulators, nationalizers, and decentralizers in the utility and financial fields, and between the "business planners" and their critics in the NRA—tended to cancel each other out and bring stalemate and confusion rather than a new synthesis. The NRA, in particular, became a study in frustration. There the agitation for reform succeeded in hampering formal cartelization, forcing Johnson out, and producing new policy statements, but the agitators were unable to reshape the code structure and use it to implement a new reform model.

During the first half of 1934, for example, those who would restore competition as the regulator did make their influence felt. Picking up support from discontented groups, academic economists, and progressive politicians, from other governmental agencies, and from such inquiries as that conducted by Clarence Darrow's National Recovery Review Board, the "market restorers" within the NRA's technical and advisory divisions were able to block various code provisions from going into effect and eventually to put through Office Memorandum 228 reaffirming faith in competitive goals and renouncing price-fixing and production control. Yet, against the entrenched opposition of the existing code authorities and their supporters, a group whose cooperation the administration seemed anxious to retain, the champions of the new policy found that they could not even revise codes that violated it, much less write new provisions to achieve its goals. The most they could do was to complain vigorously about the gap between policy and practice, thus making administrators reluctant to defend openly or enforce very actively many of the trade practice provisions. For groups needing strong government support to keep "chiselers" in check, the result was renewed competition; but for those needing only tacit cooperation, it was not. Conflicting lines of action, it seemed, although they might provide a sense of movement and involvement, had reduced the effects of government intervention to little more than an equivalent of laissez-faire.

A similar inability to translate policy into practice was also characteristic of those who would build "industrial democracy" by strengthening organized labor, particularly now by preventing the independent unionism desired by a majority of employees from being undercut by company organizations or individual bargaining. Here again, official policy, as set forth by the National Labor Board and its successor, the National Labor Relations Board, did interpret Section 7a as requiring a "majority rule," an arrangement, in other words, under which the labor organization that received a majority of employee votes would be recognized as the bargaining agent for all workers in the bargaining unit. Yet, when confronted with the antagonism of NRA administrators, the desire to avoid legal tests, and the tendency of Roosevelt to split the differences, the champions of this interpretation were unable to swing the NRA's enforcement machinery behind it or to prevent special presidential interventions from exempting key industries. Consequently, they were unable to create much of a countervailing force. Throughout the NRA period, increased unionization came chiefly in fields where strong industrial unions were already active, and employee benefits still tended to approximate those considered necessary by "enlightened" industrialists. The rise of "big labor" as a major force would await the type of law that Senator Robert Wagner would finally secure in 1935.

Even less successful and more frustrating was the experience of those who hoped to turn the NRA into an instrument for collectivist planning, one in which broad policy goals would emerge from restructured code authorities representing all interests, strong technical agencies would provide the data and "plans," and powerful "public men," using the licensing provisions if necessary and exercising control over profits and investment as well as pricing and production, would put the "plans" into effect. Only through such a system, ran the argument of men like Tugwell, Lorwin, and Galloway, could Americans have abundance, efficiency, and democracy, all at the same time, and supporting this general view now were detailed memorandums from such economists as Gardiner Means and Mordecai Ezekiel. Unlike the "market restorers," however, these "collectivists" were regarded by many of their fellow citizens as being either un-American or impractical. They lacked popular or political support; and because Roosevelt was both dubious about their approach and unwilling to antagonize the opponents of it, their influence was minimal. The licensing power expired without being invoked. Agitation for such things as profit controls, quality standards, tripartite code authorities, or systematic "expansion plans" was mostly in vain. And the limiting of code authority powers and functions that did take place seemed to stem mostly from complaints about abuse and discrimination, not from efforts to facilitate central planning.

To this agitation for change in 1934, some of the supporters of "business planning" were willing to accommodate themselves. In some fields, the need for government support was still strong enough to override the reluctance to pay a higher "price," and as some business leaders saw it, reform could still be kept in conservative channels that would promote stability and improve rather than threaten the corporate structure. More typically, however, as resentment against, or fear of, the critics mounted and as their influence with Roosevelt seemed more evident, the reaction was one of outrage, alarm, and bitter resistance. Some, still desirous of antitrust immunity and willing to pay some "price" for it, dug in along the line of the existing code structure. Some, convinced that things had already gone too far in opening the door to "socialism," "anarchy," and "labor monopolies," demanded revisions that would guarantee industrial autonomy and allow the open shop. Some, thoroughly disenchanted with the workings of the NRS or deeply frightened by the directions in which its official policies might take it, joined with those who had opposed it from the start to demand that the whole program be scrapped.

Increasingly, it seemed, as the year 1934 drew to a close, the greatest villain in business circles was becoming not "destructive competition" but "New Deal tyranny," or, for those inclined to personalize matters, "that man in the White House." Those opposed to, or disenchanted with, "business planning," those who believed that it had not been given a fair trial, and those frightened by the attacks on it could all agree that top priority now must be given to limiting or rolling back the power of a threatening, unpredictable, and potentially dangerous state bureaucracy. It was this power and its potential misuse, they decided, that were the real sources of instability, the things that frightened investors and blocked recovery. And in attacking it, they were soon invoking, with varying degrees of sincerity, either the ideals of the New Era or those of entrepreneurial capitalism, classical economics, and Jeffersonian liberalism. Many, to be sure, still felt that excessive competition and chaotic disorder were major problems; but with crisis conditions surmounted, the possibilities of solving them privately seemed greater again. Or, at least, they seemed preferable to relying upon public tools that were not properly delimited or were capable of great "abuse" when wielded by ill-informed, impractical, or hostile bureaucrats.

Such fears and beliefs also led most businessmen to oppose the deficit financing, work relief projects, and social insurance programs that might have solved most of their problems. To later generations, such measures would appear as basically conservative, designed, it seemed, to bring stable prosperity without structural change and to undercut the power bases of the system's critics. But with a few exceptions, corporate leaders in 1934 did not view them as such. Instead, they were seen as burdens upon business, as immoral departures from the "American way," as preludes to crippling taxes, capital levies, and economic disaster, or as devices to elect corrupt politicians and strengthen a menacing and wasteful bureaucracy. Recovery and security, according to numerous business speeches now, must come by shrinking government and insisting upon sound finance, not by expanding it and taking risks with the public credit. And partly in response to such criticism, partly because Roosevelt himself remained basically a "budget balancer," the administration coupled its expansion of social services and subsidies with a fiscal orthodoxy that kept the expansionary power of federal deficits far below what was needed to achieve full employment.

As the year 1935 dawned, then, the New Deal had not yet discovered the arrangements that would allow an effective corporate capitalism to function within a liberal-democratic framework. The form of business-government cooperation adopted in 1933 was under severe attack as being both unworkable and tyrannical. Yet most of its supporters, instead of modifying their model to remedy the defects, seemed bent upon resurrecting the discredited models of the 1920s or 1890s. Their rivals, moreover—the "market restorers," "collectivist planners," and "counterorganizers"—were still too weak to force a trial of their solutions. And as yet, no new philosophy had arisen capable of reconciling the conflicting thrusts into what Americans might accept as a new and superior synthesis. In a sense, to be sure, the maze of contradictory

activities, particularly those of the NRA, had brought an institutionalization of conflicting pressures; but the result for most participants was a
feeling of stalemate and frustration, not one of having broken through to
a desirable and satisfying arrangement. That Roosevelt's optimism and
"experimention" might yet produce one, the critics of "business planning" seemed convinced. But the stalemate that the NRA had become
by 1935 had few real friends, and to many the Schechter decision,
sweeping away the codes and their appendages, seemed to remove an
obstacle rather than block needed reforms. At least, it made possible
fresh starts.

   As one might expect, however, the program that eventually took
shape in 1935 clearly had its seeds in earlier developments, particularly
in the efforts of those who would limit or check business power rather
than trying to use it in the public interest. It was to these groups that
Roosevelt now swung his support, partly, it seems, because the end of
the NRA afforded him room to maneuver, partly because business hostility had led him to shift his political base toward farm and labor groups,
partly because he wished to prevent antibusiness demagogues from
making inroads on his left flank. He was limited, moreover, by the
political, legal, and ideological obstructions that now lay in the way of
other options. Business planning under government auspices, even if it
could be made to pass legal muster, was a discredited approach, not
only with the public and most "liberals" but also with the business
elements that had been frightened and irritated by their NRA experience. The small group that kept trying to revive such an arrangement
found itself unable to develop much support in either business or political circles. And "collectivist planning" was even less feasible. Although
a few of its advocates—notably, men like Tugwell, Mordecai Ezekiel,
and Jerome Frank—worked out and agitated for an "NRA in reverse,"
so constructed as to bring about "planned expansion," their chances of
implementing such a vision seemed to dwindle rather than grow.
Added to their encumbrances now was the argument that any planning
program must of necessity follow the pattern of the NRA and be dominated by "selfish monopolists."
   What emerged, then, as the "market restorers" and "counterorganizers" moved to the fore, was essentially a mixture of selective
"trustbusting," government-backed unionization, limited expansion
and nationalization of social services, and continued but disguised cartelization for "exceptional" groups willing to pay the "price" and able to
pull the right political and ideological levers. . . .
   The other major aspect of the Second New Deal was the expansion
and nationalization of social services, exemplified particularly in the

Social Security Act, the work relief program, the housing and conservation activities, and the protective labor and rural rehabilitation measures. In one sense now, "welfare capitalism," community-centered
welfare, and the patronage-oriented welfare of urban political machines
were all giving way to a larger and broader "welfare statism." Yet again,
significant as this change was, the patterns adopted worked in some
respects to strengthen rather than displace existing institutions. Local
communities still remained key units in dispersing welfare; political
machines strengthened themselves by investments or were "bribed"
into becoming "partners" along the welfare frontier; discontented elements, potentially disruptive, were converted into more conservative
citizens; and frequently, despite the humanitarianism involved, groups
needing aid and protection the most were the ones exempted. Again,
the degree of business opposition seemed disproportionate to the extent
and nature of "reform" or "socialization." Logically, the "enlightened"
group of corporate leaders willing to go along with, or join in, most of
the social program should have been much larger.

Logically, too, both corporate leaders and Second New Dealers
might have moved quickly now from the mixture taking shape in 1937 to
the "mixed economy" that seemed so satisfactory to similar groups in
the 1950s. The latter synthesis, after all, did contain many of the same
elements, particularly the same curious blend of private controls and
pressure-group "planning" with antitrust ideals, selective "trust-
busting," capitalistic labor unions, and modest measures of
seminationalized social services. What it contained beyond this was,
first of all, a general conviction that such a blend did represent a new
and superior synthesis, and second, a more effective set of techniques
for promoting and regulating economic growth. Had those shaping policy in 1937 been willing to make the required psychological adjustments,
divert somewhat more resources to trade expansion and technological
development, and seize the theory of supplementary public investment
being advanced by a few New Dealers and Keynesians, it seems possible
that the new "American system" might have come in the late 1930s
rather than the 1950s.

This development, however, was not to be. Instead, the great majority of corporate leaders and their political allies continued to blame the
lack of new investment and the failure to achieve sustained expansion
on the New Deal's "shackling," "burdening," and "frightening" of
business, whereas various groups of New Dealers continued to see a
defective corporate structure in need of income redistribution, "market
restoration," or systematic "coordination" and "balancing." By many in
both camps, Keynesianism was seen as being either counterproductive,
wasteful, dishonest, or a type of "artificial" solution, designed by their
opponents to perpetuate "unnatural" structures and controls in need of

change. And the result, since nothing done so far had really remedied the system's inability to generate the needed investment and purchasing power, was another breakdown and contraction. In the first half of 1937, as tax increases offset the expansionary effects of the Bonus Act and the administration pursued a deflationary policy, one intended to check a wage-price spiral, curb a speculative inventory boom, strengthen the market for government bonds, and bring the long-sought budget, the stage was set for a new collapse. In the fall, limited recovery and what had seemed to be an emerging equilibrium gave way to the "Roosevelt depression" and to another round of policy conflicts.

As conditions worsened in late 1937, a few business leaders began once more to urge some type of government-backed "business planning." For them, the source of instability had again become "destructive competition." For the great majority, however, the source was political in nature. It lay particularly in the undistributed profits tax of 1936, the federal labor policy, and unwarranted "attacks upon business." And the way to eliminate it and start the needed flow of new investment funds, so the argument ran, was to revise taxes, unwind much of the New Deal, and roll back federal power. Again there were exceptions, but much of organized business, it seemed, had not yet come to view the arrangements of the Second New Deal as really being "stabilizers" and "balance wheels." Nor was it ready yet to adopt the view that contraction called for larger federal deficits. Although the tax revision that business groups lobbied through Congress in early 1938 did mean a larger deficit and thus a dose of Keynesianism, this was not the intention. In the business theory of recovery, subscribed to by most supporters of the legislation, tax cuts were supposed to be accompanied by reduced governmental expenditures and a return to balanced budgets.

Meanwhile, various groups in the government were also analyzing the breakdown and urging changes in policy, again largely in terms of what they had been advocating earlier. One group, for example, represented by men like Secretary of Commerce Daniel Roper, RFC Director Jesse Jones, and Secretary of the Treasury Henry Morgenthau, Jr., seemed willing now to adopt the business formula and try to restore "confidence" by balancing the budget, revising the tax laws, and declaring a recess on reform. A second, led by Donald Richberg and other former NRA officials, wanted to check the new outbreak of "destructive competition" by setting up a new program of "business planning" through industrial codes. A third, consisting of "collectivist planners" like Ezekiel and congressional "mavericks" like Thomas Amlie, advocated an Industrial Expansion Act, a measure, in other words, that would create machinery similar to the code structure of the NRA but this time with proper safeguards and with mechanisms that would insure its use to underwrite full production rather than restricted output. A fourth, led by men like Harold Ickes, Thomas Corcoran, Leon Henderson, and antitrust chief Robert Jackson, urged that the "market restoration" activities of the Second New Deal be drastically broadened, primarily to deal with the "monopolistic" groups whose "administered" price increases had brought a new failure of purchasing power and a subsequent "strike of capital." And finally, an increasingly influential but still small group, spearheaded by men like Lauchlin Currie and Alvin Hansen, was now ready to pronounce the existing structure acceptable and use planned deficits as a way of stabilizing it. Armed now with Keynes's *General Theory*, this group had acquired a new confidence and cohesion; but much of its support in the subsequent debate still came from people who wanted to spend on humanitarian or social grounds, who saw spending as an aid to other types of reform, or who viewed it as a temporary expedient until something better could be done.

As in 1933, Roosevelt himself seemed reluctant to choose and inclined to give everyone "something." While promising a balanced budget and urging business to take up the slack, he also authorized a resumption of some spending and lending activities, encouraged those who were attacking "concentrations of economic power," discussed the need to "manage" price relationships, and talked about reviving some kind of "business planning." For a time, confusion prevailed. But gradually, some options were ruled out and others limited. "Planning," after all, was still politically unfeasible; "budget-balancing" seemed completely ineffective and would not long remain possible without tax increases; and since few could agree on just what a "decentralization" effort should include, the demands for it were channeled into the protracted studies of a Temporary National Economic Committee. This left a program consisting chiefly of the mixture of 1937 plus two major additions. One was the attempt, under Thurman Arnold's direction, to use the Sherman Act as a weapon of price control. In key areas now, where high prices and costs were felt to constitute economic "bottlenecks," an enlarged Antitrust Division set out to bring them down through highly publicized enforcement "drives" and the negotiation of numerous consent decrees. The other innovation, much more significant for the future, was Roosevelt's acceptance of planned deficits as a way of expanding the economy. Having decided in favor of a new spending program, he proceeded to justify it in Keynesian terms and to claim credit for the upturn that followed it.

As the decade drew to a close, both of these innovations engendered heated debates, and what would have happened to them had there been no World War II is difficult to say. Probably, considering the defeat of the new spending bill in 1939, it would have taken another severe recession or two before Keynesianism became the established way of regulating and stabilizing aggregate demand. And probably, considering Arnold's flair for the dramatic and the initial expansion of his program, it would have taken somewhat longer before corporate planners and other organizational leaders managed to move the antitrust enterprise back into the relatively safe areas of checking marginal abuses and protecting one business group from another. As it turned out, the war hastened both processes. The Arnold program, after coming into sharp conflict with the business-oriented war agencies, was finally shelved and forgotten, at least to the extent that there have been no subsequent efforts to use the antitrust apparatus as a major and continuing tool of price management. And Keynesianism, vindicated by the impact of the war spending, quickly became a part of the "American way," particularly since the war debt, the wartime expansion of the public sector, and the "need" for spending on armaments, technology, and foreign aid all made possible a type of fiscal management that business leaders found more palatable. Instead of being dependent on fluctuating public expenditures that could "subvert" capitalist virtues and create "competition for private enterprise," they could now rely upon a stable core of "desirable" spending and depend upon fluctuations in government revenue to regulate aggregate demand. Corporate capitalism, so "liberal" spenders seemed to think, had finally been "liberalized"; but the reverse effect, a "corporatization" of the "liberals," seemed to be somewhat closer to what had actually happened.

In the 1940s, partly because of their new "partnership" with government during the war, partly because of their subsequent success in scrapping reconversion controls and checking labor power, most corporate leaders also came to accept the other innovations of the New Deal. A mixture of properly limited "welfare statism" with "responsible" labor unions, pressure-group "planning," and devices to maintain "workable" competition, they concluded, did make for a stable environment in which corporate organizations could prosper and grow. And on the other side, deeply impressed by the wartime and postwar performance of the economy, by the changing attitudes of corporate leaders, and by the need to protect a going system from the "mindlessness" of a "radical right," those who had set out to "democratize" and "liberalize" the corporate order came to the conclusion that they had been successful. Admittedly, they noted, much power remained in the hands of a corporate elite. But now, in view of the "corporate conscience," the "workable competition," and the system of "countervailing powers" that reform had created, the power would aid rather than threaten the continued advance of liberty and democracy.

Seemingly, the tensions between corporate values and those of the liberal-democratic creed had been resolved into a new and higher synthesis, that of "democratic pluralism," the "mixed economy," or the "vital center." But the broad belief that such was the case would not endure. Deeply dissatisfied with the type of society that the new "American way" appeared to be creating, a new generation of critics would soon proclaim it to be a "new tyranny" controlled, or at least "manipulated," by an irresponsible "power elite" and a modern set of "feudal fiefdoms." "Reform," so the lament ran, had not only failed to "democratize" the area of "private government"; it had aided the "interests" and the "machine" to take over the public apparatus as well. And though the result had been prosperity for the corporation and its dependents, it had also been an expansion of "imperialism" and "exploitation," an organizational society that left the individual "alienated" and "powerless," and inaction or "repression" in the face of festering social problems. Like New Era associationalism, the pluralistic theories of the 1950s had been merely a smoke screen to hide an undemocratic system of decision-making; and like progressive reform, the New Deal had been another "triumph of conservatism."

That this tarnished image of the New Deal innovations overcompensated for the glowing view of the 1950s seems fairly obvious. The criteria of judgement, after all, were frequently unrealizable ideals or expanded definitions of what constituted "democracy," not the arrangements that preceded the New Deal, the experience of other nations, or the realistic assessment of available alternatives. Roosevelt, it must be conceded, was not the ideal philosopher-politician who might have clarified and resolved the dilemmas of industrial America, but it is hard to conceive of any political figure in the 1930s who could have filled this role. It is also difficult, considering the experience of the Hoover years and of other nations, to argue that rational systematization would have produced better results; and it is doubly difficult, considering the previous pace of reform and what preceded the New Deal innovations, to argue that the period brought a setback rather than a significant advance for democracy. Clearly, the new labor structure, despite its "corporatist" and oligarchic tendencies, was a more democratic arrangement than the company unionism of the New Era. And most believers in democracy, it would seem, would prefer the "new welfare," the expanded federal bureaucracy, and the stabilized, subsidized corporate capitalism that finally emerged, "manipulative," "elitist," and "impersonal" though they might be, to the welfare, governmental, and economic structures that existed in 1932.

The tarnished image, moreover, frequently carried with it an erroneous impression concerning the role of business groups in policymaking. Since they seemed to have benefited most from the innovations of the period, the temptation was strong to conclude that they must have planned it that way and used the New Dealers either as their tools or as camouflage for their operations. In reality, so the evidence at hand indicates, they had neither the power, the unity, nor the vision to do this. They could, to be sure, push an initial program upon the new administration, limit the efforts at structural reform, and secure desired stabilization measures for certain types of industries. But they could not make the initial program work or retain the initiative; and instead of seeing that their long-range interests lay with the pattern taking shape after 1934 and moving quickly to adopt it, most of them spent the next six years fighting a bitter and expensive delaying action. What emerged was the creation not of an omnipotent corporate elite but of a complex interaction between conflicting interest groups, resurgent liberal ideals, and the champions of competing reform models, all of which, after all, contemplated the salvation and stabilizing of corporate capitalism as well as the democratizing of it.

If the revised image overcompensated, however, it did bring into focus some glaring defects in the earlier one, particularly its magnification of the degree of change, its search for continuities only in "reform" rather than in business circles, and its assumptions that the New Deal had solved the problems of power and maldistribution, transformed corporate capitalism into an obedient servant of the people, and found the way to reconcile a technocorporate order with competitive and democratic ideals. The innovations of the 1930s, significant though they were in strengthening the economy and bringing new groups and beneficiaries into the political process, had not altered the fundamental dilemmas confronting earlier reforms. They had merely shifted them into somewhat different settings. And probably, despite the disillusionment of many critics with a "middle way," the conflicting traditions and drives that underlay the dilemmas would persist, producing, along with some "progress," another confused search for a synthesis and new but transitory claims that one had been found. Significantly, the new concern with "abuses of power," with "overorganization," and with subversion of the "public interest" was producing not only fringe rejections of liberalism and technology but also revivals of the Brandeisian model, new dreams of associationalism, and updated notions of "public men" independent of the tug and pull of interest groups. History, of course, did not run in cycles, but surely there were parallels.

9

The Coming of World War II

Avoidable or Inevitable?

During the Great Depression of the 1930s the American people and their leaders remained preoccupied for much of the period with a myriad of domestic concerns. Concentrating on solving the problems of unemployment, underproduction, agricultural distress, and an economy that seemed to be on the verge of collapse, most individuals gave relatively little thought to events on the international scene. With a few notable exceptions, the aim of Americans was to solve their internal problems; foreign relations were important only to the extent that they threatened to involve the nation in another world holocaust similar to the one that began in 1914 and ended tragically four years later. Indeed, the desire to remain isolated from developments on the international scene was so pervasive that between 1934 and 1937 the Congress enacted and the president signed a series of acts designed precisely to prevent a repetition of the events from 1914 to 1917 that eventually ended in America's participation in World War I.

The outbreak of World War II in Europe in 1939 proved to be an important turning point in the development of American foreign policy. Domestic concerns such as the Great Depression and mass unemployment receded into the background as the fear of war swept over the country. Unlike Woodrow Wilson, Roosevelt refused to ask his countrymen to remain neutral in thought as well as action. "This nation," he told the American people in a fireside chat in September 1939, "will remain a neutral nation, but I cannot ask that every American remain neutral in thought as well." From the very beginning of hostilities, Roosevelt's hope was to offer as much military aid to the Allies as he could without going to war. Upon presidential urging, Congress repealed the arms embargo that was then in effect because the two-year cash-and-carry clause of the Neutrality Act of 1937 had expired. The fall of France in the spring of 1940 intensified Roosevelt's desire to rebuild

America's military forces and to give England all aid short of war. In 1941 the program of military aid to the Allied cause was expanded considerably by the Lend-Lease Act that was passed in March. By the summer of that year, the United States was involved in an undeclared naval war with Germany as American naval forces assumed the responsibility of protecting shipping in the western half of the North Atlantic. The most dramatic gesture of American sympathy for the British cause came in August of 1941, when Roosevelt and Churchill met off the coast of Newfoundland and agreed to a joint statement on mutual war aims. Known as the Atlantic Charter, the document not only spelled out the hopes of the two leaders for a better world, but referred specifically to "the final destruction of the Nazi tyranny" as a war aim.

The situation in Asia was equally explosive. Beginning in 1937 Japan renewed her attack upon the Nationalist regime of Chiang Kai-shek. The United States, having long been committed to the preservation of the territorial integrity and independence of China, found itself facing a diplomatic crisis. Nazi victories in Europe had the effect of stimulating Japanese ambitions even further; after the fall of France, Japan occupied northern Indochina and signified its desire to establish a "coprosperity sphere" throughout eastern Asia—a euphemism for Japanese hegemony.

Roosevelt responded slowly to these developments in Asia. First, the American government adopted various forms of economic pressure. After Japan occupied southern Indochina in July of 1941, Roosevelt took the decisive step of imposing all-inclusive economic sanctions. At this point Japan faced the choice of curtailing its ambitions, particularly in China, or breaking the restrictions by resorting to armed conflict. During the remainder of the year, Japan and the United States remained on a collision course that finally culminated in the fateful attack on Pearl Harbor on December 7, 1941.

Throughout the course of World War II, few Americans expressed any doubts over the issue of war guilt or their own involvement. Faced by totalitarian regimes in Germany, Italy, and Japan—regimes committed to the goal of regional or world domination—the United States, most felt, had no choice but to defend itself and become the champion of the free world. Roosevelt tried his best to avoid war and the use of American troops overseas, but the march of events seemed to destroy his hopes. The Japanese attack on Pearl Harbor settled the issue of going to war in a conclusive manner. From that point on, America committed its industrial and military might against the forces of aggression. Such was the position taken by most contemporary scholars and writers who dealt with American diplomacy from 1937 to 1941.

The first criticisms concerning America's foreign policies in the years prior to 1941 came toward the end of World War II. Not until after the war was over, however, did the revisionists—as those critical of Roosevelt came to be known—spell out their case in great detail. The reaction against Roosevelt's policies after 1945 was not a totally unexpected or surprising development. After each of America's past wars, a debate had taken place over the question of whether the nation ought to have become involved in overt hostilities. More important in explaining the criticisms of Roosevelt's diplomacy, however, was the widespread disillusionment in the United States with the results of World War II. America had gone to war in 1941 to destroy the forces of totalitarianism and then found itself faced with an even greater menace—the Soviet Union. Germany was divided, half of Europe lay under Russian domination, and the United States and the Soviet Union entered upon a period of tense diplomatic relations in the postwar era that quickly became known as the Cold War. When the Soviet Union developed an atomic bomb of its own in 1949, America felt its physical security threatened for the first time since 1783. America's wartime allies, Britain and France, could no longer be considered first-rate powers, and the British Commonwealth was facing a severe crisis as a result of the rise of Asian and African nationalism. In the Far East the situation looked equally bleak: the destruction of Japanese power left a vacuum that was quickly filled by the Chinese Communist regime; India, gaining its independence, was weak; and Korea was left divided. At home the coming of the Cold War posed problems of internal security as some persons feared that the nation was being threatened by subversives and Communists. The result was a period of repression in the early 1950s that seriously impaired the civil rights that American citizens had traditionally enjoyed under the Constitution. All of these developments raised some doubts over the wisdom of America's participation in World War II.

Many of the major critics of Roosevelt's foreign policies, interestingly enough, had taken an isolationist position as regards America's foreign policy in the 1930s, and some even had been associated with the school of revisionist writers who opposed America's entry into World War I. Harry Elmer Barnes, the father of World War I revisionism, consistently opposed Roosevelt's diplomatic policies and addressed meetings of the America First Committee—an isolationist organization of the 1930s and early 1940s. Charles A. Beard spoke out against any American entanglements in the 1930s and testified before the Senate Foreign Relations Committee in opposition to the idea of a lend-lease program. And Charles C. Tansill, who published the leading study in the 1930s critical of Wilson's foreign policies between 1914 and 1917, also played a key role in attacking New Deal diplomacy.

One of the first scholarly attempts to discredit Roosevelt's diplomacy came in 1946 and 1948, when Charles A. Beard published *American*

Foreign Policy, 1932–1940, and *President Roosevelt and the Coming of the War, 1941,* respectively. Beard's works, receiving a good deal of attention because of the eminent reputation of their author, were quickly followed by a series of other books. Although the positions they took varied markedly, all the revisionists were in basic agreement on certain fundamental points. Moreover, most of them had nothing but contempt for historians who refused to accept their anti-Roosevelt thesis. Harry Elmer Barnes, for example, characterized those who disagreed with him as "court historians," thereby implying that they had sacrificed their scholarly integrity to gain favor in government circles.

The revisionist hypothesis was based on a number of assumptions. First, the revisionists denied that the Axis powers had threatened America's vital interests. Germany had no plans to attack the Western Hemisphere, they claimed, and the Japanese were concerned only about Asia. Roosevelt's charge that the American people were being directly threatened from abroad, therefore, had little or no substance. Secondly, Roosevelt's foreign policy was one that he knew would inevitably lead to war in Europe and Asia. Indeed, some revisionists went so far as to suggest that Roosevelt deliberately misled the American people by telling them that he was working for peace while, in reality, he was laying the foundation for war. His famous speech in Boston during the presidential campaign of 1940 in which he promised that American boys would not fight on foreign soil was simply one example of his cupidity. Finally, the revisionists emphasized that the long-term results of America's involvement in World War II were largely negative—if not disastrous; the United States, by upsetting the European balance of power and creating a power vacuum, made possible the emergence of the Soviet Union—a nation that presented a far more serious threat to American security than did Nazi Germany.

Many, though not all, of the revisionists looked upon Roosevelt as a leader who deliberately misled and lied to the American people. In his critical study of New Deal diplomacy, Charles A. Beard made this point quite explicit. Roosevelt, Beard wrote, kept reassuring the American people that he was doing everything he could to avoid war and maintain a neutral position. Yet every action that he took belied his statements. He gave military aid and assistance to Britain, first through the destroyer-base exchange, then through the lend-lease program, and finally by ordering American naval vessels to escort convoys. All of these steps were undertaken consciously; they were not forced upon a reluctant or unwilling president by events beyond his control. Roosevelt, claimed Beard, acted on the assumption that he was wiser than the American people and consequently did not feel that he had to tell them the truth. The American people, Beard concluded, were faced with the fact "that the President of the United States possesses limitless authority publicly to misrepresent and secretly to control foreign policy, foreign affairs, and the war power."[1] Beard's thesis was echoed by other revisionists. As William Henry Chamberlain put it in 1953: "One is left, therefore, with the inescapable conclusion that the promises to 'keep America out of foreign wars' were a deliberate hoax on the American people, perpetrated for the purpose of insuring Roosevelt's re-election and thereby enabling him to proceed with his plan of gradually edging the United States into war."[2]

Although the revisionists were critical of Roosevelt's European diplomacy, they usually reserved their heaviest ammunition for his Far Eastern policy. Indeed, most of the criticism of Roosevelt centered around his dealings with Japan in the period from 1937 to 1941. Reduced to its simplest form, the revisionist indictment boiled down to the fact that Roosevelt deliberately provoked the Japanese into attacking Pearl Harbor. At that point the president was able to take the American people into a war that he secretly wanted, but had not desired to ask for publicly.

Such a thesis, of course, rested on the assumption that the Japanese leaders wanted peace—but that Roosevelt's maneuverings had forced them into an untenable position that could be resolved only by war. Although not all revisionists argued along precisely the same lines, their general arguments were remarkably similar. They maintained that Japan's desire for peace was sincere and that she wished to end her four-year-old war in China. Facing a crucial shortage of oil and other resources, the Japanese hoped to end the conflict on the Asiatic mainland in order to assure themselves continued access to those materials that were indispensable to the economic well-being of the nation. To achieve these objectives, the Japanese leaders did everything within their power to arrive at a satisfactory *modus vivendi* with the United States.

President Roosevelt, according to the revisionists, was not interested in peace; he wanted war. Instead of dealing with Japan on the basis of justice and equity, he pursued a policy that he knew would ultimately provoke Japanese retaliation. During 1941 the United States increased its economic pressures upon Japan by curtailing the shipments of oil and other raw materials. At the same time, America refused to agree to any concessions to Japan regarding China. By mid-1941 all Japanese assets in the United States had been frozen, and in August Roosevelt sent a strong warning to Japan to abandon her expansionist policies. All of these

---

[1]Charles A. Beard, *President Roosevelt and the Coming of the War, 1941: A Study in Appearances and Realities* (New Haven, 1948), p. 598.

[2]William Henry Chamberlain, "The Bankruptcy of a Policy," in *Perpetual War for Perpetual Peace,* ed. Harry Elmer Barnes (Caldwell, 1953), p. 491.

moves, the revisionists claimed, were deliberately designed to provoke
Japan into some form of retaliation.

The final step, said the revisionist writers, was taken in late
November 1941, when Secretary of State Cordell Hull submitted a ten-
point proposal to Japan. This document demanded that Japan pull out of
China and Indochina. To the revisionists the document represented an
American "ultimatum" and not one that could serve as the basis for
diplomatic discussions. The perfidy of American leaders became even
clearer in the days preceding the attack on Pearl Harbor. Sometime
earlier, the United States had broken Japan's secret code. Roosevelt and
his advisers, therefore, knew that Japan really desired peace, but that
she was ready to take military action if the American government persisted in its unyielding course. High American officials, including the
President, even knew that a Japanese attack on the military and naval
installations at Pearl Harbor was imminent. According to the revisionists, the desire of the Roosevelt administration for war was so
strong that government officials did not inform the military commanders
in Hawaii of the possibility of an attack. In the end, then, Roosevelt's
harsh policies provoked the Japanese into an attack on the unprepared
military at Pearl Harbor, and gave him the declaration of war that he had
so ardently desired. To achieve his goal, some revisionists maintained,
Roosevelt knowingly sacrificed American lives as well as a large part of
the American fleet at Pearl Harbor. As Harry Elmer Barnes wrote in
Perpetual War for Perpetual Peace—a volume in which a number of leading
revisionists spelled out their case—"The net result of revisionist
scholarship applied to Pearl Harbor boils down essentially to this: In
order to promote Roosevelt's political ambitions and his mendacious
foreign policy some three thousand American boys were quite need-
lessly butchered. Of course, they were only a drop in the bucket compared to those who were ultimately slain in the war that resulted, which
was as needless, in terms of vital American interests, as the surprise
attack on Pearl Harbor."[3]

For the most part, American historians have rejected this revisionist
hypothesis. They have done so largely on the grounds that it rests upon
a simplistic conspiracy theory of history. Human beings, they claim, are
complex creatures who are affected by complex motives. To argue that
Franklin Delano Roosevelt knew the precise results of his policies would

---

[3]*Ibid.*, p. 651. By far the most detailed revisionist interpretation of the events leading up
to Pearl Harbor is Charles C. Tansill, *Back Door to War: Roosevelt Foreign Policy, 1933–1941*
(Chicago, 1952). Other revisionist accounts include George Morgenstern, *Pearl Harbor: The
Story of the Secret War* (New York, 1947); William H. Chamberlain, *America's Second Crusade*
(Chicago, 1950); and Robert A. Theobald, *The Final Secret of Pearl Harbor: The Washington
Contribution to the Japanese Attack* (New York, 1954).

be to credit him with an omniscience that no human could possibly possess. As a leading nonrevisionist historian pointed out, it is one thing to charge that the Roosevelt administration misunderstood Japan's intentions and underestimated her military strength; it is quite another matter to conclude that the tragic disaster of December 7, 1941, was a matter of calculated diplomatic planning by a scheming American president.[4]

The revisionist argument—at least in a modified version—nevertheless offers a historical thesis that cannot be easily dismissed. In the first selection in this chapter, Paul W. Schroeder discusses America's policy toward Japan in the crucial months preceding Pearl Harbor. Schroeder raises a number of issues which cast some doubt upon the wisdom of America's diplomatic moves. The major point at stake was whether the United States had been well-advised in taking a "hard" line toward Japan. The issue raised two interesting questions: Should the United States have made the liberation of China a central aim of its policy, thereby requiring the immediate evacuation of Japanese troops; and should Roosevelt have declined the invitation of the Japanese premier to a personal meeting between the two leaders to discuss their differences? To Schroeder the answer to both these questions is an emphatic "no." Until mid-1941 American planners had consistently sought two reasonable and rather limited objectives; that of splitting the three Axis powers and stopping Japan's advance with Asia. With these goals within its reach, the United States then added a third; the liberation of China. The last objective, however, was not a limited one, nor could it be attained short of war. Because of its misguided sympathy toward China, the American government drove Japan back into the arms of the Axis powers and made inevitable an armed confrontation between the two nations. American policymakers, Schroeder concluded, were not evil men determined to bring about war; they were instead men who were blinded by a sense of their own moral righteousness and had abandoned that pragmatism required of all human beings if differences between nations are not always to end in war.

Schroeder's thesis, in many respects, had already been anticipated by other writers on this subject. George F. Kennan, the former ambassador to Russia, State Department official, and historian, for example, had argued in 1951 that the United States erred grievously in the twentieth century when it committed itself to the Open Door and the preservation of the territorial and administrative integrity of China. Although a nation-state, Kennan wrote, China had many attributes which failed to coincide with the European national state that had evolved in the

---

[4]Robert H. Ferrell, "Pearl Harbor and the Revisionists," *Historian* 17 (Spring 1955): 233.

eighteenth and nineteenth centuries. Consequently, the Open Door policy was difficult to implement because it rested on the fallacious assumption that China was no different from other states. More important, Kennan insisted, the United States continuously "hacked away, year after year, decade after decade, at the positions of the other powers on the mainland of Asia, and above all the Japanese, in the unshakable belief that, if our principles were commendable, their consequences could not be other than happy and acceptable. But rarely could we be lured into a discussion of the real quantities involved: of such problems as Japan's expanding population, or the weaknesses of government in China, or the ways in which the ambitions of other powers could be practicably countered. Remember that this struck a particularly sensitive nerve in the case of countries whose interests on the Asiatic mainland were far more important to them than our interests there were to us. . . . There was always a feeling, both among the Japanese and among the British, that we were inclined to be spendthrift with their diplomatic assets in China for the very reason that our own stake in China meant so much less to us than theirs did to them."[5] The result, he concluded, was that the United States never exploited the possibility of arriving at a mutually satisfactory compromise with Japan. Like Schroeder, however, Kennan vehemently denied that the failure to reach a meaningful compromise was a deliberate choice of evil and scheming leaders.

The majority of writers dealing with America's diplomacy in the years prior to Pearl Harbor, however, took an exactly opposite point of view from the revisionists. The internationalist or interventionist school—to differentiate it from the revisionist school—based its arguments upon an entirely different set of assumptions. Writers of the internationalist school began with the proposition that the Axis powers had, in fact, posed a very serious threat to America's security and national interests. By the summer of 1940, the Nazis had conquered most of Western and Central Europe and Britain seemed to be on the verge of surrender. When Hitler invaded the Soviet Union in June 1941 a German victory appeared to be a certainty. The danger, according to the internationalist school, was that America might have to face the victorious Axis powers alone. German and Italian campaigns in North Africa created a fear that control of that continent might provide a springboard for an attack upon the Western Hemisphere. Axis successes in Europe, meanwhile, had stimulated the Japanese to increase their aggressive moves in Asia on the theory that the Allies were too preoccupied in the West to divert any forces to the Far East.

Roosevelt, according to the internationalist school, believed that

---

[5]George F. Kennan, *American Diplomacy 1900–1950* (Chicago, 1951), p. 48.

Germany represented the greatest threat to America's security. It was in the national interest, therefore, to follow a policy designed to bring about a German defeat. Thus, Roosevelt embarked upon a program of extending to England all aid short of war in the belief that such a policy might prevent a Nazi victory and contribute to the eventual downfall of Germany. Although renouncing impartial neutrality, Roosevelt hoped that aid to England would permit his nation to protect its security without committing American troops to a foreign conflict. The undeclared naval war in the North Atlantic against Germany represented the limit of America's involvement.

Roosevelt's primary interest lay in Europe—the internationalist interpretation continued—and his Far Eastern policy was designed to avert any showdown with Japan. The steps that he took in 1940 and 1941 were intended to check Japan by all means short of war. The embargo on oil and other resources, the freezing of Japanese assets in the United States, the aid to China, and the massing of the American fleet in the Pacific were aimed at deterring, not provoking, the Japanese. America's objective was to seek a peaceful settlement with Japan, but a settlement that would uphold American security and principles, protect China, and honor the British, French, and Dutch interests in the Far East. Japan's expansionist ambitions, however, proved to be too great and Roosevelt came to realize that an armed conflict between the two nations was inevitable. According to the internationalist school of writers, his policy at this point became one of stalling for time in order to permit an American military buildup.

Although the internationalist school by no means approved of all of Roosevelt's diplomatic policies, they believed that the fundamental causes for America's involvement in the war lay outside the United States and in the trend of world events over which this country had little, if any, control. Most of them were convinced that Roosevelt had sought the goal of peace with great sincerity. In fact, many argued that his desire for peace led him to overestimate the opposition to his internationalist policies, which he could have pursued even more vigorously than he did.

Almost all of the historians in the internationalist school violently rejected the revisionist point of view—particularly the insinuation that Roosevelt had plotted to provoke the Japanese assault on Pearl Harbor. While many admitted that there might have been some blundering in both Washington and Hawaii, there was general agreement that the attack came as a genuine surprise. In Washington neither civilian nor military authorities had interpreted the decoded Japanese messages correctly; virtually everyone assumed that the Japanese were moving to attack British and Dutch installations in the Southwest Pacific. Although it was true that the army and navy commanders in Hawaii were not given all of the information gained from breaking the Japanese code, most internationalist historians believed that the military officials on the spot would have interpreted the messages in the same light as their superiors in Washington. Even if they had been able to divine Japanese intentions correctly, there is some doubt as to whether a military disaster could have been avoided; the American fleet was extremely vulnerable to air attack and there were insufficient land-based planes to ward off a Japanese raid. In retrospect, then, the internationalist historians looked upon Pearl Harbor as a tragic disaster that grew out of faulty military and diplomatic planning rather than part of a presidential conspiracy.[6]

The second selection in this chapter is by Dexter Perkins, one of the deans of American diplomatic history, and represents the views of internationalist scholars while vigorously attacking the revisionist school. To Perkins historical revisionism at the close of a military conflict seems to be a common occurrence among Americans. In part, this response stems from the letdown or disillusionment that results from a failure to secure all of the goals for which the war was fought; it is related also to the inevitable reaction against the strong executive leadership that characterizes most wartime administrations. Whatever the reasons for its rise, Perkins defines such revisionism as "history by hypothesis"; it suggests that the world would have been a better place had the United States remained aloof from any involvement in World War II. Perkins goes on to argue that a victorious Germany would have been a very serious menace to America. Nor did Roosevelt deceive the American people, according to Perkins. The President was basically in accord with public opinion, for even the Republican party nominated Wendell Willkie in 1940 and took an internationalist position on foreign affairs. Although Roosevelt may have been devious in his public statements from time to time, he accurately reflected the mood and thinking of his fellow countrymen. In the final analysis, Perkins ends up with a favorable, though by no means uncritical, appraisal of Roosevelt's foreign policy prior to the war.

Other internationalist scholars have also argued strongly against the revisionist thesis that Roosevelt deliberately exposed the American fleet at Pearl Harbor in order to provoke a Japanese attack. Herbert Feis, for example, insisted that Japan was bent on dominating Asia, thus threatening America's interests in that part of the world. Had the United States not placed an embargo on trade with Japan, it would have been in the strange position of having undertaken preparations for war while at the same time strengthening the opponent it might meet in battle. Feis denied that there was conclusive evidence that Prince Konoye's offer to meet with Roosevelt in the autumn of 1941 might have averted a conflict.

---

[6]See especially Roberta Wohlstetter, *Pearl Harbor: Warning and Decision* (Stanford, 1962).

He rejected also the thesis that Secretary of State Cordell Hull's note of November 26, 1941, was in any sense an ultimatum. The basic cause of the war, concluded Feis, was Japan's insistence on becoming the dominant power in the Far East. Short of a complete surrender on America's part, the chances of avoiding war by means of diplomatic negotiations had always been remote.[7]

It should be emphasized that there are many points of disagreement among individual historians of the internationalist school even though all of them rejected the revisionist hypothesis. The differences between internationalist historians frequently reflected the same divisions that existed among Roosevelt's advisers prior to December 7, 1941. For example, Secretary of State Cordell Hull was generally cautious in his approach; he favored limiting overt action to steps short of war. Secretary of War Henry L. Stimson, on the other hand, believed that the policy of all aid short of war would not result in the defeat of the Axis powers, and that America would have to intervene sooner or later. Indeed, Stimson believed that American people would have supported Roosevelt in a declaration of war even before Pearl Harbor. Similarly, some internationalist historians, including Herbert Feis and Basil Rauch, were sympathetic to Hull and Roosevelt, while others, notably William L. Langer and S. Everett Gleason, argued that Roosevelt overestimated isolationist opposition to his policies and that the president actually lagged behind public opinion on the desirability of taking strong measures against the Axis powers.[8]

Beginning in the late 1950s, however, the internationalist school began to come under sharp attack from scholars who saw a close relationship between foreign and domestic policy, with the former growing out of the latter. These scholars took a quite different approach to the problem of war causation; rather than focusing on the immediate events that led to Pearl Harbor, they studied the long-range trends in American foreign policy and provided an alternative framework for understanding our entry into the Second World War. Perhaps the most influential scholar in this regard was William Appleman Williams, who offered in a series of important books a view of American diplomacy that was sharply at variance with his internationalist contemporaries.

The Williams thesis, in its simplest form, was that American foreign

[7]Herbert Feis, "War Came at Pearl Harbor: Suspicions Considered," *Yale Review* 45 (Spring 1956): 378–90.

[8]Herbert Feis, *The Road to Pearl Harbor: The Coming of War Between the United States and Japan* (Princeton, 1950); Basil Rauch, *Roosevelt: From Munich to Pearl Harbor* (New York, 1950); William L. Langer and S. Everett Gleason, *The Challenge to Isolation, 1937–1940* (New York, 1952) and *The Undeclared War, 1940–1941* (New York, 1953). Other internationalist works include Donald F. Drummond, *The Passing of American Neutrality* (Ann Arbor, 1955); Robert A. Divine, *The Reluctant Belligerent: American Entry into World War II* (New York, 1965); and John E. Wiltz, *From Isolation to War, 1931–1941* (New York, 1968).

policy since the late nineteenth century reflected a particular ideology
known as Open Door imperialism. A reflection of American capitalism,
this policy was based on the premise that foreign markets were indispensable for domestic prosperity and tranquility. By the 1890s, therefore, the United States had moved to acquire overseas possessions,
strategically situated so as to facilitate trade and provide naval bases but
involving few of the usual responsibilities associated with an extensive
overseas empire. The Open Door policy, argued Williams, was designed
to win victories without wars; "it was derived from the proposition that
America's overwhelming economic power would cast the economy and
the politics of the poorer, weaker, underdeveloped countries in a
pro-American mold."[9] Ultimately the ideology of the Open Door would
lead the United States into a more and more militant opposition to any
economic system—socialist, communist, totalitarian—that might diminish its overseas trade.

Williams's thesis led directly to a new interpretation of the diplomacy
of the 1930s and the coming of the Second World War. The New Deal,
according to Williams, was intended to define and institutionalize the
roles, functions, and responsibilities of three important segments of industrial society—capital, labor, government—and to do so in harmony
with the principles of capitalism. In foreign policy the New Deal continued to seek the overseas markets on which American prosperity supposedly rested; even Secretary of State Cordell Hull's reciprocal trade
program was intended to control foreign sources of raw materials while
simultaneously providing for the selling of American surpluses abroad.
The result was a strengthening of free trade imperialism, which in turn
led to a rising distrust of the United States by nations increasingly fearful
of domination by American capitalism. When Japan began to move
south into China in 1937 and Germany became more active in Latin
America, Roosevelt and his advisers moved toward an activistic and
interventionist foreign policy because of the threat to our economic
interests throughout the world. During the Second World War America's economic leaders also became enthusiastic converts to the mission
to reform the world. This crusading zeal, in conjunction with Open Door
imperialism, was in large measure responsible for the advent of the Cold
War and the disastrous course that involved the nation in two wars in
the 1950s and 1960s.[10]

The Williams thesis about the nature of foreign policy proved ex-

---

[9]William Appleman Williams, *The Tragedy of American Diplomacy* (rev. ed.: New York,
1962), p. 49. See also Williams's *The Roots of the Modern American Empire* (New York, 1969).

[10]A detailed study of New Deal diplomacy in the Williams tradition is Lloyd C. Gardner's *Economic Aspects of New Deal Diplomacy* (Madison, 1964).

traordinarily attractive to individuals and groups committed to fundamental changes in American society in the 1960s. Indeed, Williams himself concluded that the United States had to adopt a new foreign policy
that rejected the assumptions that an informal empire was necessary for
our welfare, that trade was a weapon against those nations with whom
we had disagreements or was necessary in order to pay for the costs of
military security abroad. Moreover, the United States had to stop seeing
communism in terms of an absolute evil. "Once freed from its myopic
concentration on the cold war, the United States could come to grips
with the central problem of reordering its own society so that it functions
through such a balanced relationship with the rest of the world, and so
that the labor and leisure of its own citizens are invested with creative
meaning and purpose."[11] While Williams himself was more within a
social democratic tradition, other historians—particularly those associated with the New Left—picked up where Williams had left off. In
the eyes of these scholars war, racism, and poverty were all outgrowths
of the evil nature of American capitalism, a system that rested on the
exploitation of the many by the few. Only radical changes that involved
a sharp redistribution of economic and political power would make it
possible for the American people to confront their problems and develop
appropriate solutions.[12]

Curiously enough, relatively few New Left historians have written
about the events that immediately preceded American entry into the
Second World War. While emphasizing American culpability for the
advent of the Cold War, they tended to shy away from dealing with the
Second World War, perhaps because of the difficulty of ignoring the
nature of Nazi Germany. With the exception of Williams's general interpretation of American diplomacy and Lloyd C. Gardner's study of the
economic aspects of New Deal diplomacy, relatively little has been written on the origins of the Second World War by those with an affinity for
the New Left.

Recently there has been a tendency among historians to avoid extreme interpretations of the events that led to American entry into the
Second World War. Between 1939 and 1941, according to Robert Dallek,
Roosevelt attempted to balance the nation's antiwar sentiment with the
contradictory impulse to assure a Nazi defeat. Initially he attempted to
fuse both by providing the Allies with military aid. Even when Roosevelt

---

[11]Williams, *Tragedy of American Diplomacy*, p. 306. Walter LaFeber's *America, Russia, and
the Cold War 1945–1966* (New York, 1967) and Lloyd C. Gardner's *Architects of Illusion: Men
and Ideas in American Foreign Policy 1941–1949* (Chicago, 1970) are both in the Williams
tradition.

[12]See Gabriel Kolko, *The Politics of War: The World and United States Foreign Policy 1943–
1945* (New York, 1968) and *The Roots of American Foreign Policy* (Boston, 1969).

concluded in the spring of 1941 that American involvement in the conflict was all but inevitable, according to Dallek, "he refused to force an unpalatable choice upon the nation by announcing for war." Nor did the United States provoke an attack by Japan. Roosevelt's anti-Fascist commitment made it impossible for him to discriminate between Germany and Japan; "both had to be opposed at the same time." The attack on Pearl Harbor on December 7, 1941, was an unforeseen surprise. "Seeing the fleet in Hawaii as a deterrent rather than a target, lulled by the belief that the Japanese lacked the capability to strike at Pearl Harbor and by the information or 'noise' . . . indicating that an attack might come at any one of a number of points," Dallek noted, "Roosevelt, like the rest of the nation, failed to anticipate the Pearl Harbor attack. Later contentions to the contrary had less to do with the actuality of Roosevelt's actions than with the isolationists' efforts to justify the idea that the country had never in fact been vulnerable to attack."[13]

To evaluate in a fair and objective manner the events leading up to Pearl Harbor, then, is not a simple task for scholars. The complexity of this historical problem arises from many reasons: the tangled web of interrelated events in the period before December 1941, which makes it difficult, if not impossible, to separate causes and to point to any particular one as "definitive"; the fact that some of the goals for which America went to war were not achieved by the end of the conflict; and the problem of ascertaining the precise motives of the national leaders and various interest groups of the period. Historical judgment, furthermore, rests to a considerable degree upon the starting assumptions held by various scholars; different historians approach the problem with a different set of starting assumptions and hence reach conflicting conclusions.

In contrasting the revisionist with the international school of historians, several differences are clearly discernible. First, both deal in a very different way with the issue of whether or not the Axis powers represented an immediate threat to American security. The revisionists maintained that there was no evidence that Hitler hoped to move into the Western Hemisphere. Even if he had, the revisionists held that the best policy would have been for America to have waited until Germany and Russia had destroyed each other; such a policy would have avoided the power vacuum that developed in Europe in the postwar period that enabled the Soviet Union to expand without checks. In the Far East, America also made a mistake by pushing Japan into the war by an inflexible policy and a refusal to offer any reasonable compromises. The

---

[13]Robert Dallek, *Franklin D. Roosevelt and American Foreign Policy, 1932–1945* (New York, 1979), pp. 530–32.

internationalists, on the other hand, believed that a victorious Germany posed a serious threat to American security, especially if one considers the military prowess and scientific potential of the Third Reich. Given Hitler's past behavior, there was no reason to assume that his ambitions would have been satisfied after conquering England and the Soviet Union. Insofar as the Far East was concerned, the internationalists took the view that Japan's unwillingness to abandon its imperialist policy was the prime cause of the war. Scholars within the Williams tradition tended to see the diplomacy of the 1930s as an outgrowth of American economic expansionism; they paid relatively little attention to the Axis powers and to the question whether or not American security was, in fact, threatened by developments in Europe and the Far East.[14]

A second issue that scholars dealt with was the motivation behind Roosevelt's foreign policy. Did Roosevelt deceive the American people by telling them that his policy would lead to peace when in reality he wanted war? To this question the revisionists answered in the affirmative and the internationalists in the negative. The Williams school as well as those scholars writing within the tradition of the New Left, on the other hand, tended to occupy a middle position, if only because this question was not central to their analysis. All schools had a serious problem on this score, however, because the issue revolved about the motivation and intentions of one man. How can the historian gauge the motives of any individual, particularly when so few human beings ever record their innermost convictions or are completely honest with themselves?

In many respects the most important difference separating the various schools was their judgment concerning the results of the war. To the revisionists the outcome of the war was dramatic evidence of the blundering and evil policy followed by Roosevelt and his advisers. The United States, after all, had gone to war to destroy the menace of totalitarianism. Instead, it was confronted after 1945 with the Soviet Union, a far greater menace than Nazi Germany. On the continent Russia controlled all of Eastern and a good part of Central Europe; in the Far East the destruction of Japanese power created a situation that ultimately led to a Communist takeover in China. The internationalist school, by way of comparison, readily admitted that the results of the war were anything but desirable, but its adherents also argued that these results did not necessarily make Hitler the lesser of two evils. Moreover, history suggests a tragic view of human destiny; for each

---

[14]Cf. Alton Frye, *Nazi Germany and the American Hemisphere, 1933–1941* (New Haven, 1967); James V. Compton, *The Swastika and the Eagle: Hitler, the United States, and the Origins of World War II* (Boston, 1967); and Bruce M. Russett, *No Clear and Present Danger: A Skeptical View of the United States Entry into World War II* (New York, 1972).

problem solved more arise in its place. To expect a final solution to all problems is to be unrealistic. While Roosevelt may have miscalculated in some of his policies, he did not do so knowingly or deliberately; his mistakes were due to the limitations that characterize all human beings. The Williams school and New Left historians saw in the Second World War the origins and beginnings of the Cold War, for during that time America's economic imperialism was fused with a messianic sense; the result was a crusade against any system not modeled after the example of the United States.

In general, then, the differing interpretations of America's entry into the Second World War reflect the personal faith of the historians in the particular policy they are advocating. The internationalist school believed that the United States, as a world power, could not neglect its responsibilities nor ignore events in other parts of the world. The world is far too small a place for the provincial isolationism that characterized American diplomacy in the early years of the republic. Consequently, they believed that Roosevelt was on the right track even though some of his specific moves may not have been correct ones. The revisionists, on the other hand, argued that America's national interest could have been best served by remaining aloof from conflicts that did not immediately threaten the United States. Roosevelt, therefore, made a grievous error when he committed his nation—against the will of its people—to a world conflict. The American people, the revisionists concluded, are still paying the price of that mistake. Those in the tradition of Williams or the New Left, argue by way of contrast that only a basic transformation in America's foreign policy (and hence domestic policies) can bring peace and an atmosphere conducive to meaningful social change. Consequently—with some exceptions—they see American diplomacy in the 1930s as a grievous error.

Which of these schools of thought is correct? Were the revisionists justified in their claim that the United States should have stayed out of World War II? Were they right in attributing evil and invidious motives to Roosevelt and his advisers? Or were the internationalist historians right in arguing that World War II involved vital American interests and that Roosevelt was simply trying to safeguard these interests even though it meant that the nation might eventually enter the war? Or were Williams and New Left historians correct in attributing war to Open Door imperialism? These are some of the basic issues confronting the student who is attempting to understand the background and events that led up to Pearl Harbor.

Paul W. Schroeder

PAUL W. SCHROEDER (1927–   ) is professor of history at the University of
Illinois. He is the author of several books on diplomatic history; the book
from which the present selection is taken was the recipient of the Beveridge
Prize of the American Historical Association.

In judging American policy toward Japan in 1941, it might be well to
separate what is still controversial from what is not. There is no longer
any real doubt that the war came about over China. Even an administration stalwart like Henry L. Stimson and a sympathetic critic like Herbert
Feis concur in this. Nor is it necessary to speculate any longer as to what
could have induced Japan to launch such an incredible attack upon the
United States and Great Britain as occurred at Pearl Harbor and in the
South Pacific. One need not, as Winston Churchill did in wartime,
characterize it as "an irrational act" incompatible "with prudence or
even with sanity." The Japanese were realistic about their position
throughout; they did not suddenly go insane. The attack was an act of
desperation, not madness. Japan fought only when she had her back to
the wall as a result of America's diplomatic and economic offensive.

The main point still at issue is whether the United States was wise in
maintaining a "hard" program of diplomatic and economic pressure on
Japan from July 1941 on. Along with this issue go two subsidiary questions: the first, whether it was wise to make the liberation of China the
central aim of American policy and the immediate evacuation of
Japanese troops a requirement for agreement; the second, whether it
was wise to decline Premier Konoye's invitation to a meeting of leaders
in the Pacific. On all these points, the policy which the United States
carried out still has distinguished defenders. The paramount issue between Japan and the United States, they contend, always was the China
problem. In her China policy, Japan showed that she was determined to
secure domination over a large area of East Asia by force. Apart from the
legitimate American commercial interests which would be ruined or
excluded by this Japanese action, the United States, for reasons of her
own security and of world peace, had sufficient stake in Far Eastern

questions to oppose such aggression. Finally, after ten years of Japanese expansion, it was only sensible and prudent for the United States to demand that it come to an end and that Japan retreat. In order to meet the Japanese threat, the United States had a perfect right to use the economic power she possessed in order to compel the Japanese to evacuate their conquered territory. If Japan chose to make this a cause for war, the United States could not be held responsible.

A similar defense is offered on the decision to turn down Konoye's Leaders' Conference. Historians may concede, as do Langer and Gleason, that Konoye was probably sincere in wanting peace and that he "envisaged making additional concessions to Washington, including concessions on the crucial issue of the withdrawal of Japanese troops from China." But, they point out, Konoye could never have carried the Army with him on any such concession. If the United States was right in requiring Japan to abandon the co-prosperity sphere, then her leaders were equally right in declining to meet with a Japanese premier who, however conciliatory he might have been personally, was bound by his own promises and the exigencies of Japanese politics to maintain this national aim. In addition, there was the serious possibility that much could be lost from such a meeting—the confidence of China, the cohesiveness of the coalition with Great Britain and Russia. In short, there was not enough prospect of gain to merit taking the chance.

This is a point of view which must be taken seriously. Any judgment on the wisdom or folly of the American policy, in fact, must be made with caution—there are no grounds for dogmatic certainty. The opinion here to be developed, nonetheless, is that the American policy from the end of July to December was a grave mistake. It should not be necessary to add that this does not make it treason. There is a "back door to war" theory, espoused in various forms by Charles A. Beard, George Morgenstern, Charles C. Tansill, and, most recently, Rear Admiral Robert A. Theobald, which holds that the president chose the Far East as a rear entrance to the war in Europe and to that end deliberately goaded the Japanese into an attack. This theory is quite different and quite incredible. It is as impossible to accept as the idea that Japan attacked the United States in a spirit of overconfidence or that Hitler pushed the Japanese into war. Roosevelt's fault, if any, was not that of deliberately provoking the Japanese to attack, but of allowing Hull and others to talk him out of impulses and ideas which, had he pursued them, might have averted the conflict. Moreover, the mistake (assuming that it was a mistake) of a too hard and rigid policy with Japan was, as has been pointed out, a mistake shared by the whole nation, with causes that were deeply organic. Behind it was not sinister design or warlike intent, but a sincere and uncompromising adherence to moral principles and liberal doctrines.

This is going ahead too fast, however; one needs first of all to define the mistake with which American policy is charged. Briefly, it was this. In the attempt to gain everything at once, the United States lost her opportunity to secure immediately her essential requirements in the Far East and to continue to work toward her long-range goals. She succeeded instead only in making inevitable an unnecessary and avoidable war—an outcome which constitutes the ultimate failure of diplomacy. Until July 1941, as already demonstrated, the United States consistently sought to attain two limited objectives in the Far East, those of splitting the Axis and of stopping Japan's advance southward. Both aims were in accordance with America's broad strategic interests; both were reasonable, attainable goals. Through a combination of favorable circumstance and forceful American action, the United States reached the position where the achievement of these two goals was within sight. At this very moment, on the verge of a major diplomatic victory, the United States abandoned her original goals and concentrated on a third, the liberation of China. This last aim was not in accord with American strategic interests, was not a limited objective, and, most important, was completely incapable of being achieved by peaceful means and doubtful of attainment even by war. Through her single-minded pursuit of this unattainable goal, the United States forfeited the diplomatic victory which she had already virtually won. The unrelenting application of extreme economic pressure on Japan, instead of compelling the evacuation of China, rendered war inevitable, drove Japan back into the arms of Germany for better or for worse, and precipitated the wholesale plunge by Japan into the South Seas. As it ultimately turned out, the United States succeeded in liberating China only at great cost and when it was too late to do the cause of the Nationalist Chinese much real good.

This is not, of course, a new viewpoint. It is in the main simply that of Ambassador Grew, who has held and defended it since 1941. The arguments he advances seem cogent and sensible in the light of present knowledge. Briefly summarized, they are the following: First is his insistence on the necessity of distinguishing between long-range and immediate goals in foreign policy and on the folly of demanding the immediate realization of both. Second is his contention that governments are brought to abandon aggressive policies not by sudden conversion through moral lectures, but by the gradual recognition that the policy of aggression will not succeed. According to Grew, enough awareness of failure existed in the government of Japan in late 1941 to enable it to make a beginning in the process of reversal of policy—but not nearly enough to force Japan to a wholesale surrender of her conquests and aims. Third was his conviction that what was needed on both sides was time—time in which the United States could grow stronger and in which the tide of war in Europe could be turned definitely against Germany, time in which the sense of failure could grow in Japan and in which moderates could gain better control of the situation. A victory in Europe, Grew observed, would either automatically solve the problem of Japan or make that problem, if necessary, much easier to solve by force. Fourth was his belief that Japan would fight if backed to the wall (a view vindicated by events) and that a war at this time with Japan could not possibly serve the interests of the United States. Even if one considered war as the only final answer to Japanese militarism, still, Grew would answer, the United States stood to gain nothing by seeking a decision in 1941. The time factor was entirely in America's favor. Japan could not hope to gain as much from a limited relaxation of the embargo as the United States could from time gained for mobilization; Roosevelt and the military strategists were in fact anxious to gain time by a *modus vivendi*.

There is one real weakness in Grew's argument upon which his critics have always seized. This is his contention that Konoye, faced after July 26 with the two clear alternatives of war or a genuine peace move, which would of necessity include a settlement with China, had chosen the latter course and could have carried through a policy of peace had he been given the time. "We believed," he writes, "that Prince Konoye was in a position to carry the country with him in a program of peace" and to make commitments to the United States which would "eventually, if not immediately" meet the conditions of Hull's Four Points. The answer of critics is that, even if one credits Konoye's sincerity and takes his assurances at face value, there is still no reason to believe that he could have carried even his own cabinet, much less the whole nation, with him on any program approximating that of Hull. In particular, as events show, he could not have persuaded the army to evacuate China.

The objection is well taken; Grew was undoubtedly over-optimistic about Konoye's capacity to carry through a peaceful policy. This one objection, however, does not ruin Grew's case. He countered it later with the argument that a settlement with Japan which allowed Japanese garrisons to remain in China on a temporary basis would not have been a bad idea. Although far from an ideal solution, it would have been better, for China as well, than the policy the United States actually followed. It would have brought China what was all-important—a cessation of fighting—without involving the United States, as many contended, in either a sacrifice of principle or a betrayal of China. The United States, Grew points out, had never committed herself to guaranteeing China's integrity. Further, it would not have been necessary to agree to anything other than temporary garrisons in North China which, in more favorable times, the United States could work to have removed. The great mistake was to allow American policy to be guided by a sentimental attitude toward China which in the long run could do neither the United States nor China any good. As Grew puts it:

> Japan's advance to the south, including her occupation of portions of China, constituted for us a real danger, and it was definitely in our national interest that it be stopped, by peaceful means if possible, by force of arms if necessary. American aid to China should have been regarded, as we believe it was regarded by our Government, as an indirect means to this end, and not from a sentimental viewpoint. The President's letter of January 21, 1941, shows that he then sensed the important issues in the Far East, and that he did not include China, purely for China's sake, among them. . . . The failure of the Washington Administration to seize the opportunity presented in August and September, 1941, to halt the southward advance by peaceful means, together with the paramount importance attached to the China question during the conversations in Washington, gives rise to the belief that not our Government but millions of quite understandably sympathetic but almost totally uninformed American citizens had assumed control of our Far Eastern policy.

There remains the obvious objection that Grew's solution, however plausible as it may now seem, was politically impracticable in 1941. No American government could then have treated China as expendable, just as no Japanese government could have written off the China Affair as a dead loss. This is in good measure true and goes a long way to explain, if not to justify, the hard American policy. Yet it is not entirely certain that no solution could have been found which would both have averted war and have been accepted by the American people, had a determined effort been made to find one. As F. C. Jones points out, the United States and Japan were not faced in July 1941 with an absolute dilemma of peace or war, of complete settlement or open conflict. Hull believed that they were, of course; but his all-or-nothing attitude constituted one of his major shortcomings as a diplomat. Between the two extremes existed the possibility of a *modus vivendi,* an agreement settling some issues and leaving others in abeyance. Had Roosevelt and Konoye met, Jones argues, they might have been able to agree on a relaxation of the embargo in exchange for satisfactory assurances on the Tripartite Pact and southward expansion, with the China issue laid aside. The United States would not have had to cease aid, nor Japan to remove her troops. The final settlement of the Far Eastern question, Jones concludes,

> would then have depended upon the issues of the struggle in Europe. If Germany prevailed, then the United States would be in no position to oppose Japanese ambitions in Asia; if Germany were defeated, Japan would be in no position to persist in those ambitions in the face of the United States, the USSR, and the British Commonwealth.

Such an agreement, limited and temporary in nature, would have involved no sacrifice of principle for either nation, yet would have removed the immediate danger of war. As a temporary expedient and as an alternative to otherwise inevitable and useless conflict, it could have been sold by determined effort to the public on both sides. Nor would it have been impossible, in the writer's opinion, to have accompanied or followed such an agreement with a simple truce or standstill in the China conflict through American mediation.

This appraisal, to be sure, is one based on realism. Grew's criticism of Hull's policy and the alternative he offers to it are both characterized by fundamental attention to what is practical and expedient at a given time and to limited objectives within the scope of the national interest. In general, the writer agrees with this point of view, believing that, as William A. Orton points out, it is foolish and disastrous to treat nations as morally responsible persons, "because their nature falls far short of personality," and that, as George F. Kennan contends, the right role for moral considerations in foreign affairs is not to determine policy, but rather to soften and ameliorate actions necessarily based on the realities of world politics.

From this realistic standpoint, the policy of the State Department would seem to be open to other criticisms besides those of Grew. The criticisms, which may be briefly mentioned here, are those of inconsistency, blindness to reality, and futility. A notable example of the first would be the inconsistency of a strong no-compromise stand against Japan with the policy of broad accommodation to America's allies, especially Russia, both before and after the American entrance into the war. The inconsistency may perhaps best be seen by comparing the American stand in 1941 on such questions as free trade, the Open Door in China, the territorial and administrative integrity of China, the maintenance of the prewar status quo in the Far East, and the sanctity of international agreements with the position taken on the same questions at the Yalta Conference in 1945.

The blindness to reality may be seen in the apparent inability of American policy makers to take seriously into account the gravity of Japan's economic plight or the real exigencies of her military and strategic position, particularly as these factors would affect the United States over the long run. Equally unrealistic and more fateful was the lack of appreciation on the part of many influential people and of wide sections of the public of the almost certain consequences to be expected from the pressure exerted on Japan—namely, American involvement in a war her military strategists considered highly undesirable. The attitude has been well termed by Robert Osgood, "this blind indifference toward the military and political consequences of a morally-inspired position."

The charge of futility, finally, could be laid to the practice of insisting on a literal subscription to principles which, however noble, had no chance of general acceptance or practical application. The best example is the persistent demand that the Japanese pledge themselves to carrying out nineteenth-century principles of free trade and equal access to raw materials in a twentieth-century world where economic nationalism and autarchy, trade barriers and restrictions were everywhere the order of the day, and not the least in the United States under the New Deal. Not one of America's major allies would have subscribed wholeheartedly to Hull's free-trade formula; what good it could have done to pin the Japanese down to it is hard to determine.

But these are all criticisms based on a realistic point of view, and to judge the American policy solely from this point of view is to judge it unfairly and by a standard inappropriate to it. The policy of the United States was avowedly not one of realism, but of principle. If then it is to be understood on its own grounds and judged by its own standards the main question will be whether the policy was morally right—that is, in accord with principles of peace and international justice. Here, according to its defenders, the American policy stands vindicated. For any other policy, any settlement with Japan at the expense of China, would have meant a betrayal not only of China, but also of vital principles and of America's moral task in the world.

This, as we know, was the position of Hull and his co-workers. It has been stated more recently by Basil Rauch, who writes:

> No one but an absolute pacifist would argue that the danger of war is a greater evil than violation of principle.... The isolationist believes that appeasement of Japan without China's consent violated no principle worth a risk of war. The internationalist must believe that the principle did justify a risk of war.

This is not an argument to be dismissed lightly. The contention that the United States had a duty to fulfill in 1941, and that this duty consisted in holding to justice and morality in a world given to international lawlessness and barbarism and in standing on principle against an unprincipled and ruthless aggressor, commands respect. It is not answered by dismissing it as unrealistic or by proscribing all moral considerations in foreign policy. An answer may be found, however, in a closer definition of America's moral duty in 1941. According to Hull, and apparently also Rauch, the task was primarily one of upholding principle. This is not the only possible definition. It may well be contended that the moral duty was rather one of doing the most practical good possible in a chaotic world situation and, further, that this was the main task President Roosevelt and the administration had in mind at least till the end of July 1941.

If the moral task of the United States in the Far East was to uphold a principle of absolute moral value, the principle of nonappeasement of aggressors, then the American policy was entirely successful in fulfilling it. The American diplomats proved that the United States was capable of holding to its position in disregard and even in defiance of national interests narrowly conceived. If, however, the task was one of doing concrete good and giving practical help where needed, especially to China, then the American policy falls fatally short. For it can easily be seen not only that the policy followed did not in practice help China, but also that it could not have been expected to. Although it was a pro-China and even a China-first policy in principle, it was not a practical fact designed to give China the kind of help needed.

What China required above all by late 1941 was clearly an end to the fighting, a chance to recoup her strength. Her chaotic financial condition, a disastrous inflation, civil strife with the Communists, severe hunger and privation, and falling morale all enfeebled and endangered her further resistance. Chiang Kai-shek, who knew this, could hope only for an end to the war through the massive intervention of American forces and the consequent liberation of China. It was in this hope that he pleaded so strongly for a hard American policy toward Japan. Chiang's hopes, however, were wholly unrealistic. For though the United States was willing to risk war for China's sake, and finally did incur it over the China issue, the Washington government never intended in case of war to throw America's full weight against Japan in order to liberate China. The American strategy always was to concentrate on Europe first, fighting a defensive naval war in the Far East and aiding China, as before, in order to keep the Japanese bogged down. The possibility was faced and accepted that the Chinese might have to go on fighting for some years before eventual liberation through the defeat of Japan. The vehement Chinese protests over this policy were unavailing, and the bitter disillusionment suffered by the Chinese only helped to bring on in 1942 the virtual collapse of the Chinese war effort during the later years of the war.

As a realistic appraisal of America's military capabilities and of her worldwide strategic interests, the Europe-first policy has a great deal to recommend it. But the combination of this realistic strategy with a moralistic diplomacy led to the noteworthy paradox of a war incurred for the sake of China, which could not then be fought for the sake of China and whose practical value for China at the time was, to say the least, dubious. The plain fact is that the United States in 1941 was not capable of forcing Japan out of China by means short of war and was neither willing nor, under existing circumstances, able to throw the Japanese out by war. The American government could conceivably have told the Chinese this and tried to work out the best possible program of help for China under these limitations. Instead, it yielded to Chinese importunities and followed a policy almost sure to eventuate in war, knowing that if the Japanese did attack, China and her deliverance would have to take a back seat. It is difficult to conceive of such a policy as a program of practical aid to China.

The main, though not the only, reason why this policy was followed is clearly the overwhelming importance of principle in American diplomacy, particularly the principle of nonappeasement of aggressors. Once most leaders in the administration and wide sections of the public became convinced that it was America's prime moral duty to stand hard and fast against aggressors, whatever the consequences, and once this conviction became decisive in the formulation of policy, the end result was almost inevitable: a policy designed to uphold principle and to punish the aggressor, but not to save the victim.

It is this conviction as to America's moral duty, however sincere and understandable, which the writer believes constitutes a fundamental misreading of America's moral task. The policy it gave rise to was bad not simply because it was moralistic but because it was obsessed with the wrong kind of morality—with that abstract "Let justice be done though the heavens fall" kind which so often, when relentlessly pursued, does more harm than good. It would be interesting to investigate the role which this conception of America's moral task played in the formulation of the American war aims in the Far East, with their twin goals of unconditional surrender and the destruction of Japan as a major power, especially after the desire to vindicate American principles and to punish the aggressor was intensified a hundredfold by the attack on Pearl Harbor. To pursue the later implications of this kind of morality in foreign policy, with its attendant legalistic and vindictive overtones, would, however, be a task for another volume.

In contrast, the different kind of policy which Grew advocated and toward which Roosevelt so long inclined need not really be considered immoral or unprincipled, however much it undoubtedly would have been denounced as such. A limited *modus vivendi* agreement would not have required the United States in any way to sanction Japanese aggression or to abandon her stand on Chinese integrity and independence. It would have constituted only a recognition that the American government was not then in a position to enforce its principles, reserving for America full freedom of action at some later, more favorable time. Nor would it have meant the abandonment and betrayal of China. Rather it would have involved the frank recognition that the kind of help the Chinese wanted was impossible for the United States to give at that time. It would in no way have precluded giving China the best kind of help then possible—in the author's opinion, the offer of American mediation for a truce in the war and the grant of fuller economic aid to try to help the Chinese recover—and promising China greater assistance once the crucial European situation was settled. Only that kind of morality which sees every sort of dealing with an aggressor, every instance of accommodation or conciliation, as appeasement and therefore criminal would find the policy immoral.

What the practical results of such a policy, if attempted, would have been is of course a matter for conjecture. It would be rash to claim that it would have saved China, either from her wartime collapse or from the final victory of communism. It may well be that already in 1941 the situation in China was out of control. Nor can one assert with confidence that, had this policy enabled her to keep out of war with Japan, the United States would have been able to bring greater forces to bear in Europe much earlier, thus shortening the war and saving more of Europe from communism. Since the major part of the American armed forces were always concentrated in Europe and since in any case a certain proportion would have had to stand guard in the Pacific, it is possible that the avoidance of war with Japan, however desirable in itself, would not have made a decisive difference in the duration of the European conflict. The writer does, however, permit himself the modest conclusions that the kind of policy advocated by Grew presented real possibilities of success entirely closed to the policy actually followed and that it was by no means so immoral and unprincipled that it could not have been pursued by the United States with decency and honor.

Dexter Perkins

DEXTER PERKINS (1889–   ) is emeritus professor of history at the University of
Rochester. He is the author of many books on various phases of American
diplomatic history, including three volumes on the Monroe Doctrine.

Revisionism may be defined as an after-the-event interpretation of
American participation in war, with the accent on the errors and blunders that provoked the struggle and on the folly of the whole enterprise.
If we accept this definition, we shall certainly agree that there has been
plenty of revisionism in the course of our history. The War of 1812 has
sometimes been judged to have been futile and sometimes described as
a war of intended conquest. The Mexican War has come in for harsh
treatment as a war of unnecessary aggression. James G. Randall, one of
the foremost students of the Civil War period, suggests that a less
passionate view of the sectional problem might have made the conflict
avoidable. Again and again it has been stated by reputable historians
that William McKinley might have prevented the war of 1898 had he
stressed in his message to Congress the very large concessions that had
been made by Spain. The First World War was brilliantly represented by
Walter Millis as the product of a blundering diplomacy and of economic
pressures not entirely creditable. And since 1945 we have had a crop of
historians, headed by so eminent a member of his historical generation
as Charles A. Beard, attempting to show that the maddest folly of all was
our entry into the conflict that ended less than a decade ago. Clearly,
revisionism is an American habit; though, in saying this, I do not mean
to imply that it is unknown in other lands.

The roots of the revisionist tendency are worth speculating about.
Such a point of view, I take it, is particularly apt to find expression in a
country where peace is highly treasured and where the glorification of
war is relatively uncommon. Just as many Americans easily put away
the hates and resentment of war at the end of the struggle and display a
tendency towards reconciliation with the vanquished, so they tend to
forget the passions that animated them and drove them into the conflict,
and to view what at the time seemed reasonable and natural as some-

"Was Roosevelt Wrong?," *Virginia Quarterly Review* 30 (Summer 1954): 355–72. Reprinted
with permission of the *Virginia Quarterly Review* and Dexter Perkins.

thing that with a little more forbearance or wisdom could have been avoided. And there are other factors that reinforce this point of view. Wars are apt to end in disillusionment. After the glorious hopes of the years 1917 and 1918 came the clash of national selfishness at Versailles, and a distraught and threatened world. In 1945 the defeat of Hitler and Japan was soon seen to have left grave problems ahead. In the East, the American defense of China and the hopes of a strong democratic nation in the Orient ended in the victory of the Chinese Reds. And in Europe, though the peril from the ambitions of Hitler was exorcized, the United States found itself face to face with a new totalitarianism, far-ranging in its ambitions like the old. In such a situation it was natural to forget the menace that had been defeated, and to ask whether there might not have been a better solution to the problems that ended with the capitulation ceremonies at Rheims and on the deck of the *Missouri*.

After every large-scale war, moreover, there is a reaction against that strong executive leadership which is almost inevitably associated with periods of crisis in the life of the nation. This was true in 1920; and it was true after 1945. During the conflict the personality of Mr. Roosevelt loomed large, and almost immune from attack. But under the surface there was hostility, and this was to take the form of criticism of his war policies. Sometimes this criticism came, as in the case of Frederic R. Sanborn in his "Design for War," from one who had a strong animus against the New Deal, and who approached the record of the administration in the field of foreign policy with this animus. Sometimes, on the other hand, as in the case of Charles A. Beard, it came from one who regarded the Roosevelt diplomacy as jeopardizing and perhaps wrecking far-reaching programs of internal reform. In these two cases, and in virtually every other, strong emotions entered into the account. It has been a satisfaction to the revisionists to tear down the President; and there has always been—and it was inevitable that there should be—a reading public to fall in with this point of view, either from personal dislike of Roosevelt or from partisan feeling.

Revisionism, then, has roots in the very nature of the case. But, if we analyze it coolly, what shall we think of it? This is the question I propose to examine in this essay.

It seems to me fair to say at the outset that it is impossible to avoid the conclusion that revisionism is essentially history by hypothesis. It suggests—indeed in some instances it almost claims—that the world would have been a better place, or that at any rate the present position of the United States would have been happier, if this country had not intervened in the Second World War. Such a proposition can be put forward, but it cannot be established like a theorem in geometry. We cannot go back to 1939 or 1941 and reenact the events of those stirring and tumultuous years. In a sense, we are bound by the past.

Nonetheless, it seems worthwhile, even though we are in the realm of speculation rather than scientific history, to state the revisionist point of view. First, with regard to Germany the point of view is advanced that the United States was in no essential danger from Adolf Hitler, that he demonstrated no very great interest in the American continents, that he desired until almost the day of Pearl Harbor to keep out of trouble with the United States, that there is no reliable evidence that he meditated an assault upon the New World. It is possible for the revisionist to go further. The ambitions of Hitler, it would be maintained, would have been checked and contained within limits by the presence of the great totalitarian state to the East. The two colossi would act each as a restraint on the other. It needed not the intervention of the American government to preserve the safety of the New World. As to Asia, the argument runs somewhat differently. Less emphasis is placed on the question of national security and more on a certain interpretation of national interest. The United States, we are told, had only a meager interest in China; its trade and investments there were insignificant, and were likely to remain so. They were distinctly inferior to our trade and investments in Japan. The shift in the balance of the Far East that might come about through a Japanese victory over Great Britain was no real concern of the United States. As to the Philippines, they might have been left alone had we stayed out of the war, or conversely, they were not worth the sacrifice involved in maintaining our connection with them. Such are the assumptions, implied, if not always expressed, in the revisionist view of the problem of the Orient.

Now some of the assertions in this rationale are unchallengeable. It is true that Hitler desired to avoid a clash with the United States until just before Pearl Harbor. It is true that the economic interests of the United States in China were inferior to our interests in Japan. These are facts, and must be accepted as facts. But there still remain a good many questions about the revisionist assumptions. For example, was there in 1940 and 1941 no danger of the destruction of British naval power, and would that destruction have had no unhappy consequences for the United States? Granted that the documents show great reluctance on the part of the Führer to challenge the United States, would this reluctance have outlasted the fall of Great Britain? Granted that the Kremlin might have exercised a restraining influence on the Germans, is it certain that the two powers might not have come to an understanding as they did in 1939, and had at other periods in the past? Just how comfortable a world would it have been if the psychopathic leader of Germany had emerged from the Second World War astride a large part of the Continent, with the resources of German science at his command? There are questions, too, that can be asked about the Orient. Did the United States have no responsibility for the Philippines, and would the islands have been safe for long if the Japanese had dominated the Far East? Could the United States divest itself of all concern for China, abandoning a policy of nearly forty years duration and a deep-seated American tradition? Was the destruction of British power in this part of the world a matter of no concern to this country? Could the defeat of Britain in the East be separated from the fate of Britain in the world at large? These are extremely large questions, and it is a bold man who will brush them aside as inconsequential or trivial, or who will reply to them with complete dogmatism. Indeed, it is because they raise so many problems cutting to the root of our feelings, as well as our opinions, that they arouse so much controversy. Nor is there any likelihood that we can ever arrive at a complete consensus with regard to them.

We must, I think, seek a somewhat narrower frame of reference if we are to answer the revisionists with facts, and not with speculations. One of the ways to answer them, and one particularly worth pursuing with regard to the war in Europe, is to analyze the policy of the Roosevelt administration in its relation to public sentiment.

Foreign policy, in the last analysis, depends, not upon some logical formula, but upon the opinion of the nation. No account of American diplomacy in 1940 and 1941 can pretend to authority which does not take into account the tides of sentiment which must always influence, and perhaps control, the course of government. It is not to be maintained that a president has no freedom of action whatsoever; he can, I think, accelerate or retard a popular trend. But he does not act independently of it; the whole history of American diplomacy attests the close relationship between the point of view of the masses and executive action. A peacefully-minded president like McKinley was driven to war with Spain; a president who set great store by increasing the physical power of the nation, like Theodore Roosevelt, was limited and confined in his action; and Franklin Roosevelt himself, when, in the quarantine speech of October 1937, he sought to rouse the American people against aggression, was compelled to admit failure, and to trim his sails to the popular breeze. These things are of the essence; to fail to observe them is to fail to interpret the past in the true historical spirit.

Let us apply these conceptions to the period 1939 to 1941. It will hardly be denied that from the very beginning of the war public sentiment was definitely against Germany. Indeed, even before the invasion of Poland, the public opinion polls show a strong partiality for the democratic nations. As early as January 1939, when asked the question [of] whether we should do everything possible to help England and France in case of war, 69 percent of the persons polled answered in the affirmative, and the same question in October produced a percentage of 62 percent on the same side. No doubt this sentiment did not extend to the point of actual participation in the war, but it furnished a firm foundation for the action of the President in calling Congress in special session, and in asking of it the repeal of the arms embargo on shipments of war in the interest of the Allies. The measure to this effect was introduced in the Congress towards the end of September; and it was thoroughly debated. There are several things to be said in connection with its passage. The first is that after its introduction there was a consistent majority of around 60 percent in the polls in favor of passage. The second is that, though there was a strong partisan flavor to the debate, the defections when they came were more numerous on the Republican than on the Democratic side. It is true that, without the leadership of the President, the repeal could not have been enacted. But also it did not fly in the face of public sentiment (so far as that can be measured), but on the contrary reflected it.

With the fall of France there took place a deep and significant development in public opinion. This change the revisionists usually do not mention. They prefer to treat of American policy as if it were formed in a vacuum without regard to the moving forces that have so much to do with the final decisions. Yet the evidences are ample that in June of 1940 the American people were deeply moved. Take, for example, the action of the Republican nominating convention. There were several outstanding professional politicians in the running in 1940, Senator Taft, Senator Vandenberg, Thomas E. Dewey. Each one of these men represented a policy of caution so far as Europe was concerned. Yet what did the convention do? It turned to a relatively unknown figure, to a novice in politics who had, however, more than once declared himself as advocating extensive assistance to the democracies. The choice of Wendell Willkie as the Republican candidate for the presidency is a fact the importance of which cannot be denied. It is worthwhile calling attention to other like phenomena. One of these is the overwhelming majorities by which the Congress appropriated largely increased sums for the armed forces, not only for the navy but for the army and the air force as well. Perhaps the American people, or the representatives of the American people, ought not to have been perturbed at what was happening in Europe. But the fact is that they were perturbed. They were perturbed in a big way. And the votes in the legislative halls demonstrate that fact.

Or take another example. The movement for a conscription law in time of peace developed rapidly after June of 1940. It developed with very little assistance from the White House. It cut across party lines. And it resulted in a legislative enactment which reflected the excitement of the public mind. How can we interpret the measure otherwise? Was there not a substantial body of opinion in the United States that feared a German victory?

Another important factor to be noted is the formation in June of 1940 of the Committee to Defend America by Aiding the Allies. It is highly significant that this movement arose at all. It is doubly significant that it found a leader in a Kansan Republican such as William Allen White. It is trebly significant that, once initiated, it spread like wildfire, and that by September there were more than 650 chapters in the United States. And it is also to be noted that in New York there soon came into being a more advanced group, the so-called Century Group, which advocated war if necessary to check the aggressions of Germany.

And it is further to be observed that out of the Committee to Defend America came an agitation for what was eventually to be the bases-destroyer deal of September 2, 1940. This deal, by the way, was approved by 62 percent of the persons polled on August 17, 1940, two weeks before it was actually consummated.

Let us go further. The next important step forward in American policy was the lend-lease enactment of the winter of 1941. This measure, it would appear from the polls, was based on a very distinct evolution of public sentiment. In July of 1940 59 percent of the persons polled preferred to keep out rather than to help England at the risk of war, and 36 percent took the contrary view. In October the percentages were exactly reversed: they were 36 to 59. By January of 1941 68 percent of those interviewed thought it more important to assist Great Britain than to keep out of war. And the lend-lease enactment, when presented to the Congress, passed the Lower House by the impressive vote of 317 to 71 and the Senate by 60 to 31. As in the legislation of 1939, though the vote again had a partisan flavor, there were more defections from the Republicans in favor of the measure than of Democrats against it. And there is something more to be added to the account in this instance. By the winter of 1941 the America Firsters had appeared upon the scene. A counterpropaganda was now being organized against the administration. Yet this new group, despite its vigorous efforts, failed signally to rally majority opinion. And Senator Taft, who represented the most thoughtful opposition to the administration, himself proposed a measure of assistance to Great Britain.

I shall treat a little later of the various measures requiring no legislative sanction which the President took in the course of the year 1941. But it is important to observe that throughout the period there was a strong public sentiment that believed that it was more important to defeat Germany than to keep out of war. This view was held, according to the polls, by 62 percent of those interrogated in May of 1941 and by 68 percent in December of 1941. As early as April 1941, 68 percent of the pollees believed it important to enter the war if British defeat was certain.

We should next examine the legislation of the fall of 1941. By this time the Congress was ready to authorize the arming of American merchant ships, and this by a heavy vote. The measure was passed by 259 to

138 in the House and the Senate amended it and passed it by 50 to 37. Congress was ready, more reluctantly, to repeal those provisions of the neutrality acts which excluded American vessels from the so-called war zones. It was moving in the direction of fuller and fuller engagement against Hitler. We shall never know, of course, what the next step would have been had not that step been taken by Germany. It was the dictator of the Reich who declared war on the United States, not the American national legislature that declared war on the Führer and his minions. But in the period between 1939 and 1941 it seems safe to say that the foreign policy of the Roosevelt administration was in accord with the majority opinion accepted, and pursuing a course of action which majority opinion approved.

This circumstance is naturally either ignored or obscured in the revisionist literature. And what makes it easier to forget is the undeniable fact that Franklin Roosevelt was unhappily sometimes given to equivocation and shifty conversation. Very early, it is true, as early as the quarantine speech of October 1937, he sounded the alarm against the totalitarians. Very often he stated his conviction that their continued progress presented a threat to the United States. On occasion he took his courage in his hands as, when at Charlottesville in June of 1940, in an election year, he came out frankly in favor of aid to the democracies, or in the declaration of unlimited emergency in the address of May 27, 1941. There is little doubt that he deemed the defeat of Hitler more important than the avoidance of war (as did many other Americans, as we have seen). Yet he was often less than frank in his approach, and the emphasis he laid on his devotion to peace was often excessive. He shocked even his ardent admirer, Robert Sherwood, in the election of 1940. His presentation of the case for lend-lease does not at all times suggest candor; indeed, the very phrase seems a bit of cajolery. With regard to the question of convoy, in the spring of 1941, he was clever and, though verbally correct, hardly wholly open in his approach to the problem. In the famous episode of the *Greer* (an attack by a German submarine on a vessel which was reporting its position to a British destroyer), he misrepresented the facts, or spoke without full knowledge of them. All this it is only right to admit. Yet we must not exaggerate the importance of these considerations. The country knew where it was going with regard to Germany. It accepted lend-lease as desirable. Of the patrolling of the ocean lanes which followed, the President spoke candidly in the speech of May 27, 1941. There was nothing clandestine about the occupation of Greenland or Iceland. The pattern in the fall of 1941 would most probably not have been much altered if Roosevelt had been more scrupulous with regard to the *Greer*. In the last analysis we come back to the essential fact that Roosevelt represented and expressed in action the mood of the country with regard to Germany.

The question is, I believe, more difficult when we come to examine American policy towards Japan. We can say with some assurance that the denunciation of the treaty of commerce of 1911, undertaken by the administration in July of 1939 as an indication of American displeasure with Japanese policy, was distinctly well received. Indeed, if the State Department had not acted, the legislature might have. We can also say that in August of 1939 there was an overwhelming feeling against sending war materials to Nippon. When in September of 1940, an embargo on the export of scrap iron was imposed, 59 percent of the persons polled on this issue approved the step that had been taken. And in 1941 the number of persons who believed that some check should be put on Japan even at the risk of war rose from 51 percent to 70 percent between July and September, and stood at 69 percent at the time of Pearl Harbor.

But we have fewer indications of the direction of public sentiment in the action of Congress, and no actual votes on which to base our estimate of how the representatives of the American people felt with regard to the important problem of our course of action in the Orient. We must, I think, speak less confidently on this question of public opinion than in the case of Germany. We must turn rather to an analysis of the policy of the administration, and to revisionist criticism of that policy.

First of all, let us look at some of the uncontroverted facts. We know that there were militarist elements in Japan. We know that as early as 1934 Japan proclaimed its doctrine of a Greater East Asia in the famous Amau statement. We know that in the same year it upset the naval arrangements made at Washington and London. We know that it set up a special régime in North China in 1935. We know that it became involved in a war with China in 1937. This, of course, was only prelude. The outbreak of the European conflict in Europe, and the collapse of France, offered to the sponsors of further aggressive action a great opportunity. The occupation of northern Indochina followed. In the summer of 1940, the impetuous and aggressive Matsuoka came to the Foreign Office. On September 27, 1940, there was signed a tripartite pact with Japan, which bound Nippon to come to the assistance of the Axis powers if they were attacked by a power then at peace with them. In other words, the Tokyo government sought to confine and limit American policy. In April of 1941 came a neutrality pact with Russia which freed the hands of the Japanese militarists for a policy of advance towards the South. In July came the occupation of the rest of Indochina. The occupation of *northern* Indochina made some sense from the point of view of blocking the supply route to the Chinese Nationalists. The occupation of *southern* Indochina made no sense, except as the prelude to further acts of aggression. And in due course the aggression came.

Admittedly, this is only one side of the story. The question to be examined is, did these acts take place partly as a result of American provocation? Was it possible for a wider and more prudent diplomacy to have avoided the rift that occurred in December 1941? Revisionist criticism of our Oriental policy has been expressed in a variety of ways. In its most extreme form, it suggests that the President and his advisers actually plotted war with Japan. In its less extreme form, it directs its shafts at a variety of actions, of which I shall examine the most important. They are the conversations with the British as to the defense of the Far East, the commitments made to China, the severance of commercial relations, the failure to accept the proposals of Prince Konoye for direct conversations with the President, and the breakdown of the *modus vivendi* proposal of November 1941. I shall examine each of these briefly, but let us first turn to the accusation that American policy was directed towards producing and not avoiding an armed conflict in the Orient.

It seems quite impossible to accept this view on the basis of the documentation. During the greater part of 1940 and 1941, it was certainly not the objective of the Roosevelt administration to bring about a clash in the Far East. On the contrary such a clash was regarded as likely to produce the greatest embarrassment in connection with the program of aid to Britain. The military and naval advisers of the President were opposed to it, and said so again and again. Even on the eve of Pearl Harbor this was the case. In addition, Secretary Hull was opposed to it. Ever the apostle of caution, he made his point of view quite clear almost up to the end. And as for the President, it is worth pointing out that on the occasion of the Japanese occupation of southern Indochina he came forward with a proposal for the neutralization of that territory in the interests of peace, and that in August he frankly stated it to be his purpose to "baby the Japanese along." That he feared Japanese aggression is likely, almost certain; that he desired it is something that cannot be proved.

But let us look at the various specific actions which have awakened criticism on the part of the revisionists. In the first place I cannot see that staff conversations with the British were open to any objections whatsoever. If the object of the Roosevelt administration was to limit Japanese aggression in the Far East, then it seems wholly rational to take precautions against such aggression, and surely it could reasonably be expected that such precautions would serve as a deterrent rather than as an incitement to action. It is, in my judgment, rather distorted thinking that regards such action as provocation. This is precisely the point of view of the Kremlin today with regard to the North Atlantic Treaty and the European defense pact, or, to take another example, very like the contention of the Germans when they invaded Belgium in 1914. Because the British had engaged in military conversations with the Belgians looking to the possible violation of the neutrality treaty of 1939, it was claimed by apologists for Germany that the violation of neutrality was defensible. Where is the possible justification for such reasoning?

There is more to be said with regard to the breaking off, by the United States, of commercial and financial relations with Japan on the heels of the Japanese occupation of southern Indochina in the summer of 1941. Undoubtedly this created an extraordinarily difficult situation for the government in Tokyo. Undoubtedly the cutting off of the oil supply from the United States gave great additional force to the arguments of the militarists. Undoubtedly, in the absence of a far-reaching diplomatic arrangement, it presented a strong reason for "bursting out" of the circle, and going to war. If the administration put faith in this measure of economic coercion as a substitute for physical resistance, its faith was to turn out to be groundless. For myself, I have for a long time believed that economic coercion against a strong and determined power is more likely to produce war than to prevent it. But there are circumstances that ought to be mentioned in favor of the action of the administration. It is to be emphasized that the severance of commercial and financial relations resulted not in a breach of the negotiations with Japan but in a resumption of those negotiations. It is to be remembered that Prince Konoye's proposal for a personal conference with the President came after and not before the President's action. American policy by no means put an end to the efforts of those substantial elements in Japan who feared a clash with this country and who were laboring to prevent it. It must be pointed out, also, that the alternative was by no means a pleasant one. At a time when we were deeply engaged in the Atlantic, when we were being more and more deeply committed with regard to the war in Europe, when our domestic supply of oil might have to be substantially curtailed, the continuation of our exports to the Far East to assist Japan in possible projects of aggression was a very difficult policy to follow. It may even be that it would have proven to be totally impracticable from a political point of view.

We come in the third place to the efforts of Premier Konoye to establish direct contact with President Roosevelt. It is well known that Ambassador Grew believed at that time, and that he has more than once stated since, that a good deal was to be hoped from such a meeting. And it is by no means clear why, if the objective were the postponement of a crisis, the experiment should not have been tried. Secretary Hull brought to this problem, as it seems to me, a rigidity of mind which may properly be criticized. In insisting on a previous definition of the issues before the meeting was held, he was instrumental in preventing it. While we cannot know what the result of such a meeting would have been, we are entitled, I think, to wish that it had been held. All the more is this true since it would appear likely that Prince Konoye was sincere in the effort which he made to avoid war.

But there is another side to the matter. We cannot be absolutely sure of Konoye's good faith. We can be still less sure of the willingness of the Tokyo militarists to support him in the far-reaching concessions that would have been necessary. And in the final analysis we cannot be sure of the ability of the American government to make concessions on its own part.

And here we come, as it seems to me, to the crux of the matter. It was the American policy in China that created an impassable barrier in our negotiations with Japan. It is necessary to examine that policy. From one angle of vision the patience of the American government in dealing with the China incident seems quite remarkable. There was a good deal to complain of from 1935 onward, certainly from 1937 onward, if one were to think in terms of sympathy for an aggressed people and in terms of the traditional policy of the United States with regard to this populous nation. The Roosevelt administration moved very slowly in its opposition to Japan. It made its first loan to Chiang Kai-shek in the fall of 1938. It denounced the commercial treaty of 1911 with Nippon only in the summer of 1939. And it embarked upon a policy of really substantial aid to China only contemporaneously with the signing of the tripartite pact in the fall of 1940. Its increasing assistance to Chiang is intelligible on the ground that to keep the Japanese bogged down in China was one means of checking or preventing their aggressive action elsewhere.

The fact remains, however, that it was the Chinese question which was the great and central stumbling block in the long negotiations that took place in 1941. Though the Japanese had entered into an alliance with the Axis powers, it seems not unlikely that, in 1941, as the issue of peace or war defined itself more clearly, they would have been willing to construe away their obligations under that alliance had they been able to come to terms with the United States on the Chinese problem. But by 1941 the American government was so far committed to the cause of Chiang that it really had very little freedom of maneuver. The various Japanese proposals for a settlement of the China incident would have involved a betrayal of the Chinese Nationalist leader. The proposal for a coalition government, a government of the Nationalists and the puppet régime of Wang Ching-wei, could hardly have been accepted. The proposal that America put pressure on Chiang to negotiate, and cut off aid to him if he refused, was by this time equally impracticable. And the question of the withdrawal of the Japanese troops in China presented insuperable difficulties. True it is that in October of 1941 the idea of a total withdrawal seems to have been presented to Mr. Welles by Mr. Wakasugi, Admiral Nomura's associate in the negotiations. But the idea was emphatically rejected by the militarists in Tokyo, and perhaps there was never a time when they would have agreed to any proposal that at the same time would have been acceptable to Chungking. The American government had been brought, by its policy of association with the Chinese Nationalists, to the point where understanding with Japan was practically impossible.

This fact is dramatically illustrated by the negotiations over the *modus vivendi* in November 1941. At this time, as is well known, proposals were brought forward for the maintenance of the status quo, and a gradual restoration of more normal relations through the lifting of the commercial restrictions, and through the withdrawal of the Japanese from southern Indochina. At first it seemed as if there were a possibility of working out some such proposal. But the Chinese objected most violently, and Secretary Hull dropped the idea. In the face of Chinese pressure, and of the possible popular indignation which such a policy of concession might produce, and acting either under the orders or at least with the assent of the President, he backed down. We must not exaggerate the importance of this. There is no certainty that the *modus vivendi* would have been acceptable to Tokyo, and, judging by the Japanese proposals of November 20, there is indeed some reason to think otherwise. But the fact remains that our close association with Chiang was a fundamental factor in making the breach with Japan irreparable. And it seems fair to say in addition that our hopes with regard to Nationalist China were at all times, in 1941 as later, very far removed from political reality.

Let us not, however, jump to absolute conclusions with regard to questions that, in the nature of the case, ought not to be a matter of dogmatic judgment. If there was a party in Japan, and a substantial one, which feared war with the United States and earnestly sought for accommodation, there was also a party which regarded the course of events in Europe as a heaven-sent opportunity for national self-aggrandizement. That this party might in any case have prevailed, whatever the character of American policy, does not seem by any means unlikely. It is significant that in July of 1941 the fall of Matsuoka brought no change in policy in the Far East, and that the so-called moderate, Admiral Toyoda, gave the orders for the crucial and revealing occupation of southern Indochina in the summer of 1941.

Let us not forget, either, that after all it was the Japanese who struck. The ruthless act of aggression at Pearl Harbor was no necessary consequence of the breakdown of negotiations with the United States. If new oil supplies were needed, they were, of course, to be secured by an attack on the Dutch East Indies, not by an attack on Hawaii. Though there were strategic arguments for including America in any warlike move, there were strong political reasons for not doing so. No greater miscalculation has perhaps ever been made than that made by the militarists at Tokyo in December 1941. By their own act, they unified American opinion and made their own defeat inevitable. It will always remain doubtful when the decisive involvement would have come for the United States had the bombs not dropped on Pearl Harbor on the seventh of December of 1941.

What, in conclusion, shall we say of revisionist history? There is a sense in which it is stimulating to the historian, and useful to historical science, to have the presuppositions, the conventional presuppositions, of the so-called orthodox interpreters of our foreign policy, subjected to criticism. There is surely some reason to believe that the candid examination of the views of these critics will, in the long run, result in a more accurate and a more objective view of the great events of the prewar years and in a better balanced judgment of President Roosevelt himself.

But there is another side of the question which, of course, must be recognized. It is fair to say that virtually all revisionist history (like some orthodox history) is written with a *parti pris*. It is hardly possible to speak of it as dictated by a pure and disinterested search for truth. It is, on the contrary, shot through with passion and prejudice nonetheless. It also rests upon hypotheses which, in the nature of the case, cannot be demonstrated, and assumptions that will, it is fair to say, never be generally, or perhaps even widely, accepted. As to its practical effects, there are no signs that the isolationism of the present era has important political effects, so far as foreign policy is concerned. Conceivably, it provides some reinforcement for partisan Republicanism. But even here it seems considerably less effective than the unscrupulous campaign of Senator McCarthy and his colleagues to represent the previous administration as one saturated with Communists. The urgency of present issues may make revisionism less of a force in our time than it was two decades ago. As to this, we shall have to see what the future unfolds.

10

America and the Cold War

Containment or Counterrevolution?

After the Second World War the American people faced a succession of external and internal challenges for which they had few historical precedents. By 1945 the United States had emerged as the strongest nation on earth. Having triumphed over the forces of Nazi and fascist totalitarianism, American citizens looked forward with confidence and optimism to the promise of a bright future. Such hopes and expectations were soon dashed. Within two years after the fighting ended, the United States found itself confronting the Soviet Union, its former ally. Instead of peace, the American people were plunged headlong into an era of "Cold War"—a series of crises that required economic and military mobilization even in the absence of actual hostilities.

Two developments during the war established the context within which the Cold War would be waged. One was the toppling of five major nations from the ranks of first-rate powers. America's enemies—Germany, Japan, and Italy—were defeated. Her friends—Britain and France—spent so much blood and treasure that they found it impossible to regain their prewar military and economic importance. This situation left only two superpowers—the United States and the Soviet Union. The second development was the technological revolution in warfare. With the exploding of the atomic bomb in 1945, and the capability of destroying mankind, diplomacy entered upon a new age. These two considerations led one historian to liken the relations between the United States and Russia to a scorpion and tarantula together in a bottle, each tragically committed to trying to outdo the other.[1]

---

[1]Louis Halle, *The Cold War as History* (New York, 1967), p. xiii.

Most historians, but by no means all, agreed that World War II created the setting for the Soviet-American confrontation. Although ideological differences existed between the two great powers prior to that time, the war produced suspicion, distrust, and a gap in understanding that became increasingly difficult to bridge. The Cold War, most scholars and laymen concluded, arose from two seemingly incompatible conceptions of the ideal shape of the postwar world order. The American point of view pictured the Soviet Union as a ruthless power, driven by its communist ideology, bent upon global revolution and domination, and headed by leaders like Stalin who embarked upon an aggressive policy of expansion with the ultimate aim of destroying the free world. From Russia's perspective, however, America represented the main threat to peace. The Soviet view was that the United States emerged from the war militantly committed to the idea of a capitalist world order. America, as an imperialist power, sought to encircle the Soviet Union with hostile capitalist countries, to isolate Russia from the rest of the world, and to destroy communist regimes wherever they existed. Thus, the free world and communist camp each viewed the other side as being dedicated to its destruction.

American scholars disagreed, however, when they came to evaluate the causes of the Cold War and to pass judgment on the roles of the two adversaries. Since 1945 American historians, when inquiring into the origins of the Cold War, divided into three schools: the orthodox, or traditional school; the revisionists; and the realists. Although the arguments of each school changed somewhat with the passing of time and appearance of new developments, they established the framework of the important historiographical debate that took place.

The first to appear was the orthodox school, which came into being during the immediate postwar years. At that time most of the American people, and the vast majority of scholars, were inclined to accept the official explanation of events set forth by the Truman administration in justifying its foreign policy. According to the orthodox interpretation, Soviet aggression and expansionist desires were primarily responsible for the coming of the Cold War.

The orthodox or traditional interpretation reflected closely the official view of the American and British governments at the time. Winston Churchill, speaking at Fulton, Missouri, in the spring of 1946, set forth the basic outline of this interpretation. An "iron curtain," said Churchill, had been lowered across Eastern Europe by the Soviets. No one knew for sure what secret plans for expansion were being hatched behind the iron curtain. The British leader viewed not only the Soviet Union, but communist ideology, communist parties, and "fifth column" activities as a growing peril to what he called "Christian civilization." President

Truman in 1947 echoed similar sentiments when announcing his now famous Truman Doctrine. Although the United States had made every effort to bring about a peaceful world, he said, the Soviet Union had used "indirect aggression" in Eastern Europe, "extreme pressure" in the Middle East, and had intervened in the internal affairs of many countries through "Communist parties directed from Moscow." Because of the Truman Doctrine, many scholars of the traditionalist school held that the Cold War had officially commenced in 1947.

The orthodox interpretation was presented in scholarly books and journals in the late 1940s and early 1950s by historians like Herbert Feis and policymakers such as George F. Kennan. These men, too, held that the Cold War had been brought about mainly because of Soviet actions. Motivated by the traditional desires for greater security, power, and larger spheres of influence, they said, the Soviet Union resorted to an expansionist foreign policy. Coupled with these age-old drives was the new ideological zeal of communism which made the Soviets ambitious to foment revolution and conquest in behalf of their cause. Scholars sometimes disagreed about the primary motivation of the Soviets; some favored the importance of ideology as an explanation, while others believed the main focus should be placed on Russia's traditional policy of imperialism and pursuit of national interest. But they all tended to agree that no matter what the motivation might be, Soviet objectives were expansionist in scope. The orthodox view also argued that the Soviet Union violated its agreements with the Western powers, including the Yalta accords as they concerned the political future of Eastern Europe and, to a lesser extent, the role of China in the postwar world.

America's foreign policy, according to the orthodox interpretation, was in marked contrast to that of the Soviet Union. The United States, at first, held high hopes for a peaceful postwar world. The actions of its leaders were predicated on the principles of collective security, and they looked to the newborn United Nations for the solution to any future conflicts. Faced with Soviet aggressive moves, however, America was reluctantly forced to change its views and foreign policy. To prevent the Soviet Union from spreading its influence over large parts of the world, the United States finally felt compelled to embark upon a policy of "containment." Without this containment policy, argued many, the Soviet Union would probably have become the master of all Europe— instead of dominating only Eastern Europe.

Many of the arguments of the orthodox position were set forth in an article published by George F. Kennan under the pseudonym, "Mr. X," in 1947. Kennan, an American diplomat, provided many of the insights upon which the foreign policy of the Truman administration was based. In his piece Kennan suggested, among other things, an American con-

tainment policy to check Russia's expansionist tendencies. Kennan subsequently claimed, however, that he was not thinking primarily in terms
of containment along military lines.[2]

The orthodox version, despite challenges, remains the dominant
school of thought on the origins of the Cold War. Many of its proponents, however, differ widely in their interpretations. They all place
differing emphases upon such crucial matters as the role of ideology, the
inevitability of the conflict, the presumed unintentional provocation of
the West, and the like. Although it may seem arbitrary to lump them
together, they may be identified as "orthodox" because they generally
found that responsibility for the Cold War rested to a major degree with
the Soviet Union.[3] Even this categorization remains tenuous, however,
because men like Kennan and Feis have changed their minds and shifted
their views with the passage of time. Moreover, there are significant
differences even among orthodox historians. John Lewis Gaddis, for
example, insisted that neither the Soviet Union nor the United States
was solely responsible for the Cold War. Yet he also noted that major
responsibility rested with Stalin, who had greater opportunity to adjust
to American foreign policy than Truman to Soviet policy.[4]

The roots of the revisionist interpretation, like that of the orthodox
thesis, also originated in the statements from public figures as well as
scholars. From the outset of the Cold War, the official explanation of
events had not gone unchallenged. Henry Wallace, former Vice-
President, had raised a powerful voice which questioned the soundness
of President Truman's analysis of the international situation during the
immediate postwar years. Running as a presidential candidate of a
minority party in 1948, Wallace sought to be more sympathetic towards
the Russians. But his relatively poor showing revealed how little public
support there was for this position.

Walter Lippmann, one of the nation's leading intellectuals and a
scholarly journalist, likewise refused to place the blame for international
tensions exclusively on the Soviet Union. It was Lippmann who
popularized the term "Cold War" by using it in the title of a book he

---

[2][George F. Kennan], "The Sources of Soviet Conduct," *Foreign Affairs* 25 (July 1947):
566–82.

[3]For a few examples of the orthodox interpretation see Herbert Feis's three books, *The
Road to Pearl Harbor* (Princeton, 1950), *The China Tangle* (Princeton, 1953), and *Roosevelt-
Churchill-Stalin* (Princeton, 1957); William H. McNeill, *America, Britain, and Russia: Their
Cooperation and Conflict, 1941–1946* (London, 1953); Norman Graebner, *Cold War Diplomacy:
American Foreign Policy 1945–1960* (Princeton, 1962); and André Fontaine, *History of the Cold
War from the October Revolution to the Korean War, 1917–1950*, 2 vols. (New York, 1968).

[4]John Lewis Gaddis, *The United States and the Origins of the Cold War, 1941–1947* (New
York, 1972). See also George G. Herring, Jr., *Aid to Russia, 1941–1946: Strategy, Diplomacy,
the Origins of the Cold War* (New York, 1973).

published in 1947.[5] In his work he argued that America's statesmen expended their energies assaulting Russia's vital interests in Eastern Europe. By doing so, they had furnished the Soviet Union with the reasons for rationalizing an iron rule behind the iron curtain. They also gave the Russians grounds to suspect what the Soviets had been conditioned to believe: that a capitalist coalition was being organized to destroy them. As a result of Lippmann's writings, in part, revisionist-minded historians began with one underlying assumption contrary to that of the orthodox interpretation: they were skeptical about accepting the claim that the Soviet Union was primarily or solely responsible for precipitating the Cold War.

Over the years, the revisionist approach to the origins of the Cold War gradually came to represent not merely a challenge but an antithetical position to the orthodox thesis. Many revisionists came to the conclusion that the United States and its policies—rather than Russia and communism—had brought about the Cold War. The conflict had been precipitated by Western—and especially American—moves which threatened the Soviets and compelled them to react defensively. This the Russians had done by resorting to strict control over those areas that had fallen under their influence during World War II.

It is difficult to generalize about the revisionists because of the diversity of approaches in this school of scholars. Each historian stressed different aspects of the Cold War, offered different arguments, and professed to see different motives behind the acts of the principal protagonists. Most revisionists, nevertheless, tended to agree that Russia was weak, not strong, after 1945 because of the ravages of war. Beginning with this premise, they then argued that the Soviet Union was neither willing nor able to pursue an aggressive policy after the war ended. Indeed, some revisionists maintained that while the Russians feared America's technological superiority and military power, they still viewed the United States as the main potential source of assistance to enable them to recover from the disastrous effects of the war. Other revisionists stressed that under Stalin the Soviet Union consistently pursued only cautious, defensive, and limited goals of foreign policy, despite the rhetoric of ideological bravado. Thus, the worldwide policy of aggression which the traditionalists believed they had detected in Russia's behavior seemed to the revisionists to be entirely out of character and beyond the means of the Soviet leaders.

During the 1950s and 1960s, many differing shades of revisionism appeared among American historians. Some scholars approached the

---

[5]Walter Lippmann, *The Cold War* (New York, 1947). Lippmann's book was a collection of newspaper articles written to counter Kennan's interpretation of the motivation behind Soviet policy.

problem by attempting to evaluate the degree to which the United States had been responsible for precipitating the Cold War. In tackling this issue, these writers sought to explain and justify Soviet actions since the war. Others analyzed American objectives in such a way as to show that these goals had been the basis for the postwar split. Some radical revisionists, especially those associated with the New Left, went even further: they viewed the United States as having been an aggressive power in the world not only during the Second World War, but throughout the entire twentieth century.

When revisionist-minded historians came to the matter of America's motivation, they were likewise in disagreement and offered different explanations. Some claimed that the Western powers in general, and the Truman administration in particular, tried to deny the Soviet Union its due in the matter of the Yalta agreements: the West, they said, had sought to reinterpret the meaning of these accords, and refused to recognize what Roosevelt and Churchill had been compelled by circumstances to concede at Yalta. Other historians argued that America—imbued with the missionary zeal of a latent "manifest destiny"—had hoped to reshape the world to suit its exaggerated attachment to the democratic principles of representative government. Still other scholars stressed the theme of economic expansion—postulating that America's postwar foreign policy represented a drive to capture world markets and to establish this country's economic and political influence all over the globe. Certain historians concluded that the United States used its early monopoly of nuclear weapons and economic strength to browbeat other nation-states and to force them to submit to Washington's leadership. As proof of this position, they pointed out that the Truman administration had refused major economic assistance to the Soviet Union, and that the Marshall Plan had been designed in such a way as to preclude Soviet participation in it.

Despite the complexities within the revisionist school, it is possible to distinguish two main groups in this category—the moderate revisionists and those associated with the New Left, who were more extreme. Although the revisionist scholars disagreed about the degree of responsibility they assigned to the United States in bringing on the Cold War, they all held America, in large part, accountable for the conflict because of her aggressive and menacing policy towards Russia.

One example of the moderate revisionist position was Denna F. Fleming's two-volume study, *The Cold War and its Origins, 1917–1960*, published in 1961. Fleming focused upon President Truman as the crucial figure in the coming of the Cold War. Within weeks after Roosevelt died, Fleming wrote, Truman dramatically reversed the course of America's foreign policy. Roosevelt had been dedicated to a Wilsonian "internationalism," and, recognizing that the Soviet Union would be the key to any new league of nations in the postwar period, had done his utmost to maintain good relations with Russia. But Truman adopted a tough policy toward the Russians as soon as he assumed the presidency. In April 1945, he ordered the Soviets to change their policy in Poland or else America would withdraw certain promised economic aid. Contrary to the orthodox version, which generally dated the beginning of the Cold War in 1947 with the Truman Doctrine, Fleming believed it began in 1945.

Fleming's thesis that America provoked the Cold War was amplified by the picture he presented of the postwar era. The United States was invariably portrayed as taking the initiative in relations between the two powers. Russia, on the other hand, was usually depicted as reacting to events in a defensive way. Fleming's interpretation differed greatly from the orthodox version which had pictured the Soviets as the ruthless aggressor, but his findings were suspect because they were not based on solid documentation.[6]

Writing in the same revisionist tradition was Gar Alperovitz. His book *Atomic Diplomacy: Hiroshima and Potsdam,* published in the mid-1960s, held that President Truman had helped to start the Cold War in 1945 by dropping the atomic bomb. Alperovitz added a new viewpoint to the debate by arguing that Truman resorted to "atomic diplomacy." With the United States possessing a monopoly of atomic weapons at the time, Truman adopted a hard line toward the Soviets—one which was aimed at forcing Soviet Russia's acquiescence in America's postwar plans. In short, Truman fell back upon the modern equivalent of saber-rattling to play power politics and drive Russia out of East Europe by a show of force.

Like most of the moderate revisionists, however, Alperovitz did not heap all the blame for beginning the Cold War on the United States. The Russians by their actions also helped to poison the postwar atmosphere, he said. "The cold war cannot be understood simply as an American response to a Soviet challenge," he wrote, "but rather as an insidious interaction of mutual suspicions, blame for which must be shared by all." Nevertheless, the thrust of Alperovitz's work clearly placed responsibility for the beginnings of the Cold War on American shoulders.[7]

Most New Left historians were bitter in their condemnation of the orthodox interpretation. In large part this was so because of their own ideological commitments; they were highly critical about the very nature of American society as a whole, and hence unsympathetic with the aims of the United States abroad. Moreover, where the more moderate revisionists tended to picture Roosevelt or Truman as men of limited vision who fumbled their way to disaster in the postwar period, some

[6]Denna F. Fleming, *The Cold War and Its Origins, 1917–1960,* 2 vols. (New York, 1961).

[7]Gar Alperovitz, *Atomic Diplomacy: Hiroshima and Potsdam* (New York, 1965).

New Left scholars were inclined to view developments against a much broader background. They wrote within a context that stretched far beyond the immediate postwar years: such New Left scholars held that America's foreign policy in the 1940s, 1950s, and 1960s was simply an extension of a trend that had been under way since the Spanish-American War at the turn of the century.

The most significant assault on the orthodox position came from William Appleman Williams in his books, *The Tragedy of American Diplomacy* and *The Contours of American History,* published in the late 1950s and 1960s. Although Williams never regarded himself as a member of the New Left, his writings were seized upon and extended by other radical historians. What Williams did was to provide a provocative hypothesis to explain America's diplomacy throughout our entire history. America's foreign policy was expansionist from our very beginnings, he declared. Writing from a neo-Beardian point of view, Williams went all the way back to the 1760s. He showed that even before gaining its independence, America had adopted a course to achieve economic self-sufficiency within the British empire by applying English mercantilist principles in the New World environment. Once independence had been won, the United States was committed to the idea of an independent American empire to enable the growing new nation to have markets for its products. Until the 1890s that empire lay mostly to the west on the American continent, but once the frontier was gone the search for markets led to overseas expansion. Despite the controversy between imperialists and anti-imperialists around the turn of the century, both groups agreed that economic expansion overseas was vital to the nation's prosperity and future. The debate was over means rather than ends. Imperialists felt that physical acquisition of traditional colonies was necessary; anti-imperialists, on the other hand, believed that America's economic expansion throughout the world could be achieved without the expense of maintaining a colonial empire.

The Open Door policy, according to Williams, resolved the dilemma, and ultimately became the basis for America's future foreign policy. America's Open Door policy represented an effort to achieve all the advantages of economic expansion without the disadvantages of maintaining a colonial empire. It called for an open door for trade with all foreign countries on a most-favored-nation principle—a principle that had a long tradition in American diplomacy stretching back to 1776. Although formulated originally to apply to China, the policy was expanded geographically to cover the entire globe and economically to include American investments as well as trade.[8]

---

[8]William A. Williams, *The Tragedy of American Diplomacy* (2d ed.: New York, 1962) and *The Contours of American History* (Cleveland, 1961).

Williams, operating from this premise, saw the Cold War within a different context than the orthodox school of historians. To him the postwar period represented nothing more than the extension of the Open Door policy as America, seeking markets for its goods and money, hoped to penetrate into Eastern Europe and other parts of the globe. Thus America was primarily responsible for the Cold War, for in seeking to extend its economic influence she took whatever steps were necessary to maintain or put into power governments that would do business with the United States. Counterrevolution to make the world safe for American capitalism, not containment, was the major motive behind the postwar policies of the United States.[9]

One of Williams's followers—Walter LaFeber (who in 1963 had published an important study of the origins of American expansionism in the late nineteenth century)—developed and expanded this view in a monograph that appeared in 1967. LaFeber was critical of both the United States and the Soviet Union for failing to maintain peace. Focusing upon the internal reasons behind the formulation of foreign policy in the two countries, he concluded that domestic developments played a large part in determining those foreign policies that finally emerged. In America, domestic events—presidential campaigns, economic recessions, the era of repression identified with Senator Joseph McCarthy of Wisconsin, and the struggle for power by various factions within the government—contributed as much to the making of America's foreign policy as did external events. Within Russia itself, the same was true: the machinations of Stalin and Khrushchev, problems with the Soviet economy, and power struggles within the Communist party laid the basis for most foreign policy changes. In terms of economic penetration, LaFeber found that the United States and the Soviet Union showed equal interest in exploiting foreign markets wherever possible. Both nations, he concluded, created their postwar policies with an eye to maintaining freedom of action in those areas they considered vital to their economic and strategic interests.

Conflicting aims arising from domestic concerns, LaFeber said, led to a continuing rivalry between the two giant powers as they confronted one another over two decades in many parts of the globe. America's foreign policy was based on the assumption that the nation's political, economic, and psychological needs at home dictated those commitments undertaken abroad. During the first phase of the struggle—1945 to 1953—those commitments were Europe-oriented, and even the Korean War was fought, in part, to preserve America's image as the main bulwark in the West against the Communist monolith. But after the

---

[9]Christopher Lasch, "The Cold War, Revisited and Re-Visioned," *New York Times*, Jan. 14, 1968.

mid-1950s, both America and Russia shifted their focus from Europe to the newly emerging nations all over the world, and the Cold War entered its second phase. The Vietnam War, according to LaFeber, represented a "failure" in America's foreign policy because it sought to answer the political and economic global changes posed by the newly emerging nations with military solutions. There was continuity in America's policy, concluded LaFeber, because the American people had decided to accept the responsibility of answering challenges of such a global nature as far back as 1947 with the Truman Doctrine. In a similar vein Lloyd C. Gardner, a student of Williams at the University of Wisconsin, emphasized the commitment of American leaders to a liberal world order based on the Open Door policy. Haunted by fears of depression, these leaders strove to create a world economy conducive to American capitalism and prosperity. "Responsibility for the *way* in which the Cold War developed, at least," Gardner concluded, "belongs more to the United States."[10]

Gardner's work in particular influenced a number of revisionist and New Left scholars. Athan Theoharis, for example, accepted Gardner's contention that the United States was largely responsible for the way in which the Cold War developed. Theoharis insisted that a wide variety of options were available to American policy makers in 1945; nothing compelled the adoption of policies that led to the Cold War. During the Second World War, for example, Roosevelt followed a diplomatic policy that was strikingly vacillating and ambivalent. At Yalta, on the other hand, Roosevelt pursued a conciliatory path based upon the acceptance of Soviet postwar influence and the need to arrive at an accommodation that would avert disharmony and conflict. His death, however, altered the diplomatic setting by introducing an element of uncertainty. More importantly, it brought Harry S. Truman to the White House, an individual who was more rigidly anti-Soviet. Truman's accession to the presidency, according to Theoharis, provided the opening wedge for policy advisers whose recommendations were ignored at Yalta. The result was that the opportunities for détente provided at Yalta were effectively subverted under Truman, and the stage was set for years of conflict and confrontation. The first selection in this chapter is an excerpt from an article on the origins of the Cold War by Theoharis.

While neither Williams, LaFeber, nor Gardner necessarily included themselves as members of the New Left, it was clear that their respective studies could easily serve as a point of departure for radical scholars. In

---

[10]Walter LaFeber, *America, Russia, and the Cold War, 1945–1966* (New York, 1967), and Lloyd C. Gardner, *Architects of Illusion: Men and Ideas in American Foreign Policy, 1941–1949* (Chicago, 1970). See also Thomas G. Paterson, *Soviet-American Confrontation: Postwar Reconstruction and the Origins of the Cold War* (Baltimore, 1973).

1968 Gabriel Kolko, whose earlier study of the origins of political capitalism from 1900 to 1917 had heralded the advent of the New Left school of historiography, brought out a detailed study of the origins of the Cold War that picked up where Williams and LaFeber had left off. Kolko dealt with America's foreign policy within a much narrower chronological framework; he covered only the years from 1943 to 1945. But Kolko felt that the policies forged in that crucial period were the key to the long-range plans of the United States in the postwar era. His work, *The Politics of War,* represented an attempt to document in detail and to extend the general themes introduced by Williams. Kolko advanced the thesis that the United States had acted not only to win the war in these two years, but to erect the structure for peacetime politics in the postwar world. To Kolko America's objectives were twofold: to use its military power to defeat the enemy; and to employ its political and economic power to gain leverage for extending America's influence throughout the world. Thus, Kolko, like Williams, viewed the United States as a counterrevolutionary force bent on restoring the old order in Europe and making the world safe for American capitalism.[11]

Kolko's assumptions regarding America's postwar policies were typical of many of the New Left scholars. He assumed, first of all, that the United States, not Russia, represented the greatest threat to international stability; that America was mainly responsible for bringing on the Cold War. Second, that the United States was dedicated to worldwide counterrevolution: to a policy of employing her military and economic power to extend her influence throughout the world because American capitalism was dependent upon ever-expanding foreign markets for survival. And third, that the origins of the Cold War lay not solely within World War II but stretched back to World War I and beyond.

Significantly, the revisionist view of Cold War diplomacy—both moderate and extremist—developed mainly in the 1960s. This decade was a period of deepening disillusionment among American intellectuals over the nation's foreign policy. Disenchanted by America's intervention in Cuba and Santo Domingo and the escalating involvement in Vietnam, many intellectuals had begun to question whether the United States had not taken too seriously the responsibilities of world leadership; it had involved itself unnecessarily in the internal affairs of other nations where it had no business. Moreover, they feared that this country was so conditioned to fighting totalitarianism that American leaders tended to see enemies where none existed. It is not too much to

---

[11]Gabriel Kolko, *The Politics of War: The World and United States Foreign Policy, 1943–1945* (New York, 1968). See also Joyce Kolko and Gabriel Kolko, *The Limits of Power: The World and United States Foreign Policy, 1945–1954* (New York, 1972).

suggest that this reaction among intellectuals helped to shape the unsympathetic view that the revisionists had taken toward America's foreign policy.

To some scholars neither the orthodox nor the revisionist explanations were adequate. Joseph R. Starobin—a former Communist who
broke with the American Communist party in the 1950s—insisted that
historians had ignored a key element in the origins of the Cold War,
namely, the contradictions within the communist movement itself. During and after the Second World War, the Soviet Union attempted to
overcome the diversity within a system of states and parties in which
earlier political and ideological premises had become obsolete. For Stalin, therefore, the Cold War was a struggle involving Russia's internal
objectives and the subordination of an international movement. Viewed
in this light, the struggle between the Soviet Union and the United
States was brought about by an internal crisis within the former. Starobin's article is presented as the second selection in this chapter.

If the orthodox and revisionist interpretations represented antithetical views about the origins of the Cold War, the realist school has become, in some ways, a middle-of-the-road position. The realists, unlike
the revisionists who followed them, were less likely to dismiss containment because it represented in their eyes a necessary response to Soviet
expansionism. On the other hand, they were critical of the orthodox
scholars because of the excessive moralism and legalism in the traditional interpretation. The realists were more prone to view foreign
relations in terms of *realpolitik* from which the school derived its name,
and to place more emphasis upon power politics and conflicting national
interests. Historians of the realist school were less concerned with determining the degree of moral responsibility for the Cold War and focused
their attention instead on the pragmatic political problems facing the
policymakers.

Like the other two schools of scholars, the realists could trace their
origins back to the late 1940s and early 1950s. Their writings began as a
response, in part, to the strong criticisms of Roosevelt's role in the developing East-West impasse. These criticisms held that America's supposed weakness in the postwar period had resulted either from
Roosevelt's misunderstanding of Soviet intentions or from his failure to
foresee the incompatibility of Soviet and American goals. In the eyes of
his critics, Roosevelt was responsible for the subsequent subjugation of
Eastern Europe. But the realists argued that Roosevelt, in fact, was faced
with a *fait accompli* in Eastern Europe with powerful Russian armies
occupying that area, and that the diplomatic options open to him were
severely limited as a result.

Generally speaking, the realists held that the blame for the Cold War belonged either to both sides or, more accurately, to neither. Indeed, neither the United States nor the Soviet Union had wanted to precipitate a conflict. Both had hoped that cooperation among the allies would continue—but on their own terms, of course. Each country had sought limited objectives but had expected the other to accept them as such. To be specific, the Soviet Union was motivated by fear and acted in the interests of its security rather than out of any expansionist ambitions. However, whenever one side made a move in pursuit of its limited objectives, the other side perceived the act as a threat to its existence and, in reacting accordingly, triggered a countermeasure which led to increasing escalation. As a result, small and otherwise manageable foreign crises had led inevitably to a widening conflict, which gradually assumed global proportions. In short, the realists found that both sides in pursuing their interests had sought limited goals, but the spiraling effect of such measures had inadvertently precipitated the Cold War.

The realist school tended also to view the Cold War as a traditional power conflict rather than a clash of ideologies. To many of these historians the Cold War was comparable to some of the previous struggles that had taken place to prevent a single power from dominating Europe's east-central regions. Other scholars saw the conflict within the context of the age-old battle over the European balance of power.

When viewing the situation in postwar Europe, members of the realist school took a hard look at political realities rather than indulging in speculations about diplomatic possibilities. While stressing Soviet determination to create in Eastern Europe satellite states that would enhance Russia's security, the realists also emphasized how vulnerable the countries in that part of Europe were to outside pressures because their own social, political, and economic systems had proven incapable of solving the problems of their people. These societies were ripe for revolution, the realists concluded, and an easy prey to the indigenous communist movements that existed and were Moscow-directed. The countries of Western Europe, they argued, were not susceptible to the same pressures; their social, economic, and political institutions, though weakened by the war, were still viable. Hence the realists concluded that the fear expressed in the orthodox interpretation—that Soviet influence might extend across Europe to reach the English Channel—was not only exaggerated but revealed a misunderstanding of the nature of the conflict.

The realists usually disagreed with the moderate revisionists who, like Alperovitz, claimed that the United States had used its monopoly of atomic weapons to force other nation-states into submission. On the other hand, they accepted the thesis that in employing nuclear weapons against Japan the American government was motivated not only by a desire to conclude the Pacific war, but by the hope of doing so before the Soviet Union could enter that theater of war. America, they wrote, feared that Moscow might attempt to do in the Far East what it appeared to be doing in Eastern Europe. Thus, the presence of nuclear weapons in American hands was believed by the realists to have had a psychological effect upon both the atomic "haves" and "have-nots" during the initial phases of the Cold War.

The realists likewise disagreed with those revisionists associated with the New Left. They challenged the assumptions, ideological considerations, and political misconceptions upon which they felt the New Left historians based their arguments. In his review of Kolko's *The Politics of War*, Hans J. Morgenthau (one of the leading realist scholars) charged that Kolko was reflecting the mood of his own generation in attributing blame for the origins of the Cold War. That mood, Morgenthau noted,

> ... reacts negatively to the simple and simplistic equation, obligatory during the war and postwar periods, of American interests and policies with democratic virtue and wisdom, and those of their enemies with totalitarian folly and vice. As the orthodox historiography of the Second World War and the Cold War expressed and justified that ideological juxtaposition, so the revisionism of Professor Kolko expresses and justifies the new mood of ideological sobriety. However, given the moralism behind American political thinking regardless of its content, revisionism tends to be as moralistic in its critique of American foreign policy as orthodoxy is in defending it. While the moralistic approach remains, the moral labels have been reversed: what once was right is now wrong, and vice versa. Yet as historic truth may emerge from the dialectic of opposite extremes, qualified and tempered by charity and understanding, so sound political judgment requires both the recognition of extreme positions as inevitable and of their possible transcendence through a morality which is as alien to the moralism of our political folklore as Thucydidean justice is to the compensatory justice of opposing historical schools.[12]

Morgenthau's own writings represented one of the best examples of the realist point of view. In them he was critical of what he called the legalistic-moralistic tradition which presumably prevented American statesmen from perceiving foreign policy in terms of national power and national interest in the past. His book *In Defense of the National Interest: A Critical Examination of American Foreign Policy*, published in 1951, claimed that America's foreign policies since 1776 had been much too utopian in outlook. Only in the years since World War II, he suggested, had Americans become more realistic and formulated their policy on the basis of

---

[12]Hans J. Morgenthau, "Historical Justice and the Cold War," *New York Review of Books*, July 10, 1969.

power politics and national interest.[13] Nevertheless, American policymakers had misunderstood Soviet foreign policy; they failed to see the essential continuity in the expansionist objectives sought by the czars and later by the Communists and focused instead on the new goals supposedly arising out of a revolutionary ideology. Thus, Morgenthau criticized the orthodox interpretation by suggesting that the United States had contributed to the coming of the Cold War by its long-standing tendency to view its relationship to the rest of the world in rather unrealistic terms.

Another member of the realist school, Louis Halle, took a somewhat different approach. In his book, *The Cold War as History,* published in the mid-1960s, Halle was more interested in stressing the tragic nature of the conflict. He suggested that neither side was really to blame for the Cold War. Misconceptions on both sides had led to the rise of ideological myths—myths which often had little relation to existing social realities. The West, led by the United States, was governed by the myth of a monolithic conspiracy among Communists the world over to drive for global domination, initially under the leadership of the Soviet Union. The Communists, on their part—Lenin and his associates in 1917–1918 and Mao Tse-tung a generation later in 1949–1950—were under the spell of another myth. Their world view pictured a globe divided between capitalist-imperialists, on the one hand, and exploited peasants and proletariat on the other. Each of these two Communist leaders in his own time had believed that the historical moment had come when the oppressed lower classes were about to rise up in revolution, to overthrow their upper-class masters, and to establish a utopian society of the brotherhood of man along lines predicted by Karl Marx. It was the belief in such myths which drove the free world and the Communist camp to embark upon what each side considered to be a struggle for survival.

Historical interpretations, of course, often run in cycles. Just as the revisionists challenged their more orthodox predecessors, so too did they come under scrutiny as the disillusionment of the 1960s and early 1970s gave way to new moods. Their implicit acceptance of American hegemony, moreover, seemed less tenable after the Arab-Israeli war of 1973, when an oil embargo and a subsequent quadrupling of oil prices demonstrated the vulnerability of the United States as well as its inability to use power without restraint. Some of the attacks on the revisionists were frontal in nature. In an analysis of the works of seven

---

[13]Hans J. Morgenthau, *In Defense of the National Interest: A Critical Examination of American Foreign Policy* (New York, 1951). In this same regard, it should be noted that George Kennan has come much closer to the realist school by arguing in his memoirs that the Truman administration pursued the wrong priorities in Europe by concentrating on a policy of *military* containment. George F. Kennan, *Memoirs, 1925–1950* (Boston, 1967).

leading revisionist historians, Robert J. Maddox accused them of distorting facts to prove their thesis. "Stated briefly," he noted in his introduction, "the most striking characteristic of revisionist historiography has been the extent to which New Left authors have revised the evidence itself. And if the component parts of historical interpretations are demonstrably false, what can be said about the interpretations? They may yet be valid, but in the works examined they are often irrelevant to the data used to support them. Until this fact is recognized, there can be no realistic assessment of which elements of revisionism can justifiably be incorporated into new syntheses and which must be disregarded altogether." Similarly, Robert W. Tucker insisted that New Left revisionism was based on a simple-minded explanatory mechanism that related all policy decisions to the imperatives of a capitalist economy. Charles S. Maier, on the other hand, was critical of virtually all scholars who had written on the origins of the Cold War. "Spokesmen for each side," he noted in 1970, "present the reader with a total explanatory system that accounts for all phenomena, eliminates the possibility of disproof, and thus transcends the usual process of historical reasoning. More than in most historical controversies, the questions about what happened are transformed into concealed debate about the nature of freedom and duress, exploitation and hegemony. As a result much Cold War historiography has become a confrontation *manqué*—debatable philosophy taught by dismaying example."[14]

More recently there has been a tendency for historians to avoid extremes. In a study of the decision to use the atomic bomb, Martin Sherwin explicitly rejected Gar Alperovitz's contention that the use of the bomb was largely directed at influencing Soviet postwar policy. Sherwin insisted that the decision to use the bomb was laid earlier during Franklin Delano Roosevelt's presidency. Although he conceded that the development of the bomb was predicated on the belief that it would be a diplomatic asset in the postwar era, Sherwin nevertheless insisted that Truman used the bomb to win the war against Japan and not to stop the Soviet Union from entering the war in the Far East. On the other hand, Truman hoped that Stalin would recognize American power and adopt a more conciliatory policy.[15]

Even scholars with a revisionist orientation have muted their explanations of the origins of the Cold War. In 1977 Daniel Yergin observed that wartime and postwar American diplomacy reflected two competing

---

[14]Robert J. Maddox, *The New Left and the Origins of the Cold War* (Princeton, 1973), pp. 10–11; Robert W. Tucker, *The Radical Left and American Foreign Policy* (Baltimore, 1971); Charles A. Maier, "Revisionism and the Interpretation of Cold War Origins," *Perspectives in American History* 4 (1970): 311–47.

[15]Martin J. Sherwin, *A World Destroyed: The Atomic Bomb and the Grand Alliance* (New York, 1975).

perceptions of the Soviet Union. The first—which he named the Riga axioms—was based on an image of the Soviet Union "as a world revolutionary state, denying the possibilities of coexistence, committed to unrelenting ideological warfare, powered by a messianic drive for world mastery." The second—the Yalta axioms—downplayed ideology and instead saw the Soviet Union as "behaving like a traditional Great Power within the international system, rather than trying to overthrow it." The first remained the dominant element in American foreign policy until the Nazi invasion of Russia in 1941, when Roosevelt decided to aid the beleaguered Soviets. During the war the Yalta axioms replaced the Riga axioms. At the end of the conflict the latter regained its predominance, and it was within this framework that Truman formulated his hard-line policy toward the Soviet Union. Although conceding the brutality of Stalin's regime, Yergin nevertheless insisted that the "USSR behaved as a traditional Great Power, intent upon aggrandizing itself along the lines of historic Russian goals," and that American leaders who accepted the Riga axioms "misinterpreted both the range and degree of the Soviet challenge and the character of Soviet objectives and so downplayed the possibilities for diplomacy and accommodation."[16]

In reviewing the three schools of thought—the orthodox, revisionist, and realist—students should decide for themselves the fundamental questions raised regarding America's role in world affairs since the 1940s.[17] Did the Cold War commence with the Second World War, or did it stretch back in time? Did the move of the Soviet Union into Eastern Europe represent the realization of a centuries-old Russian dream of a sphere of influence in that region? Or was it an effort by the Kremlin to extend the influence of communism in the immediate postwar period? Had the course of American diplomacy since the Spanish-American War been committed to the defense of a global status quo in an attempt to find the ever-expanding foreign markets supposedly necessary for the survival of American capitalism? Or could the roots of the Cold War crisis be traced back to the mid-1940s, when Russian military forces occupied Eastern Europe? Were America's moves dictated by a containment policy aimed at checking what was believed to be a Soviet plan for spreading communism throughout the world? Or was the United States bent upon a conservative counterrevolution that would maintain the world economic and political order in a state conducive to the purposes of American capitalism? In answering such questions, students will cope not only with the issue of the Cold War but with the very nature of American society itself.

---

[16]Daniel Yergin, *Shattered Peace: The Origins of the Cold War and the National Security State* (Boston, 1977), pp. 11–12.

[17]See the fascinating debate in Lloyd C. Gardner, Arthur Schlesinger, Jr., and Hans J. Morgenthau, *The Origins of the Cold War* (Waltham, 1970).

Athan Theoharis

ATHAN THEOHARIS (1936–   ) is professor of history at Marquette University. He has written a number of articles and books on American history since 1945, including *The Yalta Myths: An Issue in U.S. Politics, 1945–1955* (1970), and *Seeds of Repression: Harry S. Truman and the Origins of McCarthyism* (1971).

Only recently has the question of the origins of the cold war seriously divided American historians, the emergence of a revisionist school coinciding with intensive research into primary sources. Yet, revisionists do disagree over whether there existed a discontinuity between President Roosevelt's and President Truman's policies; they disagree in their evaluations of the relative influence of economic and political considerations in their estimates of the role of key advisers in shaping the decisions and priorities of the two presidents.

This paper will emphasize the tactics and personalities of Roosevelt and Truman, their specific responses to Soviet policy and influence. Focusing on Yalta, I shall examine the Truman administration's commitment to the agreements concluded at the conference and Roosevelt's and the State Department's responsibilities for the development of the cold war. Conceding that the trend of the Open Door ideology was inimical to accommodation with the Soviet Union, I, nonetheless, contend that the discretion available to policymakers did not demand the specific policies adopted after April 1945 that led to the Cold War. Put simply, the thesis of this paper is, to quote Lloyd C. Gardner, that "the United States was more responsible for the *way* in which the Cold War developed."

At issue for American diplomats during the 1940s was how to deal with the progress and consequences of World War II. Given the Soviet Union's strategic political and geographic position and its inevitable physical presence in non-Soviet territories after the war, the development of U.S. policy toward Eastern Europe, Germany, and the Far East would influence the climate of Soviet-American relations. Indeed, the diplomacy of the Roosevelt and Truman administrations in the 1941–1946 period was the product, in part, of their conceptions of the Soviet

Athan Theoharis, "Roosevelt and Truman on Yalta: The Origins of the Cold War." Reprinted with permission from the *Political Science Quarterly* 87 (June 1972): 210–41. Footnotes omitted.

involvement in the Far Eastern war and its consequences for postwar China and Japan; and of the status of postwar Germany as determined by decisions concerning the level of German reparations payments.

The dominant role of the post–New Deal presidency in the formulation of foreign policy, the consistency of Truman's policies with those of Roosevelt, and the extent to which either president determined policy or followed recommendations of ostensibly subordinate advisers, furthermore, had crucial significance for U.S.-Soviet relations. During the war, and in the postwar years, U.S. policy was made by the president or his advisers, and not simply at the major summit conferences. At best, the role of the public or of Congress had become that of a potential restraint; policymakers did operate on the premise that Congress or the public might seek to counteract policy decisions. Yet, these were possible deterrents; they did not control policy. As one result of the Executive Reorganization Act of 1939, the president had acquired a bureaucratic apparatus that increased his independence and authority. The post–New Deal president, by resorting to public relations and *fait accompli*, had, as a result, greater freedom to create public opinion and structure the policy debate.

Soviet responses, moreover, were based on an appraisal of the policies of the president, and not on the differing priorities of advisers, the Congress, the public, or the press. While, admittedly, the president, especially Roosevelt, might invoke public, congressional, or press opinion during negotiations with Soviet leaders, this bargaining ploy did not lead Stalin or other leaders in the Kremlin to view U.S. policy as determined by domestic considerations. Concessions might be made in the wording of communiques to make an agreement more palatable to the American public or press, but Soviet policymakers operated on the assumption that they were dealing with the president and that his policy was based upon understood commitments. For this reason, the nature of presidential leadership influenced immediate postwar relations between the United States and the Soviet Union. Most significantly, the Truman administration's attempts to "undo" the Yalta commitments led to the Cold War.

What was involved was not only the enigmatic and ambiguous nature of Roosevelt's policies, substantial as these ambiguities were, but the noncommitment of key personnel in the State Department to the "soft" line that Roosevelt had adopted at Yalta. . . . The rigidity of their position, in contrast to Roosevelt's at Yalta, contained the seeds of possible conflict with the Soviet Union after Truman's accession to the presidency. Truman's limited understanding, of both international affairs and Roosevelt's specific commitments, would enable policy advisers to become policymakers after April 1945 when determining the meaning of the Yalta agreements. . . .

I

During the war years, Roosevelt's policies toward the potential problems concerning the postwar status of Eastern Europe, Germany, and
the Far East were strikingly vacillating and ambivalent. The President,
like his conservative Secretary of State, Cordell Hull, sought to postpone
difficult political decisions until after the war. For a time, he refused
even to enter serious discussions with the Soviet Union over territorial
and other political matters. Roosevelt's stance on German reparations
particularly dramatizes this ambiguity of policy and preference for postponement. Thus, although Hull had agreed both to the principle of
reparations in kind and not in money at the Moscow foreign ministers
conference of October 1943 and to the establishment of an European
Advisory Commission to outline Allied policy toward postwar Germany, no efforts were made to determine the level or basis of reparations payments and to develop plans for postwar occupation. In October
1944, indeed, Roosevelt halted any planning for postwar Germany. Significantly, while the debate between Treasury and State was raging over
the level of German reparations, Roosevelt wrote to Hull that "I do not
think that at this present stage any good purpose would be served by
having the State Department or any other Department sound out the
British and Russian views on the treatment of German industry. . . ."

Throughout 1943 and 1944, Roosevelt sustained this noncommital
course, thus strengthening the resistance of the London Poles to serious
negotiations and thereby contributing to the deterioration of Soviet-
Polish relations. Following the Soviet incursion into Polish territory in
January 1944, Roosevelt offered his good offices to Mikolajczyk, the
prime minister of the London Polish government, to mediate but not
guarantee a solution of the Polish border difficulty. Roosevelt abandoned this stance of studied ambiguity only on November 17, 1944, and
then after Soviet troops had crossed the Curzon Line (July 22) and after
Moscow Radio had announced the formation of a Polish Committee on
National Liberation (July 22) and the subsequent signing of a military
and political agreement between this committee and the Soviet Union.
At that time and with the American presidential election over, Roosevelt
informed Mikolajczyk that whatever agreement the Poles and the Soviet
Union concluded would be acceptable to the United States but that the
United States could not guarantee Poland's frontiers.

U.S. policy had not been simply the product of domestic politics; key
policy advisers had continually counseled a firm stand against the
Soviets and the need to sustain the London Poles. Indeed, within State,
John Hickerson, deputy director of the office of European affairs, recommended, on January 8, 1945, that the United States secure the establishment of a Provisional Security Council, in which the United States

would have a major voice, to supervise political developments in Eastern Europe. And, on January 18, 1945, Secretary of State Stettinius made the same recommendation to Roosevelt. Significantly, Stettinius's proposal provided not only for a rotating chairmanship, thereby implying the equality of the powers, but also for establishing the headquarters in Paris. . . .

Throughout, Roosevelt attempted to secure Soviet military involvement in the war against Japan. He continued to operate on the premise that U.S. policy—to make China a great power—was correct and attainable. A Sino-Soviet accord, he believed, would minimize Soviet intervention in China and force the Chinese Communists to come to terms with Chiang Kai-shek. At the same time, Roosevelt never consistently backed General Stilwell's efforts to reform the Chinese Nationalist regime or to alter its military policy. A sense of wishfulness characterized Roosevelt's estimates of the internal strength of the Nationalist regime, of the prospects for resolving the civil conflict between the Nationalists and Communists without civil war, and of the simply military consequences of Soviet involvement in the war against Japan.

II

Roosevelt's decision to go to Yalta constituted, in essence, a change from wishful thinking and postponement. By early 1945, military developments, and prospective military and political developments, ensured that the Soviets would play a dominant role in Eastern Europe, that Soviet unilateral actions in Germany would complicate Allied occupation policy, and that the Soviet role in the Far East possibly could frustrate the attainment of U.S. objectives. To postpone matters to a postwar peace conference might contribute to the establishment of spheres of influence, to the breakdown of Allied unity and cooperation, and to the radicalization of politics throughout Europe and the Far East.

Roosevelt's diplomacy at Yalta, therefore, reflected not so much over confidence in his ability to placate Stalin through personal diplomacy, though this was a factor, as his recognition of the weakness of the U.S. diplomatic position and the reality—even legitimacy—of Soviet influence in Eastern Europe, the Far East, and Germany. Although the language is vague, the Yalta agreements did confirm this acceptance of Soviet postwar influence and the importance of accommodation to avert disharmony and conflict.

The most troublesome issue confronting the conferees was Poland. Roosevelt's phrasing of his requests at Yalta clearly conceded the weakness of the Western bargaining position. He emphasized his need to "save face" when pressing for slight territorial concessions to the Poles from the Curzon Line, emphasized the domestic importance of the Polish-American vote when urging Stalin to make other concessions over the status of the Polish government, and requested "some gesture" to satisfy the demand of the six million Polish-Americans that the United States be "in some way involved with the question of freedom of elections." By basing his requests on American domestic political considerations, Roosevelt undermined his effect on the decisions of the conference. The final communiqué could simply be worded to gloss over what in fact had been conceded. In many respects, this was the result of the negotiations on Poland: Stalin merely agreed to a formula for the formation of a Polish provisional government and the holding of free and democratic elections under tripartite supervision that would not contradict Soviet objectives yet would enable Roosevelt and Churchill to appease the public opinion that they had so regularly cited during conference proceedings.

Moreover, Roosevelt's February 6 demand that a new Polish government be established, maintaining that the Lublin government "as now composed" could not be accepted (a statement which Churchill immediately endorsed), was not pressed at the conference. The reference to Lublin "as *now* composed" and the further assurance to Stalin that the United States would never support in any way any Polish government "that would be inimical to your interests," significantly reduced the impact of this demand. Stalin replied that Poland did not involve merely honor or domestic public opinion, but the security of the Soviet Union. Second, indirectly recalling the example of the Italian surrender, Stalin also emphasized the importance for the Red Army of secure supply lines in its advance into Germany that only a stable, nonhostile local administration could provide.

The result, incorporated in the Declaration on Liberated Europe and the agreement dealing with Poland, amounted to face-saving formulas for the West. The Lublin government was not to be scrapped for a wholly new government, but rather enlarged to provide the basis for the new government. Stettinius's proposal for reorganizing the Lublin government—"fully representative Government based on all democratic forces in Poland and abroad"—was amended by Molotov to "wider democratic basis with the inclusion of democratic leaders from Poland and abroad." And, the language of the amended Declaration on Liberated Europe, by providing for unanimity even before consultations could begin, acknowledged Soviet authority and her right to veto her allies' objections. Further, the initial State Department proposal for "appropriate machinery for the carrying out of the joint responsibilities set forth in this declaration" was also amended by Molotov to provide instead that the three governments "will immediately take measures for the carrying out of mutual consultations." Nor was observation of the proposed future elections by the three governments guaranteed, since, "in effect," ambassadors alone would observe and report on elections.

The Eastern European agreements, one-sided and a tacit repudiation of earlier U.S. policy, indirectly served to create the potential for subsequent U.S.-Soviet problems. The vagueness of the language, the seeming lack (at least as existing published papers of the proceedings reveal) of intensive discussion over significant changes that amounted to U.S. acceptance of the Soviet position, as well as the exclusion of State from a central negotiating role and the implicit rejection of its policy recommendations at Yalta meant that implementation of the agreements would be determined by the commitment of U.S. policy makers to accept the reality of Soviet influence and the spirit underlying the conference.

A similar situation occurred in the Yalta discussions on Germany. Most important matters involving Germany were postponed, though even then it was implicitly agreed that the Big Three would jointly determine occupation and reparations policy. The level of German reparations payments did divide the Allies at Yalta. The final agreement, though, provided for the creation of a reparations commission to discuss this question; the commission was instructed, with Roosevelt and Stalin concurring and Churchill dissenting, that during its deliberations the figure of $20 billion with one-half going to the Soviet Union should provide "the basis for discussion."

At Yalta, Roosevelt had no clearly formulated German policy. Supporting simply a harsh peace, but no longer committed to dismemberment and sizable reparations, he nonetheless remained unwilling to force a dispute with Stalin and accepted the postponement of these issues. Roosevelt's agreement to a stated sum as the basis for discussion, however, could be construed as a commitment in a principle to a fixed figure if not to that sum. The only merit of Roosevelt's temporizing was in avoiding division and disharmony. By not providing clear guidelines for future discussions, it served to complicate future U.S.-Soviet relations.

The Yalta discussions on the Far East were characterized by the same imprecision of agreement and absence of thorough negotiations. The general terms of Soviet involvement had tacitly been agreed to at Teheran and during discussions between Stalin and Harriman in 1944. Both Roosevelt and Stalin remained interested, nonetheless, in a more specific understanding. At Stalin's insistence, the conditions for Soviet involvement were set forth in writing at Yalta and agreed to by the three powers (though Britain did not participate in the discussions). Specifically, the Soviet Union was to receive South Sakhalin and the Kurile Islands from Japan. In addition, Russia secured "lease" rights to Port Arthur; her "pre-eminent interests" were to be safeguarded in an internationalized port of Dairen and in a "jointly operated" Sino-Soviet commission for the Chinese-Eastern Railroad and the South-Manchurian Railroad; and the status of Outer Mongolia was to be "preserved." Roosevelt admitted not having discussed the matters of Outer Mongolia, the ports, or the railroads with Chiang Kai-shek and conceded that, for the moment, military considerations required continued secrecy. Stalin then informed Roosevelt that Chinese Foreign Minister T.V. Soong was coming to Moscow in April, that it might be appropriate at that time to inform him of this matter. Ultimately, it was decided that Roosevelt would take the initiative to inform the Chinese and would make his move when so directed by Stalin, the determining factor to be military developments in Europe. In return for these concessions, Roosevelt secured two qualified Soviet commitments: to enter the war against Japan two or three months after the termination of the war in Europe and to conclude a pact of "friendship and alliance" with the Nationalist government.

The Far Eastern agreements, however, had not defined the extent of the Soviet role in Manchuria, particularly in the area surrounding the ports and railroads; the reference to the "pre-eminent interests" of the Soviet Union could result in the establishment of a Soviet sphere of influence. Moreover, whether Roosevelt had accepted the German or Italian model as the basis for joint occupation policy in postwar Japan was not clear from the discussions or agreements reached at Yalta. No specific agreement had been made concerning this matter—the outright cession of South Sakhalin and the Kuriles to the Soviet Union did not establish physical occupation of Japanese territory and a right to have an equal voice in occupation policy. Roosevelt's Soviet involvement, however, and the spirit of mutual assistance and cooperation provided justification for Soviet insistence on equal participation in occupation policy.

In sum, at Yalta, Roosevelt adopted a conciliatory policy, accepting the reality of Soviet power and the legitimacy of her postwar involvement in Eastern Europe, Germany, and the Far East. . . .

III

Roosevelt's death significantly changed the diplomatic setting, by introducing, for one thing, an element of uncertainty about future U.S.-Soviet relations. More important, it introduced Harry S. Truman, a man more rigidly anti-Soviet and, given also his noninvolvement in Roosevelt's policymaking, more responsive to the suggestions of policy advisers whose recommendations had been ignored at Yalta. His personal political style would have far-reaching consequences for the Yalta understandings: Truman would not feel compelled to honor the commitments and would seek to exploit the vague language of the agreements to avoid compliance.

In part, the Truman administration in 1945 bore the legacies of Roosevelt's earlier policy of postponing and avoiding clearly defined commitments and the partial continuing of that policy at Yalta. Despite Yalta, doubt remained over Roosevelt's position on, among other things, German reparations and dismemberment, the character of the postwar governments of Eastern Europe, and the nature of the Soviet postwar role in the Far East. More important, in making concessions to the Soviet Union, Roosevelt had acted unilaterally, without securing the understanding or acquiescence of his subordinates. The imprecision of Roosevelt's administrative leadership thereby provided an opportunity for these subordinates to take advantage of the policy vacuum created by Roosevelt's death, and Truman's woeful ignorance of both international politics and the Yalta commitments, to secure the eventful adoption of their recommendations.

In April, Harriman had a conversation with Stalin that, because it coincided with Roosevelt's death, permitted him to affirm Truman's intention to continue the policies of his predecessor. Capitalizing on Stalin's statement of willingness to work with Truman as he had with Roosevelt, Harriman extracted from the premier a pledge to have Molotov, on his way to San Francisco, stop off in Washington to consult with Truman. Such a move, Harriman insisted, would promote collaboration. Stalin acceded. Intended as a friendly gesture, Molotov's trip was initiated to provide the opportunity for an exchange of views and a testing of cooperation.

Harriman's move, though not necessarily intentionally, coincided with an intensive policy reexamination in Washington involving Truman and key advisers who had urged Truman not to compromise to reach accommodation.

Truman, in fact, adopted a less conciliatory approach in April 1945. On April 16, he and Churchill sent a joint note to Stalin outlining their proposal for resolving the Polish impasse. Their note placed the Western-oriented Polish political leaders on the same basis with the Lublin Poles. Understanding that even the vague language of the Yalta agreements did not support his position, Truman, nonetheless, remained confident that a strong stand would not precipitate a break with the Soviet Union.

The same attitude also prevailed at his meeting with Molotov on April 23. Truman's language at that meeting was blunt and undiplomatic, specifically rejecting the Yugoslav formula (expanding the existing government by adding a new minister for every four already in the cabinet) as the basis for composing the new Polish provisional govern-

ment. An agreement had been concluded, Truman self-righteously affirmed, and only required Soviet compliance. In response to Molotov's
protests, Truman conceded the vagueness of the language of the
agreements (the President had earlier been advised by Leahy, among
others, that the Soviet position was consistent with the Yalta
agreements). Molotov denied that any agreement had been broken and
stressed the need for cooperation, to which Truman reiterated his insistence that the U.S. interpretation was the only one possible.

The result of this meeting, if possibly psychologically satisfying to
the frustrated Americans, did not lead to diplomatic resolution. Responding to the April 16 note and the April 23 meeting, Stalin emphasized Poland's importance to Soviet security and protested Western
efforts to dictate to the Soviet Union. Truman's refusal to accept Lublin
as the core of the new government was inconsistent with the Yalta
agreements. Soviet actions in Poland were comparable to those of Britain in Belgium and Greece; the Soviet Union had not sought to interfere
in these countries or to ascertain whether British actions made possible
representative government. The United States and Great Britain were
combining against the Soviet Union and the United States was attempting to secure Soviet renunciation of her security interests.

On May 19, in a seeming about-face, Truman consulted Stalin on
Harry Hopkins's proposed mission to Moscow for mutual consultations.
Significantly, when the Hopkins mission was first considered in early
May, Byrnes and the State Department opposed the idea, recognizing
that it meant that Truman had decided to make some concessions to the
Soviets.

Truman's objectives for the Hopkins mission remain obscure. The
trip did not eliminate the tensions that had surfaced in April, though an
agreement worked out on the composition of the Polish provisional
government did essentially follow the Yugoslav formula, and on July 5,
the Truman administration did recognize the reorganized government.

The Eastern European question, however, had not been amicably
resolved. At Potsdam, Truman refused to recognize either the Oder-
Neisse line as the western boundary of Poland or Soviet primacy in
Bulgaria, Hungary, and Romania. In his public report of August 9 on the
results of the conference, Truman declared that Bulgaria and Romania
were not to be within the sphere of influence of any one power. And
earlier on June 1, 12, and 14, the administration had instructed Harriman
to propose to Stalin that the United States and Great Britain be accorded
veto power over the actions of Soviet commanders in Hungary,
Romania, and Bulgaria.

The Truman administration's decision to accept confrontation rather
than seek accommodation also underlay its often shifting and confused,
but unbending, German policy. Thus, even though, at the time, these

decisions did not necessarily reflect a conscious strategy or policy, on May 10, 1945, Truman unilaterally approved Joint Chiefs of Staff (JCS) directive 1067 and replaced Roosevelt's representative to the Moscow Reparations Commission, Isadore Rubin, with Edwin Pauley. The vagueness of JCS 1067 and the unilateral nature of its promulgation, without consultation with the British, Russians, or French, marked a shift toward a softer policy toward Germany. The directive simply provided general discretion to U.S. military zonal authorities to determine the level of German industrial production and, indirectly thereby, German reparations payments.

During the June discussions in Moscow on reparations, Pauley had adopted an uncompromising line on Soviet requests for specific agreement on German reparations levels, thereby effectively averting progress toward any agreement. The Truman delegation adopted the same stance at Potsdam, indirectly avoiding the issue of joint policy. While paying lip service to the Yalta agreement on reparations, Secretary of State Byrnes refused to respond to Soviet efforts to determine the specific reparations sum that the United States would accept. Dismissing the Yalta figure of $10 billion as "impractical," Byrnes supported a policy whereby, in Molotov's words, "each country would have a free hand in their own zone and could act entirely independently of the others." Despite Assistant Secretary of State Clayton's warning that Byrnes's insistence that reparations come from the zone of the occupying power "would be considered by the Russians as a reversal of the Yalta position," Truman did not alter this position. Potsdam, then, contributed to the division of Germany along zonal lines. In addition, Truman's willingness to reject the Yalta formulas, while publicly proclaiming his commitment to them, added the element of distrust to diplomatic relations. The further complication to joint planning provided later by French obstruction heightened this distrust. A high Soviet official told James Warburg in the summer of 1946 that "after six months of French obstruction, we began to suspect that this was a put-up job—that you did not like the bargain you had made at Potsdam and that you are letting the French get you out of it. . . ."

The vague wording of the Far Eastern agreements presented formidable unresolved diplomatic problems for the entering Truman administration. On the surface, the concessions did not seem major. In fact, however, the extent of the postwar Soviet role in either China or Japan had not been clearly defined. Thus, as soon as he became president, Truman was beset by pressure from key advisers in State, the Foreign Service, and his cabinet to reappraise the Far Eastern agreements. At an April 23 cabinet meeting, the President himself raised the issue of reappraisal. Distressed over Soviet actions in Eastern Europe, Truman suggested that the failure of a Yalta signatory to fulfill any of its commitments might free the other signatories from fulfilling theirs. The main opposition to this position came from the military. General George C. Marshall, then chairman of the Joint Chiefs of Staff, argued that the concessions had to stand because the Far Eastern war could not be won without Soviet military assistance.

While no formal decision on the concessions was reached in the cabinet then, the German surrender on May 8 led to further administration reevaluation of Yalta. During a May 11 meeting in Forrestal's office, Harriman, who was about to return to Moscow, contended that "it was time to come to a conclusion about the necessity for the early entrance of Russia into the Japanese war." He reiterated this case at State on May 12, and it was agreed that Harriman's views should be formulated precisely "for discussion with the President. . . ."

The United States' seeming ambivalence throughout this preliminary negotiating period was indicative not of indifference but of the desire to forestall Soviet involvement in the Far East. Since the Soviet Union had declared its unwillingness to enter the war against Japan until a treaty had been concluded with China, by stalling negotiations on that treaty, the administration could avert the inevitable extension of Soviet influence in China and Japan without formally repudiating the terms laid down at Yalta.

By June, the administration's options had increased as the result of the defeat of Germany. Thereafter, the administration operated on the premise that Soviet military involvement against Japan was not imperative. This shift was revealed on June 18 in another change of position by the Joint Chiefs of Staff, who now described Soviet aid as desirable but not indispensable and recommended that the United States not bargain for Soviet involvement.

With all this in mind, Truman and Byrnes discussed the Far East with Stalin and Molotov at the Potsdam Conference on July 17. First the Soviet leaders informed Truman and Byrnes of their willingness to accept Chinese control of Manchuria as well as to recognize the Nationalists as the sole leaders of China. In reply, Byrnes affirmed that the United States held to a strict interpretation of the Yalta terms. Then, feigning ignorance of the recently concluded Soong-Stalin talks, Byrnes sounded out Stalin about the areas of Sino-Soviet disagreement. On the basis of Stalin's reply, Byrnes and Truman concluded that the differences between the Soviet and Chinese positions were so fundamental that, at least in the immediate future, a Sino-Soviet treaty was highly unlikely.

The Potsdam discussions between the U.S. and Soviet military staffs provided further assurances for the administration that a Sino-Soviet treaty was still a necessary precondition for Russia's entering the

Japanese war. Moreover, at Potsdam, the administration remained in contact with the Chinese Nationalists. On July 20, Chiang Kai-shek informed Truman about Soong's mission, arguing that the Chinese had bargained in good faith and could make no further concessions to secure the treaty. Truman agreed—in fact, he directed Chiang specifically to make no more concessions. Despite this, Truman insisted on the implementation of the Yalta terms and urged Chiang to have Soong return to Moscow to continue negotiations.

While the administration continued formally to support the Yalta commitments, in view of the July 17 meeting with Stalin and Molotov, Truman's instructions to Chiang—if Soong followed them—would effectively stymie the conclusion of a treaty. Moreover, the successful testing of the atomic bomb led Marshall to concede to Stimson and Truman on July 23 that Soviet entry into the war against Japan was no longer necessary, but Marshall again maintained that the Soviet Union could enter anyway and obtain "virtually what they wanted in the surrender terms." Byrnes came away from the discussion hoping only that the Sino-Soviet discussions might be stalled and thereby "delay Soviet entrance and the Japanese might surrender." Finally, instead of consulting the Soviets, the administration unilaterally drafted the formal declaration demanding unconditional Japanese surrender; it also decided unilaterally to accept the Japanese request of August 10 for clarification of the surrender terms.

Moreover, once the second phase of the Sino-Soviet discussions began, the United States adopted a more rigid stance, advising the Chinese to stand firm even if that firmness prevented agreement. On August 5, Byrnes asked Harriman officially to inform Soong that the United States opposed concessions beyond those agreed to at Yalta. He specifically warned the Chinese not to make further concessions over the status of Dairen or Soviet reparations demands. The essence of this new administration position was to support the Chinese at the same time that it opposed concessions needed to conclude the treaty; only if the Soviet Union reversed its attitude and radically changed its demands would a treaty result prior to Japanese surrender.

Truman's policy failed to forestall the Soviet Union's entrance into the Japanese war. Although a formal Sino-Soviet treaty had not been concluded and although the United States finally neither requested nor encouraged Soviet intervention, the Russians nonetheless declared war on Japan on August 8 and moved troops into North China and Manchuria. Simultaneously, Stalin warned Soong on August 10 that, should a formal Sino-Soviet agreement not be concluded, Chinese Communist troops would be permitted to move into Manchuria. Fearful of Soviet support of the Chinese Communists, Chiang Kai-shek acceded to the

Soviet demands on the unresolved issues. The formal Sino-Soviet treaty was then quickly concluded, and its terms announced on August 14.

The administration's indirect opposition to the Yalta provisions created the potential for U.S.-Soviet division once the war with Japan ended. The rapidity of the Japanese surrender and the last-minute Soviet entry into the war had complicated surrender proceedings. The administration had had little time to devise formal terms indicating to whom Japanese troops should surrender. Indeed, until Soviet entry, there had been no discussion about Soviet rights to direct or control Japan during the period of occupation. Thus, when unilaterally issuing General Order #1, the United States directed Japanese troops to surrender to the Nationalists in all areas of China south of Manchuria and to the Russians in Manchuria, Korea north of the thirty-eighth parallel, and Karafutu. These surrender orders were intended to achieve two purposes: to preclude Japanese surrender to Chinese Communist troops and to minimize the Soviet occupation role in China and Japan.

Immediately, on August 16, the Soviet Union protested that these surrender provisions violated the Yalta agreements. Stalin demanded that the Soviet surrender zone include the Kuriles and Hokkaido (the northern sector of Japan). Unwilling to create the opportunity for Soviet military presence in Japan, Truman on August 18 acceded to the Soviet request for the Kuriles but not for Hokkaido. At the same time he pressed for an American air base on the Kuriles. In a sharp rejoinder on August 22, Stalin reiterated his earlier demand for Hokkaido and opposed Truman's request for the air base.

This was no mere territorial conflict; it involved the more basic question of the Truman administration's policy toward the Soviet occupation of Japan. At issue was whether the administration was formally prepared for confrontation. Truman at the time hesitated to reject the prospect of a negotiated settlement and replied to Stalin's sharp note of August 22 that the United States had not sought air base but only landing rights on the Kuriles. Truman further pointed out that the Kuriles were not Soviet territory. Yalta had only permitted Soviet occupation, he said; their final status would have to be determined at a future peace conference. On August 30, Stalin acceded to the request for landing rights. He denied, however, that the status of the Kuriles was unclear, contending that the cession had been permanent and that future peace talks would merely ratify this fact.

Directly or indirectly, the objective of limiting Soviet influence in the Far East underlay administration policy toward the Yalta agreements. Truman and Byrnes cunningly, but shortsightedly, here too sought to have it both ways: to avert the effect of the agreements without formally repudiating or renegotiating them.

IV

This clearly contradictory policy required the administration to continue to refrain from publishing the Yalta agreements on the Far East. Publication would have bound the administration to fulfilling them and would have established earlier U.S. insistence on Soviet involvement, negating the limited Soviet military contribution to defeating Japan. Therefore, the Truman administration neglected to publish the Far Eastern agreements on three ostensibly favorable occasions: when the Soviet Union declared war on Japan on August 8, when the Sino-Soviet treaty was announced on August 14, or when Soviet troops occupied the Kurile Islands on August 27.

The U.S. troop withdrawal that permitted Soviet occupation of the Kuriles precipitated bitter protests by conservatives in both Congress and the press, who charged that Soviet possession of these "strategic" islands would directly threaten the security of the United States and Japan. In a September 4 press conference, on the eve of his departure for the London Foreign Ministers Conference, Byrnes attempted to allay this protest. The decision leading up to U.S. withdrawal, he informed the press, had resulted from "discussions" (as opposed to "agreements," he implied) conducted at Yalta, not Potsdam. Byrnes, claiming that his attendance at Yalta had provided him with "full" knowledge of these "discussions," attributed the responsibility for them to Roosevelt rather than Truman. He then announced his intention to review them at London; a final agreement on the status of the Kuriles, he concluded, could be made only at a forthcoming peace conference.

Byrnes dissembled in two respects at this press conference: first, in implying that the status of the Kuriles had not yet been defined and, second, in failing to report the existence of the other Far Eastern agreements. His statements were to have serious ramifications for the Truman administration.

Byrnes's secretiveness on the second point stemmed from the administration's desire to prevent the Soviets from assuming a controlling role in China and in the occupation of Japan. This objective necessarily conflicted with Soviet policy and contributed to the atmosphere of distrust that prevailed during the September meetings of the Council of Foreign Ministers in London. Although Molotov then protested the unilateral character of U.S. occupation policy in Japan, demanding the establishment of an Allied control commission, Byrnes equivocated and, in the end, succeeded in postponing any final decision on Japan.

This strategy and the attendant necessity not to publish the Far Eastern agreements—or even, for that matter, admit their existence—would seriously compromise the administration's position. The first public hint of the existence of the agreements occurred in November 1945 during the controversy surrounding the resignation of Hurley as U.S. ambassador to China. In resigning, Hurley charged that U.S. foreign policy had been subverted by "imperialists" and "communists" in both the State Department and the Foreign Service, charges which led to special hearings by the Senate Foreign Relations Committee in December.

The tone of the committee's questioning of Hurley was sharp, at times even hostile. Attempting to defend Hurley, who had repeated his charges of employee disloyalty and insubordination, a sympathetic Senator Styles Bridges asked whether at Yalta—given the absence of Chinese representatives—any agreement concerning China had been concluded. Although he had not attended the conference, Hurley claimed knowledge about the China discussions. He added that Secretary of State Byrnes was a better authority on that subject.

In his prepared statement the next day, Byrnes dismissed Hurley's charges against the personnel of the State Department and the Foreign Service as wholly unfounded. Senator Bridges, however, was much more concerned with the Truman and Roosevelt administrations' China policy. Repeating his question of the day before, he asked Byrnes whether any agreement concerning China was concluded at Yalta in the absence and without the consent of Chiang Kai-shek. Bridges's confident tone, and the possibility that he had secured access to the Yalta text through Hurley or another source in the State Department, complicated Byrnes's reply. To admit that agreements had been concluded at Yalta without advising or consulting Chiang, and had not yet been published, would put the administration on the defensive and possibly expose its earlier dissembling. Faced with this dilemma, Byrnes neither affirmed nor denied that an agreement had been made:

> I do not recall the various agreements [of the Yalta Conference]. It is entirely possible that some of the agreements arrived at at Yalta affected China some way or another, and I have told you that I would gladly furnish you the communique and then you could decide whether or not they affected China. If they were made they certainly were made by the heads of government and certainly only the three Governments were represented there.

Bridges then observed that had any agreement on China been concluded, the secretary could not have been unaware of its existence. Thus, when the administration would publish the Far Eastern agreements, it would have to offer a convincing rationale both for its earlier failure to publish them and for Byrnes's seeming ignorance of the matter.

This situation came to pass in February 1946. The event precipitating the publication of the Far Eastern agreements was the administration's announcement in January that it had turned over to an international trusteeship certain Pacific islands the United States captured from Japan during World War II. During a January 22 press conference, Acting Secretary of State Dean Acheson was asked whether the Soviet Union would similarly be required to turn over the Kuriles to an international trusteeship. In answer, Acheson pointed out that the Yalta agreements had provided only for Soviet occupation of the Kuriles; the final disposition would have to be determined at a future peace conference. Acheson conceded, however, that such a conference might simply affirm Soviet control. On January 26, Moscow Radio challenged Acheson's remarks, denying that Soviet control of these territories was temporary or that Soviet occupation was related only to the prosecution of the war against Japan.

At a press conference on January 29, Byrnes announced that the Kuriles and South Sakhalin had in fact been ceded to the Soviet Union at Yalta. He further disclosed that agreements concerning Port Arthur and Dairen had also been concluded. But these agreements would become binding only after the formal conclusion of a peace treaty with Japan.

The most dramatic aspect of Byrnes's press conference was not the disclosure of the agreements themselves but his attempts to explain the Truman administration's earlier failure to release them or indeed even to admit their existence. What Byrnes did was to tell the press that although he had been a delegate to Yalta, he had left the conference on the afternoon of February 10, before the concluding session the next day. He had not learned about the specifics of the Far Eastern agreements until August 1945, a few days after the Japanese surrender. In response to further questions, Byrnes said he did not know whether former Secretary of State Stettinius knew about the agreements or where, in fact, the text was deposited. It was not, he stated, in the State Department archives, but it might be in the White House files.

Once again, Byrnes had adroitly covered his tracks. He had shifted responsibility for both the Yalta agreements and the failure to publish them to the Roosevelt administration's tactics of secrecy. His statement did, however, raise two important questions: first, had the agreements been privately concluded by Roosevelt without the knowledge of other White House or State Department personnel and, second, where was the text.

During a January 31 press conference, Truman sought to resolve these questions. The text, he claimed, had always been in the White House files, except when under review either by members of the White House staff or other administration personnel. While he had always known the whereabouts of the text, Truman said, he had not reviewed it until he began to prepare for the Potsdam Conference. Asked when the agreements would in fact be published, Truman answered that it would be necessary first to consult the British and the Russians. Most of the agreements, he added, had already been made public; the others would be disclosed at the "proper" time.

The Truman administration's policy toward the Yalta Far Eastern agreements and other administration tactics strained the already uneasy relations between the United States and the Soviet Union. It was in the area of tactics and personality that the rigidity and moralistic tone of postwar U.S.-Soviet relations derived important substance, and not simply from conflicting ideologies and objectives. In this sense, the Cold War was an avoidable conflict: the "way" it evolved being a product of shortsighted political leadership. The opportunities for détente provided by Yalta were effectively subverted by the Truman administration, and U.S.-Soviet relations suffered until a change in presidents brought an administration less rigidly bound to the self-righteous politics of confrontation. Eisenhower's politics remained conservative; but, with the Geneva summit conference of 1955, his presidency marked a new, less militant phase of the Cold War.

Joseph R. Starobin

JOSEPH R. STAROBIN (1913–1976) was for many years a prominent member of the
American Communist Party. He broke with the party in 1954, although
never renouncing his commitment to Marxism. In his later career he was
professor of political science at the University of Toronto. Among his publications were *Paris to Peking* (1955) and *American Communism in Crisis, 1943–1957*
(1972).

It is surely a suggestive irony that just at the point when younger American historians had made serious intellectual headway with their reinterpretation of the Cold War, fixing historical responsibility in terms of
the mistakes, delusions, and imperatives of U.S. policy, the Soviet
Union astonished friends and foes by overwhelming Czechoslovakia
and turning its clock of history backwards. If the Cold War has not
revived, small thanks are due the Soviet leaders. Their extraordinary
nervousness, their maneuvers to propitiate both the outgoing and in-
coming American administrations, indicate very plainly how much they
have feared political retaliation; this in itself is a comment on where
responsibility for the cold war today should rest. That Prague should
have been the vortex in 1968 as it was in 1948 of critical problems within
communism is uncanny, but on deeper examination it may not be for-
tuitous.

After all, the least credible explanation of Moscow's desperate attempt to resolve the crisis within its own system of states and parties is
the one which pictures Czechoslovakia as the helpless Pauline at the
crossroads of Europe, about to be dishonored by West German *revan-
chards*, with agents of the CIA grinning in the background, suddenly
saved by the stalwart defenders of socialist honor and morality. Today
this type of argument is reserved within the Communist world for its
most backward members—that is, for the Soviet public and the fringes
of the most insignificant and expendable Communist parties. Yet arguments of this kind had wide currency a generation ago. New Left historians would have us believe that Stalin was simply reacting to external
challenge. In their view, the Cold War might not have set in if small-

Joseph R. Starobin, "Origins of the Cold War: The Communist Dimension," *Foreign Affairs*
47 (July 1969). 681–96. Reprinted by permission from *Foreign Affairs*. Copyright 1969 by
Council on Foreign Relations, Inc.

minded American politicians had not been determined to reverse bad bargains, if congenital imperialists had not been mesmerized by the monopoly of atomic weapons which statesmen and scientists knew to be temporary. Since all this is so plainly a half-truth when juxtaposed to events of today, then clearly the half-truth of yesteryear will hardly explain the whole of the Cold War.

Sophisticated Communists, both East and West, are asking why Czechoslovakia, which escaped the upheavals in Poland and Hungary of 1956 after a decade of Stalinist pressure, then experienced such a mounting crisis in the subsequent decade of relative détente and peaceful competition. How is it that twenty years after Communist rule had been secured in February 1948 basic verities are now placed in question—whether centralized planning may not be counterproductive, whether a one-party régime can really articulate the needs of a politically evolved people, whether the inner relations of such an unequal alliance as that administered by the Soviet Union are not so inherently antagonistic as to become explosive? Indeed, why did the rebirth of Czechoslovak political life in the first half of 1968—viewed with hope and excitement by Western Communists—raise such menacing ghosts from the past and such fearful question marks for the future that supposedly sober-minded men in Moscow took fright?

Twice within a dozen years the unmanageability of the Communist world has been revealed. The crisis which shattered the Sino-Soviet alliance after manifesting itself first in Eastern Europe now rebounds at the supposed strong-point of Czechoslovakia. And it has done so both in conditions of intense external pressure and times of relatively peaceful engagement. Perhaps it is here, in the dimension of communism as a contradictory and intractable system, that one may find the missing element in the discussions thus far on the origins of the Cold War.

II

That world history would someday polarize around two great nations, America and Russia, was a de Tocquevillean insight with which Communists were familiar a long time ago. Stalin gave it what seemed like a very clear definition back in 1927 during a talk with an American labor delegation. He envisaged that a socialist center would arise "binding to itself the countries gravitating toward socialism" and would engage the surviving capitalist center in "a struggle between them for the posession of the world economy." The fate of both would be decided by the outcome of this struggle. What appeared at first glance as a sweeping projection was, however, profoundly ambiguous on close examination. Stalin did not spell out how the countries "gravitating to socialism" would get there. Good Communists believed this could come about only by the formulas of the October Revolution; yet even Lenin, in 1922, had lamented that perhaps a "big mistake" was being made in imposing Russian precepts on foreign Communists. Nor did Stalin elucidate how new nations recruited to socialism would order their relations with Russia as the hub of the socialist center. Presumably "proletarian internationalism" would replace the domination of the weak by the strong which was, in their view, the hallmark of capitalism. Yet even by 1927 the Russification of the international movement had brought catastrophic results—in Germany and China.

Stalin did not, moreover, meet the fundamental intellectual challenge of whether "the struggle for the possession of the world economy" necessarily had to be military in character. On this crucial point, everything could be found in the Leninist grabbag. "Peaceful coexistence" is there, but so is the expectation of "frightful collisions" between the first workers' state and its opponents; the caution that socialism had to be secured in one country first is to be found along with pledges that once socialism was strong enough in Russia, it would raise up revolts in the strongholds of capitalism.

The one possibility which Leninism did not anticipate was a stalemate between rival systems, precluding a "final conflict." The notion was not even entertained that an equilibrium between contending forces might set in, that the subsequent evolution of both contenders under the impact of this equilibrium could alter their distinguishing characteristics and therefore outmode the original Leninist theorems.

Out of such doctrinal ambiguities the Second World War created policy choices affecting most of humanity. The Soviet Union and the international Communist movement found themselves allied with democratic-capitalist states among whom public power had grown drastically in an effort to overcome the Great Depression; the welfare state was expanded by the very demands of warfare while democracy was in fact enhanced. Keynes had made a serious rebuttal to Marx. Would capitalism in the West collapse in a repetition of the crisis of the 1930s after withstanding the test of war? Or had the war itself changed something vital within the workings of capitalism? Moreover, the first global war in history led to the end of colonialism and hence a new relation of metropolitan states to subject peoples. Would the former necessarily collapse because, in Lenin's analysis, they had depended so heavily on colonies? Or might they undergo transformations—short of socialism—to make them viable? Would the countries of the underdeveloped world make socialism the indispensable form of their modernization or might they, dialectically enough, find a new relation with capitalism?

Thus, the war brought on to the world stage a powerful Russia on whose survival a rival system's survival also depended. Simultaneously

America came to center stage with a greatly expanded economy no longer limited by laissez-faire economics and inwardly altered by technological change created by the war. America was indispensable to Russia as an ally but formidable as a rival in a sense far deeper than its outward power. This wartime relationship was unexpected, and it challenged ideology and practice on all sides.

Something very particular happened with communism, considered as a most uneven system of a single state and a variety of parties. The fortunes of war, thanks perhaps to Churchill's postponement of the second front, brought the Soviet armies beyond their own borders where they had to be welcomed by the West if only because their help was also being solicited on the plains of Manchuria once Hitler was defeated. Yet at the moment of Russia's greatest need and harshest difficulties, the Communist movements *least* helpful to her were those of Eastern Europe; in the one country outside of Russia where a decade before the Communists had been a real power—namely, in Germany— the party lay shattered. No anti-Hitler force of any practical significance emerged. On the East European landscape there were only two exceptions. In Yugoslavia a handful of veterans of Comintern intrigue and the hard school of the International Brigades in Spain had succeeded in establishing their power—prior to the arrival of Soviet forces in the Danubian basin. In Czechoslovakia, a Communist movement of a very different sort—that is, with a legal and parliamentary tradition—was joined by Slovak guerrillas. Both came to terms with the leadership of the government-in-exile, which both Moscow and the West recognized. A long-term cooperation of diverse social forces was implied.

On the other hand, the Communist movements underwent a spectacular resurrection in a wide arc from Greece through Italy, France, the Low Countries and Scandinavia, while in widely separated corners of Asia they also flourished—in Northwest China, in the peninsula of Indochina, in the Philippines and Malaya. All of them were successful to the degree that they identified with the defense of their nationhood and either subordinated social issues or subsumed them in national ones; where this proved too complicated, as in India, long-term disabilities resulted. But all these movements grew at a distance from the Soviet armies; their postwar fate could not depend on physical contact. Even parties at the periphery of world politics showed striking changes. They entered cabinets in Cuba and Chile, emerged from prewar disasters with great dynamism in Brazil, became legal in Canada and stood a chance of legitimizing their considerable influence in Britain and the United States. In these latter countries, they could hope to achieve "citizenship" only by ceasing to be propagandist groups reflecting Soviet prestige, and only as they grappled with the specific peculiarities of their societies in rapid change.

Yet for all this success, and perhaps because of it, communism faced the gravest problems. The peculiarity of the moment lay in the fact that some definition of Russia's relation with the West was essential to assure the most rapid conclusion of the war in Europe, and this had to precede a common strategy in Asia. Hence Moscow was obliged to define relations with the Communist parties. Simultaneously these movements—of such unequal potential and geographical relation to Russia—had to make a fresh judgment of their strategies in view of those changes within capitalism which challenged their own doctrine. Perhaps the most ambitious attempt to do this came in May 1943 with the dissolution of the Communist International.

Stalin, who had sworn at Lenin's bier to guard this "general staff of the world revolution" like the apple of his eye, was now abandoning it; and in so doing he signaled to Churchill and Roosevelt that he would project the postwar Soviet interest in essentially Russian terms. This decision was consistent with the fact that the Russian Communists had not been able to rely on ideology or internationalism in mobilizing their own peoples for the enormous sacrifices of the war. They had been forced to appeal to the Russian love of soil and the solace of the Orthodox faith. "They are not fighting for us," Stalin had once mused to Ambassador Harriman. "They are fighting for Mother Russia."

All of this would not, of course, make Russia easier to deal with. And in studying the details in the monumental accounts of Herbert Feis or W. H. McNeill, one is struck by Stalin's political opportunism and the enormous part which is played in his calculations by the need to exact material resources from friend and foe. Throughout 1944, Stalin dealt with anyone who would cease fighting, or mobilize men and matériel for the Soviet armies, safeguard their lines and pledge reparations; and everyone was suitable to Moscow in terms of these objectives—agrarians and monarchists in the Axis satellites, veteran communist haters in Finland, a Social Democratic oldtimer in Austria, Dr. Beneš in Prague or Comrade Tito in the Yugoslav mountains. Had the putsch against Hitler succeeded in July 1944, Stalin was prepared, by his committee of Nazi generals rounded up at Stalingrad, to bargain.

His only real complication arose over Poland. Here the Soviets had the tactical advantage that a generation earlier the victors at Versailles had been willing to establish the Curzon Line as Russia's western frontier. Churchill and Roosevelt were now obliged not only to ratify this line but to impose it on the intractable London Poles. Moscow's own dilemma lay in the fact that the pro-Soviet Poles, exiled in the U.S.S.R., had little political substance; they had one thing in common with their counterparts in London—lack of standing inside Poland. The Polish Communists had been decimated in the great purges and the Polish officer corps had been wiped out in the Katyn murders. Perhaps it was the need to shift the balance in his favor that led Stalin to such extraordinary measures as letting the "Home Army" be wiped out at the banks of the Vistula or continuing to murder Polish Socialists as they came to Moscow as guests. The earlier hope of some prestigious figure who would bridge the gap between Poles and yet be satisfactory to all the great powers had faded with the death in an airplane accident of General Wladislaw Sikorski.

But it is questionable whether this Soviet use of vestigial figures of Comintern experience should be viewed, as of 1944, in terms of "communization." Everything we know of the Kremlin at that time denies this. In the remarkable account by Milovan Djilas in his "Conversations with Stalin," the Kremlin was far from being a citadel of revolution, as this young Montenegrin idealist expected (like so many in Moscow for the first time, before and after him). The Kremlin was really a sort of Muscovite camping-ground such as the great Russian painter Repin might have portrayed. Crafty and boorish men, suspicious of all foreigners and of each other, contemptuous of Communists who were non-Russian but expecting their obedience, were crowded around the maps of Europe as around some Cossack camp fire, calculating how much they could extract from Churchill and Roosevelt, to whom they felt profoundly inferior.

Thus, when Ulbricht and Rakosi, Anna Pauker, and even Dmitroff were being prepared to return to the homelands where they had previously failed, Stalin advised them not to spoil their second chance by their chronic leftism and adventurism.[1] They did not go back as revolutionaries. For all of Moscow's hopes that they root themselves in native soil, they were intended to be the guarantors of control, to stabilize this backyard of Europe and mobilize its resources on Russia's behalf. The troubles with the Yugoslavs began for the very reason that as revolutionaries they would not let themselves be used.

Was Stalin already building a bloc? To be sure he was. But he also knew that the onetime *cordon sanitaire* was a veritable swamp of historic and intractable rivalries and economic backwardness, even though wealthier in immediate resources than the USSR itself. Hoping to transform this bloc, Stalin also entertained most seriously the idea of a long-term relationship with America and Britain based on some common policy toward Germany that would make its much greater resources available

---

[1]Herbert Feis is the source for the famous and revealing anecdote that when Stalin said farewell to Dr. Beneš, after signing a mutual assistance pact, he urged Beneš to help make Klement Gottwald, the Communist leader now become premier, "more worldly and less provincial"—an amazing piece of arrogance. Having themselves helped emasculate their foreign friends, the Russians now taunted them and hoped that perhaps the bourgeois world might make men of them. *Churchill, Roosevelt, Stalin* (Princeton: Princeton University Press, 1957), p. 569.

to Russia. Thus, when Churchill came to Moscow in September 1944 to work out a spheres-of-influence agreement, demanding 50:50 and 75:25 ratios in the political control of areas already liberated by the Soviet armies, Stalin agreed by the stroke of a pen. He did so without comment. He contemptuously left it to Churchill to decide whether the piece of paper should be retained by him or destroyed. The cobbler's son from Gori, the onetime seminary student, was giving a descendant of the Marlboroughs a lesson in Realpolitik.

But as he disposed of Greeks and interposed with Yugoslavs (without asking their consent) the Soviet dictator demanded no quid pro quo in Western Europe where the ultimate world balance could be determined, and where Communist movements had powerfully revived, guided by intimates of Stalin—Togliatti and Thorez—whose work he respected. Molotov is on record as inquiring about the disposition of Italian colonies, but not about the operations of the American Military Government in Italy in which Russian participation was passive. At the moment when the French Communists were debating whether to turn in their arms, Moscow recognized the Gaullist régime and invited it to sign a treaty with what de Gaulle was to call "chère et puissante Russie." Churchill's assault on Belgian and Greek Communists was reproved, in private. But no Soviet leverage was employed to help them, and the Greek Communists were advised to strike the best bargain they could to avert civil war. Only much later, when assistance was useless to them, did the Soviets reluctantly help the Greeks, though their hapless plight was useful for Cold War propaganda. Even as late as February 1945, at Yalta, Stalin pledged to renew his pact with Chiang Kai-shek in return for special treaty control of Dairen and the Manchurian railways. Half a year later, the Soviet armies ransacked the industrial installations that were by right Chinese. In central Asia they dickered with warlords, advising them against joining the Chinese Communists. Stalin shied away from the governance of Japan, asking and getting its northern islands instead. All this was accompanied by rather snide references by Molotov to Mao Tse-tung's "margarine Communists." American liberals and roving ambassadors may have been more naïve but they were also less offensive in believing the Chinese Communists to be "agrarian reformers."

III

How then did the Communist parties respond to the Comintern's dissolution? Its final document had some curious and pregnant phrases, alluding to "the fundamental differences in the historical development of the separate countries of the world"—differences, it was now discovered, which had "become apparent even before the war"; Communists were now told most authoritatively that they were "never advocates of the outmoded organizational forms." This suggests that a great watershed had been reached. The implicit self-criticism was bound to encourage those Western Communists for whom the "popular front" of the 1930s and the experience of the Spanish Republic were not defensive deceptions but major experiments in skirting the limits of Leninism. The Chinese Communists, as the specialized literature shows, saw in the disappearance of the Communist International a ratification of their own "New Democracy," in which the peasantry and the "national bourgeoisie" had been credited with revolutionary potentials for which no precedent existed in the Russian experience.

The most interesting instance of how new systems of ideas and new organizational forms were bursting the Leninist integument came in the minor party of a major country—among the American Communists. Their leader, Earl Browder, concluded that peaceful coexistence had become obligatory; he saw such coexistence as a whole historical stage in which the contradictions between antagonistic social systems would have to work themselves out—short of war; it is curious that he ruled out war as too dangerous to both sides *before* the advent of the atomic bomb. To give this very novel view some inner logic, Browder postulated a new type of state power, intermediate between capitalism and socialism, which, he thought, would prevail between the Atlantic and the Oder-Neisse Line. Thus he anticipated the "people's democracy" concept which was to have wide currency in the next few years only to be brusquely rejected by the end of 1948, when the Cold War demanded rationales of another kind.

To what extent Browder had sanction in Moscow, or only *thought* he had, or whether this sanction was even intended to be more than temporary are all fascinating matters; but for our discussion what seems more important is the fact that Browder revealed the incoherence of communism and tried to overcome it. Perhaps America was not as backward as European Communists traditionally assumed. The more advanced country was simply showing a mirror to the less advanced of the problems of their own future, to borrow an image from Marx.

One may put this dilemma in very specific terms. In 1944–1945, a quasi-revolutionary situation prevailed in key areas of Western Europe and East Asia. The Communist parties had become mass movements. They were no longer Leninist vanguards but had significant military experience. The old order had been discredited and few charismatic rivals existed. One of two options could be taken, each of them having its own logic. If the Communists seized power they might be able to hold it, as in Yugoslavia, with great good luck. But as the Greek experience was to show, the success of a prolonged civil war would involve the

rupture of the Anglo-Soviet-American coalition; and the war with Hitler
was by no means over, while the Pacific war appeared only begun. To
pursue this option meant to oblige the Soviet Union to assist revolutions
at a distance from its own armies at a moment of its own greatest weakness and when it seriously entertained the possibility of a long-range
postwar relationship with the West. Alternatively, the USSR would be
obliged to disavow its own ideological and political allies in an even
more explicit way than the dissolution of the Comintern suggested.
Stalin's entire diplomacy warned against revolution now. So did his
opinion, in a speech of November 6, 1944, that whatever disagreements
existed among the great powers could be overcome; he had said flatly
that "no accidental, transitory motive but vitally important long-term
interests lie at the basis of the alliance of our country, Great Britain and
the United States."

On the other hand, to reject the revolutionary path meant for the
Western parties (if not for the Chinese and Vietnamese) forgoing an
opportunity that might not return; for a generation this choice caused
intense misgivings and internal battles within these parties. To take part
in the wholehearted reconstruction of their societies on a less-than-
socialist basis would have involved a revision of fundamental Leninist
postulates, a fresh look at capitalism, and presumably a redefinition of
their relations with the Soviet Union. Having taken such a sharply Rus-
socentric course, could Stalin give his imprimatur to the embryonic
polycentrism of that time? The USSR was in the paradoxical position of
trying to be a great power with a shattered economic base, and of trying
to lead a world movement whose interests were quite distinct from those
of Russia, both in practice and in ideas. The ambiguities inherent in
communism, in Stalin's projections of 1927, had come home to roost.

I V

If one tries, then, to make intellectual sense and order out of the bewildering events between early 1945 and mid-1947, the least satisfactory
themes are the ones which have been so popular and have dominated
the discussion of the origins of the Cold War. The revisionist historians
are so hung up on the notion that a meticulous rediscovery of America
will reveal the clues to the Cold War that they ignore the dimensions of
communism altogether. They have little experience with communism
(and perhaps they are better off for it) but they have yet to show the
scholarship required to explore it. To say this is not to deny the value of
reappraising American policy, especially since so many of today's follies
have roots in the past. Communists, anti-Communists and ex-
Communists have all had troubles with the imperatives of coexistence.

But this is quite different from explaining the Cold War on one-sided grounds and succumbing to the elementary fallacy of *post hoc, propter hoc.*

On the other hand, the most sophisticated and persuasive rebuttal to the younger historians—that by Arthur Schlesinger, Jr., in these pages[2]—suffered from the limitations of his own major premise: the assumption that communism was a monolithic movement which disintegrated only as the Cold War was vigorously prosecuted. Certainly the monolith functioned in a pell-mell fashion after 1948, but one wonders whether its explosive decomposition in the late fifties, continuing to the events in Czechoslovakia, can be comprehended without realizing that all the elements of crisis within it were already present in its immediate postwar years. It was the futile attempts by Stalin and the Communists who everywhere followed him (even if hesitantly and in bewilderment) to stifle the nascent polycentrism and to curtail the inchoate attempts to adjust to new realities which constitute communism's own responsibility for the Cold War. Herein also is the key to communism's own disasters.

Thus, the events of 1946 and 1947 were in fact incoherent and contradictory, and for that very reason offer an important clue to the origins of Cold War. For example, Earl Browder was roundly denounced by the French Communist leader, Jacques Duclos, in an article written early in 1945 (with data that was available only in Moscow), on the grounds that the very concept of peaceful coexistence and Europe's reconstruction on a bourgeois-democratic basis was heresy; yet the curious thing is that most of the Communist parties continued to operate on Browder's assumptions—including the party led by Duclos. Such a state of affairs suggests that the Duclos article was not the tocsin of the Cold War but one of the elements of communism's incoherence. By the close of 1946, only the Yugoslavs—and William Z. Foster, who had ousted Browder in the United States—were convinced that even the "temporary stabilization" of capitalism was unlikely. This concept was of course an echo from the 1920s. "Relative and temporary stabilization" was Stalin's own justification in the late 1920s for "turning inward" and seeking a truce in external affairs. Ruling out this concept in the 1940s, Foster went even further than Tito in raising the alarm over an ever-more-imminent danger of an American attack on the Soviet Union. It is not generally known that when Browder's successor visited Europe in March 1947 he was amazed to find that few Communist leaders agreed with his views, and one of those who disagreed most sharply was Jacques Duclos.

In studying the French Communists of that period one finds unusual

[2]Arthur M. Schlesinger, Jr., "Origins of the Cold War," *Foreign Affairs* 46 (October 1967): 22–52.

emphasis on the need for a policy of "confident collaboration" with "all of the Allied nations, without exception," and a declaration by Duclos that "we are not among those who confuse the necessity and fertility of struggle with the spirit of adventurism. That is why—mark me well—we ask of a specific historic period what it can give and only what it can give . . . but we do not ask more, for we want to push ahead and not end up in abortive and disappointing failures."

In this same year of 1946, it is sometimes forgotten that the Chinese Communists negotiated seriously for a long-term coalition with Chiang Kai-shek. They did so under the aegis of General George Marshall, which suggests that their own antagonism to "American imperialism" had its limits; their view that the United States was necessarily hostile to a unified China with a large Communist component was a later development. During the recent Great Proletarian Cultural Revolution, Chinese historians blamed this coalition strategy on the now-disgraced Liu Shao Chi, alleging that he was under the influence of "Browder, Tagliatti, Thorez and other renegades to the proletariat." But the official Chinese Communist documents show that at the time Mao Tse-tung took credit for it and was himself viewed as a "revisionist"—by the Indian Communists, for example. In those same months, Ho Chi Minh led a coalition delegation to Paris, trying to work out the terms for remaining within the French Union; it is a curious but revealing detail that Ho had the previous winter dissolved his own creation, the Communist Party of Indochina, in favor of an Association of Marxist Studies, without, however, receiving a rebuke from Jacques Duclos.

Throughout 1946, almost every Communist leader in the West voiced the view that peaceful roads to socialism were not only desirable but were—because of obejctive changes in the world—now theoretically admissible. If in Eastern Europe this popularity of the "people's democracy" can be explained in terms of Stalin's attempt to stabilize a chaotic region of direct interest to Russia, in Western Europe it was part of a serious effort to implement the nonrevolutionary option which the Communists had chosen, and for which they needed a consistent justification.

Nor were the Soviet leaders immune to what was happening within communism. Stalin himself can be cited in contradictory assertions which also stimulated the diversity within the Communist world as well as baffling some of its members. Early in February 1946 Stalin declared that wars could not be abolished so long as imperialism prevailed; this came in his election campaign speech which is viewed by Sovietologists as another tocsin of the Cold War. Yet throughout 1946 Stalin gave interviews to British and American newsmen, and held a long discussion with Harold Stassen that spring, in which the key theme was the viability of peaceful coexistence. In September 1946 Stalin declared that the ruling circles of both Britain and the United States were *not* in fact oriented toward war—a view which Communists from China to Italy hailed, although it baffled Tito and William Z. Foster. Stalin also told a British Labor delegation headed by Harold Laski that socialism might well come to Britain by parliamentary means, with the monarchy remaining as a genuine institution. Earlier in the year, in a polemic with a certain Professor Razin on the significance of the doctrines of Clausewitz, Stalin is quoted as believing "it is impossible to move forward and advance science without subjecting outdated propositions and the judgments of well-known authorities to critical analysis. This applies . . . also to the classics of Marxism." Significantly, this exchange was published a full year later—in February 1947—on the eve of Cold War decisions which made such thinking heretical throughout the Communist movement.

Yet in 1946 Soviet diplomacy was in fact moving "with all deliberate speed" toward settlements of a partial kind with the West—as regards the peace treaties, the evacuation of northern Persia and other matters. Browder was cordially received in Moscow in May after his expulsion from the American party—a rather unprecedented detail in the annals of communism. The deposed Communist leader was heard out by Molotov, at the latter's request, and was given a post which enabled him to work energetically for the next two years in behalf of the proposition that Stalin wanted an American-Soviet settlement.

All students of this period have paused on the famous Varga controversy. The title of the book which the foremost Soviet economist, Eugen Varga, published in November 1946 (it was completed the year before) in itself suggests what was bothering Russian leaders, namely: *Changes in the Economy of Capitalism Resulting from the Second World War*. Within six months, Varga was under severe attack, which he resisted for the following two years. Major issues lay at the heart of the controversy. When might a crisis of overproduction be expected in the United States? How severe would it be? And to what extent would rearmament or a program for rebuilding Western Europe affect capitalism's inherent propensity for crisis, which was, of course, taken for granted. Another question was whether the new role of governmental power, so greatly enhanced by the war, might not have a bearing both on the onset of the crisis and the terrain of Communist activities. Varga did forecast an early crisis, after a brief postwar boom. In so doing, he surely misled Stalin into one of his most fundamental Cold War miscalculations. But Varga also clung to the view that something important had changed within classical capitalism; he insisted that "the question of greater or smaller participation in the management of the state will be the main content" of the political struggle in the West, and he deduced that people's democracy was in fact a transitional form between the two systems, replacing the "either-or" notions of classical Leninism. There was a plaintive protest in Varga's answer to his critics (one of whom was Vosnessensky, who would shortly disappear because of mysterious heresies of his own). "It is not a matter of enumerating all the facts so that they inevitably lead to the former conclusions of Marxism-Leninism," Varga argued, "but to use the Marxist-Leninist method in studying these facts. The world changes and the content of our work must change also."

V

In what sense, then, did all these crosscurrents determine Stalin's decision for Cold War? It would seem that the matter turned on the incompatibility between immediate Soviet objectives and the real interests of the Communist parties—or more exactly, in the particularly Stalinist answer to these incompatibilities. The Russians, it will be remembered, had set out to achieve rapid and ambitious reconstruction including, of course, the acquisition of nuclear weapons. They were most concerned with reparations. When it became plain that little help would come by loans or trade with the West (they had used up what was still in the pipelines after the abrupt cessation of lend-lease in mid-1945 and were not getting a response to their $6 billion request to Washington), they needed either the resources of Germany beyond what they could extract from their own Eastern Zone, or a desperate milking of their friends and former foes in Eastern Europe. At home, moreover, they could not rely on the ultrachauvinist themes which had served them during the war; rejecting liberalization of Soviet society, they tightened the screws and fell back on the doctrine of the primacy of the Soviet party, the purity of its doctrine and the universal validity of that doctrine. Consistent with these objectives, the Soviet leaders wanted to erase all sympathy for America which until then was widespread in the Soviet Union.[3]

These objectives, taken together, ran counter to all the tendencies among the foreign Communist parties. Both the revolutionary ambitions of the Yugoslavs, their jealous quest for autonomy as well as the emphasis on peaceful non-Soviet roads to socialism—that is, the "revisionist" themes so urgently needed by the parties in the West—could be countenanced by Moscow only if it were prepared to accept diversity

---

[3]This task was assigned to the late Ilya Ehrenburg following his 1947 visit to the States, when he deliberately oversimplified everything American with the crudest methods. The pattern for this had been set late in 1946 by Andrei Zhdanov.

within international communism. This very diversity (which they had themselves half entertained) now became an obstacle. The Stalinist premise that what was good for Russia was good for all other Communists (a notion which he himself considered abandoning) was now reaffirmed.

The origins of the Cold War lie deeper, however, than any analysis of Russia's own interest. Nor can they be understood only in terms of an attempt to prevent economic recovery and political stability in Western Europe. The Cold War's origins must be found in a dimension larger than the requirements of Soviet internal mobilization or the thrust of its foreign policy; they lie in the attempt to overcome the incipient diversity within a system of states and parties, among whom the changes produced by the war had outmoded earlier ideological and political premises. The conditions for the transformation of a monolithic movement had matured and ripened. The sources of the Cold War lie in communism's unsuccessful attempt to adjust to this reality, followed by its own abortion of this attempt. For Stalin the Cold War was a vast tug-of-war with the West, whereby not only internal objectives could be realized but the international movement subordinated; its constituent parts went along—bewildered but believing—on the assumption that in doing so, they would survive and prosper. The price of the Stalinist course was to be fearsome indeed; and by 1956 the Soviet leaders were to admit that the Cold War had damaged the USSR more than the West, that a stalemate of systems had to be acknowledged, and ineluctable conclusions had to be drawn. Thus, the Cold War arose from the failure of a movement to master its inner difficulties and choose its alternatives.

The analysis could be continued to the turning-point of mid-1947—the Marshall Plan decision and Stalin's riposte, for example, in humiliating his Czechoslovak and Polish partners, who thought in terms of what might be good for them, and indirectly for the Soviet Union. Such an analysis would take us through the near insurrections of late 1947 in France and Italy, adventurist upheavals in Asia, the Berlin blockade and the coup in Prague in 1948. But this involves another subject—how the Cold War was fought. It was indeed fought by both sides. But to say this cannot obscure the crisis within communism, where its origins lie. The record would show how recklessly entire Communist movements were expended and to what a dangerous brink the Soviet Union itself was brought. In 1956, Khrushchev was to lament these miscalculations but he did so with such a *desinvolture* as to leave a memory bank of disasters and skeletons that still rattle in communism's closets. Was the Cold War but a test of strength between systems? Or has it not also been the process whereby communism disclosed such an intellectual and political bankruptcy that a dozen years after Khrushchev's revelations, the issues still agonize—as in Czechoslovakia—all the states and parties involved? A world movement claiming to comprehend history and accepting the responsibility for "making history" still grapples with the alternatives opened by the Second World War. It has yet to face what it has tried to avoid at such a heavy cost to coexistence—namely, understanding itself.

11

Americans at Home After World War II
Consensus to Crisis?

Americans have always been ambivalent in their perceptions of their past. On the one hand, they have interpreted their history in terms of progress, growing freedom, and greater morality. On the other, they have seen their past as flawed by imperfections, goals that were not achieved, and virtues that remained unrealized. These conflicting views were often a matter of perspective, representing two sides of the same coin and constituting a differing degree of emphasis. Such was the case when American historians and other intellectuals came to evaluate developments within their society in the recent past.

In the two decades after 1945, many intellectuals looked upon American society with some degree of self-satisfaction. Generally speaking, they viewed the years from 1945 to 1965 as a period of contentment, consensus, and conformity. During these two decades there appeared to be widespread agreement among Americans on certain shared values and the distinctive features of national life. The period 1965 to 1980, on the other hand, was seen as an era characterized by unrest, crisis, and conflict. In these fifteen years, consensus seemed to be replaced by sharply divided views on foreign and domestic affairs within society. America's involvement in the Vietnam War after 1965 seemed to be the watershed event that divided the two periods.

Underlying the decades of consensus and conformity lay two of the most revolutionary developments in all of American history. First, the twenty-year period (1945–1965) constituted the longest period of sustained high prosperity in the country's past. Second, as the United States assumed the new role of leader of the free world, the Cold War reshaped America's image of itself and its relationship to the rest of the world. There were periods of anxiety during the Cold War era, to be sure, but these two changes contributed to the dominant mood of national self-confidence that marked American down in the mid-1960s.

The mood of prosperity and self-confidence was reflected in the continuity of domestic policies of the presidents in power during the 1950s and early 1960s. Whether they were Republicans or Democrats, the policies of Presidents Truman, Eisenhower, Kennedy, and Johnson symbolized a carry-over of Franklin D. Roosevelt's New Deal in many ways. These presidents did not dismantle on-going New Deal programs; they all continued to further the growth of the welfare state in America. The new role of the United States as leader of the free world fostered this development; as the powers of the federal government were expanded to meet national security needs it became easier to implement domestic social welfare programs.

There appeared to be a consensus among the American people in their willingness to accept the liberal policies of these presidents. Truman carried forward the policies inaugurated by Franklin D. Roosevelt in such legislation as the Employment Act of 1946, which committed the nation to maintaining full employment during periods of recession. Although a Republican, Eisenhower enacted programs reminiscent of the New Deal with the creation of the Department of Health, Education, and Welfare, and extension of social security to more persons, and the expansion of public housing. Kennedy proposed more federal aid to provide better medical care for the aged and expanded educational opportunities for the young. Johnson's Great Society program went the furthest of all. They provided Medicare to the aged, public housing for the poor, federal funds for depressed cities and regions, and massive federal grants for education.

American society as a result of such domestic changes seemed to grow more homogeneous and more stable during these years. The country, up to 1965—except for the McCarthy period—appeared to be less divided by conflict or by sectional and class differences than ever before. This feeling of mastery over domestic affairs was evident in the writing of many intellectuals who stressed the twin themes of consensus and conformity.

America's foreign policy during the 1950s to the mid-1960s, which was aimed at stopping the spread of communism, likewise led to conformity. The United States, viewing itself as leader of the free world, experienced great apprehension in countering Communist Russia lest a confrontation lead to a nuclear war. This sense of anxiety caused many Americans to develop a siege mentality and to become less tolerant toward anyone criticizing the American way of life. At the same time, Congress became more anxious about the issue of national security, and, at times, passed repressive laws to check on the loyalty of some American citizens.

The Cold War era heightened the conformist climate of opinion in the United States in many ways. Most Americans backed the government's foreign policy, and in the interests of national security were willing to accept more government controls and restrictions on civil liberties. Taking advantage of this prevailing mood, Senator Joseph McCarthy of Wisconsin launched a fierce anti-Communist campaign from 1950 to 1954 to rid America of supposed Soviet sympathizers in its midst. Although McCarthy's charge that American Communists or "fellow travelers" had infiltrated the national government proved false, his investigation into the presumed disloyalty of government officials did great harm. McCarthy's "Red Scare" provoked an attack on civil liberties on a scale almost unprecedented in American history.[1]

The tendency toward conformity during the 1950s and early 1960s affected many American intellectuals and none more so than the group of historians called the neoconservatives. These scholars adopted a conservative approach and emphasized consensus and continuity when interpreting American history. They rejected the older Progressive view of history which had stressed conflict and discontinuity in America's past. Responding to the great menace presumably posed by communism during the Cold War era, the neoconservatives—either consciously or subconsciously—presented to the world a historical image of an America that had been strong, stable, and united throughout most of its past.

One of the most prominent neoconservative scholars was Louis Hartz, who stressed the idea of continuity in American history. Hartz, whose book *The Liberal Tradition in America* appeared in 1955, concluded that the key fact in the nation's history was that America was founded after the age of European feudalism. Hence, America never developed the conservative social institutions that characterized the *ancien régime*. America was "born free," a liberal society at its inception, and had never known anything but a liberal tradition throughout its history. To Hartz this consensus on the liberal tradition was the single synthesis that explained all of American history.

Daniel J. Boorstin, the outstanding exponent of the neoconservative position, took a somewhat different tack. He emphasized the shared principles that gave the American way of life its distinctiveness. Boorstin

---

[1]There is a historiographical controversy regarding the origins of McCarthyism. Richard Rovere, *Senator Joseph McCarthy* (New York, 1959), attributed McCarthy's rise to his gifts as a demagogue. Earl Latham, *Communist Controversy in Washington from the New Deal to McCarthy* (Cambridge, 1966), claimed anticommunism was politically inspired by the hatred of the New Deal rather than the fear of Russia, and that the danger to national security was never serious. Daniel Bell, ed., *The Radical Right* (New York, 1955), provided a "status anxiety" explanation for the rise of McCarthyism. Richard Hofstader, *The Paranoid Style in American Politics and Other Essays* (New York, 1965), had similar insights into McCarthyism. Michael Paul Rogin, *The Intellectuals and McCarthy: The Radical Specter* (Cambridge, 1967), refuted the argument that McCarthyism grew out of earlier populism and attributed its rise to a traditional conservative heritage.

wrote two books in the 1950s which denied that European ideas or influences had any impact upon America. The American way of life, he argued, was essentially pragmatic in character, and was formed by the experience of dealing with the environment in setting and developing a huge, rich continent. In the course of time, this nontheoretical approach became a distinctive American life-style—one noted for its practicality, which enabled the American people to unite and to become a homogeneous society made up of undifferentiated men sharing the same values.[2]

But the consensus perspective was not the only view to emerge in the 1950s and 1960s, nor were historians the only intellectuals to be affected by the national mood. Some social scientists searched for the sources of the conformity that appeared to be manifest among the American people during this period. Other scholars turned to the study of the American national character in an effort to explain why Americans in the immediate postwar period seemed to be so complacent and willing to conform to the dominant values of their times. There was also a resurgence of conservative social thinkers, giving rise to the movement known as the "new conservatism."

Among the social scientists who looked for explanations of conformity was Erich Fromm, the psychoanalyst. Fromm addressed himself on a broad scale to the social and cultural forces that seemed to bring anxiety and insecurity to Western man in general in the twentieth century. In his book *Escape from Freedom*, written in 1941, Fromm had advanced the hypothesis that much of the vaunted freedom for the individual which Western society, including America, supposedly had achieved led to greater insecurity rather than to security and peace. Freedom for the individual frequently led to a terrifying sense of helplessness and inadequacy. Western man, he argued, sought to escape from freedom by fleeing into the arms of a dictator or into the mindless middle-class conformity that characterized much of Western democratic culture. In his book *The Sane Society*, written in the mid-1950s, Fromm continued to argue that modern man became a prisoner of the very institutions he had created to free himself from the past.

The renewed interest in the study of the American national character sought also to explain the apparent trend toward conformism among Americans. Some behavioral scientists developed an interpretation of the American national character that focused primarily upon culture as

---

[2]Daniel J. Boorstin, *The Genius of American Politics* (Chicago, 1953) and *The Americans: The Colonial Experience* (New York, 1958). Boorstin subsequently completed his trilogy with *The Americans: The National Experience* (New York, 1965) and *The Americans: The Democratic Experience* (New York, 1973).

the main determinant in shaping personality. Other scholars turned to a historical explanation. These scholars tended to emphasize materialistic forces—economic, environmental, or technological—as the crucial factors in the formation of national character and the development of an American value system.

The groundwork for certain studies done by the behavioral scientists in the 1950s was laid by the distinguished cultural anthropologist Margaret Mead, in one of the most significant books written about the American national character. In *And Keep Your Powder Dry*, published in 1942, Mead argued that any analysis of the American character must take into account the fact that American life is geared to success rather than to status. The average American conceived of class hierarchy as a constantly ascending ladder rather than a fixed system that would provide permanent status. From this situation came a second feature of the American character—the excessive concern for conformity. She suggested that immigrants after they had become Americanized rejected the standards of the culture from which they came and sought to perfect their conformity to American ways in order to win the approbation of their American neighbors.

David Riesman, a social psychologist, offered yet another view of the problem in his book *The Lonely Crowd: A Study of the Changing American Character*, published in 1950. In this work Riesman postulated a change in the American national character from the nineteenth-century individualist with an "inner-directed personality" to the twentieth-century conformist with an "other-directed personality." Most nineteenth-century Americans had worked in an agrarian rural society in which success depended upon their own resources in overcoming the physical environment. The development of the "other-directed personality" of the twentieth century was due in large part to technological and economic changes that made for a more interdependent world. Twentieth-century Americans were placed in types of employment where success depended more on gaining favor and interacting with other individuals. Thus, many modern Americans conducted their lives in such a way as to gain approval from the people around them. In other words, Riesman argued that, since goals in life had become externalized to a large extent, Americans sought the approval of their neighbors rather than looking to themselves and their own values for direction.

William H. Whyte, a journalist, offered an interpretation that stressed the same theme in his book *The Organization Man*, published in 1956. The "organization man," according to Whyte, was a bureaucratized individual whose conformity resulted from the fact that he lived under an imperative to succeed in corporate management where promotion and even survival depended upon effective interaction with others

432   *Americans at Home After World War II*

in a hierarchical structure. The old Protestant work ethic, said Whyte, had been replaced by a new social ethic which legitimized the pressures of society now placed on individuals. The articles of faith of this new social ethic were as follows: "a belief in the group as the source of creativity; a belief in 'belongingness' as the ultimate need of the individual; and a belief in the application of science to achieve the belongingness."[3] An essay that ultimately formed a part of Whyte's book is the first selection in this chapter.

One of the most provocative historical interpretations of the nature of the American character came from David Potter's book *People of Plenty: Economic Abundance and the American Character*, published in 1954. Although a historian, Potter made heavy use of social science concepts in approaching the problem. To Potter the most important influence in shaping the American character was the country's economic abundance, which molded its values and outlook. The abundance of goods produced from the seemingly unlimited natural resources had increased the rewards of competition in production and resulted in placing an increased premium on efficiency. The emphasis on efficiency in the process of competition favored those who were the most aggressive and eager to reap the promised rewards by taking advantage of the unrestricted latitude given to entrepreneurs. The appetite for rewards, however, outstripped the possibility of attaining them, and the desire to gain individual freedom and mobility clashed with the responsibilities and limitations of real life. The quest for abundance led Americans to abandon the system of status and to trade security for opportunity, thereby resulting in an element of anxiety within the American character.

Potter employed the concept of abundance to explain many of the peculiar traits of the American character. In the United States, for example, the idea of equality came to mean equality in competition or opportunity for social mobility. But in committing themselves to such a concept of equality, Americans deprived many people of the security inherent in the idea of status, thereby giving rise to many psychological insecurities. Potter's book, which reflected the society of plenty during the 1950s, was very much a tract of the times.

Another group of intellectuals, called the "new conservatives," sought to understand the great social and economic changes of the 1950s from a different perspective. Peter Viereck, a poet and educator, in his book *The Shame and Glory of the Intellectuals* stressed the theme of conservatism. Viereck argued that genuine freedom could exist only in an orderly setting. The truly free man was one whose life was guided by an

---

[3]William H. Whyte, *The Organization Man* (New York, 1956), p. 7.

ethical inner check and the heritage of classical philosophy and religion rather than being dependent upon the coercive restraints of society.[4]

Viereck's ideas were echoed by a whole host of like-minded men including Russell Kirk, historian-philosopher, and Clinton Rossiter, the American historian. In virtually all of this literature, the "new conservatives" relied on the principles of Edmund Burke, the English critic of the French Revolution, and reexamined them in an effort to demonstrate their applicability to the revolutionary changes of the post–World War II era. Conservatism in the Burkean sense, as Russell Kirk pointed out, was not something new in American intellectual history; it had a tradition stretching back to men like John Adams, John C. Calhoun, and Henry and Brooks Adams. What gave the movement importance in the 1950s was its attempt to judge the events of the postwar decade from a fixed vantage point rooted in Western thought. The "new conservatism," although not accepted by the majority of Americans, represented an important element in contemporary thinking during the 1950s.[5]

Early in the 1960s, Daniel Bell, a sociologist, summarized in his book *The End of Ideology* the social changes that had occurred in America during the 1950s. The decade had been marked by what he felt to be extraordinary changes: alterations in the class structure with the growth of the white-collar class; a "forced" expansion of the economy; the creation of a permanent military establishment; the buildup of an economy based on defense; and the heightening of Cold War tensions. These changes led to an exhaustion of political ideas among the intellectuals in the West in general and those in America in particular. For those persons raised in the school of Marxist polemics, the politics of the 1950s were lacking in interest for two reasons: the old rules of the dialogue and debate between rightist and leftist elements in society were gone; and the sense of excitement in the intellectual play of ideas was missing. Bell concluded that the ideas of the "Old Left," Marxist or otherwise, would no longer be able to furnish formulas for proposed social changes. Bell's work implied that the end of ideology in American politics symbolized the emergence of a consensus, and that new ideas or developments would probably originate in Cuba or the new nations in Africa rather than in America.

The decades from 1945 to 1965, in summary, were generally seen by many intellectuals as a time when there was a considerable degree of

---

[4]Peter Viereck, *The Shame and Glory of the Intellectuals* (Boston, 1953). See also his *Conservatism Revisited* (New York, 1959), and Robert Nisbet, *Quest for Community* (New York, 1953).

[5]Russell Kirk, *The Conservative Mind* (Chicago, 1953); Clinton Rossiter, *Conservative Tradition in America* (New York, 1955).

agreement within the society and a tendency among Americans to conform to this national mood. Such intellectuals tended to stress the continuities that persisted throughout the period that presumably brought about such developments—the affluence of Americans leading to a society of plenty, and the anxiety arising from American efforts to contain the spread of communism. Other intellectuals, however, disagreed with this view and felt that such a description oversimplified a complex era. They pointed to other developments that gave evidence of diversity and divisiveness within the society: the controversies over the Korean War and McCarthyism; the civil rights movement that began in the 1950s; and the poverty in America during the period of supposed affluence.[6] The generalization that these two decades were characterized by consensus and conformity appears to have considerable merit, though, like most generalizations, it needs to be qualified lest it lead to an oversimplification.

The period from 1965 to 1980, on the other hand, was often depicted as one of continuing crisis, unrest, and conflict. Dramatic developments in domestic and foreign affairs led many intellectuals to view this tumultuous era as being divided into two major crises. In each of these crises, many scholars tended to reflect in their writings the developments of each period.

The first crisis, comprising roughly the years 1965 to 1972, was social and ideological in nature. It was marked by widespread hostility and violence arising from different social movements: the civil rights movement; antiwar demonstrations against the involvement in Vietnam; and the rise of a counterculture among the youth of America.

The second crisis, beginning with Richard Nixon's second administration in 1973 and carrying through to the election of Ronald Reagan in 1980, was more political and economic in character. From a political point of view, there was a growing lack of confidence in American institutions—in political parties as voter participation continued to drop

[6]For the Korean War, see David Rees, *Korea: The Limited War* (New York, 1964) and John W. Spanier, *The Truman-MacArthur Controversy and the Korean War* (New York, 1965). Norman V. Bartley's *The Rise of Massive Resistance* (Baton Rogue, 1969) covers the issue of race and politics in the South in the 1950s. The problem of poverty is dealt with in two books by John K. Galbraith, *The Affluent Society* (Boston, 1958) and *The New Industrial State* (Boston, 1967). But the public consciousness of poverty in the period was raised more specifically by Michael Harrington, *The Other America* (New York, 1962). One of the most outspoken critics of the conservative perspective was C. Wright Mills, an outstanding radical sociologist. See his influential, *The Power Elite* (New York, 1956), in which he argued that American politics could be best understood in terms of a "power elite" within the country.

sharply; in the presidency as the result of Watergate; and in the idea that federal money and federal policy could cure any societal problem. Increasing numbers of Americans, as a result, began to question the liberal domestic politics that had characterized America since the days of the New Deal. In the economic sphere, mounting inflation caused in part by the importation of foreign oil at high prices, recessions in 1973–1974 and in 1980, and rising unemployment undermined the sense of prosperity Americans had enjoyed since the end of World War II.

The renewed drive for civil rights by blacks proved to be one of the most important social movements to emerge during the first period of crisis. Although the civil rights movement had a long history, its most recent development began in 1954 with the Supreme Court decision of *Brown et al. v. Board of Education of Topeka*. In that ruling the Court overturned the principle of "separate but equal" schools established in 1896 which had permitted the segregation of black and white children. Integration of schools proceeded very slowly, however, during the 1960s.[7]

But in the mid-1960s, the civil rights movement expanded in scope and increased in intensity. As the movement grew, black leaders became divided over goals and means. In the early part of the decade, the civil rights movement focused mainly on the continuation of the program of nonviolent activism initiated in the 1950s which sought integration and equal rights as its goal. The key spokesman and leading intellectual for this movement was the Reverend Martin Luther King, Jr., who had developed an ethic of nonviolence by borrowing ideas from Gandhi, Tolstoy, Thoreau, and the Bible. His books *Stride Toward Freedom* (1958) and *Why We Can't Wait* (1964) explained his position. King emphasized the need for redemption through Christian love and advocated peaceful tactics like boycotts and sit-ins as means of accomplishing integration.

As the 1960s progressed, however, black leaders split over the strategy to be followed in achieving racial justice.[8] Some younger black leaders rejected the goal of integration and nonviolent means, advocating instead "Black Power"—a militant term which came to symbolize the idea of separation of blacks from white society. Malcolm X and Stokely Carmichael, two prominent leaders, argued that blacks should take greater pride in their cultural heritage and color, and not seek integra-

---

[7]For the background of civil liberties gained through court decisions during the decades of the 1950s and 1960s, see: Milton Konvitz, *Expanding Liberties: Freedom's Gains in Post-War America* (New York, 1966); Anthony Lewis, *Gideon's Trumpet* (New York, 1964); and Archibald Cox, *The Warren Court, Constitutional Decision as an Instrument of Reform* (Cambridge, 1968),

[8]See Harold Cruse, *The Crisis of the Negro Intellectual* (New York, 1967); August Meier and Elliott Rudwick, eds., *Black Protest in the Sixties* (New York, 1970); and Benjamin Muse, *The American Negro Revolution* (Bloomington, 1968).

tion into American society. *The Autobiography of Malcolm X* (1967) reflected the new militancy and willingness of some younger blacks to resort to violence. This trend was best exemplified by the formation of the Black Panthers, a group of young people who armed themselves. Eldridge Cleaver's *Soul on Ice* (1967) portrayed what went into the making of a Black Panther.[9]

The second major development contributing to a sense of crisis in the years 1965–1972 was America's deepening involvement in the Vietnam War. As a result of the adverse reaction to Vietnam, many scholars began to look anew at the history of American foreign policy. William Appleman Williams in his *The Tragedy of American Diplomacy*, published in 1959, had already revised the traditional interpretation of American diplomatic history.

Williams sought to interpret America's foreign relations from the point of view of the country's domestic history. America from its origins had been expansionist, Williams argued. Before the American Revolution, the colonies had adopted a mercantilist course that would have enabled them to gain economic self-sufficiency within the British Empire. After gaining its independence, the United States committed itself to the idea of an independent American empire and pursued a policy of expansionism led by the country's agrarian interests against the Indians, Spanish, and Mexicans in North America. With the close of the frontier in the 1890s, the idea of expansion was taken over by business interests who embarked upon a policy of economic imperialism. They aimed primarily at acquiring markets for American goods, outlets for surplus capital, and raw materials for domestic manufacturers. This policy was undertaken to prevent any social unrest that might follow as a result of industrial overproduction and economic depressions. The outcome was global expansionism based upon an Open Door policy by which America sought to dominate foreign markets and resources without necessarily acquiring new territory or colonies. In short, America created an informal empire. To Williams the post–World War II period represented an extension of this Open Door policy to all parts of the world. The Cold War, according to Williams, was caused primarily by America's seeking to extend its economic influence and to maintain its informal empire.

Walter LaFeber developed and expanded Williams's thesis in a book dealing with the Cold War published in 1967. LaFeber criticized both the United States and the Soviet Union for failing to keep the peace, and focused upon domestic developments within the two countries to ex-

---

[9]For the massive resistance by white Americans in the South against racial integration of public school systems, see Bob Smith, *They Closed Their Schools: Prince Edward County, Virginia, 1951–1964* (Chapel Hill, 1965); James W. Silver, *Mississippi: The Closed Society* (New York, 1964); and Russell H. Barrett, *Integration in Old Miss* (Chicago, 1965).

plain their foreign policies. Viewing the Cold War as a struggle that began in Europe and then spread to the rest of the world, LaFeber saw it as a clash between the two powers to maintain their freedom of action in those regions they considered vital to their economic and strategic interests. The Vietnam War, LaFeber concluded, represented a failure of America's foreign policy because it sought to solve global political and economic problems by military means. During the 1960s, critics of America's Vietnam policy seized upon the writings of Williams and LaFeber to support their positions.[10]

The civil rights movement and the antiwar protests of the 1960s generated a high level of violence within the United States. Scholars writing in the 1960s who dealt with violence as a subject took issue with the neoconservative historians of the 1950s who had stressed consensus. Neoconservatives like Hartz and Boorstin had not denied that America had a violent past. But they had emphasized that America's lack of a feudal past had not given rise to the class hostilities that caused violent upheavals in Europe, and that most Americans did not take ideology seriously enough to be deeply divided by it. Scholars of the 1960s who examined collective violence in the United States came to different conclusions. One of the most notable studies on the subject was the report of the National Commission on the Causes and Prevention of Violence, entitled *Violence in America,* published in 1969. This study not only concluded that collective and individual violence was common in the nation's past, but suggested also that it was a normal aspect of American political life. Violence, it was shown, arose from the unsettled social and cultural arrangements characteristic of America, and from the difficulties of relieving the fears and satisfying the anxieties of many peoples living under fluid social circumstances. This view not only helped to explain contemporary violence, but also directly contradicted the image of a homogeneous past presented by the neoconservative scholars.[11]

The third development during the period 1965–1972 which created a sense of crisis was the renewed expression of individualism among various segments of American society. There was an increasing rejection of authority, a growing sense of social permissiveness, and a challenge to conventional cultural mores. Protest movements by blacks and antiwar demonstrators had raised the consciousness of other social groups— such as women and the youth of America—who sought greater recogni-

---

[10]Walter LaFeber, *America, Russia, and the Cold War* (New York, 1967). Not all of the criticism of America's Vietnam policy drew inspiration from the New Left. See Senator James W. Fulbright's *The Arrogance of Power* (New York, 1966) and Frances Fitzgerald, *Fire in the Lake* (Boston, 1972).

[11]Hugh D. Graham and Ted R. Gurr, eds., *Violence in America* (New York, 1969). See also Richard Hofstadter and Michael Wallace, eds., *American Violence: A Documentary History* (New York, 1970).

tion of their role in society. Both the women's liberation movement and the youth culture aimed to change the self-image and life-styles of the individuals involved in these movements.

The heightened sense of individualism among women could be seen in the rapid rise of the feminist movement, which revolutionized the way in which women thought of themselves and their place in society. Betty Friedan's book *The Feminine Mystique,* published in 1963, marked the beginning of the new feminism. Friedan argued that the "feminine mystique," which most American women accepted, could be attributed to the social conditioning to which they were exposed in their upbringing. The family, school, and mass media all conditioned women to accept the traditional roles of mothers and housewives. Women were indoctrinated to accept domesticity, their role as "sex objects," and consumerism as a way of life. American society was dominated by white males, and the social conventions they espoused prevented women from ever reaching their full potential as human beings.[12]

Another significant manifestation of individualism was the new-found self-consciousness among American youth—the counterculture. This movement represented, in part, a reaction against the conformity that seemed to have characterized much of the 1950s. The youth cult of the sixties challenged many of the accepted ideas and ideals of American society. Young people objected to what they considered to be the materialism, hypocrisy, and lack of sensitivity of the older generation. They attacked the competitiveness, status-seeking, and conformity that seemed to them to characterize American life. The result was a challenge to many of the confining standards of middle-class American society. The "straight" American of the 1950s—wearing short hair and neatly dressed—gave way to the "hippie" of the late 1960s who was often bearded, long-haired, and sometimes dressed in outlandish clothing. Turning to sex, drugs, music, and, at times, political radicalism, this segment of youth rejected an American middle-class culture that seemed alien and artificial to them.[13]

Theodore Roszak, the historian who coined the phrase "counterculture," wrote a book in 1969 called *The Making of a Counter-Culture,* which

---

[12]The literature on the women's liberation movement is voluminous, but a good general work is William Chafe, *The American Woman: 1920-1970* (New York, 1972). See also Carl Degler, *At Odds* (New York, 1980) and Lois S. Banner, *Women in Modern America* (New York, 1974). There has been no attempt made here to cover other social groups—racial minorities like the Chicanos and American Indians, or dependent groups like the poor and elderly—who were also involved in protest movements during this period.

[13]The literature on the counterculture and youth movement is vast, and much of it superficial. One serious attempt to place the phenomenon in a much broader setting is Lewis S. Feuer, *The Conflict of Generations* (New York, 1969). See also the books by Kenneth Keniston, *Youth and Dissent: The Rise of a New Opposition* (New York, 1972); *The Young Radicals* (New York, 1968); and *The Uncommitted* (New York, 1965).

sought to trace the causes of the crisis among American youth. He described America's young people as profoundly alienated from the parental generation because they questioned the conventional world-view which stressed science, logic, and reason. The young placed great emphasis instead on emotion and feeling. They were seeking a new way of life, Roszak concluded, one that rejected the hypocrisy, racism, sexism, and callousness to social problems that seemed to characterize the older generation. They rejected the discipline, hard work, and highly organized institutions of the adult world in favor of a more relaxed life-style. Roszak's reflections captured the essence of the opposition of youth to America's technocratic society.

Another work that caught the spirit of the youth movement was Charles Reich's *The Greening of America,* published in 1970. A law professor at Yale University, Reich sought to place the youth movement within a historical context by showing how a technocratic society sacrificed individualistic and humanistic values. Reich described two earlier ages—Consciousness I and Consciousness II—when earlier ideals of American enterprise, material success, and the corporation life had been fully accepted. He predicted the coming of a new age—Consciousness III—in which the corporate society would be rejected and individuals would live in a genuine communitarian spirit instead. His book created great sympathy for the rebellious younger generation, but it appeared at precisely the time when the youth movement was losing its force.

The view of the 1960s as a decade of crisis and dissent was best expressed, perhaps, in William O'Neill's informal history of the period called *Coming Apart,* published in 1971. O'Neill's aim was to describe the process of polarization in American society that occurred between Kennedy's coming to power in 1960 and the beginning of Nixon's presidency in 1969. His book depicted the 1960s as a period of great social tension, stress, and divisiveness. He chronicled the change in the climate of opinion which went from optimism and hope at the start of the decade to pessimism and despair. Domestic problems grew serious—the black struggle, student rebellions, and antiwar protests drove the American people apart in a way that would have been unimaginable in the 1950s. O'Neill emphasized especially the crucial role the Vietnam War played in bringing about the increasing fragmentation of society.[14]

The turmoil of the 1960s gave rise to a new group of radical scholars—the New Left—who attacked the neoconservative interpretation of American history. Left-wing critiques of American society had existed throughout the twentieth century, but such attacks seemed to diminish during the conformity that characterized the decade of the

---

[14]For an analysis of more formal ideas and systems of thought in the 1960s, see Ronald Berman, *America in the Sixties* (New York, 1968).

1950s. The sense of crisis generated in the 1960s—particularly by the hostility to the Vietnam War—brought with it a new condemnation of capitalism by New Left scholars. They shared a general belief that what American society needed was a thoroughgoing reformation.

Unlike the "Old Left," however, the New Left varied widely in its assessment of the problems facing the nation and the proper remedies to be employed. The New Left included a number of historians who produced revisionist studies in many fields—labor, politics, and urban history. But their most important contributions were in the area of American diplomatic history. Building on the works of the older Progressive historians as well as the volumes written by William Appleman Williams and Walter LaFeber, they produced revisionist works that reinterpreted America's role in world affairs. Most of them started from the general assumption that America's foreign policy had invariably been based on the nation's need for markets for its goods and raw materials for its manufacturers. Joyce and Gabriel Kolko, for example, were especially critical of America's part in bringing on the Cold War. Other New Left scholars were equally harsh in condemning America's involvement in the Vietnam War. The revisionist outlook of the New Left touched off a spirited historiographical controversy that affected many works written on numerous subjects.[15]

When America's political and economic institutions were subjected to severe stresses and strains during the second period of crisis—1973–1980—many scholars shifted their attention in their writings to these matters. First, confidence in the authority of America's political institutions declined perceptibly during the period. The Watergate affair of 1973–1974—during which the country faced its greatest constitutional crisis since the Civil War and Reconstruction period—helped to undermine the faith Americans had had in the political system. Second, there were persistent problems in the American economy as a result of the following conditions: the energy crisis arising from the Arab oil embargo of 1973–1974; the maldistribution of natural resources within the United States and throughout the world; and the continuing economic stagna-

---

[15]Stephen Ambrose, *The Rise of Globalism: American Foreign Policy Since 1938* (London, 1971) along with LaFeber's *America, Russia, and the Cold War* represent revisionist studies of the Cold War period in general. Joyce Kolko and Gabriel Kolko, *The Limits of Power: The World and United States Foreign Policy, 1945–1954* (New York, 1972), and Lloyd C. Gardner, *Architects of Illusion: Men and Ideas in American Foreign Policy* (Chicago, 1970) are more specific revisionist studies.

There is a burgeoning literature on the revisionists of the Cold War. Two representative works are Robert J. Maddox, *The New Left and the Origins of the Cold War* (Princeton, 1973), and Robert W. Tucker, *The Radical Left and American Foreign Policy* (Baltimore, 1971).

tion caused by excessive inflation and unemployment. Third, in the area of foreign affairs a growing sense of national insecurity among citizens as the limits of America's power were revealed by the defeat in Vietnam and the confrontation with Iran. Finally, American liberalism itself faced a state of crisis. The old liberal coalition built during the days of Franklin Delano Roosevelt fell apart; large numbers of voters increasingly rejected any identification with either party—Democratic or Republican. These political developments not only contributed to a sense of crisis after 1973 but to a growing wave of conservatism that seemingly swept the country.

The first shock to America's political system in the period came as the result of the failure in Vietnam. Despite President Nixon's claim that the end of the war brought "peace with honor," Vietnam was, in fact, a defeat for the United States. The conduct of the Vietnam War resulted eventually in the loss of public confidence in one of America's most important political institutions—the presidency. President Lyndon Johnson left office almost in disgrace in 1968 because of his Vietnam War policy, refusing to run for another term lest he be repudiated by the voters. President Richard Nixon, in turn, became so alarmed at the liberal and radical criticism of his foreign policy in Vietnam that he authorized wiretaps and break-ins allegedly to uncover leaks of classified information to the press. This disregard for constitutional and legal principles led to Nixon's undoing when members of his White House Staff became involved in the Watergate affair. Faced with impeachment proceedings for personally ordering a cover-up of the Watergate scandal, Nixon announced his resignation on August 9, 1974. His resignation marked the close of a major constitutional crisis: Nixon became the first president to resign from office and to be forced out of his post.

Arthur M. Schlesinger, Jr., however, set the Nixon presidency within a broad historical perspective in his book *The Imperial Presidency*, published in 1973. Schlesinger showed that the passivity of Congress— encouraged by the Cold War, three decades of world crises following World War II, and successive strong presidents—had eventually enabled the executive branch to gain the upper hand in governance. Two presidents—Johnson and Nixon—strengthened the warmaking powers of the executive out of all proportion to the authority exercised by their predecessors. Both these presidents had claimed an inherent executive power to send American troops into combat when there was no immediate threat to the country, and when neither Congress nor the United Nations had authorized such action. Schlesinger was particularly harsh on Nixon's political style while in office: his psychological need for regal display in dressing up the uniforms of White House guards; his penchant for seclusion; his paranoid belief that the nation was swarming with his personal enemies; and his use of federal monies for personal purposes.[16] By setting the Nixon presidency in a larger context, Schlesinger was able to demonstrate that the accretion of executive power had taken place over a much longer period of time.

The economic vulnerability of the United States was exposed during the Arab oil embargo of 1973. A number of Arab nations, as a result of the war in the Middle East with Israel, had earlier formed the Organization of Oil Exporting Countries (OPEC). When OPEC imposed its oil embargo, the United States found itself facing a critical energy crisis. Americans—a "people of plenty," as David Potter had called them— were suddenly confronted with the prospect of scarcity.

Richard Barnet, an economic and political analyst, in his book *The Lean Years,* published in 1980, discussed the coming of what he called an "age of scarcity." Barnet's book was an exposé, in part, of the important role that the great oil companies—the so-called Seven Sisters—played in America's economy after the energy crisis of 1973–1974. Barnet was interested not only in oil but in the shrinking supply of four other resources in the world—energy, food, water, and minerals. The maldistribution of these resources within the United States and in the world at large, he argued, had and would continue to have a devastating effect. Barnet predicted that the quality of life within the United States would decline sharply as these resources dwindled. A catastrophe could be averted only if there was a greater awareness of interdependence within the world economic order, more democratic planning, and the implementation of policies aimed at conserving natural resources. Unless such steps were taken, Barnet concluded, it would be impossible to maintain certain traditional human values within the United States and throughout the world.

During much of the 1970s, Americans faced the problem of "stagflation"—a combination of economic stagnation, high unemployment, and mounting inflation. One interpretation of the causes of this economic crisis was offered by Lester Thurow, an economist, in his book *The Zero-Sum Society,* published in 1980. Americans lived in a "zero-sum society," he declared, one in which every proposed economic policy which offered benefits to some groups inevitably imposed costs on other groups. Generally speaking, every suggested solution to the major economic problems facing America—rising inflation, higher unemploy-

---

[16]Much has been published about the domestic policies of the Nixon administration despite its recency, though many accounts are journalistic in nature. For more serious studies, see Alonzo Hamby, *The Imperial Years* (New York, 1976) and Raoul Berger, *Executive Privilege* (Cambridge, 1974). The link between the Watergate scandal and Nixon's fall from office is best described in three books: Bob Woodward and Carl Bernstein, *All the President's Men* (New York, 1974), Theodore H. White, *Breach of Faith* (New York, 1975), and Jonathan Schell, *The Time of Illusion* (New York, 1975).

ment, slow growth, low productivity, declining energy resources, environmental decay, economic discrimination, and economic inequality—would call for massive changes in distribution. America's political system, Thurow suggested, was simply incapable of coping with such changes.

Thurow went on to theorize that America was a "zero-sum society" in a political sense as well. In the past, political and economic power had been distributed within American society in such a way that any substantial economic losses could be imposed on various parts of the population. Economic losses had been allocated to particular powerless groups—such as blacks, other minorities, workers, women, and consumers—rather than spread across the population as a whole. These groups were no longer willing, however, to accept such losses. In fact, the political power of these previously powerless groups had increased considerably; they were now able to raise substantially the costs for those—such as the business interests—who wished to impose losses upon them. The business interests, for their part, held themselves ready to exercise an effective veto power over social policies that might adversely affect their interests. The result was a political stand-off in which the country was stalled at dead center.

To resolve the crisis, Thurow offered a number of suggestions. In the economic sphere, he suggested some serious changes: the shift of income from consumption to investment in order to modernize American industry; the integration of minorities and women into the economy on the basis of equality; an increase in social welfare expenditures; a greater reliance on market allocation but with its adverse impact on distribution tempered by governmental redistribution; a more progressive system of taxation; the guarantee of jobs for all workers; and an insured minimum standard of living. From a political point of view, he called for government leaders who would have the courage to impose such unpopular economic policies. In sum, Thurow's work proposed profound changes in both America's political and economic systems.

The three presidents responsible for America's foreign affairs from 1973 to 1980—Nixon, Ford, and Carter—found themselves facing yet another crisis: a growing sense of national insecurity among the people. Many Americans felt that the United States was slipping as a world power as a result of four developments during the 1970s decade: the defeat in Vietnam; the inability of the United States to bring lasting peace in the Middle East between Israel and the Arab states; the incapacity of America to do much when Iranian students seized more than fifty hostages after invading the American embassy in Tehran in 1979; and the failure of this country to respond in a meaningful way when Russia invaded Afghanistan the same year. Two foreign policy analysts—Charles W. Maynes and Richard H. Ullman—coeditors of the magazine

Foreign Policy—reviewed these developments and agreed that the public perception of an American decline was correct. The United States, they concluded, would be unable to regain the nation's previously dominant position in world affairs.

At the same time, however, they pointed out that the post–World War II empire of the Soviet Union was also extraordinarily fragile. The United States enjoyed certain comparative advantages over the Soviet Union in terms of its political and economic strength, they argued, but these advantages were poorly understood. As a result, America had increasingly come to rely on military means in formulating its foreign policy. This trend toward a more militarized foreign policy had arisen for several reasons: the adversary nature of American domestic politics that made it difficult for any administration to seriously propose other alternatives without risking the charge that it was threatening the nation's security; the American political system—which, unlike the parliamentary systems of many Western democratic governments, made it almost impossible to pursue consistent, coherent policies in political and economic matters; and America's preoccupation with domestic economic problems which contributed to the growing incoherence in foreign policy. What was needed, Maynes and Ullman suggested, was a more democratic foreign policy—one in which the lines of responsibility and accountability between the controlling institutions of the government and the public at large were more open.[17]

These same three presidents in dealing with domestic affairs had continued to employ many policies dating back to the tradition of American liberalism in the New Deal. There was a growing disenchantment, however, of such policies during the 1970s. American liberalism encountered a major crisis which manifested itself in several ways: the split among liberal Democrats; the growing conservatism among the electorate; the defection of a number of liberal intellectuals to the conservative ranks; and the rising skepticism among many scholars regarding the continued survival of American democracy itself.

The Nixon administration proved to be a watershed in revealing the internal division among liberal Democrats. In carrying out his policies, Nixon followed traditions with which most liberals had been sympathetic since the New Deal: the use of federal powers to solve economic problems such as wage and price controls; the increasing centralization of power in Washington; and the continuation of the trend toward a more powerful presidency. Many liberals, moreover, agreed with Nixon's foreign policy of continuing the Vietnam War. During the late 1960s and early 1970s, however, certain dissident Democrats—Eugene

---

[17]Charles W. Maynes and Richard H. Ullman. "Ten Years of Foreign Policy," *Foreign Policy* 40 (Fall 1980): 3–17.

McCarthy, Robert Kennedy, and George McGovern—disagreed with these policies. First, these dissidents were early advocates of the antiwar movement. Second, they resisted the excessive use of presidential powers for purely political purposes. Finally, they wanted to follow more liberal policies in eliminating poverty and revitalizing America's cities. These dissidents, who represented a reform wing of the Democratic party, soon discovered they were at odds with many other liberals.

The deep division among liberal politicians reflected the growing crisis of American liberalism within the electorate itself. Voters became increasingly conservative as the old New Deal political coalition began breaking apart in the late 1960s. Kevin Phillips, a political commentator, noted that this conservative trend was evident as early as the 1968 presidential election. Phillips predicted in his book *The Emerging Republican Majority*, published in 1969, that the South, West, and Middle West would grow more conservative and increasingly favor the Republican party. The trend which Phillips had observed continued and presumably resulted in the election of Ronald Reagan in 1980. Many observers interpreted Reagan's victory as a triumph of conservatism and a repudiation of the New Deal.

Another bit of evidence that supported this seeming shift to conservatism in many quarters was the defection of a number of liberal scholars and intellectuals to the ranks of the conservatives. Many of these former liberals had become less optimistic about the survival of American democracy in its present form. From their point of view, too many government regulations encroached upon the private lives of citizens. The continuing centralization of power in Washington, they said, was undermining America's democratic way of life.

In a book of essays edited by Nathan Glazer and Irving Kristol entitled *The American Commonwealth—1976* and published in the bicentennial year, certain of these liberals-turned-conservatives presented their views. Irving Kristol argued that corporate capitalism was the major force in American life, and that the future of democracy in America was intimately involved in the survival of the large corporation. Unfortunately, Kristol added, the large corporation was under attack by what he called the "antiliberal Left." James Q. Wilson, a political scientist, was critical of what he viewed as the rise of an increasingly bureaucratized state. Nathan Glazer, a sociologist, on the other hand, worried about the trend toward what he termed an "imperial judiciary." He called for more prudence by the courts, claiming that they had become too activist in dealing with certain local policies like segregation.[18]

The general pessimism regarding the prospects of American democ-

---

[18]For an example of how these ideas affected public policy during the Nixon years, see Daniel P. Moynihan, *The Politics of a Guaranteed Income* (New York, 1973).

racy found among these former scholar-liberals was echoed in the work of Robert Heilbroner, a distinguished liberal economist. Heilbroner predicted there would be some traumatic changes for the United States and the rest of the world in the near future. In his book *An Inquiry into the Human Prospect,* published in 1974, Heilbroner identified three global problems which threatened calamity: the proliferation of nuclear weapons; the runaway population growth; and the effect of rapid economic growth upon the world's natural resources. Heilbroner implied that these developments were bound to have catastrophic effects upon American democracy. His book was important not only for its findings but for reflecting the pervasive sense of crisis that affected many intellectuals.

A more direct attack upon American liberalism came from Milton Friedman, a conservative economist. Friedman hoped to maintain what he called a freer society in America—one in which the lives of citizens would be restricted less by government regulations. He challenged the ideas of Keynesian economists who had justified active government intervention in the economy since the New Deal. Friedman argued that the expansion of the government's role in the economic sphere had eroded freedom in America and undermined its prosperity. Among other policies, he proposed a program of limited taxation, reduced government spending, and far fewer laws regulating business. Such steps, he believed, would save American capitalism and prevent this country from moving in the direction of socialism and collectivism. Friedman felt that a conservative worldwide trend was turning America away from New Deal liberalism and England from Fabian socialism. His views were set forth in a book entitled *Free to Choose* written with his wife, Rose, and published in 1978.

In the continuing debate about the future course America should take—whether to follow the sentiments of a dissident liberal like George McGovern or those of a conservative like Milton Friedman—it was important to maintain some sense of historical perspective regarding the nature of social change in America's past. The United States always seems to have gone through alternating cycles of liberalism and conservatism. Forty years ago, Arthur Schlesinger, Sr., wrote an article in which he traced this cyclical phenomenon throughout American history.[19] The first two decades of the twentieth century, for example, were seen as a period of active liberalism because Presidents Theodore Roosevelt and Woodrow Wilson called upon the people to reform the national economy in the Progressive movement and then to wage a war to make the world safe for democracy. This period was followed by an

---

[19]Arthur Schlesinger, Sr., "Tides of American Politics," *Yale Review* 29 (no. 2, 1939): 217–30.

era of conservatism and inactivity during the Harding-Coolidge-Hoover presidencies of the 1920s. It was succeeded by another era of liberalism beginning with Franklin Delano Roosevelt and the New Deal.

Schlesinger's son, Arthur Schlesinger, Jr., carried forward this cyclical theory in an article, showing that the period of activism which started in the 1930s lasted for two decades: "F. D. R. and the New Deal, World War II, Truman and the Fair Deal, the Cold War, the Korean War." Once again, during the Eisenhower years in the 1950s, there was a lull. But in the 1960s, there came another burst of activism—"Kennedy and Johnson, the New Frontier and Great Society, the racial revolution and the war against poverty." The younger Schlesinger likened the 1970s to the 1950s and 1920s as a decade of rest and recuperation. Some time in the 1980s, he predicted, the cycle would return; American would embark once again upon a period of liberalism. The article by Schlesinger, Jr., written in the spring of 1980, is the second selection in this chapter.

Students trying to evaluate the pattern of domestic developments from the end of World War II to the election of Ronald Reagan remain at a grave disadvantage. There were few reflective histories to read; scholars were too close to events to have a sense of perspective. In numerous instances, the records were incomplete because participants involved in many important events were still alive and their papers were not available for research. Most important of all, the United States as a world leader had entered into the internationalist phase of its history and it was increasingly difficult to draw the line between domestic and foreign affairs. Certain questions, nevertheless, suggest themselves. Were the continuities that persisted through the era 1945 to 1980—relative prosperity and the containment of communism—more significant than the changes that took place? Could the first two postwar decades, 1945–1965, be characterized as a period of consensus and conformity? Could these decades be contrasted with the years from 1965 to 1980, which might be construed as an era of crisis, unrest, and conflict? Or was Schlesinger more correct in his periodization by calling the 1950s and 1970s decades of "rest and recuperation"? Is traditional American liberalism dead, as some intellectuals suggested, or would it revive in the near future, as Schlesinger predicted? Only by answering such questions can students determine whether the contrast between these two periods was as great as portrayed in this chapter.

William H. Whyte, Jr.

WILLIAM H. WHYTE, JR. (1917–   ) graduated from Princeton University, worked for *Fortune Magazine* from 1946 to 1959, authored many articles and books, and served on various public bodies. His best-known work is *The Organization Man* (1956).

A very curious thing has been taking place in this country—and almost without our knowing it. In a country where "individualism"—independence and self-reliance—was the watchword for three centuries, the view is now coming to be accepted that the individual himself has no meaning—except, that is, as a member of a group. "Group integration," "group equilibrium," "interpersonal relations," "training for group living," "group dynamics," "social interaction," "social physics"; more and more the notes are sounded—each innocuous or legitimate in itself, but together a theme that has become unmistakable.

In a sense, this emphasis is a measure of success. We have *had* to learn how to get along in groups. With the evolution of today's giant organizations—in business, in government, in labor, in education, in big cities—we have created a whole new social structure for ourselves, and one so complex that we're still trying to figure out just what happened. But the American genius for cooperative action has served us well. "Human relations" may not be an American invention, but in no country have people turned so wholeheartedly to the job of mastering the group skills on which our industrial society places such a premium.

But the pendulum has swung too far. Take, for example, the growing popularity of "social engineering" with its emphasis on the planned manipulation of the individual into the group role. Or, even more striking, the extraordinary efforts of some corporations to encompass the executive's wife in the organization—often with the willing acquiescence of the wife in the merger. And these, as we hope to demonstrate, are no isolated phenomena; recent public-opinion polls, slick-magazine fiction, current best-sellers, all document the same trend. Groupthink is becoming a national philosophy.

Groupthink being a coinage—and, admittedly, a loaded one—a working definition is in order. We are not talking about mere instinctive

William H. Whyte, Jr., "Groupthink," *Fortune*, 45 (March 1952): 114–17, 142, 146. Reprinted by permission of *Fortune*.

conformity—it is, after all, a perennial failing of mankind. What we are talking about is a *rationalized* conformity—an open, articulate philosophy which holds that group values are not only expedient but right and good as well. Three mutually supporting ideas form the underpinning: (1) that moral values and ethics are relative; (2) that what is important is the kind of behavior and attitudes that makes for the harmonious functioning of the group; (3) that the best way to achieve this is through the application of "scientific" techniques.

Once grasped, as the work of the social engineers makes clear, these principles lead us to an entirely new view of man. And what a dismal fellow he is! For the man we are now presented with is Social Man—completely a creature of his environment, guided almost totally by the whims and prejudices of the group, and incapable of any real self-determination of his destiny. Only through social engineering—i.e., applied groupthink—can he be saved. The path to salvation, social engineers explain, lies in a trained elite that will benevolently manipulate us into group harmony. And who's to be the elite? Social engineers modestly clear their throats.

The Vanishing Layman

This vision of a new elite guiding us to the integrated life has inspired some interesting speculations (e.g., Aldous Huxley's *Brave New World*, George Orwell's *Nineteen Eighty-Four*). The real danger, however, is something else again. It is not that the layman will be pushed around by the social engineers: it is that *he will become one himself.* Rather than the pawn of the experts, he will be the willing apprentice—and embrace groupthink as the road to security.

Is this coming to pass? Let's look for a moment at the direction American values are taking among the oncoming generations. There has been a rather disturbing amount of evidence that they are changing rapidly—and in a way that must warm social engineers' hearts. Every study made of the younger generation, every portrayal they make of themselves—from their dating habits to their artistic inclinations—uncovers one clear fact: our youth is the most group-minded we have ever had. Gregariousness, *Time's* recent study indicated, has become a necessity. "They are parts of groups," one girl shrewdly appraises her contemporaries. "When they are alone they are bored with themselves."

While youngsters are not inclined to philosophize, their attitude toward life adds up to a fairly discernible set of values. It could be described as a "practical" relativism. The old absolute moral values are disappearing. There is still black and white, to be sure, but it is no longer determined by fixed precepts; it is determined rather by what the group thinks is black and white—and if someone does things the way his group does, well, who is to censure him for his loyalty?

The colleges furnish documentation of the drift. If recent surveys are any indication, a startling swing has taken place among students to the twin ideals of group harmony and expertism. "These men," one of their mentors says in praise, "don't question the system. Their main aim is to make it work better—to get in there and lubricate the machinery. They're not rebels; they'll be social technicians for a better society."

The registrar's records bear him out. Along with a concurrent drift from the humanities, there has been a tremendous increase in specialized courses—and of specialization within specialties. Significantly, the courses that enjoyed the most phenomenal popularity among postwar classes were those connected with personnel work. "I like people" became a universal cry, and in droves students aiming for business turned thumbs down on the idea of general, executive apprenticeship in favor of personnel work; here, with stop watch and slip stick in hand, they could measure away, safe from the doubts and intangibles of the world without. The picture was a mirage, of course, but it was only by the most strenuous efforts of placement officers and corporation personnel people that students gave it up.

Does entry into business life transform these values? Apparently not. Talk with members of the younger generation of management—and we speak not of the disaffected but of the successful—and one is struck by a curious strain of resignation that often runs through their discussion. Like the heros of J. P. Marquand's perceptive novels, they are disturbed by a sense of individual impotence. Dispassionately, they describe themselves primarily as members of their environment—men more acted upon than acting. They are neither angry nor cynical about it; they are caught on a "treadmill" from which they will never escape, perhaps—but the treadmill is pleasant enough, they explain, and in the group role they find the emotional security they want so very badly.

So with their wives. No matter what problem they are discussing—from the possibility of advancement to the style of their living—they instinctively phrase their problems in terms of their relations with the group. The relations, they concede are not simple—there are the girls, the gang on Ferncrest Road, Charlie's people at the office, and a host of lesser constellations to conjure with. Tough as the job may be, however, it is a job to which they have dedicated themselves.

The System Lovers

Turn to the image of the good life in popular cultures and you find the same phenomenon at work. Slick-magazine fiction tells the story. It has never, of course, exactly called for a rebellion against the status quo, but back in the thirties it did present heroes and heroines who engaged in some kind of mild strife with their environment, told the boss off, or did something equally contentious. No longer. A *Fortune* analysis of 1935–1936 plots and 1950–1951 plots indicates that heroes and heroines have been growing remarkably submissive. Not only is the system they abide by—be it an army camp, a business office, or a small-town environment—shown as more benevolent; in some cases the system itself becomes the *deus ex machina* that solves the problems.

So in serious fiction. More and more, writers are concerning themselves with the relationship of the individual to the group, and more and more resolving it in favor of the latter. The system—and they don't mean God or the universe—is eventually revealed to the hero as bigger than any of us, and thus it is not only foolish but wrong for him not to reconcile himself to it. From the extreme of the angry, to-hell-with-the-whole-lousy-setup tracts of the 1930s we seem to be going whole hog in the opposite direction.

Let us have a look at the current best-seller, Herman Wouk's *The Caine Mutiny*. Since it is about the Navy, the system shown has some aspects peculiar to service life. The basic question posed, however—the individual's place in the system—has great universality, and in an excitingly told tale Wouk sketches one point of view with such striking overtones that the book could almost go down as a landmark in the shift of American values.

The story tells of the terrible dilemma facing the officers of a mine sweeper; their captain, one Queeg, is a neurotic, cowardly incompetent. A typhoon brings the problem to the breaking point. Through hysteria and cowardice, Queeg is about to sink the ship. In vain, Maryk, the stolid, conventional executive officer, tries to get him to keep the ship headed into the wind. Queeg refuses. In the nick of time, Maryk makes his decision. Under Article 184 of Navy regulations, he relieves Queeg of his command. The ship is saved.

What is the moral? Maryk, we find, shouldn't have done it. Says the author's protagonist, Lieutenant Willy Keith in a letter to his girl (p. 463): "... I see that we were in the wrong. ... The idea is, once you get an incompetent ass of a skipper—and it's a chance of war—there's nothing to do but serve him as though he were the wisest and the best, cover his mistakes, keep the ship going, and bear up. So I have gone all the way around Robin Hood's barn to arrive at the old platitudes, which I guess is the process of growing up."

In other times, perhaps, this definition of maturity might have been regarded as downright parody. Obedience and discipline few could have caviled at. But would they have applauded the counseling of an obedience, so abject, so *unquestioning*, that we are asked, in effect, not only to put up with the evils of a system but to regard them as right—to reach out, as Norbert Weiner's phrase goes, and kiss the whip that lashes us? Would they have joined in censuring an act to which the only logical alternative is the passive sacrifice of several hundred lives? Hardly. The executive officer's action might well have been seen as an act of great moral courage—and one, furthermore, in true allegiance to the service; it did, after all, save the ship. The other byproduct, the withdrawal of Queeg from line command, might also have been interpreted as something less than a disaster to the system.

Not so A.D. 1952. The moral, to judge from what critics and readers have been saying about it, has struck exactly the right chord. The exec, as the dust jacket has it, was merely a well-meaning man "beyond his depth," and more to be pitied than censured. It is not for the individual to question the competence of the Queegs a system may contain. Queeg was a teacher. Queegs are necessary. We needed Queegs to win the war. So goes the assent. "It is about time that more books of this sort were written," says J. P. Marquand. "The lesson the newcomer must learn is in many ways the antithesis of democracy. It is essentially a final acceptance of the doctrine that full and unquestioning obedience must be accorded a superior officer, no matter how personally odious or stupid this individual may be—and that without this individual surrender we can never win a war."

Love that system.

The Permissive Way

What makes this wave of the present particularly unsettling is the surprising fact that it is in rhythm with one of the dominant currents in contemporary American academic thought. It would be a mistake, of course, to treat the connection as cause and effect; groupthink's roots go too deep to be so summarily explained. But it would be just as much of an error to dismiss the academic underpinnings, as the layman is so tempted to do, as mere ivory-tower mumbo-jumbo. The ideology of groupthink is often incomprehensible to the uninitiated, but it is of great power nonetheless. Translated by its disciples in hundreds of lecture halls and papers, and by their disciples in turn, it has given a purpose and direction to the groupthink movement that it would otherwise lack.

The movement, in a sense, is an offshoot of the great academic revolt at the turn of the century against formalism. To Young Turks of the day the individualistic tradition of American thought needed redefinition. Too much attention, they felt, had been concentrated on the lone individual; as a consequence, the rigid values built up for his protection were inapplicable to the great social upheavals that were taking place.

What was needed was a social view of man—man as a unit of the group—and a willingness to adapt society to his needs.

Most of the credit generally goes to John Dewey, who, with William Kilpatrick, gave "progressive" education its impetus. But there were many others—Veblen in economics, for example, and Roscoe Pound in the law ("The law is social engineering"). Like a fresh breeze, through almost every field of American thought, the new concepts swept, as converts enthusiastically fell to whacking away at the restrictions of the old absolutes. Social Man was coming of age.

When the cultural anthropologists got to work on him, his final link to the old moral absolutes was severed. From their comparisons of primitive cultures, and, later, our own, many anthropologists came to the view that the ethics of a people are relative. By this they do not mean that ethics are unimportant, but rather that they are not to be judged by any abstract conceptions of "right" or "wrong." For if we realize that other cultures and ethics are "equally valid," to use Ruth Benedict's phrase, then we will be jogged into giving up all the more readily our outworn traditions and our illusions of individual autonomy. "It is not any particular set of values," another anthropologist explains, "but a way of looking at them that is important."

A half-century has gone by and the relativistic, social view of man idea is still gaining. The appetite for cultural anthropology, for example, has been growing at such a rate that Ruth Benedict's *Patterns of Culture*, first published in 1931, has reached, after a phenomenal newsstand sale, the no. 1 best-seller spot in the Mentor paperback series.

In several essentials, however, the nature of the movement against formalism has changed drastically. What started as a healthy revolt against dogmatism has produced an offshoot that has succeeded in becoming the new dogmatism itself. And since, like all dogmatisms, it promises respite from uncertainty, a society still shell-shocked by the upheavals of the twentieth century hasn't bothered yet to question its effects too closely. To be sure, those of the groupthink leaning customarily speak of themselves as rebels fighting an uphill battle against the enemy ("medievalists," "academicians," "absolutists") but the dog they are kicking is practically dead. They won that battle long ago.

Certainly so in one sector of education. Thanks to a strenuous academic controversy, the momentum of the militantly "progressive" brand was slowed down some time back. Groupthink, however, cannot be contained by a label, and to a formidable body of educators the basic ideal of adjustment to group values is so taken for granted that the only remaining job would appear to be working up better ways of bringing it about. "The American educator," writes one of them, Professor Stewart Cole, "[must] treat pupils as persons-in-groups-in-American-culture at every stage of their social learning." To do this the teacher should borrow from such disciplines as anthropology, the social sciences, psychology, and group dynamics. "The social interactions" of teachers and pupils should be "the primary channel of learning the good life for America."[1]

In this free, permissive atmosphere, the idea that the individual should be regarded as personally accountable for the way he behaves is, of course, old hat. And in the popular view as well. "If your young son sticks his tongue out at you and calls you a nasty old stinkpot," an article in *American Magazine* good-humoredly, but approvingly, counsels, "just ignore the insult and rejoice secretly that you have such a fine normal child. He is simply channeling his aggressive, aggrieved feelings harmlessly by verbal projection."

Where "social interaction" is the watchword, the attitude conditioning is left, in large part, to the child's peers. Even more than their elders, they are quick to reward deviance with hefty interaction; and thus in the natural distaste of the crowd for the individualist we now have a social tool. And this, the child learns from the books written for him, is as it should be. In these tales of fire engines and trains, as David Riesman has documented in his disturbing study, *The Lonely Crowd*, the neophyte groupthinker is taught that one wins by being directed by others—and that the most important thing in the world is to be a team player.

To further ensure that the child need never be a person-not-in-groups, the necessity for little groupthinkers to think as individuals *all by themselves* may soon be obviated altogether. Individual homework is now to be eliminated. Writes Amy Selwyn in the *Reader's Digest*, "Now authorities generally agree that children learn best if they do their learning in groups and talk out loud about lessons as they work. 'No homework' spokesmen also say if children were not required to spend their leisure studying they would not develop the resentment against study which often kills all incentive to learn anything. . . ."

Lest the layman presume to question the drift, groupthinkers explain that their work is rooted in the Scientific Method, and that now being a holy phrase, it is made plain that the debate is closed to outsiders—if indeed any grounds for debate exist at all.[2] "Because this new 'doctrine' has for its base objective findings in anthropology, social psychology, mental hygiene, and scientific child study," Professor Alain Locke of

---

[1]Educators of this bent cannot be accused of swimming against the current. As a recent Elmo Roper poll indicates, most Americans now feel the second most important reason for sending children to high school is "to teach them to get along with other people." (No. 1: to get them ready for a job.)

[2]"I should like to see teachers and professors as sure of themselves, as confident in their training and experience, as surgeons are, and as impatient of lay advice"—Margaret B. Pickel, Dean of women, Columbia University; *New York Times Magazine*, June 3, 1951.

Howard University says, "there is an authoritative consensus back of these newer educational procedures that few would care to challenge."

On the Brink of Nonsense

He is right. Many educators have seriously questioned the excesses of educational groupthink, but a large proportion of them are curiously loath to do it out loud right now. Criticism of the misapplications of science, they know, will be quickly seized as an attack on science itself. To muddy matters even more, those of the extremist fringe (notably Allen Zoll) have succeeded in putting something of the kiss of death on public discussion by their attacks on "progressive" education. They are really attacking something else, of course; their reasoning is erroneous and their motives suspect. Nevertheless, many people who have a respectable argument to make hesitate for fear they will lose their standing as liberals. The debate, however, cannot long be deferred—certainly so when it can be said, with some justification, that the best friend progressive education has today is Allen Zoll.

There are some signs that the wider implications of the groupthink movement may at last provoke a counterrevolution. Significantly, some of the most astringent critiques of groupthink are coming from the ranks of the sociologists (cf. "The Image of Man in the Social Sciences"—Reinhard Bendix in *Commentary*, February 1951). In its application to the law, Roscoe Pound himself has been led to protest the degree to which the social-utility concept has supplanted firm values. Similarly, in England—which suffers groupthink too—educator Sir Walter Moberly has been stirring the universities to a reexamination of the British variant.

But the best hope may well lie in the ambitions of the groupthinkers themselves. They stand poised, finally, on the threshold of pure nonsense. For a long time they have been growing uncomfortable over their apparent denial of ethical relevance. As the anthropologists themselves point out, man does need a firm sense of right and wrong, and an excessively relative view destroys the old firmness.

This does not mean, however, that the groupthinkers are chastened. Quite the contrary. They now propose to cure this pitfall of scientism with more scientism. Ethics are to be made "a matter of scientific investigation." To some, this merely means an objective study of ethics—certainly a proper enough task. To the groupthinker, however, it means nothing less than a theoretical apparatus for the scientific determination of what is "good" or "bad." And thus "to the innermost citadel of dogmatic thinking, the realm of values," they hopefully turn. "The conquest of the field of values," as one sounds the call, "would be almost the concluding triumph." He couldn't be more correct.

Ethics Without Tears

Why should so despairing an ideology be so popularly contagious? In a society where the old family and community ties that so long cemented it have broken down, the impulse for association is an instinctive and healthy response. But a sense of "belonging," a sense of meaningful association with others, has never required that one sacrifice his individuality as part of the bargain. Why, then, do so many rush to embrace a philosophy that tells them it *is* necessary? Why, like the moth, do we fly to the one thing that will consume us? Why, in a country with the sort of healthy political and economic base that has historically nourished individualism, are we so pathetically eager to join up in flatulent brotherhood?

To explain this impulse is to explain our blind faith in scientism as well. For their appeal is common, and many as the variations may be, they come back, eventually, to one simple, compelling theme.

They offer us freedom from moral choice.

Through the deification of group harmony, buck-passing a moral decision becomes itself a moral act; the system—as *The Caine Mutiny* advocates—attends to these things so much better than the individual, and he might just as well relax and enjoy it.

And there is freedom in another sense as well. Moral dilemmas exist because there is uncertainty. If we can now abstract a few parts from the whole of human nature and by analysis predict objectively what will make for group harmony, the intangibles that make individual decisions so poignant may be obviated altogether. Like a general who is blessed with perfect intelligence of the enemy, we will have only one valid course of action before us. We will have finally latched on to certainty.

Why Participate?

Once this denial of moral relevance is made, folly must be the consequence. For groupthinkers go on to assure themselves that in group-think itself one finds moral fulfillment. It is not put this crudely, of course; by what has now become a ritualistic explanation, our eyes are directed upward to the goal of harmony, group integration, dynamic equilibrium; upward to a golden mean in which everyone will finally attain the blessed state of—grace? No, the state of "participation."

But participation for what? As a fundamental of the democratic process, as a means of self-expression and development, participation is abundantly desirable. In this sense, *Fortune* has argued strongly for participation; it has reported its application to the problems of management and will continue to. But the word, like its blood brothers "communication" and "adjust," is assuming a sort of end-all quality. So let us put the question: *Why* participate?

In the litany of groupthink the answers describe a complete circle. One participates for the end of "social integration," for "community-centered cohesion," for better "interpersonal relations," for "group harmony," for the reduction of "social tensions," for adjustment to the environment. One participates, in other words, that he may participate. And so the end is really only a means after all. Good means, yes—but as an encompassing philosophy, somewhat less than complete.

Even as a means, participation can be a tricky concept. It is easily confused with getting a number of people to do what one did before. And in this aspect, unfortunately, it provides the resolutely pedestrian with a way of cutting down to size their up-and-coming brethren. Similarly it offers the faint of heart an alibi for ducking responsibility—if a broth is to be spoiled, it's convenient to have too many cooks participate.

Perhaps the most extraordinary aspect of groupthink is the success with which its double-talk has used the old concepts of individualism to justify their opposite. By letting others decide, one decides. By submitting oneself to a group, one becomes an individual. "It is precisely this gradual change in our mental horizon—new assumptions and hypotheses taken as factual description—that is sinister," says Lincoln Ries, professor of philosophy at Bard College. "So that while we are presented with a logical horror, we find it established and accepted widely as a fact. Nowhere vulnerable to intelligence, it is as impervious as a nightmare."

It is impervious because the ideal of unity it holds out obscures for us some disagreeable facts of life—and the necessity for facing them on moral grounds. "Communication" is a term in point. As used in its cult sense, it implies the facile premise that the conflicts that plague us are due simply to "blocks" in the communication flow, and that if we get the technical hang of it, all will be well. Up to a point this is true. But people do not always argue because they misunderstand one another; they argue because they hold different goals. These will always be a matter of debate, and attempts to evade it through "nonpartisan" communication or "education" programs simply beg the question.

Unity—or Monotony?

"Unity" is a double-edged sword. As our young corporation wife is witness, group harmony is not an unmixed blessing; conversely, neither are frustrations and tensions necessarily bad. They can be fruitful; indeed, progress is often dependent on producing rather than mitigating them. In large part, also, they stem from the scores of conflicting loyalties and allegiances we enjoy in a fluid society. Unless we forswear these in complete fealty to one embracing organization, there is no easy way to escape the moral decision they force upon us. *Nor should there be.* The danger, as Clark Kerr points out, "is not that loyalties are divided today, but that they may become undivided tomorrow."

It is precisely this smothering of the individual that the drift to group-think seems to be making more and more imminent. Few groupthinkers, to be sure, believe themselves against the individual. But in looking so intently at man as a member of the group, they have made man seem important in this role only. There is the frequent explanation, of course, that only by group participation is the individual's potential realized. But this is only a half-truth. Individual excellence must involve something more than a respect for the group and a skill in working with it. "The sphere of individual action," writes Bertrand Russell, "is not to be regarded as ethically inferior to that of social duty. On the contrary, some of the best of human activities are, at least in feeling, rather personal than social. . . . Prophets, mystics, poets, scientific discoverers, are men whose lives are dominated by a vision. . . . It . . . is such men who put into the world the things that we most value."

Few of us are potential geniuses, but the constant admonition to harmonize and integrate affects us nonetheless. Each day we are faced with a multitude of decisions. Should we trust our own judgment? Or does the group's view have an inherent rightness we cannot match?

The new values would incline us to the easy harmony of the group view, for they would have us suppose that the whole is greater than the sum of the parts; that the system has a wisdom beyond the reach of ordinary mortals. But this is not necessarily so. Man can be greater than the group, and his lone imagination worth a thousand graphs.

He is not often a creator, but even as spectator, as "the common man," he can rise in ways his past performance would not predict. To aim at his common denominators in the name of ultimate democracy is to despise him, to perpetuate his mediocrities, and to conceive him incapable of responding to anything better than the echo of his prejudices. The "equilibrium" that is the compact to be made with this boor is inevitably static, and the trouble is not solved by sticking the adjective dynamic in front of it.

Has the individual reached a low enough estate for us to become concerned? When the nation's best-selling novel advocates his abject submission without raising eyebrows; when some corporations make it policy not to hire honor graduates for fear they might not be good mixers; when it is seriously stated that "natural leaders" can be made obsolete, the time has come at least to think about the matter. For if the drift continues, man may soon cease to fret over such things at all. He will finally have engineered for himself that equilibrious society. Gelded into harmonious integration, he will be free from tensions and frustrations, content in the certainties of his special function, no longer tantalized by the sense of infinity. He will at last have become a complete bore.

The answer is not a return to a "rugged individualism" that never was. Nor is it a slackened interest in social science and "human relations." We need, certainly, to find ways of making this bewildering society of ours run more smoothly and we need all the illumination science can give us to do it. But we need something more. Lest man become an ethical eunuch, his autonomy sacrificed for the harmony of the group, a new respect for the individual must be kindled. A revival of the humanities, perhaps, a conscious, deliberate effort by the corporation not only to accommodate dissent but to encourage it—possible approaches to a problem so fundamental cannot easily be spelled out.

Only individuals can do it.

Arthur M. Schlesinger, Jr.

ARTHUR M. SCHLESINGER, JR. (1917–   ) is Albert Schweitzer Professor of the Humanities at the City University of New York. He was also a special assistant to President John F. Kennedy. Among his many published works are *The Age of Jackson* (1945), *The Age of Roosevelt* (1956–), *A Thousand Days: John F. Kennedy in the White House* (1965) and *Robert Kennedy and His Times* (1975).

Once again the cry goes out across the land that liberalism is used up, finished, a burnt-out case, and that the United States has at last become a conservative nation. Conservatism, we are told, has captured the political and ideological initiative. Liberals, it is claimed, are in retreat on every front. The latest Harris poll on the subject shows that, among Americans willing to accept either label, "conservatives" outnumber "liberals" by more than 2 to 1 (36 percent to 18; 41 percent place themselves discreetly in the middle of the road).

This poll would be more crushing if one forgets that in the midst of that stereotypically liberal decade, the 1960s, the Harris poll uncovered 35 percent conservative as against 17 percent liberal respondents (1967). By this measure, in other words, the proportion of conservatives has somewhat declined in the last dozen years, and the proportion of liberals has somewhat grown. For that matter, when Gallup first asked the question in 1939 at the high noon of the New Deal, 52 percent claimed to be conservatives—and a year later Franklin D. Roosevelt won his third term. What people mean when they style themselves conservatives or liberals evidently bears further inquiry.

The two words have bemused the democratic world for a century and a half. "Conservative" came into political use in Britain in the 1830s; "liberalism" in the 1840s. They so conclusively filled a need that by 1882 W. S. Gilbert in *Iolanthe* praised nature itself for contriving

Arthur M. Schlesinger, Jr., "Is Liberalism Dead?," *New York Times Magazine*, March 20, 1980, pp. 42, 70–73, 79. © 1980 by The New York Times Company. Reprinted by permission.

> That every boy and every gal
> That's born into the world alive,
> Is either a little Liberal,
> Or else a little Conservative.

The terms have been more indispensable, however, than their significance has been clear. For in a democratic society conservatives and liberals agree much more than they disagree. They share a commitment to individual freedom, the constitutional state and the rule of law. Still they differ over the way to secure these ends and over the nature of the threats to the free order. They differ in their constituencies—Hamilton, for example, favoring the "rich and well-born," Jefferson considering the mass of the people "the safest depository of power." They differ especially in their feelings about change.

The astute Emerson saw this as the fundamental point. "The two parties which divide the state," he wrote in 1841, "the party of Conservatism and that of Innovation, are very old, and have disputed the possession of the world ever since it was made. . . . Now one, now the other gets the day, and still the fight renews itself as if for the first time, under new names and hot personalities." Conservatives, in their satisfaction with the existing distribution of wealth and power, resist all forms of change not under their own control. Reformers, in their determination to broaden the area of individual freedom, argue the need to revise the structures of society. "The castle which conservatism is set to defend," Emerson said, "is the actual state of things, good and bad. The project of innovation is the best possible state of things."

The contrast between conservatism and innovation is rooted in temperament as well as in interest (and, as William James reminds us, temperaments "determine men in their philosophies, and always will"). The liberal sees change as inevitable in the whirling world. President Valéry Giscard d'Estaing of France put it well the other day in an interview with *Paris Match:* "It is important to understand that we have to adapt to a world in the making and not try to remain adapted to a world that is fading." For liberals, change is an adventure. For conservatives, it is a disaster. The conservative is sure that puny human efforts to control the organic currents of history will infallibly produce unanticipated consequences that will only make things worse. "The great stream of time and earthly things will sweep on just the same in spite of us . . . ," said William Graham Sumner. "That is why it is the greatest folly of which man can be capable, to sit down with a slate and pencil to plan out a new social world."

When Sumner wrote "The Absurd Effort to Make the World Over" in 1894, he might still have called himself a liberal. For in the nineteenth century a liberal was an advocate of laissez-faire in the Manchester

school of Cobden and Bright, a rigid opponent of government intervention in the economy. It was conservatives like Shaftesbury and Disraeli
who called on government to protect the poor and powerless. In the
United States the (going by constituency) "liberal" Jeffersonians thought
that government best which governed least and the "conservative"
Hamiltonians stood for the affirmative state.

But history is wayward, and, while government remains a silent
issue, liberals and conservatives have exchanged their positions. Jeffersonian antistatism served popular interests so long as the broad distribution of property in a predominantly agricultural society gave each man a
sufficiency with which to protect himself. But when industrialization
heaped up wealth in great agglomerations and created a propertyless
laboring class, new ways had to be found to protect the powerless from
the powerful. "We believe," the Populists said in their 1892 platform,
"that the powers of government—in other words, of the people—should
be expanded . . . to the end that oppression, injustice, and poverty shall
eventually cease in the land." Theodore Roosevelt saw very clearly that,
in a high-technology society of concentrated private wealth, Hamiltonian means were necessary to attain Jeffersonian ends. "Every man
holds his property," Roosevelt said, "subject to the general right of the
community to regulate its use to whatever degree the public welfare may
require it." "I feel confident," Woodrow Wilson soon added, "that if
Jefferson were living in our day he would see what we see. . . . Without
the watchful interference, the resolute interference of the government,
there can be no fair play."

As liberals moved toward an interventionist state, conservatives,
now perceiving government as a weapon that might be used against
them, moved toward laissez-faire. The two sides thus traded positions.
This process reminded Abraham Lincoln of the two drunks who "engaged in a fight with their greatcoats on, which fight, after a long and
rather harmless contest, ended in each having fought himself out of his
own coat and into that of the other."

History thus tells us that the basic differences between conservatism
and liberalism lie in their class commitments, in their feelings about
change and, in modern times, in their attitude toward government. Let
us not forget these historic distinctions, because so many contemporary
definitions of the difference are irrelevant when not positively misleading. So my neoconservative friends in their polemical zest have constructed a shameless caricature of liberalism—and I have no doubt that
in our own polemics my liberal friends and I have performed an equivalent injustice on conservatism.

A student of the writings of Irving Kristol, Henry Kissinger, Daniel
Patrick Moynihan, and Norman Podhoretz would gather, for example,
that a liberal is a person who believes in the perfectibility of man, who

regards power as intrinsically evil, who is addicted to guilt, who is filled with "self-hatred and self-contempt" (Podhoretz), whose favorite practice is "self-flagellation" (Kissinger), who has an unrequited love affair with Marxism, who assumes that Bertrand Russell used to call (ironically) the "superior virtue of the oppressed," who advocates curing criminals at home and terrorists abroad by the "therapeutic ethic" (Kristol)—i.e., compassion and the provision of social services—who is ashamed of America and supposes that "third worlders stand closer to God" (Stephen S. Rosenfeld), and who abhors geopolitics, the balance of power and the idea of a national interest.

As a bottled-in-bond liberal, one who voted as many times as constitutionally possible for Franklin Roosevelt and is now engaged in completing a history of his presidency, who served on Adlai Stevenson's staff in two campaigns, who worked in John Kennedy's White House and wrote a memoir of his administration, who was a friend and biographer of Robert Kennedy and who today is a supporter of Edward Kennedy, I subscribe to none of these propositions. Nor do most liberals I know. Someone did once remark of man that there was no "conceivable end to his march to perfection. His face is turned to the light; he stands in the sun and looks upward." But the author of these confident sentiments, far from being a liberal, was Andrew Carnegie (and his metaphor betrayed him: what happens to people who stand in the sun and look upward?). Modern liberalism has learned from Reinhold Neibuhr that the doctrine of original sin provides the only solid basis for the liberal faith. "Man's capacity for justice makes democracy possible," as Niebuhr said, "but man's inclination to injustice makes democracy necessary."

Most liberals I know do *not* regard power as intrinsically evil, are *not* filled with guilt and self-hatred, do *not* indulge in self-flagellation, reject the therapeutic ethic, have no illusions about the Third World and fully understand the vanity of human wishes. As for Marxism, I, for example, was an embattled anti-Stalinist when many neoconservatives were in their cradles. In foreign affairs, I have been a card-carrying geopolitician even since I first read Halford Mackinder and Nicholas Spykman thirty-five years ago. Some of the most powerful critics of the Vietnam War—Walter Lippmann, Hans Morgenthau, George Kennan, Niebuhr—were precisely the people who insisted most rigorously on thinking about foreign policy in terms of the national interest.

So let us have done with this attribution—by either side—of bizarre premise and motive to the other side; and let us concentrate on the basic conservative-liberal disagreement, which in the current setting of our lives is over the role of government.

Contemporary conservatives, unlike Hamilton and Disraeli, dislike government. They believe that government abridges individual scope and freedom; that it destroys self-reliance; that it is inefficient, wasteful and corrupt; that it creates an arbitrary and obnoxious bureaucracy; that it takes on too much and miscarries through overload; that it stifles enterprise with unnecessary regulation; that the people are fed up with it (hence the popularity of conservatism in the polls); that it is, beyond police functions, a burden and a menace; and that it is essentially un-creative, with no capacity to advance the quality of society. Jimmy Carter gave the conservative credo defiant expression in his 1978 State of the Union Message. In words not likely to have been uttered by say, Franklin D. Roosevelt, Carter said: "Government cannot solve our prob-lems. It can't set our goals. It cannot define our vision. Government cannot eliminate poverty, or provide a bountiful economy, or reduce inflation, or save our cities, or cure illiteracy, or provide energy."

Conservatives disparage government and other instruments of human purpose because they dream of an automatic stabilizer some-where over the rainbow that will solve our problems for us. They have appropriated the old faith of classical liberalism in Adam Smith's "in-visible hand." They see the private market as infinitely exact, sensitive, efficient, and impartial in its resolution of our social and economic perplexities. "The sole function of government," as Herbert Hoover said in the depths of the Great Depression, "is to bring about a condition of affairs favorable to the beneficial development of private enterprise."

Now, modern liberals believe in the market too. They have no wish to move to a command economy. Even some socialists have come to recognize the immense advantages of the price system. But liberals do not see the contemporary market as the perfect, frictionless, self-equilibrating mechanism imagined by conservatives. In the liberal view, industrial concentration has filled the market with rigidities. So have trade unions and beneficial social legislation. Businessmen themselves dislike competition and spend much of their time trying to escape it. In vital sectors prices are set by administrative decision, not by the law of supply and demand. Realistic analysis of the contemporary market makes liberals far more skeptical of the efficacy of the market in dealing with aggregate problems, like depression and inflation, and far more ready to invoke government in order to redress the market's distortions and compensate for its failures. In the same year that Hoover minimized the role of government, the governor of New York took a quite different view. "I assert," Franklin Roosevelt said, "that modern society, acting through its government, owes the definite obligation to prevent the starvation or the dire want of any of its fellow men and women who try to maintain themselves and cannot."

Conservatives see the confrontation between the individual and gov-ernment as a zero-sum game, in which a gain for one side means a loss for the other. Liberals feel that this may have been the case in Jefferson's rural arcadia, but that in modern society the individual dwells among so many towering centers of power that he often must turn to government in order to protect his personal space against private baronies. History leaves no doubt that this is true. It is the national government, for example, that has vindicated racial justice against private bigotry. It is the national government that has protected the Bill of Rights against private vigilantism. It is the national government that has preserved natural resources against private greed. It is the national government that has civilized our industry, that has secured the rights of labor organization, that has assured a steady income for the farmer.

It is evidently not a zero-sum game. The growth of national authority, far from diminishing the individual, has given a majority of Americans more dignity and freedom than they ever had before. The individual liberties destroyed in this century by the increase in national authority have been, in the main, the freedom to deny nonwhite Americans their constitutional rights, the freedom to work small children in mills and immigrants in sweatshops, the freedom to pay starvation wages and require barbarous working hours, the freedom to loot and waste our natural resources, the freedom to cheat in advertising and the sale of securities—all freedoms that, one supposes, a decent country can readily do without.

Government is not, in the liberal view, the enemy. It is an instrument, capable of good as well as harm. Indeed, liberals often wonder why those arms of government that have done the most damage to individual rights—the FBI and the CIA—are precisely the ones most cherished by conservatives. "Statements are made," President Kennedy said in TVA country in 1963, "labeling the Federal Government an outsider, an intruder, an adversary. The people of this area know that the United States Government is not a stranger or an enemy. It is the people of 50 states joining in a national effort. . . . Without the national Government, the people of the United States, working together, there would be no protection of the family farmer, his income and his financial independence. For he never would have been able to electrify his farm, to insure his crop, to support its price, and to stay ahead of the bugs, the boll weevils and the mortgage bankers. . . . Without the people of the United States working together with the national Government, there would be no Hill-Burton hospitals. . . . no assistance to rural libraries, no help to college dormitories, where we seek to send our children, no control of water pollution, which we must drink, or assistance to depressed areas, or help for training teachers. The list goes on and on. Only a great national effort by a great people working together can explore the mysteries of space, harvest the products at the bottom of the ocean and mobilize the human, natural and material resources of our lands."

Liberals think, moreover, that most Americans agree in favoring affirmative government. The very people who describe themselves in the abstract as conservatives endorse one concrete measure after another of government intervention. In a 1978 *New York Times*/CBS News poll, 81 percent of the self-styled liberals and 71 percent of the self-styled conservatives said that "government ought to see to it that everybody who wants a job can get one"; 91 percent of the liberals and 82 percent of the conservatives said that government should help people get doctors and hospital care at low cost. Everett Carl Ladd, Jr., reported in *Fortune* a year ago that 67 percent favor national health insurance and 61 percent mandatory price and wage controls. A majority even wants government limits on corporate profits—and this well before the oil-company bonanza.

Why then all those "conservative" hands in the air? Hadley Cantril and Lloyd A. Free cleared up that mystery a dozen years ago when their book *The Political Beliefs of Americans* elaborated on the distinction between the Ideological Spectrum and the Operational Spectrum. The Ideological Spectrum covers people's theoretical beliefs about the role of government. The Operational Spectrum covers people's practical attitudes toward specific government programs affecting their daily lives. In 1967, 16 percent registered liberal on the Ideological Spectrum, 65 percent of the Operational Spectrum. Half those professing conservatism in principle turned out to be liberals in practice. "The discrepancy between operational outlooks and ideological views," Cantril and Free concluded, "is so marked as to be almost schizoid." Schizophrenia has plainly not lessened since 1967. Proposition 13 signifies a desire on the part of voters not to renounce government benefits but to get their money's worth for their taxes. As the neoconservative James Q. Wilson recently said, "People continue to support an active, interventionist, expensive state."

This does not mean that liberals regard government as infallible; far from it. But conservative panic about "Big Government" seems exaggerated. Conservatives are chronically in a state of panic. They always oppose reform, from their nineteenth-century fights against the abolition of the imprisonment for debt and the legalization of trade unions to their modern resistance to Social Security, unemployment compensation and farm price supports. Conservativism solemnly declares that each proposed change will bring in its wake incalculable consequences that can only end by destroying the American way of life. But the Republic always turns out to be stronger than conservatives think—and the next generation of conservatives embraces the reforms their fathers so bitterly denounced.

Does government really destroy self-reliance? One recalls Winston Churchill on the British dole: "I do not sympathize with those who think that this process of compulsory mass saving will sap the virility and self-reliance of our race. There will be quite enough grindstone in human life to keep us keen." This remains as true in 1979 as when Churchill said it in 1930. It is notable, moreover, that the proposition that economic security saps self-reliance is one the rich apply only to the poor, never to themselves. Bureaucracy is unquestionably an abomination. But it is a function of large organization, not of government, and every American knows that bureaucracy is quite as arbitrary and obnoxious in the private sector as in the public. Unlike corporations, governments are at least accountable to the political process.

Government is a fallible instrument requiring constant oversight and criticism—and, on the whole, receiving them. Government interventions are often misconceived; government regulations are often foolish. If overload is a problem, reduce the load. But conservatives contend that affirmative government has been tried and has failed: back to the unfettered market! In fact, of course, liberal ideas have not governed national policy since the Indochina war diverted Lyndon Johnson from the Great Society. What has been left under Nixon, Ford, and Carter is liberal machinery run into the ground by conservative policies. The last dozen years in Washington have provided a test not of liberalism but of conservatism.

There is nothing sacrosanct about government. Still, it remains too valuable an instrument of democracy to be subjected to the cheap demagogic attack made familiar by Carter (that "horrible bloated bureaucracy," not visibly debloated since his inauguration) and by the legion of Republican presidential aspirants. A distinguished exception is Representative John Anderson of Illinois, who said of Carter: "He campaigned against Big Government and he has planted the seed of doubt in the minds of the American people on the ability of government to solve the problems. It may be almost something that comes back to haunt him." It may indeed. And the response to John Anderson's presidential campaign shows that liberalism is far from moribund, even within the Republican Party. Government, despite Carter, can define visions and set goals. As Tocqueville, a superior authority, said long ago, "Governments must apply themselves to restore to men that love of the future with which religion and the state of society no longer inspire them."

No doubt an appeal for creative government seems futile in an era the pundits have consigned to conservatism. Yet history reminds us of the inherent cyclical rhythm in our public affairs, the continuing alternation between conservatism and innovation. As a nation, we go through seasons of action, passion, idealism, reform and affirmative government, until the country is worn out. Thereupon we long for respite and enter into seasons of doldrums, drift, cynicism, hedonism and negative government. For the moment, the United States is in the depressive phase of the cycle. It will not be in that phase forever.

I inherit this cyclical perspective from my father, who sketched it out forty years ago in an article for the *Yale Review*. The theory has held up pretty well. Let us recall this century's political history. The first two decades were the years of the Progressive movement and the First World War, when two demanding presidents, Theodore Roosevelt and Wilson, exhorted the American people first to reform our national economy and then to make the world safe for democracy. After two decades of activism, the people were emotionally exhausted. Their capacity for further response to crisis was drained. They were tired of discipline and sacrifice. They were tired of abstract and intangible objectives. They wanted to be let off from public affairs. They longed to immerse themselves in the privacies of life. They yearned for what the new president, Warren G. Harding, called "normalcy." The politics of purpose gave way to the politics of fatigue.

Then, after the do-nothing twenties, came two more decades of action and passion: FDR and the New Deal, World War II, Truman and the Fair Deal, the Cold War, the Korean War—and once again the people found themselves tired and drained. So we had the Eisenhower lull in the 1950s. Eisenhower became president, Walter Lippmann perceptively noted, when "this country and the Western world had had all the dynamism, all the innovation, all the crusading human nature can take." The Eisenhower years provided a needed interlude.

But in due course Americans wanted to get their country moving again. So, as the 1920s led into the '30s, the '50s led into the '60s. We had a new season of activism—Kennedy and Johnson, the New Frontier and the Great Society, the racial revolution and the war against poverty. This time desperate events gave the cyclical swing an ominous turn, an edge of hysteria—first the assassination at Dallas, then the war in Vietnam. There followed riots in the cities, turmoil on the campuses, two more terrible assassinations, drugs and violence, Watergate, the near impeachment of a president. The result, in less than the usual two decades, was national exhaustion. In the 1970s the United States became, as it had been in the '50s and the '20s, a spent nation, self-absorbed and cynical, the "me" decade, a people in search of rest and recuperation.

The issue is evidently not so much conservatism versus liberalism as it is weariness versus vitality. "A good deal of our politics," Emerson said, "is physiological." And several things happen during the seasons of recuperation. The changes wrought in the previous activist period are digested by the social organism and penetrate the framework of society. So conservatives, who had savagely resisted the New Deal in the age of Roosevelt, accepted it in the age of Eisenhower. Moreover, the national energies begin to be replenished, the national batteries start to recharge themselves. Most important of all, the problems neglected in the years of cynicism and apathy become acute and threaten to become unmanageable.

Each period of activism has a detonating issue—a problem growing in size and menace and plainly beyond the capacity of the market's invisible hand to contain or mitigate. As the Republic gathers its forces to meet such problems, it discharges energies across the board. In the early decades of the century, the detonating issue was the concentration of private economic power in the trusts. In the thirties it was the depression. In the sixties it was racial justice. In tackling such problems, government becomes for a moment a vehicle for public idealism. And in such times the national Government is relatively free of those disquieting phenomena of corruption, graft, private rip-off. There were no great problems of corruption during the New Deal or the New Frontier. Corruption is characteristic of the periods of apathy and cynicism; not of the periods of idealism and purpose.

Yet activism and idealism have their dangers too. For, once released to deal with problems at home, the activist impulse tends to spill over into foreign affairs. When government takes an affirmative role at home, it is likely also to take an affirmative role in the world. The great domestic reformers have also been the great foreign-policy activists—TR, Wilson, FDR, Truman, Kennedy, Johnson. There is a disturbing tendency for the United States to get involved in war during activist times. But this point cannot be pushed too far. Obviously reform crusades in the United States did not produce the Kaiser or Hitler or the Japanese imperialists. Still, there is good reason for Americans to exercise special circumspection in foreign policy when the Republic girds itself up once again to confront the urgent problems of the domestic community.

For that time is bound to come, and soon. Sometime in the 1980s the dam will break, as it broke at the turn of the century, in the 1930s and in the 1960s. The detonating issues this time will be inflation and energy—two problems before which the conventional wisdom is that Americans no longer will stand for the remorseless rise in prices—or for the Ford-Carter policy of using recession as the remedy for inflation (and then using inflation as the remedy for recession). And Americans will call for a strong energy policy covering both the development of new sources and the fair allocation of existing supplies. Only the national government can meet these demands. One may speak of the *inevitability* of liberalism, for inflation and energy make affirmative government a technical imperative, a functional necessity, in the years ahead. These are problems that the market is structurally incapable of solving. As the nation turns to meet them with a politics of purpose, our sense of adventure and idealism will return. Our blood will start flowing. There will be a breakthrough into a new political epoch, a new conviction of social possibility, a new hunger for dynamism, innovation, crusading, new efforts to redeem the promise of American life.

And so the cycle will continue, until the nation grows tired again of commitment and uplift. The cyclical rhythm is a physiological process, like the systole and diastole of the heart. For, as Emerson pointed out, both conservatism and liberalism easily rush to excess. The conservative party, he wrote, "vindicates no right, it aspires to no real good, it brands no crime, it proposes no generous policy, it does not build, nor write, nor cherish the arts, nor foster religion, nor establish schools, nor encourage science, nor emancipate slaves, nor befriend the poor, or the Indian, or the immigrant." On the other hand, reform "runs to egotism and bloated self-conceit." The spirit of American radicalism "is destructive and aimless; it is not loving; it has no ulterior and divine ends; but is destructive only out of hatred and selfishness."

Both conservatism and liberalism have their function in preserving the health of the body politic. Both have their indispensable roles in the rhythm of public policy. Both must be restrained from pressing their points too far. Emerson, as usual, said it best: "It may be safely affirmed of these two metaphysical antagonists, that each is a good half, but an impossible whole. Each exposes the abuses of the other, but in a true society, in a true man, both must combine."

Index